ULTIMATE
VISUAL
DICTIONARY
2001

A Dorling Kindersley Book

CONTENTS

ARTIFICIALLY GROWN
CARTILAGE

OETZI

SYDNEY OLYMPIC VILLAGE

ARECIBO RADIO TELESCOPE

LEFT: INSIDE REICHSTAG DOME

BREITLING ORBITER

REICHSTAG

AIRBUS A3XX COCKPIT

VELOCIRAPTOR FOREARM

Probing the universe

IT IS JANUARY 2, 2004. The Stardust spacecraft is plowing through the billowing cloud of gas and dust that is Comet Wild 2. Two years later, the craft will home in on the Earth, ejecting a capsule that contains its dust collector and its precious cargo. What scientists hope to find when they investigate is hard evidence to confirm that comets carry the building blocks of life all over the universe. Other space probes, such as Cassini and Deep Space 1, are on just as important scientific missions. However, the most exciting quest of them all is undoubtedly the search for extraterrestrial life.

BACK TO BASICS

Like Pathfinder and other probes in the Discovery series, Stardust is as stripped back to basics as it can be. All that it carries are solar panels, a camera, a radio, a spectrometer to analyze sunlight bouncing off the comet, some sensors, and its all-important sample collection system. On its outward voyage to Comet Wild 2, this will be collecting interstellar dust grains; on arrival, the dust collector will flip around and start to scoop up dust from the comet's tail.

Protective capsule

Delta 2 launch vehicle

THE STARDUST PROJECT

Stardust began its mission on February 7, 1999. Its return is scheduled for January 2006, when it will eject its recovery capsule. This will parachute to the ground on the salt flats in the Utah desert.

Launch gantry

Collecting arm

CLOSE ENCOUNTER

As Stardust meets Comet Wild 2, an arm shaped something like a tennis racquet will be mechanically deployed by the craft to catch the precious samples of comet dust. This is the job of tiny cells filled with aerogel, a substance that will slow down and trap the incoming dust particles as they impact at ten times the speed of a rifle bullet. Stardust will go on to probe the comet's nucleus before turning for home.

CASSINI
Launched in October 1997, the Cassini spacecraft is scheduled to release the Huygens probe into the hazy atmosphere of Titan, Saturn's largest moon, in July 2004. It will take Cassini seven years to reach Titan, the only one of Saturn's moons that is known to possess a thick atmosphere. After releasing Huygens, Cassini will go on to orbit Saturn and study the planet itself, its other moons, and its celebrated rings.

ION POWER
Another deep-space probe intended to examine asteroids and other space phenomena, Deep Space 1's first port of call was the tiny Braille asteroid, which it reached in July 1999. The probe is powered by an ion engine, which uses charged particles of xenon gas to create a propulsive jet. The innovation is a foretaste of the future. Though the new engine does not possess the same raw power of a conventional rocket, it can maintain its thrust for far longer.

UTILIZING GRAVITY
Four gravity-assists helped Cassini to reach its target: it flew past Venus twice, and Earth and Jupiter once. Each time, the gravitational pull increased the probe's velocity, flinging it like a slingshot into a more distant orbit. Stardust uses the same technique, as it would take too much fuel to intercept Comet Wild 2 directly.

SETI AT WORK
The multigigabytes of signal data flooding into the Arecibo radio telescope means that SETI (Search for Extra Terrestrial Intelligence) can no longer rely solely on the professionals for signal analysis. In May 1999, researchers at the University of California at Berkeley launched a project called SETI@home. Part of a research program called SERENDIP, it allows anyone with a personal computer to play a part in the search for extra-terrestrial intelligence. All that is needed to participate is a special screensaver and Internet access. When it is in screen-saver mode, the PC starts work analyzing SETI signals downloaded to it via the Internet. It transmits its results back to Berkeley and SETI in the same way.

RADIO "EAR"
SETI research is currently centered on Arecibo Observatory, Puerto Rico, home of the world's largest radio telescope.

LISTENING TO THE STARS
The telescope's dish targets Sunlike stars, which scientists consider are the most likely to possess planets where intelligent life might exist. It checks nearly 2 billion radio channels per star before moving on.

Hubble Space Telescope

ORBITING 360 MILES ABOVE the Earth, the Hubble Space Telescope bypasses the blurring effects of the atmosphere to give astronomers some of the clearest and deepest views of space ever witnessed. During 1995, Hubble sent back images that significantly improved our understanding of the Universe. Scientists believed that there were about 10 billion galaxies in the Universe, until studies of Hubble's deep field view enabled them to calculate that this figure is closer to 50 billion. Details of the stunning photographs of the interstellar cloud and dust columns found in the Eagle Nebula have documented, for the first time, the way in which newly-formed stars are revealed by a process called "photo-evaporation," where ultraviolet light from nearby stars erodes surrounding clouds of gas into space. Close-ups of the Orion Nebula provide the best evidence so far that the dark "splotches" found within it are discs of dust swirling around protostars (baby stars). These are believed to be solar systems in the making, which increases the chance of finding life elsewhere in the Universe.

HUBBLE SPACE TELESCOPE

When Hubble was first launched from the Space Shuttle in April 1990, NASA scientists discovered several structural flaws, including a fault with the 2.4 m mirror. A repair mission was successfully performed by astronauts in December 1993.

DEEP FIELD VIEW

In December 1995, a team of astronomers studied this section of sky, which begins near the handle of the Big Dipper and stretches as far as the visible horizon of the Universe. At least 1,500 galaxies in total were counted. Extrapolating from this figure, they calculated that there is probably a total of 50 billion galaxies in the Universe.

Light has left the oldest, most distant galaxies (shown in red) up to 9 billion years ago

This view, assembled from separate images taken in blue, red, and infrared light, approximates true color

High-gain antenna

Aperture door

Solar panel

Light shield

Primary mirror housing

Aft shell

Crew handrail

Access panel

Solar panel

This apparently foreground star is 400,000 times fainter than the naked eye limit

Bluer galaxies contain young stars and are relatively close

The farthest galaxies are up to 4 billion times fainter than the limits of human vision

ORION NEBULA

A sequence of close-up images of the Orion Nebula (a cloud of dust and gas within our Galaxy) revealed that the mysterious set of dark "splotches" are, in fact, dust clouds swirling around very young stars. Scientists believe that these could be embryonic solar systems.

Four massive young stars known as "The Trapezium"

Molecular cloud

The "Great Wall" or "Bright Bar," made up of luminous gas

The Orion Nebula is 1,500 light years away, and spreads across 90 million million miles

Ultraviolet radiation from stars ionizes gas, causing it to glow

STAR DEATH (MYCN18)

The fine detail shown in Hubble images of the star MYCN18 has helped scientists understand how a star like the sun will die. Over several thousands of years, a dying star expands, becoming cooler and redder, and gently puffs its layers of gas into space.

Dust clouds glowing with ultraviolet radiation

Vigorous ejection of star's internal layers

Episodic ejections of star's outer layers produces concentric shells

Hot central core cools off to become a white dwarf (a collapsed, cooling star)

Dramatic illumination is caused by nearby stars

EGGs appear as tiny bumps on the column surface

Foreground star

Smaller columns form, protected from photoevaporation by the shadow of EGGs

INTERSTELLAR GAS AND DUST IN THE EAGLE NEBULA

Over six million million miles high and 7,000 light years away (one light year equals 6 million million miles), these columns of interstellar dust and gas are found in the Eagle Nebula. Projecting from their surfaces are small fingerlike projections called EGGs (Evaporating Gas Globules). Within these extra-dense regions of gas – which are approximately the size of our solar system – young stars develop. Over millions of years, the surrounding gas globules evaporate to reveal the newly formed stars.

Molecular hydrogen gas dispersing into space

PHOTOEVAPORATION

The whiteish haze surrounding each column represents the dispersal of hydrogen into space. This process of erosion, called photoevaporation, is caused by UV light from nearby stars.

Columns are formed by very dense clouds of gas and dust that will eventually erode away

An EGG that has been eroded from the main surface of column

Galileo spacecraft

IN DECEMBER 1995, the Galileo spacecraft finally arrived at the planet Jupiter. More than six years after it had been launched by NASA, the spacecraft's atmospheric probe, which had separated from the orbiter four months earlier, plunged through the gas giant's intense radiation belts and deep into its atmosphere. The onboard electronic systems had to be heavily shielded to protect them against the radiation

PLANET JUPITER

and temperatures twice as hot as the Sun's surface. As the probe parachuted into Jupiter's atmosphere, pulled in by the enormous gravity, the orbiter passed close to the planet, receiving and storing information for later relay back to Earth. This was just the start of the Galileo mission – since 1995, the orbiter has been circling Jupiter and recording information about its weather and its planet-sized moons. Before arriving at Jupiter, Galileo photographed the impact of Comet P/Shoemaker-Levy 9 with Jupiter, the largest explosion ever seen in the Solar System. More recently, the spacecraft has photographed volcanic activity on the moon Io, and found evidence of water beneath the icy crust of another moon, Europa.

GALILEO'S JOURNEY

As it began its six-year flight, Galileo moved away from Earth towards Venus, then doubled back, using the gravitational fields of Venus and Earth to propel it toward Jupiter.

Jupiter

Jupiter's orbit

Long boom carrying magnetic sensors

Low-gain antenna

Double-dish antenna

Retro propulsion module

Atmospheric sampling instrument

Atmospheric descent module

Atmospheric descent probe module

Camera package

Instruments package

Radioisotope thermoelectric generator

LIFE ON MARS?

Organic molecules thought to be from Mars were recently found in a 4.5 billion-year-old rock that fell into the Antarctic 13,000 years ago. Mineral features suggesting biological activity and possible microscopic fossils of bacterialike organisms were discovered.

Composition matches Martian rock

Water-penetrated cracks

MARTIAN METEORITE

Hydrocarbon deposits

Possible microfossil

Rock structure

MICROSCOPIC VIEW OF METEORITE

GALILEO

The main body of the spacecraft circling Jupiter is known as the orbiter. The probe, on the left of the diagram, descended into Jupiter's atmosphere. The probe consists of a descent module and a deceleration module; the latter protects the former from excessive heat, separating off and slowing the probe's descent.

Earth

Mars

Venus

The Sun

Asteroid belt

Galileo's flight path

GALILEO CIRCLING
The orbiter and the probe split apart and the orbiter circles Jupiter, making approaches to all the planet's large moons. It uses their gravity to change course and pick up speed with very little fuel.

COMET SHOEMAKER-LEVY 9
From July 16 to 22, 1994, pieces of a comet designated P/Shoemaker-Levy 9 collided with the planet Jupiter. This was the first collision of two Solar System bodies ever to be observed. While other comets revolve around the Sun, Shoemaker-Levy 9 – named after its discoverers, Eugene and Carolyn Shoemaker and David Levy – moved around Jupiter in a very unusual elongated orbit within a period of just over two years. It became clear that the comet had recently been "captured" by the gravitational field of the planet and would soon collide with it.

Close encounter with Jupiter in 1992 broke comet apart

The gravities of Jupiter and the Sun string fragments out

Pieces consist of fragments of ice and dust

Antenna transmits data back to Earth

Erupting volcano on the moon Io

Io, Jupiter's largest moon

Jupiter

Fragment up to two kilometers in diameter

Surrounding debris cloud

Fragment a few hundred meters in diameter

TRAVELLING COMET
The comet consisted of at least 21 discernible icy fragments with diameters estimated at up to two kilometers. The fragments stretched across 710,000 miles (1.1 million km) of space, almost three times the distance between Earth and the Moon.

Scars formed by dark gases rising to Jupiter's surface

Impact scars larger than Earth

Light cloud zones

Darker cloud belts

Main parachute

Descent module

Protective shield of deceleration module

THE PROBE DESCENDING
The probe descended through Jupiter's atmosphere gathering data. The descent module split from the deceleration module and a parachute slowed its rate of descent. The module descended for 57 minutes before burning out.

POINT OF IMPACT
The impacts of the comet on Jupiter's atmosphere have been spectacular, with plumes thousands of miles high, hot "bubbles" of gas in the atmosphere, and large dark "scars."

Very Large Telescope

THE WORLD'S LARGEST telescope system, the Very Large Telescope (VLT), is located at Cerro Paranal in the Atacama desert, Chile. It is used to study visible light and to collect and analyze infrared heat energy and ultraviolet radiation. During a one hour exposure, each telescope can photograph objects that are four billion times fainter than can be seen with the naked eye. The VLT consists of four telescope units, each with a mirror of 27 ft (8.2 m) in diameter. These units can be used individually or in parallel; together they simulate one large telescope with a mirror of 52 ft (16 m) in diameter. Working in parallel, a process known as interferometry, the VLT allows celestial objects to be seen in much finer detail than with the Hubble Space Telescope. On May 22, 1998, one of the telescope units took its first photograph of a celestial object, an event that astronomers call "first light." The VLT will be used principally to search for small, Earthlike planets around other stars.

SPACE PROBES

In addition to telescopes, new space probes continue to explore the Solar System. In 1997, the Mars Pathfinder successfully surveyed an ancient flood plain on Mars. In the same year, the Galileo space probe discovered strong evidence for a global ocean under the ice sheets of Europa, one of Jupiter's 16 moons. Future space probes will investigate the possible existence of alien microbes on both Mars and Europa.

Ramp from the Pathfinder *Research buggy inspects the rock, Yogi*

MARS PATHFINDER MISSION

Natural color of ice floes *Enhanced color shows ice composition*

EUROPA AS SEEN FROM GALILEO

TELESCOPE UNIT
The four telescopes of the VLT are precisely engineered structures. Each individual telescope was assembled and tested in Europe, before being taken apart and carefully transported to Chile. Final assembly took place inside the telescope enclosures on the mountain.

Small secondary mirror used to focus starlight

Tilting mechanism adjusts altitude of telescope

Primary mirror sits horizontally

Adjustable structure allows telescope to rotate

Flaw exaggerated by computer

REOSC
OPTIQUE

17/06/97
14:07:58

406.0
nm

COMPUTER MAPPING OF MIRROR DEFECT
The four mirrors of the VLT were cast in Germany and polished in France. The shape of each mirror was checked at regular intervals using laser beams, and laser data was formulated into a map of the mirror's surface. Defects (see right), perhaps only a millionth of a millimeter in diameter, were exaggerated by the computer so that they could be located and corrected.

TELESCOPE SITE
The VLT is located at the summit of Cerro Paranal, a mountain in the Atacama desert, Chile. At 8,635 ft (2,632 m) above sea level, the site is one of the driest places on Earth, despite being situated only 7.5 miles (12 km) from the Pacific coast. The mountaintop site provides remarkable conditions for observation and photography. There are up to 350 cloud-free nights per year, and images are stable owing to the lack of water vapor in the atmosphere.

Telescope unit

Telescope enclosure

Surface of mirror

IMAGE QUALITY

The atmosphere of the Earth blurs light from distant celestial objects. The VLT is able to compensate for this using a computerized system known as adaptive optics. Every one hundredth of a second, a computer analyzes a tiny fraction of light from a star being observed by the VLT. It then measures the effect that the Earth's atmosphere is having on the light, and calculates how to compensate for that effect. The computer sends signals to a set of activators, which support the flexible mirror. This then refocuses the light from the telescope. The worst effects of the atmosphere are eliminated and sharp images, comparable with those taken by the Hubble Space Telescope, are produced. Images taken by a ground-based telescope (above right) and the VLT (right), show different views of the same planetary nebula.

PLANETARY NEBULA I
This image of the Dumbbell Nebula shows the cloud of gas that has drifted away into space from the remains of a dead star. It was taken by a ground-based telescope.

Dust and gas of the nebula

PLANETARY NEBULA II
Taken by the VLT, this view of the Dumbbell Nebula shows the center of the gas cloud in far more detail. Complex patterns can reveal the way that gas is moving within the cloud.

Colors indicate the types of gas

International Space Station

IN 1998, THE FIRST components of the International Space Station (ISS) were launched from Russia and the US. The ISS will provide a unique place to study the Earth, and to see how the Sun's violent eruptions affect the operation of communications satellites, and the weather on Earth. The effects of gravity inside the station will be minuscule and scientists will be able to study a myriad of subtle biological, physical, and chemical reactions which are impossible to duplicate on Earth. Complete construction will require a total of 45 space missions and many hours of space-walking by astronauts. The station is scheduled to be permanently crewed from the eighth mission onward, due to take place in 2000. Astronauts will spend many months at a time on the station, testing equipment for future space exploration missions.

MIR SPACE STATION
Now referred to as Phase One of the International Space Station, Mir was home to American, Russian, and European astronauts as they learned to work together in space.

ARTIST'S IMPRESSION OF THE ISS
The most ambitious space project since the Apollo missions to land man on the Moon, the ISS is the next step in the human exploration of the Solar System. It is a joint venture between 16 nations, and the largest scientific cooperative program in history. All power on the space station will be generated by the large arrays of solar panels connected to the main structure of the station. Also attached to this framework are corrugated panels, which act as radiators dispersing excess heat from the station into space. Astronauts will live and work in the cylindrical modules between the solar panel arrays, and will eventually be able to spend many years at a time in space.

SPACE HAZARDS

Dust grains traveling through space at speeds of up to 230 ft (70 m) per second can "sandblast" spacecraft and astronauts. Subatomic particles travel close to the speed of light, and can cause severe damage to living cells. Space stations therefore provide shields to protect astronauts from dust and particle storms and solar flares.

DAMAGE CRATER
This tiny crater in a window of the Space Shuttle was caused by a fleck of paint. It is 0.64mm wide and 0.63mm deep.

SOLAR FLARE
These violent eruptions from the photosphere (the visible surface of the Sun) cause major disruptions to communications satellites that orbit the Earth.

Solar panels provide energy

Zaraya control module

Russian Soyuz spacecraft

US MODULES
The US modules of the
ISS were built in Alabama.
Astronauts will eat and
sleep in the habitat module
and work in the laboratory
module. A connecting unit
called Node 1 will join these
two modules together.

Laboratory module

Node 1 connecting unit

Habitat module

SLEEPING IN SPACE
Astronauts sleep in an upright
position so that they receive
a constant flow of air. If they
slept horizontally, the effects
of weightlessness could result
in suffocation from exhaled
carbon dioxide. This astro-
naut remains stationary by
crossing his arms and using
straps to anchor himself to
the wall of the module.

Radiators for cooling

Exposure platform

LABORATORY MODULES
The European Columbus
Orbital Facility is one of
many laboratory modules
that contain computer
and scientific equipment
for running a vast range of
experiments. Some modules
have access to robotic arms
that will be able to conduct
experiments on exposure
platforms outside the station.

*European Columbus
Orbital Facility*

*Connecting
module*

*Japanese
Experiment Module*

Giganotosaurus

THE BONES OF A GIANT new dinosaur, *Giganotosaurus carolinii*, were recently excavated by two scientists in Argentina. *Giganotosaurus* ("giant reptile of the south") is believed to be one of the largest carnivorous dinosaurs ever found. With a body length of 42 ft (12.5 m) and an estimated weight of between 6 and 8 tons, it is believed to have been even larger than the *Tyrannosaurus rex*. Like T-Rex, the *Giganotosaurus* is classified in the *Theropoda* – a suborder of the Saurischia (lizard-hipped) group of dinosaurs that were characterized by short forelimbs and an S-shaped neck. It existed an estimated 100 million years ago during the Cretaceous period, and appears to be quite closely related to a theropod that lived 50 million years previously, *Allosaurus*.

CARCHARODONTOSAURUS SAHARICUS

Another theropod rivaling the great size of T-Rex is the Moroccan-found *Carcharodontosaurus saharicus* ("shark-toothed reptile from the Sahara"). In May 1996 the discovery of a 5.4 ft (1.65 m) skull was announced by scientists from the University of Chicago. The dinosaur is estimated at being 45 ft (13.7 m) long, 12 ft (3.65 m) high, and weighing 8.3 tons. The skull reveals razor-sharp teeth that would have enabled this formidable dinosaur to slash and slice its prey with the greatest of ease.

RECONSTRUCTING THE SKELETON

The skeleton was actually discovered in 1993 by Ruben D. Carolini, who is credited within the full name of the dinosaur, *Giganotosaurus carolinii*. Paleontologists Rodolfo A. Coria and Leonardo Salgado then began the work of excavating, piecing together, and studying the bones. They waited until they had completed a full examination before announcing their findings in the September 1995 issue of the journal *Nature*.

ARTIST'S IMPRESSION OF THE FULL SKELETON

More than 70 percent of the skeleton has been unearthed so far and a clear idea of the full skeleton can be gained from this artist's impression.

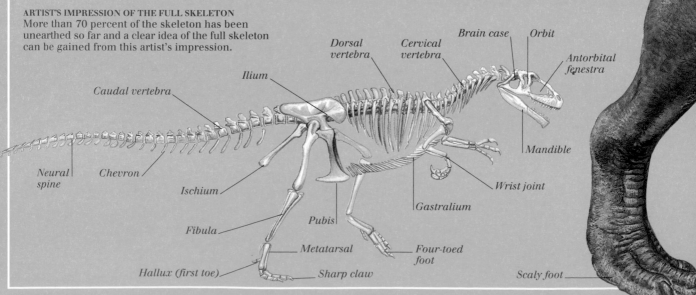

Long heavy tail

Hind limb

Dorsal vertebra

Cervical vertebra

Brain case

Orbit

Antorbital fenestra

Ilium

Caudal vertebra

Neural spine

Chevron

Ischium

Fibula

Pubis

Metatarsal

Hallux (first toe)

Sharp claw

Gastralium

Four-toed foot

Wrist joint

Mandible

Scaly foot

Both *Giganotosaurus* and *Tyrannosaurus* existed during the Cretaceous period, which spanned the time between 65 and 144 million years ago and saw the end of the Age of Dinosaurs. Preceding *Tyrannosaurus* by 30 million years, *Giganotosaurus* is thought to have evolved independently. The fact that both meat-eaters shared the same enormous dimensions suggests that both were equally equipped to tackle large plant-eating dinosaurs.

THEROPOD TIMELINE

MILLION YEARS AGO
248   208   144   65

TRIASSIC   JURASSIC   CRETACEOUS

Possibly striped for camouflage

Scaly skin

Shoulder

Head 5 ft (1.53 m) long

Eye

Nostril

Thick, stocky neck

Tongue

Powerful jaws

Sharp teeth up to 8 in (20 cm) long

Short forelimb

RELATIVE DIMENSIONS
Giganotosaurus shares many of the physical characteristics of *Allosaurus*. Its skull, measuring 1.53 m long, is more than twice as big as the skull of *Allosaurus* (75 cm), while the entire length of the skeleton (12.5 m) is one meter longer than "Sue," the largest *Tyrannosaurus* found, and, because its bones are so dense, the animal could have been at least 4,000 lb (1,800 kg) heavier.

Strong thighs to support and power the body

Claw

Finger

Ankle

First toe turned backward

Large toe-claw

15A

From dinosaurs to birds?

WHERE THE FIRST BIRDS CAME FROM is a question that continues to baffle the experts. Although the most famous fossil bird is still *Archaeopteryx*, which dates from near the end of the Jurassic period about 155 to 150 million years ago, fossil discoveries in China from 1995 onward have started to transform the picture. In the eyes of some experts, these "feathered" dinosaurs undoubtedly seem to strengthen the case for some form of evolutionary link between dinosaurs and birds. The recent Chinese finds also suggest that feathers could have first evolved from scales for reasons other than flying, with the ability to fly only developing later as a secondary role.

WHY FEATHERS?

If the Chinese dinosaurs had feathers, the as-yet unanswered question is: why did the change occur? Feathers, say some of the experts, may have evolved as camouflage, to attract mates, or simply as a means of retaining body warmth (but this would imply these dinosaurs were warm-blooded, not reptilian).

Sharp, cutting teeth

Tail feathers for display

Hairlike downy feathers

Clawed hand

CAUDIPTERYX

From 1995, fossil finds in China, particularly in Liaoning province, have led to a major rethinking of the story of bird evolution. However, some of the finds have caused more problems than they solved. Though *Caudipteryx* fossils apparently showed the imprints of feathers, the preserved bones suggest that it was too heavy to get off the ground into flight.

Long, winglike arms

Elongated leg and foot bones

Clawed foot

FALSE TRAIL

In August 1999, the discovery of *Archaeoraptor liaonongensis* was hailed as finally establishing the missing link in the dinosaur-bird saga. The fossil was identified as being around 130 million years old. Head, body, and wings were those of a true bird, but the tail was that of a true dinosaur. However, further investigation revealed that the fossil was a composite of at least two creatures and that it was a deliberate fake.

BEFORE THE DINOSAURS

Some experts believe that the origins of birds date back to the Permian period some 250 million years ago, well before the dinosaurs themselves emerged. What they argue is that dinosaurs, birds, pterosaurs (the flying reptiles known as pterodactyls), and the forerunners of modern crocodiles, such as *Gracilisuchus* and *Terrestrisuchus*, may well share one common ancestor and that the most likely candidates are the ancient reptiles known as thecodonts. The most likely thecodonts to fit the bill are the ornithosuchian group, so-called because of their birdlike features, but hard factual fossil evidence to support the theory is lacking.

STARTING POINT
Four very different creatures may have had one common ancestor.

BIRDS

PTEROSAURS

THECODONTS

DINOSAURS

CROCODILIANS

WRISTS IN COMMON

Fossil evidence suggests that maniraptorans, a group of medium-sized dinosaurs, had the same ability to swivel their wrists as modern birds. The bones in a bird's wrist are adapted to help twist and flap the whole forelimb and also to fold the wing against the body at rest. The long arms, swiveling wrists, and grasping claws of the maniraptorans were suited to snapping the hands forward suddenly to catch prey.

VELOCIRAPTOR FOREARM (SKELETON)
First digit
Second digit
Forearm
Wrist joint
Third digit
Elbow joint

First digit
Long forearm
BIRD WING (SKELETON)
Wrist joint
Second and third digits fused
Elbow joint

HALFWAY HOUSE

First discovered in the 1860s, only six fossil specimens of *Archaeopteryx* exist. A halfway stage between dinosaurs and birds, its similarity to small theropod dinosaurs like *Compsognathus*, one of its contemporaries, led to the view that smallish, as yet unknown, theropods, dating from earlier in the Jurassic period, must have been the original ancestors of the first birds.

Arms have evolved into feathered wings

ARCHAEOPTERYX

PIGEON

Arms tucked into body

AVIMIMUS

Front limbs serve as arms

Changed digit pattern

Large hind legs for standing and running

COMPSOGNATHUS

EARLIEST BIRD
Fully dinosaurian features of *Archaeopteryx* included teeth in the beak and a long tail made of a chain of vertebrae. Others were almost fully avian: the arms had evolved into wings and feathers, and were obviously adapted for flight.

Preserved in the ice

ONE OF THE MOST EXCITING PREHISTORIC FINDS of recent years was the discovery of a 23,000-year-old wooly mammoth mummified apparently intact in a block of ice deep in the frozen wastes of Siberia. In fall 1999, the mammoth, still embedded in the ice that had preserved it, was airlifted by helicopter to the nearest town, where it is to be kept in a specially-built ice-laboratory, ready for scientists to study. This is the most ambitious attempt yet made to preserve such a long-dead animal so it can be analyzed in detail.

UP AND AWAY
Buigues organized an expedition to cut into the ice around the frozen mammoth. In October 1999, the whole find was airlifted like a giant hairy ice cube to the Khatanga airstrip. Its eventual resting place will be an icy cellar-laboratory dug underground.

Small ears helped prevent heat loss

HOW BIG WERE MAMMOTHS?
Wooly mammoths, with a shoulder height of 8 ft (2.3 m), had shaggy coats to protect them against the cold. The broad ivory tusks may have been used to sweep snow away from the grass the mammoths ate.

Ivory tusk

AN EXCITING DISCOVERY
The Jarkov mammoth is named after the reindeer-herding family who discovered its tusks poking from the ice in 1997. They removed the tusks to sell at a local market where the French explorer Bernard Buigues saw them. He visited the site and took samples from the head and teeth. These showed it was a male aged about 47 when it died.

BIG PLANS FOR THE BIG BEAST
If the mammoth's sex organs are well-enough preserved, one idea is to extract frozen sperm from them, which hopefully could be used to fertilize eggs taken from an Asian elephant, the mammoth's closest living relative. If the process works, the result could be a hybrid that was half-mammoth and half-elephant. Further selective breeding among the offspring might eventually produce almost pure mammoths.

ARCTIC OCEAN

Khatanga

RUSSIA

AT KHATANGA
Work on the Jarkow mammoth may take 50 years to omplete. One fear is that, if its temperature has risen above -4°F (-20°C), the DNA may be too fragmented for use. However, the Jarkov mammoth is the best candidate yet to emerge in the quest to recreate a living creature from prehistoric times.

MAMMOTH CLONES

Cloning is another idea under active consideration once tissue samples taken from the mammoth have been analyzed. Mammoth DNA would be injected into suitable cells, such as elephant egg cells, which have had their own genetic material removed. Using the instructions in their new genes, the eggs would develop into baby mammoths.

DEATH IN THE ANDES

In early 1999, the frozen remains of three children – two girls and a boy – were discovered at an Inca burial site high in the Argentinian Andes. The ice had done its work well: two bodies were almost perfectly preserved, while the third seems to have been damaged by lightning. The freezing itself had taken place within hours of burial. It was clear that the children had been ritually sacrificed. Examination of the bodies and of the wealth of rich artifacts found with them will give scientists an unprecedented chance of finding out more about the Inca way of life.

Thick insulating coat

DEFROSTING THE MAMMOTH

The plan is to thaw out the mammoth and the ice that encases it using nothing more complicated than home hairdryers. Thousands of samples will be taken as the creature is slowly defrosted in hundreds of slow stages.

OETZI'S SECRETS REVEALED

Oetzi (Ötzi), the Austro-Italian iceman, was another exciting discovery of the 1990s. His remains were found by accident in 1991, thawing from the ice high in an Alpine pass between Austria and Italy. Along with his clothes and tools, Oetzi's mummified body had been preserved almost intact for a staggering 5,300 years. Investigations revealed that he was around 46 years old when he died, 5 ft 3 in (1.65 m) tall and weighed 130 pounds (60 kg). In 1998 Oetzi was moved to a new home in a refrigerated case at the South Tyrol Museum of Archaeology in Bolzano.

AUSTRIA

Solden

ITALY

Bolzano

The valley after which Oetzi was named

Small tail

Wooly underhair

OETZI'S REMAINS

WHAT OETZI WORE

When he died, Oetzi was wearing a plaited grass waterproof cloak, a loincloth, a goat's hide tunic and leggings, a pouched belt, a bearskin hat, and deerskin boots lined with grass for extra warmth.

Large feet support body weight

Medical Research

SOME SIGNIFICANT BREAKTHROUGHS have recently been made in DNA research, with enormous implications for controlling and curing diseases, reproducing identical organisms (cloning), and "decoding," or listing, the sequence of the genes that compose an organism's DNA ("genome sequencing"). In May 1996, Oxford University scientists announced that they had identified the regulatory "switch" for the gene CFTR, which, when defective, causes cystic fibrosis. The discovery will potentially enable healthy copies of the gene to be introduced into a patient's body and activated in relevant cells. Geneticists have, for the first time, sequenced the genome of an organism larger than a bacterium, with enormous consequences for the future study into human genetics. Other areas of development include the use of highly specialized computer technology to provide long-distance medical care, and virtual-reality environments for medical practice, training, and research.

THE COMPOSITION OF DNA (DEOXYRIBONUCLEIC ACID)

Human cell

Nucleus

Nucleolus

GENETIC CODING

A chromosome is a condensed strand of DNA. There are 23 pairs of chromosomes in the human cell and together they contain about 100,000 genes. Every gene is a tiny segment of DNA, made up of paired nucleotide bases arranged in triplets. The above computer display shows the base-pair structure of adjacent genes. The entire sequence of these bases forms the specific genetic code (genome) of an organism. A world-wide research effort, known as the Human Genome Project, has been set up to identify and code all of the genes in human DNA.

Nucleosome

Sugar phosphate backbone

Chromosome (human cells have 23 pairs)

DNA wraps around a core of binding proteins

Unraveled double helix of DNA

A DNA SEGMENT

This computer representation shows the double helix (blue) of the DNA linked together by the base pairs (yellow and red).

DNA GENOME SEQUENCING

Saccharomyces cerevisiae, or brewer's yeast, is the first organism more complex than a bacterium to have its entire genome sequenced. Three hundred scientists worked over a period of six years to sequence the 12,071 base pairs. Their achievement was announced at the European Commission in April 1996.

YEAST CELLS

WORM DNA

Another subject of genetic research is the *Caenorhabditis elegans*, a soil-dwelling nematode worm. Scientists have already mapped out its genes and have embarked on identifying the specific sequence of the 100 million base pairs in its genome.

NEMATODE WORM

KEY TO BASES

Adenine

Guanine

Thymine

Cytosine

CLONING

A breakthrough in efforts to genetically engineer species of animals was announced in March 1996. Pictured here at nine months old, these two Welsh mountain sheep were successfully cloned by using an electric current to fuse a lab-cultured cell with an unfertilized egg (one emptied of all its chromosomes). This stimulus also fertilized the cell, which then divided, developed into an embryo, and was transferred to a surrogate mother.

CLONED SHEEP, MEGAN AND MORAG

BASE PAIRS

The four chemical compounds or bases, are paired in "rungs" and grouped in triplets, forming the double helix "ladder". The sequence of these base pairs contains the inherited coded instructions (genes) responsible for the development of an organism.

Nucleotide base

Paired nucleotide base

Gene is made up of sections of base triplets (3 successive pairs of bases)

TISSUE ENGINEERING

An artificial human ear, developed by growing human cartilage in a biodegradable polyester scaffold mold, was grafted onto the back of a mouse to see whether outer skin would form and the blood would circulate. This experiment, successfully carried out at the Massachusetts Institute of Technology by Dr. C. Vacanti, is a vital step towards using such structures in future human transplant surgery.

COMPUTER TECHNOLOGY AND MEDICINE

TELEMEDICINE

Telemedicine – the practice of medicine at a distance using computer networks – was pioneered by NASA to provide medical support to astronauts. Not only can it be used for consulting with patients in rural or widespread geographical areas but it can also provide emergency care in remote and disaster situations.

TELEMEDICAL ANALYSIS OF BRAIN SCAN

VIRTUAL REALITY

Virtual reality environments are being developed to provide realistic training for certain surgical procedures, much as flight simulators are used to train pilots to fly. The highly specialized techniques performed in minimally invasive "keyhole" surgery, using such instruments as the gastroscope (above), can be practiced using a virtual environment that simulates tissue properties. A virtual environment developed to simulate eye surgery is shown below. The surgeon is able to experience both the visual and mechanical sensations associated with performing the operation.

Surgeon's eyepiece

Keyhole surgery instruments feed back video images

Controls

GASTROSCOPE

VIRTUAL ENVIRONMENT FOR SIMULATION OF EYE SURGERY

STRESS CONTOURS SHOWN AS INCISION IS MADE IN CORNEA

Diamond guarded scalpel

Surgeon's tremor power spectrum

Patient's vital signs

Ocular fixation ring

Target of incision

INTERACTION OF SURGICAL INSTRUMENTS WITH VIRTUAL EYE

Genetic advances

HUMAN HEART

DEVELOPMENTS IN CLONING are among the most important advances in recent genetic science. A clone is a group of genes, cells, or complete organisms in which all of the group's members have the same genetic constitution. The term is also used to refer to individual members of a clone. Clones occur in nature, especially in the case of simple organisms, such as bacteria and viruses, which reproduce merely by splitting (asexual reproduction) after their DNA has replicated itself. They also occur in humans and other animals when a single fertilized egg divides and separates to form two or more identical individuals. Artificial cloning of selected genes is one of the most significant breakthroughs ever made in biology and has powerful implications for both science and industry. Once the desired gene is obtained, the cloning can be left to organisms such as bacteria, which, under suitable conditions, reproduce almost indefinitely. In this way, enormous quantities of the particular gene may be produced. Gene cloning is most commonly done in the laboratory by means of the polymerase chain reaction (PCR), which can produce millions of copies of a single gene in a matter of hours. Far more daunting an enterprise than gene cloning is the cloning of whole animals (see below right), only recently shown to be practicable. A further key genetic advance is the creation of transgenic animals, in particular pigs, which are currently being used for the "manufacture" of human-compatible organs, such as hearts.

CREATING A TRANSGENIC ANIMAL

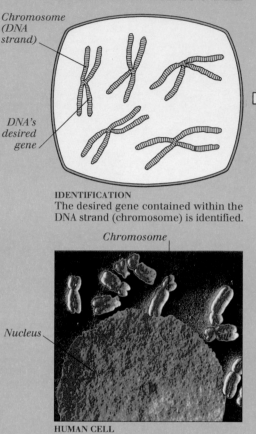

Chromosome (DNA strand)

DNA's desired gene

IDENTIFICATION
The desired gene contained within the DNA strand (chromosome) is identified.

Chromosome

Nucleus

HUMAN CELL
After cell division, perfect copies of each of its chromosomes are passed to each of the daughter cells.

BSE

Among the more worrying aspects of biological research is the discovery that the brain disease bovine spongiform encephalopathy (BSE) is identical to the fatal human condition Creutzfeldt-Jakob disease (CJD). There is general agreement that the introduction of bovine tissue from affected animals into the food chain was the cause of the recent BSE epidemic. Although the genetic modification of animals is unlikely to involve the genes active in BSE, the number of unanswered questions has caused much concern about the propriety of the procedure.

GENETICALLY MODIFIED FOODS

An increasingly controversial practice in the food industry is the genetic modification of foodstuffs in order to extend their shelf life. This means that not only foods, for example fruit and vegetables, but also food ingredients and additives that contain genes derived from animals, fish, insects, and viruses, will appear in stores unlabeled as such.

Rotting is far more visible

A little decay is apparent

GENETICALLY MODIFIED TOMATO

"NATURAL" TOMATO OF THE SAME AGE

ANIMAL CLONING

To produce a clone of an animal, a sample of its DNA must be used. Since each body cell contains a complete DNA genome, this is easily obtained. This DNA has to be introduced into an ovum (egg) of another animal of the same species after the ovum's original DNA is extracted. The egg is then inserted into a surrogate animal's womb and the pregnancy proceeds as normal. Although every body cell contains a complete genome, it will normally activate only those genes necessary for its own body part – for example kidney, brain, or bone. The other genes are not needed and are not "switched on." However, if the cell is starved of nutrients, development can be stopped at an early stage, at which point all the genes can be operative. The ovum into which the DNA is inserted will then behave as if the DNA were its own.

A donor provides the cell for cloning, e.g., mammary cell

CELL DONOR

A ewe provides an egg

EGG DONOR

Special enzymes called restriction enzymes snip the DNA at specific points to isolate and free the gene

TRANSGENIC ANIMALS

A transgenic animal is not a clone, but an animal whose genes contain DNA taken from another source. It is now possible to create transgenic pigs in order to provide organs for human transplant. If, for example, a human gene is introduced at the one-cell stage of pig embryo development, the organ taken from the resulting pig will be less likely to be rejected by the human. The gene must be introduced at the one-cell stage so that it is incorporated into all of the grown specimen's cells. The diagram (left) shows the commonest way to create a transgenic pig. However, following a recent discovery that pigs carry a virus that can infect human cells, some researchers are calling for the practice to be banned.

Restriction enzyme

FREEING THE GENE

Chromosome arm

HUMAN CHROMOSOME
This photograph of a human chromosome shows its irregular structure.

THE FREED GENE

PCR machine

Cloned cells produced in a PCR machine

PCR MACHINE
The polymerase chain reaction is carried out automatically in machines such as this.

Syringe needle

Pig's egg

The egg is secured while the gene is injected

MICROSCOPIC VIEW OF CELL INSERTION
Once introduced into the pig's egg, the gene develops as normal. The result, after birth, is a transgenic piglet.

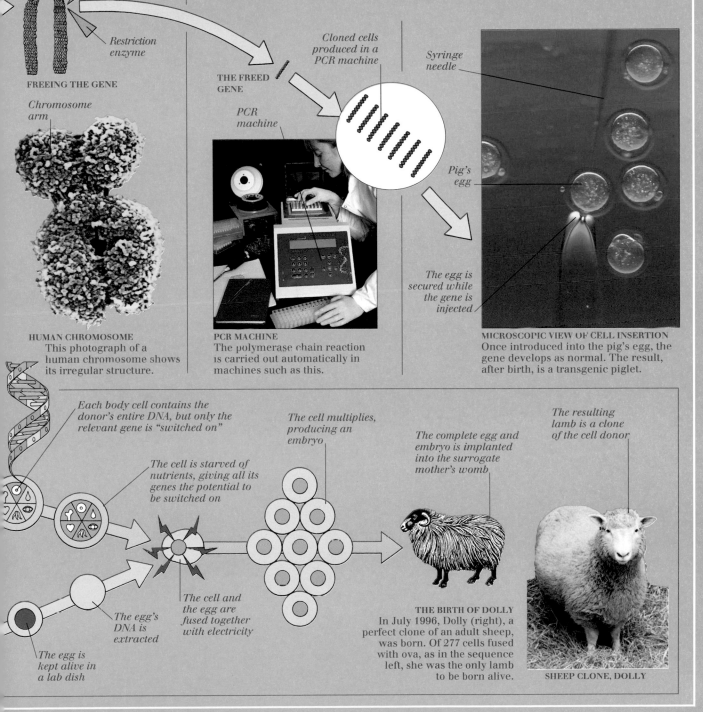

Each body cell contains the donor's entire DNA, but only the relevant gene is "switched on"

The cell is starved of nutrients, giving all its genes the potential to be switched on

The cell multiplies, producing an embryo

The complete egg and embryo is implanted into the surrogate mother's womb

The resulting lamb is a clone of the cell donor

The cell and the egg are fused together with electricity

The egg's DNA is extracted

The egg is kept alive in a lab dish

THE BIRTH OF DOLLY
In July 1996, Dolly (right), a perfect clone of an adult sheep, was born. Of 277 cells fused with ova, as in the sequence left, she was the only lamb to be born alive.

SHEEP CLONE, DOLLY

Modern surgery

WITH NEW DISCOVERIES AND advancing technology, medicine is constantly evolving. Developments in technical expertise have resulted in a successful hand transplant and the repair of a congenital defect in a fetus while still in the womb. Advances in technology have also been far-reaching, providing a glimpse of what might be achieved in the future. The application of virtual reality in medicine has already enabled progress in both the teaching and practice of surgery, and may soon be used in the treatment of eating disorders and agoraphobia. Minimally invasive and robot- and computer-aided surgery allow delicate and complex surgical procedures to be carried out with the precision of a thousandth of a millimeter. This means that surgery has become safer, and patient pain and recovery time have been reduced.

MRI SCAN OF A FEMALE BODY
This color-enhanced Magnetic Resonance Image (MRI) is the product of a number of MRI scans made along the length of the body, which have been collated by the scanner's computer.

Headset   Dataglove   Virtual leg

VIRTUAL SURGERY
Medical imaging such as X-ray, Computerized Tomography (CT), and Magnetic Resonance Imaging (MRI), allows visual access to the internal anatomy and functions of the human body. The precise anatomical information provided by these images can be used to create a virtual patient, on which surgeons and medical students can practice procedures. To study the anatomy of the human leg, these surgeons wear headsets equipped with a 3-D video display to view an image, and a black rubber glove (dataglove) that has woven optical fiber sensors. The glove relays details of the body part to the computer, which then generates the image.

Surgical clamp   Muscular wall of mother's womb

INTRAUTERINE SURGERY
The repair of birth defects through fetal surgery has so far been mostly experimental. However, groundbreaking advances were made in 1998 with the treatment of a case of spina bifida, a developmental defect in the posterior wall of the spinal canal. With this condition, the delicate tissue of the spinal cord may be exposed to varying degrees of damage, depending on the severity of the defect. This can result in paralysis of the lower limbs and incontinence. A team of surgeons in the US corrected the defect in a 23-week-gestation fetus, after the condition had been detected during a routine ultrasound. Follow-up at the walking and toilet-training stages will be necessary to judge the success of the operation.

ROBOTS IN SURGERY

Recent advances in biomedical engineering have led to the increasing use of robots in surgery. Once a robot has been correctly programmed, it will be more accurate than a human in performing many precise but repetitive tasks. Robots may soon act as surgeons' assistants during operations, holding instruments such as an endoscope (for viewing internal parts of the body), and making incisions when required.

ROBOT-AIDED BRAIN SURGERY
A robot performs simulated brain surgery on a model head (right). The surgeon views the operation on a large screen and uses a joystick to control the robot's movements.

Robotic arm   Model head

COMPUTER-AIDED BRAIN SURGERY
A surgeon uses a computer-assisted microscope to locate a brain tumour in a patient. The microscope uses MRI scans to plot the position of the tumor, and maps it in 3-D virtual reality. The surgeon can then locate and destroy the tumor using a laser integrated into the microscope.

Digital
artery

Blood
capillary
network

Distal
flexor
tendon

Nerve to
finger

Vein

Flexor
retinaculum

Deep flexor
tendons

Superficial
flexor tendon

Pronator
muscle

Radial
artery

Radius

Median
nerve

Palmaris
longus tendon

Ulnar
nerve

Ulnar
artery

Ulna

Skin

Fatty layer

Flexed finger

Muscle

ROBOTIC HAND

This battery-operated robotic hand needs only three fingers to perform 85 percent of the functions of a normal hand. The hand will be covered in artificial skin that contains tiny pressure sensors to aid use (see below). Artificial hands will eventually be powered by energy generated by the movement of tendons in the upper arm.

Adjustable
finger
manipulation

ROBOT SENSOR CHIP

Sensors built into artificial skin react to pressure on the fingertips caused by the manipulation of objects. The sensors enable the hand to maintain a grip on objects of all shapes and sizes.

HAND TRANSPLANT

In 1998, a multinational team of surgeons performed the first successful hand transplant in France. The transplant recipient had lost his hand in a circular saw accident nine years previously. Arteries and veins in the arm and hand were connected to supply vital nutrients to, and remove waste products from, the skin and tissues of the hand. Regeneration of nerve tissue, even after reconstruction, was more gradual and, three months after the operation, the patient started to regain sensation in his fingertips.

Bursa protecting tendons

Superficial flexor tendons

Deep flexor tendons

Median nerve

Radial artery

Pronator
muscle

Radius

Tendons
stabizing radial
and ulnar bones

Ulnar artery

Ulna

Ulnar
nerve

TRANSVERSE SECTION THROUGH WRIST

This diagram shows the arteries, veins, and nerves that travel through the arm and hand. At the wrist joint, bones in the arm articulate with bones in the hand to allow movement.

Body healing

MODERN MEDICINE AND STATE-OF-THE-ART TECHNOLOGY are working hand in hand to transform the way in which a whole range of medical problems and conditions are treated. Microsurgery, where doctors are now able to connect blood vessels and nerves thinner than human hair, is only one area of exciting progress. Developments in tissue engineering mean that it is now possible to "grow" replacement skin and cartilage in the laboratory, while microchips and advanced computer electronics are playing a vitally important part in restoring full body movement and in helping people cope with the problems of damaged hearing and sight.

Internal microcircuitry

DETECTING SOUND PATTERNS

Cochlear implants are designed to help the profoundly deaf hear. A receiver in the skull receives signals from a microphone, via a sound processor and transmitter, using them to activate electrodes implanted in the cochlear nerve. They stimulate the nerve to send electric impulses to the brain.

Implanted receiver

External transmitter

Electrode

Cochlea

Wire to sound processor

Sound processor

FIGHTING DEAFNESS

Modern microtechnology means that hearing aids have taken major steps forward with the development of tiny hearing aid shells called Deep Canal, MicroCanal, or CIC (completely-in-the-canal). The aids are inserted deep within the ear canal and have the ability to adjust automatically to compensate for varying noise conditions. They also need less power because of their nearness to the eardrum.

ARTIFICIAL SIGHT

Though "Jerry" is blind, he can walk around chairs, through doorways, and read letters at a distance thanks to special glasses equipped with a small digital camera and rangefinder. These send fast-updated images as electronic signals to a computer on his waist. This processes the signals and feeds them along wires that pass through his skin and skull directly to the visual cortex of the brain, which is where nerve impulses from the eyes are normally processed. The signals pass to the brain via 68 platinum electrodes.

Wires taking signals to brain

Digital camera

Implanted electrodes

Wires from waist minicomputer

MAGIC MICROCHIPS

Microchip implants are now being used to provide artificial retinas for the eyes, mainly using CCDs (charge couple devices) of the kind installed in video camcorders. What they do is to detect light rays, turning them into a pattern of electronic signals. These are fed through ultra-fine implanted electrodes into the retinal ganglion, or optic nerve fibers that lead to the visual centers of the brain. In another system, a retinal encoder outside the eye has the job of detecting light rays and processing them. Converted into electromagnetic waves, these are sent to a retinal stimulator that is physically implanted in the eye, sending signals direct to the brain.

MAMMOTH OPERATION

In 2000, Edouard Herriot Hospital in Lyons, France, saw the world's first successful double-hand transplant operation. The operation, which took 17 hours to complete, involved a 50-strong team of doctors, nurses, technicians, and surgeons, led by specialists Jean-Michel Dubernard and Earl Owen. The surgical procedures themselves were extremely complicated. Each part and tissue in the region of the forearm, including bones, muscles, tendons, nerves, and blood vessels, had to be connected separately. By the time he left hospital, the patient, Denis Chatelier, could wiggle his fingertips and his fingernails had started to grow. Two years before, the team had performed the first-ever single hand transplant on Australian Clint Hallam. Though the transplant was successful, the hand has not attained full dexterity.

SURGICAL SUCCESS
Denis Chatelier, the world's first double-hand transplant recipient, leaves hospital in Lyons in February 2000, holding his bandaged arms aloft to greet his wellwishers.

Culture of human skin

Protective clothing preserves sterility

Synthetic fibers

Cartilage tissue

ARTIFICIAL CARTILAGE

Growing replacement cartilage is a new medical technique, which eliminates the risk of tissue rejection. In it, artificial fibers form a template for cells that then grow and multiply to form new cartilage tissue.

LABORATORY REPLACEMENT

Tissue engineering uses a combination of artificial plasticlike fibers called biopolymers and real human cells, which are produced by genetic engineering or obtained from human embryos. The cells are treated to make them "think" that they are in a very early, developing embryo in the phase of growth called organogenesis, which occurs in nature during the first eight weeks after conception. What actually happens is that the cells are grown in the laboratory onto a biopolymer "scaffold" to give them a physical framework. Then, various chemicals, including special nutrients, can be added to stimulate and direct the course of cell development. As a result, the cells multiply and start to build their own tissue, such as skin or cartilage. This can be transplanted into the body, where the biopolymers naturally biodegrade, or dissolve away, leaving no traces behind. For their part, the cells continue to multiply, moving, shaping, or modeling their tissue, which then integrates naturally with the recipient's own tissues.

LOOKING TO THE FUTURE

The use of tissue-engineered skin was pioneered in the US in 1999 to treat people suffering from certain types of burns, ulcers, and other medical problems. The notion of smart bandaging was pioneered at the University of Glasgow, in Scotland. Substitute tendon, bone, and heart valve tissues are also being researched, while further down the line whole organs, such as kidneys, the liver, and even the heart, may be originated. Such part-living, part-synthetic spare parts are known medically as neoorgans. They do not use microchips, nor should they provoke rejection once they have been implanted. Such developments could help scientists achieve their goal of making sure no one should have to suffer for lack of a compatible implant.

Cut tendons on layers of bandage

Replacement tendon cells growing

Diagonal groove etched in bandage

SMART BANDAGING

When this biodegradable bandage is placed between a tendon's broken ends, the tiny diagonal grooves in it direct the growth of new tissue. When fully developed from its current experimental stage, the technology may supply templates for hip replacements and all kinds of other cell engineering projects.

El Niño and La Niña

ALSO REFERRED TO AS the El Niño-Southern Oscillation (ENSO) Cycle, El Niño and La Niña are extreme instances of the natural climate cycle of the tropical Pacific. Although scientists have been aware of the oscillation for several decades, the public has only become aware of its increasingly destructive effects in more recent years. These warm and cold seasonal variations occur due to interaction between the ocean surface, the atmosphere, and trade winds (general wind patterns). The resulting rise and fall in ocean temperature has been linked with severe weather conditions in parts of South America, Indonesia, and Australia. The cycle oscillates between warm (El Niño) to neutral or cold (La Niña) conditions every 3–7 years. Meteorologists use information provided by weather satellites in the prediction and tracking of these events, which have had a dramatic effect on climate patterns around the world since at least the last century. It is not known how the ENSO Cycle will be affected if the global climate grows warmer.

NORMAL CONDITIONS
Normally, southeasterly trade winds drive water westward across the equatorial South Pacific, causing warm surface water to form a deep pool near Indonesia. The Peru Current flows northward along the South American coast, and cold water wells up to the surface, carrying oxygen and nutrients that sustain fish and birds.

INTERPRETING INFORMATION

Weather forecasts in newspapers and on radio and television begin as observations. Thousands of surface stations on land and hundreds of weather ships at sea – many of them are fully automated – monitor visibility, air pressure, wind direction and speed, temperature, humidity, and the amount, type, and height of cloud. Together with information received from weather balloons and satellites, data is collated at weather centers to produce synoptic charts (see below). These enable meteorologists to prepare forecasts.

FORECAST PREPARATION

Center of low pressure   *Isobar*

SYNOPTIC WEATHER CHART

Trade winds slacken   *Cool water is suppressed*

Pacific

Ocean

Sea current changes direction and flows east

Warm surface water

EL NIÑO CONDITIONS
During an El Niño episode, trade winds slacken or even reverse. Warm surface water flows from west to east, increasing the depth of warm water off the South American coast. Heavy rainfall follows the warm water, leading to flooding in Peru and drought in parts of Indonesia and Australia.

EL NIÑO SEA CURRENTS
The normal sea current reverses and warm water forms a pool near South America. This pool suppresses the nutrient-rich water of the Peru Current and, starved of nutrients, fish and sea birds move away or die.

Trade winds drive warm water toward Asia

Current carries water westward

Cool water of Peru Current wells to the surface

Warm water

Pacific

Ocean

WEATHER SATELLITE
Five satellites in equally spaced geostationary orbits about 22,000 miles (35,400 km) above the equator, observe the whole of the Earth. They transmit data that is shared under the supervision of the World Meteorological Organization. Satellites in lower orbits pass over the poles every 90 minutes.

Casing encloses transmission equipment

South America

NORMAL SEA CURRENTS
Sea currents flow westward and carry warm water across the ocean. The body of water near South America remains relatively cool.

Pool of warm water grows larger and deeper

A tiny spark can cause fierce flames

LA NIÑA CONDITIONS
During a La Niña episode, trade winds strengthen and warm surface water accumulates in a deep pool near Asia. Rainfall follows the warm water, bringing heavy rain to parts of Australia and Indonesia. The upwelling of the Peru Current increases and cool water flows north and then west, flowing as a surface current part of the way across the ocean.

Pacific

Ocean

Trade winds strengthen

Cool surface water

South America

Cool ocean current

BUSH FIRE
El Niño episodes affect weather over a large area. They have been linked to droughts in Indonesia and Australia, where vegetation becomes so dry that the smallest spark can ignite it. The result is a fierce bush fire, as shown above.

Storm surge at high tide

Sea level rises due to low pressure

LA NIÑA SEA CURRENTS
The cold upwelling intensifies and sea-surface temperatures drop by up to 4°C. This brings nutrients and improves fishing across a wide area.

HURRICANE AND FLOODING
Hurricanes have been linked to La Niña episodes. As well as ferocious winds and torrential rain, hurricanes can cause coastal flooding. The sea level rises due to very low pressure, and strong winds drive water toward the shore. If the hurricane coincides with a high tide, the resulting storm surge can cause severe damage.

House of the future

SOHO TRANSFORMABLE APARTMENT
This Central London flat can be used as one large living space, or partitioned with freestanding boxes to provide bedrooms. It was designed by architect Mark Guard.

IN THE LAST FEW decades, the environmentally friendly or sustainable house has been associated with green enthusiasts who built homes to both blend in with the natural landscape and harness renewable energy resources. As we enter the new millennium, environmental concerns will become a matter of expediency. Architects, developers, and homeowners will be pressed to take a more pragmatic approach to where they build, and the more economic use of space and energy supplies. Extreme climates currently present architects with the greatest challenge in energy conservation. In urban areas, there is a growing trend for disused buildings that can be converted into housing, and for dwellings that can be easily adapted to accommodate different types of residents.

CONVERTED WATER TOWER
This structure on the outskirts of Antwerp, Belgium, was originally built in the early 20th century. It was converted into a dramatic and unusual dwelling by architect Jo Crepain in 1998.

Winter garden

Columns form main structure of house

Opaque glass

Platform of original tower

Drum where water originally collected

MEZZANINE VIEW
A mezzanine level in the base of the tower overlooks the living room and creates a cosy space for watching television. The natural, wooded setting of the tower is emphasized by the great expanse of glass.

TOP-FLOOR WINTER GARDEN
The use of buildings that were not originally intended for domestic purposes often results in an unconventional house layout. Here, rooms inside the glass-encased water tower are stacked on top of one other. The winter garden is located below the disused water drum.

INTERIOR OF THE BASE
The architect used the original structure to divide the concrete base of the tower. The sitting area is located at the rear, and the kitchen on the street front.

OYSTER HOUSE

Nigel Coates' Oyster House was the winning entry in the Concept House competition at the 1998 *Daily Mail* Ideal Home Exhibition in London. It was designed to provide a new model for the speculative home in a typical suburban community. With this design, Coates extended the idea of loft living to the family home. The ground floor is open plan with flexible partitions, enabling the living space to adapt as children grow up, and to incorporate friends, work, and guests. There are two staircases, which allow for separation and privacy upstairs. Each stairway leads to a bathroom, with a double bedroom on each side of the house.

EXTERIOR VIEW

INTERIOR VIEW OF GROUND FLOOR

MONOLITHIC WALLS

Among the most distinctive features of the Burnette house are its concrete walls with narrow glass slits. These walls filter the sun on the north and south walls, while the glass slits act as a giant sundial that charts the movement of the sun throughout the day.

Glass front of east elevation has low-emissivity surface

Narrow glass slit

East block contains living spaces

WENDELL BURNETTE HOUSE

This house and studio were built by the architect Wendell Burnette in 1995. The house is situated in a desert landscape on the west face of the Phoenix Mountain Preserve in Arizona. Burnette's innovative design takes a truly inspired approach to environmental concerns. It proposes imaginative solutions to both the extreme desert climate, and the existence of unsightly housing in the surrounding area.

Fully shaded evaporative pool

Internal court divides living area and studio

Carport

Stairway to terrace

MICROCLIMATE IN THE INTERNAL COURT

Burnette's inspiration for a water-cooling system was drawn from the naturally occurring "canyon seats" or springs found in the Arizona desert. Here, his water-cooled internal court supports a lush microclimate at the entrance to the house, and divides the east and west blocks. A fully shaded evaporative pool located below the studio floor overflows into a trough. Water runs down the natural slope of the site, cooling the internal court and improving ventilation throughout the house.

Airbus A3XX

A DOUBLE-DECKER AIRLINER with up to 1,000 seats is the response of Airbus Industrie, the European aircraft manufacturer, to the ever-growing global demand for air travel. The number of airline passengers is rising by an estimated five percent every year, which means that the number of people traveling by air will double in 15 years and nearly triple in 20. Many existing airways, however, are already congested, while most major airports are struggling to cope with existing traffic levels. There is also environmental opposition to further expansion. The A3XX is intended to resolve the dilemma by carrying many more passengers in far fewer aircraft.

FLIGHT EFFICIENCY
The A3XX will burn up to 20 percent less fuel per passenger than the Boeing 747-400, thus reducing pollution in the upper atmosphere. The giant new engines being designed for the new super-jumbo are more fuel- and weight-efficient.

Economy seats on upper deck

Electrically-controlled flaps

Economy seats on lower deck

Business-class seats on upper deck

255 ft (80 m) wing span

Fuel tanks

Cargo deck

First-class seats on main deck

New engines reduce weight and lower fuel consumption

BIGGER AND BETTER
Massive development costs and uncertainty about demand deterred other major aircraft manufacturers like Boeing from going ahead with similar plans, while some airlines argued that, to make air-travel pay, what was needed were fewer passengers paying more, rather than more paying less. Nevertheless, Airbus expects to sell at least 650 aircraft by 2020.

AIRLINER EVOLUTION
Passenger air travel started to take off in the mid-1930s with the introduction of aircraft like the Douglas DC-3, with its revolutionary retractable undercarriage. Long-haul flight began with flying boats and entered the jet age with the De Havilland Comet.

CHINA CLIPPER
1936

STRATOCRUISER
1947

| 1930 | 1940 | 1950 |

JUNKER JU52
1933

DOUGLAS DC-3
1936

COMET 1
1949

FLYING IN STYLE
Carrying more passengers does not necessarily mean reducing leg room, as this mock-up of the A3XX's upper deck Business Class cabin demonstrates. Other amenities, such as beds and exercise machines, are planned for the main deck.

Galleys and other passenger facilities

COCKPIT TECHNOLOGY
The A3XX's cockpit, located between the two passenger decks, features eight large interactive screens. Along with other data, they will show pictures from external cameras, so the pilots can monitor what is going on during taxiing.

Wide stairs make deck access easy

FASTER AND FARTHER

For decades, aircraft manufacturers and aerospace researchers have been working on plans to produce a bigger successor to the supersonic Concorde which would be commercially viable and, at the same time, environmentally acceptable. To be cost-effective, it has to carry 300 passengers more than 6,215 miles (10,000 km) at twice the speed of sound with halved per-passenger fuel consumption. To satisfy environmentalists, it would also be essential to eliminate the sonic boom that restricts Concorde's maximum-speed operation to over the ocean. Assuming the design gets the final go-ahead, Airbus estimates that the aircraft could be in worldwide passenger service by the 2020s.

JOINT EFFORT
French, British, and German aerospace companies pooled research to produce plans for the new supersonic airliner. It could carry up to 300 passengers across the Pacific in a few hours.

TOO FAR, TOO FAST
Boeing abandoned work on its variable-geometry 2707 as a result of technical problems and consequent cost overruns. These led to a withdrawal of official support for the project.

BOEING 707
1954

BOEING 747
1969

SUPER CONCORDE
2010

1960   1970   1980   1990   2000   2010

CONCORDE
1969

AIRBUS A3XX
2005

Tilting trains

SWEDISH TILTING TRAIN (1990)

ALTHOUGH TILTING TRAINS have been in use since the 1960s, it is only recent technological developments that have been able to prevent much of the passenger discomfort caused by cornering at high speeds. As a train goes into a curve, it produces substantial centrifugal force toward the outside of the curve. By tilting the train (the equivalent of leaning into a curve on a bicycle), this centrifugal force is balanced by a force into the inner curve, and passenger discomfort is reduced. Current computer-controlled active tilting systems operate from self-steering trucks (the wheeled undercarriage of the train). Improvements in design enhance the operation of the train by reducing track forces, and radial self-steering trucks with "soft" suspension have been introduced. Modern tilting trains allow operators to achieve higher speeds on existing curved routes without costly track improvements or the need to consider completely new high-speed lines.

NORMAL TRAIN CARRIAGE

Centrifugal force pushes the car contents toward the outside of the curve

CENTRIFUGAL FORCE

As the train enters the curve, a strong centrifugal force is produced

Banking is limited to 6°

NORMAL TRAIN ON CURVE
The normal train is "banked" slightly and slows as it goes into the bend, but the car body does not tilt.

Fiat's Pendolino – "Little Pendulum" – tilting train

PENDOLINO
Fiat's Pendolino is the prototype for most recent European tilting trains. The French tilting train shown in the main diagram (opposite) will be based on similar technology.

Train approaches at an angle

Track

Strong sideways force outward

STIFF-WHEEL AXLES
The inability of the axles to move means that high forces are taken by the axles themselves and then by the track.

Axle

HIGH-SPEED TRAINS

The Japanese pioneered modern high-speed rail travel with their *Shinkansen* (High-Speed Line) trains, which entered service in 1964. On a special new line between Tokyo and Osaka, they achieved speeds of up to 130 mph (210 km/h). The line was reserved for high-speed trains, so there was no slower moving, conflicting traffic to interfere with operations. The latest Bullet Train, *Nozomi*, pictured here, has also broken speed records. Since the early 1980s, similar trains have been developed in France, intitially running between Paris and Lyon and, like the Japanese train, running on priority "dedicated" tracks. German Railways have also developed high-speed links since 1991.

Pantograph to collect electric current

Single-level passenger cabin

Driver's cab has streamlined profile

TILTING TRAIN CARRIAGE

Force produced by train's tilting motion

SIDEWAYS FORCE

Reduced forces lead to less disturbance

CENTRIFUGAL FORCE

Passenger suffers less discomfort

Force is reduced by tilt of car body

Car body can tilt up to 8°

Air suspension units

Wheel axles respond individually to curves, adopting a radial attitude

Forces on track are reduced

Pneumatic suspension

RADIALLY SELF-STEERING WHEEL AXLES
These axles reduce the greater track forces produced by the higher speeds.

Truck frame

Sprung wheel sets

Hydraulic system tilts car body on receiving signals from detector/ computer

Track still banked to angle of 6°

Axle

Track

TILTING TRAIN ON CURVE

Signals from an accelerometer that measures train speed and curvature are analyzed by a computer, which tilts the individual cars as the first car goes into the curve. This active passenger-car tilting minimizes the passengers' discomfort and allows higher speeds (up to 30 percent) on traditional tracks. A tilt of eight degrees will compensate for 70 percent of the centrifugal forces.

Electronic signal/speed detection equipment in train nose

BULLET TRAIN
The train can carry 1,324 passengers and features 64 separate traction motors, each producing 285kw of power. The body shells are made of aluminum alloy.

RECORD BREAKER
The latest prototype Bullet Train has reached speeds of 214 mph (345 km/h), but the French TGV holds the world railspeed record of 320 mph (515 km/h).

Electric Car / Le Shuttle

IN 1995, PEUGEOT LAUNCHED their first electrically powered vehicle designed for the private motorist – the Peugeot 106 Electric. Unlike conventional gas-driven cars, the electric car has the advantage of being a "zero emission" vehicle that does not pollute or damage the environment. Other advantages include an engine that is durable, quiet, and mechanically almost trouble-free. With a top speed of 56 mph (90 km/h) and a capacity of 50 miles (80 km) per battery, the 106 Electric goes a long way toward overcoming the customary disadvantages of the electric car (low speeds and short range of distance), which had limited its use to specific commercial applications. This new vehicle represents a significant step towards the development of an alternative to petrol-driven cars. Other "zero-emission" vehicles, such as solar-powered cars (top right), are still in the experimental stages of development.

THE PEUGEOT 106 ELECTRIC
After a series of trials held throughout France, the Peugeot 106 Electric went on sale to the public. Using the body of an existing Peugeot model, it looks no different to other cars and is suited to motorists who use their vehicles for short urban journeys.

THE BATTERY
The 20-battery pack has a combined acceleration rate of 30 mph (0–50 km/h) in 8.3 seconds, a top speed of 56 mph (90 km/h) and a maximum mileage of 50 miles (80 km).

RECHARGING
The battery can be recharged from any 220v/16-amp socket. It takes up to 6 hours to fully recharge the battery, at a rate of 1 hour for every 12.5 miles (20 km).

Block of 11 batteries

Tinted electric window

Wheel shaft

Fiberglass body

Connector for charge plug

Connects to 220v/16-amp socket

Plugs into connector on side of car

THE CHARGING PLUG

SOLAR-POWERED CARS

Solar power is an even better solution to the problem of air pollution than is the electric car. It represents a renewable source of energy and, unlike fossil fuels, can be generated without seriously depleting the world's finite resources. Solar-powered vehicles have external solar cell panels that can absorb sunlight and convert its energy into electricity. This prototype of a solar-powered racing car, the "Swatchmobile," was recently developed in Switzerland by the Biel Engineering School.

THE "SWATCHMOBILE"

SHUTTLE SERVICE
Since Spring 1995, cars and heavy freight vehicles have been able to travel between England and France through the Channel Tunnel. The train that transports them, at speeds of up to 100 mph (160 km/h), is "Le Shuttle."

Wagon containing cars — Service tunnel — Running tunnel

Le Shuttle car train — Eurostar passenger train

LOADING THE CARS
Cars are loaded onto enclosed wagons at terminals in Folkestone, England, and Coquelles, France. Once inside, the drivers and the passengers stay with their vehicles for the duration of the 35-minute journey under the Channel.

CROSS-SECTION OF THE TUNNEL
Construction of the 32 mile- (51.8 km-) long tunnels housing the rail link was completed in 1994. They are lined with reinforced concrete rings and equipped with complex draining, cooling, and ventilation systems.

Cars — Main lighting — Handrail

Cooling water pipes — Drains — Evacuation walkway

Cooling system

Box containing 3 batteries

Electric motor

Electrical unit

Fun

Radiator

Drive shaft

Batteries stored below

Record breakers

JUST AFTER DAWN on March 21, 1999, after an epic flight lasting 19 days, 21 hours, and 47 minutes, a silvery balloon as tall as an 18-story building floated down to make its landing in the Sahara. It had won the race to become the first balloon to fly around the world. Piloting Breitling Orbiter 3 were Bertrand Piccard from Switzerland and Brian Jones from England. Lifting off from the Swiss Alps, they had flown south to the Sahara to pick up the powerful jet streams they needed for their onward journey. This required a measure of luck as well as piloting skills – Piccard and Jones had to avoid no-fly zones and locate new jet streams – but fortune was with them. Precisely at 9.54 GMT on March 20, the two fliers crossed the longitude that ran through their starting point; the next day, with their last tank of propane – the gas that powered the balloon's burners – nearly empty, they touched down at the landing site that had been prepared for them just outside the Egyptian town of Mut.

INFLATION
Nonflammable helium is held in a cell in the upper part of the balloon, within an outer skin of Mylar plastic. The air in the cone-shaped area beneath the helium cell is heated by a battery of burners mounted on the crew capsule. The fuel used is propane, supplied by cylinders strapped to the sides of the capsule.

Supporting gantry

Observation blister

Pressurized capsule

Cooking facilities

Navigational equipment

Pilot position

Burner flames heat air to make balloon rise

Burners

Air recycling equipment

Toilet

Bed with special insulating cover

Gas cylinders

THE CABIN
Pressurizing the cabin meant that the crew could fly safely at up to 49,000 feet (13,000 m). The air in the cabin was constantly recycled, with fresh oxygen being added and carbon dioxide removed via a hydroxide filter.

THRUST SSC

On October 15, 1997, British Royal Air Force pilot Andy Green smashed the existing world land speed record in the aptly-named Thrust SSC (SuperSonic Car) on the broad expanse of the Black Rock Desert in Nevada. His average speed over the two runs was 763 mph (1227.985 km/h). The car's power came from two Rolls-Royce Spey jet engines, which developed a thrust equal to that of 140 Formula 1 Grand Prix racers.

OVER THE ALPS
Even high over the Alps, the cabin temperature was kept at about 53° F (15°C). Power for vital instruments was provided by batteries recharged by solar power. The crew's link to ground control was through Inmarsat satellites, while Global Positioning Satellites (GPS) helped to pinpoint their position to within a few feet.

UNDERSEA ADVENTURE
US oceanographer Robert Ballard holds the record for the number of explorations he has led to probe the ocean's depths. Using state-of-the-art submersibles, he discovered the wreck of the legendary liner *Titanic* (*right*). In 2000, he embarked on a quest to discover the real location of Noah's ark.

Helium balloon in upper "tent"

Vent

Decompression valves

Insulating outer skin

Helium cell

ORBITER ESSENTIALS
The 180-foot (55-m) high Oribiter is as tall as the Leaning Tower of Pisa when fully inflated, but, with a takeoff weight of 8 tons, it weighs only as much as a modern jet fighter. From takeoff to landing during its voyage around the world, the balloon and its two-man crew traveled a total of 28,415 miles (45,720 km) at an average altitude of 22,274 feet (7,000 m).

Rising hot air cone

180 ft
55m

Rip panel

THE BALLOON
The Orbiter's design is known as a Roziere, after the first human ever to fly in a balloon. This was the Frenchman Jean Pilatre de Rozier, in 1783. It was he who first conceived the notion of combining the advantages of gas and hot-air balloons – the one offering greater buoyancy, the other greater flexibility.

Burners

TOUCH DOWN
With only four fuel tanks left out of 32, it was touch and go whether Piccard and Jones would cross the Atlantic safely. Luckily, they picked up a steady jet stream, and in the early hours of March 20, crossed the African coast. Soon, they crossed the line of longitude that marked the official end of their circumnavigation, flying on for a few more hours to reach their final landing site.

Gas cylinders

AROUND THE WORLD
It was not all plain sailing for the two-man crew. Flying south to the Sahara, their effective starting line, consumed precious fuel, and they had to avoid no-fly zones in Yemen, Egypt, and China. They sometimes lost the jet streams as well, relying on computer modeling of weather patterns at ground control in Geneva to predict where and when other jet streams might occur.

Raising Alexandria

IN NOVEMBER 1996, the stunning revelation was made that marine archaeologists had discovered remains of the vanished royal quarter of the ancient city of Alexandria. Founded by Alexander the Great in 331BC, Alexandria was a celebrated center of culture and learning in ancient times, as well as the scene of legendary events involving Cleopatra, Mark Antony, and the Caesars. The discovery was made just 20–26 ft (6–8 m) under the Mediterranean Sea on the eastern side of modern Alexandria's harbor. A team of 16 divers made 3,500 dives over a period of four months and discovered some 9,000 blocks and pieces, including material from pavements, quays, columns, and statues. Using a satellite-based global positioning system (GPS), the team mapped out a two-acre area. Selected finds were then hoisted to the surface using air-filled balloons and cables lowered by cranes. Among the pieces raised were portions of the mighty Pharos lighthouse, once the tallest building on earth and one of the Seven Wonders of the ancient world.

MAP OF ALEXANDRIA HARBOR
(ANCIENT CITY IN RED)

MARINE ENCRUSTATION
Underwater archaeologists often remove marine encrustation from material while it is still on the seabed. Here, the diver begins the task of uncovering an engraved stone.

Specially adapted underwater scraping tool

A huge concave mirror reflected light up to 31 miles (50 km) out to sea

Airlift hose

The total height of the building was 384 ft (117 m)

The lighthouse was covered in white marble

RECONSTRUCTION OF PHAROS LIGHTHOUSE
Although the lighthouse was toppled by an earthquake in the 14th century, it is possible to combine historical information with the results of the search campaign to render three-dimensional computer images of its structure.

AIRLIFT HOSE
Among the specialized equipment used in the project was this airlift hose. Here, the sand is sucked away to unearth a magnificent sphinx statue.

MEASURING ON SITE
The puzzle of the sunken city was pieced together without the excavation of every find. The team precisely drew and measured material on site, before transferring the information to computer.

The diver records the exact dimensions of the find

Scale bar

Two-ton
sphinx

Block
inscribed with
hieroglyphics

Underwater
breathing
apparatus

Rose granite
statue head

POSITIONING THE HARNESS
Using harness equipment, the
diver prepares this statue head
for removal to the surface.

*This 1.5-ton head
completes the statue
of the Ptolemy king*

THE STATUE OF THE PTOLEMY KING
The colossal bust of the Ptolemy king is
one of the great discoveries of sunken
Alexandria. The dynasty ruled Egypt
from the death of Alexander the Great
(323BC) until the death of Cleopatra (30BC).

FROM WATER TO DRY LAND
The mighty granite bust is hoisted clear
of the water and transported to the dock
using cables lowered from a crane.

SECURING THE STATUE
Even when stationary on the dock, the
priceless statue must be kept carefully
secured with sturdy ropes and cables.

EXAMINING THE STONE
Before the process of desalinization
takes place, archaeologists make an
initial examination of the stone's surface.

Rebuilding Berlin

THE WALL THAT DIVIDED EAST AND WEST BERLIN

SINCE THE BERLIN WALL'S FALL in November 1989, the capital of newly reunified Germany has been architecturally transformed, with particular concentration on East Berlin, where Communist restrictions had left large areas dilapidated. In the city's center, many of the world's great architects have been at work: outstanding buildings there include Nicholas Grimshaw's Stock Exchange, Jean Nouvell's Gallerie Lafayette store complex, Daniel Libeskind's Jewish Museum, Zaha Hadid's apartments, and, above all, Sir Norman Foster's Reichstag, with its huge glass dome.

THE BRANDENBURG TOR

Built in 1791 as a triumphal arch to celebrate Prussia's military prowess, the Brandenburg Tor saw many national celebrations up to World War II, including the parade of the *Das Reich* division to celebrate its victorious return from France in 1940. Following the war, however, particularly after the building of the Wall, which left it standing in the no-man's land between west and east, the Brandenburg Tor became the symbol of a divided city. Now, Berliners again see it as a token of German unity.

THE BRANDENBURG TOR AT NIGHT

THE REICHSTAG REBORN
Sir Norman Foster's plans, which won the international competition held to find an architect for the new building, were based on his respect for Paul Wallot's original 1894 design. The focal point is the huge circular debating chamber, which sits under the building's dome.

REBUILDING THE REICHSTAG
During the years that Berlin was sliced in half by the Wall, the ruined Reichstag found itself stranded. Although physically just inside the Western sector, it was virtually isolated from the rest of the city by the Spree River, the Wall, and the vast central parkland of the Tiergarten. Once the wall came down, however, the crumbling building regained its symbolic importance, especially after Berlin's confirmation as Germany's new capital.

Reichstag

The Brandenburg Tor

Potsdamer Platz

CITY CENTER
The Reichstag stands in the heart of Berlin, close to the Brandenburg Tor with Potsdamer Platz a little farther away. The original Reichstag was the German parliament's meeting place until 1933, when the interior was destroyed in an arson attack, leaving just the shell behind.

UNDER THE DOME

The new Reichstag's 1990s refurbishment and rebuilding is truly awesome and inspired in scale. Its crowning glory, the huge glass dome, which Sir Norman Foster intended as a symbol of the open nature of German democracy, gives native Berliners and visitors to the city alike the chance to watch politicians at work. Construction started in summer 1995 and was completed in 1999.

Ventilation chimney

Angled mirrors reflect light

Shiny reflective fabric

Seating for members of the parliament

WRAPPING THE REICHSTAG

In June 1995, after two decades of planning and lobbying, the conceptual artists Christo and his wife Jeanne-Claude "wrapped" the old Reichstag building in fabric. By July 8, when the process of dismantling started, an estimated 2 million people had visited the site. The wrapping, according to the artists, got rid of the dark ghosts of the past, while the unwrapping symbolized people's hopes for a new, brighter future.

POTSDAMER PLATZ

A glittering center for fashionable Berliners during the 1920s, Potsdamer Platz became a virtual wasteland as a result of devastating Allied bombing raids in World War II and the area's neglect during the decades of division that followed. Once the Berlin Wall that ran through the square finally toppled, however, Potsdamer Platz was soon well on the way to regaining much of its former glory. Working to an overall masterplan conceived by the Italian architect Renzo Piano, the area became Europe's greatest construction site. Its eye-catching, stylish buildings included imposing corporate headquarters for a string of leading multinational companies, such as Daimler-Benz and Sony. Embedded at the roots of these great towers is a sparkling new subway station delivering visitors to a vast shopping mall, which itself has proved to be a huge public attraction. The complex also houses a massive IMAX theater, 30 restaurants, a casino, and a concert hall.

SONY BUILDING

Work on the headquarters building for Sony Europe was finished in 1999. As well as 26 floors of office space, it contains entertainment centers and a multiplex cinema. Designed by architect Helmut Jahn, it is just one of the many elements that are transforming the Berlin skyline.

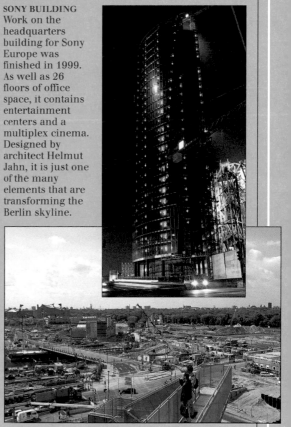

EUROPE'S BIGGEST CONSTRUCTION SITE

Construction work gets into full swing in the heart of Potsdamer Platz, as a new city quarter of 19 massive buildings starts to take shape. Planning the building program for the area began in the early 1990s, shortly after the fall of the Berlin Wall, which, since 1961, had been a mini Iron Curtain, separating East Berlin from the west.

Kansai Airport

AERIAL VIEW OF KANSAI

OPEN FOR BUSINESS since 4 September 1994, Kansai International Airport (KIX) is one of only two artificial structures visible from space – the other is the Great Wall of China. The purpose of this project was to build Japan's first 24-hour international airport, in order to respond to the increased demand for air transport not only in Kansai but in the whole of the country. Three mountains in the southeastern part of Japan's Osaka Bay had to be leveled to provide the landmass, and transport bridges from the harbor 3 miles (5 km) away also had to be built. The cost and constructional difficulties of this ambitious undertaking were outweighed by the ideal of an isolated flight-site with future expansion possibilities and without the need for noise restrictions. Although the island is fully operational, this is only the end of Phase 1. Plans for Phase 2 include increasing the size of the island and adding a further two runways.

Each year, the runway handles 160,000 takeoffs and landings

Taxiing area

Passenger boarding bridge

Check-in points

The roof comprises 90,000 stainless-steel panels – all identical in size

CROSS-SECTION OF THE TERMINAL
In the cross-section above, the aerodynamic shape of the terminal building's roof is clearly defined. Italian architect Renzo Piano developed this design to combat the local hazard – hurricanes. The central terminal uses a tiered system, which allows passengers quick and easy transfers between flights.

The island measures ¼ x 2¾ miles (1.25 x 4.37 km)

The transport bridge from the mainland has a six-lane highway and a two-way rail link

AIR CIRCULATION
This computer-rendered image illustrates the gentle, aerodynamic curve of the building's roof. This design is echoed on the ceiling inside the building, allowing the fresh air, introduced through vents, to move around freely.

**AERIAL VIEW OF
AIRPORT SITE**

Control
tower

Terminal
building

The rail line
from the mainland
runs right up to the
terminal building

Airplane
parking bays

Air foil-
shaped
wing

THE CONTROL TOWER
The roof of the terminal building is low enough for the control tower
to have a clear view of the airplanes' tails, while its shape means that
maximum use can be made of the island for taxiing and for the runway.

DEPARTURE AREA
The terminal building is supported by
900 steel columns. These are repeatedly
adjusted by computer-controlled
hydraulic jacks, which compensate
for continual site settlement.

The two departure
area "wings" are
identical in length

Phase 2 will see the
island's area increase
from 511 to 1,380
hectares (1,263 to
3,410 acres)

Railway
line

Pont de Normandie

THE PONT DE NORMANDIE, which spans the estuary of the Seine River, was officially opened in January 1995. Built using state-of-the-art engineering, this stunning cable-stayed bridge is the longest of its kind in the world. Its central span, measuring 2,808 ft (856 m), crosses the estuary at 170.6 ft (52 m) above water level to enable shipping traffic to pass beneath it. The team of engineers, led by Michel Virlogeux of the French road administration, SETRA, designed every aspect of the bridge to withstand fierce coastal winds, which can reach 112 mph (180 km/h). Carrying an average of 6,000 vehicles a day, the bridge cuts 31 miles (50 km) from the journey between Le Havre and Honfleur, and forms part of "The Road of the Estuaries" motorway project, designed to link Belgium with Spain.

THE FOUNDATION

At the foundation of each tower are 28 piles, bored to a depth of between 164–197 ft (50–60 m). Layers of clay and large boulders caused major problems during construction.

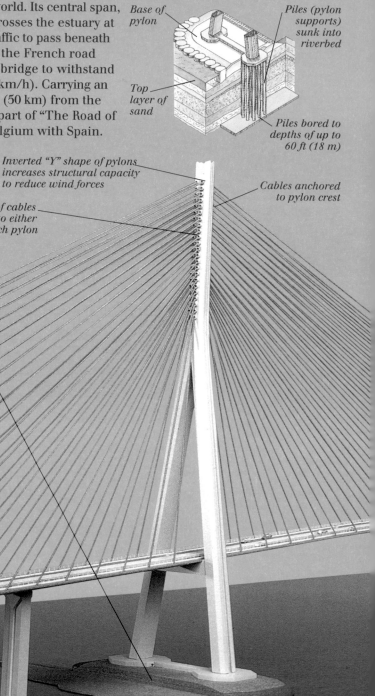

Base of pylon

Piles (pylon supports) sunk into riverbed

Top layer of sand

Piles bored to depths of up to 60 ft (18 m)

CABLE-STAYED BRIDGE DESIGN

The deck of cable-stayed bridges is supported by straight cables attached to both sides of one or more towers (pylons). The side spans may have additional suport from piers. One of the reasons why this design was chosen is because the marshy banks of the Seine estuary could not support the huge anchorage needed for a suspension bridge.

Inverted "Y" shape of pylons increases structural capacity to reduce wind forces

Cables anchored to pylon crest

23 pairs of cables attached to either side of each pylon

Artificial island created to support northern shore pylon

4 lanes of traffic

Piers support side spans

DESIGN OF THE VEHICLE DECK

The deck is aerodynamic in design, tapering at either edge. It is made of reinforced concrete, covering the outer sectional steel box-girders of the central span. This streamlined design reduced the weight and increased the stability of the Pont de Normandie, enabling it to exceed other cable-stayed bridges by 40 percent.

75 ft (23 m) wide vehicle deck

Tapered edges minimize the force of wind

10 ft (3 m) deep

Steel box-girder

Aerodynamic design was developed for the construction of the first Severn Bridge in the UK

BASIC PRINCIPLES OF BRIDGE ENGINEERING

BEAM (OR GIRDER) BRIDGE
The most basic bridge type has compression (pushing together) and tension (pulling apart) balanced within a single rigid beam, or girder, supported at each end.

ARCH BRIDGE
As heavy loads put all the material of an arch into compression, the forces have to be channeled downward and outward into the supporting abutments.

CANTILEVER BRIDGE
This develops the principle of the beam bridge by using balanced supports that extend and rise from both sides of the piers, attached to the central span.

SUSPENSION BRIDGE
This type of bridge principally exploits tension. The deck is hung from hanger cables or chains that are draped over the towers and anchored at each end.

BRIDGE DIMENSIONS

2,810 ft (856 m) from pylon to pylon

2,047 ft (624 m) steel box-girder

7,025 ft (2141.25 m) length of entire bridge

Aerodynamic vehicle deck

Ships can pass beneath the deck, which is 170 ft (52 m) above water level

Southern shore pylon

23 pairs of cables

THE CABLES
Each one of the 184 cables is made up of between 30 and 51 steel strands. The cables are protected from corrosion by polypropylene sheaths. Designed to prevent the collection of rain droplets, they also create additional wind resistance.

Guggenheim, Bilbao

AT THE BEGINNING OF the 20th century, modern architects hailed the coming of a new "age of the machine" when buildings would become as innovative as the most technically advanced cars, ships, and planes. As we enter the new millennium, computer technology, rather than engineering, is having the most impact on the form of buildings and the way that they are used. The fantastic curves and fractured planes of Frank Gehry's Guggenheim Museum in Bilbao, Spain (1997) would have been impossible to realize without the aid of computers in the design and construction processes. Technology has allowed the architect to realize what is, effectively, an enormous sculpture. Like an artist, Gehry made models out of sheets of paper and tape, which were then translated on screen into working drawings for the building's construction. Not all futuristic architectural designs have a sculptural look. Sir Norman Foster's proposal for the Millennium Tower in Tokyo, Japan (1989) brings together all the features of a city in one megastructure that was to be the highest in the world.

MILLENNIUM TOWER
In contrast to the sculptural curves of the Guggenheim, the complex structure of Sir Norman Foster's proposal for the Millennium Tower resembles a rocket.

"Sky centers" were to house public areas

GUGGENHEIM MUSEUM
Los Angeles architect Frank Gehry is well known for his striking and inventive creations. For Bilbao, he has designed a truly iconic building that now represents the city on postcards and in photographs around the world. The decision to locate the Guggenheim Foundation's modern art collection in Bilbao was part of a conscious attempt by the authorities to revitalize the city.

GUGGENHEIM ANIMATED MODEL
Gehry's office used a computer program called CATIA to construct onscreen models that could be worked on in an animated form.

COMPUTER RENDERING
Geometric mathematical formulas were used to define each of the building's surfaces and elements.

MONUMENTAL FISH SCULPTURE

The monumental fish sculpture was designed by Gehry's practice for a hotel in Barcelona, Spain. It was the first structure the office completed using the CATIA program, a specialized computer application developed by the French aeronautical industry. Like the Guggenheim Museum, the fish sculpture was developed directly on screen from a model. It also has a curvilinear surface with metal cladding. The CATIA computer model was the principal reference for its development, and there was little need for traditional architectural or technical drawings. The program enabled the 180 ft- (55 m-) long and 115 ft- (35 m-) high sculpture to be designed and built in just over eight months.

Curvilinear surface

CATIA COMPUTER MODEL

Exposed structure   *Metal cladding*

WATERFRONT MONUMENT
For many years, Frank Gehry has explored movement in architecture, often using fishlike shapes. Located on the waterfront, this sculpture may also be a reference to Barcelona as a port city.

The structure crowning the museum resembles an artichoke heart

The titanium sheets were milled on site

A slight pillow effect softens the appearance of the building

INTERIOR VESTIBULE
The large central atrium connects the main entrance with three floors of galleries via a system of curvilinear bridges, glass elevators, and stair towers. A soaring space over 164 ft (50 m) high, it has a sculptural roof with forms that have been likened to the billowing shapes of Marilyn Monroe's skirt.

Olympics 2000

To PROVIDE A FITTINGLY MODERN setting for the 24th Olympiad – the first Olympic Games of the new millennium – Sydney created a feast of inspired architecture in a lavish building program that took the city firmly into the 21st century. More than a dozen dazzling new stadiums and sporting venues formed the core of Australia's largest-ever urban renewal project, which, by the time it was completed, had rescued Homebush Bay and the area around it from near dereliction. The catalyst for the development was the city's successful 1995 bid to host the Olympics and the identification of Homebush Bay as the ideal setting for many of the events. It was within easy reach of the city center, had good water as well as road access, and was large enough to accommodate all the varied facilities that a successful modern Olympic staging demands. It also gave Australians the opportunity to develop world-class expertise in the reclamation of decaying industrial sites in an ambitious drive to stage what were claimed to be the first "green" Olympic Games.

Baseball Stadium *Sydney Showground* *Aquatic Center* *Athletics Center*

Multi-Use Arena *Stadium Australia*

STADIUM AUSTRALIA
Designed to accommodate 110,000 spectators, Stadium Australia is the largest outdoor venue in Olympic history. It is distinguished by its pair of lightweight flanking "wings" arching up over the long sides of the auditorium. Suspended from these, the roof is covered in translucent polycarbonate to shield spectators from the harsh sun, while still allowing natural light to filter through into the stadium below.

KEEPING IT GREEN
Stadium Australia was designed by Bligh Lobb Sports Architecture to conform to the Sydney Olympics brief of being as ecologically sensitive as possible. All the building materials were selected for their green qualities. Much use was made of natural light, while all back-up lighting conformed to energy-efficient green standards.

FROM WEST AND EAST

Two new sports - Triathlon and Taekwondo - made their official Olympic debuts at Sydney 2000. Triathlon is an exciting multievent sport involving swimming, cycling and running; it is a continuous race against the clock and fellow competitor. The origins of the sport date back to around 1974 in southern California, when a group of runners, swimmers, and cyclists began to train together. Taekwondo, a martial art from Korea, can trace its origins as far back as 37 B.C. Today, it is one of the world's fastest-growing participation sports.

TRIATHLON

TAEKWONDO

Floodlight tower

Permanent grandstand

Temporary open Olympic grandstand

Supporting wing

Bars, restaurants, and other facilities

Access to enclosed concourses for each seating tier

Pedestrian walkway around stadium

DUNC GRAY VELODROME
Another simple, but stunning, design was produced to house the Olympic cycling events, which took place in the western Sydney suburb of Bankstown. The metal roof of the velodrome has glazed central skylights equipped with light-control slats to allow in optimum natural light, while rainwater from the roof is fed into a pond alongside. Inside, surrounding the Baltic pine banked cycling track, is permanent seating for 5,000 spectators. The stadium is named after the famous cyclist who won the country's first gold medal in cycling at the Los Angeles Olympics of 1932.

INSIDE THE STADIUM
Stadium Australia is already in use, hosting prestigious sports events. One of the features of the design is the ability to alter the seating configuration easily. After the Olympics are over, for instance, the open grandstands are to be dismantled and seating capacity cut to 80,000.

Translucent roof reducing glare and shadow

Lower seating bowl

Temporary open Olympic grandstand

Roof-mounted solar cells generate power

ARCHERY CENTER
Although one of the smallest stadiums at the 2000 Olympics, the Archery Center in Homebush Bay is one of the most delightful. A simple rectangular building was offset by a large "fly roof" – a tilted wing held at an angle on inclined column supports. The beautiful sweep of the roof is a modern interpretation of Australian vernacular shelters and provided welcome shade for the building and spectators. The center was designed by architecture practice Stutchbury & Pape.

OLYMPIC VILLAGE
Sydney's Olympic Village is the first urban community in the world to be totally solar-powered. Its roof-mounted solar cells have the capacity to generate more than 1 million kilowatt hours of electric power a year. With accommodation for 15,300 athletes and officials, this is the first time that all the participants in the Olympics have been housed on one site.

Global telecommunications

CONSTELLATIONS OF LOW-ORBITING satellites hold the key to today's flexible global telephone networks. These systems integrate satellite communications with existing land-line and cellular networks to provide truly global coverage from a mobile phone. This enables people in remote areas, even those on tiny Pacific islands or high in the Himalayas, to keep in touch with the rest of the world. Satellite systems are the next logical step in the mobile-phone revolution that swept the world in the late 1990s. Iridium® was the first system to offer a commercial service. It was conceived and developed by the US electronics company Motorola, and began operation on 1 November 1998. The system was named after the 77th chemical element in the Periodic Table, as there were originally to be 77 satellites in the network. Other networks offering a similar service include Globalstar, which operates with a constellation of 48 satellites.

Communication aerial receieves and transmits signals

IRIDIUM HANDSET
Early satellite phones required briefcase-sized units to receive and process signals from communication satellites. The Iridium handset has similar features to a conventional mobile phone but is slightly larger in size. It is also more expensive to purchase and operate but, unlike an ordinary mobile phone, can be used in any location on Earth.

LCD display panel

Lightweight main body

Processing unit

Satellite sends signal to ground-based gateway

Gateway connects with land-line system

IRIDIUM SATELLITE ORBITAL NETWORK
The Iridium network consists of 66 satellites, each providing a coverage of 6 million square miles (16 million square km). It offers a constant service, as there will always be one or more satellites over the horizon. Thenetwork operates as a constellation, which means that a failed or malfunctioning satellite will not impede the system's ability to provide global coverage. When a call is made it is routed to the nearest satellite, and then relayed around the world to its destination. If the destination is a land-based telephone, the last satellite in the chain feeds the signal to a "gateway" ground station. This gateway then connects with the existing land-line telephone system.

Connection is achieved in remote location *Message is relayed between satellites* *Call is routed to nearest satellite*

MICROWAVE RELAY TOWER
The Iridium communications system can route calls through an ordinary mobile telephone network, if available, and also interconnect with conventional telephone networks. Land links, such as this microwave relay tower, are often needed to route calls to their final destination.

Satellites pass over the Poles

Satellite orbits the Earth

ORBITAL PLANES
The 66 satellites of the Iridium network circle the Earth in six different orbital planes. They pass over the North and South Poles at a height of 485 miles (780 km), circling the Earth once every 100 minutes.

ENVIRONMENTAL CONCERNS

Mobile phones operate using radio signals. They have a transmitter that sends a signal to an aerial, which is part of a nationwide communications network. These radios work at low power, so mobile phone users need to be within a few kilometres of an aerial for their signal to be received. The mobile-phone revolution of the late 1990s has resulted in hundreds of millions of users worldwide, and thousands of aerials have been built, both in town and country, to receive the ever-increasing number of signals. In environmentally sensitive areas, unsightly aerial masts are sometimes disguised as trees (right) or flagpoles. They have also been sited on buildings and church towers, and then camouflaged.

APS and Digital Photography

THE ADVANCED PHOTO SYSTEM was announced in 1995 as a breakthrough in photographic technology. Developed over five years by a consortium of film and camera manufacturers (Kodak, Nikon, Fuji, Canon, Minolta), the APS was designed to maximize the quality of images taken by amateur photographers, and to overcome some of the most common problems encountered. The key to this new system is the "smart" film with its drop-in and automatic-load cassette. The film contains a magnetic strip, which records information specific to each shot, such as lighting conditions, magnification, date and time, and communicates this data to the processing equipment in the minilab. Once processed, the photographer receives a set of index prints, the photographs in any one of three different print sizes, and the developed film stored within the original cassette. APS film can be directly scanned and digitized, allowing the new system to bridge the gap between conventional 35mm film and digital photography.

PRINT FORMATS

A great advantage of APS is the variety it allows in the format of the print. When taking a picture there are three different formats which can be selected: C (Classic) gives a normal 35mm print, H (HDTV) is for a wider view and P (Panorama) provides the extra-wide landscape shot.

H and P

C

P

H and C

PRINT FORMATS

INFORMATION EXCHANGE ("IX")

Information about each frame – such as lighting conditions, selected print format, and exposure speed – is recorded on magnetic data strips. In a process called "information exchange" this data is read by processing equipment, which adjusts itself to produce the best results for each individual picture.

IX DATA TRACKS

Photofinishing magnetic data

Manufacturer's optical leader data

Camera optical data

Camera magnetic data

Manufacturer's optical frame data

THE MINOLTA VECTIS-40

View finder

Diopter adjuster

Subject program pointer

PRINT

SEL TITLE

ADJ DATE

For title backprinting

For date and time imprinting

Flash mode indicator

Fill-flash

APS FILM AND CARTRIDGE

To avoid misfeeding, the cassette loads, advances, and retracts the film automatically, and is also used to store processed film. A data disc tells the camera the film speed, type, and exposure length.

Magnetic recording area

Optical data

24mm film

Light lock opening mechanism

Data disk located at this side of cassette

FUJICOLOR A200

25 EXP.

FUJIFILM

Cassette spool

Film status indicator

○ *Unexposed*

◗ *Partially exposed*

✚ *Fully exposed but unprocessed*

☐ *Processed*

DIGITAL IMAGE SCANNER

The digital image scanner allows users to input developed APS film cartridges into their personal computer. The Index view instantly displays thumbnail versions of all the images stored on the roll.

Film cassette slots in here

Cartridge eject

Power switch

INFORMATIVE DATA AND INDEX PRINTS

IX allows a variety of information to be imprinted on the back of each photo. Not only is the date and time given, but a title for each shot can be chosen. At-a-glance index prints are also provided showing the C, H, or P format of each frame plus the print number.

INDEX PRINT

Individual index print

Frame type

Frame number

Barcode

ID178-734

95.12.21-96.02/2

(No.124> 95.12.21 FZG06

Frame number

Subject program selection

Date/time

Cartridge ID

Automatic flash

LCD panel

Frame counter

Drop-in loading and film chamber

Film chamber door below

Self-timer

Close-ups

Film cartridge loaded

DIGITAL IMAGE WORKSTATION

Photographs are digitized and placed on templates for printing out on a color printer. The workstation can also store the images on floppy disks or send them online to other locations.

Monitor

Floppy disk drive

2 Gigabyte hard disk drive

Cartridge slots in here

100-Megabyte Zip™ disk drive

DIGITAL CAMERA
NO FILM OR PROCESSING REQUIRED

Filmless digital cameras are a technological advancement in the photography world. Within minutes a picture can be taken and transmitted anywhere in the world, via email or the World Wide Web. Digital cameras are also ideal for desktop publishing, business presentations, and a variety of scientific or industrial applications.

KODAK DC50

CANON EOS-1 WITH KODAK DCS 5C

Accessory shoe for flash

Shutter release button

Lens release button

Zoom lens

PCMCIA card slots in back

TRANSMITTING LIGHT INTO DIGITAL DATA

Electronic sensors inside the camera transmit the different levels of light, which enter through the red, green, and blue filters (seen in this order below), onto a CCD (photosensitive semiconductor). The CCD digitally records the image and stores it onto a PCMCIA card – a tiny disk drive.

Red filter

Green filter

Green filter

Blue filter

FROM DATA TO ON-SCREEN IMAGE

Digital cameras can be plugged into a computer's serial port and the pictures can be instantly transferred from the camera's hard disk into popular graphics or publishing applications.

Interactive television

THE FUTURE OF TELEVISION is undoubtedly digital. Television or video signals can be converted from their normal analog form (continuously varying) into a digital form, which consists of a series of definite pulses. Digital signals can be transmitted, compressed, and manipulated by computers without any unwanted "noise" affecting the data. One of the advantages of digital technology is that video data can be manipulated to make interactive television possible. Interactive "video-on-demand" (VOD) services allow users to watch the material of their choice from a large central video "vault." A digital server enables many users to watch the same film, starting at different times, by sending the video data in small "packets" to them. Other services include news programs, games, music, and electronic shopping. With the latter, the user "strolls" through a virtual store and uses a credit card to buy items, which are then delivered to the home within days.

VIDEO-ON-DEMAND

Allowing viewers to choose a film or television program from a vast selection whenever desired, video-on-demand comes complete with all the flexibility of a video recorder (including fast-forward, rewind, and pause facilities). A typical VOD system consists of video vaults containing compressed digital video data, a sophisticated digital server that sends the requested material to the correct destination, and decoder and remote control units in the home.

REMOTE CONTROL
As well as offering the standard features, the remote control enables the user to operate the VOD, play games, and buy goods from home-shopping services.

The Fin button returns the viewer to normal cable television service

Video-on-demand button

Select button

Remote controls for interactive television are simple and user-friendly in format

VJB 02

SET-TOP BOX
The set-top box sends the user's choices to the digital server and decodes video data entering the home system. Depending on the system used, the digital video data from the server is converted to an analog signal for the television either by a junction box outside the home or by the set-top box.

Direction buttons for navigating on-screen menus

These keys allow quick selection of color-coded, on-screen choices

On-screen menus

Many new set-top boxes have considerable computing power

CATEGORIES

Drama 1
Comedy 2
Childrens 3
Natural History 4
Travel and Arts 5
What's On 6

To return to cable TV,
press 'FIN' twice on your remote control

HELP   MAIN   BACK

SONY

The television is an analog device

Coaxial cable carries the video data as an electrical signal

NEIGHBORHOOD NODE
The junction box, or neighborhood node, converts the fiber-optic cable's optical signal into an electrical signal, which is transmitted via coaxial cable to different homes in the neighborhood.

ATM stands for
"Asynchronous
Transfer Mode"

ATM SWITCH
The ATM switch passes
data from the server to the
modulator at incredible speed.

*The server is
the "brains"
of the system*

*Fiber-optic cable carries
the digital video data in
the form of light pulses*

*The modulator
changes the
data's frequency*

MODULATOR
The information
received by the
modulator is
converted to the
correct frequency
for its journey to
the home.

DIGITAL SERVER
The digital server
locates the viewer's
selection in the
storage vaults and
divides the data into
"packets." It then
addresses the packets
before sending them
back to the ATM
switch.

*Each vault can
store enough data
for over 500 movies*

STORAGE VAULTS
Digital video data
is compressed
before being
stored in vaults.
A typical vault
may house up
to 100 magnetic
hard drives.

DIGITAL VIDEO DISC

The video format set to replace tapes
and laserdiscs in the home looks
exactly like an audio compact disc
(CD) – a silver platter $4^3/_4$ in (12 cm)
in diameter. (To avoid a repetition of
the 1980s VHS/Beta videocassette war,
electronics companies involved have agreed
on one format.) However, the digital video disc
can hold up to 9 hours of data on its 2 sides, with
each side containing 133 minutes of program
time. This is compared with the 74 minutes held
by a CD. In addition, DVD's interactivity means
that certain programs can be viewed from a
variety of camera angles.

COMPACT DISC

CD "tracks"

DIGITAL VIDEO DISC

*DVD tracks are
packed more tightly*

CD CROSS-SECTION

*CD has one
layer of data*

DVD CROSS-SECTION

*DVD has two layers
of data on each side*

MOVIES BY COMPUTER

Disney Productions' *Toy Story* (1995) was
the world's first feature film to be generated
entirely on computer. A team of 27 animators
worked on the film, producing an average of
$3^1/_2$ minutes of footage per week. Some of the
characters and scenes were created solely
on computer, while others were set up with
models and props before being scanned into
the computer for digitization.

BUZZ LIGHTYEAR AND WOODY IN *TOY STORY*

Measuring time

ALL TIMEKEEPING DEVICES depend on counting a regularly repeated phenomenon. The earliest timekeeping devices were based on daily, monthly, or yearly cycles of the sun or moon. Most modern clocks are based on repeated mechanical or electronic oscillations (vibrations). The more frequent the vibrations, the greater the potential accuracy of the clock. The crystal in a quartz watch typically vibrates at 32,768 hertz (32,768 times a second), so it keeps better time than a pendulum clock, whose pendulum typically swings twice a second.

The most accurate timekeeping devices are atomic fountains, which are based on oscillations of cesium atoms. Global communication technologies, such as computer networks and broadcasting, rely on the world using one accurate time standard. This is called UCT (Universal Coordinated Time), and is based on the average time signal received from over 200 atomic clocks worldwide. The more we rely on high technology for precise timekeeping, the more vulnerable we become to problems with that technology – for example, the bug that threatens to strike at the beginning of the new millennium.

Microwave cavity

E

Trapping coils help keep the ball of atoms together

Mechanism advances the hands

Pendulum swings back and forth

PENDULUM CLOCK
In the 16th century, Italian scientist Galileo Galilei used the regular swing of a pendulum to measure periods of time. He suggested that a pendulum could be connected to the hands of a clock to turn them in regular steps.

THE ATOMIC FOUNTAIN
At present, the most accurate time-keeping device is the atomic fountain. It was developed by Nobel prize-winning scientists in the early 1990s and is far more accurate than a standard atomic clock, such as NIST-7 (see below, left). The atomic fountain enables us to measure time with greater accuracy, mainly because it uses cooler, slower-moving atoms than an atomic clock. Atomic fountain devices are accurate to within one ten-billionth of a second per day.

C

Goggles protect eyes from radiation

Laser components held in place by an optical bench

Detector laser source

Detector laser

NIST-7 ATOMIC CLOCK
This laser forms part of an early 1990s atomic clock developed by the US National Institute of Standards and Technology. At that time, the clock was the most accurate timekeeping device in the world, precise to within one billionth of a second per day (one second in three million years). Above, a scientist observes the laser as it "excites" cesium atoms. The atoms oscillate between two energy states, and the clock counts the oscillations.

Laser source

A

Ball of atoms
is launched
upward by
detuning
the lasers

②

③

Atoms change
state as they
fall through
the cavity

D

①

Ball of cesium atoms
just above absolute
zero (the lowest
possible temperature)

F

Trapping and
cooling laser beam

Fluorescence
given off by
cesium atoms

④

Detector counts
how many atoms
have been excited
into changing
energy state

B

Trapping and
cooling laser beam

MEASURING THE SECOND
Atomic devices keep time using
cesium atoms, which flip between
two energy states when they are
hit with microwave radiation of a
specific, fixed frequency – called
the resonant frequency. One
second is defined as exactly
9,192,631,770 oscillations of this
radiation. Atomic clocks measure
time by producing radiation
with a frequency as
close as possible
to the resonant
frequency of the
cesium atom, and
then counting
the oscillations.

⑤ ⑥

HOW THE ATOMIC FOUNTAIN WORKS

① THREE PAIRS OF LASER BEAMS (AB, CD, EF) TRAP AND COOL A BALL OF SEVERAL MILLION CESIUM ATOMS, ALL IN ONE OF TWO ENERGY STATES

② THE LASERS ARE DETUNED SLIGHTLY TO SLOWLY LAUNCH THE BALL UPWARD THROUGH A FIELD OF MICROWAVE RADIATION

③ AS THE ATOMS FALL THROUGH THE MICROWAVE CAVITY, MANY OF THEM ARE "EXCITED" AND CHANGE ENERGY STATE

④ A DETECTOR UNIT MEASURES THE FLUORES-CENCE OF THE ATOMS AND CALCULATES HOW MANY HAVE CHANGED STATE

⑤ THE MICROWAVE FREQUENCY IS FINE-TUNED TO EXCITE A GREATER PROPORTION OF THE ATOMS TO CHANGE ENERGY STATE

⑥ WHEN THIS PROPORTION IS GREATEST, THE MICROWAVE FREQUENCY IS CLOSEST TO THE TRUE RESONANT FREQUENCY OF THE ATOM

THE MILLENNIUM BUG

The millennium or Y2K (Year 2000) bug
was a threat to computer systems that store
dates using just two digits. Thus, the year
after 1999 would be represented as 00, which
could be interpreted as 99 years earlier
rather than one year later. Systems that store
dates in this way were considered in danger
of crashing on January 1, 2000. Although
it was thought that the millennium bug could
affect personal computers, the greatest threat
it posed was to embedded systems – custom-
built computers that are used in vital service
industries such as banking, utilities,
transportation, telecommunications, and air
traffic control. Severe problems were
predicted if equipment that could be affected
by the bug was not modified. The efforts
made to tackle the problem proved successful
and January 1, 2000 passed without incident.

AIR TRAFFIC CONTROL ROOM

Network computers

THE INTERNET LINKS MILLIONS of computers worldwide, and anybody with a personal computer (PC) and basic communication tools can become a part of it. The ever-expanding "Net" is becoming a vital resource for business, education, and entertainment. The huge multimedia database of the World Wide Web, which is one aspect of the Net, is so sophisticated that users can meet in "virtual worlds." As the Net evolves, so new ways of computing are made possible. Network computing is one possible development which promises greater compatibility and efficiency than personal computing. At present, the Net consists mainly of PCs with large amounts of processing power and disk space (called "fat client computers") connected to servers (other computers that distribute data). The idea behind network computing is to replace the PC, or fat client, with a network computer (NC), or "thin client." A thin client computer has a processor, like a PC, but less memory and no disk storage, and so is much cheaper. Instead of storing application programs and data on a local hard disk (as a PC does), an NC simply downloads programs and data from a server into its RAM as needed. Network computing promises economies of scale and centralization, since all the data is stored on a few servers, and any software developments that need to be made apply to these servers only.

DATA SERVER

Data server stores data from many users

JAVA APPLET SERVER

Java applet server stores a wide range of compact, downloadable programs

MODEM

High-speed Internet links via modems and other devices

THIN CLIENT COMPUTER
The thin client NC is halfway between a PC and a dumb terminal, used on mainframe computers. A dumb terminal consists only of a keyboard and a monitor – all processing and data storage is carried out centrally by the mainframe. Like dumb terminals, NCs have no local disk storage, but like PCs, they do have a processor. In addition to being smaller and cheaper than PCs, NCs should be more reliable, since they do not have complex peripherals with moving parts, such as disk drives.

Monitor

Thin client computer consists of a basic processor and input/output devices

Thin client

Mouse

Keyboard

Monitor

Applet developers write software for the servers

Server

APPLET DEVELOPERS' SYSTEM

Different regions of the network are separated for security purposes by firewalls

FIREWALL

Firewalls limit access to authorized users

DISTRIBUTED COMPUTING

Network computing has been made possible because the computer industry has agreed hardware and software standards, including a new language, Java. When a thin client – or a fat client acting as a Java station – is switched on, its basic boot-up software connects to a network and downloads the full Java operating system. The user can then download Java application programs (called applets) and data required, paying any fee with a smart card. High-speed links between client and server mean that processing tasks can be distributed between computers, so the applets can be relatively small. In network computing, the main burden falls not on the client machines but on the network. Whether the present Internet infrastructure (phone lines, cables, etc.) has the required capacity, speed, and reliability to support network computing remains to be seen.

VIRTUAL WORLDS ON THE NET

The World Wide Web has brought multimedia – graphics, animations, sound, and hyperlinking – to the Internet. The Virtual World Wide Web (VWWW), with virtual environments, is a further development where users can interact graphically with each other. Typical VWWW environments are spread across sites on the Net and on a CD-ROM. The basic program runs from the CD, but "interactions" between users occur at VWWW sites.

VIRTUAL PARIS

3D ENVIRONMENTS
All three-dimensional virtual worlds must first be rendered in ink, as shown below, after which the illustrations are digitized by a computer.

3D drawing of Paris buildings

The CD-ROM is based on a series of detailed sketches

CITIZENS OF A VIRTUAL WORLD
When a user logs on to a virtual world, he or she chooses a graphical identity; this is how they will appear on other users' screens around the world. These virtual people stroll around and meet in virtual streets – although the real users might be thousands of miles apart.

Style and measurement categories

Users can choose their appearance and their personality

REAL SERVICES IN A VIRTUAL SOCIETY
Some features of a virtual world are purely fictional, like a user's graphical identity, while the streets or environment may be based on a real place. But, as in the real Paris, you can "walk" into a store, shop using your real credit card, and have the real goods delivered.

Virtual transport takes the user to other worlds

Home shopping services are located around the virtual city

World Wide Web

SINCE 1993, THE WORLD WIDE WEB (WWW) has become one of the fastest growing communication systems in history. Consisting of an expanding pool of "pages" created by companies, associations, and individuals, it is accessible to anyone connected to the Internet. Two features of the Web make it appealing. The first is the nonlinear method of presenting information known as "hypertext." This enables users to jump between documents of subject-related material at the click of the mouse. The second is the multimedia format of Web pages, which can be designed using sophisticated graphics, sound, and animation, and displayed on-screen by a program called a browser. Since the development of the browser, the Web has become more sophisticated and easier to use and interest in the WWW has exploded.

THE INTERNET AND THE WEB

Tim Berners-Lee, the physics researcher who first conceived the Web in 1989, compared the Internet and the Web to the difference between the brain and the mind; where the Internet is the physical method of communication and the Web is the information itself.

1. Web page broken down into packets of binary data for transmission

Original Web page

2. Data is sent to destination via the Internet

5. Web page is downloaded onto user's screen

4. Packets of binary data are translated into a readable message

3. Analog audio signal received and converted into binary data via modem

Web site

WEB SITES

A web site is a collection of linked documents stored on a single computer, anywhere in the world. Sites can be linked up to each other using hyperlinks.

NAVIGATING THE WEB

There are millions of pages available on the Web and graphical browsers, such as Netscape Navigator, provide a window in the computer screen on which these pages are displayed in fine detail. Keyword searches can be performed using a facility called a search engine; particular topics can be explored using directories called subject trees; and specific pages can be accessed by typing the exact address, or URL (Universal Resource Locator). Other browser tools include history lists, hot lists, and bookmarks.

WELCOME PAGE

UNIVERSAL RESOURCE LOCATOR (URL)

Prefix "http://" (hyper-text transfer protocol) indicates a Web site or page is being accessed

Locates particular folder and file

`http://` | `www.astro.uva.nl` | / | `michielb/sun` | / | `kaft.htm.`

Commands browser to look for Web pages stored at this computer

Indicates name of document to be retrieved

CHOICE AND VARIETY ON THE INTERNET

CHILDREN'S WEB SITES
From finding an email pen-pal to linking up to educational resources, the Web provides information and enjoyment for children.

COMMERCE ON THE WEB
Placing sites on the World Wide Web is becoming an increasingly popular marketing strategy for many companies around the world.

MUSIC PAGES
Musicians are able to present themselves and their music to the public, and fans can find more information on their favorite bands.

NEWS AND INFORMATION
Many newspapers and magazines now have regularly updated online editions, such as the UK's *Daily Telegraph*.

HYPERTEXT AND HYPERMEDIA

Using a format called hypertext or hypermedia, Web documents contain links to other pages of text, pictures, sound recordings, or videos, which can be activated by clicking on highlighted or underlined text and picture icons, known as hyperlinks or hotspots. These links are created by the programming language HTML (HyperText Mark-up Language), which also defines how the text and graphics will appear on the page.

URL or Web page address

Netscape browser menu contains navigation buttons

The welcome page (the first screen) usually contains an introduction or a contents list

Browser icon

Web pages can contain clips of film, animation, and sound (which is why hypertext is now often referred to as hypermedia)

Embedded beneath hyperlinks or hotspots lies a command to get the relevant document or node

Sound node

The contents of many Web sites are illustrated with colorful graphics

This Web site, called "Virtual Sun," was authored by a graduate student in Astronomy at the University of Amsterdam

Nonlinear organization of information allows user to pursue areas of particular interest

A page can contain direct links to several other pages of related information, as well as other Web sites

Index

ACKNOWLEDGMENTS

2001 EDITION
Designer Hugh Schermuly
Editor Jeremy Harwood
Deputy Art Director Bryn Walls
Category Publisher Jonathan Metcalf

Picture researcher Franziska Marking, Anna Grapes
Picture Librarians Sally Hamilton, Diane LeGrande
Production Michelle Thomas
Indexer Jill Ford

ALL EDITIONS
Project Editors Kirstie Hills, Julie Oughton, Nichola Thomasson
Art Editors Paul Greenleaf, Sasha Howard, Joanne Mitchell, Dawn Terrey
Editors Caroline Hunt, David Tombesi-Walton
DTP Designers Mark Bracey, Rob Campbell

Consultants Michael Allaby (El Niño and La Niña), Anita Bardhan-Roy (World Wide Web), David
Brown (Pont de Normandie), Helen Castle (Guggenheim, Bilbao; House of the future), Stuart Clarke
(International Space Station; Very Large Telescope), John Coiley (Tilting trains), Heather Couper
(Hubble Space Telescope), Bernie Fitzsimons (Airbus A3XX), Robin Kerrod (Probing the universe;
Record breakers; Global telecommunications), David Lambert (Giganotosaurus), Michael Langford
(APS and Digital Photography), Colin Lewis (Electric Car/Le Shuttle), Angela Marlow (Medical
research), Dr. Gabrielle Murphy (Modern surgery), Steve Parker (From dinosaurs to birds; Preserved
in the ice; Body healing), Mukul Patel (Interactive television; Measuring time; Network computers),
Dr. Tony Smith (Medical research), Giles Sparrow (Galileo spacecraft), Fay Sweet (Rebuilding Berlin;
Olympics 2000), Dr. Robert Youngsen (Genetic advances)

Senior Editors Louise Candlish, Peter Jones
Senior Art Editors Tracy Hambleton-Miles, Heather McCarry
Managing Editors Gwen Edmonds, Christine Winters
Senior Managing Editor Anna Kruger
Senior Managing Art Editor Steve Knowlden
Deputy Art Director Tina Vaughan
Category Publisher Sean Moore

Illustrations Andy Burton, Rob Campbell, Geoff Denney, Mick Gillah, Tony Graham, Nicholas H. T. Hall,
Steve Kirk, Chris D. Orr, Jim Robins, Richard Tibbits, Matthew Wallis, John Woodcock
Model making Jonathan Hateley
Photography Andy Crawford, Bob Gathany, Gary Ombler, Kim Taylor, Frank Greenaway,
Dave King, Tim Ridley, Philip Dowell, Mike Dunning
Picture Research Angela Anderson, Katherine Mesquita, Sam Ruston, Mariana Sonnenberg

Production Sarah Coltman, David Proffit, Meryl Silbert

Copyright © 2000 Dorling Kindersley Limited, London

Dorling Kindersley would like to thank: Christine Baker, Jonathan Biggington, Laura Buller, Brian
Cooper, Nicola Erdpresser, Mike Flynn, Alan Greenwood, Steve Howard, Neil Lockley, Tim Mann,
Simon Murrell, Eric Pierrat (Gallimard), Nicola Powling, Clare Ryder, Richard Shellabear, Richard
Sinclair, Nigel Spencer (British Library/Holborn Reading Room), Sylvia Tombesi -

The publisher would like to thank the following for their kind permission to reproduce
photographs and artworks:

(a=above, b=bottom, c=centre, l=left, r=right, t=top)

Adtranz: 24A tl; *Amateur Photographer*: 39A bl; **Agence France Presse**: 27A tr; **Airbus Industrie**:
3A crb, 32A tr, 52-53A, 33A cra, 33A c. **Allsport**: Scott Barbour 51A c, Shaun Botterill 50A bl,
Mark Dadswell 50A clb, Nick Wilson 1A bl, 3A clb, 50A tr, 50-51A, 51A br; **1996 American Association
for the Advancement of Science**: Excerpt from Science reprinted with permission: 12A cl; **Arcaid**:
Paul Raffery, Architect: Stutchbury and Pape 51A cr. **Associated Press**: JPL/NASA 5A cr; Keystone 58A
cl; NASA 4A tr; National Geographic Society 16A tc; RTRS 59A cr; **Austin Brown/Aviation Picture
Library**: 53A crb; **BBC Tomorrow's World**: 15A bc; **Michiel Berger (Astronomical Institute,
University of Amsterdam):** 43A bl, 47A c, cla, bl, bc, br; **Boeing/Genesis Space Photo Library**: 4A bl;
Breitling SA: 3A tr, 39A c; **Wendell Burnette Architects**: 23A cr, 23A tr, 23A bc; **Canal Plus**: 45A tr,
tcr, bcr, br; **Canon (UK) Limited**: 59A cra; **Branson Coates Architecture**: Branson Coates 23A cla,
Philip Vile 23A cl; **Corbis UK Ltd**: AFP 3A cra, 27A tc, 42A cl, 43A t; Bettmann 42A tl; Dave G. Houser
43A br; Gregor Schmidt 2A; Ralph White 59A tr; Reuters Newmedia Inc 1A br, 18A tr, 19A tr, 26A tr,
26A bc, 33A tl; **EPA/DPA**: 42-43A; **Eumetsat (European Organisation for the Exploitation of
Meteorological Satellites)**: 21A tr, 21A tr; **Fuji Photo Film**: 38A cl, bl, 39A c; **Galaxy Picture
Library**: 6A tl, 7A br; **Galaxy Picture Library**: 9A crb, 9A br; Victor Gedris / Ken Adams: 47A tc;
Genesis Space Photo Library: 12-13A ca; **Mark Guard Associates**: 22A tl; **Guggenheim Museum,
Bilbao:** Erika Barahona Ede 34-35a, 35A br; **K. Hiwatashi**: 34A tr; **Institut Amatller D'Art Hispanic**:
35A tr; Shunji Ishiba 30-31A cr; **Kansai International Airport Co. Ltd**: 50-51A c, 51A tr; **KeyMed
(Medical & Industrial Equipment) Ltd:**15A cra; **1996 Knowledge Adventure Inc.** all rights reserved.
JumpStart, Knowledge Land and Knowledge Adventure are trademarks of Knowledge Adventure, Inc:
47A tl; **The Kodak Library**: 39A tr; **Brigitte Lafaille**: F. Latrielle 19A c; 19A tl; **Magnum Photos**:
Jean Gaumy 52A tl, 53A br; **Michelin**: 27A tl, tr; **Minolta (UK) Ltd**: 38A tl, 38-39A c; **NASA**: 4A tl, 6A
bl, 6-7A tc, cr, bc, bcl, bl; 8A bl, 10A bc, tl, 10-11a, 11A tl, tr; **The Natural History Museum, London**:
J. Sibbick 17A bl-cr; **Netscape Communications Corporation**: Netscape and Netscape Navigator are
trademarks of Netscape Communications, all rights reserved 46A bl; **Panasonic UK Ltd**: 41A tr;
Peugeot: 26A tl, cl, bl, 26-27a; **Popperfoto**: Reuters 1A tr, 3A cla, 18A bl, 19A br, 38-59A, 38A b, 39A br,
39A clb2; **Press Association**: 17A br; **Profile Public Relations**: 36A l; **QA Photos Ltd**: 27A tr, crb,
Channel Tunnel Group Ltd: 27A cra, br; **Renzo Piano Building Workshop**: 30A l; **Rex Features**:
Paul Felix 37A br; SNCF: 24A tr, 25A tl; **Mark Sagar**: 15A c, crb, br; **Science Museum**: 5A crb; **Science
Photo Library**: 16-17A cr, cl, crb, 5A cl, Jim Amos 17A br, David Bewsey, Ethicon Ltd and University
of Glasgow 27A crb, David Ducros 1A tl, 45A, Simon Fraser 27A cr, David Mooney 5A cl, 27A clb,
David Parker 5A bl, 5A br, J.C. Revy 27A cl, Dr Seth Schostak 5A cb,; NASA 4A cr, Volker Steger,
Peter Arnold Inc 26A crb, c, 8-9A, David Ducros 11A br, Simon Fraser 15A tr, Carlos Goldin 12A tl, tr,
Patrice Loiez 2A c, Will & Deni McIntryre 14A br, Peter Menzel 43A br, Motorola 36-57A, 57A bl,
Carlos Munoz-Yague 20A bl, N.A.S.A: 8A clb, 10A clb, David Parker 20A clb, 57A tr, JC Revy 14A tr,
David Scharf 14A bc, Space Telescope Science Institute 4A cr, 5A b, tl, tr, r; Sinclair Stammers 14A
bl, Alexander Tsiaras 42A bl; **National Museums of Scotland**: 17A cl; **Frank Spooner Pictures**:
Gamma: Clare Aaron 15A ca, 21A cr, 40A br; **Sporting Pictures (uk) Ltd**: 51A t; **Tony Stone Images**:
16A tl; **Sun Microsystems**: 44A bl, 44/45A tc; **Sygma**: 3A br, 28-29A (all except Stephanie Compoint
28A bl © Gedeon-Exmachina) Warren Winter 16A bl; © **The Telegraph plc. London 1996**: 47A tr;
Topham Picturepoint: 42A tr, 43A cr, 43A cb; **Verne Fotografie**: 22A clb, br, c, cra; **West Japan
Railways**: 24A bl, 25A br, 24-25A clb; **Westminster Cable**: 40A bl, 40-41A cl.

EXTERNAL FEATURES OF A BUTTERFLY

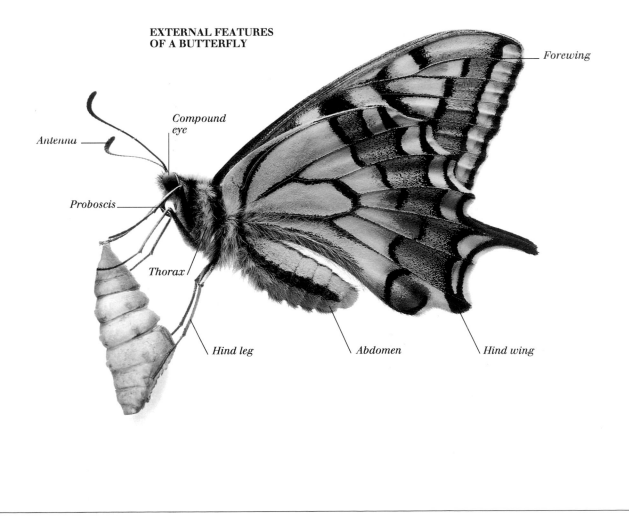

Forewing

Compound eye

Antenna

Proboscis

Thorax

Hind leg

Abdomen

Hind wing

INTERNAL FEATURES
OF BRACHIOSAURUS

First
electron
shell

Second
electron
shell

Nucleus

ANATOMY OF A
FLUORINE–19 ATOM

Location of
Solar System

Nucleus

OVERHEAD VIEW OF OUR GALAXY

Cervical
musculature

Lung

Ovary

Bract

Pith

LONGITUDINAL SECTION THROUGH
SUNFLOWER INFLORESCENCE

Fault plane

Dip of
fault plane

Hade of
fault
plane

STRUCTURE OF A FAULT

Gizzard

Exhaust port

Floral
design

VELOCETTE OHV ENGINE

MOSAIC DESIGN

Metacarpal

DORLING KINDERSLEY
ULTIMATE
VISUAL
DICTIONARY

Figurehead

Cat block

Catted anchor

Frame

Riband

BOW OF A 74–GUN SHIP

Ankle joint

A Dorling Kindersley Book

Dorling Kindersley

LONDON, NEW YORK, SYDNEY, DELHI, PARIS
MUNICH, AND JOHANNESBURG

PROJECT ART EDITORS HEATHER McCARRY, JOHNNY PAU, CHRIS WALKER, KEVIN WILLIAMS
DESIGNER SIMON MURRELL
PROJECT EDITORS LUISA CARUSO, PETER JONES, JANE MASON, GEOFFREY STALKER
EDITOR JO EVANS
US EDITOR JULEE BINDER

DTP DESIGNER ZIRRINIA AUSTIN
PICTURE RESEARCHER CHARLOTTE BUSH

MANAGING ART EDITOR TONI KAY
SENIOR EDITOR ROGER TRITTON
MANAGING EDITOR SEAN MOORE

PRODUCTION MANAGER HILARY STEPHENS

ANATOMICAL AND BOTANICAL MODELS SUPPLIED BY SOMSO MODELLE, COBURG, GERMANY

ACOUSTIC GUITAR

PUBLISHED IN THE UNITED STATES BY
DORLING KINDERSLEY PUBLISHING, INC.
95 MADISON AVENUE
NEW YORK, NEW YORK 10016

REVISED AMERICAN EDITION © 2000
2 4 6 8 10 9 7 5 3

DORLING KINDERSLEY BOOKS ARE AVAILABLE AT SPECIAL DISCOUNTS FOR BULK PURCHASES FOR SALES PROMOTIONS OR PREMIUMS SPECIAL EDITIONS,
INCLUDING PERSONALIZED COVERS, EXCERPTS OF EXISTING GUIDES, AND CORPORATE IMPRINTS CAN BE CREATED IN LARGE QUANTITIES FOR SPECIFIC NEEDS.
FOR MORE INFORMATION, CONTACT SPECIAL MARKETS DEPT./DORLING KINDERSLEY PUBLISHING, INC./95 MADISON AVE./NEW YORK, NY 10016/FAX: 800-600-9098

LIBRARY OF CONGRESS CATALOGING-IN-PUBLICATION DATA
DORLING KINDERSLEY ULTIMATE VISUAL DICTIONARY. - - REVISED AMERICAN ED.
INCLUDES INDEX
ISBN 0-7894-6111-0
1. PICTURE DICTIONARIES, ENGLISH. I. DORLING KINDERSLEY. INC.
PE 1629.D67 1994   94-11173
423 ' . 1- -dc20   CIP

REPRODUCED BY COLOURSCAN, SINGAPORE
PRINTED AND BOUND BY MONDADORI, ITALY

SEE OUR COMPLETE
CATALOG AT
www.dk.com

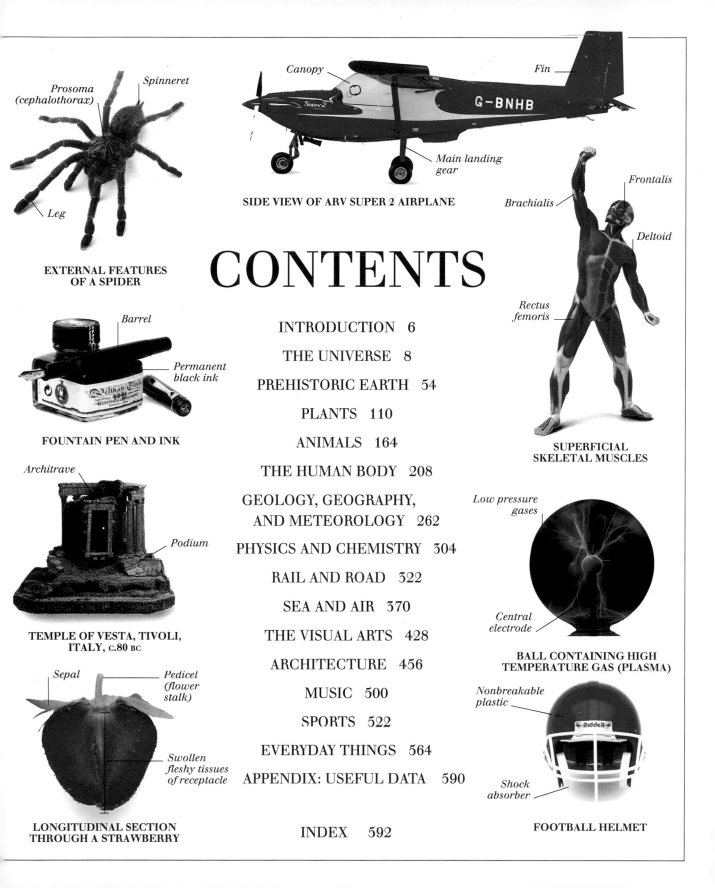

Prosoma (cephalothorax) — *Spinneret*

Leg

EXTERNAL FEATURES OF A SPIDER

Canopy — *Fin*

G-BNHB

Super2

Main landing gear

SIDE VIEW OF ARV SUPER 2 AIRPLANE

Frontalis

Brachialis — *Deltoid*

Rectus femoris

SUPERFICIAL SKELETAL MUSCLES

Barrel

Permanent black ink

FOUNTAIN PEN AND INK

Architrave

Podium

TEMPLE OF VESTA, TIVOLI, ITALY, c.80 BC

Low pressure gases

Central electrode

BALL CONTAINING HIGH TEMPERATURE GAS (PLASMA)

Sepal — *Pedicel (flower stalk)*

Swollen fleshy tissues of receptacle

LONGITUDINAL SECTION THROUGH A STRAWBERRY

Nonbreakable plastic

Shock absorber

FOOTBALL HELMET

CONTENTS

Introduction

THE ULTIMATE VISUAL DICTIONARY is a completely new kind of reference book. It provides a link between pictures and words in a way that no ordinary dictionary ever has. Most dictionaries simply tell you what a word means, but the *Ultimate Visual Dictionary* shows you — through a combination of detailed annotations, explicit photographs, and illustrations. In the *Ultimate Visual Dictionary*, pictures define the annotations around them. You do not read definitions of the annotated words, you see them. The highly accessible format of the *Ultimate Visual Dictionary*, the thoroughness of its annotations, and the range of its subject matter make it a unique and helpful reference tool.

***How to use the* Ultimate Visual Dictionary**
You will find the *Ultimate Visual Dictionary* simple to use. It is divided by subject into 14 sections— The Universe, Prehistoric Earth, Plants, Animals, The Human Body, etc. Each section begins with a table of contents listing the major entries within that section. For example, The Visual Arts section contains entries on *Drawing, Tempera, Fresco, Oils, Watercolor, Pastels, Acrylics, Calligraphy, Printmaking, Mosaic,* and *Sculpture*. Every entry includes a short introduction explaining the purpose of the photographs and illustrations, and the significance of the annotations.

If you know what something looks like, but don't know its name, turn to the annotations surrounding the pictures; if you know a word, but don't know what it refers to, use the comprehensive index to direct you to the appropriate page.

Suppose you want to know what the bone at the end of your little finger is called. With a standard dictionary, you wouldn't know where to begin. But with the *Ultimate Visual Dictionary* you simply turn to the entry called *Hands*—within The Human Body section—and you will find four fully annotated color photographs showing the skin, muscles, and bones of the human hand. In this entry you will quickly find that the bone you are searching for is called the distal phalanx. In addition, you will discover that it is attached to the middle phalanx by the distal interphalangeal joint.

Perhaps you want to know what a catalytic converter looks like. If you look up "catalytic converter" in an ordinary dictionary, you will be told what it is and possibly what it does—but you will not be able to tell what shape it is or what it is made of. However, if you look up "catalytic converter" in the index of the *Ultimate Visual Dictionary*, you will be directed to the *Modern engines* entry on page 344—where the introduction gives you basic information about what a catalytic converter is—and to page 350—where there is a spectacular exploded-view photograph of the mechanics of a Renault Clio. From these pages you will find out not only what a catalytic converter looks like, but also that it is attached at one end to an exhaust downpipe and at the other to a silencer.

Whatever it is that you want to find a name for, or whatever name you want to find a picture for, you will find it quickly and easily in the *Ultimate Visual Dictionary*. Perhaps you need to know where the vamp on a shoe is; or how to tell obovate and lanceolate leaves apart; or what a spiral galaxy looks like; or whether birds have nostrils. With the *Ultimate Visual Dictionary* close by, the answers to each of these questions, and thousands more, are readily available.

The *Ultimate Visual Dictionary* does not just tell you what the names of the different parts of an object are. The photographs, illustrations, and annotations are all specially arranged to help you understand which parts relate to one another and how objects function.

With the *Ultimate Visual Dictionary*, in seconds you can find the words or pictures that you are looking for; or you can simply browse. The *Ultimate Visual Dictionary* is not intended to replace a standard dictionary or encyclopedia, but is instead a stimulating and valuable companion to ordinary reference volumes. Giving you access to the language that is used by astronomers and architects, musicians and mechanics, pilots and professional athletes, it is the ideal reference book for experts and novices of all ages.

Sections of the ULTIMATE VISUAL DICTIONARY

The 14 sections of the *ULTIMATE VISUAL DICTIONARY* contain a total of more than 30,000 terms, encompassing a wide range of topics:

- In the first section, THE UNIVERSE, spectacular photographs and illustrations are used to show the names of the stars and planets and to explain the structure of solar systems, galaxies, nebulae, comets, and black holes.

- PREHISTORIC EARTH tells the story of how our own planet has evolved since its formation. It includes examples of prehistoric flora and fauna, and fascinating dinosaur models— some with parts of the body stripped away to show anatomical sections.

- PLANTS covers a huge range of species— from the familiar to the exotic. In addition to the color photographs of plants included in this section, there is a series of micrographic photographs illustrating plant details—such as pollen grains, spores, and cross-sections of stems and roots.

- In the ANIMALS section, skeletons, anatomical diagrams, and different parts of animals' bodies have been meticulously annotated. This section provides a comprehensive guide to the vocabulary of zoological classification and animal physiology.

- The structure of the human body, its parts, and its systems are presented in THE HUMAN BODY. The section includes lifelike, three-dimensional models and the latest false-color images. Clear and authoritative annotations indicate the correct anatomical terms.

- GEOLOGY, GEOGRAPHY, AND METEOROLOGY describes the structure of the Earth—from the inner core to the exosphere—and the physical phenomena, such as volcanoes, rivers, glaciers, and climate, that shape its surface.

- PHYSICS AND CHEMISTRY is a visual journey through the fundamental principles underlying the physical universe, that provides the essential vocabulary of these sciences.

- In RAIL AND ROAD, a wide range of trains, trolleys and buses, cars, bicycles, and motorcycles are described. Exploded-view photographs show mechanical details with striking clarity.

- SEA AND AIR illustrates hundreds of parts of ships and airplanes. The section includes civil and fighting craft, both historical and modern.

- THE VISUAL ARTS shows the equipment and materials used by painters, sculptors, printers, and other artists. Well-known compositions have been chosen to illustrate specific artistic techniques and effects.

- ARCHITECTURE includes photographs of exemplary architectural models and illustrates dozens of additional features such as columns, domes, and arches.

- MUSIC provides a visual introduction to the special language of music and musical instruments. It includes clearly annotated photographs of each of the major groups of traditional instruments—brass, woodwind, strings, and percussion—together with modern electronic instruments.

- The SPORTS section is a guide to the playing areas, formations, equipment, and techniques needed for many of today's most popular sports.

- In EVERYDAY THINGS, familiar objects, such as shoes, clocks, and toasters, are taken apart—down to the very last screw or length of thread—to show their inner workings and to give a special insight into the language that is used by their manufacturers.

THE UNIVERSE

Anatomy of the Universe

Fireball of rapidly expanding, extremely hot gas lasting about one million years

THE UNIVERSE CONTAINS EVERYTHING that exists, from the tiniest subatomic particles to galactic superclusters (the largest structures known). Nobody knows how big the Universe is, but astronomers estimate that it contains about 100 billion galaxies, each comprising an average of 100 billion stars. The most widely accepted theory about the origin of the Universe is the Big Bang theory, which states that the Universe came into being in a huge explosion—the Big Bang—that took place between 10 and 20 billion years ago. The Universe initially consisted of a very hot, dense fireball of expanding, cooling gas. After about one million years, the gas probably began to condense into localized clumps called protogalaxies. During the next five billion years, the protogalaxies continued condensing, forming galaxies in which stars were being born. Today, billions of years later, the Universe as a whole is still expanding, although there are localized areas in which objects are held together by gravity; for example, many galaxies are found in clusters. The Big Bang theory is supported by the discovery of faint, cool background radiation coming evenly from all directions. This radiation is believed to be the remnant of the radiation produced by the Big Bang. Small "ripples" in the temperature of the cosmic background radiation are thought to be evidence of slight fluctuations in the density of the early Universe, which resulted in the formation of galaxies. Astronomers do not yet know if the Universe is "closed," which means it will eventually stop expanding and begin to contract, or if it is "open," which means it will continue expanding forever.

COMPUTER-ENHANCED MICROWAVE MAP OF COSMIC BACKGROUND RADIATION

Pink indicates "warm ripples" in background radiation

Pale blue indicates "cool ripples" in background radiation

Deep blue indicates background radiation corresponding to -454.5°F (remnant of the Big Bang)

Red and pink band indicates radiation from our galaxy

Low-energy microwave radiation corresponding to about -454°F

High-energy gamma radiation corresponding to about 5,400°F

ORIGIN AND EXPANSION OF THE UNIVERSE

Quasar (probably the center of a galaxy containing a massive black hole)

Universe one to five billion years after Big Bang

Protogalaxy (condensing gas cloud)

Galaxy spinning and flattening to become spiral shaped

Dark cloud (dust and gas condensing to form a protogalaxy)

Elliptical galaxy in which stars form rapidly

Universe today (10–20 billion years after Big Bang)

Cluster of galaxies held together by gravity

Elliptical galaxy containing old stars and little gas and dust

Irregular galaxy

Spiral galaxy containing gas, dust, and young stars

OBJECTS IN THE UNIVERSE

CLUSTER OF GALAXIES IN VIRGO

COLOR-ENHANCED IMAGE OF 3C273 (QUASAR)

NGC 4406 (ELLIPTICAL GALAXY)

NGC 5236 (SPIRAL GALAXY)

NGC 6822 (IRREGULAR GALAXY)

THE ROSETTE NEBULA (EMISSION NEBULA)

THE JEWEL BOX (STAR CLUSTER)

THE SUN (MAIN SEQUENCE STAR)

EARTH

THE MOON

Galaxies

SOMBRERO,
A SPIRAL GALAXY

A GALAXY IS A HUGE MASS OF STARS, nebulae, and interstellar material. The smallest galaxies contain about 100,000 stars, while the largest contain up to 3,000 billion stars. There are three main types of galaxy, classified according to their shape: elliptical, which are oval shaped; spiral, which have arms spiraling outward from a central bulge; and irregular, which have no obvious shape. Sometimes, the shape of a galaxy is distorted by a collision with another galaxy. Quasars (quasi-stellar objects) are thought to be galactic nuclei but are so far away that their exact nature is still uncertain. They are compact, highly luminous objects in the outer reaches of the known Universe; while the farthest known "ordinary" galaxies are about 10 billion light-years away, the farthest known quasar is about 15 billion light-years away. Active galaxies, such as Seyfert galaxies and radio galaxies, emit intense radiation. In a Seyfert galaxy, this radiation comes from the galactic nucleus; in a radio galaxy, it also comes from huge lobes on either side of the galaxy. The radiation from active galaxies and quasars is thought to be caused by black holes (see pp. 28-29).

OPTICAL IMAGE OF NGC 4486 (ELLIPTICAL GALAXY)

Globular cluster containing very old red giants

Central region containing old red giants

Less densely populated region

Neighboring galaxy

OPTICAL IMAGE OF LARGE MAGELLANIC CLOUD (IRREGULAR GALAXY)

Tarantula Nebula

Dust cloud obscuring light from stars

Emission nebula

Light from stars

OPTICAL IMAGE OF NGC 2997 (SPIRAL GALAXY)

Glowing nebula in spiral arm

Spiral arm containing young stars

Galactic nucleus containing old stars

Dust in spiral arm reflecting blue light from hot young stars

Hot, ionized hydrogen gas emitting red light

Dust lane

**OPTICAL IMAGE OF CENTAURUS A
(RADIO GALAXY)**

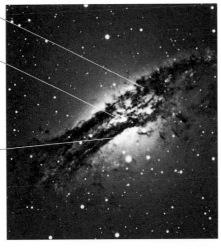

Dust lane crossing
elliptical galaxy

Galactic nucleus
containing
powerful source
of radiation

Light from
old stars

**COLOR-ENHANCED RADIO
IMAGE OF CENTAURUS A**

Red indicates
high-intensity
radio waves

Radio
lobe

Blue indicates
low-intensity
radio waves

Radiation from
galactic nucleus

Outline of
optical image
of Centaurus A

Radio
lobe

Yellow indicates
medium-intensity
radio waves

COLOR-ENHANCED RADIO IMAGE OF 3C273 (QUASAR)

Radiation from jet
of high-energy
particles moving
away from quasar

Quasar nucleus

Blue indicates
low-intensity
radio waves

White indicates high-
intensity radio waves

**OPTICAL IMAGE OF NGC 1566
(SEYFERT GALAXY)**

Nebula in
spiral arm

Compact nucleus
emitting intense
radiation

Spiral arm

**COLOR-ENHANCED OPTICAL IMAGE OF
NGC 5754 (TWO COLLIDING GALAXIES)**

Blue indicates low-
intensity radiation

Red indicates
medium-intensity
radiation

Spiral arm distorted
by gravitational
influence of smaller
galaxy

Large spiral
galaxy

Smaller galaxy
colliding with
larger galaxy

Yellow indicates
high-intensity
radiation

The Milky Way

**VIEW TOWARD
GALACTIC CENTER**

THE MILKY WAY IS THE NAME GIVEN TO THE FAINT BAND OF LIGHT that stretches across the night sky. This light comes from stars and nebulae in our galaxy, known as the Milky Way Galaxy or simply as "the Galaxy." The Galaxy is shaped like a spiral, with a dense central bulge that is encircled by four arms spiraling outward and surrounded by a less dense halo. We cannot see the spiral shape because our Solar System is in one of the spiral arms, the Orion Arm (also called the Local Arm). From our position, the center of the Galaxy is completely obscured by dust clouds; as a result, optical maps give only a limited view of the Galaxy. However, a more complete picture can be obtained by studying radio, infrared, and other radiation. The central bulge of the Galaxy is a relatively small, dense sphere that contains mainly older red and yellow stars. The halo is a less dense region in which the oldest stars are situated; some of these stars may be as old as the Galaxy itself (possibly 15 billion years). The spiral arms contain mainly hot, young, blue stars, as well as nebulae (clouds of dust and gas, inside which stars are born). The Galaxy is vast—about 100,000 light-years across (a light-year is about 5,879 billion miles); in comparison, the Solar System seems small, at about 12 light-hours across (about 8 billion miles). The entire Galaxy is rotating in space, although the inner stars travel faster than those further out. The Sun, which is about two-thirds out from the center, completes one lap of the Galaxy about every 220 million years.

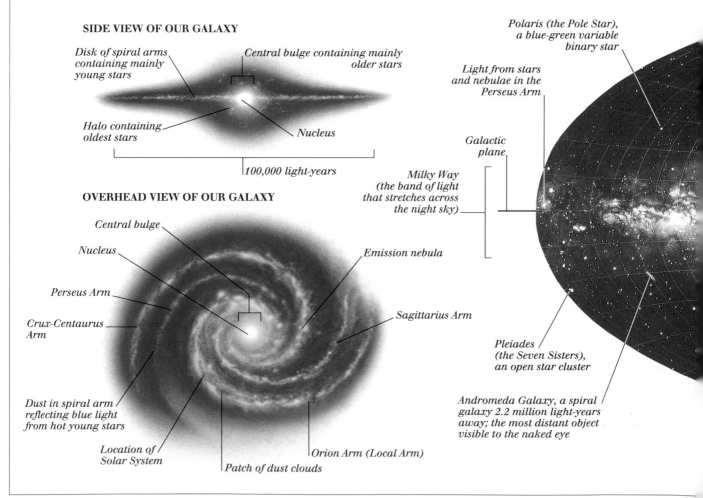

SIDE VIEW OF OUR GALAXY

Disk of spiral arms containing mainly young stars

Central bulge containing mainly older stars

Halo containing oldest stars

Nucleus

100,000 light-years

OVERHEAD VIEW OF OUR GALAXY

Central bulge

Nucleus

Perseus Arm

Crux-Centaurus Arm

Emission nebula

Sagittarius Arm

Dust in spiral arm reflecting blue light from hot young stars

Location of Solar System

Patch of dust clouds

Orion Arm (Local Arm)

PANORAMIC OPTICAL MAP OF OUR GALAXY AND NEARBY GALAXIES

Polaris (the Pole Star), a blue-green variable binary star

Light from stars and nebulae in the Perseus Arm

Galactic plane

Milky Way (the band of light that stretches across the night sky)

Pleiades (the Seven Sisters), an open star cluster

Andromeda Galaxy, a spiral galaxy 2.2 million light-years away; the most distant object visible to the naked eye

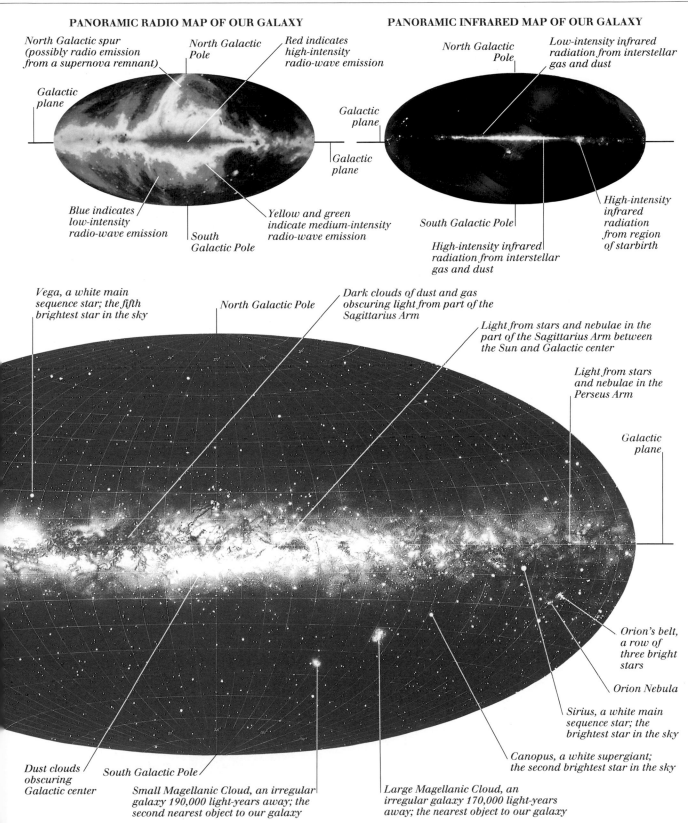

PANORAMIC RADIO MAP OF OUR GALAXY

North Galactic spur (possibly radio emission from a supernova remnant)

North Galactic Pole

Red indicates high-intensity radio-wave emission

Galactic plane

Galactic plane

Galactic plane

Blue indicates low-intensity radio-wave emission

South Galactic Pole

Yellow and green indicate medium-intensity radio-wave emission

PANORAMIC INFRARED MAP OF OUR GALAXY

North Galactic Pole

Low-intensity infrared radiation from interstellar gas and dust

High-intensity infrared radiation from region of starbirth

South Galactic Pole

High-intensity infrared radiation from interstellar gas and dust

Vega, a white main sequence star; the fifth brightest star in the sky

North Galactic Pole

Dark clouds of dust and gas obscuring light from part of the Sagittarius Arm

Light from stars and nebulae in the part of the Sagittarius Arm between the Sun and Galactic center

Light from stars and nebulae in the Perseus Arm

Galactic plane

Orion's belt, a row of three bright stars

Orion Nebula

Sirius, a white main sequence star; the brightest star in the sky

Canopus, a white supergiant; the second brightest star in the sky

Large Magellanic Cloud, an irregular galaxy 170,000 light-years away; the nearest object to our galaxy

Small Magellanic Cloud, an irregular galaxy 190,000 light-years away; the second nearest object to our galaxy

South Galactic Pole

Dust clouds obscuring Galactic center

Nebulae and star clusters

**HODGE 11, A
GLOBULAR CLUSTER**

A NEBULA IS A CLOUD OF DUST AND GAS inside a galaxy. Nebulae become visible if the gas glows or if the cloud reflects starlight or obscures light from more distant objects. Emission nebulae shine because their gas emits light when it is stimulated by radiation from hot young stars. Reflection nebulae shine because their dust reflects light from stars in or around the nebula. Dark nebulae appear as silhouettes because they block light from shining nebulae or stars behind them. Two types of nebula are associated with dying stars: planetary nebulae and supernova remnants. Both consist of expanding shells of gas that were once the outer layers of a star. A planetary nebula is a gas shell drifting away from a dying stellar core. A supernova remnant is a gas shell moving away from a stellar core at great speed following a violent explosion called a supernova (see pp. 26-27). Stars are often found in groups known as clusters. Open clusters are loose groups of a few thousand young stars that were born in the same cloud and are drifting apart. Globular clusters are densely packed, roughly spherical groups of hundreds of thousands of older stars.

TRIFID NEBULA (EMISSION NEBULA)

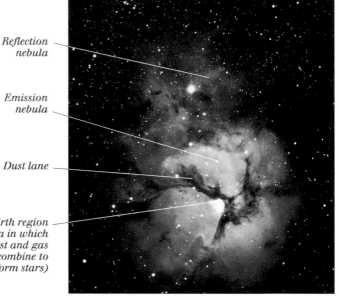

Reflection nebula

Emission nebula

Dust lane

Starbirth region (area in which dust and gas combine to form stars)

**PLEIADES (OPEN STAR CLUSTER)
WITH A REFLECTION NEBULA**

Wisps of dust and hydrogen gas remaining from cloud in which stars formed

Young star in an open cluster of 300–500 stars

Reflection nebula

HORSEHEAD NEBULA (DARK NEBULA)

Glowing filament of hot, ionized hydrogen gas

Alnitak (star in Orion's belt)

Dust lane

Emission nebula

Star near southern end of Orion's belt

Emission nebula

Horsehead Nebula

Reflection nebula

Dark nebula obscuring light from distant stars

ORION NEBULA (DIFFUSE EMISSION NEBULA)

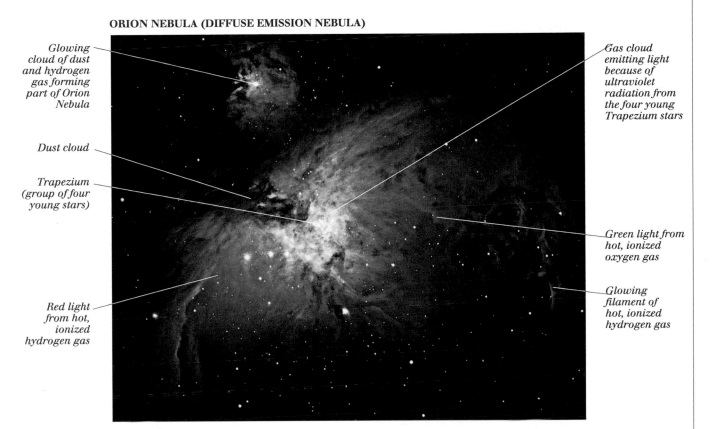

Glowing cloud of dust and hydrogen gas forming part of Orion Nebula

Gas cloud emitting light because of ultraviolet radiation from the four young Trapezium stars

Dust cloud

Trapezium (group of four young stars)

Green light from hot, ionized oxygen gas

Glowing filament of hot, ionized hydrogen gas

Red light from hot, ionized hydrogen gas

VELA SUPERNOVA REMNANT

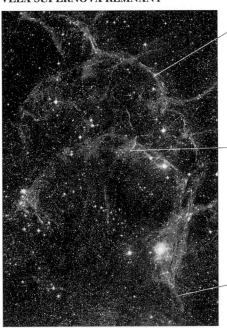

Supernova remnant (gas shell consisting of outer layers of star thrown off in supernova explosion)

Hydrogen gas emitting red light due to being heated by supernova explosion

HELIX NEBULA (PLANETARY NEBULA)

Planetary nebula (gas shell expanding outward from dying stellar core)

Stellar core at a temperature of about 180,000°F

Red light from hot, ionized hydrogen gas

Blue-green light from hot, ionized oxygen and nitrogen gases

Glowing filament of hot, ionized hydrogen gas

Stars of northern skies

WHEN YOU LOOK AT THE NORTHERN SKY, you look away from the densely populated Galactic center, so the northern sky generally appears less bright than the southern sky (see pp. 20-21). Among the best-known sights in the northern sky are the constellations Ursa Major (the Great Bear) and Orion. Some ancient civilizations believed that the stars were fixed to a celestial sphere surrounding the Earth, and modern maps of the sky are based on a similar idea. The North and South Poles of this imaginary celestial sphere are directly above the North and South Poles of the Earth, at the points where the Earth's axis of rotation intersects the sphere. The celestial North Pole is at the center of the map shown here, and Polaris (the Pole Star) lies very close to it. The celestial equator marks a projection of the Earth's equator on the sphere. The ecliptic marks the path of the Sun across the sky as the Earth orbits the Sun. The Moon and planets move against the background of the stars because the stars are much more distant; the nearest star outside the Solar System (Proxima Centauri) is more than 50,000 times farther away than the planet Jupiter.

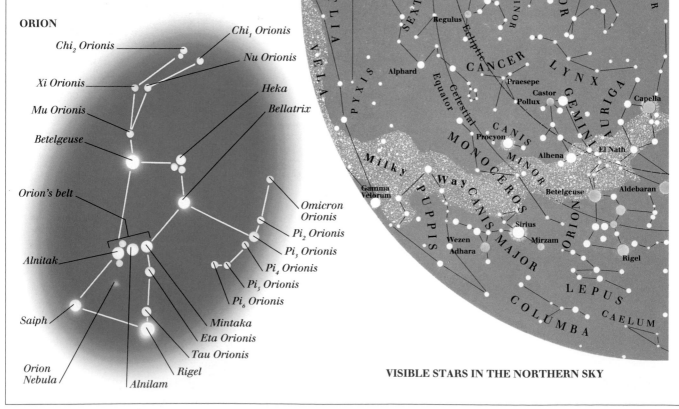

ORION

Chi₂ Orionis — Chi₁ Orionis — Nu Orionis — Xi Orionis — Heka — Mu Orionis — Bellatrix — Betelgeuse — Orion's belt — Omicron Orionis — Pi₂ Orionis — Pi₃ Orionis — Pi₄ Orionis — Pi₅ Orionis — Pi₆ Orionis — Alnitak — Saiph — Mintaka — Eta Orionis — Tau Orionis — Orion Nebula — Rigel — Alnilam

VISIBLE STARS IN THE NORTHERN SKY

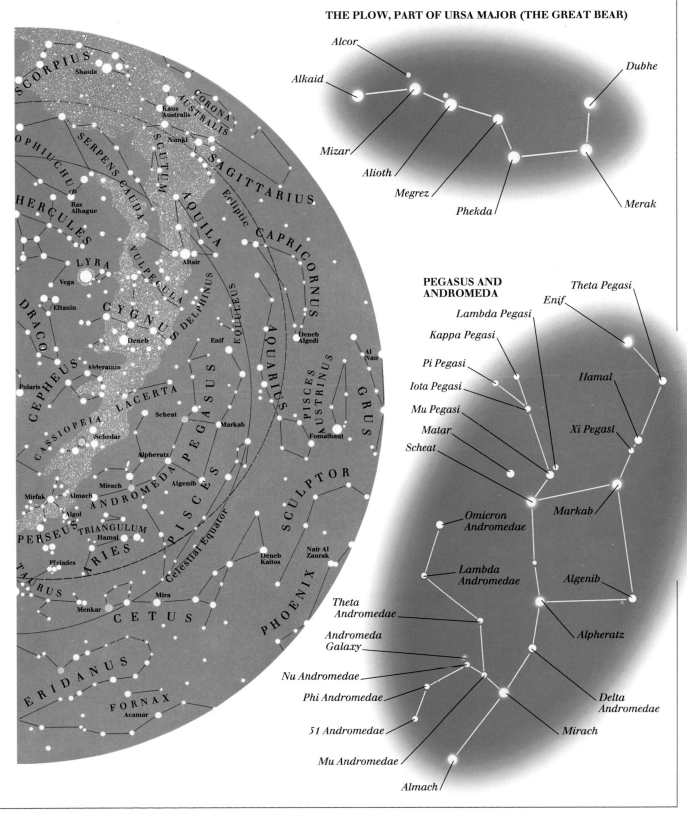

THE PLOW, PART OF URSA MAJOR (THE GREAT BEAR)

Alcor
Alkaid
Dubhe
Mizar
Alioth
Megrez
Phekda
Merak

SCORPIUS
Shaula
CORONA AUSTRALIS
Kaus Australis
Nunki
OPHIUCHUS
SERPENS CAUDA
SCUTUM
SAGITTARIUS
AQUILA
CAPRICORNUS
Ras Alhague
HERCULES
VULPECULA
Altair
Ecliptic
LYRA
Vega
DELPHINUS
EQUULEUS
AQUARIUS
Deneb Algedi
Al Nair
Eltanin
CYGNUS
Enif
DRACO
Deneb
PISCES AUSTRINUS
GRUS
Alderamin
LACERTA
PEGASUS
Scheat
Polaris
CEPHEUS
Markab
Fomalhaut
CASSIOPEIA
Schedar
Alpheratz
ANDROMEDA
Algenib
SCULPTOR
Mirfak
Mirach
Almach
PISCES
Algol
PERSEUS
TRIANGULUM
Hamal
ARIES
Deneb Kaitos
Nair Al Zaurak
Pleiades
TAURUS
Mira
Menkar
CETUS
PHOENIX
ERIDANUS
FORNAX
Acamar
Celestial Equator

PEGASUS AND ANDROMEDA

Theta Pegasi
Enif
Lambda Pegasi
Kappa Pegasi
Pi Pegasi
Hamal
Iota Pegasi
Mu Pegasi
Xi Pegasi
Matar
Scheat
Markab
Omicron Andromedae
Lambda Andromedae
Algenib
Theta Andromedae
Alpheratz
Andromeda Galaxy
Nu Andromedae
Phi Andromedae
Delta Andromedae
51 Andromedae
Mirach
Mu Andromedae
Almach

Stars of southern skies

WHEN YOU LOOK AT THE SOUTHERN SKY, you look toward the Galactic center, which has a huge population of stars. As a result, the Milky Way appears brighter in the southern sky than in the northern sky (see pp. 18-19). The southern sky is rich in nebulae and star clusters. It contains the Large and Small Magellanic Clouds, which are the two nearest galaxies to our own. Stars make fixed patterns in the sky called constellations. The constellations, however, are only apparent groupings of stars, because the distances to the stars in a constellation may vary enormously. The shapes of constellations may change over many thousands of years because of the relative motions of stars. The apparent movement of entire constellations across the sky is due to the Earth's motion in space. The daily rotation of the Earth causes the constellations to move across the sky from east to west, and the orbit of the Earth around the Sun causes different areas of sky to be visible in different seasons. The visibility of areas of sky also depends on the location of the observer. For instance, stars near the celestial equator may be seen from either hemisphere at some time during the year, while stars close to the celestial poles (the celestial South Pole is at the center of the map shown here) can never be seen from the opposite hemisphere.

HYDRUS (THE WATER SNAKE) AND MENSA (THE TABLE)

Small Magellanic Cloud

Beta Hydri

Delta Hydri

Gamma Hydri

Alpha Hydri

Gamma Mensae

Alpha Mensae

Eta Mensae

Epsilon Hydri

Beta Mensae

Large Magellanic Cloud

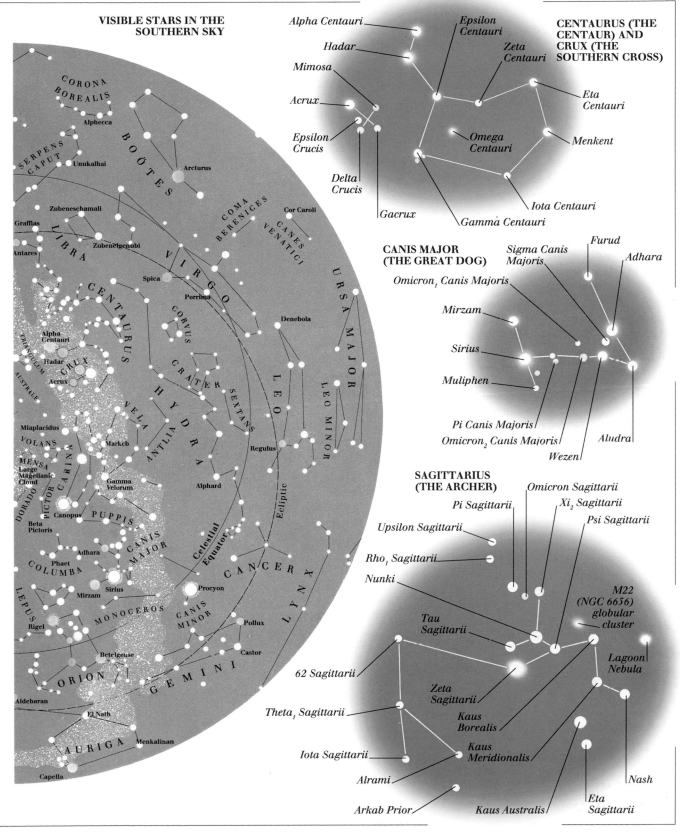

VISIBLE STARS IN THE SOUTHERN SKY

CORONA BOREALIS
Alphecca
BOÖTES
SERPENS CAPUT
Unukalhai
Arcturus
COMA BERENICES
Cor Caroli
CANES VENATICI
Zubeneschamali
Graffias
LIBRA
Zubenelgenubi
VIRGO
Antares
URSA MAJOR
Spica
Porrima
CENTAURUS
Denebola
CORVUS
LEO MINOR
Alpha Centauri
CRATER
SEXTANS
LEO
Hadar
CRUX
HYDRA
Acrux
TRIANGULUM AUSTRALE
VELA
ANTLIA
Miaplacidus
VOLANS
Markeb
Regulus
MENSA
Large Magellanic Cloud
CARINA
Gamma Velorum
PICTOR
Alphard
DORADO
Canopus
PUPPIS
Celestial Equator
Ecliptic
Beta Pictoris
CANIS MAJOR
CANCER
Adhara
COLUMBA
Phaet
MONOCEROS
Mirzam
Sirius
CANIS MINOR
Procyon
LYNX
Pollux
LEPUS
Rigel
Castor
Betelgeuse
ORION
GEMINI
Aldebaran
El Nath
Menkalinan
AURIGA
Capella

CENTAURUS (THE CENTAUR) AND CRUX (THE SOUTHERN CROSS)

Alpha Centauri
Epsilon Centauri
Hadar
Zeta Centauri
Mimosa
Eta Centauri
Acrux
Epsilon Crucis
Omega Centauri
Menkent
Delta Crucis
Iota Centauri
Gacrux
Gamma Centauri

CANIS MAJOR (THE GREAT DOG)

Sigma Canis Majoris
Furud
Omicron₁ Canis Majoris
Adhara
Mirzam
Sirius
Muliphen
Pi Canis Majoris
Omicron₂ Canis Majoris
Aludra
Wezen

SAGITTARIUS (THE ARCHER)

Omicron Sagittarii
Pi Sagittarii
Xi₂ Sagittarii
Psi Sagittarii
Upsilon Sagittarii
Rho₁ Sagittarii
Nunki
M22 (NGC 6656) globular cluster
Tau Sagittarii
Lagoon Nebula
62 Sagittarii
Zeta Sagittarii
Theta₁ Sagittarii
Kaus Borealis
Iota Sagittarii
Kaus Meridionalis
Alrami
Arkab Prior
Kaus Australis
Eta Sagittarii
Nash

21

Stars

OPEN STAR CLUSTER AND DUST CLOUD

STARS ARE BODIES of hot glowing gas that are born in nebulae (see pp. 24-27). They vary enormously in size, mass, and temperature: diameters range from about 450 times smaller to over 1,000 times bigger than that of the Sun; masses range from about a twentieth to over 50 solar masses; and surface temperatures range from about 5,500°F to over 90,000°F. The color of a star is determined by its temperature: the hottest stars are blue and the coolest are red. The Sun, with a surface temperature of 10,000°F, is between these extremes and appears yellow. The energy emitted by a shining star is produced by nuclear fusion in the star's core. The brightness of a star is measured in magnitudes—the brighter the star, the lower its magnitude. There are two types of magnitude: apparent magnitude, which is the brightness seen from Earth, and absolute magnitude, which is the brightness that would be seen from a standard distance of 10 parsecs (32.6 light-years). The light emitted by a star may be split to form a spectrum containing a series of dark lines (absorption lines). The patterns of lines indicate the presence of particular chemical elements, enabling astronomers to deduce the composition of the star's atmosphere. The magnitude and spectral type (color) of stars may be plotted on a graph called a Hertzsprung-Russell diagram, which shows that stars tend to fall into several well-defined groups. The principal groups are main sequence stars (those which are fusing hydrogen to form helium), giants, supergiants, and white dwarfs.

STAR SIZES

Red giant (diameters between about 10 million and 100 million miles)

The Sun (main sequence star with diameter about 870,000 miles)

White dwarf (diameters between about 2,000 and 30,000 miles)

ENERGY EMISSION FROM THE SUN

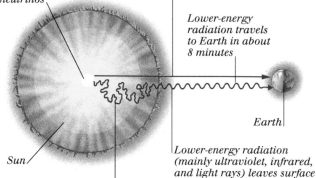

Nuclear fusion in core produces gamma rays and neutrinos

Neutrinos travel to Earth directly from Sun's core in about 8 minutes

Lower-energy radiation travels to Earth in about 8 minutes

Earth

Sun

Lower-energy radiation (mainly ultraviolet, infrared, and light rays) leaves surface

High-energy radiation (gamma rays) loses energy while traveling to surface over 2 million years

STAR MAGNITUDES

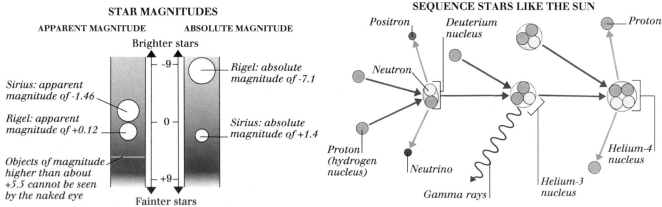

APPARENT MAGNITUDE   **ABSOLUTE MAGNITUDE**

Brighter stars

-9

0

+9

Fainter stars

Sirius: apparent magnitude of -1.46

Rigel: apparent magnitude of +0.12

Objects of magnitude higher than about +5.5 cannot be seen by the naked eye

Rigel: absolute magnitude of -7.1

Sirius: absolute magnitude of +1.4

NUCLEAR FUSION IN MAIN SEQUENCE STARS LIKE THE SUN

Positron

Deuterium nucleus

Proton

Neutron

Proton (hydrogen nucleus)

Neutrino

Gamma rays

Helium-3 nucleus

Helium-4 nucleus

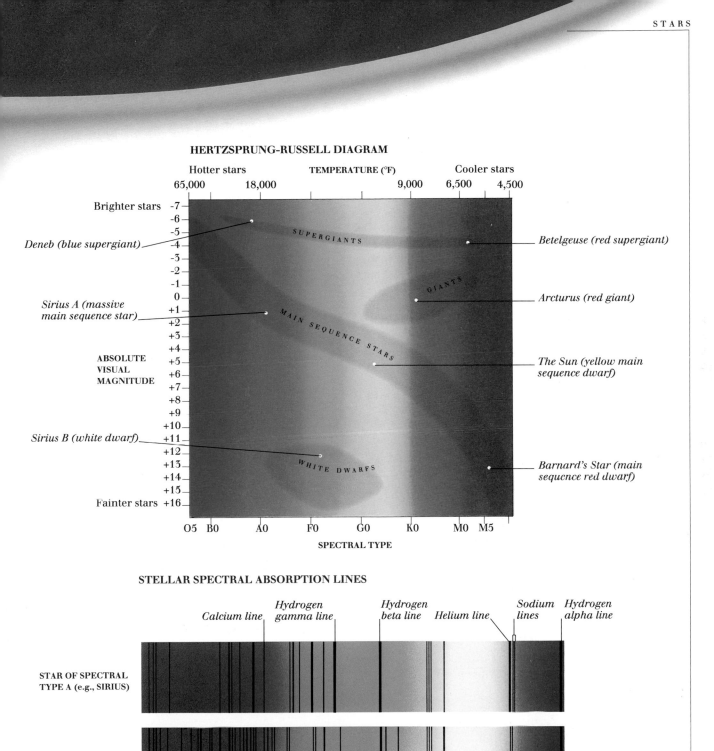

HERTZSPRUNG-RUSSELL DIAGRAM

Hotter stars   TEMPERATURE (°F)   Cooler stars

65,000   18,000   9,000   6,500   4,500

Brighter stars -7
-6
-5
Deneb (blue supergiant) -4
-3
-2
-1
0
Sirius A (massive +1
main sequence star) +2
+3
+4
ABSOLUTE +5
VISUAL +6
MAGNITUDE +7
+8
+9
+10
+11
Sirius B (white dwarf) +12
+13
+14
+15
Fainter stars +16

SUPERGIANTS

GIANTS

MAIN SEQUENCE STARS

WHITE DWARFS

Betelgeuse (red supergiant)

Arcturus (red giant)

The Sun (yellow main
sequence dwarf)

Barnard's Star (main
sequence red dwarf)

O5 B0   A0   F0   G0   K0   M0 M5

SPECTRAL TYPE

STELLAR SPECTRAL ABSORPTION LINES

Calcium line   Hydrogen   Hydrogen   Helium line   Sodium   Hydrogen
                gamma line   beta line   lines   alpha line

STAR OF SPECTRAL
TYPE A (e.g., SIRIUS)

STAR OF SPECTRAL
TYPE G (e.g., THE SUN)

Hydrogen   Magnesium   Sodium   Hydrogen
beta line   lines   lines   alpha line

Small stars

**REGION OF
STAR FORMATION
IN ORION**

SMALL STARS HAVE A MASS of up to about one and a half times that of the Sun. They begin to form when a region of higher density in a nebula condenses into a huge globule of gas and dust that contracts under its own gravity. Within a globule, regions of condensing matter heat up and begin to glow, forming protostars. If a protostar contains enough matter, the central temperature reaches about 27 million °F. At this temperature, nuclear reactions in which hydrogen fuses to form helium can start. This process releases energy, which prevents the star from contracting further, and also causes it to shine; it is now a main sequence star. A star of about one solar mass remains in the main sequence for about 10 billion years, until the hydrogen in the star's core has been converted into helium. The helium core then contracts again, and nuclear reactions continue in a shell around the core. The core becomes hot enough for helium to fuse to form carbon, while the outer layers of the star expand, cool, and shine less brightly. The expanding star is known as a red giant. When the helium in the core runs out, the outer layers of the star may drift off as an expanding gas shell called a planetary nebula. The remaining core (about 80 percent of the original star) is now in its final stages. It becomes a white dwarf star that gradually cools and dims. When it finally stops shining altogether, the dead star will become a black dwarf.

STRUCTURE OF A MAIN SEQUENCE STAR

*Core containing hydrogen
fusing to form helium*

*Radiative
zone*

*Convective
zone*

*Surface temperature
about 10,000°F*

*Core temperature
about 27 million °F*

STRUCTURE OF A NEBULA

*Young main
sequence star*

*Dense region of dust and
gas (mainly hydrogen)
condensing under gravity
to form globules*

*Hot, ionized hydrogen
gas emitting red light
due to stimulation by
radiation from hot
young stars*

*Dark globule of dust and
gas (mainly hydrogen)
contracting to form protostars*

LIFE OF A SMALL STAR OF ABOUT ONE SOLAR MASS

*Cool cloud of
gas (mainly
hydrogen)
and dust*

*Dense globule
condensing to
form protostars*

NEBULA

*Glowing
ball of gas
(mainly
hydrogen)*

*Natal cocoon
(shell of dust
blown away by
radiation from
protostar)*

PROTOSTAR
Duration: 50 million years

About 870,000 miles

*Star
producing
energy by
nuclear fusion
in core*

MAIN SEQUENCE STAR
Duration: 10 billion years

STRUCTURE OF A RED GIANT

Cooling, expanding
outer layers glow red

Surface temperature
about 6,300°F

Outer envelope consisting
mainly of hydrogen

Shell where hydrogen is
fusing to form helium

Intermediate layer
consisting mainly
of helium

Shell where
helium is fusing
to form carbon

Carbon core
temperature
about
180 million °F

At least 40 million miles

Cooling,
expanding
outer layers

RED GIANT
Duration: 100 million years

Outer layers form
expanding
gas shell

Dense,
contracting
core

About 8,000 miles

PLANETARY NEBULA
Duration: 35,000 years

Very dense core (one
teaspoonful weighs
about five tons)

WHITE DWARF

Cooling core
glows red

Cold,
dead core

**COOLING
WHITE DWARF**

BLACK DWARF

Massive stars

MASSIVE STARS HAVE A MASS AT LEAST THREE TIMES that of the Sun, and some stars are as massive as about 50 Suns. A massive star evolves in a similar way to a small star until it reaches the main sequence stage (see pp. 24-25). During the main sequence, a star shines steadily until the hydrogen in its core has fused to form helium. This process takes billions of years in a small star, but only millions of years in a massive star. A massive star then becomes a red supergiant, which initially consists of a helium core surrounded by outer layers of cooling, expanding gas. Over the next few million years, a series of nuclear reactions form different elements in shells around an iron core. The core eventually collapses in less than a second, causing a massive explosion called a supernova, in which a shock wave blows away the outer layers of the star. Supernovae shine brighter than an entire galaxy for a short time. Sometimes, the core survives the supernova explosion. If the surviving core is between about one and a half and three solar masses, it contracts to become a tiny, dense neutron star. If the core is considerably greater than three solar masses, it contracts to become a black hole (see pp. 28-29).

SUPERNOVA

TARANTULA NEBULA BEFORE SUPERNOVA

STRUCTURE OF A RED SUPERGIANT

Outer envelope consisting mainly of hydrogen

Layer consisting mainly of helium

Layer consisting mainly of carbon

Layer consisting mainly of oxygen

Layer consisting mainly of silicon

Shell of hydrogen fusing to form helium

Shell of helium fusing to form carbon

Shell of carbon fusing to form oxygen

Shell of oxygen fusing to form silicon

Shell of silicon fusing to form iron core

Surface temperature about 5,500°F

Cooling, expanding outer layers glow red

Core of mainly iron at a temperature of 5.4–9 billion °F

LIFE OF A MASSIVE STAR OF ABOUT 10 SOLAR MASSES

Dense globule condensing to form protostars

Cool cloud of gas (mainly hydrogen) and dust

NEBULA

Glowing ball of gas (mainly hydrogen)

Natal cocoon (shell of dust blown away by radiation from protostar)

PROTOSTAR
Duration: a few hundred thousand years

About 2 million miles

Star producing energy by nuclear fusion in core

MAIN SEQUENCE STAR
Duration: 10 million years

FEATURES OF A SUPERNOVA

TARANTULA NEBULA SHOWING SUPERNOVA IN 1987

Ejecta (outer layers of star thrown off during explosion) travels at speeds of up to 6,000 miles/sec

Shock wave travels outward from core at speeds of up to 20,000 miles/sec

Reverse shock wave moves inward and heats ejecta, causing it to shine

Heavy chemical elements are scattered through space by explosion

Contracting core consisting mainly of neutrons remains after explosion

Light energy of a billion Suns emitted during explosion

Central temperature more than 18 billion °F

Extremely dense core (one teaspoonful weighs about a billion tons)

About 6 miles

Core mass of less than three solar masses

NEUTRON STAR

About 60 million miles

Cooling, expanding outer layers

RED SUPERGIANT
Duration: 4 million years

Outer layers of star blown off in explosion

Contracting stellar core may remain after supernova

SUPERNOVA
Duration of visibility: 1–2 years

Core of mass greater than three solar masses continues contracting to become black hole

Accretion disk

BLACK HOLE

Neutron stars and black holes

NEUTRON STARS AND BLACK HOLES form from the stellar cores that remain after stars have exploded as supernovae (see pp. 26-27). If the remaining core is between about one and a half and three solar masses, it contracts to form a neutron star. If the remaining core is considerably greater than about three solar masses, it contracts to form a black hole. Neutron stars are typically only about six miles in diameter and consist almost entirely of subatomic particles called neutrons. These stars are so dense that a teaspoonful would weigh about a billion tons. Neutron stars are observed as pulsars, so-called because they rotate rapidly and emit two beams of radio waves, which sweep across the sky and are detected as short pulses. Black holes are characterized by their extremely strong gravity, which is so powerful that not even light can escape; as a result, black holes are invisible. However, they may be detected if they have a close companion star. The gravity of the black hole pulls gas from the other star, forming an accretion disk that spirals around the black hole at high speed, heating up and emitting radiation. Eventually, the matter spirals in to cross the event horizon (the boundary of the black hole), finally disappearing from the visible Universe.

X-ray emission from pulsar (neutron star rotating 30 times each second)

X-ray emission from center of nebula

X-RAY IMAGE OF THE CRAB NEBULA (SUPERNOVA REMNANT)

PULSAR (ROTATING NEUTRON STAR)

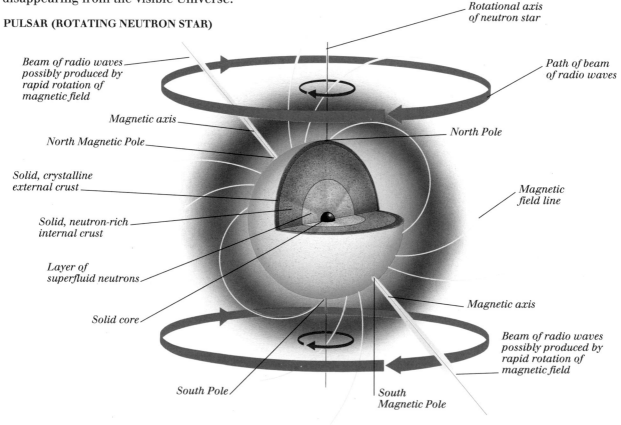

Rotational axis of neutron star

Beam of radio waves possibly produced by rapid rotation of magnetic field

Path of beam of radio waves

Magnetic axis

North Magnetic Pole

North Pole

Solid, crystalline external crust

Magnetic field line

Solid, neutron-rich internal crust

Layer of superfluid neutrons

Magnetic axis

Solid core

Beam of radio waves possibly produced by rapid rotation of magnetic field

South Pole

South Magnetic Pole

STELLAR BLACK HOLE

Blue supergiant star

Gas current (outer layers of nearby blue supergiant pulled toward black hole by gravity)

Singularity (theoretical region of infinite density, pressure, and temperature)

Hot spot (region of intense friction where gas current joins accretion disk)

Gas in outer part of accretion disk emitting low-energy radiation

Event horizon (boundary of black hole)

Hot gas in inner part of accretion disk emitting high-energy X-rays

Accretion disk (matter spiraling around black hole)

Black hole

Gas at temperatures of millions °F spiraling at close to the speed of light

FORMATION OF A BLACK HOLE

Stellar core remains after supernova explosion

Light rays increasingly bent by gravity as core collapses

Core shrinks beyond its event horizon to become a black hole

Light rays cannot escape because gravity is so strong

Outer layers of massive star thrown off in explosion

Core greater than three solar masses collapses under its own gravity

Density, pressure, and temperature of core increase as core collapses

Event horizon

Singularity (theoretical region of infinite density, pressure, and temperature)

SUPERNOVA

COLLAPSING STELLAR CORE

BLACK HOLE

The Solar System

THE SUN

THE SOLAR SYSTEM consists of a central star (the Sun) and the bodies that orbit it. These bodies include nine planets and their 61 known moons, asteroids, comets, and meteoroids. The Solar System also contains interplanetary gas and dust. Most of the planets fall into two groups: four small rocky planets near the Sun (Mercury, Venus, Earth, and Mars), and four planets farther out, the gas giants (Jupiter, Saturn, Uranus, and Neptune). Pluto belongs to neither group—it is very small, solid, and icy. Pluto is the outermost planet, except when it passes briefly inside Neptune's orbit. Between the rocky planets and gas giants is the asteroid belt, which contains thousands of chunks of rock orbiting the Sun. Most of the bodies in the Solar System move around the Sun in elliptical orbits located in a thin disk around the Sun's equator. All the planets orbit the Sun in the same direction (counterclockwise when viewed from above) and all but Venus, Uranus, and Pluto also spin around their axes in this direction. Moons also spin as they, in turn, orbit their planets. The entire Solar System orbits the center of our galaxy, the Milky Way (see pp. 14-15).

Perihelion (orbital point closest to Sun)

Sun

Elliptical orbit

Planet orbiting Sun

Direction of planetary rotation

Aphelion (orbital point farthest from Sun)

Aphelion of Neptune: 2,819 million miles

ORBITS OF INNER PLANETS

Average orbital speed of Venus: 21.8 miles/sec

Average orbital speed of Mercury: 29.8 miles/sec

Average orbital speed of Earth: 18.5 miles/sec

Average orbital speed of Mars: 15 miles/sec

Perihelion of Mercury: 28.5 million miles

Perihelion of Venus: 66.7 million miles

Perihelion of Earth: 91.4 million miles

Mercury

Mars

Perihelion of Mars: 128.4 million miles

Earth

Venus

Sun

Aphelion of Mercury: 43.3 million miles

Aphelion of Venus: 67.7 million miles

Aphelion of Pluto: 4,583 million miles

Asteroid belt

Aphelion of Earth: 94.5 million miles

Aphelion of Mars: 154.8 million miles

MERCURY
Year: 87.97 Earth days
Mass: 0.055 Earth masses
Diameter: 3,031 miles

VENUS
Year: 224.7 Earth days
Mass: 0.81 Earth masses
Diameter: 7,521 miles

EARTH
Year: 365.26 days
Mass: 1 Earth mass
Diameter: 7,926 miles

MARS
Year: 1.88 Earth years
Mass: 0.11 Earth masses
Diameter: 4,217 miles

JUPITER
Year: 11.86 Earth years
Mass: 318 Earth masses
Diameter: 88,850 miles

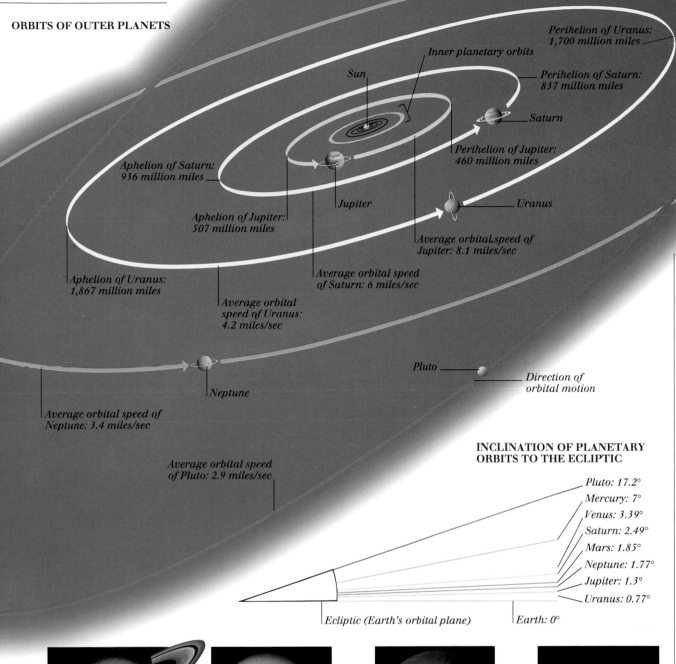

ORBITS OF OUTER PLANETS

Perihelion of Uranus:
1,700 million miles

Inner planetary orbits

Perihelion of Saturn:
837 million miles

Sun

Saturn

Aphelion of Saturn:
936 million miles

Perihelion of Jupiter:
460 million miles

Aphelion of Jupiter:
507 million miles

Jupiter

Uranus

Average orbital speed of
Jupiter: 8.1 miles/sec

Aphelion of Uranus:
1,867 million miles

Average orbital speed
of Saturn: 6 miles/sec

Average orbital
speed of Uranus:
4.2 miles/sec

Pluto

Direction of
orbital motion

Neptune

Average orbital speed of
Neptune: 3.4 miles/sec

INCLINATION OF PLANETARY ORBITS TO THE ECLIPTIC

Average orbital speed
of Pluto: 2.9 miles/sec

Pluto: 17.2°
Mercury: 7°
Venus: 3.39°
Saturn: 2.49°
Mars: 1.85°
Neptune: 1.77°
Jupiter: 1.3°
Uranus: 0.77°

Ecliptic (Earth's orbital plane)   *Earth: 0°*

SATURN
Year: 29.46 Earth years
Mass: 95.18 Earth masses
Diameter: 74,901 miles

URANUS
Year: 84.01 Earth years
Mass: 14.5 Earth masses
Diameter: 31,765 miles

NEPTUNE
Year: 164.79 Earth years
Mass: 17.14 Earth masses
Diameter: 30,777 miles

PLUTO
Year: 248.54 Earth years
Mass: 0.0022 Earth masses
Diameter: 1,429 miles

The Sun

SOLAR PHOTOSPHERE

THE SUN IS THE STAR AT THE CENTER of our Solar System. It is about five billion years old and will probably continue to shine as it does now for about another five billion years. The Sun is a yellow main sequence star (see pp. 22-23) about 870,000 miles in diameter. It consists almost entirely of hydrogen and helium. In the Sun's core, hydrogen is converted to helium by nuclear fusion, releasing energy in the process. The energy travels from the core through the radiative and convective zones to the photosphere (visible surface), where it leaves the Sun in the form of heat and light. On the photosphere there are often dark, relatively cool areas called sunspots. These usually appear in pairs or groups and are thought to be caused by magnetic fields. Other types of solar activity are flares, which are usually associated with sunspots, and prominences. Flares are sudden discharges of high-energy radiation and atomic particles. Prominences are huge loops or filaments of gas extending into the solar atmosphere; some last for hours, others for months. Beyond the photosphere is the chromosphere (inner atmosphere) and the extremely rarified corona (outer atmosphere), which extends millions of miles into space. Tiny particles that escape from the corona give rise to the solar wind, which streams through space at hundreds of miles per second. The chromosphere and corona can be seen from Earth when the Sun is totally eclipsed by the Moon.

Sun

Moon passes between Sun and Earth

Umbra (inner, total shadow) of Moon

Region of Earth from which total eclipse is visible

Penumbra (outer, partial shadow) of Moon

Region of Earth from which partial eclipse is visible

Earth

Umbra (inner, total shadow) of Earth

Penumbra (outer, partial shadow) of Earth

SURFACE FEATURES

Gas loop (looped prominence)

Prominence (jet of gas at edge of Sun's disk up to hundreds of thousands of miles high)

Spicule (vertical jet of gas)

Photosphere (visible surface)

Chromosphere (inner atmosphere)

TOTAL SOLAR ECLIPSE

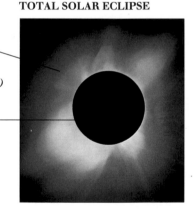

Corona (outer atmosphere of extremely hot diffuse gas)

Moon covers Sun's disk

SUNSPOTS

Granulated surface of Sun

Penumbra (lighter, outer region) containing radial fibril

Umbra (darker, inner region) temperature about 7,200°F

Photosphere temperature about 9,900°F

**EXTERNAL FEATURES AND
INTERNAL STRUCTURE OF THE SUN**

Chromosphere (inner
atmosphere) up to
6,000 miles thick

Convective zone about
90,000 miles thick

Radiative zone about
230,000 miles thick

Chromosphere
temperature about
18,000°F

Photosphere
temperature
about 9,900°F

Corona
(outer atmosphere)

Corona temperature
about 3.6 million °F

Core temperature
about 27 million °F

Photosphere
(visible surface)

Filament
(prominence visible
against photosphere)

Supergranule
(convection cell)

Granulated
surface

Prominence
(jet of gas at edge of
Sun's disk up to hundreds
of thousands of miles high)

Macrospicule
(vertical jet of gas
about 25,000 miles high)

Spicule (vertical jet of
gas about 6,000 miles high)

Sunspot
(cool region)

Solar flare
(sudden release
of energy associated
with sunspots)

Gas loop
(looped prominence)

Mercury

MERCURY

MERCURY IS THE NEAREST PLANET to the Sun, orbiting at an average distance of about 36 million miles. Because Mercury is the closest planet to the Sun, it moves faster than any other planet, traveling at an average speed of nearly 30 miles per second and completing an orbit in just under 88 days. Mercury is very small (only Pluto is smaller) and rocky. Most of the surface has been heavily cratered by the impact of meteorites, although there are also smooth, sparsely cratered plains. The Caloris Basin is the largest crater, measuring about 800 miles across. It is thought to have been formed when a rock the size of an asteroid hit the planet and is surrounded by concentric rings of mountains thrown up by the impact. The surface also has many ridges, called rupes, that are thought to have been formed when the hot core of the young planet cooled and shrank about four billion years ago, buckling the planet's surface in the process. The planet rotates about its axis very slowly, taking nearly 59 Earth days to complete one rotation. As a result, a solar day (sunrise to sunrise) on Mercury is about 176 Earth days—twice as long as the 88-day Mercurian year. Mercury has extreme surface temperatures, ranging from a maximum of 800°F on the sunlit side to -270°F on the dark side. At nightfall, the temperature drops very quickly because the planet's atmosphere is almost nonexistent. It consists only of minute amounts of helium and hydrogen captured from the solar wind, plus traces of other gases.

TILT AND ROTATION OF MERCURY

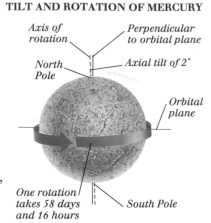

Axis of rotation

Perpendicular to orbital plane

North Pole

Axial tilt of 2°

Orbital plane

One rotation takes 58 days and 16 hours

South Pole

DEGAS AND BRONTË (RAY CRATERS)

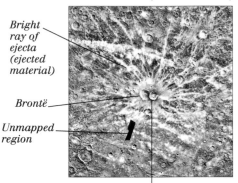

Bright ray of ejecta (ejected material)

Brontë

Unmapped region

Degas with central peak

FORMATION OF A RAY CRATER

Debris thrown out by impact

Path of meteorite colliding with planet

Wall of rock thrown up around crater

Impact forms saucer-shaped crater

Fractured rock

METEORITE IMPACT

Path of rocky ejecta (ejected material)

Ejecta forms secondary craters

Loose debris on crater floor

SECONDARY CRATERING

Wall of rock forms ring of mountains

Ray of ejecta (ejected material)

Small secondary crater

Loose ejected rock

Central mountain rings form if floor of large crater recoils from meteorite impact

Falling debris forms ridges on side of wall

RAY CRATER

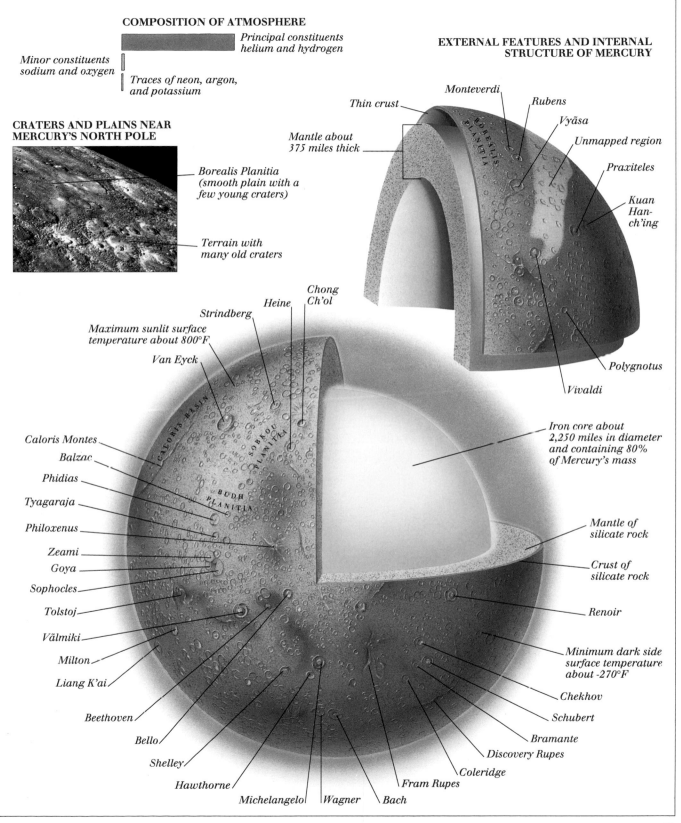

COMPOSITION OF ATMOSPHERE

Principal constituents helium and hydrogen

Minor constituents sodium and oxygen

Traces of neon, argon, and potassium

EXTERNAL FEATURES AND INTERNAL STRUCTURE OF MERCURY

Thin crust

Mantle about 375 miles thick

Monteverdi

Rubens

Vyāsa

Unmapped region

Praxiteles

Kuan Han-ch'ing

Polygnotus

Vivaldi

CRATERS AND PLAINS NEAR MERCURY'S NORTH POLE

Borealis Planitia (smooth plain with a few young craters)

Terrain with many old craters

Chong Ch'ol

Heine

Strindberg

Maximum sunlit surface temperature about 800°F

Van Eyck

Caloris Montes

Balzac

Phidias

Tyagaraja

Philoxenus

Zeami

Goya

Sophocles

Tolstoj

Vālmiki

Milton

Liang K'ai

Beethoven

Bello

Shelley

Hawthorne

Michelangelo

Wagner

Bach

Coleridge

Fram Rupes

Discovery Rupes

Bramante

Schubert

Chekhov

Minimum dark side surface temperature about -270°F

Renoir

Crust of silicate rock

Mantle of silicate rock

Iron core about 2,250 miles in diameter and containing 80% of Mercury's mass

Venus

RADAR IMAGE OF VENUS

VENUS IS A ROCKY PLANET and the second planet from the Sun. Venus spins slowly backward as it orbits the Sun, causing its rotational period to be the longest in the Solar System, at about 243 Earth days. It is slightly smaller than Earth and probably has a similar internal structure, consisting of a semisolid metal core surrounded by a rocky mantle and crust. Venus is the brightest object in the sky after the Sun and Moon because its atmosphere reflects sunlight strongly. The main component of the atmosphere is carbon dioxide, which traps heat in a greenhouse effect far stronger than that on Earth. As a result, Venus is the hottest planet, with a maximum surface temperature of about 900°F. The thick cloud layers contain droplets of sulfuric acid and are driven around the planet by winds at speeds of up to 220 miles per hour. Although the planet takes 243 Earth days to rotate once, the high-speed winds cause the clouds to circle the planet in only four Earth days. The high temperature, acidic clouds, and enormous atmospheric pressure (about 90 times greater at the surface than that on Earth) make the environment extremely hostile. However, orbiting satellites have managed to land on Venus and photograph its dry, dusty surface. The Venusian surface has also been mapped by probes with radar equipment that can "see" through the cloud layers. Such radar maps reveal a terrain with craters, mountains, volcanoes, and areas where craters have been covered by plains of solidified volcanic lava. There are two large highland regions called Aphrodite Terra and Ishtar Terra.

TILT AND ROTATION OF VENUS

Axis of rotation

Perpendicular to orbital plane

North Pole

Axial tilt of 2°

Orbital plane

One rotation takes 243 days and 14 minutes

South Pole

CLOUD FEATURES

Polar hood

Dark, mid-latitude band

Cloud features swept around planet by winds of up to 220 mph

Dirty yellow hue due to sulfuric acid in atmosphere

Bright polar band

VENUSIAN CRATERS

Danilova

Ejecta (ejected material)

Central peak

Howe

COMPUTER-ENHANCED RADAR MAP OF THE SURFACE OF VENUS

Metis Regio

Maxwell Montes

Bell Regio

Tethus Regio

Sedna Planitia

Eisila Regio

Guinevere Planitia

Phoebe Regio

Alpha Regio

Themis Regio

Lavinia Planitia

Helen Planitia

ISHTAR TERRA

APHRODITE TERRA

Atalanta Planitia

Leda Planitia

Tellus Regio

Niobe Planitia

Ovda Regio

Thetis Regio

Aino Planitia

Lada Terra

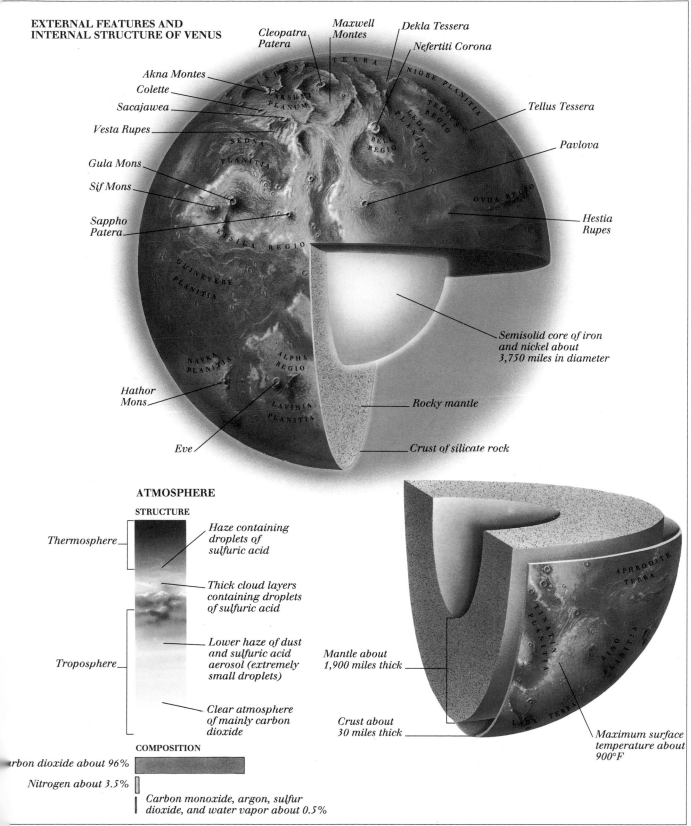

EXTERNAL FEATURES AND INTERNAL STRUCTURE OF VENUS

Cleopatra Patera

Maxwell Montes

Dekla Tessera

Nefertiti Corona

Akna Montes

Colette

Sacajawea

Vesta Rupes

Tellus Tessera

Gula Mons

Sif Mons

Pavlova

Sappho Patera

Hestia Rupes

Semisolid core of iron and nickel about 3,750 miles in diameter

Rocky mantle

Hathor Mons

Crust of silicate rock

Eve

ATMOSPHERE

STRUCTURE

Thermosphere

Haze containing droplets of sulfuric acid

Thick cloud layers containing droplets of sulfuric acid

Lower haze of dust and sulfuric acid aerosol (extremely small droplets)

Troposphere

Mantle about 1,900 miles thick

Clear atmosphere of mainly carbon dioxide

Crust about 30 miles thick

COMPOSITION

Maximum surface temperature about 900°F

Carbon dioxide about 96%

Nitrogen about 3.5%

Carbon monoxide, argon, sulfur dioxide, and water vapor about 0.5%

The Earth

THE EARTH IS THE THIRD of the nine planets that orbit the Sun. It is the largest and densest rocky planet, and the only one known to support life. About 70 percent of the Earth's surface is covered by water, which is not found in liquid form on the surface of any other planet. There are four main layers: the inner core, the outer core, the mantle, and the crust. At the heart of the planet the solid inner core has a temperature of about 7,230°F.

THE EARTH

The heat from this inner core causes material in the molten outer core and mantle to circulate in convection currents. It is thought that these convection currents generate the Earth's magnetic field, which extends into space as the magnetosphere. The Earth's atmosphere helps screen out some of the harmful radiation from the Sun, stops meteorites from reaching the planet's surface, and traps enough heat to prevent extremes of cold. The Earth has one natural satellite, the Moon, which is large enough for both bodies to be considered a double-planet system.

TILT AND ROTATION OF THE EARTH

Axis of rotation

Axial tilt of 23.4°

North Pole

Orbital plane

South Pole

One rotation takes 23 hours and 56 minutes

Perpendicular to orbital plane

THE FORMATION OF THE EARTH

The heat of the collisions caused the planet to glow red

The cloud broke up into particles of ice and rock, which stuck together to form planets

Microorganisms began to photosynthesize, creating a supply of oxygen

4,600 YEARS AGO, THE SOLAR SYSTEM FORMED FROM A CLOUD OF GAS AND DUST

THE EARTH WAS FORMED FROM COLLIDING ROCKS

4,500 YEARS AGO THE SURFACE COOLED TO FORM THE CRUST

THE CONTINENTS BROKE UP AND REFORMED, GRADUALLY TAKING THEIR PRESENT POSITIONS

Solar wind enters atmosphere and produces aurora

Magnetosphere (magnetic field)

Solar wind (stream of electrically charged particles)

THE EARTH'S MAGNETOSPHERE

Van Allen radiation belt

Earth

Axis of geographic poles

Axis of magnetic poles

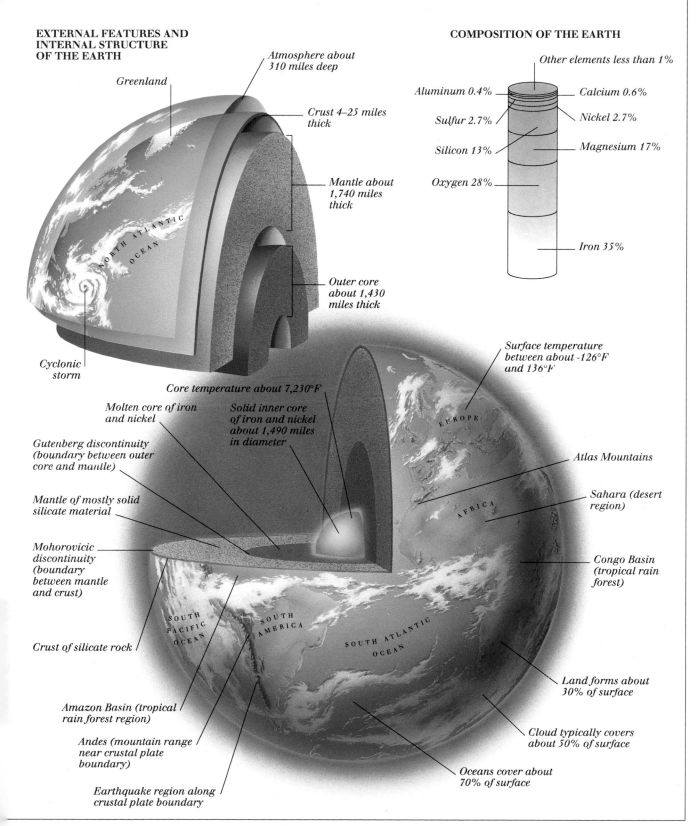

EXTERNAL FEATURES AND
INTERNAL STRUCTURE
OF THE EARTH

Greenland

Atmosphere about
310 miles deep

Crust 4–25 miles
thick

Mantle about
1,740 miles
thick

Outer core
about 1,430
miles thick

Cyclonic
storm

NORTH ATLANTIC OCEAN

COMPOSITION OF THE EARTH

Other elements less than 1%

Aluminum 0.4%

Calcium 0.6%

Sulfur 2.7%

Nickel 2.7%

Silicon 13%

Magnesium 17%

Oxygen 28%

Iron 35%

Surface temperature
between about -126°F
and 136°F

Core temperature about 7,230°F

Molten core of iron
and nickel

Solid inner core
of iron and nickel
about 1,490 miles
in diameter

Gutenberg discontinuity
(boundary between outer
core and mantle)

Atlas Mountains

Sahara (desert
region)

Mantle of mostly solid
silicate material

Mohorovicic
discontinuity
(boundary
between mantle
and crust)

Congo Basin
(tropical rain
forest)

Crust of silicate rock

EUROPE

AFRICA

SOUTH
PACIFIC
OCEAN

SOUTH
AMERICA

SOUTH ATLANTIC
OCEAN

Land forms about
30% of surface

Amazon Basin (tropical
rain forest region)

Andes (mountain range
near crustal plate
boundary)

Earthquake region along
crustal plate boundary

Cloud typically covers
about 50% of surface

Oceans cover about
70% of surface

39

The Moon

THE MOON FROM EARTH

THE MOON IS THE EARTH'S only natural satellite. It is relatively large for a moon, with a diameter of about 2,155 miles—just over a quarter that of the Earth. The Moon takes the same time to rotate on its axis as it takes to orbit the Earth (27.3 days), and so the same side (the near side) always faces us. However, the amount of the surface we can see—the phase of the Moon—depends on how much of the near side is in sunlight. The Moon is dry and barren, with no atmosphere or water. It consists mainly of solid rock, although its core may contain molten rock or iron. The surface is dusty, with highlands covered in craters caused by meteorite impacts, and lowlands in which large craters have been filled by solidified lava to form dark areas called maria or "seas." Maria occur mainly on the near side, which has a thinner crust than the far side. Many of the craters are rimmed by mountain ranges that form the crater walls and can be thousands of feet high.

TILT AND ROTATION OF THE MOON

Axis of rotation
Perpendicular to orbital plane
North Pole
Axial tilt of 6.7°
Orbital plane
One rotation takes 27 Earth days and 8 hours
South Pole

CRATERS ON OCEANUS PROCELLARUM

Aristarchus
Cobra Head (head of Schröter's Valley)
Herodotus

NEAR SIDE OF THE MOON

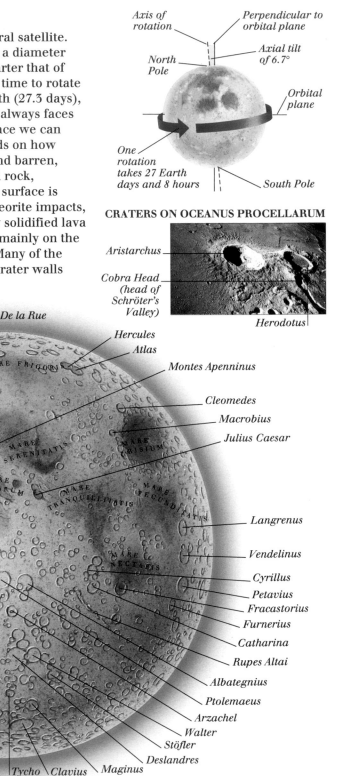

Aristoteles
De la Rue
Aristillus
Hercules
Plato
Atlas
Archimedes
Montes Apenninus
Montes Jura
Sinus Iridum
Cleomedes
Bright rays of ejected material
Macrobius
Copernicus
Julius Caesar
Aristarchus
Kepler
Langrenus
Encke
Vendelinus
Flamsteed
Cyrillus
Fra Mauro
Petavius
Grimaldi
Fracastorius
Letronne
Furnerius
Gassendi
Catharina
Mersenius
Rupes Altai
Albategnius
Ptolemaeus
Arzachel
Walter
Pitatus
Stöfler
Schickard
Deslandres
Alphonsus
Bailly
Tycho
Clavius
Maginus

MARE FRIGORIS
MARE IMBRIUM
MARE SERENITATIS
MARE CRISIUM
MARE VAPORUM
MARE TRANQUILLITATIS
MARE FECUNDITATIS
OCEANUS PROCELLARUM
MARE NECTARIS
MARE NUBIUM
MARE HUMORUM

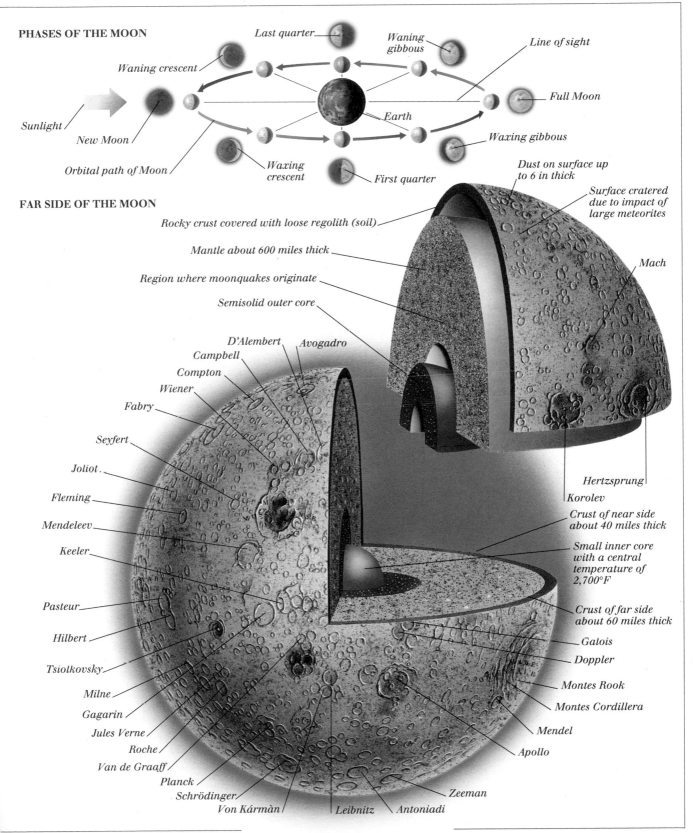

PHASES OF THE MOON

Last quarter

Waning gibbous

Waning crescent

Line of sight

Sunlight

New Moon

Full Moon

Earth

Orbital path of Moon

Waxing gibbous

Waxing crescent

First quarter

Dust on surface up to 6 in thick

Surface cratered due to impact of large meteorites

FAR SIDE OF THE MOON

Rocky crust covered with loose regolith (soil)

Mantle about 600 miles thick

Region where moonquakes originate

Semisolid outer core

Mach

D'Alembert

Avogadro

Campbell

Compton

Wiener

Fabry

Seyfert

Joliot

Hertzsprung

Korolev

Fleming

Mendeleev

Crust of near side about 40 miles thick

Keeler

Small inner core with a central temperature of 2,700°F

Pasteur

Hilbert

Crust of far side about 60 miles thick

Tsiolkovsky

Galois

Milne

Doppler

Gagarin

Montes Rook

Jules Verne

Montes Cordillera

Roche

Mendel

Van de Graaff

Apollo

Planck

Schrödinger

Zeeman

Von Kármàn

Leibnitz

Antoniadi

41

Mars

MARS

MARS, KNOWN AS THE RED PLANET, is the fourth planet from the Sun and the outermost rocky planet. In the 19th century, astronomers first observed what were thought to be signs of life on Mars. These signs included apparent canal-like markings on the surface, and dark patches that were thought to be vegetation. It is now known that the canals are an optical illusion and the dark patches are areas where the red dust that covers most of the planet has blown away. The fine dust particles are often whipped up by winds into dust storms that occasionally obscure almost all Mars's surface. Residual dust in the atmosphere gives the Martian sky a pinkish hue. The northern hemisphere of Mars has many large plains formed of solidified volcanic lava, while the southern hemisphere has many craters and large impact basins. There are also several huge, extinct volcanoes, including Olympus Mons, which at 370 miles wide and 15 miles high is the largest known volcano in the Solar System. The surface also has many canyons and branching channels. The canyons were formed by movements of the surface crust, but the channels are thought to have been formed by flowing water that has now vaporized almost completely and escaped from the atmosphere. The Martian atmosphere is much thinner than Earth's, with only a few clouds and morning mists. Mars has two tiny irregularly shaped moons, Phobos and Deimos. Their small size indicates that they may be asteroids that have been captured by the gravity of Mars.

TILT AND ROTATION OF MARS

Axis of rotation

Axial tilt of 24°

Perpendicular to orbital plane

North Pole

Orbital plane

One rotation takes 24 hours and 37 minutes

South Pole

SURFACE FEATURES OF MARS

Bright water-ice fog

Fog in canyon about 12 miles wide at end of Valles Marineris

Syria Planum

NOCTIS LABYRINTHUS (CANYON SYSTEM)

Summit caldera consisting of overlapping collapsed volcanic craters

Crater

Gentle slope produced by lava flow

Cloud formation

OLYMPUS MONS (EXTINCT SHIELD VOLCANO)

THE SURFACE OF MARS

Dark area where dust has been blown away by wind

South polar ice cap

Surface covered with red-colored iron oxide dust

MOONS OF MARS

PHOBOS
Average diameter: 14 miles
Average distance from planet: 5,800 miles

DEIMOS
Average diameter: 8 miles
Average distance from planet: 14,600 miles

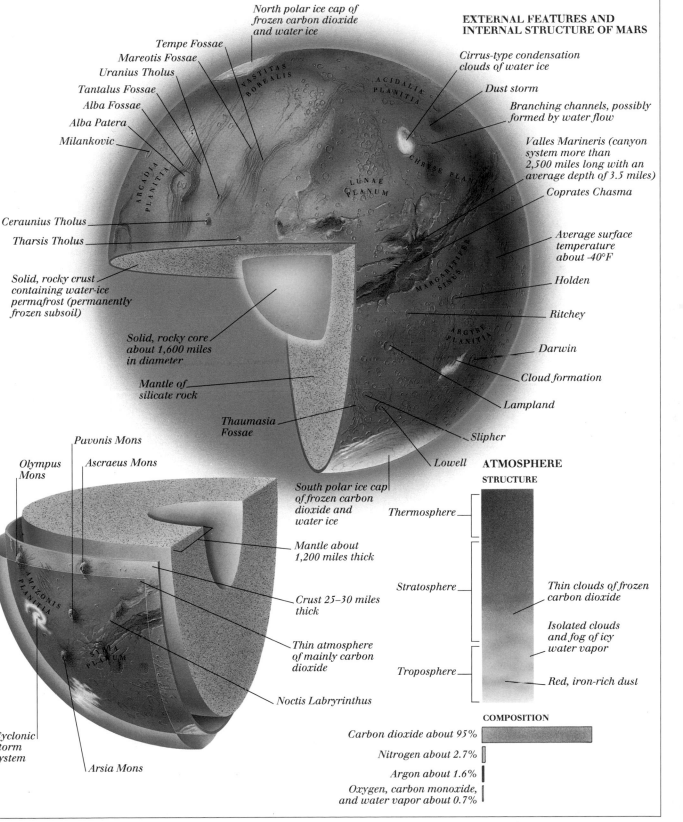

North polar ice cap of
frozen carbon dioxide
and water ice

Tempe Fossae

Mareotis Fossae

Uranius Tholus

Tantalus Fossae

Alba Fossae

Alba Patera

Milankovic

Ceraunius Tholus

Tharsis Tholus

Solid, rocky crust
containing water-ice
permafrost (permanently
frozen subsoil)

Solid, rocky core
about 1,600 miles
in diameter

Mantle of
silicate rock

Thaumasia
Fossae

**EXTERNAL FEATURES AND
INTERNAL STRUCTURE OF MARS**

Cirrus-type condensation
clouds of water ice

Dust storm

Branching channels, possibly
formed by water flow

Valles Marineris (canyon
system more than
2,500 miles long with an
average depth of 3.5 miles)

Coprates Chasma

Average surface
temperature
about -40°F

Holden

Ritchey

Darwin

Cloud formation

Lampland

Slipher

Lowell

South polar ice cap
of frozen carbon
dioxide and
water ice

Olympus
Mons

Pavonis Mons

Ascraeus Mons

Mantle about
1,200 miles thick

Crust 25–30 miles
thick

Thin atmosphere
of mainly carbon
dioxide

Noctis Labryrinthus

Cyclonic
storm
system

Arsia Mons

ATMOSPHERE

STRUCTURE

Thermosphere

Stratosphere

Troposphere

Thin clouds of frozen
carbon dioxide

Isolated clouds
and fog of icy
water vapor

Red, iron-rich dust

COMPOSITION

Carbon dioxide about 95%

Nitrogen about 2.7%

Argon about 1.6%

Oxygen, carbon monoxide,
and water vapor about 0.7%

43

Jupiter

JUPITER

JUPITER IS THE FIFTH PLANET from the Sun and the first of the four gas giants. It is the largest and the most massive planet, with a diameter about 11 times that of the Earth and a mass about 2.5 times the combined mass of the eight other planets. Jupiter is thought to have a small rocky core surrounded by an inner mantle of metallic hydrogen (liquid hydrogen that acts like a metal). Outside the inner mantle is an outer mantle of liquid hydrogen and helium that merges into the gaseous atmosphere. Jupiter's rapid rate of rotation causes the clouds in its atmosphere to form belts and zones that encircle the planet parallel to the equator. Belts are dark, low-lying, relatively warm cloud layers. Zones are bright, high-altitude, cooler cloud layers. Within the belts and zones, turbulence causes the formation of cloud features such as white ovals and red spots, both of which are huge storm systems. The most prominent cloud feature is a storm called the Great Red Spot, which consists of a spiraling column of clouds three times wider than the Earth that rises about five miles above the upper cloud layer. Jupiter has one thin, faint, main ring, inside of which is a halo ring of tiny particles extending toward the planet. There are 16 known Jovian moons. The four largest moons (called the Galileans) are Ganymede, Callisto, Io, and Europa. Ganymede and Callisto are cratered and probably icy. Europa is smooth and icy and may contain water. Io is covered in bright red, orange, and yellow splotches. This coloring is caused by sulfurous material from active volcanoes that shoot plumes of lava hundreds of miles above the surface.

RINGS OF JUPITER

Main ring

Halo ring

TILT AND ROTATION OF JUPITER

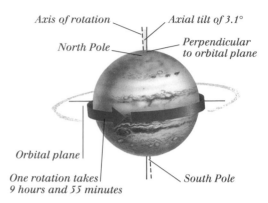

Axis of rotation

Axial tilt of 3.1°

North Pole

Perpendicular to orbital plane

Orbital plane

One rotation takes 9 hours and 55 minutes

South Pole

GREAT RED SPOT AND WHITE OVAL

Great Red Spot (anticyclonic storm system)

Red color probably due to phosphorus

White oval (temporary anticyclonic storm system)

GALILEAN MOONS OF JUPITER

EUROPA
Diameter: 1,950 miles
Average distance from planet: 416,900 miles

CALLISTO
Diameter: 2,983 miles
Average distance from planet: 1,168,200 miles

GANYMEDE
Diameter: 3,270 miles
Average distance from planet: 664,900 miles

IO
Diameter: 2,263 miles
Average distance from planet: 262,100 miles

ATMOSPHERE

STRUCTURE

EXTERNAL FEATURES AND INTERNAL STRUCTURE OF JUPITER

Stratosphere

Troposphere

White clouds of ammonia crystals

Dark orange clouds of ammonium hydrosulfide crystals

Bluish clouds of water ice and water droplets

Atmosphere of mainly hydrogen and helium

Outer mantle merging into atmosphere

Inner mantle about 18,500 miles thick

Zone (high-pressure region of rising gases)

Red spot

Plume (trailing cloud)

High-altitude white cloud

COMPOSITION

Hydrogen about 90%

Helium about 10%

Traces of ammonia, methane, and water vapor

North polar aurora

North Temperate Zone

North Temperate Belt

North Tropical Zone

North Equatorial Belt

Equatorial Zone

South Equatorial Belt

South Tropical Zone

South Temperate Belt

South Temperate Zone

Flash of lightning

Great Red Spot (anticyclonic storm system)

Outer mantle of liquid hydrogen and helium

Inner mantle of metallic hydrogen

Rocky core about 17,500 miles in diameter

Core temperature about 54,000°F

Belt (low-pressure region of sinking gases)

White oval (temporary anticyclonic storm system)

Cloud-top temperature about -180°F

Saturn

SATURN IS THE SIXTH PLANET from the Sun. It is
a gas giant almost as big as Jupiter, with an
equatorial diameter of about 74,900 miles. Saturn
is thought to consist of a small core of rock and ice
surrounded by an inner mantle of metallic hydrogen
(liquid hydrogen that acts like a metal). Outside the
inner mantle is an outer mantle of liquid hydrogen
that merges into a gaseous atmosphere. Saturn's
clouds form belts and zones similar to those on
Jupiter, but obscured by overlying haze. Storms and eddies,
seen as red or white ovals, occur in the clouds. Saturn has
an extremely thin but wide system of rings that is less than
one mile thick but extends outward to about 260,000 miles
from the planet's surface. The main rings comprise
thousands of narrow ringlets, each made of icy lumps that
range in size from tiny particles to chunks several yards
across. The D, E, and G rings are very faint, the F ring is
brighter, and the A, B, and C rings are bright enough to
be seen from Earth with binoculars. Saturn has 18 known
moons, some of which orbit inside the rings and are thought
to exert a gravitational influence on the shapes of the rings.
Unusually, seven of the moons are co-orbital—they share
an orbit with another moon. Astronomers believe that
such co-orbital moons may have originated from
a single satellite that broke up.

TILT AND ROTATION OF SATURN

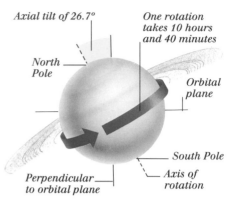

Axial tilt of 26.7°

One rotation takes 10 hours and 40 minutes

North Pole

Orbital plane

South Pole

Axis of rotation

Perpendicular to orbital plane

COLOR-ENHANCED IMAGE OF SATURN'S CLOUD FEATURES

Ribbon-shaped striation caused by winds of up to 335 mph

Oval (rotating storm system)

INNER RINGS OF SATURN

D ring

C ring ("crepe ring")

B ring

Cassini Division

A ring

Encke Division

F ring

MOONS OF SATURN

ENCELADUS
Diameter: 309 miles
Average distance from
planet: 148,000 miles

TETHYS
Diameter: 652 miles
Average distance from
planet: 183,000 miles

DIONE
Diameter: 695 miles
Average distance from
planet: 234,000 miles

MIMAS
Diameter: 247 miles
Average distance from
planet: 115,600 miles

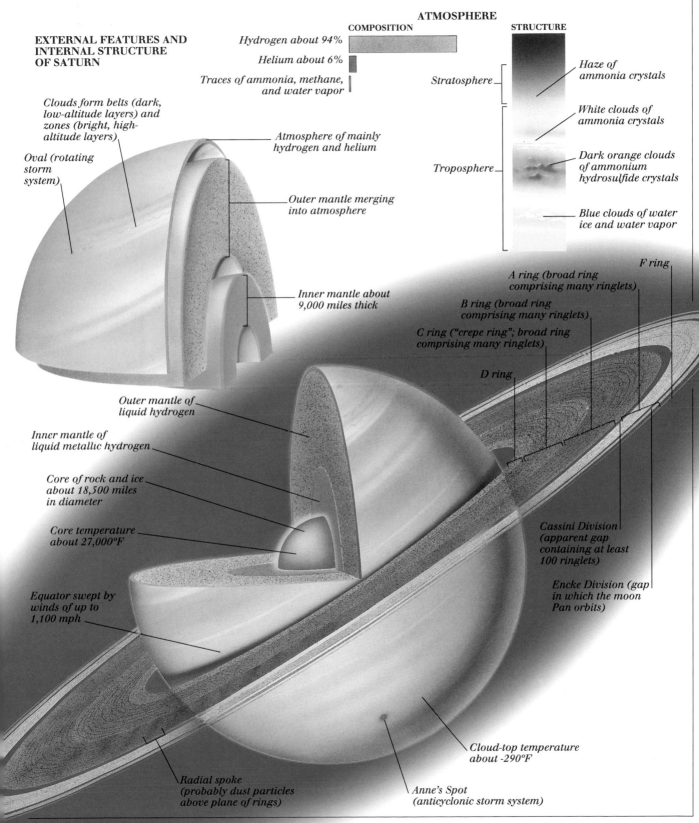

ATMOSPHERE

EXTERNAL FEATURES AND INTERNAL STRUCTURE OF SATURN

COMPOSITION

Hydrogen about 94%

Helium about 6%

Traces of ammonia, methane, and water vapor

STRUCTURE

Stratosphere

Troposphere

Haze of ammonia crystals

White clouds of ammonia crystals

Dark orange clouds of ammonium hydrosulfide crystals

Blue clouds of water ice and water vapor

Clouds form belts (dark, low-altitude layers) and zones (bright, high-altitude layers)

Oval (rotating storm system)

Atmosphere of mainly hydrogen and helium

Outer mantle merging into atmosphere

Inner mantle about 9,000 miles thick

Outer mantle of liquid hydrogen

Inner mantle of liquid metallic hydrogen

Core of rock and ice about 18,500 miles in diameter

Core temperature about 27,000°F

Equator swept by winds of up to 1,100 mph

F ring

A ring (broad ring comprising many ringlets)

B ring (broad ring comprising many ringlets)

C ring ("crepe ring"; broad ring comprising many ringlets)

D ring

Cassini Division (apparent gap containing at least 100 ringlets)

Encke Division (gap in which the moon Pan orbits)

Cloud-top temperature about -290°F

Radial spoke (probably dust particles above plane of rings)

Anne's Spot (anticyclonic storm system)

Uranus

COLOR-ENHANCED IMAGE OF URANUS

URANUS IS THE SEVENTH PLANET from the Sun and the third largest, with a diameter of about 32,000 miles. It is thought to consist of a dense mixture of different types of ice and gas around a solid core. Its atmosphere contains traces of methane, giving the planet a blue-green hue, and the temperature at the cloud tops is about -350°F. Uranus is the most featureless planet to have been closely observed: only a few icy clouds of methane have been seen so far. Uranus is unique among the planets in that its axis of rotation lies close to its orbital plane. As a result of its strongly tilted rotational axis, Uranus rolls on its side along its orbital path around the Sun, while other planets spin more or less upright. Uranus is encircled by 11 rings that consist of rocks interspersed with dust lanes. The rings contain some of the darkest matter in the Solar System. They are extremely narrow, making them difficult to detect: nine of them are less than six miles wide, whereas most of Saturn's rings are thousands of miles in width. There are 15 known Uranian moons, all of which are icy and most of which are farther out than the rings. The 10 inner moons are small and dark, with diameters of less than 100 miles, and the five outer moons are between about 290 and 1,000 miles in diameter. The outer moons have a wide variety of surface features. Miranda has the most varied surface, with cratered areas broken up by huge ridges and cliffs 12 miles high.

TILT AND ROTATION OF URANUS

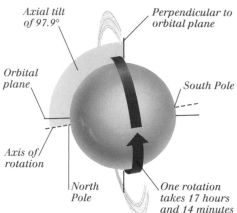

Axial tilt of 97.9°

Perpendicular to orbital plane

Orbital plane

South Pole

Axis of rotation

North Pole

One rotation takes 17 hours and 14 minutes

OUTER MOONS

MIRANDA
Diameter: 293 miles
Average distance from planet: 80,700 miles

ARIEL
Diameter: 720 miles
Average distance from planet: 118,800 miles

TITANIA
Diameter: 981 miles
Average distance from planet: 270,900 miles

UMBRIEL
Diameter: 726 miles
Average distance from planet: 165,300 miles

OBERON
Diameter: 946 miles
Average distance from planet: 362,000 miles

RINGS OF URANUS

RINGS AND DUST LANES

Epsilon ring

Ring 1986 U1R

Delta ring

Gamma ring

Eta ring

Beta ring

Alpha ring

Rings 4 and 5

Ring 6

Ring 1986 U2R

EXTERNAL FEATURES AND INTERNAL STRUCTURE OF URANUS

COMPOSITION OF ATMOSPHERE

Hydrogen 85%

Helium 12%

Methane 3%

Atmosphere of hydrogen, helium, and methane gases

Dense mantle of icy and gaseous water, ammonia, and methane

Core temperature about 12,600°F

Solid rocky core up to 10,500 miles in diameter

Mantle about 6,000 miles thick

Atmosphere merging into mantle

Icy clouds of frozen methane blown by winds of up to 185 mph

Sharply defined outer Epsilon ring

Blue-green hue due to presence of methane in atmosphere

South Pole

Cloud-top temperature about -350°F

Rings of dark rocks interspersed with dust lanes

49

Neptune and Pluto

COLOR-ENHANCED IMAGE OF NEPTUNE

NEPTUNE AND PLUTO are the two farthest planets from the Sun, at an average distance of about 2,800 million miles and 3,700 million miles, respectively. Neptune is a gas giant and is thought to consist of a small rocky core surrounded by a mixture of liquids and gases. The atmosphere contains several prominent cloud features. The largest of these are the Great Dark Spot, which is as wide as the Earth, the Small Dark Spot, and the Scooter. The Great and Small Dark Spots are huge storms that are swept around the planet by winds of about 1,200 miles per hour. The Scooter is a large area of cirrus cloud. Neptune has four tenuous rings and eight known moons. Triton is the largest Neptunian moon and the coldest object in the Solar System, with a temperature of -391°F. Unlike most moons in the Solar System, Triton orbits its mother planet in the opposite direction to the planet's rotation. Pluto is usually the outermost planet, but its elliptical orbit causes it to pass inside the orbit of Neptune for 20 years of its 248-year orbit. Pluto is so small and distant that little is known about it. It is a rocky planet, probably covered with ice and frozen methane. Pluto's only known moon, Charon, is large for a moon, at half the size of its parent planet. Because of the small difference in their sizes, Pluto and Charon are sometimes considered to be a double-planet system.

TILT AND ROTATION OF NEPTUNE

Axial tilt of 28.8°
Axis of rotation
Perpendicular to orbital plane
North Pole
Orbital plane
South Pole
One rotation takes 16 hours and 7 minutes

CLOUD FEATURES OF NEPTUNE

Great Dark Spot (anticyclonic wind storm)

Scooter (cirrus cloud)

Small Dark Spot (cyclonic wind storm)

RINGS OF NEPTUNE

Adams ring
Plateau
Le Verrier ring
Galle ring

HIGH-ALTITUDE CLOUDS

Methane cirrus clouds 25 miles above main cloud deck
Cloud shadow
Main cloud deck blown by winds at speeds of about 1,200 mph

MOONS OF NEPTUNE

TRITON
Diameter: 1,681 miles
Average distance from planet: 220,500 miles

PROTEUS
Diameter: 259 miles
Average distance from planet: 73,100 miles

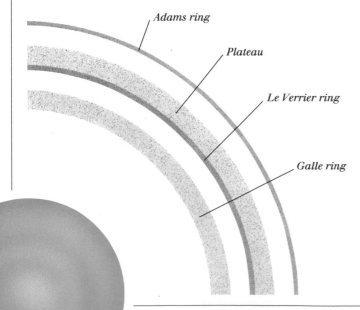

EXTERNAL FEATURES AND INTERNAL STRUCTURE OF NEPTUNE

COMPOSITION OF ATMOSPHERE

Hydrogen 85%

Helium 13%

Methane 2%

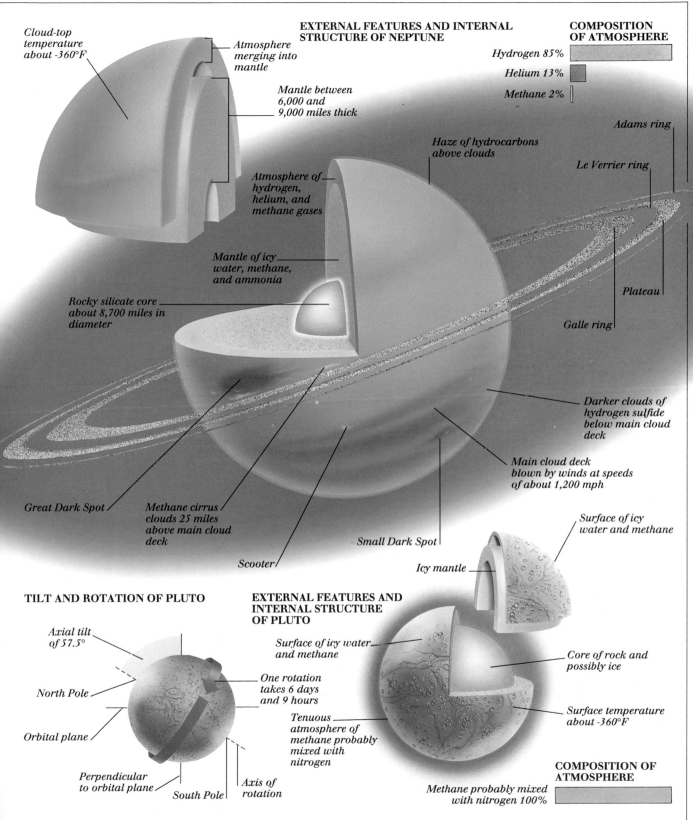

Cloud-top temperature about -360°F

Atmosphere merging into mantle

Mantle between 6,000 and 9,000 miles thick

Haze of hydrocarbons above clouds

Adams ring

Le Verrier ring

Atmosphere of hydrogen, helium, and methane gases

Mantle of icy water, methane, and ammonia

Plateau

Rocky silicate core about 8,700 miles in diameter

Galle ring

Darker clouds of hydrogen sulfide below main cloud deck

Main cloud deck blown by winds at speeds of about 1,200 mph

Great Dark Spot

Methane cirrus clouds 25 miles above main cloud deck

Scooter

Small Dark Spot

Surface of icy water and methane

Icy mantle

TILT AND ROTATION OF PLUTO

EXTERNAL FEATURES AND INTERNAL STRUCTURE OF PLUTO

Axial tilt of 57.5°

North Pole

Orbital plane

Perpendicular to orbital plane

South Pole

Axis of rotation

One rotation takes 6 days and 9 hours

Surface of icy water and methane

Tenuous atmosphere of methane probably mixed with nitrogen

Core of rock and possibly ice

Surface temperature about -360°F

COMPOSITION OF ATMOSPHERE

Methane probably mixed with nitrogen 100%

Asteroids, comets, and meteoroids

ASTEROID 951 GASPRA

ASTEROIDS, COMETS, AND METEOROIDS are all debris remaining from the nebula in which the Solar System formed 4.6 billion years ago. Asteroids are rocky bodies up to several hundred miles in diameter, although most are much smaller. Most of them orbit the Sun in the asteroid belt, which lies between the orbits of Mars and Jupiter. Comets may originate in a huge cloud, called the Oort Cloud, that is thought to surround the Solar System. They are made of frozen gases and dust, and are a few miles in diameter. Occasionally, a comet is deflected from the Oort Cloud to orbit the Sun in a long, elliptical path. As the comet approaches the Sun, the comet's surface starts to vaporize in the heat, producing a brightly shining coma (a huge sphere of gas and dust around the nucleus), a gas tail, and a dust tail. Meteoroids are small chunks of stone or stone and iron, some of which are fragments of asteroids or comets. Meteoroids range in size from tiny dust particles to objects tens of yards across. If a meteoroid enters the Earth's atmosphere, it is heated by friction and appears as a glowing streak of light called a meteor (also known as a shooting star). Meteor showers occur when the Earth passes through the trail of dust particles left by a comet. Most meteors burn up in the atmosphere. The few that are large enough to reach the Earth's surface are termed meteorites.

COLOR-ENHANCED IMAGE OF HALLEY'S COMET

High-intensity light emission

Nucleus

Medium-intensity light emission

Low-intensity light emission

COLOR-ENHANCED IMAGE OF A LEONID METEOR SHOWER

METEORITES

DEVELOPMENT OF COMET TAILS

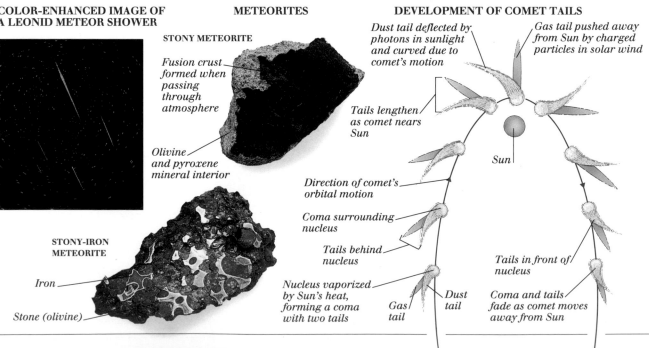

STONY METEORITE

Fusion crust formed when passing through atmosphere

Olivine and pyroxene mineral interior

STONY-IRON METEORITE

Iron

Stone (olivine)

Dust tail deflected by photons in sunlight and curved due to comet's motion

Gas tail pushed away from Sun by charged particles in solar wind

Tails lengthen as comet nears Sun

Sun

Direction of comet's orbital motion

Coma surrounding nucleus

Tails behind nucleus

Nucleus vaporized by Sun's heat, forming a coma with two tails

Gas tail

Dust tail

Tails in front of nucleus

Coma and tails fade as comet moves away from Sun

FEATURES OF A COMET

Thin, straight
gas tail

Broad, curved
dust tail

Gas molecules
heated by Sun
and emitting
light

Comet tails up to
62 million miles long

Thin, straight gas
tail blown by
solar wind

Head (coma and nucleus)

Coma
surrounding
nucleus

Nucleus a few
miles across

STRUCTURE OF
A COMET

Glowing coma
up to 600,000
miles across
surrounding
nucleus

Possible
core of
silicate
dust

Crust
with active
areas emitting
jets of gas
and dust

Jet of gas
and dust produced
by vaporization on
sunlit side of nucleus

Ices, including
water ice, and frozen carbon
dioxide, methane, and ammonia

Broad dust
tail curved along
comet's orbital path

Dust particles
reflecting sunlight

PREHISTORIC EARTH

The changing Earth

THE EARTH FORMED FROM A CLOUD OF DUST and gas drifting through space about 4,600 million years ago. Dense minerals sank to the center while lighter ones formed a thin rocky crust. However, the first known life forms—bacteria and blue-green algae—did not appear until about 3,400 million years ago, and it was only about 700 million years ago that more complex plants and animals began to develop. Since then, thousands of animal and plant species have evolved. Some, such as the dinosaurs, survived for millions of years, while others died out quickly. The Earth itself is continually changing. Although continents neared their present locations about 50 million years ago, they are still drifting slowly over the planet's surface, and mountain ranges such as the Himalayas—which began to form 40 million years ago—are continually being built up and worn away. Climate is also subject to change: the Earth has undergone a series of ice ages interspersed with warmer periods (the most recent ice age was at its height about 20,000 years ago).

Small mammals appeared (e.g., Crusafontia)

Dinosaurs became extinct

Global mountain building occurred

Multicellular soft-bodied animals appeared (e.g., worms and jellyfish)

Shelled invertebrates appeared (e.g., trilobites)

Marine plants flourished

Land plants appeared (e.g., Cooksonia)

Unicellular organisms appeared (e.g., blue-green algae)

Earth formed

Coral reefs appeared

Vertebrates appeared (e.g., Hemicyclaspis)

More complex types of algae appeared

Amphibians appeared (e.g., Ichthyostega)

GEOLOGICAL TIMESCALE

MILLIONS OF
YEARS AGO (MYA)

4,600	570	510	439	409	363	323	290

PRECAMBRIAN TIME	CAMBRIAN	ORDOVICIAN	SILURIAN	DEVONIAN	MISSISSIPPIAN (NORTH AMERICA)	PENNSYLVANIAN (NORTH AMERICA)
					CARBONIFEROUS	

PALEOZOIC

EVOLUTION OF THE EARTH

Birds appeared (e.g., Archaeopteryx)

Dinosaurs flourished

Marine reptiles appeared (e.g., Mixosaurus)

JURASSIC

TRIASSIC

Flowering plants appeared (e.g., Magnolia)

Oil and gas deposits formed

Himalayas began to form

Coal-forming forests flourished

Large mammals appeared (e.g., Arsinoitherium)

Early desertification occurred

PERMIAN

Conifers appeared

TERTIARY

BONIFEROUS

Last glacial period occurred

Colorado River began to cut out the Grand Canyon

Uplift of the Sierra Nevada began

QUATERNARY

Modern humans (Homo sapiens) appeared

65	56.5	35.5	23.5	5.2	1.64		0.01	0	MYA
PALEOCENE	EOCENE	OLIGOCENE	MIOCENE	PLIOCENE		PLEISTOCENE		HOLOCENE	EPOCH

290	245	208	146			
PERMIAN	TRIASSIC	JURASSIC	CRETACEOUS	TERTIARY	QUATERNARY	PERIOD
	MESOZOIC			CENOZOIC		ERA

57

The Earth's crust

THE EARTH'S CRUST IS THE SOLID outer shell of the Earth. It includes continental crust (about 25 miles thick) and oceanic crust (about four miles thick). The crust and the topmost layer of the mantle form the lithosphere. The lithosphere consists of semi-rigid plates that move relative to each other on the underlying asthenosphere (a partly molten layer of the mantle). This movement is known as plate tectonics and helps explain continental drift. Where two plates move apart, there are rifts in the crust. In mid-ocean, this movement results in seafloor spreading and the formation of ocean ridges; on continents, crustal spreading can form rift valleys. When plates move toward each other, one may be subducted beneath (forced under) the other. In mid-ocean, this causes ocean trenches, seismic activity, and arcs of volcanic islands. Where oceanic crust is subducted beneath continental crust or where continents collide, land may be uplifted and mountains formed (see pp. 62–63). Plates may also slide past each other—along the San Andreas fault, for example. Crustal movement on continents may result in earthquakes, while movement under the seabed can lead to tidal waves.

ELEMENTS IN THE EARTH'S CRUST

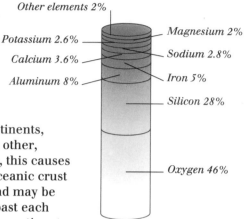

Other elements 2%

Potassium 2.6%

Calcium 3.6%

Aluminum 8%

Magnesium 2%

Sodium 2.8%

Iron 5%

Silicon 28%

Oxygen 46%

FEATURES OF PLATE MOVEMENTS

Ocean trench formed where oceanic crust is forced under continental crust

Subduction zone

Ridge where magma is rising to form new oceanic crust

Region of seafloor spreading

Rift formed where two plates are moving apart

Magma (molten rock) erupts at rift

Magma rises to form a hot spot

Volcano develops over hot spot and builds up to form an island

Volcanic island that originally formed over hot spot

Oceanic crust melts

Magma rises to form a volcano

MAJOR PLATES OF THE EARTH'S CRUST

North American plate

Hellenic plate

Eurasian plate

Plates sliding past each other

Pacific plate

Cocos plate

Philippine plate

Caribbean plate

Plates converging

Nazca plate

South American plate

African plate

Indo-Australian plate

Plates moving apart

MOVEMENT OF LAND ALONG OCEANIC RIDGES

Boundary along which two plates slide past each other

Land moves apart at a constant rate, perpendicular to ridge

Mountain range uplifted where subducting oceanic crust compresses and deforms edge of continental crust

STRAIGHT OCEANIC RIDGE

Land moves apart at a constant rate, perpendicular to curve

CURVED OCEANIC RIDGE

Staggered parallel ridge sections take shape of curve

Transform fault

Lithosphere (crust and topmost layer of mantle)

Asthenosphere (upper part of mantle)

STRESSES RESOLVE INTO SECTIONS

Faults and folds

THE CONTINUOUS MOVEMENT of the Earth's crustal plates (see pp. 58–59) can squeeze, stretch, or break rock strata, deforming them and producing faults and folds. A fault is a fracture in a rock along which there is movement of one side relative to the other. The movement can be vertical, horizontal, or oblique (vertical and horizontal). Faults develop when rocks are subjected to compression or tension. They tend to occur in hard, rigid rocks, which are more likely to break than bend. The smallest faults occur in single mineral crystals and are microscopically small, while the largest —the Great Rift Valley in Africa, which formed between 5 million and 100,000 years ago—is more than 6,000 miles long. A fold is a bend in a rock layer caused by compression. Folds occur in elastic rocks, which tend to bend rather than break. The two main types of fold are anticlines (upfolds) and synclines (downfolds). Folds vary in size from a few millimeters long to folded mountain ranges hundreds of miles long, such as the Himalayas (see pp. 62–63) and the Alps, which are repeatedly folding. In addition to faults and folds, other features associated with rock deformations include boudins, mullions, and *en échelon* fractures.

STRUCTURE OF A FOLD

Axial plane

Crest

Limb

Angle of plunge

Hingeline

STRUCTURE OF A FAULT

Fault plane

Dip of fault plane (angle from horizontal)

Upthrow

Throw (vertical displacement of fault)

Downthrow

Hade of fault plane (angle from vertical)

STRUCTURE OF A SLOPE

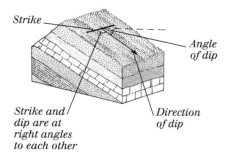

Strike

Angle of dip

Strike and dip are at right angles to each other

Direction of dip

FOLDED ROCK

Steeply dipping limbs

Crest of anticline

Plunge

SECTION THROUGH FOLDED ROCK STRATA THAT HAVE BEEN ERODED

Dipping bed

Anticlinal fold

Monoclinal fold

Mineral-filled fault

Upper Carboniferous Millstone Grit

Lower Carboniferous Limestone

EXAMPLES OF FOLDS

Anticlinorium
Monocline
Syncline
Overturned fold
Overthrust fold
Chevron fold

Synclinorium
Anticline
Isocline
Recumbent fold
Fan fold
Box fold
Cuspate fold

EXAMPLES OF FAULTS

Sinistral strike-slip (lateral) fault
Dextral strike-slip (lateral) fault
Horst
Tear fault

Normal dip-slip fault
Reverse dip-slip fault
Thrust fault
Oblique-slip fault
Graben
Cylindrical fault

SMALL-SCALE ROCK DEFORMATIONS

Competent bed (rocks that break)
Tension
Incompetent bed
Tension
Tension
Tension
Masses of rock shear past each other
En échelon fracture

Tension
Incompetent bed (rocks that bend)
Competent bed breaks into sections
Competent bed
Competent bed splits into prisms
Tension
Joint opened by stress

BOUDIN
MULLION
EN ECHELON FRACTURE

Mineral-filled fault
Dipping bed
Gently folded bed
Horizontal bed
Mineral-filled fault
Dipping bed

Upper Carboniferous Millstone Grit
Upper Carboniferous Coal Measures

Mountain building

THE PROCESSES INVOLVED in mountain building—termed orogenesis—occur as a result of the movement of the Earth's crustal plates (see pp. 58-59). There are three main types of mountains: volcanic mountains, fold mountains, and block mountains. Most volcanic mountains have been formed along plate boundaries where plates have come together or moved apart and lava and other debris have been ejected onto the Earth's surface. The lava and debris may have built up to form a dome around the vent of a volcano. Fold mountains are formed where plates push together and cause the rock to buckle upward. Where oceanic crust meets less dense continental crust, the oceanic crust is forced under the continental crust. The continental crust is buckled by the impact. This is how folded mountain ranges, such as the Appalachian Mountains in North America, were formed. Fold mountains are also formed where two areas of continental crust meet. The Himalayas, for example, began to form when India collided with Asia, buckling the sediments and parts of the oceanic crust between them. Block mountains are formed when a block of land is uplifted between two faults as a result of compression or tension in the Earth's crust (see pp. 60-61). Often, the movement along faults has taken place gradually over millions of years. However, two plates may cause an earthquake by suddenly sliding past each other along a faultline.

BHAGIRATHI PARBAT,
HIMALAYAS

Asia

Himalayas formed by buckling of sediment and part of the oceanic crust between two colliding continents

India moves north

India collides with Asia about 40 million years ago

EXAMPLES OF MOUNTAINS

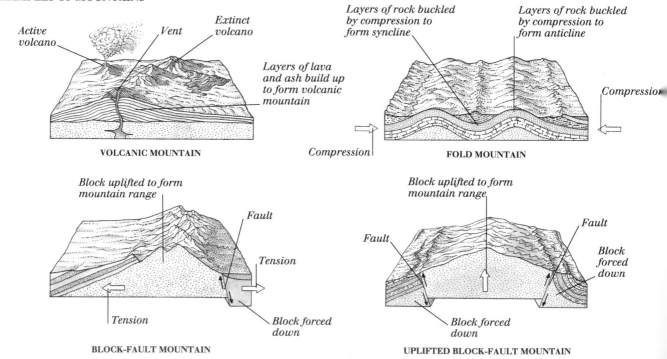

Active volcano

Vent

Extinct volcano

Layers of lava and ash build up to form volcanic mountain

VOLCANIC MOUNTAIN

Layers of rock buckled by compression to form syncline

Layers of rock buckled by compression to form anticline

Compression

Compression

FOLD MOUNTAIN

Block uplifted to form mountain range

Fault

Tension

Tension

Block forced down

BLOCK-FAULT MOUNTAIN

Block uplifted to form mountain range

Fault

Fault

Block forced down

Block forced down

UPLIFTED BLOCK-FAULT MOUNTAIN

STAGES IN THE FORMATION OF THE HIMALAYAS

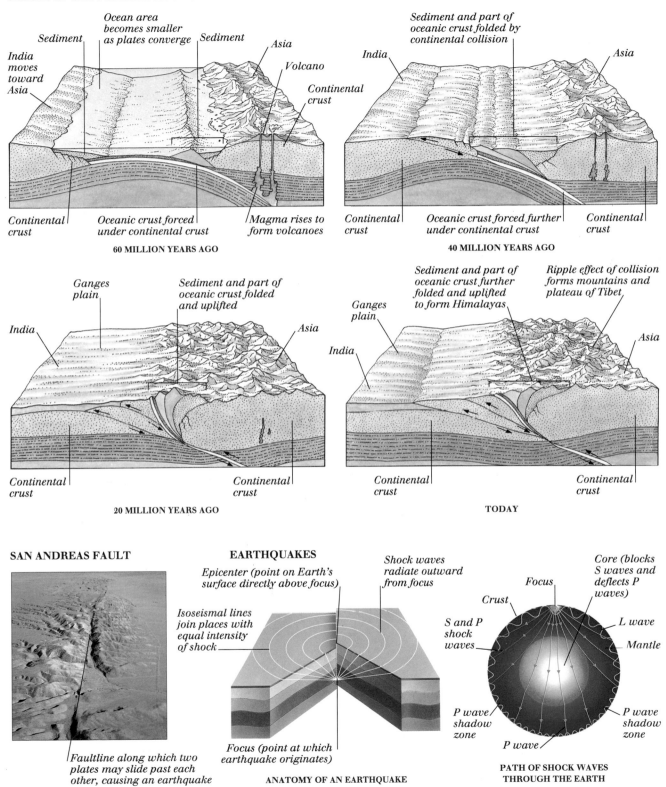

Sediment

Ocean area becomes smaller as plates converge

Sediment

Asia

Volcano

India moves toward Asia

Continental crust

Continental crust

Oceanic crust forced under continental crust

Magma rises to form volcanoes

60 MILLION YEARS AGO

Sediment and part of oceanic crust folded by continental collision

India

Asia

Continental crust

Oceanic crust forced further under continental crust

Continental crust

40 MILLION YEARS AGO

Ganges plain

Sediment and part of oceanic crust folded and uplifted

India

Asia

Continental crust

Continental crust

20 MILLION YEARS AGO

Sediment and part of oceanic crust further folded and uplifted to form Himalayas

Ripple effect of collision forms mountains and plateau of Tibet

Ganges plain

India

Asia

Continental crust

Continental crust

TODAY

SAN ANDREAS FAULT

Faultline along which two plates may slide past each other, causing an earthquake

EARTHQUAKES

Epicenter (point on Earth's surface directly above focus)

Isoseismal lines join places with equal intensity of shock

Shock waves radiate outward from focus

Focus (point at which earthquake originates)

ANATOMY OF AN EARTHQUAKE

Focus

Core (blocks S waves and deflects P waves)

Crust

S and P shock waves

L wave

Mantle

P wave shadow zone

P wave shadow zone

P wave

PATH OF SHOCK WAVES THROUGH THE EARTH

Precambrian to Devonian periods

WHEN THE EARTH FORMED about 4,600 million years ago, its atmosphere consisted of volcanic gases with little oxygen, making it hostile to most forms of life. One large supercontinent, Gondwanaland, was situated over the southern polar region, while other smaller continents were spread over the rest of the world. Constant movement of the earth's crustal plates carried continents across the earth's surface. The first primitive life-forms emerged around 3,400 million years ago in shallow, warm seas. The build up of oxygen began to form a shield of ozone around the earth, protecting living organisms from the sun's harmful rays and helping to establish an atmosphere in which life could sustain itself. The first vertebrates appeared about 470 million years ago, during the Ordovician period (510–439 million years ago), the first land plants appeared around 400 million years ago during the Devonian period (409–363 million years ago), and the first land animals about 30 million years later.

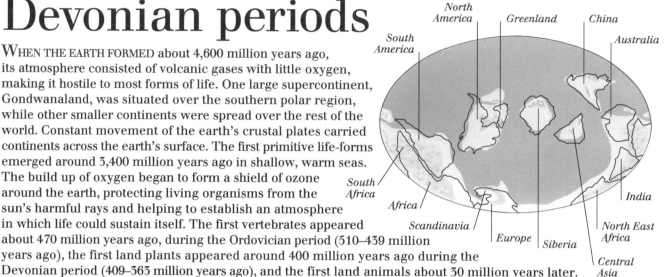

MIDDLE ORDOVICIAN POSITIONS OF PRESENT-DAY LANDMASSES

North America
South America
Greenland
China
Australia
South Africa
Africa
Scandinavia
Europe
Siberia
India
North East Africa
Central Asia

EXAMPLES OF PRECAMBRIAN TO DEVONIAN PLANT GROUPS

A PRESENT-DAY CLUBMOSS
(*Lycopodium sp.*)

A PRESENT-DAY LAND PLANT
(*Asparagus setaceous*)

FOSSIL OF AN EXTINCT LAND PLANT
(*Cooksonia hemisphaerica*)

FOSSIL OF AN EXTINCT SWAMP PLANT
(*Zosterophyllum llanoveranum*)

EXAMPLES OF PRECAMBRIAN TO DEVONIAN TRILOBITES

ACADAGNOSTUS
Family: Agnostidae
Length: ¹/₅ in (8 mm)

PHACOPS
Family: Phacopidae
Length: 1³/₄ in (4.5 cm)

OLENELLUS
Family: Olenellidae
Length: 2¹/₂ in (6 cm)

ELRATHIA
Family: Ptychopariidae
Length: ³/₄ in (2 cm)

THE EARTH DURING THE MIDDLE ORDOVICIAN PERIOD

Siberia

Laurentia

China

Kazakstania

Gondwanaland

Baltica

EXAMPLES OF EARLY MARINE INVERTEBRATES

FOSSIL NAUTILOID
(Estonioceras perforatum)

FOSSIL BRACHIOPOD
(Dicoelosia bilobata)

TRACE FOSSIL
(Mawsonites spriggi)

FOSSIL GRAPTOLITE
(Monograptus convolutus)

EXAMPLES OF DEVONIAN FISH

RHAMPHODOPSIS
Family: Ptyctodontidae
Length: 6 in (15 cm)

PTERASPIS
Family: Pteraspidae
Length: 10 in (25 cm)

COCCOSTEUS
Family: Coccosteidae
Length: 14 in (35 cm)

BOTHRIOLEPIS
Family: Bothriolepidae
Length: 16 in (40 cm)

CHEIRACANTHUS
Family: Acanthodidae
Length: 12 in (30 cm)

PTERICHTHYODES
Family: Asterolepidae
Length: 6 in (15 cm)

CHEIROLEPIS
Family: Cheirolepidae
Length: 6³/₄ in (17 cm)

CEPHALASPIS
Family: Cephalaspidae
Length: 8³/₄ in (22 cm)

Carboniferous to Permian periods

LATE CARBONIFEROUS POSITIONS OF PRESENT-DAY LANDMASSES

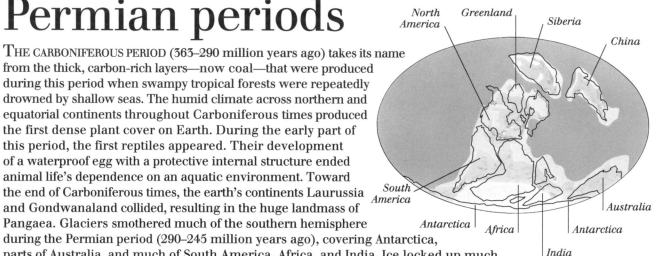

North America — Greenland — Siberia — China — South America — Antarctica — Africa — India — Antarctica — Australia

THE CARBONIFEROUS PERIOD (363–290 million years ago) takes its name from the thick, carbon-rich layers—now coal—that were produced during this period when swampy tropical forests were repeatedly drowned by shallow seas. The humid climate across northern and equatorial continents throughout Carboniferous times produced the first dense plant cover on Earth. During the early part of this period, the first reptiles appeared. Their development of a waterproof egg with a protective internal structure ended animal life's dependence on an aquatic environment. Toward the end of Carboniferous times, the earth's continents Laurussia and Gondwanaland collided, resulting in the huge landmass of Pangaea. Glaciers smothered much of the southern hemisphere during the Permian period (290–245 million years ago), covering Antarctica, parts of Australia, and much of South America, Africa, and India. Ice locked up much of the world's water and large areas of the northern hemisphere experienced a drop in sea-level. Away from the poles, deserts and a hot dry climate predominated. As a result of these conditions, the Permian period ended with the greatest mass extinction of life on earth ever.

EXAMPLES OF CARBONIFEROUS AND PERMIAN PLANT GROUPS

A PRESENT-DAY FIR
(Abies concolor)

FOSSIL OF AN EXTINCT FERN
(Zeilleria frenzlii)

FOSSIL OF AN EXTINCT HORSETAIL
(Equisetites sp.)

FOSSIL OF AN EXTINCT CLUBMOSS
(Lepidodendron sp.)

EXAMPLES OF CARBONIFEROUS AND PERMIAN TREES

PECOPTERIS
Family: Marattiaceae
Height: 13 ft (4 m)

PARIPTERIS
Family: Medullosaceae
Height: 16 ft 6 in (5 m)

MARIOPTERIS
Family: Unclassified
Height: 16 ft 6 in (5 m)

MEDULLOSA
Family: Medullosaceae
Height: 16 ft 6 in (5 m)

THE EARTH DURING THE LATE CARBONIFEROUS PERIOD

Siberia

Laurussia

China

Ural Mountains

Caledonian Mountains

Appalachian Mountains

Gondwanaland

EXAMPLES OF CARBONIFEROUS AND PERMIAN ANIMALS

SKULL OF AN EXTINCT SYNAPSID REPTILE
(Dimetrodon loomisi)

FOSSIL TEETH OF AN EXTINCT SHARK
(Helicoprion bessonowi)

MODEL OF AN EXTINCT CARBONIFEROUS REPTILE
(Westlothiana lizziae)

LEPIDODENDRON
Family: Lepidodendraceae
Height: 100 ft (30 m)

CORDAITES
Family: Cordaitacea
Height: 33 ft (10 m)

GLOSSOPTERIS
Family: Glossopteridaceae
Height: 26 ft (8 m)

ALETHOPTERIS
Family Medullosaceae
Height: 16 ft 6 in (5 m)

Triassic period

THE TRIASSIC PERIOD (245–208 million years ago) marked the beginning of what is known as the Age of the Dinosaurs (the Mesozoic era). During this period, the present-day continents were massed together, forming one huge continent known as Pangaea. This landmass experienced extremes of climate, with lush green areas around the coast or by lakes and rivers, and arid deserts in the interior. The only forms of plant life were nonflowering plants, such as conifers, ferns, cycads, and ginkgos; flowering plants had not yet evolved. The principal forms of animal life included primitive amphibians, rhynchosaurs ("beaked lizards"), and primitive crocodilians. Dinosaurs first appeared about 230 million years ago, at the beginning of the Late Triassic period. The earliest known dinosaurs were the carnivorous (flesh-eating) herrerasaurids and staurikosaurids, such as *Herrerasaurus* and *Staurikosaurus*. Early herbivorous (plant-eating) dinosaurs first appeared in Late Triassic times and included *Plateosaurus* and *Technosaurus*. By the end of the Triassic period, dinosaurs dominated Pangaea, possibly contributing to the extinction of many other reptiles.

North America
Europe
Asia
South America
Africa
Antarctica
India
Australia

EXAMPLES OF TRIASSIC PLANT GROUPS

A PRESENT-DAY CYCAD
(*Cycas revoluta*)

A PRESENT-DAY GINKGO
(*Ginkgo biloba*)

A PRESENT-DAY CONIFER
(*Araucaria araucana*)

FOSSIL OF AN EXTINCT FERN
(*Pachypteris* sp.)

FOSSIL LEAF OF AN EXTINCT CYCAD
(*Cycas* sp.)

EXAMPLES OF TRIASSIC DINOSAURS

MELANOROSAURUS
A melanorosaurid
Length: 40 ft (12.2 m)

MUSSAURUS
A plateosaurid
Length: 6 ft 6 in–10 ft (2–3 m)

HERRERASAURUS
A herrerasaurid
Length: 10 ft (3 m)

PISANOSAURUS
A primitive ornithischian
Length: 3 ft (90 cm)

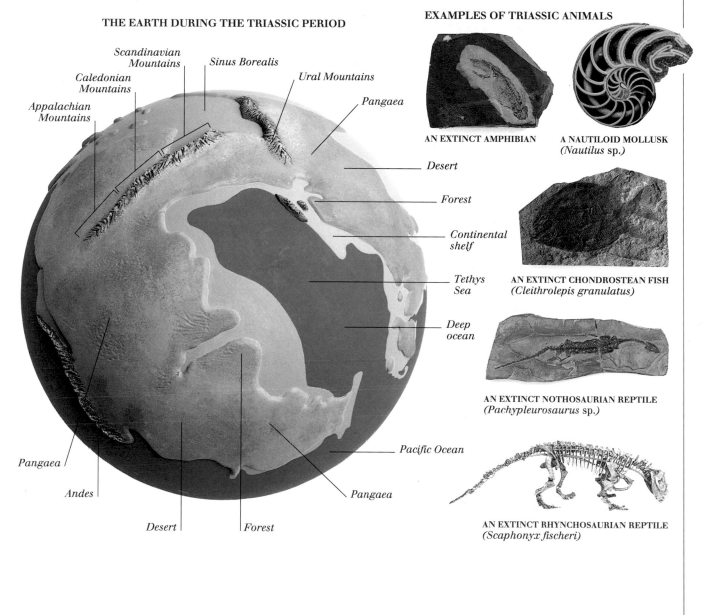

THE EARTH DURING THE TRIASSIC PERIOD

Scandinavian Mountains

Caledonian Mountains

Sinus Borealis

Ural Mountains

Appalachian Mountains

Pangaea

Desert

Forest

Continental shelf

Tethys Sea

Deep ocean

Pacific Ocean

Pangaea

Pangaea

Andes

Desert

Forest

EXAMPLES OF TRIASSIC ANIMALS

AN EXTINCT AMPHIBIAN

A NAUTILOID MOLLUSK
(*Nautilus* sp.)

AN EXTINCT CHONDROSTEAN FISH
(*Cleithrolepis granulatus*)

AN EXTINCT NOTHOSAURIAN REPTILE
(*Pachypleurosaurus* sp.)

AN EXTINCT RHYNCHOSAURIAN REPTILE
(*Scaphonyx fischeri*)

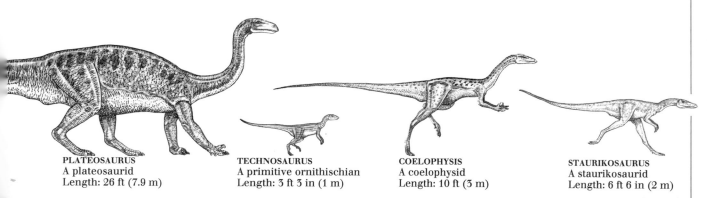

PLATEOSAURUS
A plateosaurid
Length: 26 ft (7.9 m)

TECHNOSAURUS
A primitive ornithischian
Length: 3 ft 3 in (1 m)

COELOPHYSIS
A coelophysid
Length: 10 ft (3 m)

STAURIKOSAURUS
A staurikosaurid
Length: 6 ft 6 in (2 m)

Jurassic period

THE JURASSIC PERIOD, the middle part of the Mesozoic era, lasted from 208 to 146 million years ago. During the Jurassic period, the landmass of Pangaea broke up into the continents of Gondwanaland and Laurasia, and sea-levels rose, flooding areas of lower land. The Jurassic climate was warm and moist. Plants such as ginkgos, horsetails, and conifers thrived, and giant redwood trees appeared, as did the first flowering plants. The abundance of plant food coincided with the proliferation of herbivorous (plant-eating) dinosaurs, such as the large sauropods (e.g., *Diplodocus*) and stegosaurs (e.g., *Stegosaurus*). Carnivorous (flesh-eating) dinosaurs, such as *Compsognathus* and *Allosaurus*, also flourished by hunting the many animals that existed—among them other dinosaurs. Further Jurassic animals included shrewlike mammals, and pterosaurs (flying reptiles), as well as plesiosaurs and ichthyosaurs (both marine reptiles).

JURASSIC POSITIONS OF PRESENT-DAY LANDMASSES

North America
Europe
Arabia
Asia
Australia
South America
Afric
India
Antarctica

EXAMPLES OF JURASSIC PLANT GROUPS

A PRESENT-DAY FERN
(Dicksonia antarctica)

A PRESENT-DAY HORSETAIL
(Equisetum arvense)

A PRESENT-DAY CONIFER
(Taxus baccata)

FOSSIL LEAF OF AN EXTINCT CONIFER
(Taxus sp.)

FOSSIL LEAF OF AN EXTINCT REDWOOD
(Sequoiadendron affinis)

EXAMPLES OF JURASSIC DINOSAURS

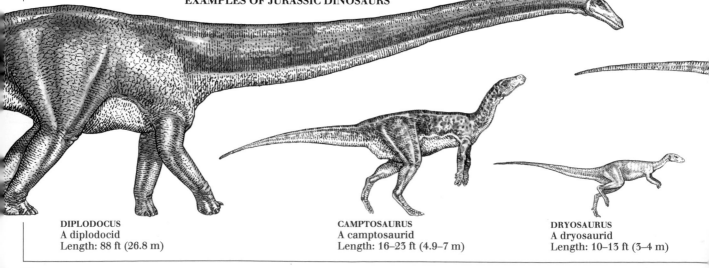

DIPLODOCUS
A diplodocid
Length: 88 ft (26.8 m)

CAMPTOSAURUS
A camptosaurid
Length: 16–23 ft (4.9–7 m)

DRYOSAURUS
A dryosaurid
Length: 10–13 ft (3–4 m)

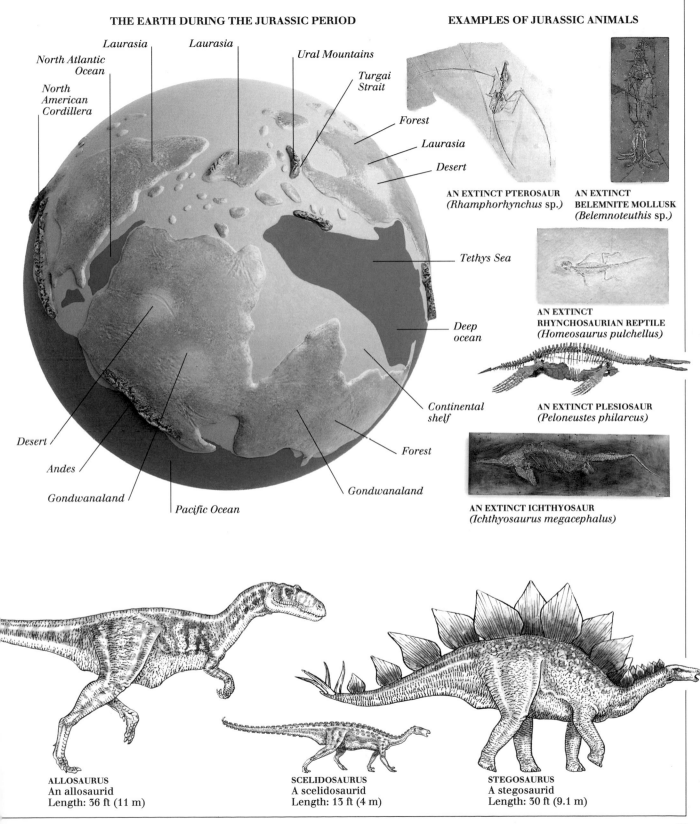

THE EARTH DURING THE JURASSIC PERIOD

North Atlantic Ocean

Laurasia

Laurasia

Ural Mountains

Turgai Strait

North American Cordillera

Forest

Laurasia

Desert

Tethys Sea

Deep ocean

Continental shelf

Desert

Forest

Andes

Gondwanaland

Gondwanaland

Pacific Ocean

EXAMPLES OF JURASSIC ANIMALS

AN EXTINCT PTEROSAUR
(*Rhamphorhynchus* sp.)

AN EXTINCT BELEMNITE MOLLUSK
(*Belemnoteuthis* sp.)

AN EXTINCT RHYNCHOSAURIAN REPTILE
(*Homeosaurus pulchellus*)

AN EXTINCT PLESIOSAUR
(*Peloneustes philarcus*)

AN EXTINCT ICHTHYOSAUR
(*Ichthyosaurus megacephalus*)

ALLOSAURUS
An allosaurid
Length: 36 ft (11 m)

SCELIDOSAURUS
A scelidosaurid
Length: 13 ft (4 m)

STEGOSAURUS
A stegosaurid
Length: 30 ft (9.1 m)

Cretaceous period

THE MESOZOIC ERA ENDED WITH the Cretaceous period, which lasted from 146 to 65 million years ago. During this period, Gondwanaland and Laurasia were breaking up into smaller landmasses that more closely resembled those of the modern continents. The climate remained mild and moist, but the seasons became more marked. Flowering plants, including deciduous trees, replaced many cycads, seed ferns, and conifers. Animal species became more varied, with the evolution of new mammals, insects, fish, crustaceans, and turtles. Dinosaurs evolved into a wide variety of species during Cretaceous times; more than half of all known dinosaurs—including *Iguanodon, Deinonychus, Tyrannosaurus,* and *Hypsilophodon*—lived during this period. At the end of the Cretaceous period, however, large dinosaurs became extinct. The reason for this mass extinction is unknown but it is thought to have been caused by climatic changes due to either a catastrophic meteor impact with the Earth or extensive volcanic eruptions.

North America   Europe   Arabia   Asia   Australia   India   Antarctica   Africa   South America

EXAMPLES OF CRETACEOUS PLANT GROUPS

A PRESENT-DAY CONIFER
(Pinus muricata)

**A PRESENT-DAY
DECIDUOUS TREE**
(Magnolia sp.*)*

**FOSSIL OF AN
EXTINCT FERN**
(Sphenopteris latiloba)

**FOSSIL OF AN
EXTINCT GINKGO**
(Ginkgo pluripartita)

**FOSSIL LEAVES
OF AN EXTINCT
DECIDUOUS TREE**
(Cercidyphyllum sp.*)*

EXAMPLES OF CRETACEOUS DINOSAURS

SALTASAURUS
A titanosaurid
Length: 40 ft (12.2 m)

TOROSAURUS
A ceratopsid
Length: 25 ft (7.6 m)

HYPSILOPHODON
A hypsilophodontid
Length: 4 ft 6 in–7 ft 6 in (1.4–2.3 m)

THE EARTH DURING THE CRETACEOUS PERIOD

EXAMPLES OF CRETACEOUS ANIMALS

West Africa

Greenland

North America

Africa

Europe

Continental Sea

Rocky Mountains

Ural Mountains

Desert

Tethys Sea

Asia

India

Indian Ocean

Australia

Pacific Ocean

North Atlantic Ocean

Andes

South America

South Atlantic Ocean

Antarctica

Forest

AN EXTINCT INSECT
(*Libellulium longialatum*)

AN EXTINCT MARINE TURTLE
(*Plesiochelys latiscutata*)

AN EXTINCT CRUSTACEAN
(*Homarus* sp.)

AN EXTINCT CROCODILIAN

AN EXTINCT HOLOSTEAN FISH
(*Lepidotes maximus*)

TYRANNOSAURUS
A tyrannosaurid
Length: 40 ft (12.2 m)

DEINONYCHUS
A dromaeosaurid
Length: 8–11 ft (2.4–3.4 m)

IGUANODON
An iguanodontid
Length: 30 ft (9.1 m)

73

Tertiary period

FOLLOWING THE DEMISE OF THE DINOSAURS at the end of the Cretaceous period, the Tertiary period (65–1.6 million years ago), which formed the first part of the Cenozoic era (65 million years ago–present), was characterized by a huge expansion of mammal life. Placental mammals nourish and maintain their young in the mother's uterus; only three orders of placental mammals existed during Cretaceous times, compared with 25 orders during the Tertiary period. One of these 25 included the first hominid (see pp.108–109), *Australopithecus*, which appeared in Africa. By the beginning of the Tertiary period, the continents had almost reached their present position. The Tethys Sea, which had separated the northern continents from Africa and India, began to close up, forming the Mediterranean Sea and allowing the migration of terrestrial animals between Africa and western Europe. India's collision with Asia led to the formation of the Himalayas. During the middle part of the Tertiary period, the forest-dwelling and browsing mammals were replaced by mammals such as the horse, better suited to grazing the open savannahs that began to dominate. Repeated cool periods throughout the Tertiary period established the Antarctic as an icy island continent.

**TERTIARY POSITIONS OF
PRESENT-DAY LANDMASSES**

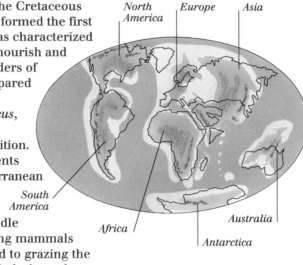

North America

Europe

Asia

South America

Africa

Antarctica

Australia

EXAMPLES OF TERTIARY PLANT GROUPS

A PRESENT-DAY OAK
(*Quercus palustris*)

A PRESENT-DAY BIRCH
(*Betula grossa*)

**FOSSIL LEAF OF AN
EXTINCT BIRCH**
(*Betulites sp.*)

**FOSSIL STEM OF AN
EXTINCT PALM**
(*Palmoxylon*)

**EXAMPLES OF TERTIARY
ANIMAL GROUPS**

HYAENODON
An hyaenodontid
Length: 6 ft 6 in (2 m)

TITANOHYRAX
A pliohyracid
Length: 6 ft 6 in (2 m)

PHORUSRHACUS
A phorusrhacid
Length: 5 ft (1.5 m)

SAMOTHERIUM
A giraffid
Length: 10 ft (3 m)

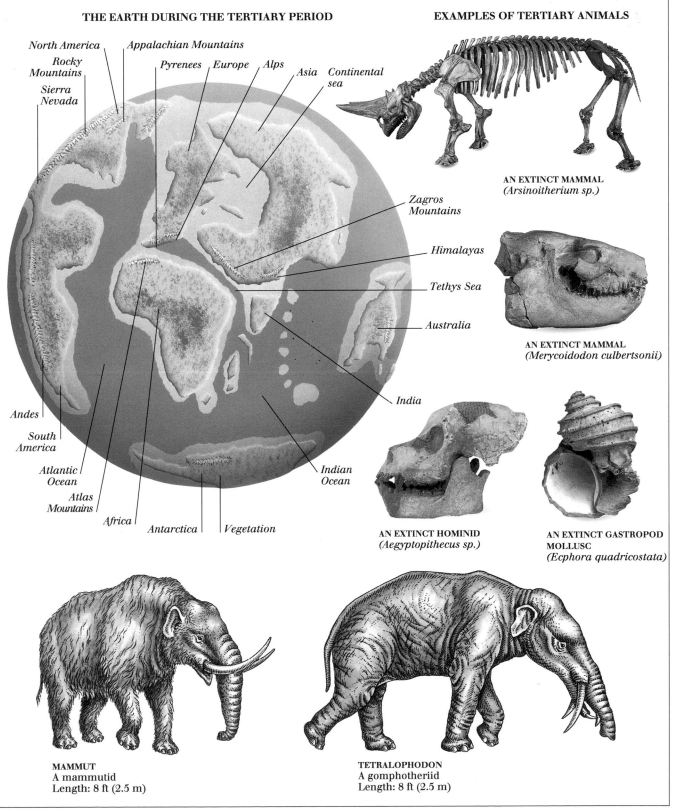

THE EARTH DURING THE TERTIARY PERIOD

North America
Rocky Mountains
Sierra Nevada
Appalachian Mountains
Pyrenees
Europe
Alps
Asia
Continental sea
Zagros Mountains
Himalayas
Tethys Sea
Australia
India
Andes
South America
Atlantic Ocean
Atlas Mountains
Africa
Antarctica
Vegetation
Indian Ocean

EXAMPLES OF TERTIARY ANIMALS

AN EXTINCT MAMMAL
(Arsinoitherium sp.)

AN EXTINCT MAMMAL
(Merycoidodon culbertsonii)

AN EXTINCT HOMINID
(Aegyptopithecus sp.)

AN EXTINCT GASTROPOD MOLLUSC
(Ecphora quadricostata)

MAMMUT
A mammutid
Length: 8 ft (2.5 m)

TETRALOPHODON
A gomphotheriid
Length: 8 ft (2.5 m)

Quaternary period

THE QUATERNARY PERIOD (1.6 million years ago–present) forms the second part of the Cenozoic era (65 million years ago–present): it has been characterized by alternating cold (glacial) and warm (interglacial) periods. During cold periods, ice sheets and glaciers have formed repeatedly on northern and southern continents. The cold environments in North America and Eurasia, and to a lesser extent in southern South America and parts of Australia, have caused the migration of many life forms toward the Equator. Only the specialized ice-age mammals such as *Mammuthus* and *Coelodonta*, with their thick wool and fat insulation, were suited to life in very cold climates. Humans developed throughout the Pleistocene period (1.6 million–10,000 years ago) in Africa and migrated northward into Europe and Asia. Modern humans, *Homo sapiens*, lived on the cold European continent 30,000 years ago and hunted mammals. The end of the last ice age and the climatic changes that occurred about 10,000 years ago brought extinction to many Pleistocene mammals, but enabled humans to flourish.

QUATERNARY POSITIONS OF PRESENT-DAY LANDMASSES

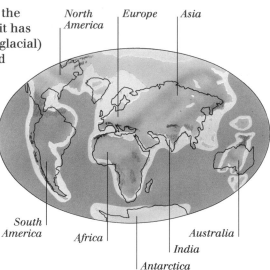

North America · Europe · Asia · South America · Africa · India · Antarctica · Australia

EXAMPLES OF QUATERNARY PLANT GROUPS

A PRESENT-DAY BIRCH
(*Betula lenta*)

A PRESENT-DAY SWEEETGUM
(*Liquidambar styraciflua*)

FOSSIL LEAF OF A SWEETGUM
(*Liquidambar europeanum*)

FOSSIL LEAF OF A BIRCH
(*Betula sp.*)

EXAMPLES OF QUATERNARY ANIMAL GROUPS

PROCOPTODON
A macropodid
Length: 10 ft (3 m)

DIPROTODON
A diprotodontid
Length: 10 ft (3 m)

TOXODON
A toxodontid
Length: 10 ft (3 m)

MAMMUTHUS
An elephantid
Length: 10 ft (3 m)

THE EARTH DURING THE QUATERNARY PERIOD

EXAMPLES OF QUATERNARY ANIMALS

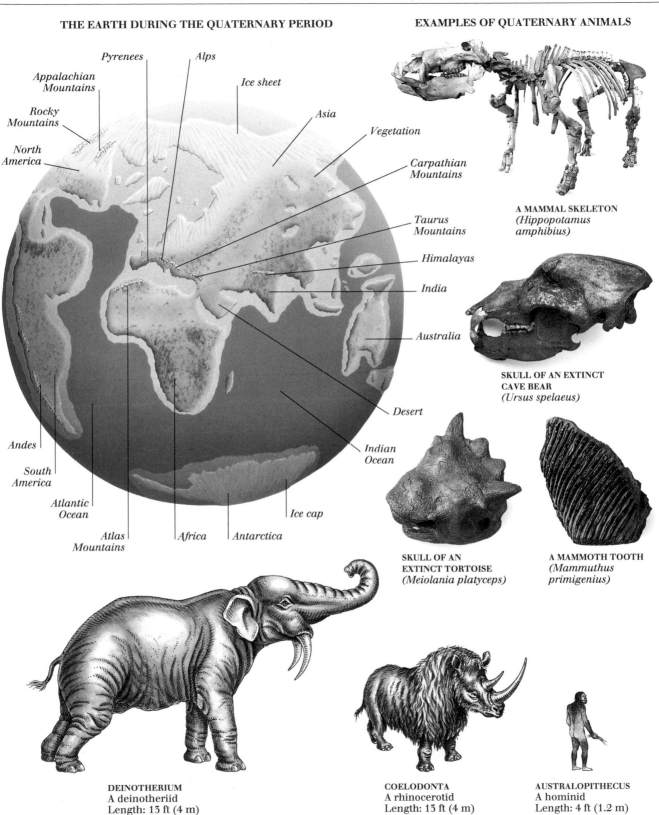

Appalachian Mountains
Rocky Mountains
North America
Pyrenees
Alps
Ice sheet
Asia
Vegetation
Carpathian Mountains
Taurus Mountains
Himalayas
India
Australia
Desert
Indian Ocean
Andes
South America
Atlantic Ocean
Atlas Mountains
Africa
Antarctica
Ice cap

A MAMMAL SKELETON
(*Hippopotamus amphibius*)

SKULL OF AN EXTINCT CAVE BEAR
(*Ursus spelaeus*)

SKULL OF AN EXTINCT TORTOISE
(*Meiolania platyceps*)

A MAMMOTH TOOTH
(*Mammuthus primigenius*)

DEINOTHERIUM
A deinotheriid
Length: 13 ft (4 m)

COELODONTA
A rhinocerotid
Length: 13 ft (4 m)

AUSTRALOPITHECUS
A hominid
Length: 4 ft (1.2 m)

Early signs of life

FOR ALMOST A THOUSAND MILLION YEARS after its formation, there was no known life on Earth. The first simple, sea-dwelling organic structures appeared about 3,400 years ago; they may have formed when certain chemical molecules joined together. Prokaryotes, single-celled micro-organisms such as blue-green algae, were able to photosynthesize (see pp. 138–139), and thus produce oxygen. A thousand million years later, sufficient oxygen had built up in the earth's atmosphere to allow multicellular organisms to proliferate in the Precambrian seas (before 570 million years ago). Soft-bodied jellyfish, corals, and seaworms flourished about 700 million years ago. Trilobites, the first animals with hard body frames, developed during the Cambrian period (570–510 million years ago). However, it was not until the beginning of the Devonian period (409–363 million years ago) that early land plants, such as *Asteroxylon*, formed a water-retaining cuticle, which ended their dependence on an aquatic environment. About 363 million years ago, the first amphibians (see pp. 80–81) crawled onto the land, although they still returned to the water to lay their soft eggs. Not until the emergence of the first reptiles would animals appear that were not dependent on water in this way.

STROMATOLITIC LIMESTONE

Alternate layers of mud and sand

Layers bound by algae

Layered structure

Limestone

Long, beaklike snout

Growth line

Dorsal plate

Dorsal spine base

FOSSILIZED JAWLESS FISH

Glabella

Eye

Thoracic pleurae

Fixed lateral plate

Bony dorsal shield

Tail shield

Tail area

FOSSILIZED TRILOBITE

Ambulacral groove

Small ossicles of upper surface

Disk

Iron pyrites

FOSSILIZED STARFISH

Row of ossicles

Broad disk

UPPER SURFACE OF FOSSILIZED STARFISH

Row of ossicles

Short arm

LOWER SURFACE OF FOSSILIZED STARFISH

Jointed leg

Chelicera (jointed pincer)

Jointed leg with oar-shaped paddle

Segmented abdomen

UNDERSIDE OF FOSSILIZED EURYPTERID

Telson (tail spine)

Abdominal segments

Shell contains eight somites (thoracic segments)

Hingeless, bivalved shell

FOSSIL OF AN EXTINCT SHRIMP

Growing tip

Disk-shaped sporangium (spore-case)

Leaflike scale

Stem

RECONSTRUCTION OF ASTEROXYLON

Amphibians and reptiles

THE EARLIEST KNOWN AMPHIBIANS, such as *Acanthostega* and *Ichthyostega*, lived about 363 million years ago at the end of the Devonian period (409–363 million years ago). Their limbs may have evolved from the muscular fins of lungfish. These fish can use their fins to push themselves along the bottom of lakes and some can breathe at the water's surface. While amphibians (see pp. 182–183) can exist on land, they are dependent on a wet environment because their skin does not retain moisture and they must return to the water to lay their eggs. Evolving from amphibians, reptiles (see pp. 184–187) first appeared during the Carboniferous period (363–290 million years ago): *Westlothiana*, the earliest known reptile, lived on land 338 million years ago. The development of the amniotic egg, with an embryo enclosed in its own wet environment (the amnion) and protected by a waterproof shell, freed reptiles from the amphibian's dependence on a wet habitat. A scaly skin protected the reptile from desiccation on land and enabled it to exploit ways of life closed to its amphibian ancestors. Reptiles include the dinosaurs, which came to dominate life on land during the Mesozoic era (245–65 million years ago).

FOSSIL SKULL OF ACANTHOSTEGA

Orbit
Sculpted or pitted bone surface
Spiracle to draw in water
Pocket enclosing nostril
Mandible
Small tooth

MODEL OF ICHTHYOSTEGA

Muscular back
Scaly skin
Shoulder girdle
Finned tail
Hip girdle

SKELETON OF ERYOPS

Dorsal vertebra
Scapula
Cleithrum
Cervical vertebra
Cranium
Orbit
Maxilla
Naris
Mandible
Sharp tooth
Clavicle
Phalanges
Glenoid cavity
Humerus
Rib
Elbow joint
Radius
Ulna
Metacarpals

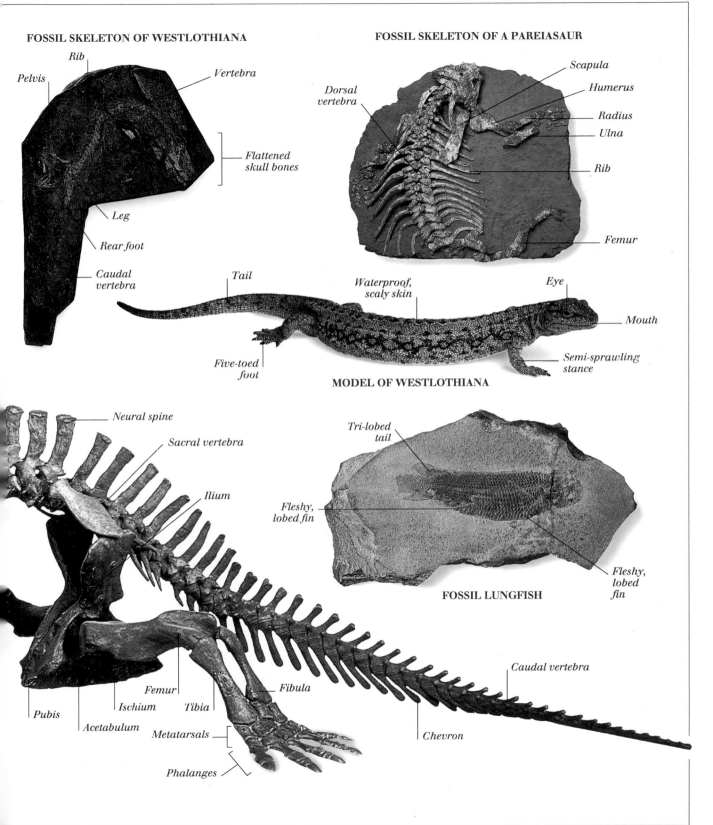

FOSSIL SKELETON OF WESTLOTHIANA

Rib

Pelvis

Vertebra

Flattened
skull bones

Leg

Rear foot

Caudal
vertebra

FOSSIL SKELETON OF A PAREIASAUR

Dorsal
vertebra

Scapula

Humerus

Radius

Ulna

Rib

Femur

Tail

Waterproof,
scaly skin

Eye

Mouth

Five-toed
foot

Semi-sprawling
stance

MODEL OF WESTLOTHIANA

Neural spine

Sacral vertebra

Ilium

Tri-lobed
tail

Fleshy,
lobed fin

Fleshy,
lobed
fin

FOSSIL LUNGFISH

Caudal vertebra

Femur

Fibula

Pubis

Ischium

Tibia

Acetabulum

Metatarsals

Chevron

Phalanges

81

The dinosaurs

THE DINOSAURS WERE A LARGE GROUP of reptiles that were the dominant land vertebrates (animals with backbones) for most of the Mesozoic era (245–65 million years ago). They appeared some 230 million years ago and were distinguished from other scaly, egg-laying reptiles by an important feature: dinosaurs had an erect limb stance. This enabled them to keep their bodies well above the ground, unlike the sprawling and semi-sprawling stance of other reptiles. The head of the dinosaur's femur (thighbone) fits into a socket in its pelvis (hipbone), producing efficient and mobile locomotion. Dinosaurs are categorized into two groups according to the structure of their pelvis: saurischian (lizard-hipped) and ornithischian (bird-hipped) dinosaurs. In the case of most saurischians, the pubis (part of the pelvis) jutted forward, while in ornithischians it slanted back, parallel to the ischium (another part of the pelvis). The enormous variety of dinosaur species equals that of mammals. The Dinosauria were the most successful land vertebrates ever, and survived for 165 million years, until their extinction 65 million years ago.

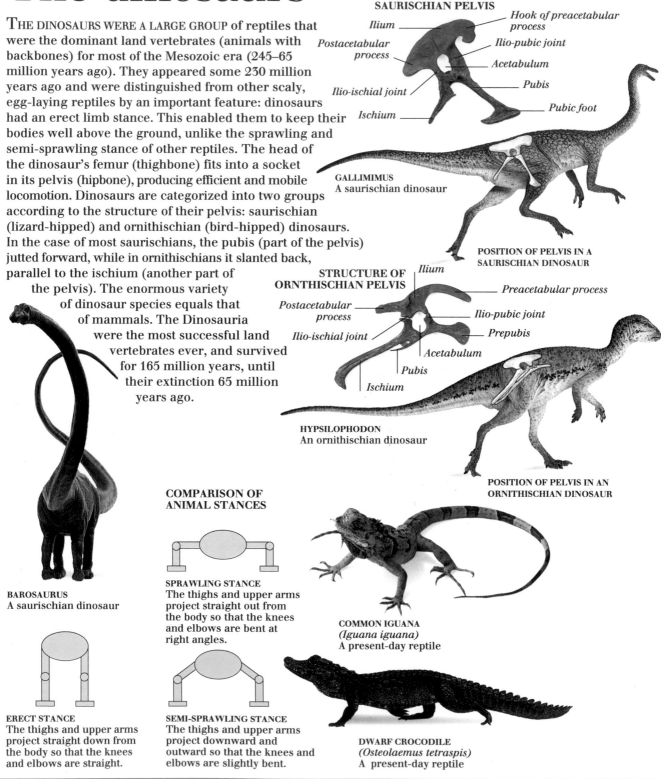

STRUCTURE OF SAURISCHIAN PELVIS
Ilium
Hook of preacetabular process
Postacetabular process
Ilio-pubic joint
Acetabulum
Pubis
Ilio-ischial joint
Pubic foot
Ischium

GALLIMIMUS
A saurischian dinosaur

POSITION OF PELVIS IN A SAURISCHIAN DINOSAUR

STRUCTURE OF ORNITHISCHIAN PELVIS
Ilium
Preacetabular process
Postacetabular process
Ilio-pubic joint
Prepubis
Ilio-ischial joint
Acetabulum
Pubis
Ischium

HYPSILOPHODON
An ornithischian dinosaur

POSITION OF PELVIS IN AN ORNITHISCHIAN DINOSAUR

BAROSAURUS
A saurischian dinosaur

COMPARISON OF ANIMAL STANCES

SPRAWLING STANCE
The thighs and upper arms project straight out from the body so that the knees and elbows are bent at right angles.

COMMON IGUANA
(Iguana iguana)
A present-day reptile

ERECT STANCE
The thighs and upper arms project straight down from the body so that the knees and elbows are straight.

SEMI-SPRAWLING STANCE
The thighs and upper arms project downward and outward so that the knees and elbows are slightly bent.

DWARF CROCODILE
(Osteolaemus tetraspis)
A present-day reptile

82

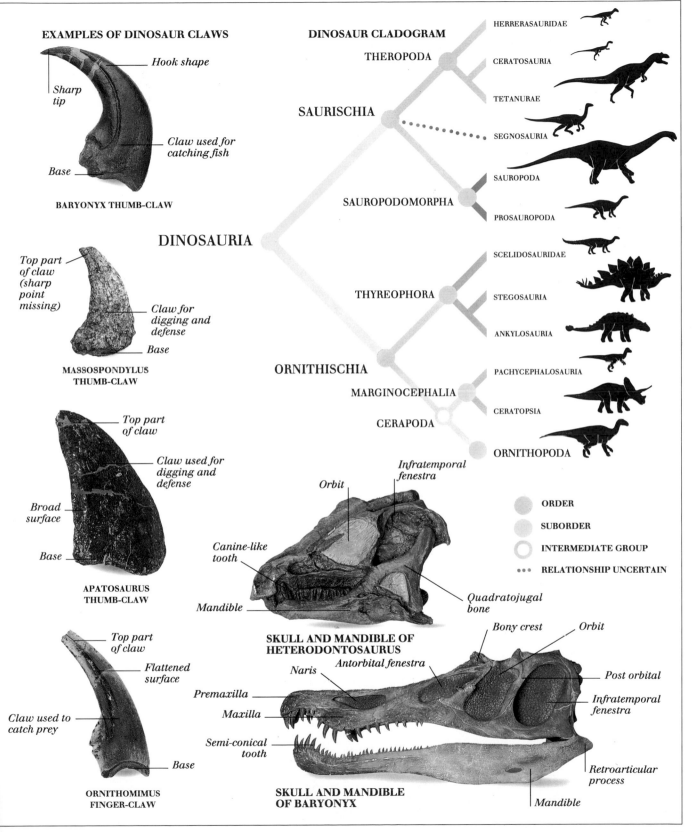

EXAMPLES OF DINOSAUR CLAWS

Hook shape

Sharp tip

Claw used for catching fish

Base

BARYONYX THUMB-CLAW

Top part of claw (sharp point missing)

Claw for digging and defense

Base

MASSOSPONDYLUS THUMB-CLAW

Top part of claw

Claw used for digging and defense

Broad surface

Base

APATOSAURUS THUMB-CLAW

Top part of claw

Flattened surface

Claw used to catch prey

Base

ORNITHOMIMUS FINGER-CLAW

DINOSAUR CLADOGRAM

HERRERASAURIDAE

THEROPODA

CERATOSAURIA

SAURISCHIA

TETANURAE

SEGNOSAURIA

SAUROPODA

SAUROPODOMORPHA

PROSAUROPODA

DINOSAURIA

SCELIDOSAURIDAE

THYREOPHORA

STEGOSAURIA

ANKYLOSAURIA

PACHYCEPHALOSAURIA

ORNITHISCHIA

MARGINOCEPHALIA

CERATOPSIA

CERAPODA

ORNITHOPODA

● ORDER

● SUBORDER

○ INTERMEDIATE GROUP

••• RELATIONSHIP UNCERTAIN

Infratemporal fenestra

Orbit

Canine-like tooth

Quadratojugal bone

Mandible

SKULL AND MANDIBLE OF HETERODONTOSAURUS

Bony crest

Orbit

Naris

Antorbital fenestra

Post orbital

Premaxilla

Infratemporal fenestra

Maxilla

Semi-conical tooth

Retroarticular process

Base

SKULL AND MANDIBLE OF BARYONYX

Mandible

Theropods 1

AN ENORMOUSLY SUCCESSFUL SUBORDER of the Saurischia, the bipedal (two-footed) theropods ("beast feet") emerged 230 million years ago in Late Triassic times; the oldest known example comes from South America. Theropods spanned the whole of the Age of the Dinosaurs (230–65 million years ago) and included most known predatory dinosaurs. The typical theropod had small arms with sharp, clawed fingers; powerful jaws lined with sharp teeth; an S-shaped neck; long, muscular hind limbs; and clawed, usually four-toed feet. Many theropods may have been warm-blooded; most were exclusively carnivorous. Theropods ranged from animals no larger than a chicken to huge creatures, such as *Tyrannosaurus* and *Baryonyx*. The group also included ostrichlike omnivores and herbivores with toothless beaks, such as *Struthiomimus* and *Gallimimus*. Many scientists believe that birds are the closest living relatives to the dinosaurs, and share a common ancestor with the theropods. *Archaeopteryx*, small and feathered, was the first known bird and lived alongside its dinosaur relatives.

INTERNAL ANATOMY OF ALBERTOSAURUS LEG

SKELETON OF TYRANNOSAURUS

EXTERNAL FEATURES OF TYRANNOSAURUS

FOSSIL SKELETON OF ARCHAEOPTERYX

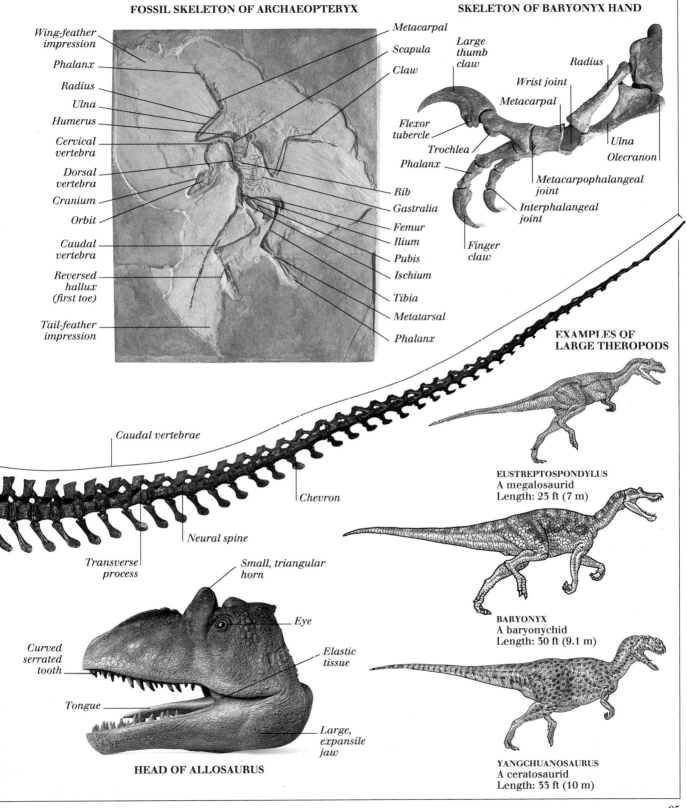

Wing-feather impression

Phalanx

Radius

Ulna

Humerus

Cervical vertebra

Dorsal vertebra

Cranium

Orbit

Caudal vertebra

Reversed hallux (first toe)

Tail-feather impression

Metacarpal

Scapula

Claw

Rib

Gastralia

Femur

Ilium

Pubis

Ischium

Tibia

Metatarsal

Phalanx

SKELETON OF BARYONYX HAND

Large thumb claw

Flexor tubercle

Trochlea

Phalanx

Radius

Wrist joint

Metacarpal

Ulna

Olecranon

Metacarpophalangeal joint

Interphalangeal joint

Finger claw

Caudal vertebrae

Chevron

Neural spine

Transverse process

EXAMPLES OF LARGE THEROPODS

EUSTREPTOSPONDYLUS
A megalosaurid
Length: 23 ft (7 m)

BARYONYX
A baryonychid
Length: 30 ft (9.1 m)

YANGCHUANOSAURUS
A ceratosaurid
Length: 33 ft (10 m)

Small, triangular horn

Eye

Curved serrated tooth

Elastic tissue

Tongue

Large, expansile jaw

HEAD OF ALLOSAURUS

Theropods 2

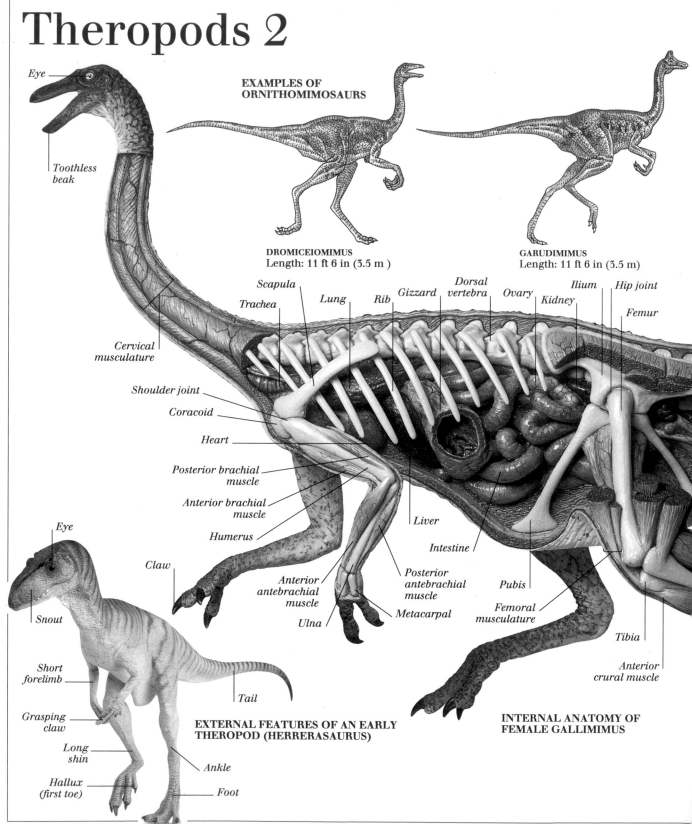

Eye

Toothless
beak

**EXAMPLES OF
ORNITHOMIMOSAURS**

DROMICEIOMIMUS
Length: 11 ft 6 in (3.5 m)

GARUDIMIMUS
Length: 11 ft 6 in (3.5 m)

Cervical
musculature

Scapula

Trachea

Lung

Rib

Gizzard

Dorsal
vertebra

Ovary

Kidney

Ilium

Hip joint

Femur

Shoulder joint

Coracoid

Heart

Posterior brachial
muscle

Anterior brachial
muscle

Humerus

Liver

Intestine

Anterior
antebrachial
muscle

Posterior
antebrachial
muscle

Pubis

Femoral
musculature

Ulna

Metacarpal

Tibia

Anterior
crural muscle

Eye

Snout

Short
forelimb

Claw

Grasping
claw

Long
shin

Tail

Hallux
(first toe)

Ankle

Foot

**EXTERNAL FEATURES OF AN EARLY
THEROPOD (HERRERASAURUS)**

**INTERNAL ANATOMY OF
FEMALE GALLIMIMUS**

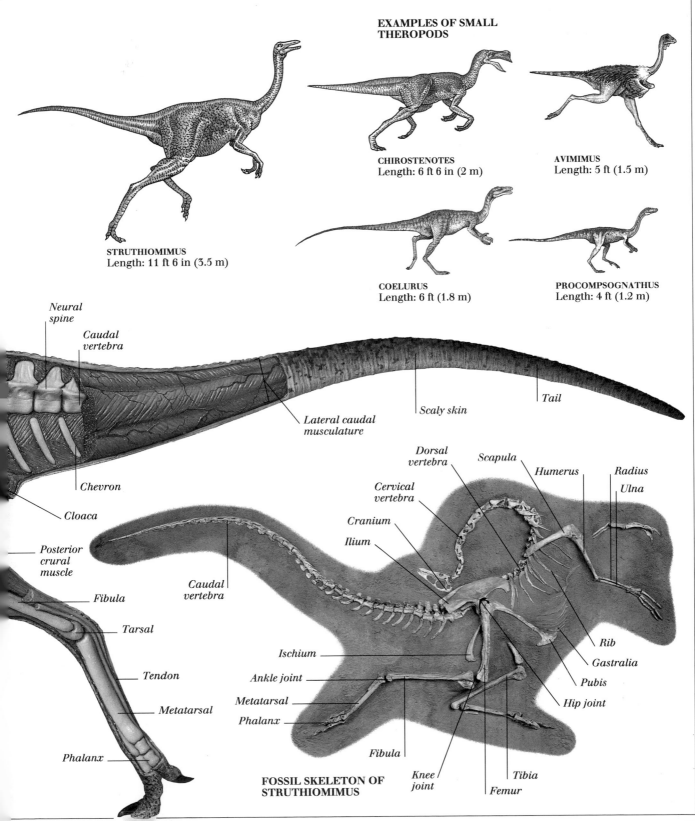

EXAMPLES OF SMALL THEROPODS

CHIROSTENOTES
Length: 6 ft 6 in (2 m)

AVIMIMUS
Length: 5 ft (1.5 m)

STRUTHIOMIMUS
Length: 11 ft 6 in (3.5 m)

COELURUS
Length: 6 ft (1.8 m)

PROCOMPSOGNATHUS
Length: 4 ft (1.2 m)

Neural spine

Caudal vertebra

Lateral caudal musculature

Scaly skin

Tail

Chevron

Cloaca

Dorsal vertebra

Scapula

Humerus

Radius

Ulna

Cervical vertebra

Cranium

Ilium

Posterior crural muscle

Caudal vertebra

Fibula

Tarsal

Tendon

Rib

Metatarsal

Gastralia

Ischium

Pubis

Ankle joint

Hip joint

Metatarsal

Phalanx

Phalanx

Fibula

Knee joint

Tibia

Femur

FOSSIL SKELETON OF STRUTHIOMIMUS

Sauropodomorphs 1

THE SAUROPODOMORPHA ("lizard-feet forms") were herbivorous, usually quadrupedal (four-footed) dinosaurs. A suborder of the Saurischia, they were characterized by small heads, bulky bodies, and long necks and tails. There were two infraorders: prosauropods and sauropods.

THECODONTOSAURUS

Prosauropods lived from Late Triassic to Early Jurassic times (225–180 million years ago) and included beasts such as the small *Anchisaurus* and one of the first very large dinosaurs, *Melanosaurus*. By Middle Jurassic times (about 165 million years ago), sauropods had replaced prosauropods and spread worldwide. They included the heaviest and longest land animals ever, such as *Diplodocus* and *Brachiosaurus*. Sauropods persisted to the end of the Cretaceous period (65 million years ago). Many of these dinosaurs moved in herds, protected from predatory theropods by their huge bulk and powerful tails, which they could use to lash out at attackers. Sauropodomorphs were the most common large herbivores until Late Jurassic times (about 145 million years ago), and appear to have survived in southern continents long after they had disappeared from the north.

SKULL AND MANDIBLE OF PLATEOSAURUS

Naris

Antorbital fenestra

Orbit

Mandible

Infratemporal fenestra

Paroccipital process

Serrated, leaf-shaped tooth

Mandibular fenestra

SKELETON OF PLATEOSAURUS

Dorsal vertebrae

Sacral vertebrae

Cervical vertebrae

Ilium

Humerus

Scapula

Shoulder joint

Rib

Pubis

Hip joint

Femur

Ischium

Curved thumb claw

Elbow joint

Knee joint

Tail

Radius

Tibia

Wrist joint

Ulna

Fibula

Metacarpal

Ankle joint

Metatarsals

Cranium

Phalanx

Orbit

Mandible

Phalanges

Naris

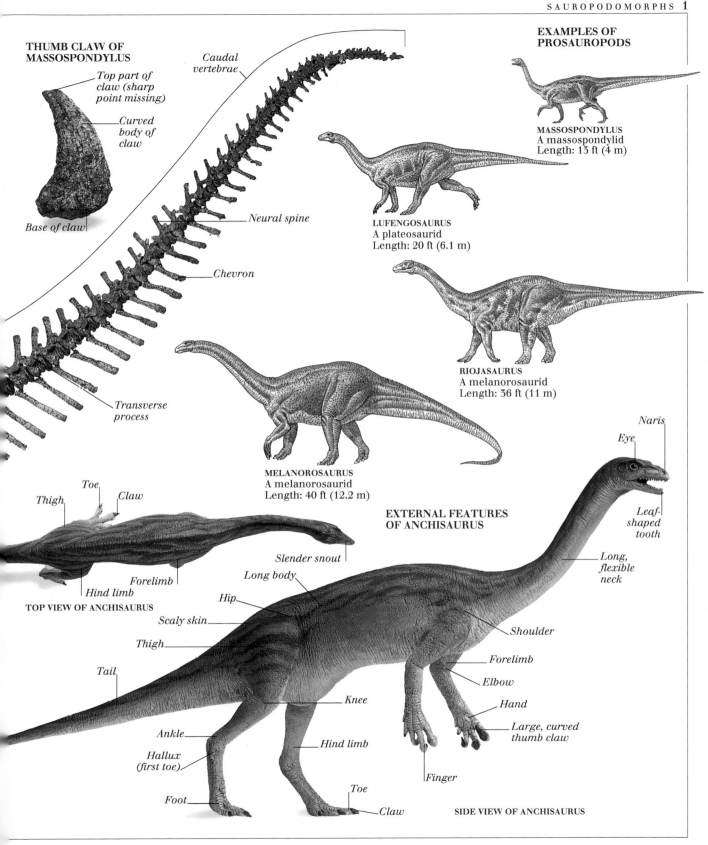

THUMB CLAW OF MASSOSPONDYLUS

Top part of claw (sharp point missing)

Curved body of claw

Base of claw

Caudal vertebrae

Neural spine

Chevron

Transverse process

EXAMPLES OF PROSAUROPODS

MASSOSPONDYLUS
A massospondylid
Length: 13 ft (4 m)

LUFENGOSAURUS
A plateosaurid
Length: 20 ft (6.1 m)

RIOJASAURUS
A melanorosaurid
Length: 36 ft (11 m)

MELANOROSAURUS
A melanorosaurid
Length: 40 ft (12.2 m)

EXTERNAL FEATURES OF ANCHISAURUS

Thigh
Toe
Claw
Slender snout
Long body
Forelimb
Hip
Hind limb
Scaly skin
Thigh
Tail
Knee
Ankle
Hind limb
Hallux (first toe)
Finger
Foot
Toe
Claw

TOP VIEW OF ANCHISAURUS

Naris
Eye
Leaf-shaped tooth
Long, flexible neck
Shoulder
Forelimb
Elbow
Hand
Large, curved thumb claw

SIDE VIEW OF ANCHISAURUS

Sauropodomorphs 2

SKULL AND MANDIBLE OF DIPLODOCUS

Cranium
Orbit
Antorbital fenestra
Maxillary fenestra
Maxilla
Peg-shaped tooth
Sclerotic ring
Infratemporal fenestra
Mandible

FOREFOOT OF ELEPHANT

Wrist
Nail

FOREFOOT BONES OF ELEPHANT

Radius
Ulna
Carpals
Metacarpals
Phalanges

COMPARISON OF THE FOREFEET OF AN ELEPHANT AND DIPLODOCUS

FOREFOOT BONES OF DIPLODOCUS

Radius
Ulna
Carpals
Metacarpals
Phalanges

MIDDLE SECTION OF DIPLODOCUS SKELETON

Coracoid
Scapula
Dorsal vertebra
Sacral vertebra
Ilium
Caudal vertebra
Humerus
Rib
Elbow joint
Ulna
Radius
Wrist joint
Phalanges
Metacarpals
Knee joint
Tibia
Fibula
Hip joint
Femur
Ischium
Ankle joint
Cloaca
Caudal musculature

Neural spine
Small intestine
Dorsal vertebra
Ovary
Kidney
Rib
Large intestine
Hip joint
Cecum
Pubis
Femur
Oviduct
Thigh musculature
Posterior crural musculature
Fibula
Ankle joint
Metatarsal
Anterior crural muscle

FOSSIL EGG OF TITANOSAURID

Fossil eggshell fragment

Fossil egg

Fossil eggshell fragment

Outer ear

Naris

Eye

Mouth

Orbit

Antorbital fenestra

Naris

Maxilla

Cranium

Infratemporal fenestra

Mandible

Spoon-shaped tooth

SKULL AND MANDIBLE OF CAMARASAURUS

INTERNAL ANATOMY OF FEMALE BRACHIOSAURUS

Cervical vertebra

Scapula

Trachea

Esophagus

Intercostal muscle

Scapular muscle

Shoulder joint

Lung

Humerus

Gizzard

Anterior brachial muscle

Posterior brachial musculature

Elbow joint

Radius

Ulna

Posterior antebrachial musculature

Wrist joint

Metacarpal

CETIOSAURUS
A cetiosaurid
Length: 59 ft (18 m)

SHUNOSAURUS
A cetiosaurid
Length: 33 ft (10 m)

SALTASAURUS
A titanosaurid
Length: 40 ft (12.2 m)

DIPLODOCUS
A diplodocid
Length: 90 ft (27.4 m)

Thyreophorans 1

THYREOPHORANS ("SHIELD BEARERS") were a group
of quadrupedal armored dinosaurs. A suborder of the
Ornithischia (bird-hipped dinosaurs), they were characterized
by rows of bony studs, plates, or spikes along the back, which
protected some from predators and may have helped others regulate
body temperature. Up to 30ft (9m) long, with a small head and small cheek
teeth, Thyreophorans had shorter forelimbs than hind limbs and probably
browsed on low-level vegetation. The earliest thyreophorans were
small and lived in Early Jurassic times (about 200 million
years ago) in Europe, North America, and
China. Stegosaurs, such as *Stegosaurus*
and *Kentrosaurus*, replaced these older
forms. The earliest stegosaur remains
come from England and China. Several genera
of stegosaurs survived into the Early Cretaceous period
(146–100 million years ago), but only in India did they persist
into Late Cretaceous times (97–65 million years ago).
Ankylosaurs, with their toothless beaks and cheek
teeth adapted for cropping vegetation,
appeared later than stegosaurs.
They originated in the Late
Jurassic period (155 million
years ago) and in North
America survived until the
extinction of the dinosaurs,
65 million years ago.

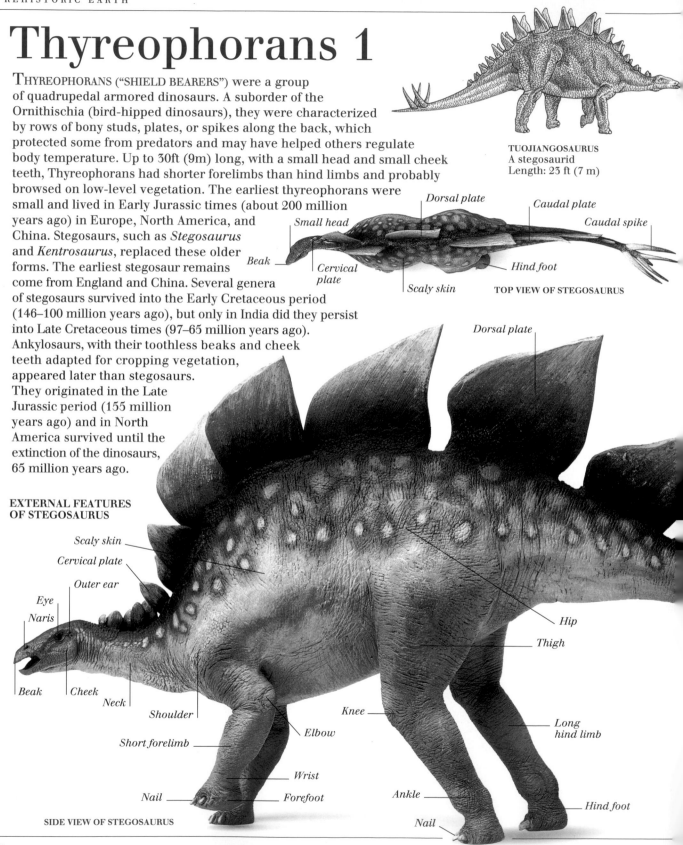

TUOJIANGOSAURUS
A stegosaurid
Length: 23 ft (7 m)

Dorsal plate

Caudal plate

Caudal spike

Small head

Beak

Cervical plate

Hind foot

Scaly skin

TOP VIEW OF STEGOSAURUS

Dorsal plate

**EXTERNAL FEATURES
OF STEGOSAURUS**

Scaly skin

Cervical plate

Outer ear

Eye

Naris

Hip

Thigh

Beak

Cheek

Neck

Shoulder

Elbow

Knee

Long
hind limb

Short forelimb

Wrist

Nail

Forefoot

Ankle

Hind foot

Nail

SIDE VIEW OF STEGOSAURUS

EXAMPLES OF STEGOSAURS

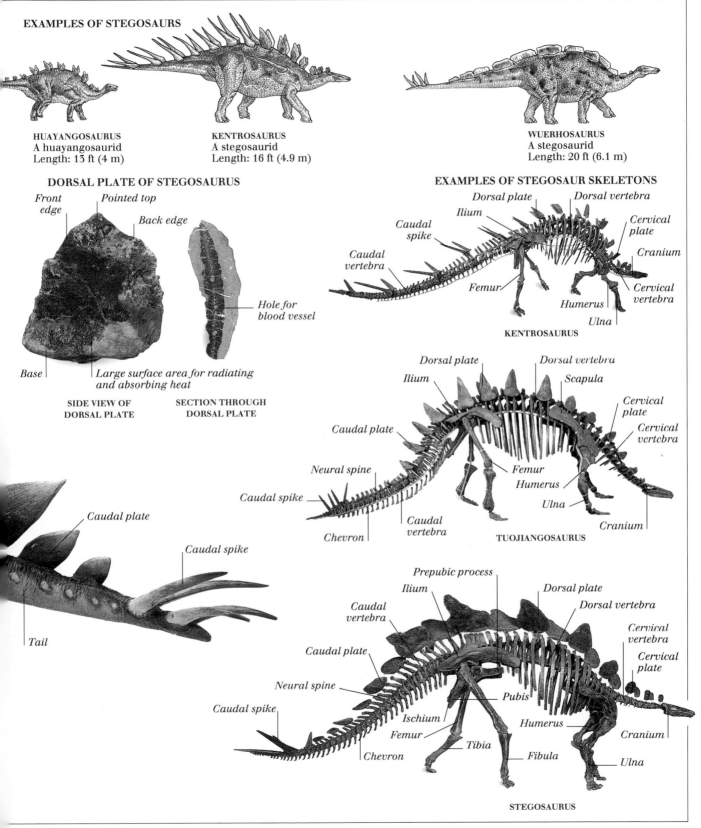

HUAYANGOSAURUS
A huayangosaurid
Length: 13 ft (4 m)

KENTROSAURUS
A stegosaurid
Length: 16 ft (4.9 m)

WUERHOSAURUS
A stegosaurid
Length: 20 ft (6.1 m)

DORSAL PLATE OF STEGOSAURUS

Front edge

Pointed top

Back edge

Base

Large surface area for radiating and absorbing heat

Hole for blood vessel

SIDE VIEW OF DORSAL PLATE

SECTION THROUGH DORSAL PLATE

Caudal plate

Caudal spike

Tail

EXAMPLES OF STEGOSAUR SKELETONS

Dorsal plate

Ilium

Caudal spike

Caudal vertebra

Dorsal vertebra

Cervical plate

Cranium

Femur

Cervical vertebra

Humerus

Ulna

KENTROSAURUS

Dorsal plate

Ilium

Dorsal vertebra

Scapula

Cervical plate

Caudal plate

Cervical vertebra

Neural spine

Caudal spike

Femur

Humerus

Chevron

Caudal vertebra

Ulna

Cranium

TUOJIANGOSAURUS

Prepubic process

Ilium

Caudal vertebra

Dorsal plate

Dorsal vertebra

Cervical vertebra

Caudal plate

Cervical plate

Neural spine

Caudal spike

Ischium

Femur

Pubis

Humerus

Cranium

Chevron

Tibia

Fibula

Ulna

STEGOSAURUS

Thyreophorans 2

EXAMPLES OF ANKYLOSAUR SKULLS

Maxilla

Orbit

Posterolateral horn

Naris

Cranium

Beak

Tooth

Mandible

Jugal plate

SKULL AND MANDIBLE OF EUOPLOCEPHALUS

Posterolateral horn

Nasal bone

Maxilla

Orbit

Cranium

Naris

Beak

Tooth

Mandible

SKULL AND MANDIBLE OF ANKYLOSAURUS

Beak

Nasal bone

Orbit

Naris

Cranium

Infratemporal fenestra

Mandible

SKULL AND MANDIBLE OF PANOPLOSAURUS

Dorsal vertebra

Small intestine

Iliotibial muscle

Rib

Gizzard

Ilium

Reproductive canal

Scapula

Lung

Ischium

Shoulder spike

Coracoid

Cervical musculature

Head horn

Humerus

Radius

Wrist joint

Heart

Iliotibial muscle

Femur

Metacarpal

Liver

Fibula

Knee joint

Toothless beak

Large intestine

Gastrocnemius muscle

Ventral antebrachial muscle

Ulna

Elbow joint

Digital extensor muscle

Ankle joint

Metatarsal

INTERNAL ANATOMY OF FEMALE EUOPLOCEPHALUS

EXTERNAL FEATURES OF EDMONTONIA

Hind limb

Flank spike

Dorsal scute

Dermal armor

Scaly skin

Nuchal ring

Shoulder spike

Broad, flat snout

Naris

Ankle

Elbow

Forelimb

Forefoot

Blunt nail

Caudal vertebra

Neural spine

Ureter

Terminal plate

Chevron

Cloaca

Lateral caudal musculature

Lateral plate

EXAMPLES OF ANKYLOSAURS

PINACOSAURUS
An ankylosaurid
Length: 16 ft 6 in (5 m)

MINMI
A nodosaurid
Length: 8 ft (2.4 m)

POLACANTHUS
A nodosaurid
Length: 13 ft (4 m)

FOSSIL OF ANKYLOSAURUS TAIL CLUB

Ossified caudal vertebra

Tail club

Ornithopods 1

IGUANODON TOOTH

ORNITHOPODS ("BIRD FEET") were a group of ornithischian ("bird-hipped") dinosaurs. These bipedal and quadrupedal herbivores had a horny beak, plant-cutting or grinding cheek teeth, and a pelvic and tail region stiffened by bony tendons. They evolved teeth and jaws adapted to pulping vegetation and flourished from the Middle Jurassic to the Late Cretaceous period (165–65 million years ago) in North America, Europe, Africa, China, Australia, and Antarctica. Some ornithopods were no larger than a dog, while others were immense creatures up to 49 ft (15 m) long. Iguanodonts, an ornithopod group, had a broad, toothless beak at the end of a long snout, large jaws with long rows of ridged, closely packed teeth for grinding vegetation, a bulky body, and a heavy tail. *Iguanodon* and some other iguanodonts had large thumb-spikes that were strong enough to stab attackers. Another group, the hadrosaurs, such as *Gryposaurus* and *Hadrosaurus,* lived in Late Cretaceous times (97–65 million years ago) and with their broad beaks are sometimes known as "duckbills." They were characterized by their deep skulls and closely packed rows of teeth, while some, such as *Corythosaurus* and *Lambeosaurus,* had tall, hollow, bony head crests.

SKELETON OF IGUANODON

Orbit
Cranium
Naris
Mandible
Cervical rib
Cervical vertebra
Scapula
Humerus
Sternal bone
Radius
Ulna
Prepubic process
Femur
Pubis
Tibia
Fibula
Metatarsal
Dorsal vertebra
Sacral vertebra
Caudal vertebra
Neural spine
Ilium
Chevron
Ischium

Thigh
Heavy, stiff tail
Knee
Hind limb
Ankle
Toe
Foot
Hooflike nail

SKULL AND MANDIBLE OF YOUNG IGUANODON

Cheek tooth
Orbit
Cranium
Maxilla
Premaxilla
Paroccipital process
Jugal bone
Coronoid process
Predentary bone
Dentary bone
Mandible

EXAMPLES OF IGUANODONTS

OURANOSAURUS
An iguanodontid
Length: 23 ft (7 m)

CAMPTOSAURUS
A camptosaurid
Length: 16–23 ft (4.9–7 m)

MUTTABURRASAURUS
A camptosaurid
Length: 23 ft (7 m)

PROBACTROSAURUS
An iguanodontid
Length: 20 ft (6.1 m)

EXTERNAL FEATURES OF IGUANODON

Eye

Naris

Shoulder

Neck

Tongue

Beak

Scaly skin

Forelimb

Elbow

Wrist

Hand

Finger

Thumb-spike

Hooflike nail

**INTERNAL ANATOMY OF
HIND LEG OF IGUANODON**

Iliofemoral
muscle

Ilium

Iliotibial
muscle

Ambiens
muscle

Short
caudo-
femoral
muscle

External pubo-ischio-
femoral muscle

Tibial flexor
muscle

Femur

Iliofibular
muscle

Common digital
extensor muscle

Gastrocnemius
muscle

Anterior tibial
muscle

Tibia

Fibula

Tarsal

Metatarsal

Toe

Hooflike nail

Ornithopods 2

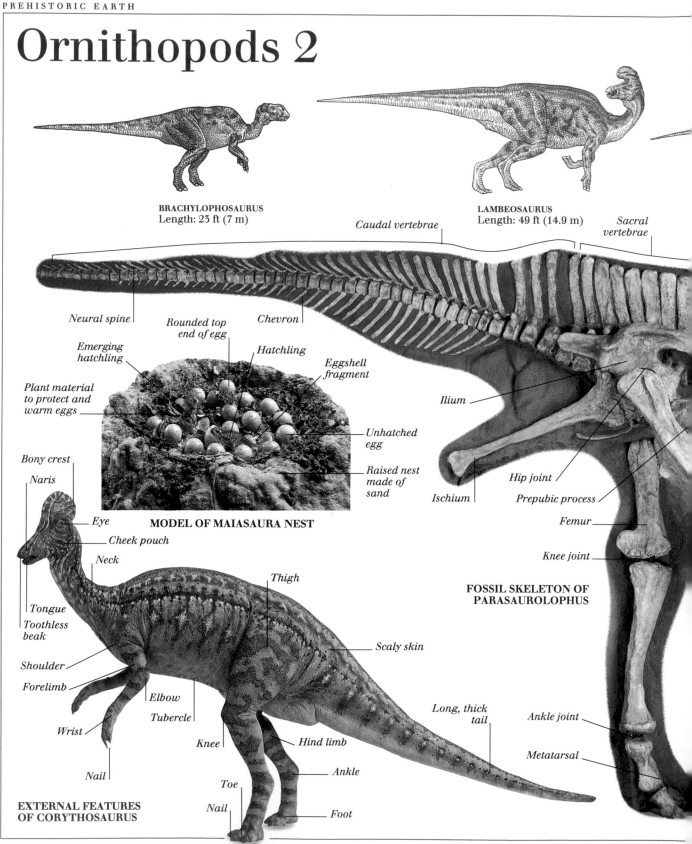

BRACHYLOPHOSAURUS
Length: 23 ft (7 m)

LAMBEOSAURUS
Length: 49 ft (14.9 m)

Caudal vertebrae

Sacral vertebrae

Neural spine

Rounded top end of egg

Chevron

Emerging hatchling

Hatchling

Eggshell fragment

Plant material to protect and warm eggs

Ilium

Bony crest

Naris

Unhatched egg

Eye

Raised nest made of sand

Cheek pouch

Hip joint

Ischium

Prepubic process

MODEL OF MAIASAURA NEST

Neck

Femur

Knee joint

Tongue

Thigh

**FOSSIL SKELETON OF
PARASAUROLOPHUS**

Toothless beak

Shoulder

Scaly skin

Forelimb

Elbow

Tubercle

Wrist

Knee

Long, thick tail

Ankle joint

Hind limb

Nail

Ankle

Metatarsal

Toe

Nail

Foot

**EXTERNAL FEATURES
OF CORYTHOSAURUS**

EXAMPLES OF HADROSAURS

HYPACROSAURUS
Length: 30 ft (9.1 m)

HADROSAURUS
Length: 26–33 ft (7.9–10 m)

GRYPOSAURUS
Length: 26–33 ft (7.9–10 m)

Dorsal vertebrae

Bony crest

Air passage

Cranium

Infratemporal fenestra

Orbit

Cervical vertebrae

Mandible

Naris

Orbit

Infratemporal fenestra

Air passage

Naris

Mandible

Tooth

**SKULL AND MANDIBLE
OF JUVENILE
LAMBEOSAURUS**

Scapula

Shoulder joint

Tibia

Rib

Fibula

Humerus

Elbow joint

Radius

Ulna

Wrist joint

Phalanges

Metacarpal

Phalanges

Sclerotic ring

Cranium

Bony crest

Orbit

Naris

Infratemporal fenestra

Mandible

Premaxilla

**SKULL AND MANDIBLE
OF ADULT
LAMBEOSAURUS**

Marginocephalians 1

MARGINOCEPHALIA ("margined heads") were a group of bipedal and quadrupedal ornithischian dinosaurs with a narrow shelf or deep, bony frill at the back of the skull. Marginocephalians were probably descended from the same ancestor as the ornithopods and lived in what are now North America, Africa, Asia, and Europe during the Cretaceous period (146–65 million years ago). They were divided into two infraorders: Pachycephalosauria ("thick-headed lizards"), such as *Pachycephalosaurus* and *Stegoceras*, and Ceratopsia ("horned faces"), such as *Triceratops* and *Psittacosaurus*. The thick skulls of Pachycephalosauria protected their brains during head-butting contests fought to win territory and mates; their hips and spines were also strengthened to withstand the shock. The bony frill of Ceratopsia would have added to their frightening appearance when charging; the neck was strengthened for impact and to support the huge head, with its snipping beak and powerful slicing toothed jaws. A charging ceratops would have been a formidable opponent for even the largest predators. Ceratopsia were among the most abundant herbivorous dinosaurs of the Late Cretaceous period (97–65 million years ago).

HEAD-BUTTING PRENOCEPHALES

Thick, high-domed cranium
Supraorbital ridge
Orbit
Naris
Mandible
Neural spine
Cervical rib
Humerus
Ulna
Radius
Prepubis
Wrist joint
Metacarpal
Phalanx
Ilium
Ischium
Metatarsals
Phalanges

EXAMPLES OF SKULLS OF PACHYCEPHALOSAURS

Orbit
Thickened dome of cranium
Maxilla
Bony ridge
Tooth
Mandible
SKULL AND MANDIBLE OF STEGOCERAS

Orbit
Thickened dome of cranium
Maxilla
Bony nodule
SKULL OF PRENOCEPHALE

Thickened dome of cranium
Bony spike
Maxilla
Orbit
Bony nodule
SKULL OF PACHYCEPHALOSAURUS

EXTERNAL FEATURES OF PACHYCEPHALOSAURUS

Scaly skin
Bony nodule
Domed head
Eye
Bony spike
Neck
Snout
Forelimb
Finger
Hand
Claw
Toe
Foot
Ankle
Hind limb
Knee
Tail

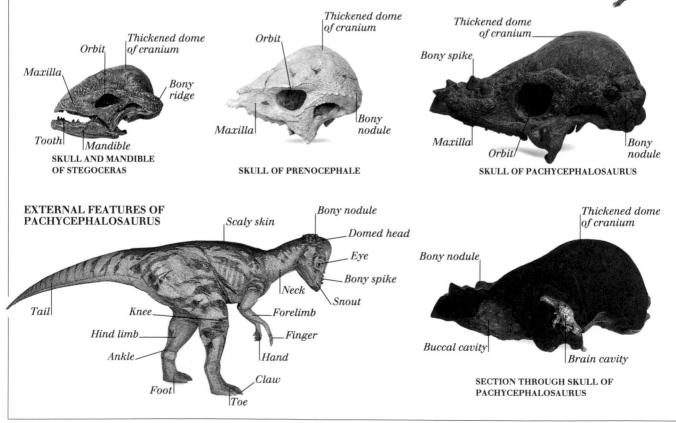

Thickened dome of cranium
Bony nodule
Buccal cavity
Brain cavity
SECTION THROUGH SKULL OF PACHYCEPHALOSAURUS

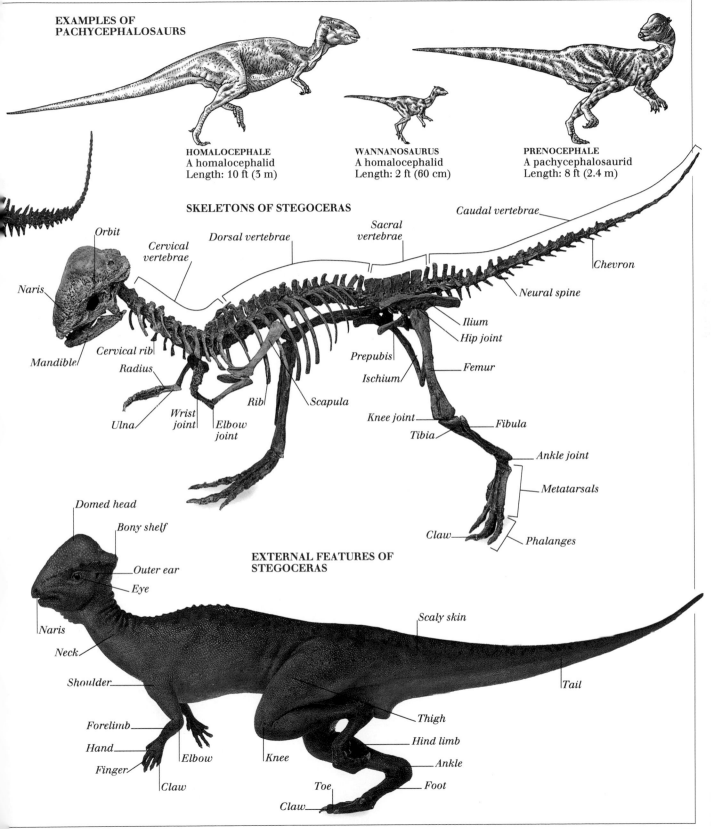

**EXAMPLES OF
PACHYCEPHALOSAURS**

HOMALOCEPHALE
A homalocephalid
Length: 10 ft (3 m)

WANNANOSAURUS
A homalocephalid
Length: 2 ft (60 cm)

PRENOCEPHALE
A pachycephalosaurid
Length: 8 ft (2.4 m)

SKELETONS OF STEGOCERAS

Orbit

Cervical
vertebrae

Dorsal vertebrae

Sacral
vertebrae

Caudal vertebrae

Chevron

Naris

Neural spine

Ilium

Hip joint

Mandible

Cervical rib

Radius

Prepubis

Femur

Ischium

Rib

Scapula

Wrist
joint

Elbow
joint

Ulna

Knee joint

Fibula

Tibia

Ankle joint

Metatarsals

Claw

Phalanges

Domed head

Bony shelf

Outer ear

Eye

**EXTERNAL FEATURES OF
STEGOCERAS**

Scaly skin

Naris

Neck

Tail

Shoulder

Forelimb

Thigh

Hand

Hind limb

Finger

Elbow

Knee

Ankle

Claw

Toe

Foot

Claw

Marginocephalians 2

Parietosquamosal frill

Brow horn

Nose horn

Epoccipital bone

Thick, scaly skin

Thigh

Tail

Ankle

Hind limb

Nail

Elbow

Forelimb

Wrist

Eye

Naris

Toothless beak

EXTERNAL FEATURES OF TRICERATOPS

Parietal fenestra

Epoccipital bone

Parietosquamosal frill

Nose-horn core

Supraorbital ridge

Orbit

Naris

Cranium

Mandible

SKULL AND MANDIBLE OF STYRACOSAURUS

Parietosquamosal frill

Cranium

Postorbital bone

Nasal bone

Orbit

Lacrimal bone

Parietal fenestra

Naris

Infratemporal fenestra

Beak

Rostral bone

Jugal bone

Predentary bone

Surangular bone

Dentary bone

Tooth

Angular bone

Mandible

SKULL AND MANDIBLE OF PROTOCERATOPS

Prepubis

Ilium

Hip joint

Dorsal vertebrae

Caudal vertebra

Chevron

Neural spine

Ischium

Femur

Knee joint

Fibula

Tibia

Ankle joint

Metatarsals

Phalanges

Rib

Scapula

Humerus

Elbow joint

Ulna

Sternal bone

Coracoid

Shoulder joint

Radius

SKELETON OF TRICERATOPS

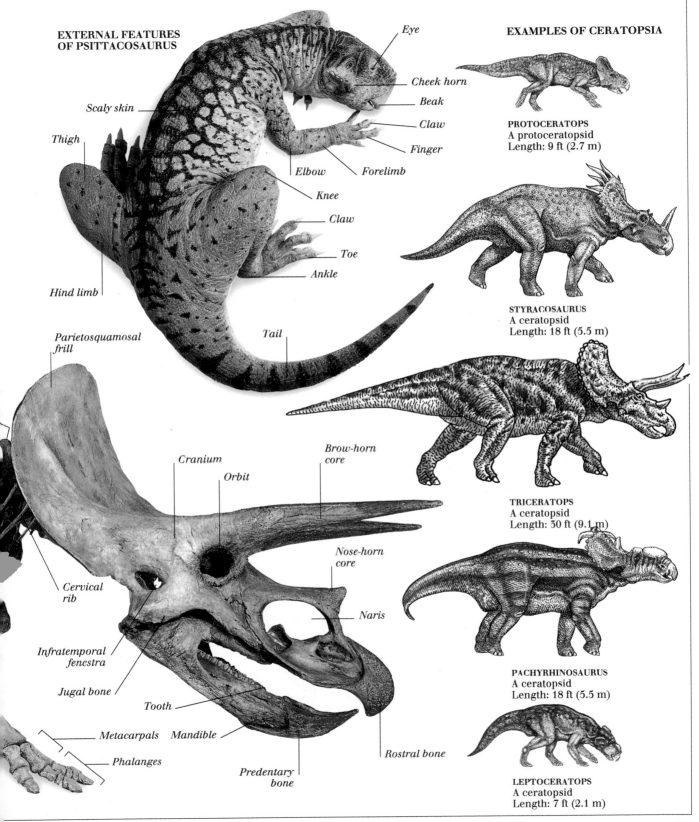

**EXTERNAL FEATURES
OF PSITTACOSAURUS**

Eye

Cheek horn

Beak

Claw

Finger

Scaly skin

Thigh

Elbow

Forelimb

Knee

Claw

Toe

Ankle

Hind limb

Parietosquamosal
frill

Tail

Cranium

Orbit

Brow-horn
core

Nose-horn
core

Naris

Cervical
rib

Infratemporal
fenestra

Jugal bone

Tooth

Metacarpals   Mandible

Phalanges

Predentary
bone

Rostral bone

EXAMPLES OF CERATOPSIA

PROTOCERATOPS
A protoceratopsid
Length: 9 ft (2.7 m)

STYRACOSAURUS
A ceratopsid
Length: 18 ft (5.5 m)

TRICERATOPS
A ceratopsid
Length: 30 ft (9.1 m)

PACHYRHINOSAURUS
A ceratopsid
Length: 18 ft (5.5 m)

LEPTOCERATOPS
A ceratopsid
Length: 7 ft (2.1 m)

Mammals 1

TETRALOPHODON CHEEK TEETH

SINCE THE EXTINCTION of the dinosaurs 65 million years ago, mammals have been the dominant vertebrates on Earth and include terrestrial, aerial, and aquatic forms. Having developed from the reptilian Therapsids, the first true mammals—small, nocturnal, rodentlike creatures, such as *Megazostrodon*—appeared over 200 million years ago during the Triassic period (245–208 million years ago). Mammals had several features that improved on those of their reptilian ancestors: an efficient four-chambered heart allowed these warm-blooded animals to sustain high levels of activity; a covering of hair helped them maintain a constant body temperature; an improved limb structure gave them more efficient locomotion; and the birth of live young and the immediate supply of food from the mother's milk aided their rapid growth. Since the end of the Mesozoic era (65 million years ago), the number of different mammal orders and the abundance of species in each order have varied dramatically. For example, the Perissodactyla (the order that includes *Coelodonta* and modern horses) was the most common group during the Early Tertiary period (about 54 million years ago). Today, the mammalian orders with the most populous species are the Rodentia (rats and mice), the Carnivora (bears, cats, and dogs), and the Artiodactyla (cattle, deer, and pigs), while the Proboscidea order, which included many genera, such as *Phiomia, Moeritherium, Tetralophodon,* and *Mammuthus*, now has only one member: the modern elephant. In Australia and South America, millions of years of continental isolation led to the development of the marsupials, a group of mammals distinct from the placentals (see p. 74) that existed elsewhere.

MODEL OF A MEGAZOSTRODON

Long tail aids balance

Insulating hair

Neural spine

Scapula

Cervical vertebra

Humerus

Nasal horn

Naris

Predentary bone

Orbit

Mandible

Radius

Ulna

Chisel-edged molar

Metacarpal

Phalanx

UPPER JAWBONE (MAXILLA) OF A HORSE

Molars

Premolars

HOOFBONE (THIRD PHALANX) OF A HORSE

Articular surface

Tendon insertion

Cranium

Naris

Predentary bone

Molar tooth

SKULL AND MANDIBLE OF A MOERITHERIUM

Nasal tusk

Molar tooth

Shovel-shaped tusk

SKULL AND MANDIBLE OF A PHIOMIA

Trunk

Thick hide

Short tusk used for rooting up plants

MODEL OF A PHIOMIA

Dorsal vertebra

Ilium

Ball and socket joint

Pubis

Rib

Caudal vertebra

Femur

Tibia

Fibula

Metatarsal

Phalanx

SKELETON OF AN ARSINOITHERIUM

Mandible

Cranium

Teeth

Elongated digit

Humerus

Hind limb bone

FOSSIL SKELETON OF A BAT

Mammals 2

LOWER JAW OF A BEAR

Articulation with skull

Large canine

Diastema

Low cusp

Molar

Premolar

SKELETON OF A TOXODON

Scapula

Neural spine

Cervical vertebra

Cranium

Coronoid process

Zygomatic arch

Orbit

Maxilla

Nasal bone

Incisor

Canine

Mandible

Molar

Humerus

Radius

Ulna

Large breastbone

Metacarpals

SKULL OF AN OPOSSUM

Orbit

Cranium

Naris

Occipital region

Canine

Infraorbital foramen

Molar

**FOSSIL SKULL OF
AN HYAENODON**

Orbit

Naris

Canine

*Infraorbital
foramen*

Mandible

Molar

Sagittal crest

Cranium

*Neck
insertion*

**LOWER JAW OF AN
AUSTRALOPITHECUS**

*Expanded
occlusal
surface*

Premolar

Molar

Ilium

Rib

Femur

*Knee
joint*

Tibia

Fibula

Metatarsals

Phalanx

SKULL OF A SMILODON

Orbit

Naris

*Infraorbital
foramen*

Muscle scar

Sagittal crest

*Occipital
condyle*

Canine

*Dentary
bone*

*Slicing
tooth*

*Zygomatic
arch*

*Thick,
insulating
coat*

Ivory tusk

*Woolly
underhair*

Hairy trunk

RECONSTRUCTION OF A MAMMOTH

The first hominids

MODERN HUMANS BELONG TO THE MAMMALIAN order of primates (see pp. 202–203), which originated about 55 million years ago; they comprise the only extant hominid species. The earliest hominid was *Australopithecus* ("southern ape"), a small-brained intermediate between apes and humans that was capable of standing and walking upright. *Homo habilis*, the first known human appeared at least 2 million years ago. This larger-brained "handy man" began making tools for hunting. *Homo erectus* first appeared in Africa about 1.8 million years ago and spread into Asia about 800,000 years later. Smaller toothed than *Homo habilis*, it developed fire as a tool, which enabled it to cook food. Neanderthals, a near relative of modern humans, originated about 200,000 years ago, and *Homo sapiens* (modern humans) appeared in Africa about 100,000 years later. The two coexisted for thousands of years, but by 30,000 years ago, *Homo sapiens* had become dominant and the Neanderthals had died out. Classification of *Homo sapiens* in relation to its ancestors is enormously problematic: modern humans must be classified not only by bone structure, but also by specific behavior—the ability to plan future action; to follow traditions; and to use symbolic communication, including complex language and the ability to use and recognize symbols.

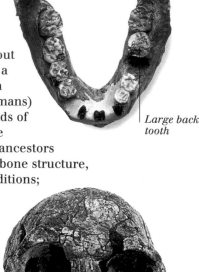

JAWBONE OF AUSTRALOPITHECUS (SOUTHERN APE)

Larger jawbone than modern human

Large back tooth

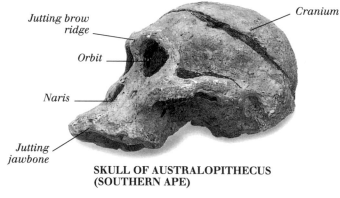

Jutting brow ridge

Orbit

Naris

Jutting jawbone

Cranium

SKULL OF AUSTRALOPITHECUS (SOUTHERN APE)

Orbit

Naris

SKULL OF HOMO HABILIS (FIRST KNOWN HUMAN)

Larger braincase than Australopithecus

Orbit

Naris

External auditory meatus

SKULL OF HOMO ERECTUS (UPRIGHT MAN)

Well-rounded cranium

Small brow ridge

Orbit

Naris

Small tooth

External auditory meatus

SKULL OF HOMO SAPIENS (MODERN HUMAN)

FLINT TOOL MADE ABOUT 250,000 YEARS AGO

Point

Sharp edge used to cut meat

Flint may have been carved by Homo erectus

FLINT HANDAXE

FLINT FLAKE

EXAMPLES OF TOOLS USED BY HOMO SAPIENS

Axe used to clear land

Leather binding

FIRE-MAKING TOOLS

Wooden mouthpiece held drill securely

WOODEN MOUTHPIECE

Wooden drill turned in drill hole to create spark

Bone

Leather bow kept drill upright

BOW DRILL

Drill hole

DRY STRAW

WOODEN HEARTH

Hammer head used to detach chips of flint

Head used to mine flint

Handle

Handle

Handle

ANTLER HAMMER

RED DEER ANTLER HAMMER

FARMING AXE

EXAMPLES OF PREHISTORIC FOODS

MINT

WHEAT GRAINS

SALMON

SPEAR AND ARROW HEADS

Antler

HARPOON POINT

Twine binding

FISHING TACKLE

Wooden point hardened by fire

WOODEN ARROW

Flint glued into groove cut in shaft

FLINT ARROW

109

Plants

Plant varieties

THERE ARE MORE THAN 300,000 SPECIES of plants. They
show a wide diversity of forms, ranging from delicate liverworts, adapted for life
in a damp habitat, to cacti, capable of surviving in the desert. The plant kingdom includes
herbaceous plants, such as corn, which completes its life cycle in one year, to the giant redwood tree, which
can live for thousands of years. This diversity reflects the adaptations of plants to survive in a wide range of
habitats. This is seen most clearly in the flowering plants (phylum Angiospermophyta), which are the most
numerous, with over 250,000 species. They are also the most widespread, being found from the tropics to the
arctic. Despite their diversity, plants share certain characteristics. Typically, plants are green, and make their
food by photosynthesis. Most plants live in or on a substrate, such as soil, and do not actively move. Algae
(kingdom Protista) and fungi (kingdom Fungi) have some plantlike characteristics and are
often studied alongside plants, although they are not true plants.

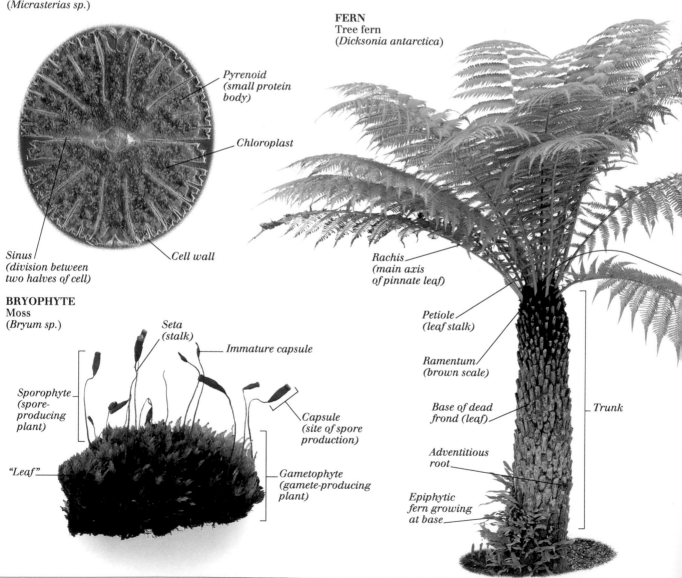

GREEN ALGA
Micrograph of desmid
(*Micrasterias sp.*)

Pyrenoid
(small protein
body)

Chloroplast

Sinus
(division between
two halves of cell)

Cell wall

FERN
Tree fern
(*Dicksonia antarctica*)

Rachis
(main axis
of pinnate leaf)

Petiole
(leaf stalk)

Ramentum
(brown scale)

Base of dead
frond (leaf)

Trunk

Adventitious
root

Epiphytic
fern growing
at base

BRYOPHYTE
Moss
(*Bryum sp.*)

Seta
(stalk)

Immature capsule

Sporophyte
(spore-
producing
plant)

Capsule
(site of spore
production)

"Leaf"

Gametophyte
(gamete-producing
plant)

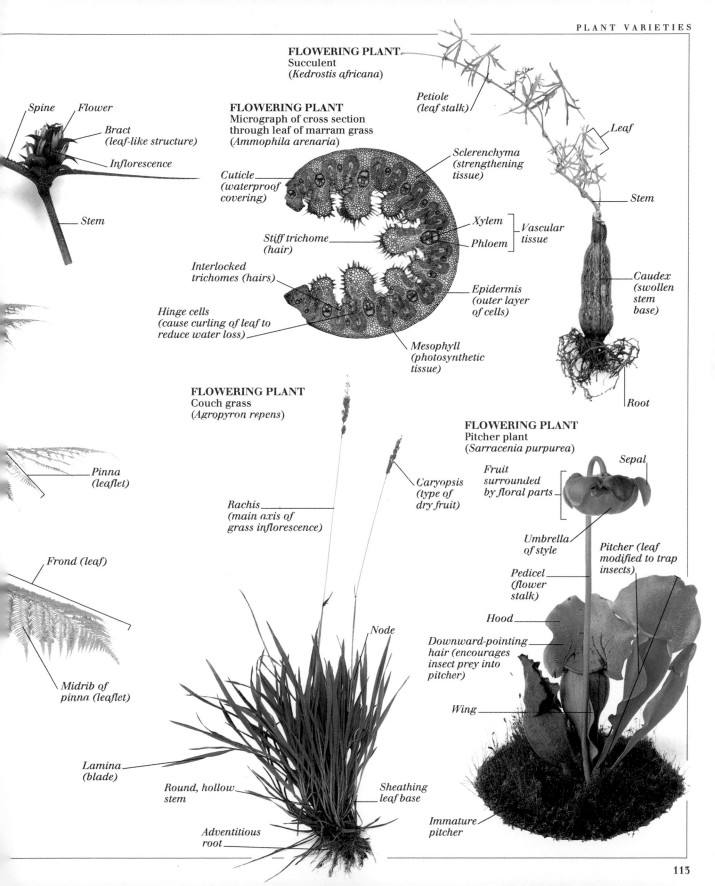

FLOWERING PLANT
Succulent
(*Kedrostis africana*)

Petiole
(leaf stalk)

Leaf

Stem

Caudex
(swollen
stem
base)

Root

Spine

Flower

Bract
(leaf-like structure)

Inflorescence

Stem

FLOWERING PLANT
Micrograph of cross section
through leaf of marram grass
(*Ammophila arenaria*)

Cuticle
(waterproof
covering)

Sclerenchyma
(strengthening
tissue)

Xylem
Phloem
} Vascular
tissue

Stiff trichome
(hair)

Interlocked
trichomes (hairs)

Hinge cells
(cause curling of leaf to
reduce water loss)

Epidermis
(outer layer
of cells)

Mesophyll
(photosynthetic
tissue)

FLOWERING PLANT
Couch grass
(*Agropyron repens*)

Caryopsis
(type of
dry fruit)

Rachis
(main axis of
grass inflorescence)

Node

Pinna
(leaflet)

Frond (leaf)

Midrib of
pinna (leaflet)

Lamina
(blade)

Round, hollow
stem

Sheathing
leaf base

Adventitious
root

FLOWERING PLANT
Pitcher plant
(*Sarracenia purpurea*)

Sepal

Fruit
surrounded
by floral parts

Umbrella
of style

Pitcher (leaf
modified to trap
insects)

Pedicel
(flower
stalk)

Hood

Downward-pointing
hair (encourages
insect prey into
pitcher)

Wing

Immature
pitcher

113

Fungi and lichens

FUNGI WERE ONCE THOUGHT OF AS PLANTS but are now classified as a separate kingdom. This kingdom includes not only the familiar mushrooms, puffballs, stinkhorns, and molds, but also yeasts, smuts, rusts, and lichens. Most fungi are multicellular, consisting of a mass of thread-like hyphae that together form a mycelium. However, the simpler fungi, like yeasts, are microscopic, single-celled organisms. Typically, fungi reproduce by means of spores. Most fungi feed on dead or decaying matter or on living organisms. A few fungi obtain their food from plants or algae, with which they have a symbiotic (mutually advantageous) relationship. Lichens are a symbiotic partnership between algae and fungi. Of the six types of lichens the three most common are crustose (flat and crusty), foliose (leafy), and fruticose (shrub-like). Some lichens (such as *Cladonia floerkeana*) are a combination of types. Lichens reproduce by means of spores or soredia (powdery vegetative fragments).

Emerging sporophore (spore-bearing structure)

Pileus (cap) continuous with stipe (stalk)

Bark of dead beech tree

Inrolled margin of pileus (cap)

Gill (site of spore production)

Sporophore (spore-bearing structure)

Stipe (stalk)

Hyphae (fungal filaments)

OYSTER FUNGUS
(*Pleurotus pulmonarius*)

EXAMPLES OF LICHENS

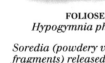

Secondary fruticose thallus

Branched, hollow stem

Apothecium (spore-producing body)

FRUTICOSE
Cladonia portentosa

Soredia (powdery vegetative fragments) produced at end of lobe

Tree bark

Foliose thallus

FOLIOSE
Hypogymnia physodes

Gleba (spore-producing tissue found in this type of fungus)

Sporophore (spore-bearing structure)

Porous stipe (stalk)

Volva (remains of universal veil)

STINKHORN
(*Phallus impudicus*)

Toothed branchlet

Branch

Sporophore (spore-bearing structure)

Stipe (stalk)

RAMARIA FORMOSA

Soredia (powdery vegetative fragments) released onto surface of squamulose thallus

Apothecium (spore-producing body)

Basal scale of primary squamulose thallus

Moss

Podetium (granular stalk) of secondary fruticose thallus

SQUAMULOSE (SCALY) AND FRUTICOSE THALLUS
Cladonia floerkeana

SECTION THROUGH FOLIOSE LICHEN SHOWING REPRODUCTION BY SOREDIA

Algal cell

Soredium (powdery vegetative fragment involved in propagation) released from lichen

Fungal hypha

Upper cortex

Algal layer

Medulla of fungal hyphae (mycelium)

Lower cortex

Rhizine (bundle of absorptive hyphae)

Soralium (pore in upper surface of thallus)

Upper surface of thallus

Exoperidium

Endoperidium

Peridium (wall surrounding spore-producing tissue)

Gleba (spore-producing tissue found in this type of fungus)

Scale on exoperidium (outer part of peridium)

Stipe (stalk)

Underground mycelium (mass of hyphae)

Substratum of woodland soil and leaf litter

COMMON PUFFBALL
(Scleroderma citrinum)

Fan-shaped pileus (cap)

Sporophore (spore-bearing structure)

Stipe (stalk)

Gill (site of spore production)

HOHENBUEHELIA PETALOIDES

FRINGED CRUMBLE CAP
(Psathyrella candolleana)

Pileus (cap)

Stipe (stalk)

Sporophore (spore-bearing structure)

Substratum of woodland soil and leaf litter

Hyphae (fungal filaments)

LIFE CYCLE OF A MUSHROOM

Velar scale (remains of universal veil)

Pileus (cap)

Gill (site of spore production)

Annulus (ring)

Stipe (stalk)

Underground mycelium

MATURE SPOROPHORE (SPORE-BEARING STRUCTURE)

Sporophore (spore-bearing structure)

Basidium (spore-producing structure)

Discharged spore

SECTION OF GILL

Primary mycelium develops from spore

Spore

Septum (cross wall)

Hypha

Primary mycelia fuse to produce secondary mycelium

Nucleus

SPORES GERMINATE AND PRODUCE MYCELIUM

Immature sporophore

Mycelium

MYCELIUM FORMS SPOROPHORE

Universal veil (membrane enclosing developing sporophore)

Pileus (cap)

Gill

Underground mycelium

Stipe (stalk)

SPOROPHORE GROWS ABOVE GROUND

Expanding pileus (cap)

Partial veil (joins pileus to stipe)

Annulus (ring) being formed as partial veil breaks

Stipe (stalk)

Underground mycelium

Volva (remains of universal veil)

UNIVERSAL VEIL BREAKS

Algae and seaweed

ALGAE ARE NOT TRUE PLANTS. They form a diverse group
of plantlike organisms that belong to the kingdom Protista.
Like plants, algae possess the green pigment chlorophyll
and make their own food by photosynthesis (see pp. 138-139).
Many algae also possess other pigments by which they can be
classified. For example, the brown pigment fucoxanthin is
found in brown algae. Some of the ten phyla of algae are
exclusively unicellular (single-celled); others also contain
aggregates of cells in filaments or colonies. Three phyla—
the Chlorophyta (green algae), Rhodophyta (red algae),
and Phaeophyta (brown algae)—contain larger, multicellular,
thalloid (flat), marine organisms commonly known as seaweed.
Most algae can reproduce sexually. For
example, in brown seaweed
Fucus vesiculosus, gametes
(sex cells) are produced in
conceptacles (chambers) in
the receptacles (fertile tips
of fronds); after their release
into the sea, antherozoids
(male gametes) and oospheres
(female gametes) fuse. The
resulting zygote settles on a rock
and develops into a new seaweed.

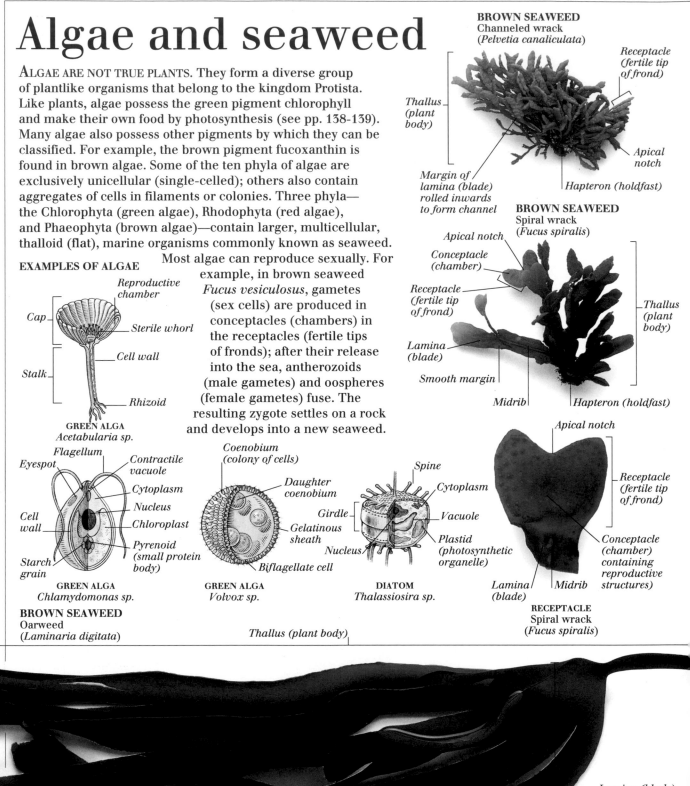

EXAMPLES OF ALGAE

Reproductive chamber
Cap
Sterile whorl
Cell wall
Stalk
Rhizoid
GREEN ALGA
Acetabularia sp.

Flagellum
Eyespot
Contractile vacuole
Cytoplasm
Cell wall
Nucleus
Chloroplast
Pyrenoid (small protein body)
Starch grain
GREEN ALGA
Chlamydomonas sp.

Coenobium (colony of cells)
Daughter coenobium
Girdle
Gelatinous sheath
Nucleus
Biflagellate cell
GREEN ALGA
Volvox sp.

Spine
Cytoplasm
Vacuole
Plastid (photosynthetic organelle)
DIATOM
Thalassiosira sp.

BROWN SEAWEED
Oarweed
(*Laminaria digitata*)

Thallus (plant body)

BROWN SEAWEED
Channeled wrack
(*Pelvetia canaliculata*)
Receptacle (fertile tip of frond)
Thallus (plant body)
Apical notch
Margin of lamina (blade) rolled inwards to form channel
Hapteron (holdfast)

BROWN SEAWEED
Spiral wrack
(*Fucus spiralis*)
Apical notch
Conceptacle (chamber)
Receptacle (fertile tip of frond)
Lamina (blade)
Smooth margin
Midrib
Thallus (plant body)
Hapteron (holdfast)

Apical notch
Receptacle (fertile tip of frond)
Conceptacle (chamber) containing reproductive structures
Lamina (blade)
Midrib
RECEPTACLE
Spiral wrack
(*Fucus spiralis*)

Lamina (blade) palmately divided

GREEN SEAWEED
Enteromorpha linza

Crinkled margin

Thallus
(plant
body)

Unbranched,
spirally twisted
frond

Small hapteron
(holdfast) attaching
seaweed to mussel

RED SEAWEED
Dilsea carnosa

Thallus
(plant
body)

Lamina
(blade)

Hapteron
(holdfast)

RED SEAWEED
Corallina officinalis

Branch

Branched,
hard thallus
(plant body)

Hapteron
(holdfast)

Main
stem

LIFE CYCLE OF BROWN SEAWEED
Bladder wrack
(*Fucus vesiculosus*)

Male
receptacle

Female
receptacle

Air bladder

Lamina
(blade)

Hapteron
(holdfast)

Stipe
(stalk)

MALE AND FEMALE SEAWEEDS

Male
receptacle

Female
receptacle

Conceptacle

Ostiole
(opening to
conceptacle)

MALE AND FEMALE RECEPTACLES

Paraphysis
(sterile hair)

Ostiole
(opening to
conceptacle)

Antheridium
(male sex
organ)

Oogonium
(female sex organ)

**SECTIONS THROUGH MALE AND FEMALE
CONCEPTACLES**

Antherozoid
(male gamete)

Oogonium

Antheridium
(male sex organ)

Oosphere
(female
gamete)

PRODUCTION OF GAMETES

Antherozoid (male
gamete) swims
toward oosphere

Flagellum

Oosphere
(female
gamete) is
fertilized by
antherozoid
to produce
a zygote

FERTILIZATION

GREEN ALGA
Spirogyra sp.

Cytoplasm

End wall
of cell

Cell (cylindrical)

Cell wall

Filament
(strand of
linked cells)

Two filaments
linked for
conjugation
(sexual
reproduction)

Spirally
wound
chloroplast

Conjugation
tube

End wall of conjugation
tube still in place

Flexible stipe
(stalk)

Hapteron
(holdfast)

Young thallus
(plant body)

Hapteron
(holdfast)

**ZYGOTE DEVELOPS INTO
A YOUNG SEAWEED**

Liverworts and mosses

LIVERWORTS AND MOSSES ARE SMALL, LOW-GROWING PLANTS that belong to the phylum Bryophyta. Bryophytes do not have true stems, leaves, or roots (they are anchored to the ground by rhizoids), nor do they have the vascular tissues (xylem and phloem) that transport water and nutrients in higher plants. With no outer, waterproof cuticle, bryophytes are susceptible to dehydration, and most grow in moist habitats. The bryophyte life cycle has two stages. In stage one, the green plant (gametophyte) produces male and female gametes (sex cells), which fuse to form a zygote. In stage two, the zygote develops into a sporophyte that remains attached to the gametophyte. The sporophyte produces spores, which are released and germinate into new green plants. Liverworts (class Hepaticae) grow horizontally and may be thalloid (flat and ribbon-like) or "leafy." Mosses (class Musci) typically have an upright "stem" with spirally arranged "leaves."

A LEAFY LIVERWORT
Scapania undulata

"Stem"

"Leaf"

Rhizoid

A THALLOID LIVERWORT
Marchantia polymorpha

Gemma cup

Gemma (detachable tissue that produces new plants)

Thallus (plant body)

Toothed margin of cup

DETAIL OF GEMMA CUP

Archegoniophore (stalked structure carrying archegonia)

Disk
Lobe
Stalk

Thallus (plant body)

Rhizoid

FEMALE GAMETOPHYTE

Disk

Lobe

Stalk

SIDE VIEW OF ARCHEGONIOPHORE

Lobe

Ray (radial groove)

Stalk

Disk

ARCHEGONIOPHORE FROM BELOW

Pore

Ray (radial groove)

MICROGRAPH OF LOBE

Gemma cup

Thallus (plant body)

Apical notch

Midrib

Archegoniophore (stalked structure carrying archegonia)

MICROGRAPH OF THALLUS
Conocephalum conicum

Position of air chamber

Pore for exchange of gases

Upper surface

Rhizoid

A COMMON MOSS
Polytrichum commune

"Stem"

Branch of conducting tissue to "leaf"

Cortex

Epidermis

"Leaf"

Central strand of conducting tissue

Midrib

MICROGRAPH OF CROSS SECTION THROUGH STEM AND LEAF

MICROGRAPH OF MOSS SPORE
Funaria hygrometrica

Epidermis of capsule

Spore-containing space

Columella (central tissue of capsule)

Remains of spore-forming tissue

CROSS SECTION THROUGH CAPSULE

LIFE CYCLE OF MOSS
Funaria sp.

Female rosette ("leaves" around archegonia)

Male rosette ("leaves" around antheridia)

Main "stem"

Lateral branch of "stem"

Rhizoid

Archegonium (female sex organ)

GAMETOPHYTE

Antherozoids (male gametes) released from antheridium

Antheridium (male sex organ)

SECTION THROUGH MATURE MALE APEX

SECTION THROUGH MATURE FEMALE APEX

Neck

Venter

Flagellum

Antherozoid (male gamete swims to oosphere)

Oosphere (female gamete fertilized by antherozoid)

FERTILIZATION

Capsule

Apophysis (swollen area between seta and capsule)

Columella (central tissue of capsule)

Operculum (lid)

Beak

Calyptra (hood covering capsule)

Seta (stalk)

"Leaf"

Young aerial "stem"

Male apex ("leaves" surrounding antheridia)

"Leaf"

"Stem"

Sporophyte grows from fertilized oosphere

Capsule

Seta (stalk)

Gametophyte

SPOROPHYTE

Capsule

Apophysis

Seta (stalk)

Air space

Operculum (lid)

Peristome tooth opens

Spores dispersed

RIPE CAPSULE

Young gametophyte

Protonema (branched green filament)

Rhizoid

Bud

Spore

DEVELOPING GAMETOPHYTE

"Stem"

EXTERNAL VIEW OF MOSS

Horsetails, club mosses, and ferns

HORSETAILS, CLUB MOSSES, AND FERNS are primitive land plants, which, like higher plants, have stems, roots, leaves, and vascular systems that transport water, minerals, and food. Unlike higher plants, however, they do not produce seeds when reproducing. Their life cycles involve two stages. In stage one, the sporophyte (green plant) produces spores in sporangia. In stage two, the spores germinate, developing into small, short-lived gametophyte plants that produce male and female gametes (sex cells). The gametes fuse to form a zygote from which a new sporophyte plant develops. Horsetails (phylum Sphenophyta) have erect green stems with branches arranged in whorls. Some stems are fertile and have a single spore-producing strobilus (group of sporangia) at the tip. Club mosses (phylum Lycopodophyta) typically have small leaves arranged spirally around the stem, with spore-producing strobili at the tip of some stems. Ferns (phylum Filicinophyta) usually have large, pinnate leaves called fronds. Sporangia, grouped together in sori, develop on the underside of fertile fronds.

FROND
Male fern
(*Dryopteris filix-mas*)

Stem with spirally arranged leaves

Branch

Strobilus (group of sporangia)

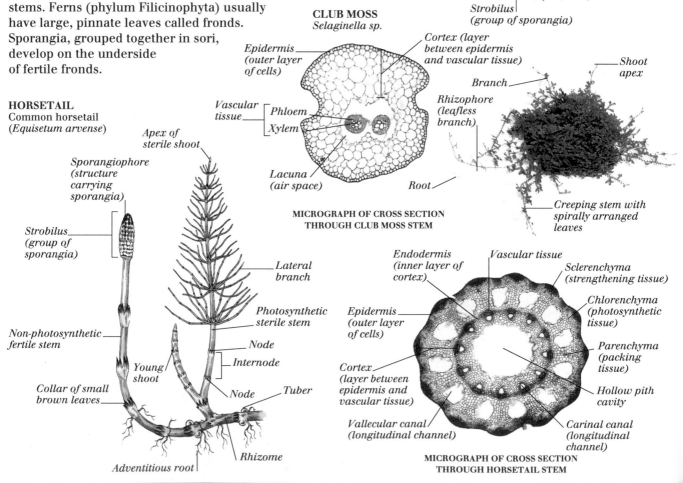

CLUB MOSS
Selaginella sp.

Epidermis (outer layer of cells)

Cortex (layer between epidermis and vascular tissue)

Vascular tissue — Phloem / Xylem

Lacuna (air space)

MICROGRAPH OF CROSS SECTION THROUGH CLUB MOSS STEM

Shoot apex

Branch

Rhizophore (leafless branch)

Root

Creeping stem with spirally arranged leaves

HORSETAIL
Common horsetail
(*Equisetum arvense*)

Apex of sterile shoot

Sporangiophore (structure carrying sporangia)

Strobilus (group of sporangia)

Non-photosynthetic fertile stem

Collar of small brown leaves

Young shoot

Lateral branch

Photosynthetic sterile stem

Node

Internode

Node

Tuber

Rhizome

Adventitious root

Endodermis (inner layer of cortex)

Vascular tissue

Sclerenchyma (strengthening tissue)

Chlorenchyma (photosynthetic tissue)

Epidermis (outer layer of cells)

Parenchyma (packing tissue)

Cortex (layer between epidermis and vascular tissue)

Hollow pith cavity

Vallecular canal (longitudinal channel)

Carinal canal (longitudinal channel)

MICROGRAPH OF CROSS SECTION THROUGH HORSETAIL STEM

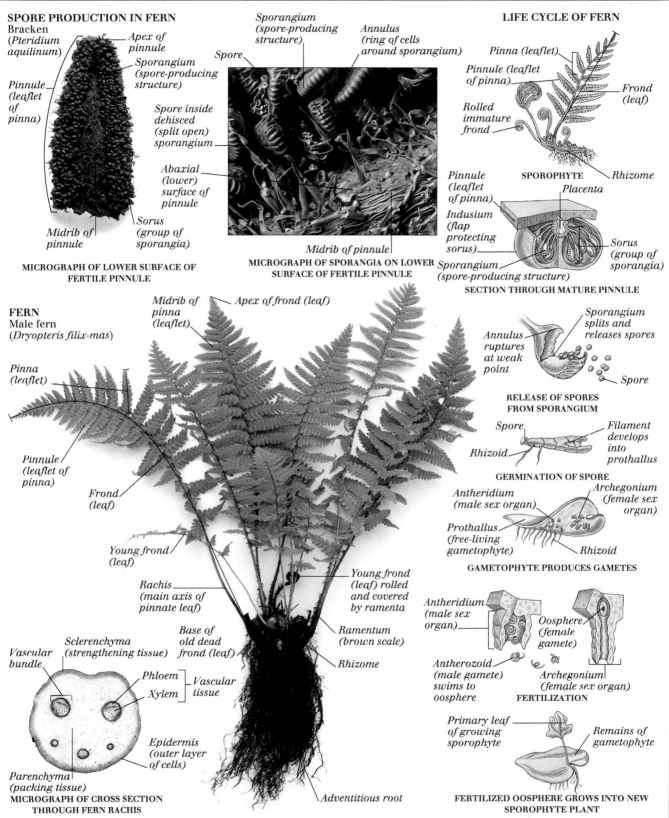

SPORE PRODUCTION IN FERN
Bracken
(*Pteridium aquilinum*)

Apex of pinnule

Sporangium (spore-producing structure)

Pinnule (leaflet of pinna)

Spore inside dehisced (split open) sporangium

Abaxial (lower) surface of pinnule

Midrib of pinnule

Sorus (group of sporangia)

MICROGRAPH OF LOWER SURFACE OF FERTILE PINNULE

Sporangium (spore-producing structure)

Spore

Annulus (ring of cells around sporangium)

Midrib of pinnule

MICROGRAPH OF SPORANGIA ON LOWER SURFACE OF FERTILE PINNULE

LIFE CYCLE OF FERN

Pinna (leaflet)

Pinnule (leaflet of pinna)

Frond (leaf)

Rolled immature frond

SPOROPHYTE

Rhizome

Pinnule (leaflet of pinna)

Placenta

Indusium (flap protecting sorus)

Sorus (group of sporangia)

Sporangium (spore-producing structure)

SECTION THROUGH MATURE PINNULE

Sporangium splits and releases spores

Annulus ruptures at weak point

Spore

RELEASE OF SPORES FROM SPORANGIUM

Spore

Filament develops into prothallus

Rhizoid

GERMINATION OF SPORE

Antheridium (male sex organ)

Archegonium (female sex organ)

Prothallus (free-living gametophyte)

Rhizoid

GAMETOPHYTE PRODUCES GAMETES

Antheridium (male sex organ)

Oosphere (female gamete)

Antherozoid (male gamete) swims to oosphere

Archegonium (female sex organ)

FERTILIZATION

Primary leaf of growing sporophyte

Remains of gametophyte

FERTILIZED OOSPHERE GROWS INTO NEW SPOROPHYTE PLANT

FERN
Male fern
(*Dryopteris filix-mas*)

Midrib of pinna (leaflet)

Apex of frond (leaf)

Pinna (leaflet)

Pinnule (leaflet of pinna)

Frond (leaf)

Young frond (leaf)

Rachis (main axis of pinnate leaf)

Base of old dead frond (leaf)

Young frond (leaf) rolled and covered by ramenta

Ramentum (brown scale)

Rhizome

Vascular bundle

Sclerenchyma (strengthening tissue)

Phloem

Xylem

Vascular tissue

Epidermis (outer layer of cells)

Parenchyma (packing tissue)

MICROGRAPH OF CROSS SECTION THROUGH FERN RACHIS

Adventitious root

121

Gymnosperms 1

THE GYMNOSPERMS ARE FOUR RELATED PHYLA of seed-producing plants: Their seeds, however, lack the protective outer covering which surrounds the seeds of flowering plants. Typically, gymnosperms are woody, perennial shrubs or trees, with stems, leaves, roots, and a well-developed vascular (transport) system. The reproductive structures in most gymnosperms are cones. Male cones produce microspores in which male gametes (sex cells) develop; female cones produce megaspores in which female gametes develop. Microspores are blown by the wind to female cones, male and female gametes fuse during fertilization, and a seed develops. The four gymnosperm phyla are the conifers (phylum Coniferophyta), mostly tall trees; cycads (phylum Cycadophyta), small palm-like trees; the ginkgo or maidenhair tree (phylum Ginkgophyta), a tall tree with bilobed leaves; and gnetophytes (phylum Gnetophyta), a diverse group of plants, mainly shrubs, but also including the horizontally growing welwitschia.

LIFE CYCLE OF SCOTS PINE
(*Pinus sylvestris*)

Needle (foliage leaf)

Cone

Ovuliferous scale (ovule-/seed-bearing structure)

MALE CONES

YOUNG FEMALE CONE

Pollen grain in micropyle (entrance to ovule)

Ovuliferous scale

Pollen grain

Nucleus

Air sac

Ovule (contains female gamete)

POLLINATION

Integument (outer part of ovule)

Archegonium (containing female gamete)

Pollen tube (carries male gamete from pollen grain to ovum)

FERTILIZATION

Seed

Seed

Ovuliferous scale (ovule-/seed-bearing structure)

Wing

MATURE FEMALE CONE AND WINGED SEED

SCALE AND SEEDS
Pine
(*Pinus sp.*)

Ovuliferous scale (ovule-/seed-bearing structure)

Wing scar

Wing of seed derived from ovuliferous scale

Seed

Seed

Point of attachment to axis of cone

Seed scar

OVULIFEROUS SCALE FROM THIRD-YEAR FEMALE CONE

Microsporangium (structure in which pollen grains are formed)

Microsporophyll (modified leaf carrying microsporangia)

Axis of cone

Scale leaf

Ovuliferous scale (ovule-/seed-bearing structure)

MICROGRAPH OF LONGITUDINAL SECTION THROUGH YOUNG MALE CONE

Ovule (contains female gametes)

Bract scale

Axis of cone

MICROGRAPH OF LONGITUDINAL SECTION THROUGH SECOND-YEAR FEMALE CONE

Plumule (embryonic shoot)

Cotyledon (seed leaf)

Root

GERMINATION OF PINE SEEDLING

WELWITSCHIA
(*Welwitschia mirabilis*)

Frayed end of leaf

SMOOTH CYPRESS
(*Cupressus glabra*)

Immature female cone

Ovuliferous scale (ovule-/seed-bearing structure)

Mature female cone

Immature male cone

Scalelike leaf

Ovuliferous scale

Ovule (contains female gamete)

CROSS SECTION THROUGH IMMATURE CONE

Ovuliferous scale (ovule-/seed-bearing structure)

Seed

CROSS SECTION THROUGH MATURE CONE

Woody scale

Opening between woody scales through which seeds are released

DISCARDED CONE

YEW
(*Taxus baccata*)

Single ovule (contains female gamete)

Scale

Female "cone"

Scale

Developing seed

Scale

FEMALE "CONES" AT VARIOUS STAGES OF DEVELOPMENT

Seed

Aril (fleshy outgrowth from seed)

Stem

Needle (foliage leaf)

CYCAD
Sago palm
(*Cycas revoluta*)

Pinna (leaflet)

Pinnate leaf

Scale leaf

Old leaf base

Stem covered by scale leaves

GINKGO
(*Ginkgo biloba*)

Stem

Girdle scar

Petiole (leaf stalk)

Bilobed leaf

Continuously growing leaf

Site of cone growth

Immature cone

Stalk scar

Woody stem

Adaxial (upper) surface of leaf

Abaxial (lower) surface of leaf

Frayed end of leaf

Gymnosperms 2

BRANCH OF BISHOP PINE
(*Pinus muricata*)

Second-year female cone

Ovuliferous scale
(ovule-/seed-bearing
structure)

*Needle
(foliage leaf)*

*Ovuliferous scale
(ovule-/seed-bearing
structure)*

*Bud
scale*

Cone

Cone stalk

Stem

Dwarf shoot

Scale leaf scar

FEMALE CONE (FIRST YEAR)

Apical bud

Stem

Needle (foliage leaf)

Dwarf shoot

Male cone

*Upper surface
of needle
(foliage leaf)*

*Margin
of needle
(foliage leaf)*

*Needle
(foliage leaf)*

Apical bud

*Scar of
dwarf shoot*

Stem

Dwarf shoot

TERMINAL ZONE OF BRANCH

*Stoma
(pore)*

Vascular tissue

Phloem   Xylem

*Mesophyll
(photosynthetic tissue)*

*Epidermis
(outer
layer of
cells)*

*Stoma
(pore)*

*Female
cone*

*Woody ovuliferous
scale (ovule-/seed-
bearing structure)*

*Endodermis
(inner layer
of cortex)*

Resin canal

*Cuticle
(waterproof
covering)*

FEMALE CONE (THIRD YEAR)

**MICROGRAPH OF CROSS SECTION
THROUGH NEEDLE (FOLIAGE LEAF)**

**MICROGRAPH OF NEEDLE
(FOLIAGE LEAF) OF PINE
(*Pinus sp.*)**

CROSS SECTION THROUGH MATURE STEM OF BISHOP PINE
(Pinus muricata)

Apical bud scale

Apical bud

Shoot apex

Immature needle (foliage leaf)

Needle (foliage leaf) bud

Bud scale

Scale leaf

MICROGRAPH OF LONGITUDINAL SECTION THROUGH SHOOT APEX OF PINE
(Pinus sp.)

Annual ring

Heartwood (supportive, inactive secondary xylem)

Branch trace (vascular bundle supplying branch)

Pith

Medullary ray (extension of pith)

Pith

Hypodermis (cell layer below epidermis)

Cortex (layer between epidermis and vascular tissue)

Base of dwarf shoot

Dwarf shoot trace (vascular bundle supplying dwarf shoot)

Secondary xylem

Phloem

Epidermis (outer layer of cells)

Vascular tissue

Primary xylem

Resin canal

Sapwood (active secondary xylem)

Phloem

Bark

Periderm (outer layer of bark)

MICROGRAPH OF CROSS SECTION THROUGH YOUNG STEM OF PINE
(Pinus sp.)

Cortex (layer between phellem and vascular tissue)

Resin canal

Cortex (layer between phellem and vascular tissue)

Secondary xylem

Primary xylem

Endodermis (inner layer of cortex)

Phellem (protective outer layer)

Secondary xylem

Phloem

Phellem (protective outer layer)

Primary xylem

Phloem

Resin canal

MICROGRAPH OF CROSS SECTION THROUGH YOUNG ROOT OF PINE
(Pinus sp.)

MICROGRAPH OF CROSS SECTION THROUGH MATURE ROOT OF PINE
(Pinus sp.)

Monocotyledons and dicotyledons

CROSS SECTION THROUGH MONOCOTYLEDONOUS LEAF BASES

FLOWERING PLANTS (PHYLUM ANGIOSPERMOPHYTA) are divided into two classes: monocotyledons (class Monocotyledoneae) and dicotyledons (class Dicotyledoneae). Typically, monocotyledons have seeds with one cotyledon (seed leaf); their foliage leaves are narrow with parallel veins; the flower components occur in multiples of three; sepals and petals are indistinguishable and are known as tepals; vascular (transport) tissues are scattered in random bundles throughout the stem; and, because they lack stem cambium (actively dividing cells that produce wood), most monocotyledons are herbaceous (see pp. 128-129). Dicotyledons have seeds with two cotyledons; leaves are broad with a central midrib and branched veins; flower parts occur in multiples of four or five; sepals are generally small and green; petals are large and colorful; vascular bundles are arranged in a ring around the edge of the stem; and, because many dicotyledons possess wood-producing stem cambium, there are woody forms (see pp. 130-131) as well as herbaceous ones.

COMPARISONS BETWEEN MONOCOTYLEDONS AND DICOTYLEDONS

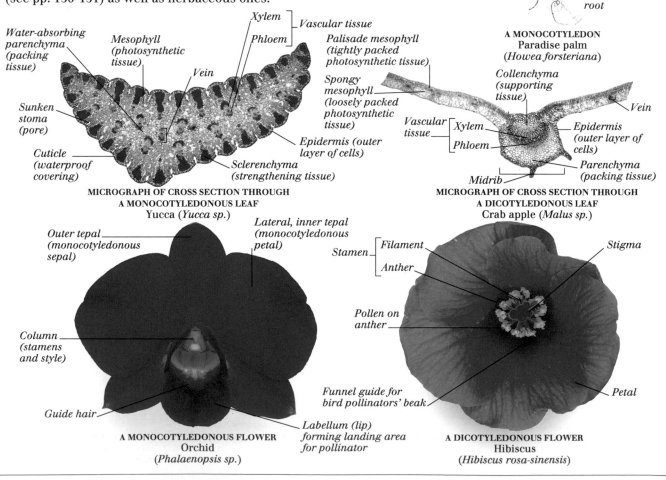

Vein (parallel venation)

Leaflet

Petiole (leaf stalk)

Emerging leaf

Leaf base

Adventitious root

A MONOCOTYLEDON
Paradise palm
(*Howea forsteriana*)

Water-absorbing parenchyma (packing tissue)

Mesophyll (photosynthetic tissue)

Xylem

Phloem

Vascular tissue

Vein

Sunken stoma (pore)

Cuticle (waterproof covering)

Sclerenchyma (strengthening tissue)

Epidermis (outer layer of cells)

MICROGRAPH OF CROSS SECTION THROUGH A MONOCOTYLEDONOUS LEAF
Yucca (*Yucca sp.*)

Palisade mesophyll (tightly packed photosynthetic tissue)

Spongy mesophyll (loosely packed photosynthetic tissue)

Vascular tissue

Xylem

Phloem

Collenchyma (supporting tissue)

Vein

Epidermis (outer layer of cells)

Parenchyma (packing tissue)

Midrib

MICROGRAPH OF CROSS SECTION THROUGH A DICOTYLEDONOUS LEAF
Crab apple (*Malus sp.*)

Outer tepal (monocotyledonous sepal)

Lateral, inner tepal (monocotyledonous petal)

Column (stamens and style)

Guide hair

Labellum (lip) forming landing area for pollinator

A MONOCOTYLEDONOUS FLOWER
Orchid
(*Phalaenopsis sp.*)

Stamen

Filament

Anther

Pollen on anther

Funnel guide for bird pollinators' beak

Stigma

Petal

A DICOTYLEDONOUS FLOWER
Hibiscus
(*Hibiscus rosa-sinensis*)

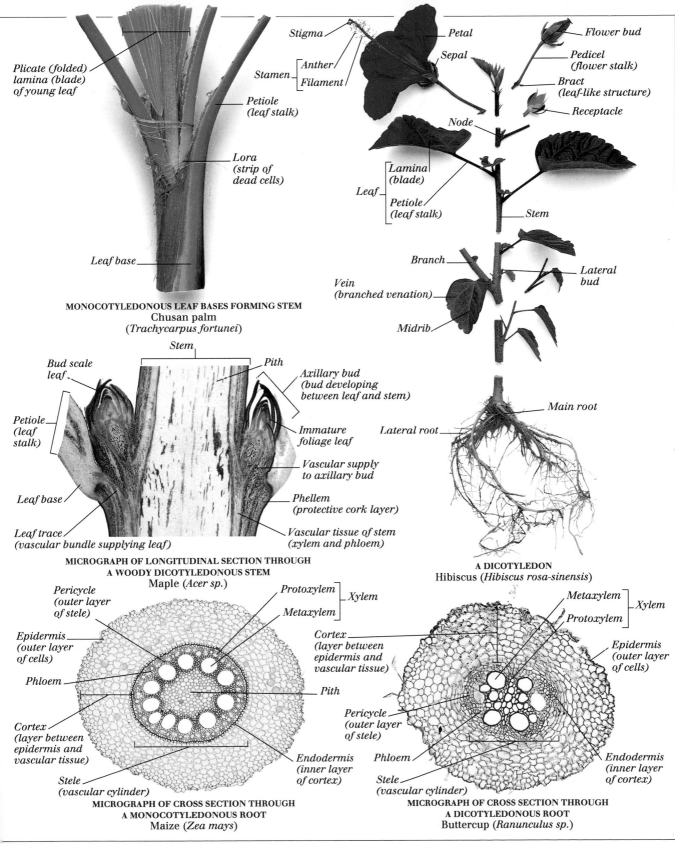

Plicate (folded) lamina (blade) of young leaf

Petiole (leaf stalk)

Lora (strip of dead cells)

Leaf base

MONOCOTYLEDONOUS LEAF BASES FORMING STEM
Chusan palm
(*Trachycarpus fortunei*)

Stigma

Stamen { Anther / Filament }

Petal

Sepal

Flower bud

Pedicel (flower stalk)

Bract (leaf-like structure)

Receptacle

Node

Lamina (blade)

Leaf { Lamina (blade) / Petiole (leaf stalk) }

Stem

Branch

Lateral bud

Vein (branched venation)

Midrib

Stem

Pith

Bud scale leaf

Axillary bud (bud developing between leaf and stem)

Petiole (leaf stalk)

Immature foliage leaf

Vascular supply to axillary bud

Leaf base

Leaf trace (vascular bundle supplying leaf)

Phellem (protective cork layer)

Vascular tissue of stem (xylem and phloem)

MICROGRAPH OF LONGITUDINAL SECTION THROUGH A WOODY DICOTYLEDONOUS STEM
Maple (*Acer sp.*)

Lateral root

Main root

A DICOTYLEDON
Hibiscus (*Hibiscus rosa-sinensis*)

Pericycle (outer layer of stele)

Protoxylem

Metaxylem
} Xylem

Epidermis (outer layer of cells)

Phloem

Cortex (layer between epidermis and vascular tissue)

Pith

Cortex (layer between epidermis and vascular tissue)

Stele (vascular cylinder)

Endodermis (inner layer of cortex)

MICROGRAPH OF CROSS SECTION THROUGH A MONOCOTYLEDONOUS ROOT
Maize (*Zea mays*)

Metaxylem

Protoxylem
} Xylem

Cortex (layer between epidermis and vascular tissue)

Epidermis (outer layer of cells)

Pericycle (outer layer of stele)

Phloem

Stele (vascular cylinder)

Endodermis (inner layer of cortex)

MICROGRAPH OF CROSS SECTION THROUGH A DICOTYLEDONOUS ROOT
Buttercup (*Ranunculus sp.*)

Herbaceous flowering plants

HERBACEOUS FLOWERING PLANTS TYPICALLY HAVE GREEN NON-WOODY STEMS, and tend to be relatively short-lived. Many herbaceous plants live for only one or two years. Annuals (such as sweet peas) grow from seed, produce flowers and then seeds, and die within a single year. Biennials (like carrots) have a two-year life cycle. In the first year, seeds grow into plants, which produce leaves and store food in underground storage organs; the stems and foliage then die in winter. In the second year, new stems grow from the storage organs, produce leaves, flowers, and seeds, and then die. Some herbaceous plants (such as potatoes) are perennial. They grow back year after year, producing shoots and flowers in spring, storing food in underground tubers or rhizomes during summer, dying in autumn, and surviving underground during winter.

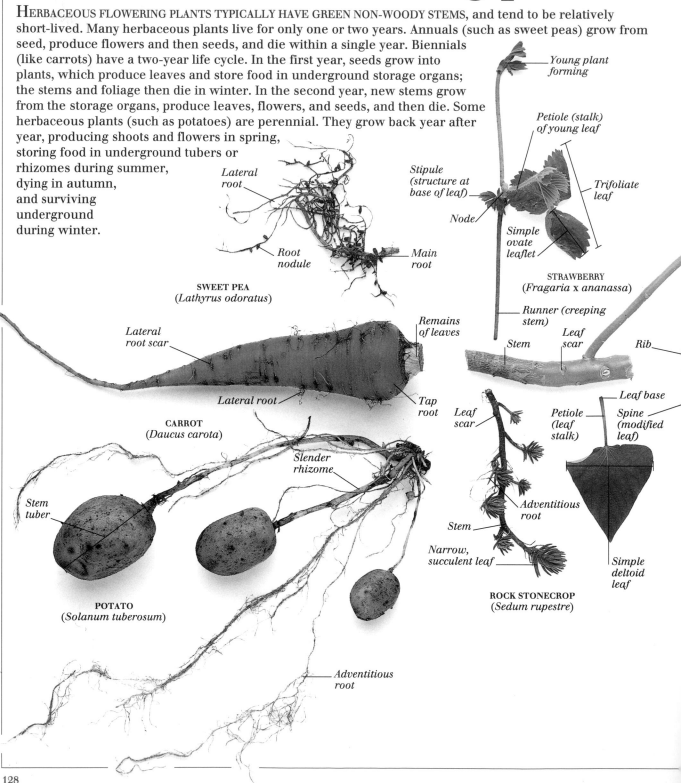

Lateral root

Root nodule

Main root

SWEET PEA
(Lathyrus odoratus)

Young plant forming

Petiole (stalk) of young leaf

Stipule (structure at base of leaf)

Trifoliate leaf

Node

Simple ovate leaflet

STRAWBERRY
(Fragaria x ananassa)

Runner (creeping stem)

Lateral root scar

Remains of leaves

Stem

Leaf scar

Rib

Lateral root

Tap root

CARROT
(Daucus carota)

Leaf scar

Leaf base

Petiole (leaf stalk)

Spine (modified leaf)

Slender rhizome

Stem tuber

Adventitious root

Stem

Narrow, succulent leaf

Simple deltoid leaf

POTATO
(Solanum tuberosum)

ROCK STONECROP
(Sedum rupestre)

Adventitious root

PARTS OF HERBACEOUS FLOWERING PLANTS

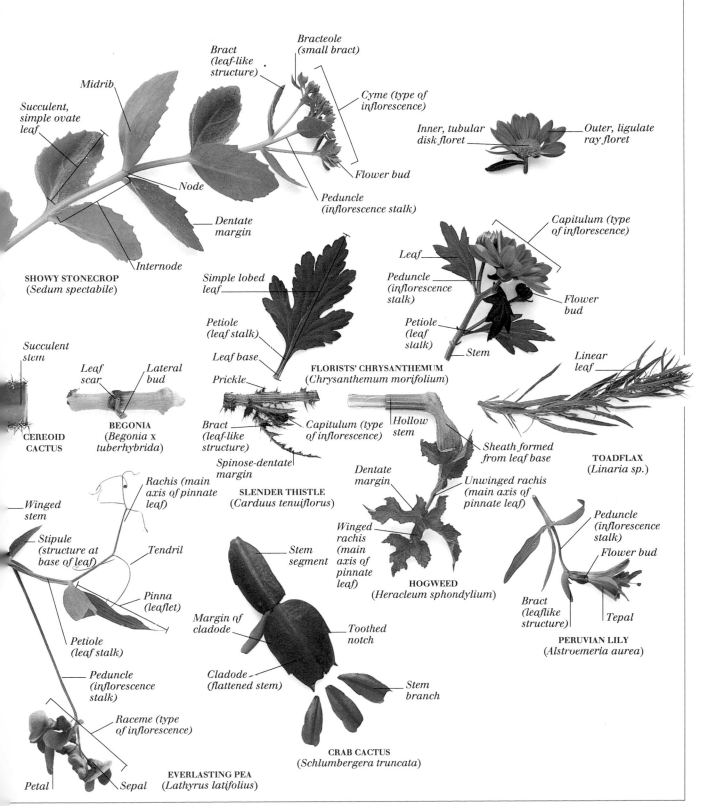

Succulent, simple ovate leaf

Midrib

Bract (leaf-like structure)

Bracteole (small bract)

Cyme (type of inflorescence)

Inner, tubular disk floret

Outer, ligulate ray floret

Flower bud

Node

Peduncle (inflorescence stalk)

Dentate margin

Internode

SHOWY STONECROP
(Sedum spectabile)

Capitulum (type of inflorescence)

Leaf

Peduncle (inflorescence stalk)

Flower bud

Petiole (leaf stalk)

Stem

Succulent stem

Leaf scar

Lateral bud

Simple lobed leaf

Petiole (leaf stalk)

Leaf base

Prickle

FLORISTS' CHRYSANTHEMUM
(Chrysanthemum morifolium)

Linear leaf

CEREOID CACTUS

BEGONIA
(Begonia x tuberhybrida)

Bract (leaf-like structure)

Capitulum (type of inflorescence)

Hollow stem

Sheath formed from leaf base

TOADFLAX
(Linaria sp.)

Spinose-dentate margin

Dentate margin

Unwinged rachis (main axis of pinnate leaf)

Winged stem

Stipule (structure at base of leaf)

Rachis (main axis of pinnate leaf)

SLENDER THISTLE
(Carduus tenuiflorus)

Tendril

Stem segment

Winged rachis (main axis of pinnate leaf)

Peduncle (inflorescence stalk)

Flower bud

Pinna (leaflet)

HOGWEED
(Heracleum sphondylium)

Petiole (leaf stalk)

Margin of cladode

Toothed notch

Bract (leaflike structure)

Tepal

Peduncle (inflorescence stalk)

Cladode (flattened stem)

Stem branch

PERUVIAN LILY
(Alstroemeria aurea)

Raceme (type of inflorescence)

CRAB CACTUS
(Schlumbergera truncata)

Petal

Sepal

EVERLASTING PEA
(Lathyrus latifolius)

129

Woody flowering plants

WOODY FLOWERING PLANTS ARE PERENNIAL: They continue to grow and reproduce for many years. They have one or more permanent stems above ground and numerous smaller branches. The stems and branches have a strong woody core that supports the plant and contains vascular tissue for transporting water and nutrients. Outside the woody core is a layer of tough, protective bark, which has lenticels (tiny pores) to allow gases to pass through. Woody flowering plants may be shrubs, which have several stems rising from the soil; bushes, which are shrubs with dense branching and foliage; or trees, which typically have a single upright stem (the trunk) that bears branches. Deciduous woody plants (like roses) shed all their leaves once a year and remain leafless during winter. Evergreen woody plants (such as holly) shed their leaves gradually, so they retain full leaf cover throughout the year.

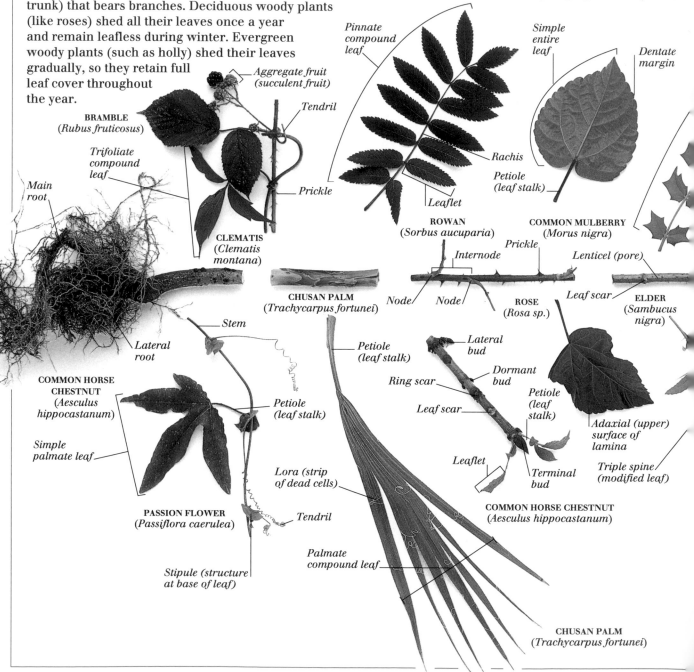

Pinnate compound leaf

Simple entire leaf

Dentate margin

Aggregate fruit (succulent fruit)

Tendril

BRAMBLE
(Rubus fruticosus)

Trifoliate compound leaf

Prickle

Rachis

Petiole (leaf stalk)

Main root

Leaflet

ROWAN
(Sorbus aucuparia)

COMMON MULBERRY
(Morus nigra)

CLEMATIS
(Clematis montana)

Internode

Prickle

Lenticel (pore)

CHUSAN PALM
(Trachycarpus fortunei)

Node

Node

ROSE
(Rosa sp.)

Leaf scar

ELDER
(Sambucus nigra)

Stem

Petiole (leaf stalk)

Lateral bud

Lateral root

Dormant bud

COMMON HORSE CHESTNUT
(Aesculus hippocastanum)

Petiole (leaf stalk)

Ring scar

Leaf scar

Petiole (leaf stalk)

Adaxial (upper) surface of lamina

Simple palmate leaf

Lora (strip of dead cells)

Leaflet

Terminal bud

Triple spine (modified leaf)

PASSION FLOWER
(Passiflora caerulea)

Tendril

COMMON HORSE CHESTNUT
(Aesculus hippocastanum)

Stipule (structure at base of leaf)

Palmate compound leaf

CHUSAN PALM
(Trachycarpus fortunei)

PARTS OF WOODY FLOWERING PLANTS

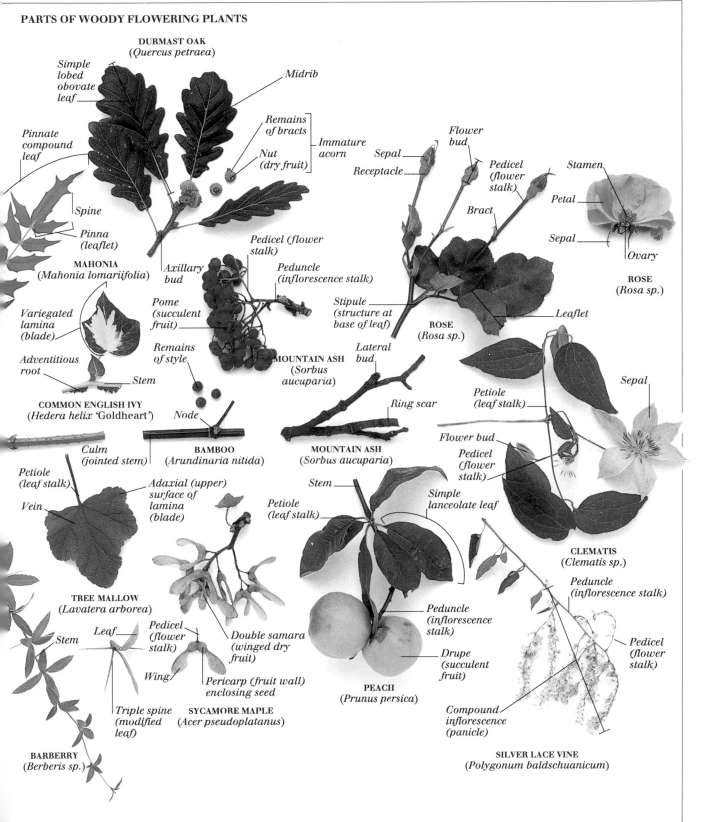

DURMAST OAK
(Quercus petraea)

Simple lobed obovate leaf

Midrib

Pinnate compound leaf

Remains of bracts

Nut (dry fruit)

Immature acorn

Spine

Pinna (leaflet)

MAHONIA
(Mahonia lomariifolia)

Axillary bud

Pedicel (flower stalk)

Peduncle (inflorescence stalk)

Pome (succulent fruit)

Variegated lamina (blade)

Adventitious root

Stem

COMMON ENGLISH IVY
(Hedera helix 'Goldheart')

Remains of style

Node

Culm (jointed stem)

BAMBOO
(Arundinaria nitida)

MOUNTAIN ASH
(Sorbus aucuparia)

Stipule (structure at base of leaf)

ROSE
(Rosa sp.)

Flower bud

Sepal

Receptacle

Pedicel (flower stalk)

Bract

Stamen

Petal

Sepal

Ovary

ROSE
(Rosa sp.)

Leaflet

Lateral bud

Ring scar

MOUNTAIN ASH
(Sorbus aucuparia)

Petiole (leaf stalk)

Sepal

Flower bud

Pedicel (flower stalk)

CLEMATIS
(Clematis sp.)

Stem

Petiole (leaf stalk)

Simple lanceolate leaf

Petiole (leaf stalk)

Vein

Adaxial (upper) surface of lamina (blade)

TREE MALLOW
(Lavatera arborea)

Stem

Leaf

Pedicel (flower stalk)

Wing

Double samara (winged dry fruit)

Pericarp (fruit wall) enclosing seed

Peduncle (inflorescence stalk)

Drupe (succulent fruit)

PEACH
(Prunus persica)

Peduncle (inflorescence stalk)

Pedicel (flower stalk)

Compound inflorescence (panicle)

SILVER LACE VINE
(Polygonum baldschuanicum)

Triple spine (modified leaf)

SYCAMORE MAPLE
(Acer pseudoplatanus)

BARBERRY
(Berberis sp.)

Roots

ROOTS ARE THE UNDERGROUND PARTS OF PLANTS. They have three main functions. First, they anchor the plant in the soil. Second, they absorb water and minerals from the spaces between soil particles. The roots' absorptive properties are increased by root hairs, which grow behind the root tip, allowing maximum absorption of vital substances. Third, the root is part of the plant's transport system. Xylem carries water and minerals from the roots to the stem and leaves, and phloem carries nutrients from the leaves to all parts of the root system. In addition, some roots (like carrots) are food stores. Roots have an outer epidermis covering a cortex of parenchyma (packing tissue), and a central cylinder of vascular tissue. This arrangement helps the roots resist the forces of compression as they grow through the soil.

MICROGRAPH OF PRIMARY ROOT DEVELOPMENT
Cabbage (*Brassica sp.*)

Split in testa as seed germinates

Cotyledon (seed leaf)

Primary root

Testa (seed coat)

Root hair

CARROT (*Daucus carota*)

Root tip (region of cell division)

FEATURES OF A TYPICAL ROOT
Buttercup (*Ranunculus sp.*)

Stele (vascular cylinder)

Phloem sieve tube (through which nutrients are transported)

Pericycle (outer layer of stele)

Companion cell (cell associated with phloem sieve tube)

Root hair

Cortex (layer between epidermis and vascular tissue)

Air space (allowing gas diffusion in the root)

Root hair

Epidermis (outer layer of cells)

Xylem vessel (through which water and minerals are transported)

Endodermis (inner layer of cortex)

Cell wall

Nucleus

Cytoplasm

Parenchyma (packing) cell

PRIMARY ROOT AND MICROGRAPHS OF SECTIONS THROUGH ROOTS

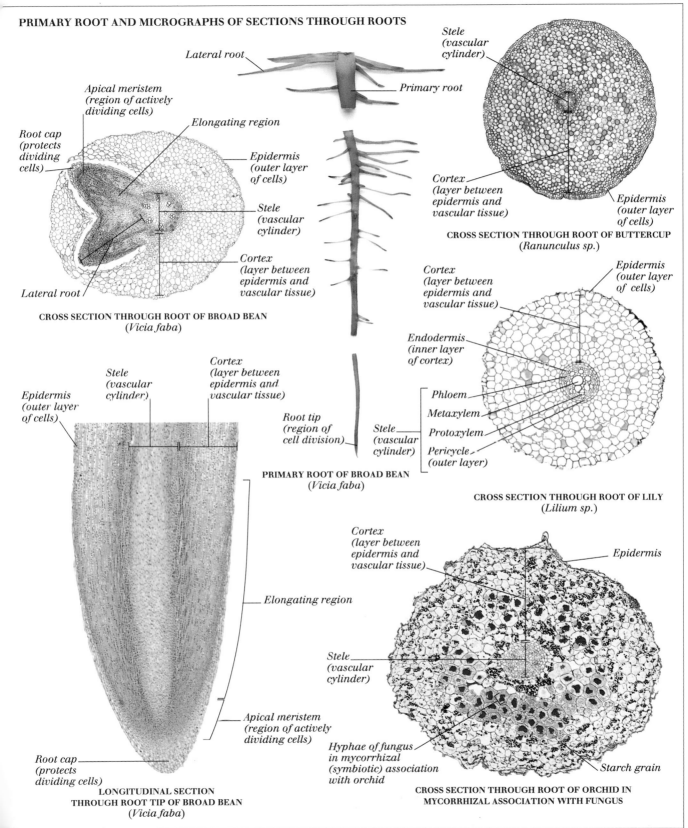

Lateral root

Primary root

Apical meristem
(region of actively
dividing cells)

Elongating region

Root cap
(protects
dividing
cells)

Epidermis
(outer layer
of cells)

Stele
(vascular
cylinder)

Cortex
(layer between
epidermis and
vascular tissue)

Lateral root

CROSS SECTION THROUGH ROOT OF BROAD BEAN
(Vicia faba)

Stele
(vascular
cylinder)

Cortex
(layer between
epidermis and
vascular tissue)

Epidermis
(outer layer
of cells)

CROSS SECTION THROUGH ROOT OF BUTTERCUP
(Ranunculus sp.)

Cortex
(layer between
epidermis and
vascular tissue)

Epidermis
(outer layer
of cells)

Endodermis
(inner layer
of cortex)

Phloem

Metaxylem

Protoxylem

Pericycle
(outer layer)

Stele
(vascular
cylinder)

CROSS SECTION THROUGH ROOT OF LILY
(Lilium sp.)

Root tip
(region of
cell division)

PRIMARY ROOT OF BROAD BEAN
(Vicia faba)

Stele
(vascular
cylinder)

Cortex
(layer between
epidermis and
vascular tissue)

Epidermis
(outer layer
of cells)

Elongating region

Apical meristem
(region of actively
dividing cells)

Root cap
(protects
dividing cells)

**LONGITUDINAL SECTION
THROUGH ROOT TIP OF BROAD BEAN**
(Vicia faba)

Cortex
(layer between
epidermis and
vascular tissue)

Epidermis

Stele
(vascular
cylinder)

Hyphae of fungus
in mycorrhizal
(symbiotic) association
with orchid

Starch grain

**CROSS SECTION THROUGH ROOT OF ORCHID IN
MYCORRHIZAL ASSOCIATION WITH FUNGUS**

Stems

THE STEM IS THE MAIN SUPPORTIVE PART OF A PLANT that grows above ground. Stems bear leaves (organs of photosynthesis), which grow at nodes; buds (shoots covered by protective scales), which grow at the stem tip (apical or terminal buds) and in the angle between a leaf and the stem (axillary or lateral buds); and flowers (reproductive structures). The stem forms part of the plant's transport system. Xylem tissue in the stem transports water and minerals from the roots to the aerial parts of the plant, and phloem tissue transports nutrients manufactured in the leaves to other parts of the plant. Stem tissues are also used for storing water and food. Herbaceous (nonwoody) stems have an outer protective epidermis covering a cortex that consists mainly of parenchyma (packing tissue) but also has some collenchyma (supporting tissue). The vascular tissue of such stems is arranged in bundles, each of which consists of xylem, phloem, and sclerenchyma (strengthening tissue). Woody stems have an outer protective layer of tough bark, which is perforated with lenticels (pores) to allow gas exchange. Inside the bark is a ring of secondary phloem, which surrounds an inner core of secondary xylem.

MICROGRAPH OF LONGITUDINAL SECTION THROUGH APEX OF STEM
Coleus sp.

Apical meristem (region of actively dividing cells)

Procambial strand (cells that produce vascular tissue)

Leaf primordium (developing leaf)

Developing bud

Cortex (layer between epidermis and vascular tissue)

Vascular tissue

Epidermis (outer layer of cells)

Pith

YOUNG WOODY STEM
Linden
(*Tilia sp.*)

EMERGENT BUDS
Maple
(*Acer*)

Secondary phloem

Pith

Phellem (protective cork layer)

Cortex (layer between phellem and vascular tissue)

Xylem vessel (through which water and minerals are transported)

Xylem fiber (supporting tissue)

Ray (parenchyma cells)

Phloem sieve tube (through which nutrients are transported)

Phloem fiber (supporting tissue)

Lenticel (pore)

Vascular cambium (actively dividing cells that produce xylem and phloem)

Summer wood

Spring wood

Secondary xylem

Companion cell (cell associated with phloem sieve tube)

Young leaves emerging

Terminal bud

Lateral bud

Node

Internode

Inner bud scale

Outer bud scale

Node

Leaf scar

Lenticel (pore)

Woody stem

MICROGRAPHS OF CROSS SECTIONS THROUGH VARIOUS STEMS

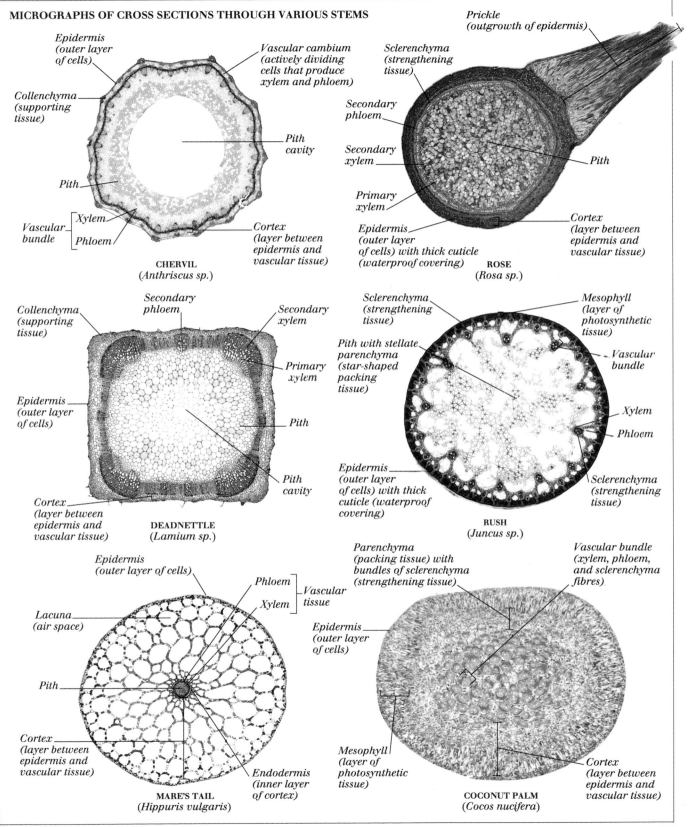

Epidermis
(outer layer
of cells)

Vascular cambium
(actively dividing
cells that produce
xylem and phloem)

Collenchyma
(supporting
tissue)

Pith
cavity

Pith

Xylem

Vascular
bundle

Phloem

Cortex
(layer between
epidermis and
vascular tissue)

CHERVIL
(Anthriscus sp.)

Prickle
(outgrowth of epidermis)

Sclerenchyma
(strengthening
tissue)

Secondary
phloem

Secondary
xylem

Pith

Primary
xylem

Epidermis
(outer layer
of cells) with thick cuticle
(waterproof covering)

Cortex
(layer between
epidermis and
vascular tissue)

ROSE
(Rosa sp.)

Collenchyma
(supporting
tissue)

Secondary
phloem

Secondary
xylem

Primary
xylem

Epidermis
(outer layer
of cells)

Pith

Pith
cavity

Cortex
(layer between
epidermis and
vascular tissue)

DEADNETTLE
(Lamium sp.)

Sclerenchyma
(strengthening
tissue)

Mesophyll
(layer of
photosynthetic
tissue)

Pith with stellate
parenchyma
(star-shaped
packing
tissue)

Vascular
bundle

Xylem

Phloem

Epidermis
(outer layer
of cells) with thick
cuticle (waterproof
covering)

Sclerenchyma
(strengthening
tissue)

RUSH
(Juncus sp.)

Epidermis
(outer layer of cells)

Phloem

Xylem

Vascular
tissue

Lacuna
(air space)

Pith

Cortex
(layer between
epidermis and
vascular tissue)

Endodermis
(inner layer
of cortex)

MARE'S TAIL
(Hippuris vulgaris)

Parenchyma
(packing tissue) with
bundles of sclerenchyma
(strengthening tissue)

Vascular bundle
(xylem, phloem,
and sclerenchyma
fibres)

Epidermis
(outer layer
of cells)

Mesophyll
(layer of
photosynthetic
tissue)

Cortex
(layer between
epidermis and
vascular tissue)

COCONUT PALM
(Cocos nucifera)

Leaves

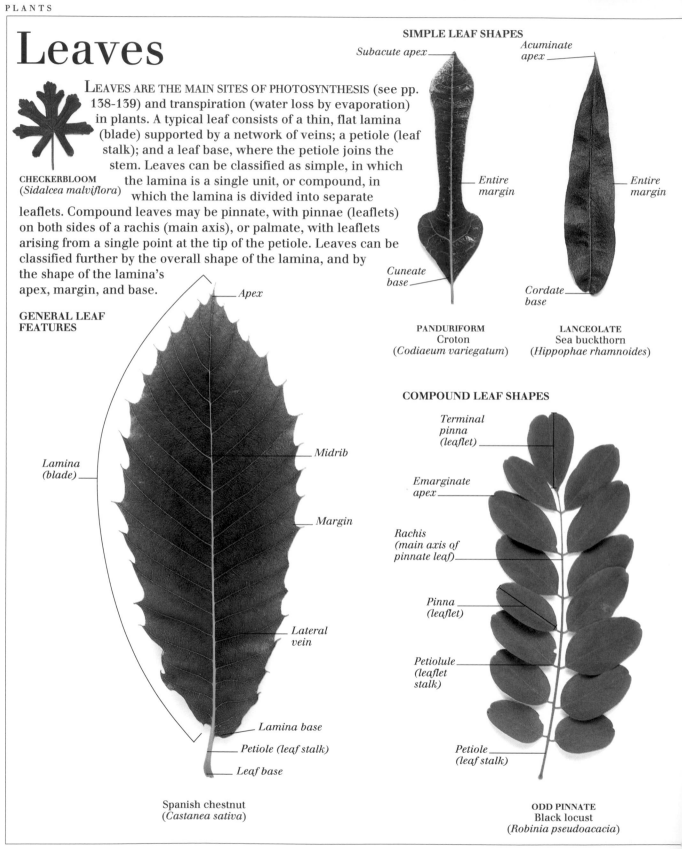

CHECKERBLOOM
(*Sidalcea malviflora*)

LEAVES ARE THE MAIN SITES OF PHOTOSYNTHESIS (see pp. 138-139) and transpiration (water loss by evaporation) in plants. A typical leaf consists of a thin, flat lamina (blade) supported by a network of veins; a petiole (leaf stalk); and a leaf base, where the petiole joins the stem. Leaves can be classified as simple, in which the lamina is a single unit, or compound, in which the lamina is divided into separate leaflets. Compound leaves may be pinnate, with pinnae (leaflets) on both sides of a rachis (main axis), or palmate, with leaflets arising from a single point at the tip of the petiole. Leaves can be classified further by the overall shape of the lamina, and by the shape of the lamina's apex, margin, and base.

SIMPLE LEAF SHAPES

Subacute apex

Acuminate apex

Entire margin

Entire margin

Cuneate base

Cordate base

PANDURIFORM
Croton
(*Codiaeum variegatum*)

LANCEOLATE
Sea buckthorn
(*Hippophae rhamnoides*)

GENERAL LEAF FEATURES

Apex

Midrib

Margin

Lamina (blade)

Lateral vein

Lamina base

Petiole (leaf stalk)

Leaf base

Spanish chestnut
(*Castanea sativa*)

COMPOUND LEAF SHAPES

Terminal pinna (leaflet)

Emarginate apex

Rachis (main axis of pinnate leaf)

Pinna (leaflet)

Petiolule (leaflet stalk)

Petiole (leaf stalk)

ODD PINNATE
Black locust
(*Robinia pseudoacacia*)

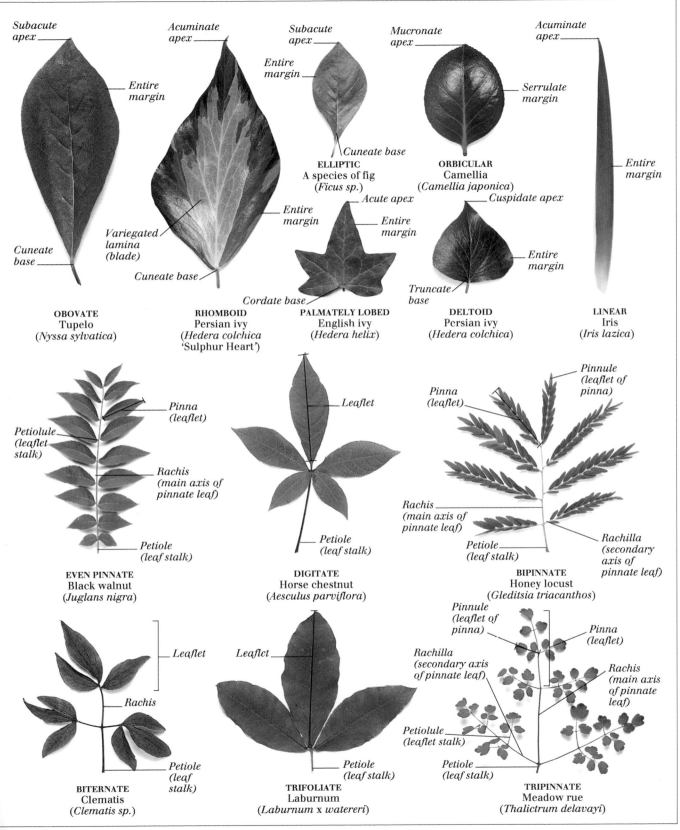

Subacute apex

Entire margin

Acuminate apex

Entire margin

Variegated lamina (blade)

Cuneate base

Cuneate base

OBOVATE
Tupelo
(*Nyssa sylvatica*)

RHOMBOID
Persian ivy
(*Hedera colchica*
'Sulphur Heart')

Subacute apex

Entire margin

Cuneate base

ELLIPTIC
A species of fig
(*Ficus sp.*)

Acute apex

Entire margin

Cordate base

PALMATELY LOBED
English ivy
(*Hedera helix*)

Mucronate apex

Serrulate margin

ORBICULAR
Camellia
(*Camellia japonica*)

Cuspidate apex

Entire margin

Truncate base

DELTOID
Persian ivy
(*Hedera colchica*)

Acuminate apex

Entire margin

LINEAR
Iris
(*Iris lazica*)

Pinna (leaflet)

Petiolule (leaflet stalk)

Rachis (main axis of pinnate leaf)

Petiole (leaf stalk)

EVEN PINNATE
Black walnut
(*Juglans nigra*)

Leaflet

Petiole (leaf stalk)

DIGITATE
Horse chestnut
(*Aesculus parviflora*)

Pinnule (leaflet of pinna)

Pinna (leaflet)

Rachis (main axis of pinnate leaf)

Petiole (leaf stalk)

Rachilla (secondary axis of pinnate leaf)

BIPINNATE
Honey locust
(*Gleditsia triacanthos*)

Leaflet

Rachis

Petiole (leaf stalk)

BITERNATE
Clematis
(*Clematis sp.*)

Leaflet

Petiole (leaf stalk)

TRIFOLIATE
Laburnum
(*Laburnum* x *watereri*)

Pinnule (leaflet of pinna)

Pinna (leaflet)

Rachilla (secondary axis of pinnate leaf)

Rachis (main axis of pinnate leaf)

Petiolule (leaflet stalk)

Petiole (leaf stalk)

TRIPINNATE
Meadow rue
(*Thalictrum delavayi*)

Photosynthesis

PHOTOSYNTHESIS IS THE PROCESS by which plants make their food using sunlight, water, and carbon dioxide. It takes place inside special structures in leaf cells called chloroplasts. The chloroplasts contain chlorophyll, a green pigment that absorbs energy from sunlight. During photosynthesis, the absorbed energy is used to join together carbon dioxide and water to form the sugar glucose, which is the energy source for the whole plant. Oxygen, a waste product, is released into the air. Leaves are the main sites of photosynthesis and have various adaptations for that purpose. Flat laminae (blades) provide a large surface for absorbing sunlight; stomata (pores) in the lower surface of the laminae allow gases (carbon dioxide and oxygen) to pass into and out of the leaves; and an extensive network of veins brings water into the leaves and transports the glucose produced by photosynthesis to the rest of the plant.

MICROGRAPH OF LEAF
Lily (*Lilium sp.*)

Stoma
(pore)

Guard cell
(controls
opening
and closing
of stoma)

Lower
surface of
lamina
(blade)

THE PROCESS OF PHOTOSYNTHESIS

Glucose molecule

Oxygen atom

Carbon atom

Hydrogen atom

Glucose is a high-energy product of photosynthesis. It travels to all parts of the plant through the phloem

Sunlight, which is absorbed by chloroplasts in the leaf, provides the energy for photosynthesis

The leaf is the main site of photosynthesis. Its broad, thin lamina (blade) is an adaptation for this process

Hydrogen atom

Oxygen atom — Water molecule

Hydrogen atom

Carbon dioxide molecule

Oxygen atom

Carbon atom

Oxygen atom

Oxygen atom

Oxygen atom — Oxygen molecule

Water, a raw material in the soil, travels to the leaf from the roots via the xylem

Carbon dioxide, a raw material in the air, enters the leaf through stomata on the lower surface of the lamina (blade)

Oxygen, a waste product of photosynthesis, leaves the leaf through stomata on the lower surface of the lamina (blade)

CROSS SECTION THROUGH LEAF
Christmas rose
(*Helleborus niger*)

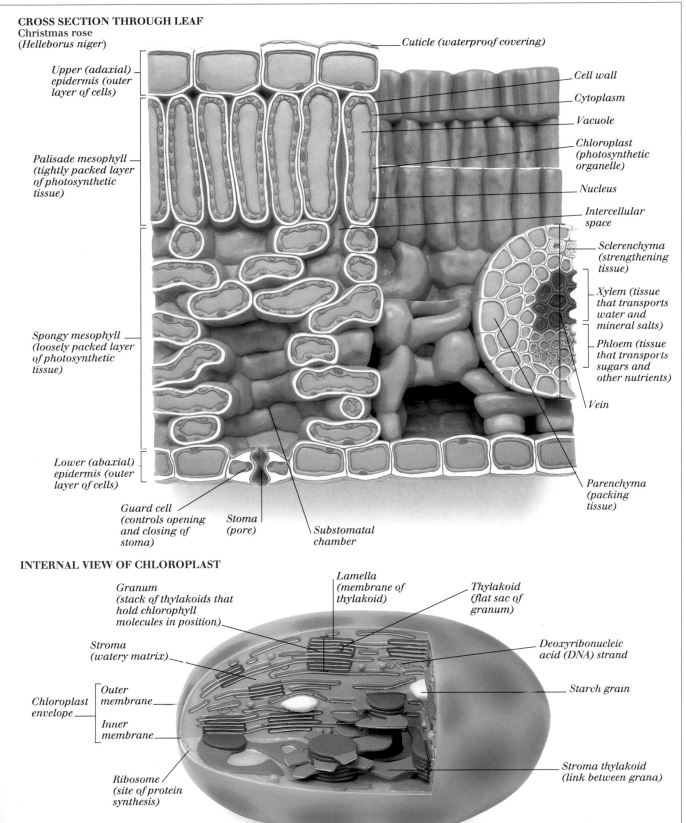

Cuticle (waterproof covering)

Upper (adaxial)
epidermis (outer
layer of cells)

Cell wall

Cytoplasm

Vacuole

Chloroplast
(photosynthetic
organelle)

Palisade mesophyll
(tightly packed layer
of photosynthetic
tissue)

Nucleus

Intercellular
space

Sclerenchyma
(strengthening
tissue)

Xylem (tissue
that transports
water and
mineral salts)

Spongy mesophyll
(loosely packed layer
of photosynthetic
tissue)

Phloem (tissue
that transports
sugars and
other nutrients)

Vein

Lower (abaxial)
epidermis (outer
layer of cells)

Parenchyma
(packing
tissue)

Guard cell
(controls opening
and closing of
stoma)

Stoma
(pore)

Substomatal
chamber

INTERNAL VIEW OF CHLOROPLAST

Granum
(stack of thylakoids that
hold chlorophyll
molecules in position)

Lamella
(membrane of
thylakoid)

Thylakoid
(flat sac of
granum)

Stroma
(watery matrix)

Deoxyribonucleic
acid (DNA) strand

Chloroplast
envelope

Outer
membrane

Starch grain

Inner
membrane

Ribosome
(site of protein
synthesis)

Stroma thylakoid
(link between grana)

Flowers 1

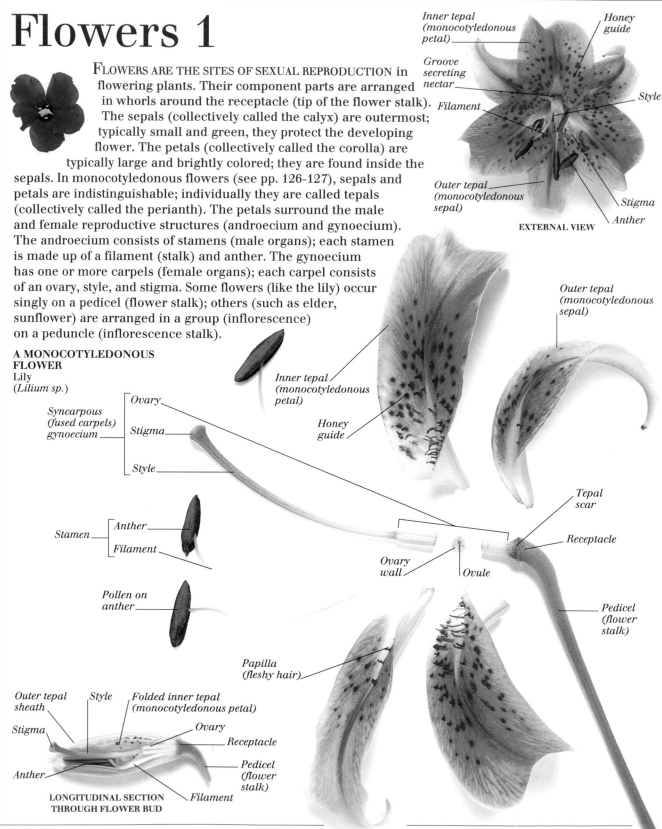

FLOWERS ARE THE SITES OF SEXUAL REPRODUCTION in flowering plants. Their component parts are arranged in whorls around the receptacle (tip of the flower stalk). The sepals (collectively called the calyx) are outermost; typically small and green, they protect the developing flower. The petals (collectively called the corolla) are typically large and brightly colored; they are found inside the sepals. In monocotyledonous flowers (see pp. 126-127), sepals and petals are indistinguishable; individually they are called tepals (collectively called the perianth). The petals surround the male and female reproductive structures (androecium and gynoecium). The androecium consists of stamens (male organs); each stamen is made up of a filament (stalk) and anther. The gynoecium has one or more carpels (female organs); each carpel consists of an ovary, style, and stigma. Some flowers (like the lily) occur singly on a pedicel (flower stalk); others (such as elder, sunflower) are arranged in a group (inflorescence) on a peduncle (inflorescence stalk).

EXTERNAL VIEW

Inner tepal (monocotyledonous petal)

Honey guide

Groove secreting nectar

Filament

Style

Stigma

Anther

Outer tepal (monocotyledonous sepal)

A MONOCOTYLEDONOUS FLOWER
Lily
(*Lilium sp.*)

Syncarpous (fused carpels) gynoecium

Ovary

Stigma

Style

Inner tepal (monocotyledonous petal)

Honey guide

Outer tepal (monocotyledonous sepal)

Tepal scar

Receptacle

Stamen

Anther

Filament

Pollen on anther

Ovary wall

Ovule

Pedicel (flower stalk)

Papilla (fleshy hair)

Outer tepal sheath

Style

Folded inner tepal (monocotyledonous petal)

Stigma

Ovary

Receptacle

Anther

Pedicel (flower stalk)

LONGITUDINAL SECTION THROUGH FLOWER BUD

Filament

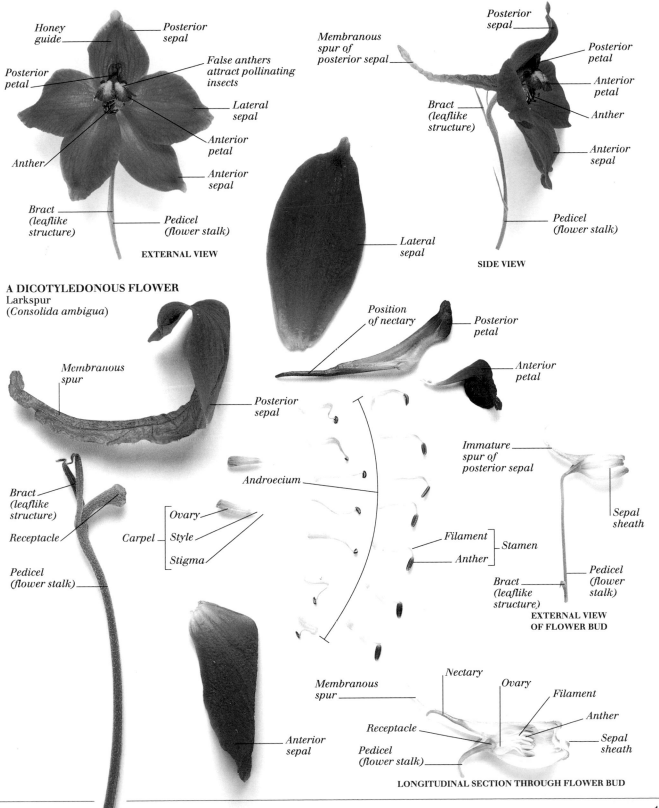

Honey guide

Posterior sepal

Posterior petal

False anthers attract pollinating insects

Lateral sepal

Anterior petal

Anther

Anterior sepal

Bract (leaflike structure)

Pedicel (flower stalk)

EXTERNAL VIEW

Posterior sepal

Membranous spur of posterior sepal

Posterior petal

Anterior petal

Anther

Bract (leaflike structure)

Anterior sepal

Pedicel (flower stalk)

SIDE VIEW

Lateral sepal

A DICOTYLEDONOUS FLOWER
Larkspur
(*Consolida ambigua*)

Membranous spur

Position of nectary

Posterior petal

Anterior petal

Posterior sepal

Androecium

Bract (leaflike structure)

Receptacle

Pedicel (flower stalk)

Carpel
- Ovary
- Style
- Stigma

Filament
Anther
Stamen

Immature spur of posterior sepal

Sepal sheath

Bract (leaflike structure)

Pedicel (flower stalk)

EXTERNAL VIEW OF FLOWER BUD

Membranous spur

Anterior sepal

Nectary

Ovary

Filament

Anther

Receptacle

Sepal sheath

Pedicel (flower stalk)

LONGITUDINAL SECTION THROUGH FLOWER BUD

Flowers 2

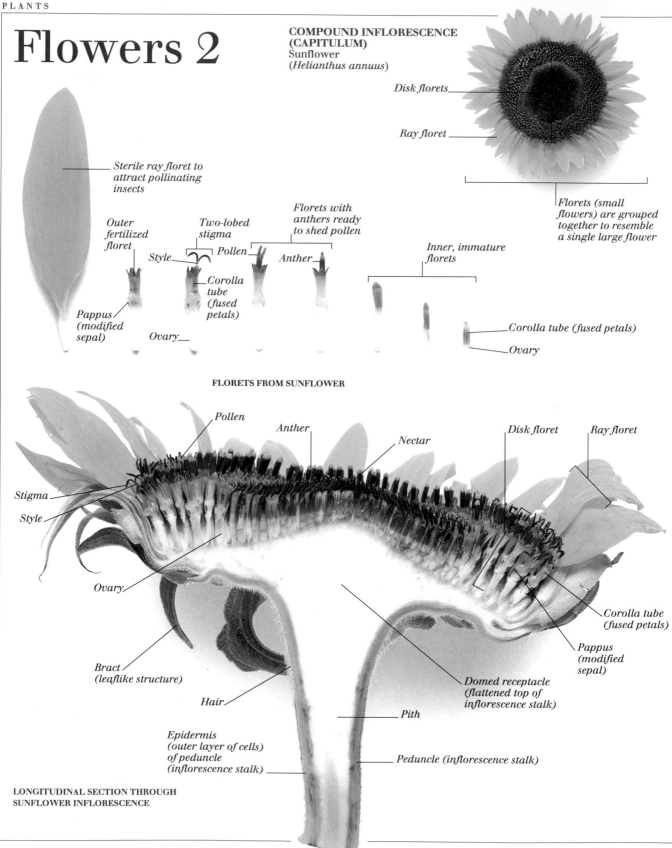

COMPOUND INFLORESCENCE (CAPITULUM)
Sunflower
(*Helianthus annuus*)

Disk florets

Ray floret

Florets (small flowers) are grouped together to resemble a single large flower

Sterile ray floret to attract pollinating insects

Outer fertilized floret

Two-lobed stigma

Style

Pollen

Florets with anthers ready to shed pollen

Anther

Inner, immature florets

Corolla tube (fused petals)

Pappus (modified sepal)

Ovary

Corolla tube (fused petals)

Ovary

FLORETS FROM SUNFLOWER

Pollen

Anther

Nectar

Disk floret

Ray floret

Stigma

Style

Ovary

Bract (leaflike structure)

Hair

Epidermis (outer layer of cells) of peduncle (inflorescence stalk)

Corolla tube (fused petals)

Pappus (modified sepal)

Domed receptacle (flattened top of inflorescence stalk)

Pith

Peduncle (inflorescence stalk)

LONGITUDINAL SECTION THROUGH SUNFLOWER INFLORESCENCE

ARRANGEMENT OF FLOWERS ON STEM

Bract
(leaflike
structure)

Flower

Ovary

Peduncle
(inflorescence
stalk)

Remains of tepals
(monocotyledonous
petals and sepals)

INFLORESCENCE (SPIKE)
Heliconia peruviana

Flower

Petal

Peduncle
(inflorescence
stalk)

Pedicel
(flower
stalk)

**INFLORESCENCE
(COMPOUND UMBEL)**
European elder
(*Sambucus nigra*)

Spathe
(large bract) to
attract pollinating
insects

Spadix (fleshy
axis) carrying
male and female
flowers

Peduncle
(inflorescence
stalk)

INFLORESCENCE (SPADIX)
Flamingo Flower
(*Anthurium andreanum*)

Stigma

Anther

Style

Filament

Stamen

Flower
bud

Pedicel
(flower
stalk)

Bract
(leaflike
structure)

Peduncle
(inflorescence
stalk) fused
to bract

**INFLORESCENCE
(DICHASIAL CYME)**
Common linden
(*Tilia x europaea*)

Three-lobed
stigma

Inner tepal
(monocotyledonous
petal)

Style

Ovary

Filament

Anther

Stamen

Outer tepal
(monocotyledonous
sepal)

Pedicel
(flower stalk)

SINGLE FLOWER
Glory lily
(*Gloriosa superba*)

Flower

Peduncle
(inflorescence
stalk)

Corolla

Calyx

Bract
(leaflike
structure)

**SINGLE
FLOWER**

**INFLORESCENCE
(SPHERICAL UMBEL)**
Echinops sp.

Pollination

POLLINATION IS THE TRANSFER OF POLLEN (which contains the male sex cells) from an anther (part of the male reproductive organ) to a stigma (part of the female reproductive organ). This process precedes fertilization (see pp. 146-147). Pollination may occur within the same flower (self-pollination), or between flowers on separate plants of the same species (cross-pollination). In most plants, pollination is carried out either by insects (entomophilous pollination) or by the wind (anemophilous pollination). Less commonly, birds, bats, or water are the agents of pollination. Insect-pollinated flowers are typically scented and brightly colored. They also produce nectar, on which insects feed. Such flowers also tend to have patterns that are visible only in ultraviolet light, which many insects can see but which humans cannot. These features attract insects, which become covered with the sticky pollen grains when they visit one flower, and then transfer the pollen to the next flower they visit. Wind-pollinated flowers are generally small, relatively inconspicuous, and unscented. They produce large quantities of light pollen grains that are easily blown by the wind to other flowers.

REPRODUCTIVE STRUCTURES IN WIND-POLLINATED PLANT
Sweet chestnut
(*Castanea sativa*)

Flower bud

Prominent stigma protrudes from flower

Female flower

Petiole (leaf stalk)

Bract (leaflike structure)

Peduncle (inflorescence stalk)

FEMALE

Male flower

Part of male catkin (inflorescence adapted for wind pollination)

Peduncle (inflorescence stalk)

Filament

Anther

MALE

REPRODUCTIVE STRUCTURES IN INSECT-POLLINATED PLANTS

Stigma

Style

Dehisced (split open) pollen sac

Boundary between two fused carpels (each carpel consists of a stigma, style, and ovary)

Ovary

Endothecium (pollen sac wall)

Pollen grain

Anther

Filament

Stamen

Calyx (whorl of sepals)

MICROGRAPH OF CARPELS (FEMALE ORGANS)
Yellow-wort
(*Blackstonia perfoliata*)

MICROGRAPH OF STAMENS (MALE ORGANS)
Common centaury
(*Centaurium erythraea*)

MICROGRAPHS OF POLLEN GRAINS

Exine (outer coat of pollen grain)

Colpus (furrow-shaped aperture)

Pore

EUROPEAN FIELD ELM
(*Ulmus minor*)

Exine (outer coat of pollen grain)

JUSTICIA AUREA

Exine (outer coat of pollen grain)

Pore

Baculum (rod-shaped structure)

MEADOW CRANESBILL
(*Geranium pratense*)

Colpus (furrow-shaped aperture)

Exine (outer coat of pollen grain)

Equatorial furrow

BOX-LEAVED MILKWORT
(*Polygala chamaebuxus*)

INSECT POLLINATION OF MEADOW SAGE

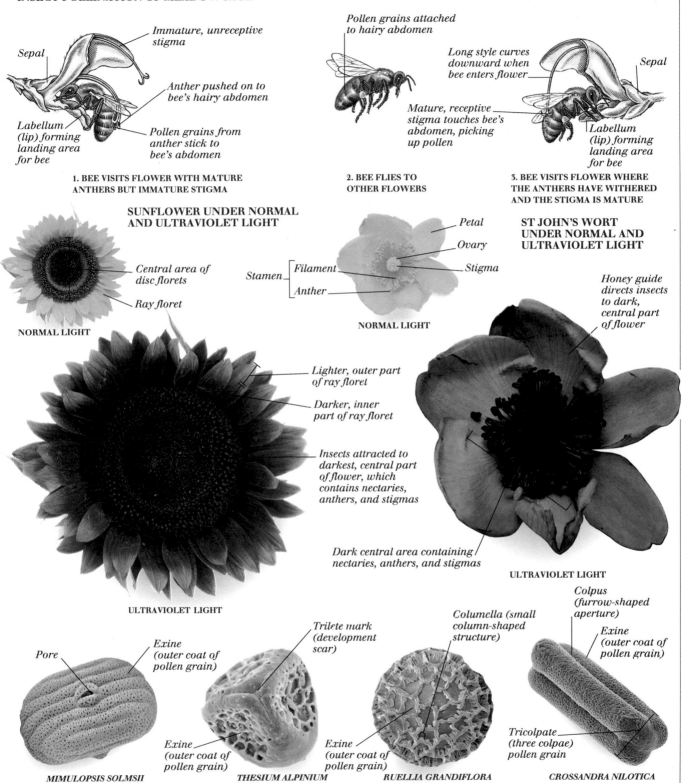

Immature, unreceptive stigma

Sepal

Anther pushed on to bee's hairy abdomen

Labellum (lip) forming landing area for bee

Pollen grains from anther stick to bee's abdomen

1. BEE VISITS FLOWER WITH MATURE ANTHERS BUT IMMATURE STIGMA

Pollen grains attached to hairy abdomen

2. BEE FLIES TO OTHER FLOWERS

Long style curves downward when bee enters flower

Sepal

Mature, receptive stigma touches bee's abdomen, picking up pollen

Labellum (lip) forming landing area for bee

3. BEE VISITS FLOWER WHERE THE ANTHERS HAVE WITHERED AND THE STIGMA IS MATURE

SUNFLOWER UNDER NORMAL AND ULTRAVIOLET LIGHT

Central area of disc florets

Ray floret

NORMAL LIGHT

Petal

Ovary

Stamen { Filament, Anther }

Stigma

NORMAL LIGHT

ST JOHN'S WORT UNDER NORMAL AND ULTRAVIOLET LIGHT

Honey guide directs insects to dark, central part of flower

Lighter, outer part of ray floret

Darker, inner part of ray floret

Insects attracted to darkest, central part of flower, which contains nectaries, anthers, and stigmas

Dark central area containing nectaries, anthers, and stigmas

ULTRAVIOLET LIGHT

ULTRAVIOLET LIGHT

Pore

Exine (outer coat of pollen grain)

Exine (outer coat of pollen grain)

MIMULOPSIS SOLMSII

Trilete mark (development scar)

Exine (outer coat of pollen grain)

THESIUM ALPINIUM

Columella (small column-shaped structure)

Exine (outer coat of pollen grain)

RUELLIA GRANDIFLORA

Colpus (furrow-shaped aperture)

Exine (outer coat of pollen grain)

Tricolpate (three colpae) pollen grain

CROSSANDRA NILOTICA

Fertilization

FERTILIZATION IS THE FUSION of male and female gametes (sex cells) to produce a zygote (embryo). Following pollination (see pp. 144-145), the pollen grains that contain the male gametes are on the stigma, some distance from the female gamete (ovum) inside the ovule. To enable the gametes to meet, the pollen grain germinates and produces a pollen tube, which grows down and enters the embryo sac (the inner part of the ovule that contains the ovum). Two male gametes, traveling at the tip of the pollen tube, enter the embryo sac. One gamete fuses with the ovum to produce a zygote that will develop into an embryo plant. The other male gamete fuses with two polar nuclei to produce the endosperm, which acts as a food supply for the developing embryo. Fertilization also initiates other changes: the integument (outer part of ovule) forms a testa (seed coat) around the embryo and endosperm; the petals fall off; the stigma and style wither; and the ovary wall forms a layer (called the pericarp) around the seed. Together, the pericarp and seed form the fruit, which may be succulent (see pp. 148-149) or dry (see pp. 150-151). In some species (such as blackberry), apomixis can occur: The seed develops without fertilization of the ovum by a male gamete, but endosperm formation and fruit development take place as in other species.

BANANA
(*Musa 'Lacatan'*)

DEVELOPMENT OF A SUCCULENT FRUIT
Blackberry
(*Rubus fruticosus*)

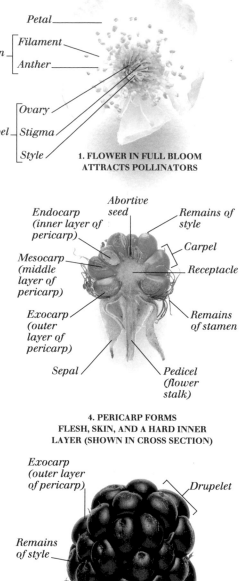

Petal

Stamen
- Filament
- Anther

Carpel
- Ovary
- Stigma
- Style

**1. FLOWER IN FULL BLOOM
ATTRACTS POLLINATORS**

Endocarp (inner layer of pericarp)

Abortive seed

Remains of style

Carpel

Mesocarp (middle layer of pericarp)

Receptacle

Exocarp (outer layer of pericarp)

Remains of stamen

Sepal

Pedicel (flower stalk)

**4. PERICARP FORMS
FLESH, SKIN, AND A HARD INNER
LAYER (SHOWN IN CROSS SECTION)**

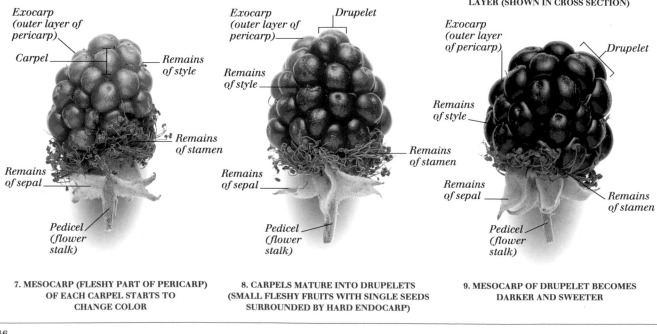

Exocarp (outer layer of pericarp)

Carpel

Remains of style

Remains of stamen

Remains of sepal

Pedicel (flower stalk)

**7. MESOCARP (FLESHY PART OF PERICARP)
OF EACH CARPEL STARTS TO
CHANGE COLOR**

Exocarp (outer layer of pericarp)

Drupelet

Remains of style

Remains of stamen

Remains of sepal

Pedicel (flower stalk)

**8. CARPELS MATURE INTO DRUPELETS
(SMALL FLESHY FRUITS WITH SINGLE SEEDS
SURROUNDED BY HARD ENDOCARP)**

Exocarp (outer layer of pericarp)

Drupelet

Remains of style

Remains of sepal

Remains of stamen

Pedicel (flower stalk)

**9. MESOCARP OF DRUPELET BECOMES
DARKER AND SWEETER**

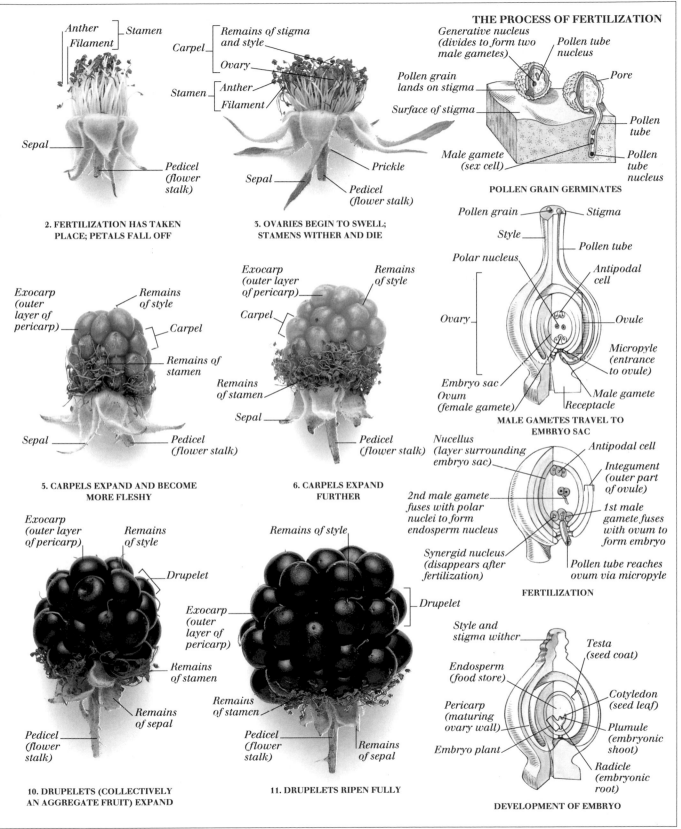

Anther
Filament
Stamen

Sepal

Pedicel
(flower
stalk)

**2. FERTILIZATION HAS TAKEN
PLACE; PETALS FALL OFF**

Carpel
Remains of stigma
and style
Ovary
Stamen
Anther
Filament

Prickle
Sepal
Pedicel
(flower stalk)

**3. OVARIES BEGIN TO SWELL;
STAMENS WITHER AND DIE**

THE PROCESS OF FERTILIZATION

Generative nucleus
(divides to form two
male gametes)
Pollen tube
nucleus
Pollen grain
lands on stigma
Pore
Surface of stigma
Pollen
tube
Male gamete
(sex cell)
Pollen
tube
nucleus

POLLEN GRAIN GERMINATES

Exocarp
(outer
layer of
pericarp)
Remains
of style
Carpel
Remains of
stamen

Sepal
Pedicel
(flower stalk)

**5. CARPELS EXPAND AND BECOME
MORE FLESHY**

Exocarp
(outer layer
of pericarp)
Remains
of style
Carpel
Remains
of stamen
Sepal
Pedicel
(flower stalk)

**6. CARPELS EXPAND
FURTHER**

Pollen grain
Stigma
Style
Pollen tube
Polar nucleus
Antipodal
cell
Ovary
Ovule
Micropyle
(entrance
to ovule)
Embryo sac
Ovum
(female gamete)
Male gamete
Receptacle

**MALE GAMETES TRAVEL TO
EMBRYO SAC**

Nucellus
(layer surrounding
embryo sac)
Antipodal cell
Integument
(outer part
of ovule)
2nd male gamete
fuses with polar
nuclei to form
endosperm nucleus
1st male
gamete fuses
with ovum to
form embryo
Synergid nucleus
(disappears after
fertilization)
Pollen tube reaches
ovum via micropyle

FERTILIZATION

Exocarp
(outer layer
of pericarp)
Remains
of style
Drupelet
Remains
of stamen
Remains
of sepal
Pedicel
(flower
stalk)

**10. DRUPELETS (COLLECTIVELY
AN AGGREGATE FRUIT) EXPAND**

Remains of style
Exocarp
(outer
layer of
pericarp)
Drupelet
Remains
of stamen
Pedicel
(flower
stalk)
Remains
of sepal

11. DRUPELETS RIPEN FULLY

Style and
stigma wither
Testa
(seed coat)
Endosperm
(food store)
Cotyledon
(seed leaf)
Pericarp
(maturing
ovary wall)
Plumule
(embryonic
shoot)
Embryo plant
Radicle
(embryonic
root)

DEVELOPMENT OF EMBRYO

Succulent fruits

A FRUIT IS A FULLY DEVELOPED and ripened ovary—the seed-producing part of a plant's female reproductive organs. Fruits may be succulent or dry (see pp. 150-151). Succulent fruits are fleshy and brightly colored, making them attractive to animals, which eat them and disperse the seeds away from the parent plant. The wall (pericarp) of a succulent fruit has three layers: an outer exocarp, a middle mesocarp, and an inner endocarp. These three layers vary in thickness and texture in different types of fruits and may blend into each other. Succulent fruits can be classed as simple (derived from one ovary) or compound (derived from several ovaries). Simple succulent fruits include berries, which typically have many seeds, and drupes, which typically have a single stone or pit (such as cherry and peach). Compound succulent fruits include aggregate fruits, which are formed from many ovaries in one flower, and multiple fruits, which develop from the ovaries of many flowers. Some fruits, known as false fruits or pseudocarps, develop from parts of the flower in addition to the ovaries. For example, the flesh of the apple is formed from the receptacle (the upper end of the flower stalk).

BERRY
Cocoa
(*Theobroma cacao*)

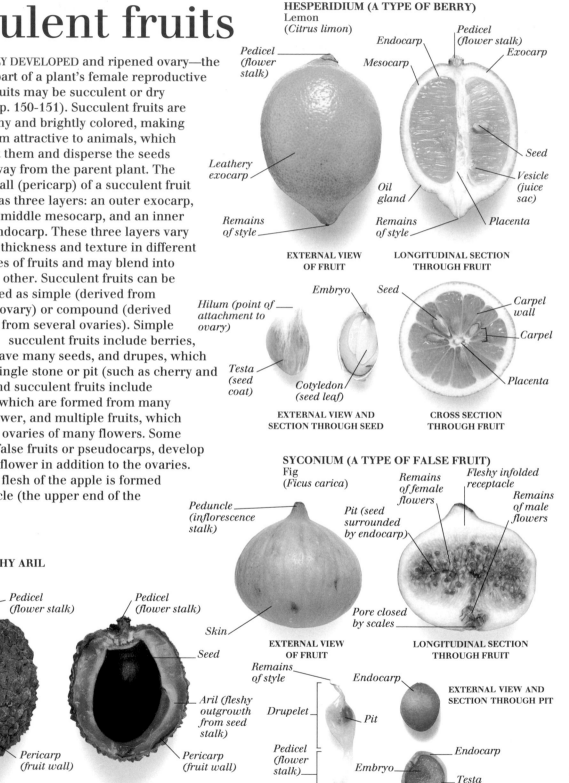

HESPERIDIUM (A TYPE OF BERRY)
Lemon
(*Citrus limon*)

Pedicel (flower stalk)

Endocarp

Mesocarp

Pedicel (flower stalk)

Exocarp

Leathery exocarp

Oil gland

Seed

Vesicle (juice sac)

Remains of style

Remains of style

Placenta

EXTERNAL VIEW OF FRUIT

LONGITUDINAL SECTION THROUGH FRUIT

Hilum (point of attachment to ovary)

Embryo

Seed

Carpel wall

Carpel

Testa (seed coat)

Cotyledon (seed leaf)

Placenta

EXTERNAL VIEW AND SECTION THROUGH SEED

CROSS SECTION THROUGH FRUIT

SYCONIUM (A TYPE OF FALSE FRUIT)
Fig
(*Ficus carica*)

Peduncle (inflorescence stalk)

Remains of female flowers

Fleshy infolded receptacle

Remains of male flowers

Pit (seed surrounded by endocarp)

Skin

Pore closed by scales

EXTERNAL VIEW OF FRUIT

LONGITUDINAL SECTION THROUGH FRUIT

FRUIT WITH FLESHY ARIL
Lychee
(*Litchi chinensis*)

Pedicel (flower stalk)

Pedicel (flower stalk)

Seed

Aril (fleshy outgrowth from seed stalk)

Pericarp (fruit wall)

Pericarp (fruit wall)

Remains of style

Drupelet

Pit

Pedicel (flower stalk)

Endocarp

EXTERNAL VIEW AND SECTION THROUGH PIT

Embryo

Cotyledon (seed leaf)

Endocarp

Testa (seed coat)

EXTERNAL VIEW OF FRUIT

LONGITUDINAL SECTION THROUGH FRUIT

REMAINS OF A SINGLE FEMALE FLOWER

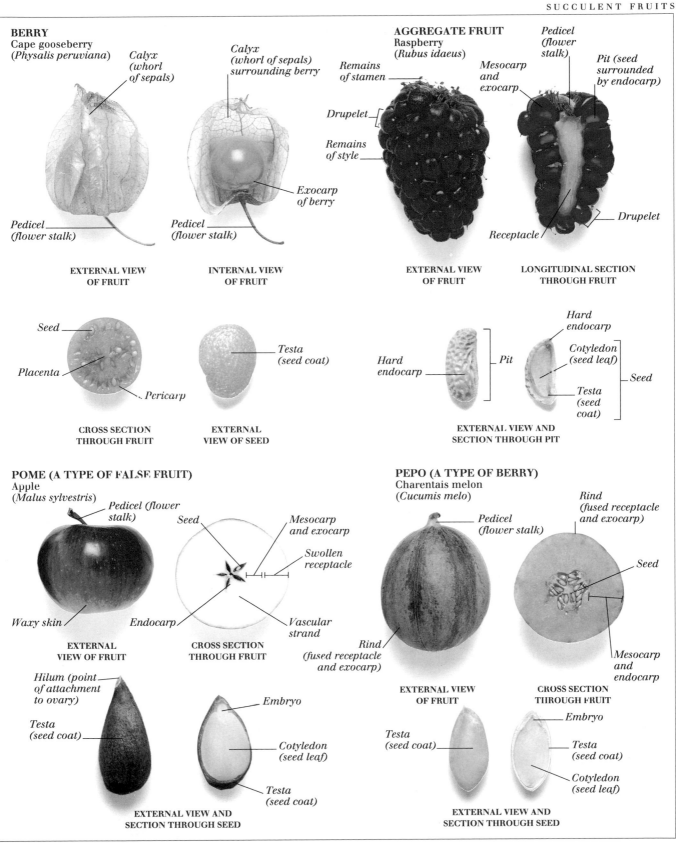

BERRY
Cape gooseberry
(*Physalis peruviana*)

Calyx (whorl of sepals)

Calyx (whorl of sepals) surrounding berry

Exocarp of berry

Pedicel (flower stalk)

Pedicel (flower stalk)

EXTERNAL VIEW OF FRUIT

INTERNAL VIEW OF FRUIT

Seed

Placenta

Pericarp

Testa (seed coat)

CROSS SECTION THROUGH FRUIT

EXTERNAL VIEW OF SEED

AGGREGATE FRUIT
Raspberry
(*Rubus idaeus*)

Remains of stamen

Drupelet

Remains of style

Pedicel (flower stalk)

Mesocarp and exocarp

Pit (seed surrounded by endocarp)

Drupelet

Receptacle

EXTERNAL VIEW OF FRUIT

LONGITUDINAL SECTION THROUGH FRUIT

Hard endocarp

Hard endocarp

Cotyledon (seed leaf)

Pit

Seed

Testa (seed coat)

EXTERNAL VIEW AND SECTION THROUGH PIT

POME (A TYPE OF FALSE FRUIT)
Apple
(*Malus sylvestris*)

Pedicel (flower stalk)

Seed

Mesocarp and exocarp

Swollen receptacle

Waxy skin

Endocarp

Vascular strand

EXTERNAL VIEW OF FRUIT

CROSS SECTION THROUGH FRUIT

Hilum (point of attachment to ovary)

Embryo

Testa (seed coat)

Cotyledon (seed leaf)

Testa (seed coat)

EXTERNAL VIEW AND SECTION THROUGH SEED

PEPO (A TYPE OF BERRY)
Charentais melon
(*Cucumis melo*)

Pedicel (flower stalk)

Rind (fused receptacle and exocarp)

Seed

Rind (fused receptacle and exocarp)

Mesocarp and endocarp

EXTERNAL VIEW OF FRUIT

CROSS SECTION THROUGH FRUIT

Testa (seed coat)

Embryo

Testa (seed coat)

Cotyledon (seed leaf)

EXTERNAL VIEW AND SECTION THROUGH SEED

Dry fruits

DRY FRUITS HAVE A HARD, DRY PERICARP (fruit wall) around their seeds, unlike succulent fruits, which have fleshy pericarps (see pp. 148-149). Dry fruits are divided into three types: dehiscent, in which the pericarp splits open to release the seeds; indehiscent, which do not split open; and schizocarpic, in which the fruit splits but the seeds are not exposed. Dehiscent dry fruits include capsules (for example, love-in-a-mist), follicles (delphinium), legumes (pea), and silicles (honesty). Typically, the seeds of dehiscent fruits are dispersed by the wind. Indehiscent dry fruits include nuts (sweet chestnut), nutlets (goose grass), achenes (strawberry), caryopses (wheat), samaras (elm), and cypselas (dandelion). Some indehiscent dry fruits are dispersed by the wind, assisted by "wings" (elm) or "parachutes" (dandelion); others (goose grass) have hooked pericarps to aid dispersal on animals' fur. Schizocarpic dry fruits include cremocarps (hogweed), and double samaras (sycamore maple); these are dispersed by the wind.

NUTLET
Goose grass
(*Galium aparine*)

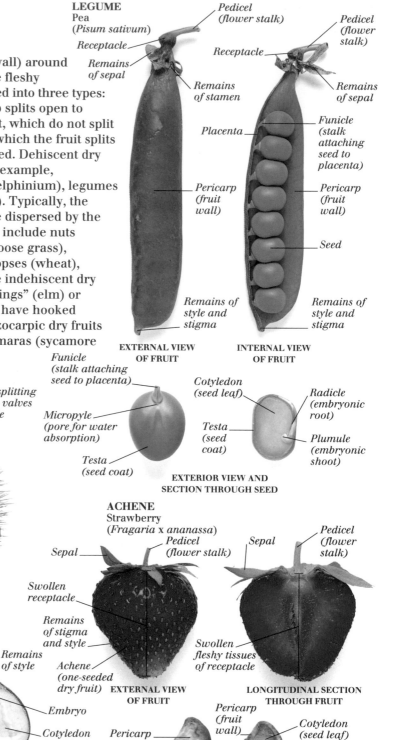

LEGUME
Pea
(*Pisum sativum*)

Pedicel (flower stalk)
Receptacle
Remains of sepal
Remains of stamen

Pedicel (flower stalk)
Receptacle
Remains of sepal

Placenta
Funicle (stalk attaching seed to placenta)

Pericarp (fruit wall)

Pericarp (fruit wall)

Seed

Remains of style and stigma

Remains of style and stigma

EXTERNAL VIEW OF FRUIT

INTERNAL VIEW OF FRUIT

Funicle (stalk attaching seed to placenta)
Micropyle (pore for water absorption)
Testa (seed coat)

Cotyledon (seed leaf)
Radicle (embryonic root)
Testa (seed coat)
Plumule (embryonic shoot)

EXTERIOR VIEW AND SECTION THROUGH SEED

NUT
Spanish chestnut
(*Castanea sativa*)

Line of splitting between valves of cupule

Peduncle (inflorescence stalk)

Remains of male inflorescence

Nut (indehiscent fruit)

Spiky cupule (husk around fruit formed from bracts)

EXTERNAL VIEW OF FRUIT WITH SURROUNDING CUPULE

Remains of stigma
Remains of style

Remains of stigma
Remains of style

Nut (indehiscent fruit)

Embryo

Cotyledon (seed leaf)

Testa (seed coat)

Woody pericarp (fruit wall)

Woody pericarp (fruit wall)

EXTERNAL VIEW AND SECTION THROUGH FRUIT

ACHENE
Strawberry
(*Fragaria x ananassa*)

Sepal
Pedicel (flower stalk)

Sepal
Pedicel (flower stalk)

Swollen receptacle

Remains of stigma and style

Achene (one-seeded dry fruit)

Swollen fleshy tissues of receptacle

EXTERNAL VIEW OF FRUIT

LONGITUDINAL SECTION THROUGH FRUIT

Pericarp (fruit wall)

Pericarp (fruit wall)

Cotyledon (seed leaf)

Testa (seed coat)

EXTERNAL VIEW AND SECTION THROUGH SEED

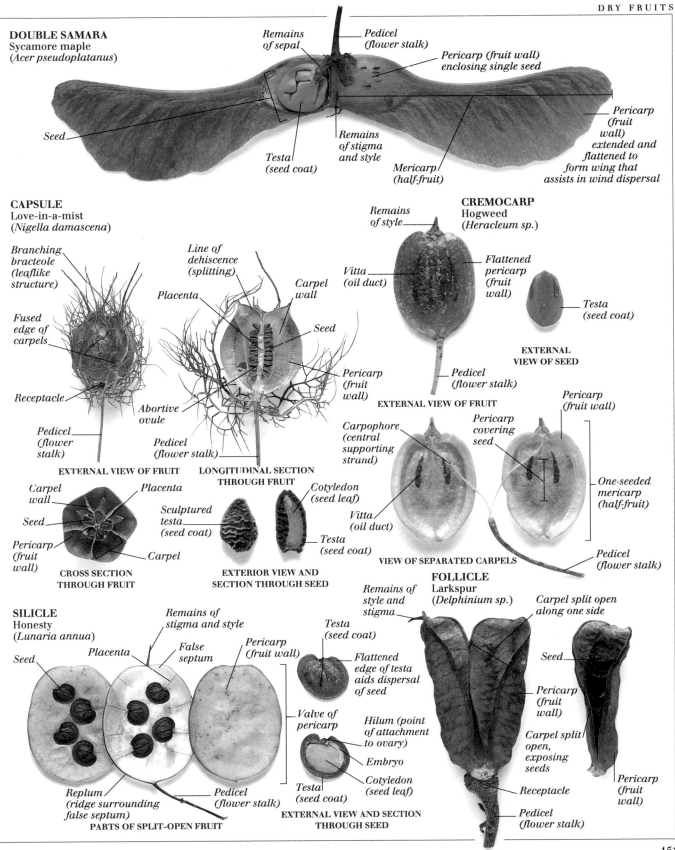

DOUBLE SAMARA
Sycamore maple
(*Acer pseudoplatanus*)

Remains of sepal

Pedicel (flower stalk)

Pericarp (fruit wall) enclosing single seed

Seed

Testa (seed coat)

Remains of stigma and style

Mericarp (half-fruit)

Pericarp (fruit wall) extended and flattened to form wing that assists in wind dispersal

CAPSULE
Love-in-a-mist
(*Nigella damascena*)

Branching bracteole (leaflike structure)

Fused edge of carpels

Receptacle

Pedicel (flower stalk)

Line of dehiscence (splitting)

Placenta

Carpel wall

Seed

Pericarp (fruit wall)

Abortive ovule

Pedicel (flower stalk)

EXTERNAL VIEW OF FRUIT

LONGITUDINAL SECTION THROUGH FRUIT

Carpel wall

Placenta

Seed

Pericarp (fruit wall)

Carpel

CROSS SECTION THROUGH FRUIT

Sculptured testa (seed coat)

Cotyledon (seed leaf)

Testa (seed coat)

EXTERIOR VIEW AND SECTION THROUGH SEED

CREMOCARP
Hogweed
(*Heracleum sp.*)

Remains of style

Vitta (oil duct)

Flattened pericarp (fruit wall)

Testa (seed coat)

EXTERNAL VIEW OF SEED

Pedicel (flower stalk)

EXTERNAL VIEW OF FRUIT

Carpophore (central supporting strand)

Vitta (oil duct)

Pericarp covering seed

Pericarp (fruit wall)

One-seeded mericarp (half-fruit)

Pedicel (flower stalk)

VIEW OF SEPARATED CARPELS

SILICLE
Honesty
(*Lunaria annua*)

Seed

Placenta

Remains of stigma and style

False septum

Pericarp (fruit wall)

Replum (ridge surrounding false septum)

Pedicel (flower stalk)

PARTS OF SPLIT-OPEN FRUIT

Testa (seed coat)

Flattened edge of testa aids dispersal of seed

Valve of pericarp

Hilum (point of attachment to ovary)

Embryo

Testa (seed coat)

Cotyledon (seed leaf)

EXTERNAL VIEW AND SECTION THROUGH SEED

FOLLICLE
Larkspur
(*Delphinium sp.*)

Remains of style and stigma

Carpel split open along one side

Seed

Pericarp (fruit wall)

Carpel split open, exposing seeds

Receptacle

Pedicel (flower stalk)

Pericarp (fruit wall)

Germination

GERMINATION IS THE GROWTH OF SEEDS INTO SEEDLINGS. It starts when seeds become active below ground, and ends when the first foliage leaves appear above ground. A seed consists of an embryo and its food supply, surrounded by a testa (seed coat). The embryo is made up of one or two cotyledons (seed leaves) attached to a central axis. The upper part of the axis consists of an epicotyl, which has a plumule (embryonic shoot) at its tip. The lower part of the axis consists of a hypocotyl and a radicle (embryonic root). After dispersal from the parent plant, the seeds dehydrate and enter a period of dormancy. Germination begins, following this dormant period, as long as the seeds have enough water, oxygen, warmth, and, in some cases, light. In the first stages of germination, the seed takes in water; the embryo starts to use its food store; and the radicle swells, breaks through the testa, and grows downward. Germination then proceeds in one of two ways, depending on the type of seed. In epigeal germination, the hypocotyl lengthens, pulling the plumule and its protective cotyledons out of the soil. In hypogeal germination, the cotyledons remain below ground and the epicotyl lengthens, pushing the plumule upward.

HYPOGEAL GERMINATION
Broad bean
(*Vicia faba*)

Cotyledon (seed leaf)

Cotyledon (seed leaf)

Plumule (embryonic shoot)

Testa (seed coat)

Epicotyl (upper part of axis)

Hypocotyl (region between epicotyl and radicle)

Radicle (embryonic root)

SEED AT START OF GERMINATION

Cotyledon (seed leaf)

Foliage leaf

Cotyledon (seed leaf)

Stipule (structure at base of leaf)

Epicotyl increases in length and turns green

Cataphyll (scale leaf of plumule)

Epicotyl (upper part of axis)

Hypocotyl (region between epicotyl and radicle)

FOLIAGE LEAVES APPEAR

Cotyledons (seed leaves) remain food source for the seedling

Primary root

Radicle (embryonic root)

Lateral root system

Split in testa (seed coat) due to expanding cotyledons

Young shoot

Cataphyll (scale leaf of plumule)

Testa (seed coat)

Epicotyl (upper part of axis) lengthens

Plumule (embryonic shoot)

Hilum (point of attachment to ovary)

Cortex

Vascular tissue (xylem and phloem)

Epidermis

Root tip (region of cell division)

Cotyledons (seed leaves) remain within testa (seed coat) below soil's surface

SHOOT APPEARS ABOVE SOIL

Primary root

Lateral root

RADICLE BREAKS THROUGH TESTA

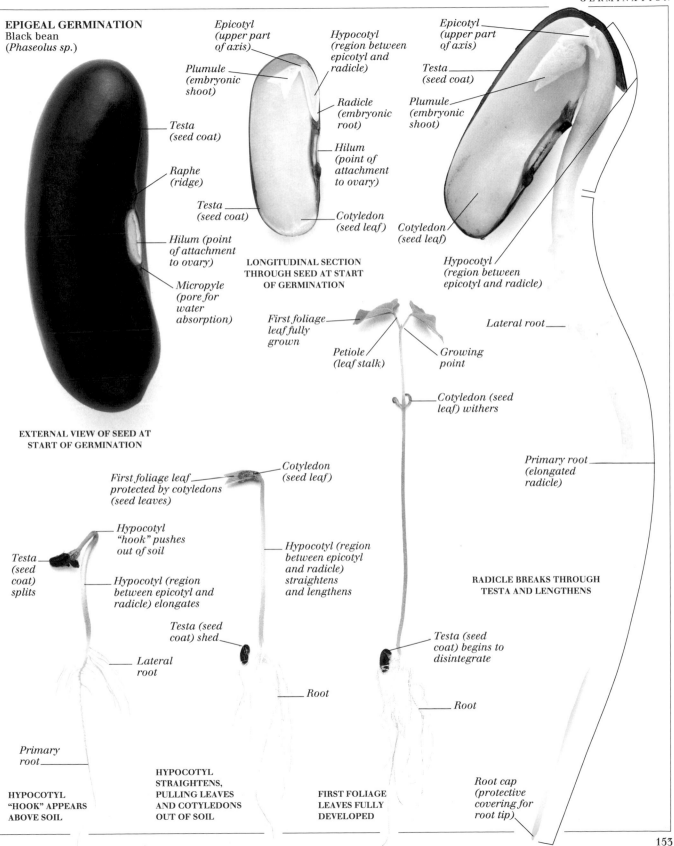

EPIGEAL GERMINATION
Black bean
(*Phaseolus sp.*)

Epicotyl (upper part of axis)

Plumule (embryonic shoot)

Hypocotyl (region between epicotyl and radicle)

Radicle (embryonic root)

Hilum (point of attachment to ovary)

Testa (seed coat)

Testa (seed coat)

Cotyledon (seed leaf)

Epicotyl (upper part of axis)

Testa (seed coat)

Plumule (embryonic shoot)

Cotyledon (seed leaf)

Hypocotyl (region between epicotyl and radicle)

Testa (seed coat)

Raphe (ridge)

Hilum (point of attachment to ovary)

Micropyle (pore for water absorption)

LONGITUDINAL SECTION THROUGH SEED AT START OF GERMINATION

First foliage leaf fully grown

Petiole (leaf stalk)

Growing point

Lateral root

Cotyledon (seed leaf) withers

EXTERNAL VIEW OF SEED AT START OF GERMINATION

Primary root (elongated radicle)

Cotyledon (seed leaf)

First foliage leaf protected by cotyledons (seed leaves)

Hypocotyl "hook" pushes out of soil

Testa (seed coat) splits

Hypocotyl (region between epicotyl and radicle) elongates

Hypocotyl (region between epicotyl and radicle) straightens and lengthens

RADICLE BREAKS THROUGH TESTA AND LENGTHENS

Testa (seed coat) shed

Lateral root

Root

Testa (seed coat) begins to disintegrate

Root

Primary root

HYPOCOTYL "HOOK" APPEARS ABOVE SOIL

HYPOCOTYL STRAIGHTENS, PULLING LEAVES AND COTYLEDONS OUT OF SOIL

FIRST FOLIAGE LEAVES FULLY DEVELOPED

Root cap (protective covering for root tip)

Vegetative reproduction

MANY PLANTS CAN PROPAGATE THEMSELVES by vegetative reproduction. In this process, part of a plant separates, takes root, and grows into a new plant. Vegetative reproduction is a type of asexual reproduction; it involves only one parent and there is no fusion of gametes (sex cells). Plants use various structures to reproduce vegetatively. Some plants use underground storage organs. Such organs include rhizomes (horizontal, underground stems), the branches of which produce new plants; bulbs (swollen leaf bases) and corms (swollen stems), which produce daughter bulbs or corms that separate from the parent; and stem tubers (thickened underground stems) and root tubers (swollen adventitious roots), which also separate from the parent. Other propagative structures include runners and stolons, creeping horizontal stems that take root and produce new plants; bulbils, small bulbs that develop on the stem or in the place of flowers, and then drop off and grow into new plants; and adventitious buds, miniature plants that form on leaf margins before dropping to the ground and growing into mature plants.

CORM
Gladiolus
(*Gladiolus sp.*)

ADVENTITIOUS BUD
Mexican hat plant
(*Kalanchoe
daigremontiana*)

*Apex of
leaf*

*Lamina
(blade) of
leaf*

*Leaf
margin*

*Notch in leaf
margin containing
meristematic
(actively dividing)
cells*

*Adventitious bud
(detachable bud
with adventitious
roots) drops
from leaf*

*Petiole
(leaf stalk)*

BULBIL IN PLACE OF FLOWER
Orange lily
(*Lilium bulbiferum*)

*Scar left
by flower*

Leaf

*Pedicel
(flower stalk)*

*Detachable
bulbil formed
in place of
flower*

*Peduncle
(inflorescence
stalk)*

STOLON
Ground ivy
(*Glechoma hederacea*)

*Terminal
bud*

Internode

Node

Node

*Parent
plant*

*Stolon
(creeping stem)*

*Adventitious root
of daughter plant*

*Daughter plant
developed from
lateral bud*

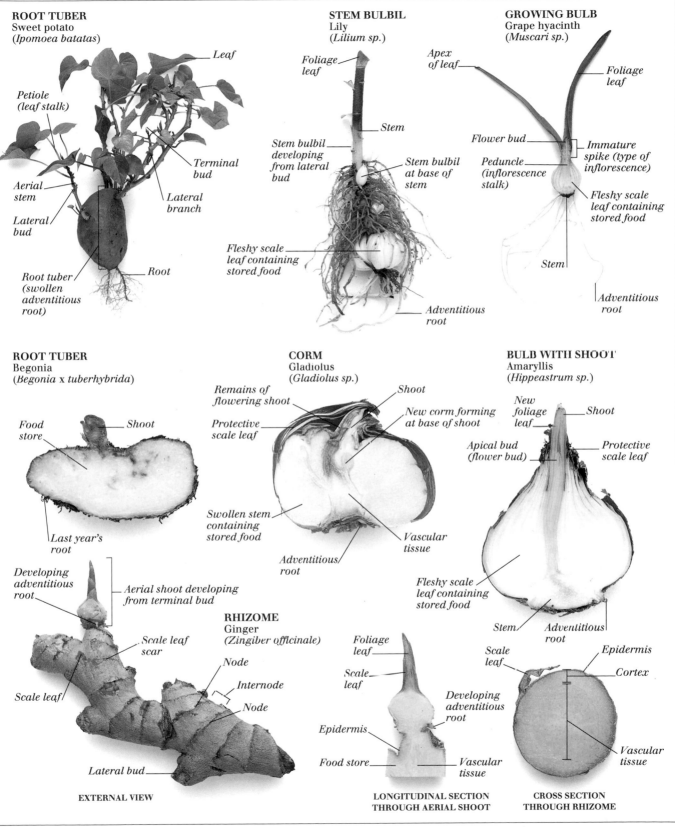

ROOT TUBER
Sweet potato
(*Ipomoea batatas*)

Leaf

Petiole
(leaf stalk)

Terminal
bud

Aerial
stem

Lateral
branch

Lateral
bud

Root tuber
(swollen
adventitious
root)

Root

STEM BULBIL
Lily
(*Lilium sp.*)

Foliage
leaf

Stem

Stem bulbil
developing
from lateral
bud

Stem bulbil
at base of
stem

Fleshy scale
leaf containing
stored food

Adventitious
root

GROWING BULB
Grape hyacinth
(*Muscari sp.*)

Apex
of leaf

Foliage
leaf

Flower bud

Immature
spike (type of
inflorescence)

Peduncle
(inflorescence
stalk)

Fleshy scale
leaf containing
stored food

Stem

Adventitious
root

ROOT TUBER
Begonia
(*Begonia* x *tuberhybrida*)

Food
store

Shoot

Last year's
root

Developing
adventitious
root

Aerial shoot developing
from terminal bud

Scale leaf
scar

Scale leaf

Node

Internode

Node

Lateral bud

EXTERNAL VIEW

CORM
Gladiolus
(*Gladiolus sp.*)

Remains of
flowering shoot

Shoot

New corm forming
at base of shoot

Protective
scale leaf

Swollen stem
containing
stored food

Vascular
tissue

Adventitious
root

RHIZOME
Ginger
(*Zingiber officinale*)

Foliage
leaf

Scale
leaf

Developing
adventitious
root

Epidermis

Food store

Vascular
tissue

**LONGITUDINAL SECTION
THROUGH AERIAL SHOOT**

BULB WITH SHOOT
Amaryllis
(*Hippeastrum sp.*)

New
foliage
leaf

Shoot

Apical bud
(flower bud)

Protective
scale leaf

Fleshy scale
leaf containing
stored food

Stem

Adventitious
root

Scale
leaf

Epidermis

Cortex

Vascular
tissue

**CROSS SECTION
THROUGH RHIZOME**

155

Dryland plants

DRYLAND PLANTS (XEROPHYTES) are able to survive in unfavorable habitats. All are found in places where little water is available; some live in high temperatures that cause excessive loss of water from the leaves. Xerophytes show a number of adaptations to dry conditions. These include reduced leaf area, rolled leaves, sunken stomata, hairs, spines, and thick cuticles. One group, succulent plants, stores water in specially enlarged spongy tissues found in leaves, roots, or stems. Leaf succulents have enlarged, fleshy, water-storing leaves. Root succulents have a large underground water-storage organ with short-lived stems and leaves above ground. Stem succulents are represented by the cacti (family Cactaceae). Cacti stems are fleshy, green, and photosynthetic. They are typically ribbed or covered by tubercles in rows, with leaves being reduced to spines or entirely absent.

LEAF SUCCULENT
Lithops sp.

STEM SUCCULENT
Golden barrel cactus
(*Echinocactus grusonii*)

Areole (modified lateral shoot)

Trichome (hair)

Spine (modified leaf)

Waxy cuticle (waterproof covering)

Water-storing parenchyma (packing tissue)

Sinuous (wavy) cell wall

Stoma (pore) controlling exchange of gases

Tubercle (projection from stem surface)

Vascular cylinder (transport tissue)

Spine (modified leaf)

Tubercle (projection from stem surface)

Root

EXTERNAL VIEW

MICROGRAPH OF STEM SURFACE

Spine (modified leaf)

Areole (modified lateral shoot)

Tubercle (projection from stem surface)

Waxy cuticle (waterproof covering)

Root

DETAIL OF STEM SURFACE

LONGITUDINAL SECTION THROUGH STEM

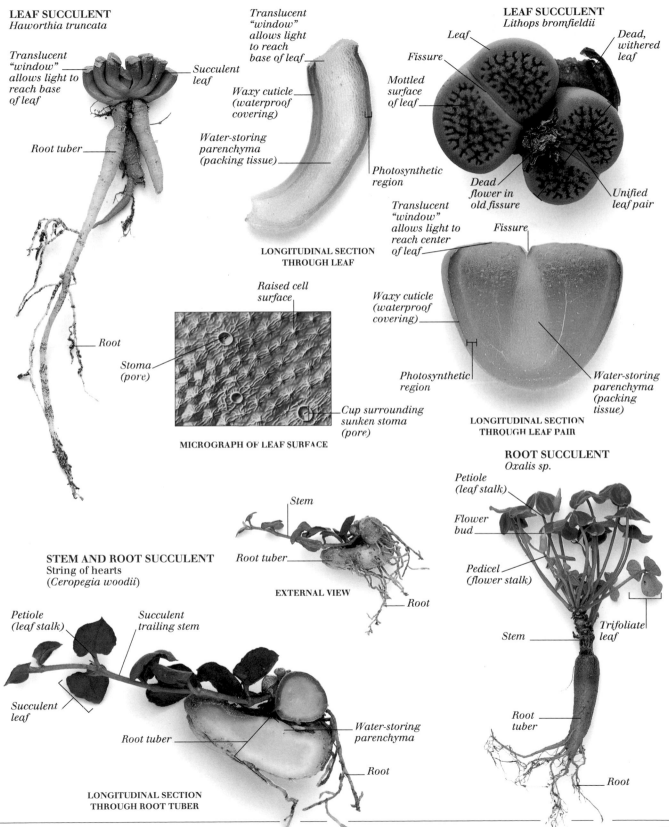

LEAF SUCCULENT
Haworthia truncata

Translucent "window" allows light to reach base of leaf

Succulent leaf

Root tuber

Root

Translucent "window" allows light to reach base of leaf

Waxy cuticle (waterproof covering)

Water-storing parenchyma (packing tissue)

Photosynthetic region

LONGITUDINAL SECTION THROUGH LEAF

Raised cell surface

Stoma (pore)

Cup surrounding sunken stoma (pore)

MICROGRAPH OF LEAF SURFACE

LEAF SUCCULENT
Lithops bromfieldii

Leaf

Fissure

Mottled surface of leaf

Dead, withered leaf

Dead flower in old fissure

Unified leaf pair

Translucent "window" allows light to reach center of leaf

Fissure

Waxy cuticle (waterproof covering)

Photosynthetic region

Water-storing parenchyma (packing tissue)

LONGITUDINAL SECTION THROUGH LEAF PAIR

ROOT SUCCULENT
Oxalis sp.

Petiole (leaf stalk)

Flower bud

Pedicel (flower stalk)

Stem

Trifoliate leaf

Root tuber

Root

STEM AND ROOT SUCCULENT
String of hearts
(*Ceropegia woodii*)

Stem

Root tuber

Root

EXTERNAL VIEW

Petiole (leaf stalk)

Succulent trailing stem

Succulent leaf

Root tuber

Water-storing parenchyma

Root

LONGITUDINAL SECTION THROUGH ROOT TUBER

Wetland plants

WETLAND PLANTS GROW SUBMERGED IN WATER, either partially, like the water hyacinth, or completely, like the pondweeds, and show various adaptations to this habitat. Typically, there are numerous air spaces inside the stems, leaves, and roots; these aid gas exchange and buoyancy. Submerged parts generally have no cuticle (waterproof covering), allowing the plants to absorb minerals and gases directly from the water. Also, because they are supported by the water, wetland plants need little of the supportive tissue found in land plants. Stomata, the gas exchange pores, are absent from plants that are completely submerged. In partially submerged plants with floating leaves, such as water lilies, stomata are found on the upper leaf surfaces, where they cannot be flooded.

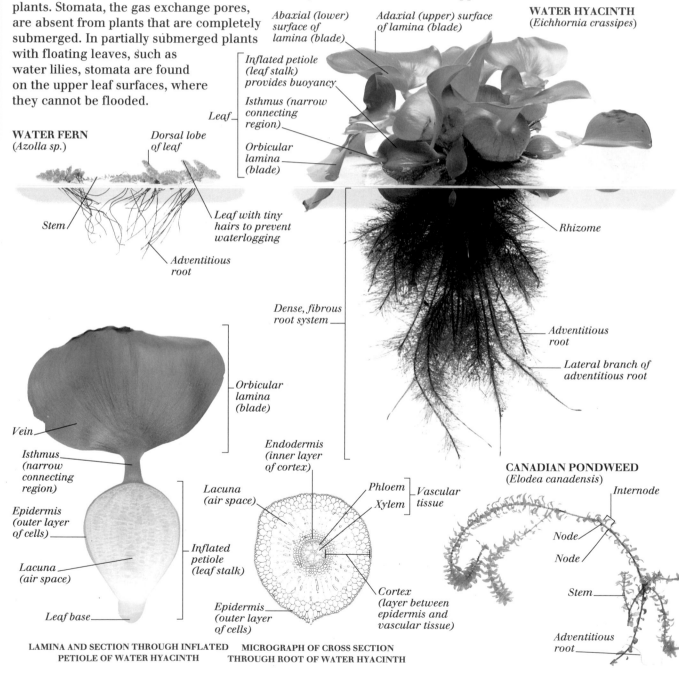

WATER HYACINTH
(*Eichhornia crassipes*)

Abaxial (lower) surface of lamina (blade)

Adaxial (upper) surface of lamina (blade)

Inflated petiole (leaf stalk) provides buoyancy

Isthmus (narrow connecting region)

Leaf

Orbicular lamina (blade)

Rhizome

WATER FERN
(*Azolla sp.*)

Dorsal lobe of leaf

Stem

Leaf with tiny hairs to prevent waterlogging

Adventitious root

Dense, fibrous root system

Adventitious root

Lateral branch of adventitious root

Orbicular lamina (blade)

Vein

Isthmus (narrow connecting region)

Epidermis (outer layer of cells)

Lacuna (air space)

Leaf base

Endodermis (inner layer of cortex)

Lacuna (air space)

Phloem

Xylem

Vascular tissue

Inflated petiole (leaf stalk)

Epidermis (outer layer of cells)

Cortex (layer between epidermis and vascular tissue)

CANADIAN PONDWEED
(*Elodea canadensis*)

Internode

Node

Node

Stem

Adventitious root

LAMINA AND SECTION THROUGH INFLATED PETIOLE OF WATER HYACINTH

MICROGRAPH OF CROSS SECTION THROUGH ROOT OF WATER HYACINTH

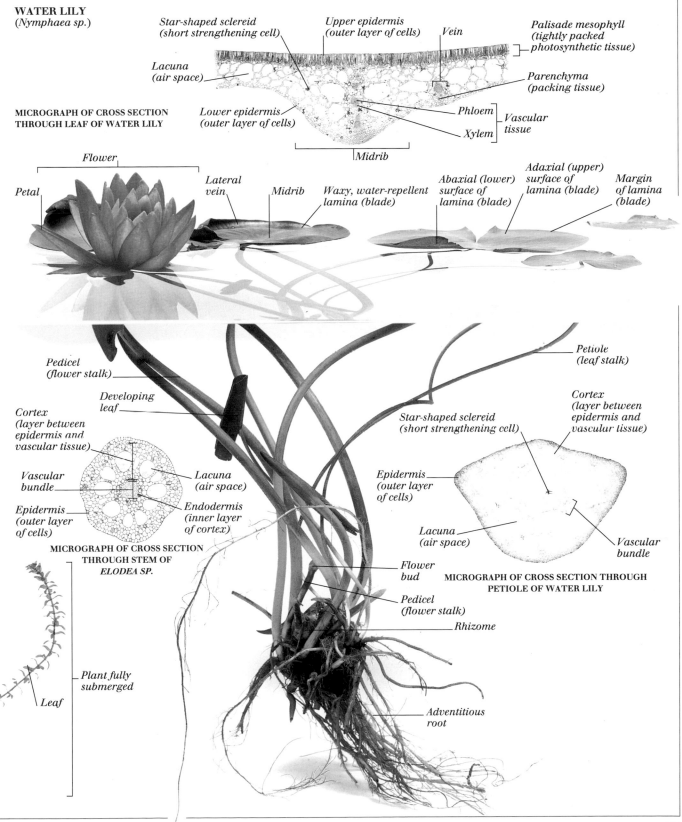

WATER LILY
(*Nymphaea sp.*)

Star-shaped sclereid
(short strengthening cell)

Upper epidermis
(outer layer of cells)

Vein

Palisade mesophyll
(tightly packed
photosynthetic tissue)

Lacuna
(air space)

Parenchyma
(packing tissue)

MICROGRAPH OF CROSS SECTION
THROUGH LEAF OF WATER LILY

Lower epidermis
(outer layer of cells)

Phloem

Xylem

Vascular
tissue

Midrib

Flower

Petal

Lateral
vein

Midrib

Waxy, water-repellent
lamina (blade)

Abaxial (lower)
surface of
lamina (blade)

Adaxial (upper)
surface of
lamina (blade)

Margin
of lamina
(blade)

Pedicel
(flower stalk)

Developing
leaf

Petiole
(leaf stalk)

Cortex
(layer between
epidermis and
vascular tissue)

Star-shaped sclereid
(short strengthening cell)

Cortex
(layer between
epidermis and
vascular tissue)

Vascular
bundle

Lacuna
(air space)

Epidermis
(outer layer
of cells)

Epidermis
(outer layer
of cells)

Endodermis
(inner layer
of cortex)

Lacuna
(air space)

Vascular
bundle

MICROGRAPH OF CROSS SECTION
THROUGH STEM OF
ELODEA SP.

MICROGRAPH OF CROSS SECTION THROUGH
PETIOLE OF WATER LILY

Flower
bud

Pedicel
(flower stalk)

Rhizome

Plant fully
submerged

Leaf

Adventitious
root

Carnivorous plants

CARNIVOROUS (INSECTIVOROUS) PLANTS FEED ON INSECTS and other small animals in addition to producing food in their leaves by photosynthesis. The nutrients absorbed from trapped insects allow carnivorous plants to thrive in acid, boggy soils that lack essential minerals, especially nitrates, where most other plants could not survive.

All carnivorous plants have some leaves modified as traps. Many use bright colors and scented nectar to attract prey, and most use enzymes to digest the prey. There are three types of traps. Pitcher plants, such as the monkey cup and cobra lily, have leaves modified as pitcher-shaped pitfall traps, half-filled with water. Once lured inside the mouth of the trap, insects lose their footing on the slippery surface, fall into the liquid, and either decompose or are digested. Venus flytraps use a spring-trap mechanism; when an insect touches trigger hairs on the inner surfaces of the leaves, the two lobes of the trap snap shut. Butterworts and sundews entangle prey by sticky droplets on the leaf surface, while the edges of the leaves slowly curl over to envelop and digest the prey.

A PITCHER PLANT
Cobra lily (*Darlingtonia californica*)

Areola ("window" of transparent tissue)

Fishtail nectary

Wing

Hood

Pitcher

Tubular petiole (leaf stalk)

Areola ("window" of transparent tissue)

Smooth surface

Nectar roll

Dome-shaped hood develops

Fishtail nectary appears

Immature pitcher

Wing

Mouth

Downward-pointing hair

DEVELOPMENT OF MODIFIED LEAF IN COBRA LILY

Immature trap

Interlocked teeth

Closed trap

Red color of trap attracts insects

VENUS FLYTRAP
(*Dionaea muscipula*)

Phyllode (flattened petiole)

Summer petiole (leaf stalk)

Nectary zone (glands secrete nectar)

Digestive zone (glands secrete digestive enzymes)

Tooth

Lobe of trap

Midrib (hinge of trap)

Trigger hair

Spring petiole (leaf stalk)

Trap (twin-lobed leaf blade)

Sensory hinge

Trigger hair

Inner surface of trap

Digestive gland

MICROGRAPH OF LOBE OF VENUS FLYTRAP

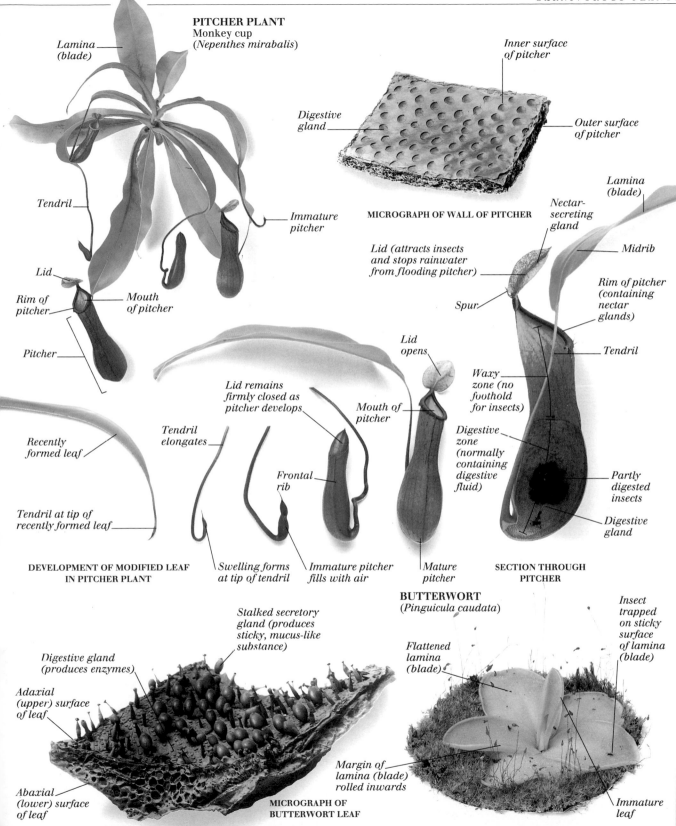

PITCHER PLANT
Monkey cup
(*Nepenthes mirabalis*)

Lamina (blade)

Tendril

Immature pitcher

Lid

Rim of pitcher

Mouth of pitcher

Pitcher

Inner surface of pitcher

Digestive gland

Outer surface of pitcher

MICROGRAPH OF WALL OF PITCHER

Nectar-secreting gland

Lamina (blade)

Lid (attracts insects and stops rainwater from flooding pitcher)

Midrib

Spur

Rim of pitcher (containing nectar glands)

Tendril

Waxy zone (no foothold for insects)

Digestive zone (normally containing digestive fluid)

Partly digested insects

Digestive gland

SECTION THROUGH PITCHER

Recently formed leaf

Tendril elongates

Lid remains firmly closed as pitcher develops

Mouth of pitcher

Lid opens

Frontal rib

Tendril at tip of recently formed leaf

Swelling forms at tip of tendril

Immature pitcher fills with air

Mature pitcher

DEVELOPMENT OF MODIFIED LEAF IN PITCHER PLANT

BUTTERWORT
(*Pinguicula caudata*)

Stalked secretory gland (produces sticky, mucus-like substance)

Insect trapped on sticky surface of lamina (blade)

Digestive gland (produces enzymes)

Flattened lamina (blade)

Adaxial (upper) surface of leaf

Abaxial (lower) surface of leaf

Margin of lamina (blade) rolled inwards

Immature leaf

MICROGRAPH OF BUTTERWORT LEAF

Epiphytic and parasitic plants

EPIPHYTIC AND PARASITIC PLANTS GROW ON OTHER LIVING PLANTS. Typically, epiphytic plants are not rooted in the soil. Instead, they live above ground level on the stems and branches of other plants. Epiphytes obtain water from trapped rainwater and from moisture in the air. They obtain minerals from organic matter that has accumulated on the surface of the plant on which they are growing. Like other green plants, epiphytes produce their food by photosynthesis. Epiphytes include tropical orchids and bromeliads (air plants) and some mosses that live in temperate regions. Parasitic plants obtain all their nutrient requirements from the host plants on which they grow. The parasites produce haustoria, root-like organs that penetrate the stem or roots of the host and grow inward to merge with the host's vascular tissue. These extract water, minerals, and manufactured nutrients. Because they have no need to produce their own food, parasitic plants lack chlorophyll, the green photosynthetic pigment, and they have no foliage leaves. Partial parasitic plants, like mistletoe, obtain water and minerals from the host plant but have green leaves and stems and are therefore able to produce their own food by photosynthesis.

EPIPHYTIC BROMELIAD
Aechmea miniata

Inflorescence (spike)

Peduncle (inflorescence stalk)

Flower bud

Strap-shaped arching leaf (part of rosette of leaves)

Leaf margin with spines

Overlapping leaf bases in which rainwater is trapped

Mass of adventitious roots

Stem

Bark of tree to which epiphyte is attached

EPIPHYTIC ORCHID
Brassavola nodosa

Peduncle (inflorescence stalk)

Pedicel (flower stalk)

Flower

Scale leaf

Leaf

Aerial root

Node

Stem

Bark of tree to which epiphyte is attached

Velamen (multilayered epidermis capable of absorbing water from rain or condensation)

Cortex (layer between epidermis and vascular tissue)

Cortex cell containing chloroplasts

Vascular tissue { Xylem / Phloem

Exodermis (outer layer of cortex)

Pith

Endodermis (inner layer of cortex)

MICROGRAPH OF CROSS SECTION THROUGH AERIAL ROOT OF EPIPHYTIC ORCHID

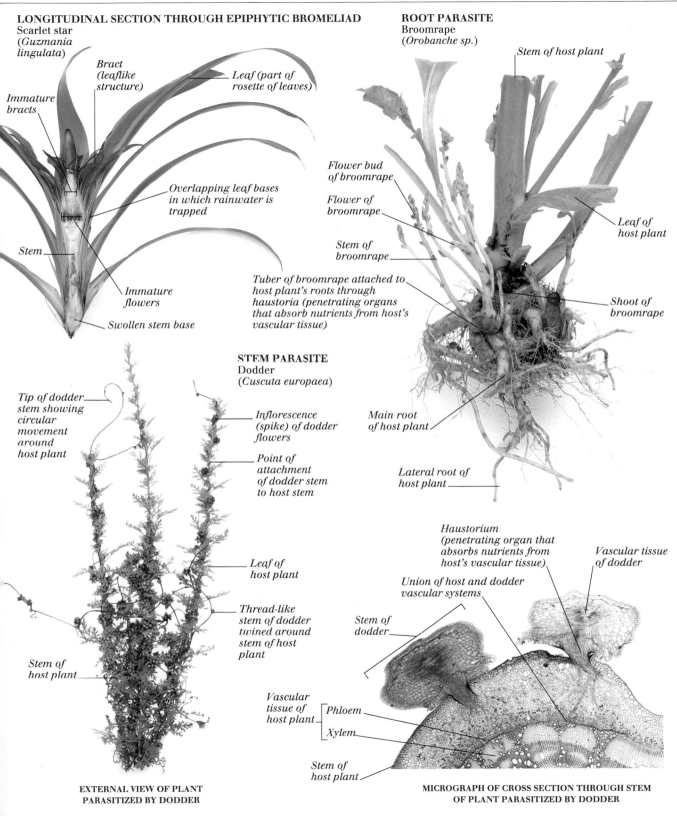

LONGITUDINAL SECTION THROUGH EPIPHYTIC BROMELIAD
Scarlet star (*Guzmania lingulata*)

Immature bracts

Bract (leaflike structure)

Leaf (part of rosette of leaves)

Overlapping leaf bases in which rainwater is trapped

Stem

Immature flowers

Swollen stem base

ROOT PARASITE
Broomrape (*Orobanche sp.*)

Stem of host plant

Flower bud of broomrape

Flower of broomrape

Stem of broomrape

Tuber of broomrape attached to host plant's roots through haustoria (penetrating organs that absorb nutrients from host's vascular tissue)

Leaf of host plant

Shoot of broomrape

Main root of host plant

Lateral root of host plant

STEM PARASITE
Dodder (*Cuscuta europaea*)

Tip of dodder stem showing circular movement around host plant

Inflorescence (spike) of dodder flowers

Point of attachment of dodder stem to host stem

Leaf of host plant

Thread-like stem of dodder twined around stem of host plant

Stem of host plant

EXTERNAL VIEW OF PLANT PARASITIZED BY DODDER

Haustorium (penetrating organ that absorbs nutrients from host's vascular tissue)

Vascular tissue of dodder

Union of host and dodder vascular systems

Stem of dodder

Vascular tissue of host plant

Phloem

Xylem

Stem of host plant

MICROGRAPH OF CROSS SECTION THROUGH STEM OF PLANT PARASITIZED BY DODDER

163

ANIMALS

Sponges, jellyfish, and sea anemones

SPONGES ARE MAINLY MARINE animals that make up the phylum Porifera. They are among the simplest of all animals, having no tissues or organs. Their bodies consist of two layers of cells separated by a jelly-like layer (mesohyal) that is strengthened by mineral spicules or protein fibers. The body is perforated by a system of pores and water channels called the aquiferous system. Special cells (choanocytes) with whip-like structures (flagella) draw water through the aquiferous system, thereby bringing tiny food particles to the sponge's cells. Jellyfish (class Scyphozoa), sea anemones (class Anthozoa), and corals (also class Anthozoa) belong to the phylum Cnidaria, also known as Coelenterata. More complex than sponges, coelenterates have simple tissues, such as nervous tissue; a radially symmetrical body; and a mouth surrounded by tentacles with unique stinging cells (cnidocytes).

INTERNAL ANATOMY OF A SPONGE

Amebocyte

Osculum (excurrent pore)

Choanocyte (collar cell)

Ostium (incurrent pore)

Porocyte (pore cell)

Mesohyal

Spongocoel (atrium; paragaster)

Spicule

Pinacocyte (epidermal cell)

Ostium (incurrent pore)

SKELETON OF A SPONGE

Protein matrix

Pore

EXTERNAL FEATURES OF A SEA ANEMONE

Tentacle

EXAMPLES OF SEA ANEMONES

JEWEL ANEMONE (*Corynactis viridis*)

PARASITIC ANEMONE (*Calliactis parasitica*)

PLUMOSE ANEMONE (*Metridium senile*)

MEDITERRANEAN SEA ANEMONE (*Condylactis sp.*)

GREEN SNAKELOCK ANEMONE (*Anemonia viridis*)

BEADLET ANEMONE (*Actinia equina*)

GHOST ANEMONE (*Actinothoe sphyrodeta*)

Sagartia elegans

EXTERNAL APPEARANCE OF A JELLYFISH

INTERNAL ANATOMY OF A JELLYFISH

Stomach

Filament

Gonad

Ectoderm

Endoderm

Mesoglea

Radial canal

Hood

Tentacle

Subgenital pit

Rhopalium

Oral arm

Mouth

EXAMPLES OF CORALS

HONEYCOMB CORAL
(Goniastrea aspera)

MUSHROOM CORAL
(Fungia fungites)

STAR CORAL
(Balanophyllia regia)

STRUCTURE OF A CNIDOCYTE

Operculum

Cnidocil (trigger)

Barb (stylet)

Thread

Nucleus

BEFORE DISCHARGE

Thread

Spine

Cnidocil (trigger)

Barb (stylet)

Operculum

Nucleus

AFTER DISCHARGE

INTERNAL ANATOMY OF A SEA ANEMONE

Oral disk

Mouth

Ostium (mesenteric perforation)

Tentacle

Sphincter muscle

Collar

Siphonoglyph

Mesenteric filament

Complete mesentery

Incomplete mesentery

Retractor muscle

Gonad

Basal disk (pedal disk)

Pharynx

Gastrovascular cavity

Oral disk

Mouth

Insects

PUPA (CHRYSALIS)

THE WORD INSECT REFERS to small invertebrate creatures, especially those with bodies divided into sections. Insects, including beetles, ants, bees, butterflies, and moths, belong to various orders in the class Insecta, which is a division of the phylum Arthropoda. Features common to all insects are an exoskeleton (external skeleton); three pairs of jointed legs; three body sections (head, thorax, and abdomen); and one pair of sensory antennae. Beetles (order Coleoptera) are the biggest group of insects, with about 300,000 species (about 30 percent of all known insects). They have a pair of hard elytra (wing cases), which are modified front wings. The principal function of the elytra is to protect the hind wings, which are used for flying. Ants, together with bees and wasps, form the order Hymenoptera, which contains about 200,000 species. This group is characterized by a marked narrowing between the thorax and abdomen. Butterflies and moths form the order Lepidoptera, which has about 150,000 species. They have wings covered with tiny scales, hence the name of their order (Lepidoptera means "scale wings"). The separation of lepidopterans into butterflies and moths is largely artificial as there are no features that categorically distinguish one group from the other. In general, however, most butterflies fly by day, whereas most moths are night flyers. Some insects, including butterflies and moths, undergo complete metamorphosis (transformation) during their life cycle. A butterfly metamorphoses from an egg to a larva (caterpillar), then to a pupa (chrysalis), and finally to an imago (adult).

EXAMPLES OF INSECTS

BUMBLEBEE

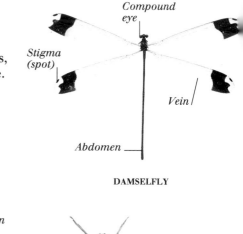

DAMSELFLY

EXTERNAL FEATURES OF A BEETLE

CRICKET

ANT

FLY

EARWIG

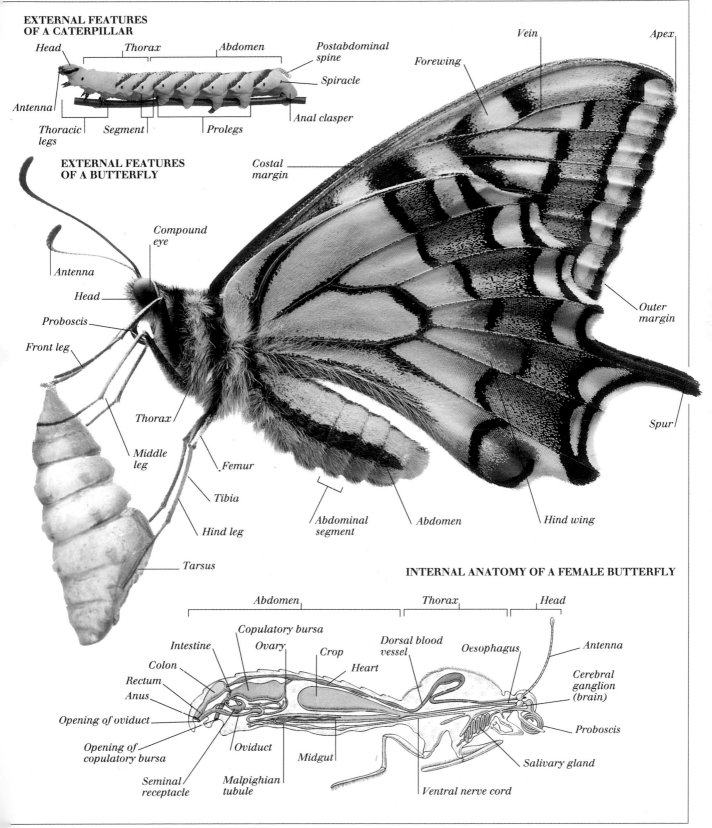

EXTERNAL FEATURES OF A CATERPILLAR

Head

Thorax

Abdomen

Postabdominal spine

Spiracle

Antenna

Thoracic legs

Segment

Prolegs

Anal clasper

EXTERNAL FEATURES OF A BUTTERFLY

Vein

Apex

Forewing

Costal margin

Compound eye

Antenna

Head

Proboscis

Front leg

Thorax

Middle leg

Femur

Tibia

Hind leg

Tarsus

Outer margin

Spur

Abdominal segment

Abdomen

Hind wing

INTERNAL ANATOMY OF A FEMALE BUTTERFLY

Abdomen

Thorax

Head

Copulatory bursa

Intestine

Ovary

Crop

Dorsal blood vessel

Oesophagus

Antenna

Colon

Heart

Rectum

Cerebral ganglion (brain)

Anus

Proboscis

Opening of oviduct

Opening of copulatory bursa

Oviduct

Midgut

Salivary gland

Seminal receptacle

Malpighian tubule

Ventral nerve cord

169

Arachnids

THE CLASS ARACHNIDA INCLUDES SPIDERS (order Araneae) and scorpions (order Scorpiones). The class is part of the phylum Arthropoda, which also includes insects and crustaceans. Spiders and scorpions are characterized by having four pairs of walking legs; a pair of pincer-like mouthparts called chelicerae; another pair of frontal appendages called pedipalps, which are sensory in spiders but used for grasping in scorpions; and a body divided into two sections (a combined head and thorax called a cephalothorax, or prosoma, and an abdomen, or opisthosoma). Unlike other arthropods, spiders and scorpions lack antennae. Spiders and scorpions are carnivorous. Spiders poison prey by biting with the fanged chelicerae, scorpions by stinging with the end of the metasoma (tail).

MEXICAN TRUE RED-LEGGED TARANTULA
(*Euathlus emilia*)

INTERNAL ANATOMY OF A FEMALE SPIDER

Anterior aorta
Ostium
Pumping stomach
Heart
Digestive gland
Posterior aorta
Malpighian tubule
Intestine
Cloaca
Ovary
Anus
Spinneret
Silk gland
Trachea
Spermatheca (seminal receptacle)
Oviduct
Vagina
Book lung
Spiracle
Gut cecum
Esophagus
Mouth
Fang
Chelicera
Poison duct
Poison gland
Simple eye
Brain

EXTERNAL FEATURES OF A SCORPION

Chela (claw of pedipalp)
Pedipalp
Prosoma (cephalothorax)
Opisthosoma (abdomen)
Stinger
Metasoma (tail)
Chelicera
Median eye
Patella
Tibia
Tarsus
Coxa
Femur
4th walking leg
1st walking leg
3rd walking leg
Metatarsus
Trochanter
2nd walking leg
Claw

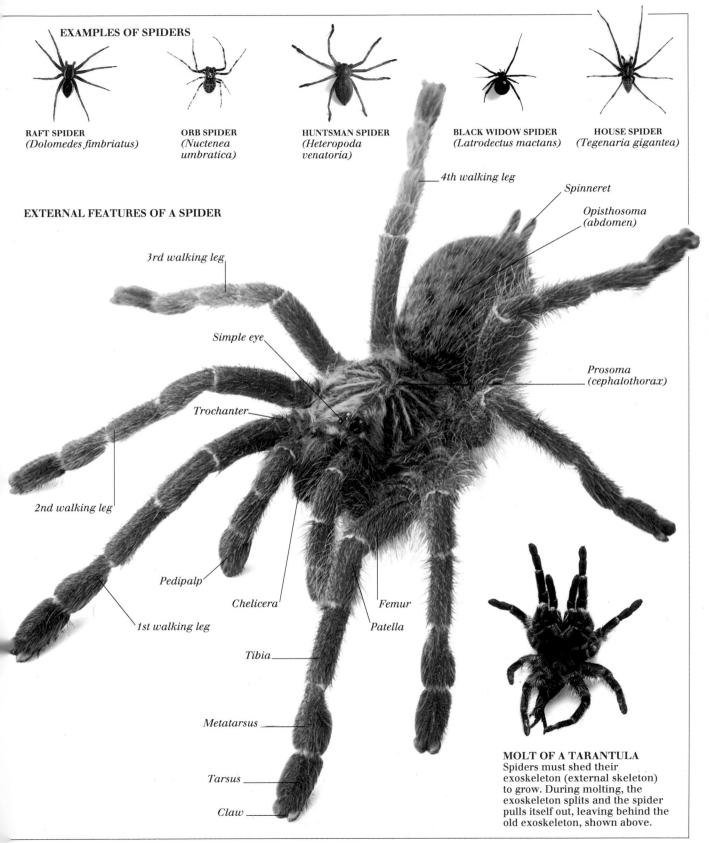

EXAMPLES OF SPIDERS

RAFT SPIDER
(*Dolomedes fimbriatus*)

ORB SPIDER
(*Nuctenea umbratica*)

HUNTSMAN SPIDER
(*Heteropoda venatoria*)

BLACK WIDOW SPIDER
(*Latrodectus mactans*)

HOUSE SPIDER
(*Tegenaria gigantea*)

EXTERNAL FEATURES OF A SPIDER

4th walking leg

Spinneret

Opisthosoma (abdomen)

3rd walking leg

Simple eye

Prosoma (cephalothorax)

Trochanter

2nd walking leg

Pedipalp

Chelicera

Femur

Patella

1st walking leg

Tibia

Metatarsus

Tarsus

Claw

MOLT OF A TARANTULA
Spiders must shed their
exoskeleton (external skeleton)
to grow. During molting, the
exoskeleton splits and the spider
pulls itself out, leaving behind the
old exoskeleton, shown above.

171

Crustaceans

THE SUBPHYLUM CRUSTACEA is one of the largest groups in the phylum Arthropoda. The subphylum is divided into several classes, the most important of which are Malacostraca and Cirripedia. The class Malacostraca includes crayfish, crabs, lobsters, and shrimps. Typical features of malacostracans include a body divided into two sections (a combined head and thorax called a cephalothorax, and an abdomen); an exoskeleton (external skeleton) with a large plate (carapace) covering the cephalothorax; stalked, compound eyes; and two pairs of antennae. The class Cirripedia includes barnacles, which, unlike other crustaceans, spend their adult lives attached to a surface, such as a rock. Other characteristics of cirripedes include an exoskeleton of overlapping calcareous plates; a body consisting almost entirely of thorax (the abdomen and head are minute); and six pairs of thoracic appendages (cirri) used for filter feeding.

1st swimmeret (1st pleopod)

2nd swimmeret (2nd pleopod)

3rd swimmeret (3rd pleopod)

4th swimmeret (4th pleopod)

5th swimmeret (5th pleopod)

Telson

Abdomen

Endopod

Exopod

Uropod

Abdominal segment

3rd leg (3rd pereopod)

5th leg (5th pereopod)

4th leg (4th pereopod)

2nd leg (2nd pereopod)

EXTERNAL FEATURES OF A CRAB

Propodus

Carpus

Dactylus

Compound eye

Antenna

Cheliped (chela; claw; 1st leg; 1st pereopod)

Carapace (shell)

Merus

Abdomen

2nd leg (2nd pereopod)

3rd leg (3rd pereopod)

4th leg (4th pereopod)

5th leg (5th pereopod)

EXTERNAL FEATURES OF A SHRIMP

Compound eye

Cephalothorax

Abdomen

Antenna

Leg (pereopod)

Swimmeret (pleopod)

Uropod

Exopod

Endopod

Telson

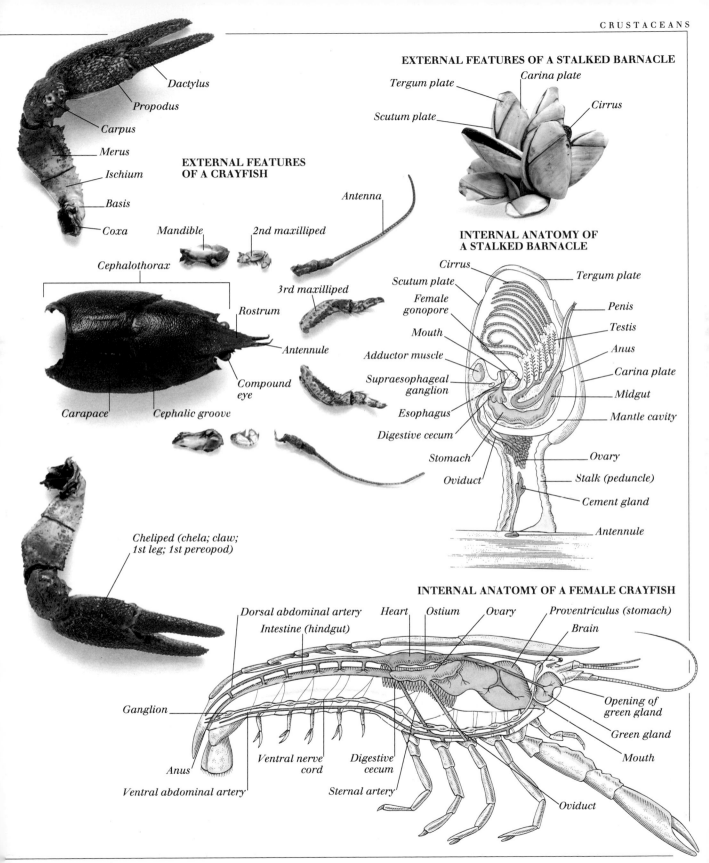

EXTERNAL FEATURES OF A STALKED BARNACLE

Tergum plate
Carina plate
Scutum plate
Cirrus

Dactylus
Propodus
Carpus
Merus
Ischium
Basis
Coxa

EXTERNAL FEATURES OF A CRAYFISH

Mandible
2nd maxilliped
Antenna

Cephalothorax
3rd maxilliped
Rostrum
Antennule
Compound eye

Carapace
Cephalic groove

INTERNAL ANATOMY OF A STALKED BARNACLE

Cirrus
Scutum plate
Female gonopore
Mouth
Adductor muscle
Supraesophageal ganglion
Esophagus
Digestive cecum
Stomach
Oviduct

Tergum plate
Penis
Testis
Anus
Carina plate
Midgut
Mantle cavity
Ovary
Stalk (peduncle)
Cement gland
Antennule

Cheliped (chela; claw; 1st leg; 1st pereopod)

INTERNAL ANATOMY OF A FEMALE CRAYFISH

Dorsal abdominal artery
Heart
Ostium
Ovary
Proventriculus (stomach)
Intestine (hindgut)
Brain

Ganglion
Opening of green gland
Green gland
Mouth

Anus
Ventral nerve cord
Digestive cecum
Ventral abdominal artery
Sternal artery
Oviduct

Starfish and sea urchins

STARFISH, SEA URCHINS, AND THEIR relatives (including feather stars, brittle stars, basket stars, sea daisies, sea lilies, and sea cucumbers) make up the phylum Echinodermata. A unique feature of echinoderms is the water vascular system, which consists of a series of water-filled canals from which protrude thousands of tiny tube feet. The tube feet may be used for movement, feeding, or respiration. Other features include pentaradiate symmetry (that is, the body can be divided into five parts radiating from the center); no head; a diffuse, decentralized nervous system that lacks a brain; and no excretory organs. Typically, echinoderms also have an endoskeleton (internal skeleton) consisting of hard calcite ossicles embedded in the body wall and often bearing protruding spines or tubercles. The ossicles may fit together to form a test (as in sea urchins) or remain separate (as in sea cucumbers).

EXTERNAL FEATURES OF A STARFISH (UPPER, OR ABORAL, SURFACE)

Disk

Madreporite

Spine

Arm

INTERNAL ANATOMY OF A STARFISH

Rectum

Pyloric stomach

Madreporite

Stone canal

Anus

Rectal cecum

Tube foot

Ring canal

Lateral canal

Radial canal

Ampulla

Cardiac stomach

Pyloric duct

Pyloric cecum

Mouth

Esophagus

Gonad

Gonopore

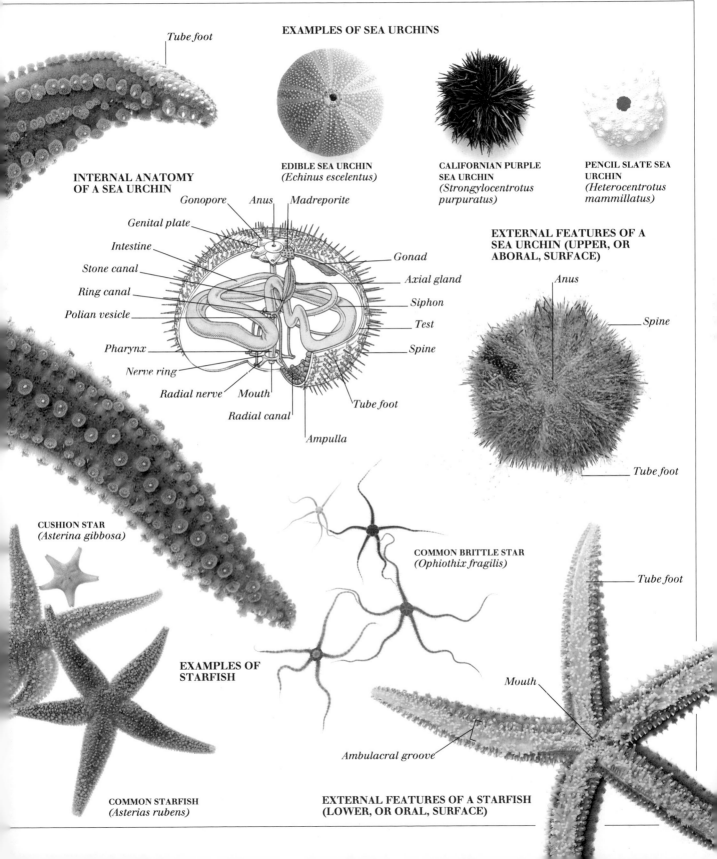

Tube foot

EXAMPLES OF SEA URCHINS

EDIBLE SEA URCHIN
(*Echinus escelentus*)

CALIFORNIAN PURPLE
SEA URCHIN
(*Strongylocentrotus
purpuratus*)

PENCIL SLATE SEA
URCHIN
(*Heterocentrotus
mammillatus*)

**INTERNAL ANATOMY
OF A SEA URCHIN**

Gonopore   *Anus*   *Madreporite*

Genital plate

Intestine

Stone canal

Ring canal

Polian vesicle

Pharynx

Nerve ring

Radial nerve   *Mouth*

Radial canal

Ampulla

Gonad

Axial gland

Siphon

Test

Spine

Tube foot

**EXTERNAL FEATURES OF A
SEA URCHIN (UPPER, OR
ABORAL, SURFACE)**

Anus

Spine

Tube foot

CUSHION STAR
(*Asterina gibbosa*)

COMMON BRITTLE STAR
(*Ophiothix fragilis*)

Tube foot

**EXAMPLES OF
STARFISH**

Mouth

Ambulacral groove

COMMON STARFISH
(*Asterias rubens*)

**EXTERNAL FEATURES OF A STARFISH
(LOWER, OR ORAL, SURFACE)**

Mollusks

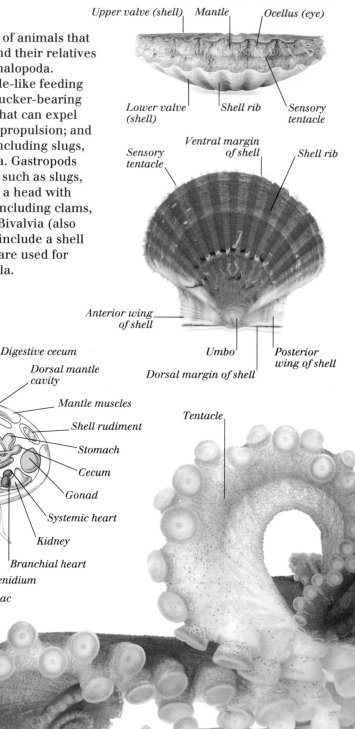

Upper valve (shell)   Mantle   Ocellus (eye)

Lower valve (shell)   Shell rib   Sensory tentacle

Sensory tentacle   Ventral margin of shell   Shell rib

Anterior wing of shell

Umbo   Posterior wing of shell

Dorsal margin of shell

THE PHYLUM MOLLUSCA (MOLLUSKS) is a large group of animals that includes octopuses, snails, and scallops. Octopuses and their relatives —including squid and cuttlefish—form the class Cephalopoda. Cephalopods typically have a head with a radula (a file-like feeding organ) and beak; a well-developed nervous system; sucker-bearing tentacles; a muscular mantle (part of the body wall) that can expel water through the siphon, enabling movement by jet propulsion; and a small shell or no shell. Snails and their relatives—including slugs, limpets, and abalones—make up the class Gastropoda. Gastropods typically have a coiled external shell, although some, such as slugs, have a small internal shell or no shell; a flat foot; and a head with tentacles and a radula. Scallops and their relatives—including clams, mussels, and oysters—make up the class Bivalvia (also called Pelecypoda). Features of bivalves include a shell with two halves (valves); large gills that are used for breathing and filter feeding; and no radula.

INTERNAL ANATOMY OF AN OCTOPUS

Cephalic vein

Skull

Brain

Siphon (funnel)

Buccal mass

Beak

Poison gland

Crop

Digestive cecum

Dorsal mantle cavity

Mantle muscles

Shell rudiment

Stomach

Cecum

Gonad

Systemic heart

Kidney

Branchial heart

Ctenidium

Ink sac

Anus

Muscular septum

Tentacle

Sucker

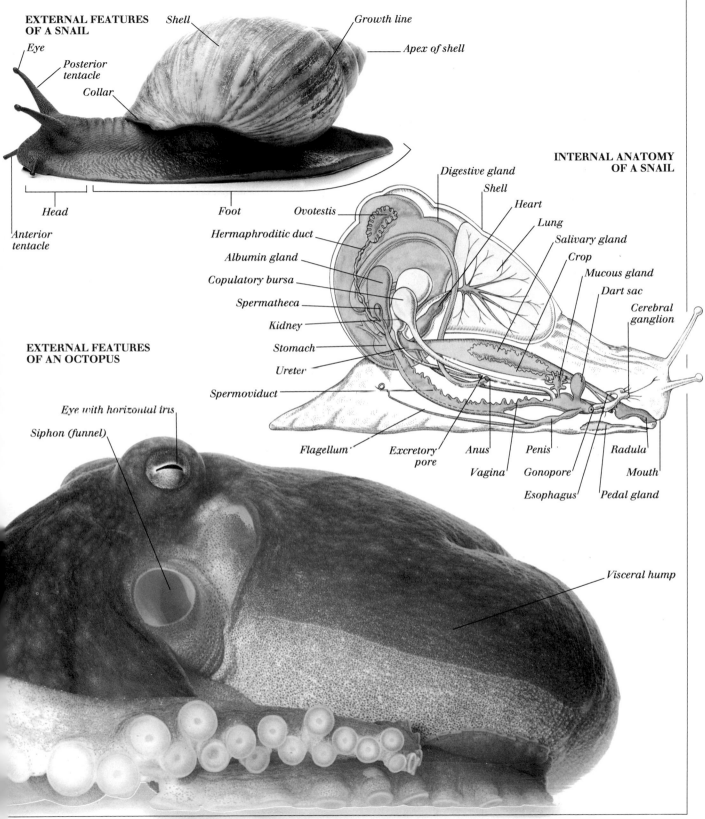

EXTERNAL FEATURES OF A SNAIL

Eye

Posterior tentacle

Collar

Shell

Growth line

Apex of shell

Head

Anterior tentacle

Foot

INTERNAL ANATOMY OF A SNAIL

Digestive gland

Shell

Heart

Lung

Salivary gland

Crop

Mucous gland

Dart sac

Cerebral ganglion

Ovotestis

Hermaphroditic duct

Albumin gland

Copulatory bursa

Spermatheca

Kidney

Stomach

Ureter

Spermoviduct

Flagellum

Excretory pore

Anus

Vagina

Penis

Gonopore

Esophagus

Radula

Mouth

Pedal gland

EXTERNAL FEATURES OF AN OCTOPUS

Eye with horizontal iris

Siphon (funnel)

Visceral hump

Sharks and jawless fish

SHARKS, DOGFISH (WHICH ARE actually small sharks), skates, and rays belong to a class of fish called Chondrichthyes, which is a division of the superclass Gnathostomata (meaning "jawed mouths"). Also sometimes known as elasmobranchs, sharks and their relatives have a skeleton made of cartilage (hence their common name, cartilaginous fish), a characteristic that distinguishes them from bony fish (see pp. 180-181). Other important features of cartilaginous fish are extremely tough, tooth-like scales, and lack of a swim bladder. Jawless fish—lampreys and hagfish—are primitive, eel-like fish that make up the order Cyclostomata (meaning "round mouths"), a division of the superclass Agnatha (meaning "without jaws"). In addition to their characteristic round, sucker-like mouths and lack of jaws, cyclostomes also have smooth, slimy skin without scales, and unpaired fins.

SHARKS' JAWS

Jaws of an adult tiger shark

Jaws of a young tiger shark

EXTERNAL FEATURES OF A DOGFISH

Snout

Eye

Gill slit

Pectoral fin

Anterior dorsal fin

Posterior dorsal fin

FEATURES OF A LAMPREY'S HEAD

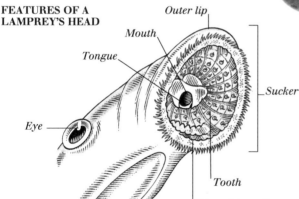

Outer lip

Mouth

Tongue

Sucker

Eye

Tooth

Fringed inner lip

EXTERNAL FEATURES OF A LAMPREY

Eye

Gill opening

Sucker

Anal fin

Caudal fin

EXAMPLES OF CARTILAGINOUS FISH

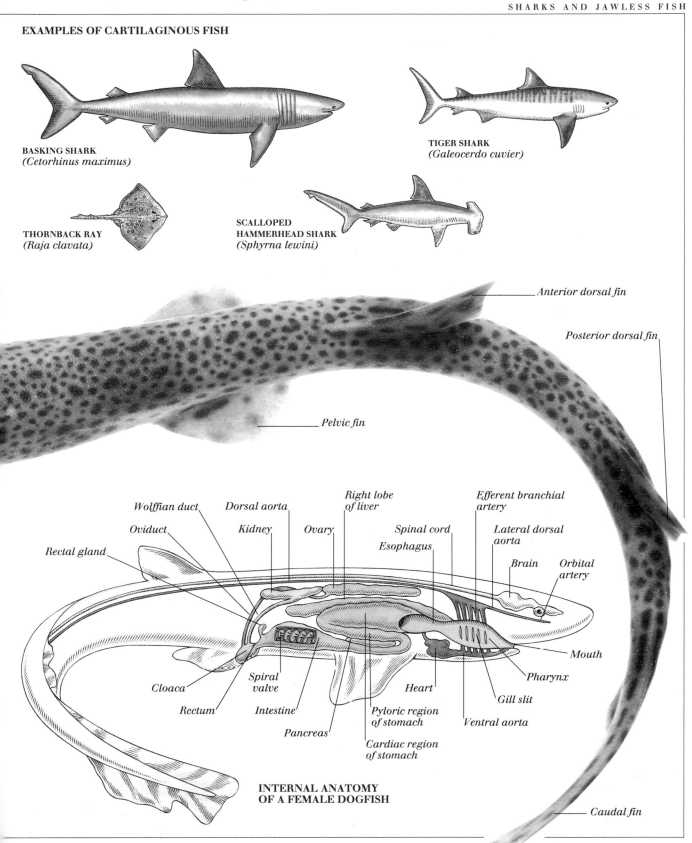

BASKING SHARK
(Cetorhinus maximus)

TIGER SHARK
(Galeocerdo cuvier)

THORNBACK RAY
(Raja clavata)

**SCALLOPED
HAMMERHEAD SHARK**
(Sphyrna lewini)

Anterior dorsal fin

Posterior dorsal fin

Pelvic fin

Wolffian duct

Dorsal aorta

*Right lobe
of liver*

*Efferent branchial
artery*

Oviduct

Kidney

Ovary

Spinal cord

*Lateral dorsal
aorta*

Rectal gland

Esophagus

Brain

*Orbital
artery*

Cloaca

*Spiral
valve*

Rectum

Intestine

Pancreas

*Cardiac region
of stomach*

*Pyloric region
of stomach*

Heart

Pharynx

Gill slit

Ventral aorta

Mouth

**INTERNAL ANATOMY
OF A FEMALE DOGFISH**

Caudal fin

179

Bony fish

BONY FISH, SUCH AS CARP, TROUT, SALMON, perch, and cod, are by far the best known and largest group of fish, with more than 20,000 species (over 95 percent of all known fish). As their name suggests, bony fish have skeletons made of bone, in contrast to the cartilaginous skeletons of sharks, jawless fish, and their relatives (see pp. 178-179). Other typical features of bony fish include a swim bladder, which functions as a variable-buoyancy organ, enabling a fish to remain effortlessly at whatever depth it is swimming; relatively thin, bone-like scales; a flap (called an operculum) covering the gills; and paired pelvic and pectoral fins. Scientifically, bony fish belong to the class Osteichthyes, which is a division of the superclass Gnathostomata (meaning "jawed mouths").

HOW FISH BREATHE

Fish "breathe" by extracting oxygen from water through their gills. Water is sucked in through the mouth; simultaneously, the opercula close to prevent the water from escaping. The mouth is then closed, and muscles in the walls of the mouth, pharynx, and opercular cavity contract to pump the water inside over the gills and out through the opercula. Some fish rely on swimming with their mouths open to keep water flowing over the gills.

Gill raker

Pharynx

Water out

Gill slit

Mouth

Water in

Gill filament

Operculum

EXAMPLES OF BONY FISH

MANDARINFISH
(Synchiropus splendidus)

ANGLERFISH
(Caulophryne jordani)

OCEANIC SEAHORSE
(Hippocampus kuda)

LIONFISH
(Pterois volitans)

STURGEON
(Acipenser sturio)

SNOWFLAKE MORAY EEL
(Echidna nebulosa)

Vertebra

Neural spine

Hypural

Hemal spine

Caudal fin ray

Anal fin ray

Radial cartilage

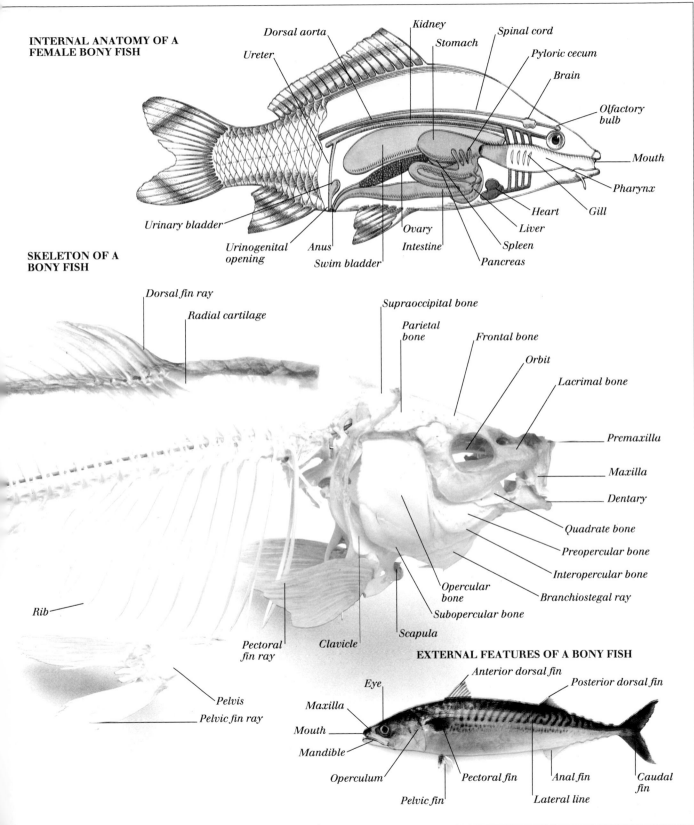

INTERNAL ANATOMY OF A FEMALE BONY FISH

Dorsal aorta

Ureter

Kidney

Stomach

Spinal cord

Pyloric cecum

Brain

Olfactory bulb

Mouth

Pharynx

Gill

Heart

Liver

Spleen

Pancreas

Ovary

Intestine

Swim bladder

Anus

Urinogenital opening

Urinary bladder

SKELETON OF A BONY FISH

Dorsal fin ray

Radial cartilage

Supraoccipital bone

Parietal bone

Frontal bone

Orbit

Lacrimal bone

Premaxilla

Maxilla

Dentary

Quadrate bone

Preopercular bone

Interopercular bone

Branchiostegal ray

Subopercular bone

Opercular bone

Scapula

Clavicle

Pectoral fin ray

Rib

Pelvis

Pelvic fin ray

EXTERNAL FEATURES OF A BONY FISH

Anterior dorsal fin

Posterior dorsal fin

Eye

Maxilla

Mouth

Mandible

Operculum

Pelvic fin

Pectoral fin

Anal fin

Lateral line

Caudal fin

Amphibians

THE CLASS AMPHIBIA INCLUDES FROGS and toads (which make up the order Anura) and newts and salamanders (which make up the order Urodela). Amphibians typically have moist, scaleless, hairless skin; lungs; and are cold-blooded. They also undergo complete metamorphosis, from eggs laid in water through various water-living larval stages (such as the tadpole stage) to land-living adults. Typical features of adult frogs and toads include a squat body with no tail; long, powerful hind legs; and large, often bulging, eyes. Adult newts and salamanders typically have a long body with a well-developed tail; and relatively short legs of equal size. However, newts and salamanders show considerable variation; for example, in some species the adults have minute legs, external gills rather than lungs, and spend their entire lives in water.

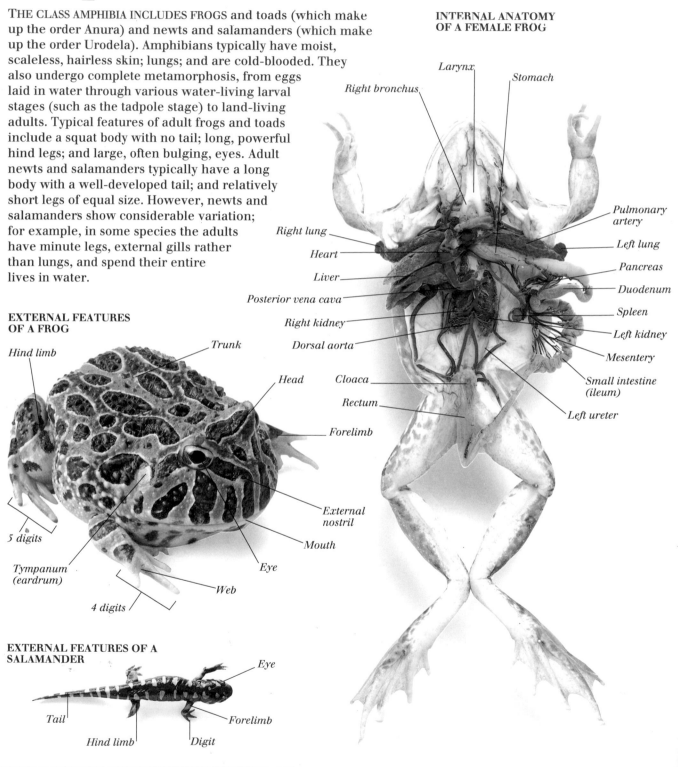

INTERNAL ANATOMY OF A FEMALE FROG

Larynx

Right bronchus

Stomach

Pulmonary artery

Right lung

Left lung

Heart

Pancreas

Liver

Duodenum

Posterior vena cava

Spleen

Right kidney

Left kidney

Dorsal aorta

Mesentery

Cloaca

Small intestine (ileum)

Rectum

Left ureter

EXTERNAL FEATURES OF A FROG

Hind limb

Trunk

Head

Forelimb

5 digits

External nostril

Tympanum (eardrum)

Mouth

Web

Eye

4 digits

EXTERNAL FEATURES OF A SALAMANDER

Eye

Tail

Forelimb

Hind limb

Digit

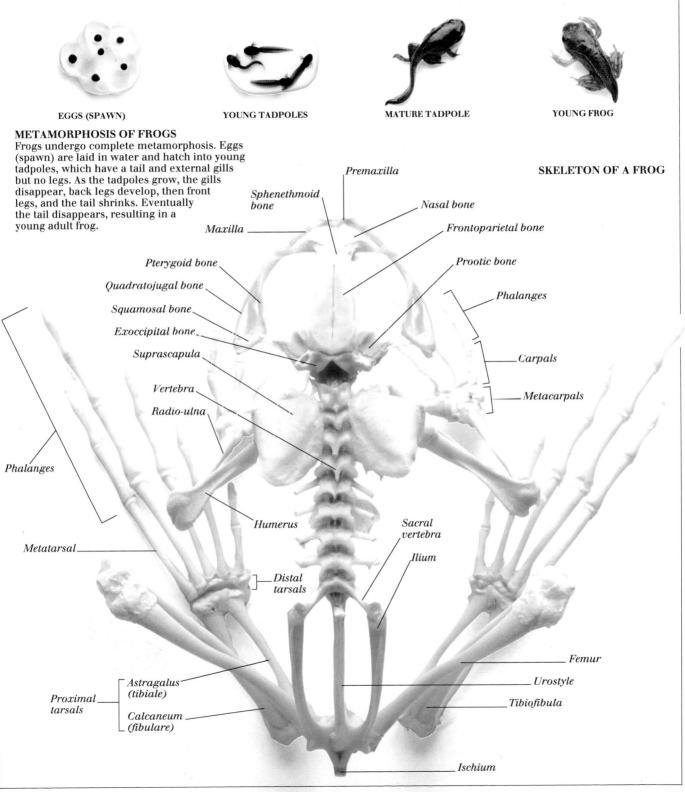

EGGS (SPAWN)   **YOUNG TADPOLES**   **MATURE TADPOLE**   **YOUNG FROG**

METAMORPHOSIS OF FROGS
Frogs undergo complete metamorphosis. Eggs (spawn) are laid in water and hatch into young tadpoles, which have a tail and external gills but no legs. As the tadpoles grow, the gills disappear, back legs develop, then front legs, and the tail shrinks. Eventually the tail disappears, resulting in a young adult frog.

SKELETON OF A FROG

Premaxilla

Sphenethmoid bone

Nasal bone

Frontoparietal bone

Maxilla

Prootic bone

Pterygoid bone

Phalanges

Quadratojugal bone

Squamosal bone

Exoccipital bone

Carpals

Suprascapula

Metacarpals

Vertebra

Radio-ulna

Phalanges

Humerus

Sacral vertebra

Ilium

Metatarsal

Distal tarsals

Femur

Urostyle

Astragalus (tibiale)

Proximal tarsals

Calcaneum (fibulare)

Tibiofibula

Ischium

Lizards and snakes

LIZARDS AND SNAKES BELONG to the order Squamata, a division of the class Reptilia. Characteristic reptilian features include scaly skin, lungs, and cold-bloodedness. Most reptiles lay leathery-shelled eggs, although some hatch the eggs inside their bodies and give birth to live young. Lizards belong to the suborder Lacertilia. Typically, they have long tails, and shed their skin in several pieces. Many lizards can regenerate a tail if it is lost; some can change color; and some are limbless. Snakes make up the suborder Ophidia (also called Serpentes). All snakes have long, limbless bodies; can dislocate their lower jaw to swallow large prey; and have eyelids that are joined together to form a single transparent covering over the front of the eye. Most snakes shed their skin in a single piece. Constrictor snakes kill their prey by squeezing; venomous snakes poison their prey.

EXAMPLES OF SNAKES

MEXICAN
MOUNTAIN
KING SNAKE
(*Lampropeltis triangulum annulata*)

EXTERNAL FEATURES OF A LIZARD

BANDED MILK
SNAKE
(*Lampropeltis ruthveni*)

SKELETON OF A LIZARD

Skull
Orbit
Scapula
Cervical vertebrae
Phalanges
Carpals
Metacarpal
Ulna
Humerus
Radius
Rib
Thoracolumbar vertebrae
Pelvis
Femur
Sacrum
Tibia
Fibula
Tarsals
Metatarsal
Caudal vertebrae
Phalanges
Toe
Claw

Eye
Mouth
External nostril
Crest
Eardrum
Masseteric scale
Dorsal scale
Dewlap
Foreleg
Belly
Ventral scale

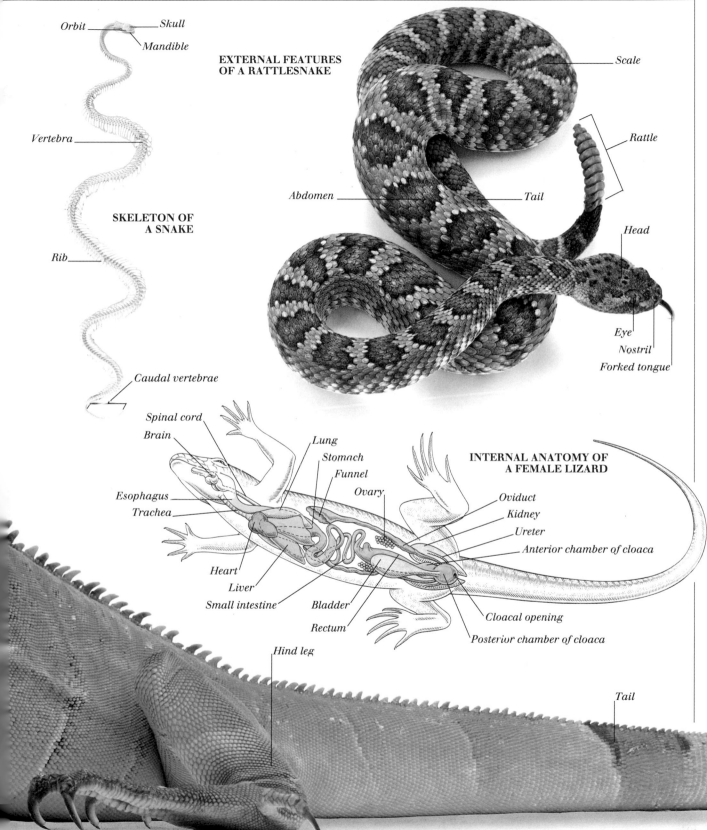

Orbit

Skull

Mandible

**EXTERNAL FEATURES
OF A RATTLESNAKE**

Scale

Vertebra

Rattle

**SKELETON OF
A SNAKE**

Abdomen

Tail

Head

Rib

Eye

Nostril

Forked tongue

Caudal vertebrae

Spinal cord

Brain

Lung

Stomach

**INTERNAL ANATOMY OF
A FEMALE LIZARD**

Funnel

Esophagus

Ovary

Oviduct

Trachea

Kidney

Ureter

Anterior chamber of cloaca

Heart

Liver

Bladder

Small intestine

Cloacal opening

Rectum

Posterior chamber of cloaca

Hind leg

Tail

185

Crocodilians and turtles

GHARIAL
(Gavialis gangeticus)

NILE CROCODILE
(Crocodylus niloticus)

MISSISSIPPI ALLIGATOR
(Alligator mississippiensis)

CROCODILIANS AND TURTLES BELONG to different orders in the class Reptilia. The order Crocodilia includes crocodiles, alligators, caimans, and gharials. Typically, crocodilians are carnivores (flesh-eaters), and have a long snout, sharp teeth for gripping prey, and hard, square scales. All crocodilians are adapted to living on land and in water: they have four strong legs for moving on land; a powerful tail for swimming; and their eyes and nostrils are high on the head so that they stay above water while the rest of the body is submerged. The order Chelonia includes marine turtles, freshwater turtles (terrapins), and land turtles (tortoises). Characteristically, chelonians have a short, broad body encased in a bony shell with an outer horny covering, into which the head and limbs can be withdrawn; and a horny beak instead of teeth.

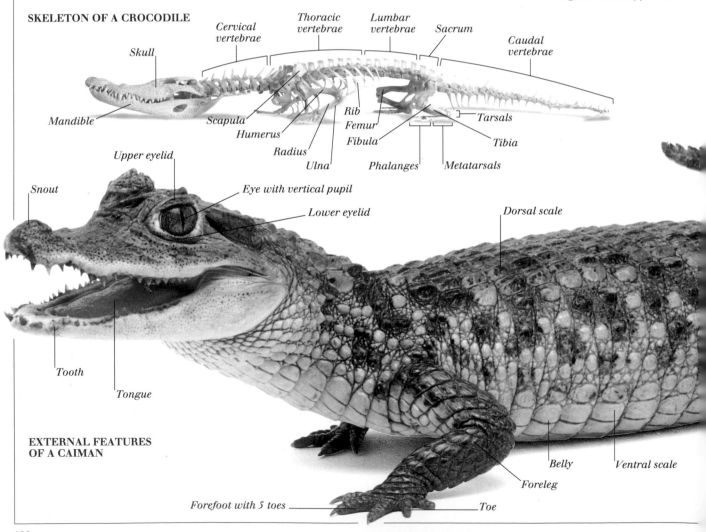

SKELETON OF A CROCODILE

Skull · Cervical vertebrae · Thoracic vertebrae · Lumbar vertebrae · Sacrum · Caudal vertebrae

Mandible · Scapula · Humerus · Radius · Ulna · Rib · Femur · Fibula · Phalanges · Metatarsals · Tarsals · Tibia

Snout · Upper eyelid · Eye with vertical pupil · Lower eyelid · Dorsal scale

Tooth · Tongue

EXTERNAL FEATURES OF A CAIMAN

Forefoot with 5 toes · Toe · Foreleg · Belly · Ventral scale

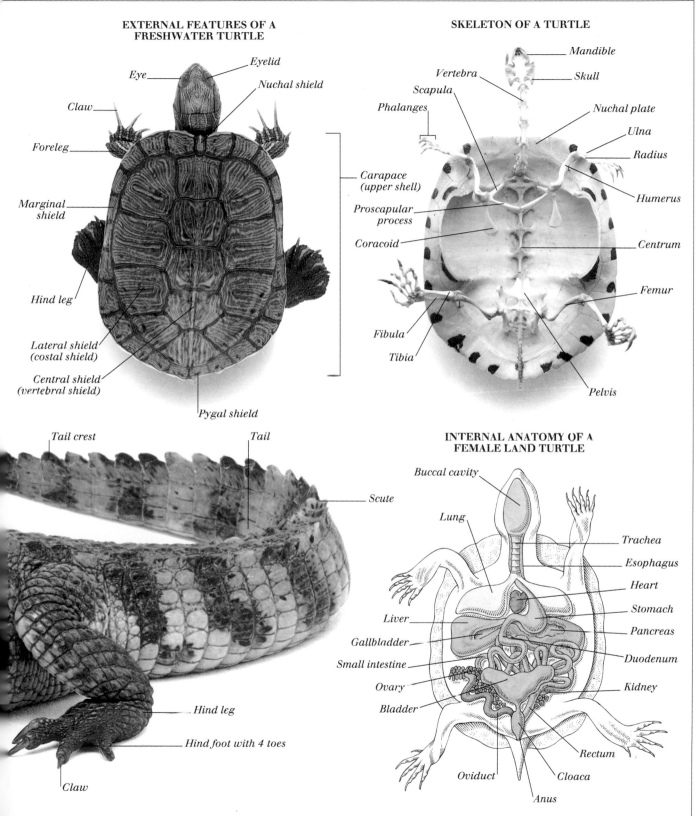

**EXTERNAL FEATURES OF A
FRESHWATER TURTLE**

Eye

Eyelid

Claw

Nuchal shield

Foreleg

Marginal
shield

Hind leg

Lateral shield
(costal shield)

Central shield
(vertebral shield)

Pygal shield

Carapace
(upper shell)

Proscapular
process

Coracoid

SKELETON OF A TURTLE

Mandible

Vertebra

Skull

Scapula

Phalanges

Nuchal plate

Ulna

Radius

Humerus

Centrum

Femur

Fibula

Tibia

Pelvis

Tail crest

Tail

Scute

Hind leg

Hind foot with 4 toes

Claw

**INTERNAL ANATOMY OF A
FEMALE LAND TURTLE**

Buccal cavity

Lung

Trachea

Esophagus

Heart

Stomach

Pancreas

Liver

Gallbladder

Duodenum

Small intestine

Kidney

Ovary

Bladder

Rectum

Oviduct

Cloaca

Anus

187

Birds 1

BIRDS MAKE UP THE CLASS AVES. There are more than 9,000 species, almost all of which can fly (the only flightless birds are penguins, ostriches, rheas, cassowaries, and kiwis). The ability to fly is reflected in the typical bird features: forelimbs modified as wings, a streamlined body, and hollow bones to reduce weight. All birds lay hard-shelled eggs, which the parents incubate. Birds' beaks and feet vary according to diet and way of life. Beaks range from general purpose types suitable for a mixed diet (those of thrushes, for example), to types specialized for particular foods (such as the large, curved, sieving beaks of flamingos). Feet range from the webbed "paddles" of ducks, to the talons of birds of prey. Plumage also varies widely, and in many species the male is brightly colored for courtship display whereas the female is drab.

EXTERNAL FEATURES OF A BIRD

Forehead
Eye
Crown
Nostril
Nape
Upper mandible
Beak
Lower mandible
Chin
Throat

EXAMPLES OF BIRDS

MALE TUFTED DUCK
(Aythya fuligula)

WHITE STORK
(Ciconia ciconia)

MALE OSTRICH
(Struthio camelus)

Minor coverts
Lesser wing coverts
Median wing coverts

Greater wing coverts (major coverts)

Secondary flight feathers (secondary remiges)

Primary flight feathers (primary remiges)

Breast
Belly
Flank
Thigh
Claw
Toe
Under tail coverts
Tarsus
Tail feathers (retrices)

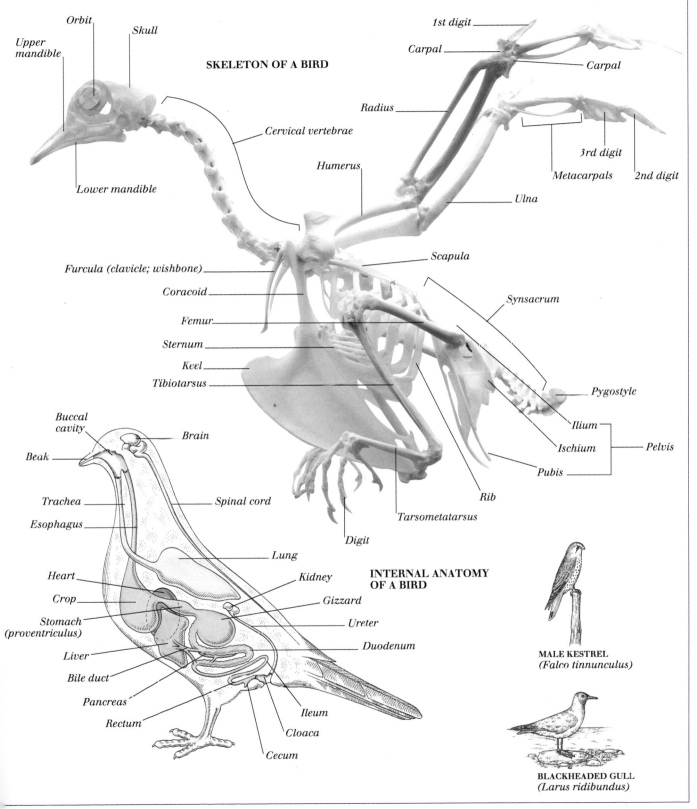

SKELETON OF A BIRD

Orbit

Skull

Upper mandible

Lower mandible

Cervical vertebrae

1st digit

Carpal

Carpal

Radius

3rd digit

Metacarpals

2nd digit

Humerus

Ulna

Scapula

Furcula (clavicle; wishbone)

Coracoid

Synsacrum

Femur

Sternum

Keel

Tibiotarsus

Pygostyle

Ilium

Ischium

Pelvis

Pubis

Rib

Tarsometatarsus

Digit

INTERNAL ANATOMY OF A BIRD

Buccal cavity

Brain

Beak

Spinal cord

Trachea

Esophagus

Lung

Heart

Kidney

Crop

Gizzard

Stomach (proventriculus)

Ureter

Duodenum

Liver

Bile duct

Pancreas

Ileum

Rectum

Cloaca

Cecum

MALE KESTREL
(Falco tinnunculus)

BLACKHEADED GULL
(Larus ridibundus)

189

Birds 2

EXAMPLES OF BIRDS' FEET

KITTIWAKE
(Rissa tridactyla)
The webbed feet are
adapted for paddling
through water.

LITTLE GREBE
(Tachybaptus ruficollis)
The lobed, flattened feet
are adapted for swimming
underwater.

TAWNY OWL
(Strix aluco)
The clawed feet are adapted
for gripping prey.

EXAMPLES OF BIRDS' BEAKS

KING VULTURE
(Sarcorhamphus papa)
The hooked beak is adapted
for pulling apart flesh.

GREATER FLAMINGO
(Phoenicopterus ruber)
In the living bird, the large,
curved beak contains a
cartilaginous "sieve" for
filtering food particles
from water.

MAVIS, OR MISTLE THRUSH
(Turdus viscivorus)
The all-purpose beak is suitable
for gathering a wide range of
animal and plant foods.

BLUE-AND-YELLOW MACAW
(Ara ararauna)
The broad, powerful, hooked beak
is adapted for crushing seeds and
eating fruit.

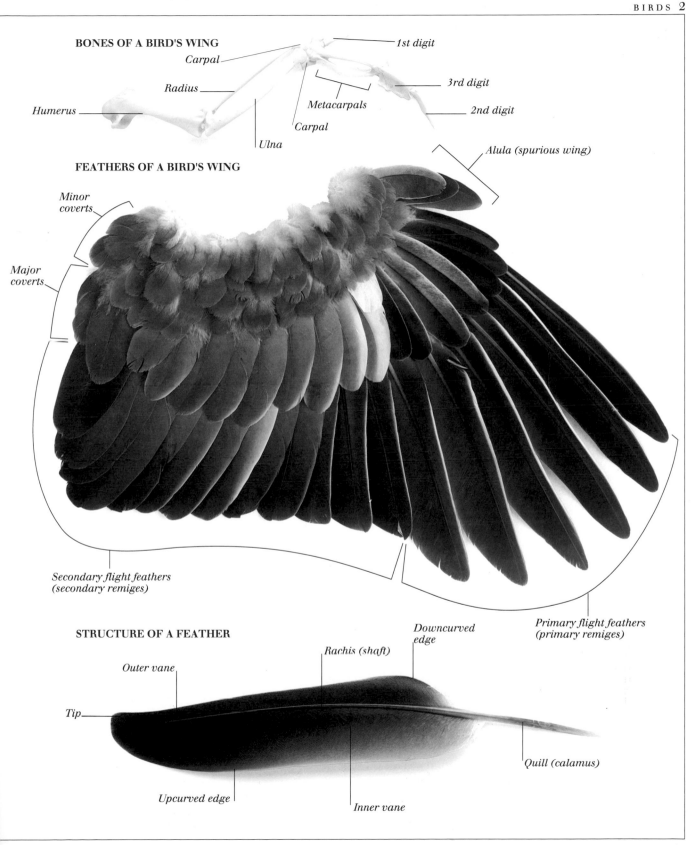

BONES OF A BIRD'S WING

1st digit

Carpal

Radius

3rd digit

Humerus

Metacarpals

Carpal

2nd digit

Ulna

Alula (spurious wing)

FEATHERS OF A BIRD'S WING

Minor coverts

Major coverts

Secondary flight feathers (secondary remiges)

Primary flight feathers (primary remiges)

STRUCTURE OF A FEATHER

Downcurved edge

Rachis (shaft)

Outer vane

Tip

Quill (calamus)

Upcurved edge

Inner vane

Eggs

AN EGG IS A SINGLE CELL, produced by the female, with the capacity to develop into a new individual. Development may take place inside the mother's body (as in most mammals) or outside, in which case the egg has a protective covering such as a shell. Egg yolk nourishes the growing young. Eggs developing inside the mother generally have little yolk, because the young are nourished from her body. Eggs developing outside may also have little yolk if they are produced by animals whose young go through a larval stage (such as a caterpillar) that feeds itself while developing into the adult form. The shelled eggs of birds and reptiles contain enough yolk to sustain the young until it hatches into a juvenile version of the adult.

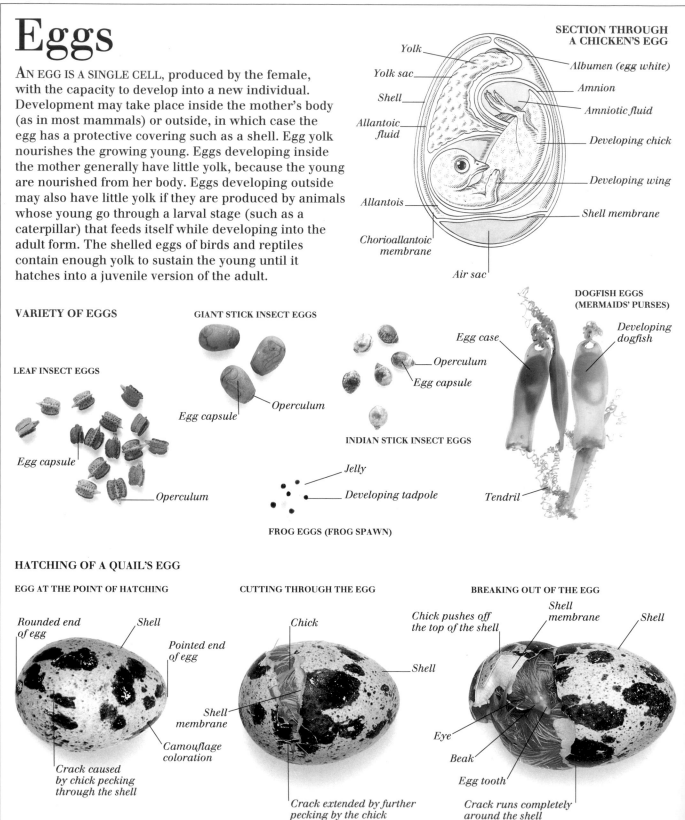

SECTION THROUGH A CHICKEN'S EGG

Yolk
Yolk sac
Shell
Allantoic fluid
Allantois
Chorioallantoic membrane
Air sac
Albumen (egg white)
Amnion
Amniotic fluid
Developing chick
Developing wing
Shell membrane

VARIETY OF EGGS

GIANT STICK INSECT EGGS

LEAF INSECT EGGS

Egg capsule
Operculum

Egg capsule
Operculum

Operculum
Egg capsule

INDIAN STICK INSECT EGGS

DOGFISH EGGS (MERMAIDS' PURSES)

Egg case
Developing dogfish
Tendril

Jelly
Developing tadpole

FROG EGGS (FROG SPAWN)

HATCHING OF A QUAIL'S EGG

EGG AT THE POINT OF HATCHING

Rounded end of egg
Shell
Pointed end of egg
Camouflage coloration
Crack caused by chick pecking through the shell

CUTTING THROUGH THE EGG

Chick
Shell
Shell membrane
Crack extended by further pecking by the chick

BREAKING OUT OF THE EGG

Chick pushes off the top of the shell
Shell membrane
Shell
Eye
Beak
Egg tooth
Crack runs completely around the shell

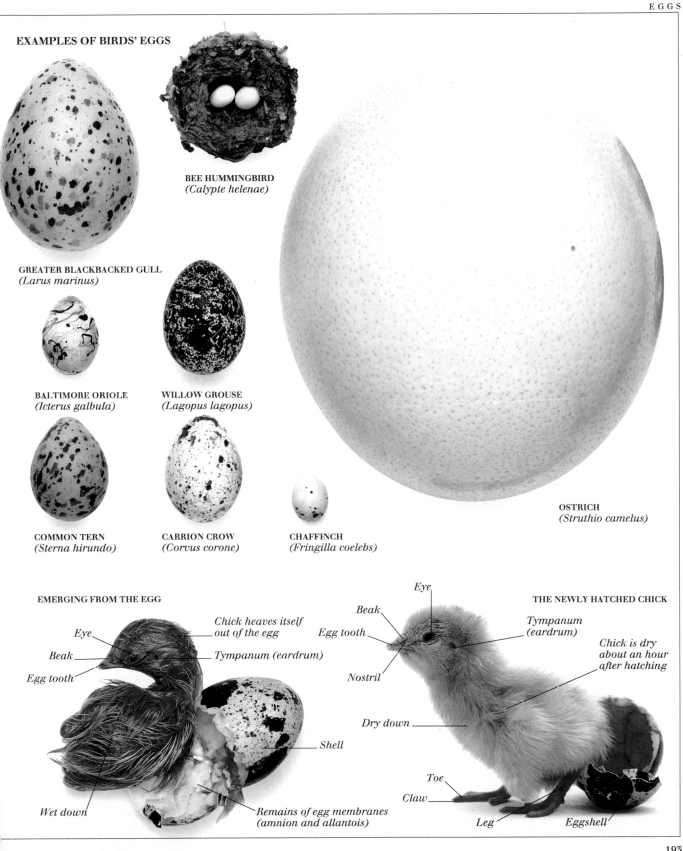

EXAMPLES OF BIRDS' EGGS

BEE HUMMINGBIRD
(Calypte helenae)

GREATER BLACKBACKED GULL
(Larus marinus)

BALTIMORE ORIOLE
(Icterus galbula)

WILLOW GROUSE
(Lagopus lagopus)

COMMON TERN
(Sterna hirundo)

CARRION CROW
(Corvus corone)

CHAFFINCH
(Fringilla coelebs)

OSTRICH
(Struthio camelus)

EMERGING FROM THE EGG

Eye
Beak
Egg tooth
Chick heaves itself out of the egg
Tympanum (eardrum)
Shell
Wet down
Remains of egg membranes (amnion and allantois)

THE NEWLY HATCHED CHICK

Eye
Beak
Egg tooth
Nostril
Tympanum (eardrum)
Chick is dry about an hour after hatching
Dry down
Toe
Claw
Leg
Eggshell

193

Carnivores

THE MAMMALIAN ORDER CARNIVORA includes cats, dogs, bears, raccoons, pandas, weasels, badgers, skunks, otters, civets, mongooses, and hyenas. The order's name is derived from the fact that most of its members are carnivores (flesh-eaters). Typical carnivore features therefore reflect a hunting lifestyle: speed and agility; sharp claws and well-developed canine teeth for holding and killing prey; carnassial teeth (cheek teeth) for cutting flesh; and forward-facing eyes for good distance judgment. However, some members of the order—bears, badgers, and foxes, for example—have a more mixed diet, and a few are entirely herbivorous (plant-eating), notably pandas. Such animals have no carnassial teeth and tend to be slower-moving than pure flesh-eaters.

EXTERNAL FEATURES OF A MALE LION

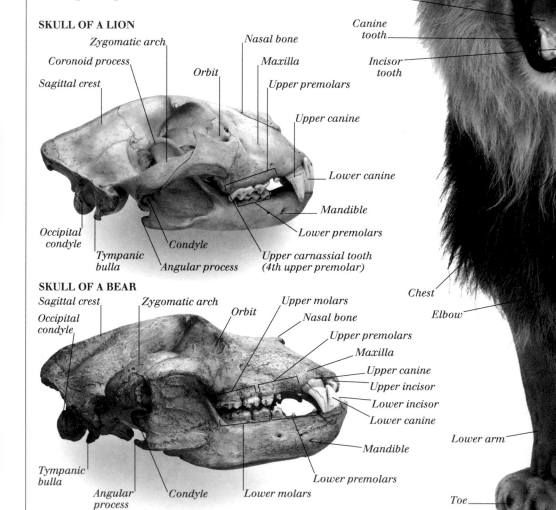

Nose

Eye

Mane

Nostril

Vibrissa (whisker)

Tongue

Canine tooth

Incisor tooth

Chest

Elbow

Lower arm

Toe

SKULL OF A LION

Zygomatic arch

Coronoid process

Sagittal crest

Orbit

Nasal bone

Maxilla

Upper premolars

Upper canine

Lower canine

Mandible

Lower premolars

Occipital condyle

Tympanic bulla

Condyle

Angular process

Upper carnassial tooth (4th upper premolar)

SKULL OF A BEAR

Sagittal crest

Occipital condyle

Zygomatic arch

Orbit

Upper molars

Nasal bone

Upper premolars

Maxilla

Upper canine

Upper incisor

Lower incisor

Lower canine

Mandible

Tympanic bulla

Angular process

Condyle

Lower molars

Lower premolars

EXAMPLES OF CARNIVORES

GERMAN SHEPHERD DOG
(Canis familiaris)

MANED WOLF
(Chrysocyon brachyurus)

RACCOON
(Procyon lotor)

AMERICAN BLACK BEAR
(Ursus americanus)

SKELETON OF A DOMESTIC CAT

Back
Rump
Hip
Rib cage
Belly
Thigh
Knee
Hock
Paw
Tail

Caudal vertebrae
Sacrum
Lumbar vertebrae
Thoracic vertebrae
Cervical vertebrae
Skull
Pelvis
Femur
Patella
Fibula
Tibia
Metatarsals
Tarsals
Phalanges
Rib
Ulna
Radius
Scapula
Sternum
Humerus
Carpals
Metacarpals

INTERNAL ANATOMY OF A MALE DOMESTIC CAT

Brain
Spinal cord
Diaphragm
Stomach
Liver
Kidney
Ureter
Large intestine
Small intestine
Anus
Testis
Nasal cavity
Buccal cavity
Nostril
Tongue
Trachea
Esophagus
Lung
Hock
Paw
Tail
Heart
Gallbladder
Pancreas
Spleen
Bladder
Urethra
Vas deferens (sperm duct)

195

Rabbits and rodents

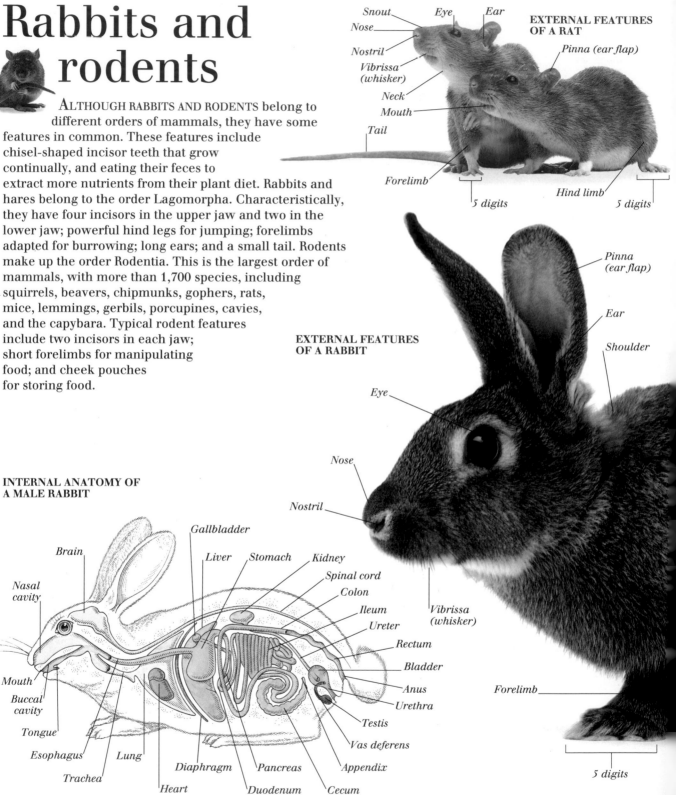

ALTHOUGH RABBITS AND RODENTS belong to different orders of mammals, they have some features in common. These features include chisel-shaped incisor teeth that grow continually, and eating their feces to extract more nutrients from their plant diet. Rabbits and hares belong to the order Lagomorpha. Characteristically, they have four incisors in the upper jaw and two in the lower jaw; powerful hind legs for jumping; forelimbs adapted for burrowing; long ears; and a small tail. Rodents make up the order Rodentia. This is the largest order of mammals, with more than 1,700 species, including squirrels, beavers, chipmunks, gophers, rats, mice, lemmings, gerbils, porcupines, cavies, and the capybara. Typical rodent features include two incisors in each jaw; short forelimbs for manipulating food; and cheek pouches for storing food.

EXTERNAL FEATURES OF A RAT

Snout
Eye
Ear
Nose
Pinna (ear flap)
Nostril
Vibrissa (whisker)
Neck
Mouth
Tail
Forelimb
5 digits
Hind limb
5 digits

EXTERNAL FEATURES OF A RABBIT

Pinna (ear flap)
Ear
Shoulder
Eye
Nose
Nostril
Vibrissa (whisker)
Forelimb
5 digits

INTERNAL ANATOMY OF A MALE RABBIT

Brain
Gallbladder
Liver
Stomach
Kidney
Spinal cord
Colon
Ileum
Ureter
Rectum
Bladder
Anus
Urethra
Testis
Vas deferens
Appendix
Cecum
Duodenum
Pancreas
Heart
Diaphragm
Lung
Trachea
Esophagus
Tongue
Buccal cavity
Mouth
Nasal cavity

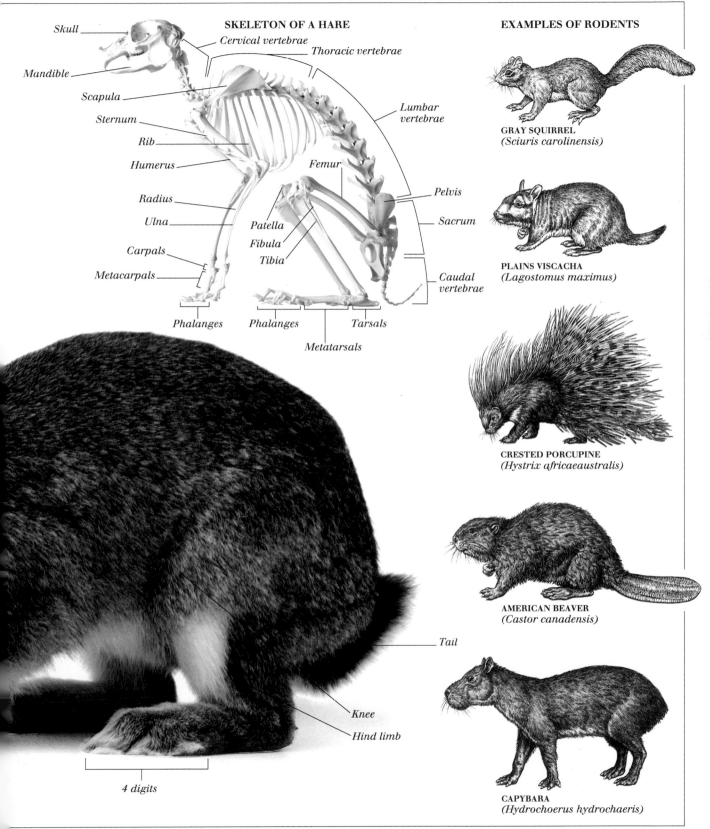

SKELETON OF A HARE

Skull
Mandible
Cervical vertebrae
Thoracic vertebrae
Scapula
Sternum
Rib
Humerus
Radius
Ulna
Carpals
Metacarpals
Phalanges
Femur
Patella
Fibula
Tibia
Phalanges
Metatarsals
Tarsals
Lumbar vertebrae
Pelvis
Sacrum
Caudal vertebrae

Tail
Knee
Hind limb
4 digits

EXAMPLES OF RODENTS

GRAY SQUIRREL
(*Sciuris carolinensis*)

PLAINS VISCACHA
(*Lagostomus maximus*)

CRESTED PORCUPINE
(*Hystrix africaeaustralis*)

AMERICAN BEAVER
(*Castor canadensis*)

CAPYBARA
(*Hydrochoerus hydrochaeris*)

Ungulates

UNGULATES IS A GENERAL TERM FOR a large, varied group of mammals that includes horses, cattle, and their relatives. The ungulates are divided into two orders on the basis of the number of toes. Members of the order Perissodactyla (odd-toed ungulates) have one or three toes. Perissodactyls include horses, asses, and zebras (all of which are one-toed), and rhinoceroses and tapirs (which are three-toed). Members of the order Artiodactyla (even-toed ungulates) have two or four toes. Most artiodactyls have two toes, which are typically encased in hooves to give the so-called cloven hoof. Two-toed, cloven-hoofed artiodactyls include cows and other cattle, sheep, goats, antelopes, deer, and giraffes. The other main two-toed artiodactyls are camels and llamas. Most two-toed artiodactyls are ruminants; that is, they have a four-chambered stomach and chew the cud. The principal four-toed artiodactyls are hogs and hippopotamuses.

DIGESTIVE SYSTEM OF A COW

Chambers of stomach
Rumen Omasum Abomasum Reticulum
Colon
Anus
Rectum
Mouth
Cecum
Tongue
Esophagus
Small intestine
Duodenum

COMPARISON OF THE FRONT FEET OF A HORSE AND A COW

SKELETON OF THE LEFT FRONT FOOT OF A HORSE

SKELETON OF THE RIGHT FRONT FOOT OF A COW

Croup
Back
Loin
Root of tail
Buttock
Tail
Thigh
Flank
Belly
Stifle
Gaskin
Hock
Shannon bone (cannon bone)
Pastern
Heel
Coronet
Hoof

2nd metacarpal (splint bone)
3rd metacarpal (cannon bone)
Fused 3rd and 4th metacarpals
Sesamoid bone
Sesamoid bone
Phalanges of 3rd digit
Phalanges of 3rd digit
Hoof bone
Phalanges of 4th digit
Hoof bone of 3rd digit
Hoof bone of 4th digit

**EXAMPLES OF
UNGULATES**

MALE WAPITI
(Cervus elephas)
An even-toed ungulate
(order Artiodactyla)

BACTRIAN CAMEL
(Camelus ferus)
An even-toed ungulate
(order Artiodactyla)

GIRAFFE
(Giraffa camelopardalis)
An even-toed ungulate
(order Artiodactyla)

BLACK RHINOCEROS
(Diceros bicornis)
An odd-toed ungulate
(order Perissodactyla)

**EXTERNAL FEATURES
OF A HORSE**

Mane

Poll

Crest

Ear

Forelock

Forehead

Withers

Eye

Muzzle

Nose

Nostril

Cheek

Throatlatch

Mouth

Neck

*Chin
groove*

Shoulder

Breast

SKELETON OF A HORSE

Orbit

Atlas

Skull

Lumbar vertebrae

Thoracic vertebrae

Axis

Sacrum

*Caudal
vertebrae*

Pelvis

*Cervical
vertebrae*

Scapula

Elbow

Mandible

Forearm

Femur

Sternum

Fibula

Humerus

Tibia

Patella

Knee

Radius

Calcaneum

Rib

Ulna

Carpals

Cannon bone

2nd metatarsal

Tarsals

*3rd metacarpal
(cannon bone)*

4th metatarsal

Fetlock

3rd metatarsal

Phalanges of 3rd digit

Pastern

*Phalanges of
3rd digit*

Elephants

THE TWO SPECIES OF elephants—African
and Asian—are the only members of the
mammalian order Proboscidea. The
bigger African elephant is the largest
land animal: a fully grown male may
be up to 13 ft (4m) tall and weigh as
much as 7.7 tons (7 tonnes). A fully
grown male Asian elephant may be
11 ft (3.3 m) tall and weigh 6 tons
(5.4 tonnes). The muscular trunk—an
extension of the nose and upper lip—is
the elephant's most obvious feature.
It is used for manipulating and lifting,
feeding, drinking and spraying water,
smelling, touching, and producing
trumpeting sounds. Other characteristic
features of this mighty plant-eater
include a pair of ivory tusks, used for
defense and for crushing vegetation;
thick, pillar-like legs and broad feet to
support the massive body; and large ear
flaps that act as radiators to keep the
elephant cool.

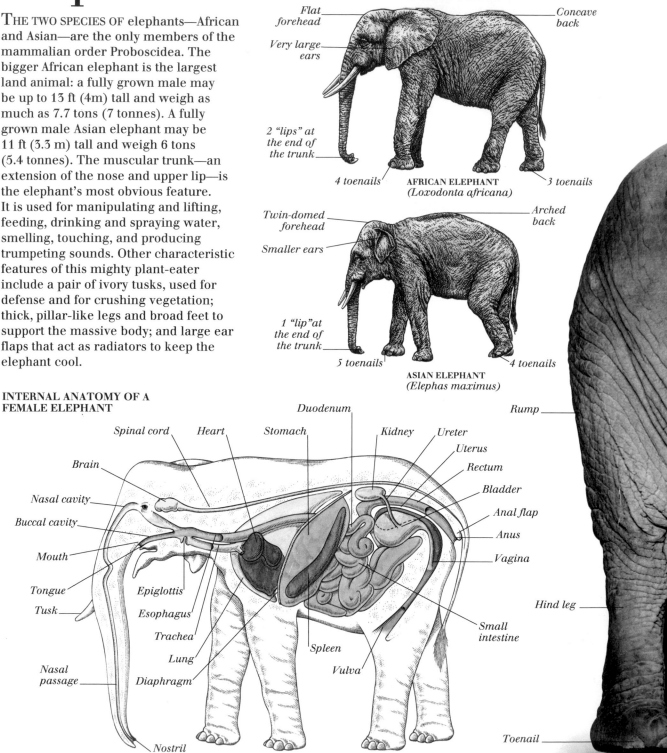

DIFFERENCES BETWEEN AFRICAN AND ASIAN ELEPHANTS

Flat forehead · Concave back · Very large ears · 2 "lips" at the end of the trunk · 4 toenails · 3 toenails

AFRICAN ELEPHANT (*Loxodonta africana*)

Twin-domed forehead · Arched back · Smaller ears · 1 "lip" at the end of the trunk · 5 toenails · 4 toenails

ASIAN ELEPHANT (*Elephas maximus*)

INTERNAL ANATOMY OF A FEMALE ELEPHANT

Spinal cord · Heart · Stomach · Duodenum · Kidney · Ureter · Uterus · Rectum · Bladder · Anal flap · Anus · Vagina · Rump · Brain · Nasal cavity · Buccal cavity · Mouth · Tongue · Tusk · Epiglottis · Esophagus · Trachea · Lung · Diaphragm · Nasal passage · Nostril · Spleen · Vulva · Small intestine · Hind leg · Toenail

EXTERNAL FEATURES OF A FEMALE AFRICAN ELEPHANT (TUSKS REMOVED)

Flat forehead

Eye

Pinna (ear flap)

SKULL OF AN ASIAN ELEPHANT

Orbit

Cranium

Maxilla

Jugal bone

Premaxilla

Upper molars

Tusk (upper incisor)

Lower molars

Mandible

Annulus (ring) of trunk

SKELETON OF AN AFRICAN ELEPHANT (TUSKS REMOVED)

Cervical vertebrae

Thoracolumbar vertebrae

Skull

Sacrum

Caudal vertebrae

Mandible

Scapula

Pelvis

Sternum

Rib

Femur

Humerus

Patella

Radius

Ulna

Tibia

Belly

Fibula

Foreleg

Carpals

Trunk (proboscis)

Metacarpals

Upper "lip" of trunk

Phalanx

Lower "lip" of trunk

Phalanx

Tarsals

Metatarsals

Primates

THE MAMMALIAN ORDER PRIMATES consists of monkeys, apes, and their relatives (including humans). There are two suborders of primates: Prosimii, the primitive primates, which include lemurs, tarsiers, and lorises; and Anthropoidea, the advanced primates, which include monkeys, apes, and humans. The anthropoids are divided into New World monkeys, Old World monkeys, and hominids. New World monkeys typically have widespread nostrils that open to the side; and long tails, which are prehensile (grasping) in some species. This group of monkeys lives in South America, and includes marmosets, tamarins, and howler monkeys. Old World monkeys typically have close-set nostrils that open forward or downward and nonprehensile tails. This group of monkeys lives in Africa and Asia, and includes langurs, mandrills, macaques, and baboons. Hominids typically have large brains and no tail. This group includes the apes—chimpanzees, gibbons, gorillas, and orangutans—and humans.

INTERNAL ANATOMY OF A FEMALE CHIMPANZEE

Buccal cavity
Brain
Nasal cavity
Tongue
Spinal cord
Trachea
Esophagus
Lung
Heart
Diaphragm
Liver
Stomach
Pancreas
Spleen
Small intestine
Large intestine
Cecum
Rectum
Appendix
Bladder
Ovary
Urethra
Uterus
Vagina

SKELETON OF A RHESUS MONKEY

Skull
Orbit
Cervical vertebrae
Mandible
Thoracic vertebrae
Clavicle
Scapula
Rib
Humerus
Lumbar vertebrae
Radius
Ulna
Sacrum
Femur
Patella
Tibia
Carpals
Metacarpals
Fibula
Pelvis
Phalanges
Caudal vertebrae
Tarsals
Metatarsals
Phalanges

SKULL OF A CHIMPANZEE

Temporal bone
Suture
Frontal bone
Parietal bone
Supraorbital ridge
Orbit
Occipital bone
Maxilla
Premaxilla
Auditory meatus
Zygomatic arch
Incisor tooth
Mandible
Canine tooth
Molar tooth
Premolar tooth

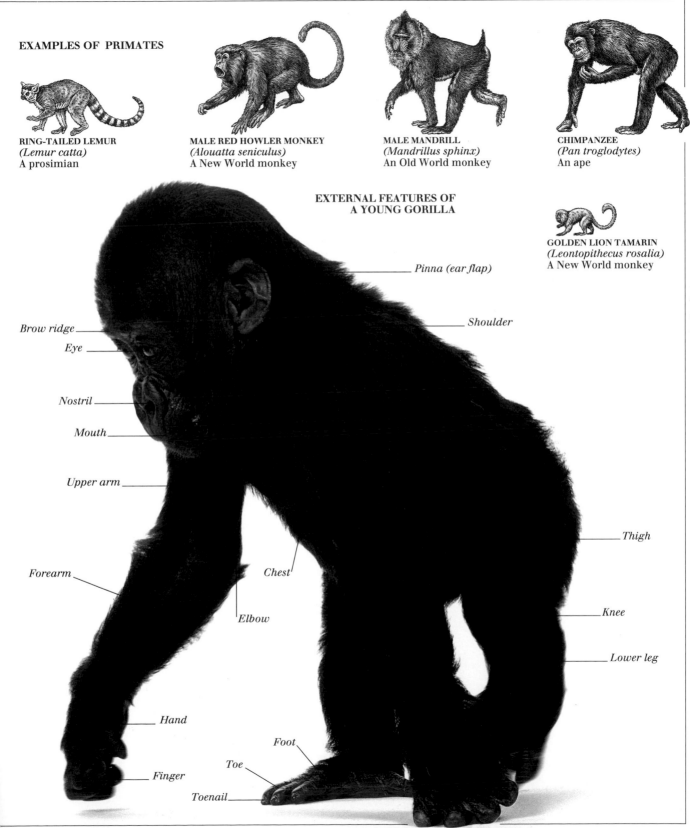

EXAMPLES OF PRIMATES

RING-TAILED LEMUR
(Lemur catta)
A prosimian

MALE RED HOWLER MONKEY
(Alouatta seniculus)
A New World monkey

MALE MANDRILL
(Mandrillus sphinx)
An Old World monkey

CHIMPANZEE
(Pan troglodytes)
An ape

**EXTERNAL FEATURES OF
A YOUNG GORILLA**

GOLDEN LION TAMARIN
(Leontopithecus rosalia)
A New World monkey

Pinna (ear flap)

Shoulder

Brow ridge

Eye

Nostril

Mouth

Upper arm

Thigh

Forearm

Chest

Elbow

Knee

Lower leg

Hand

Foot

Toe

Finger

Toenail

Dolphins, whales, and seals

DOLPHINS, WHALES, AND SEALS belong to two orders of mammals adapted to living in water. Dolphins and whales make up the order Cetacea. Typical cetacean features include a streamlined, fish-like shape; forelimbs in the form of flippers; no visible hind limbs; a horizontally flattened tail; and thick blubber under the skin. There are two groups of cetaceans: toothed whales, including sperm whales, white whales, beaked whales, dolphins, and porpoises; and the larger whalebone (baleen) whales, including rorquals, gray whales, and right whales. The blue whale—a rorqual—is the largest living animal: an adult may be up to 100 ft (30m) long and weigh 145 tons (130 tonnes). Seals and their relatives—sea lions and walruses—make up the order Pinnipedia. Characteristically, they have a streamlined, torpedo-shaped body; forelimbs and hind limbs modified as flippers; thick blubber; and no external ears.

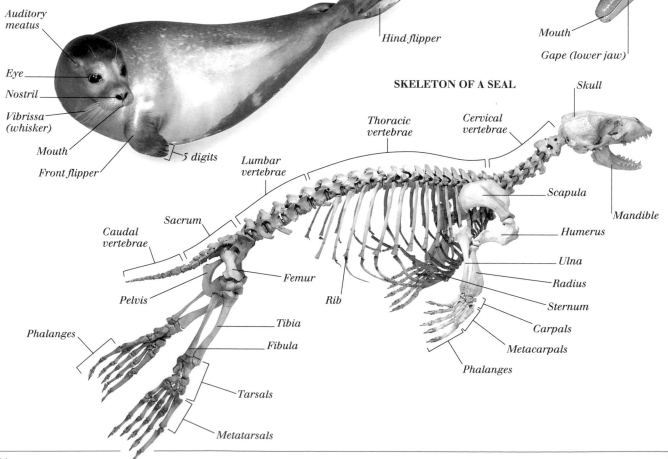

Forehead

Rostrum (beak)

Mouth

Gape (lower jaw)

Eye

Flipper

Belly

Mouth

Gape (lower jaw)

5 digits

Hind flipper

EXTERNAL FEATURES OF A SEAL

Auditory meatus

Eye

Nostril

Vibrissa (whisker)

Mouth

Front flipper

5 digits

SKELETON OF A SEAL

Skull

Thoracic vertebrae

Cervical vertebrae

Mandible

Scapula

Humerus

Ulna

Radius

Sternum

Carpals

Metacarpals

Phalanges

Lumbar vertebrae

Sacrum

Caudal vertebrae

Pelvis

Femur

Rib

Tibia

Fibula

Phalanges

Tarsals

Metatarsals

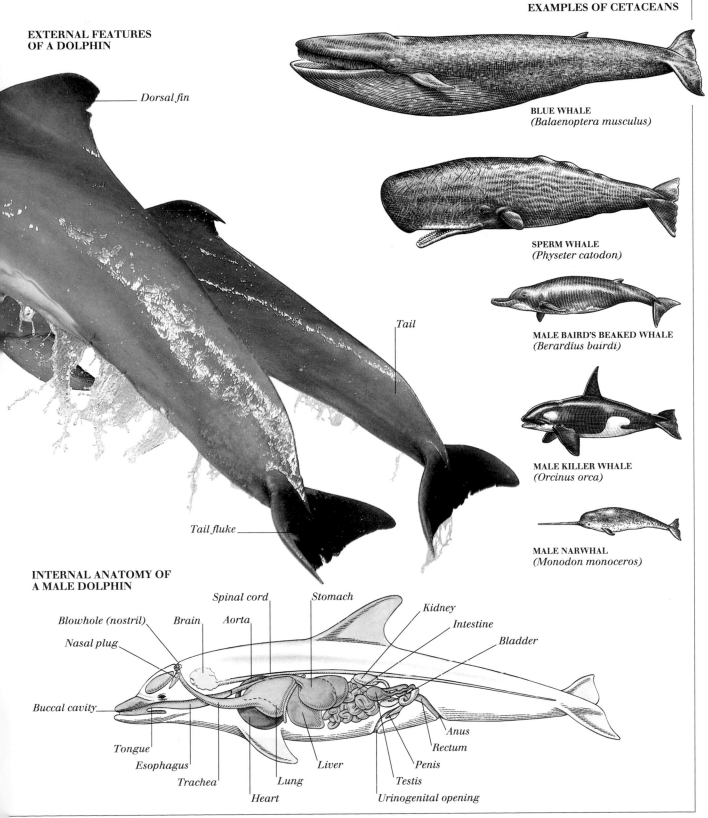

EXAMPLES OF CETACEANS

**EXTERNAL FEATURES
OF A DOLPHIN**

Dorsal fin

Tail

Tail fluke

BLUE WHALE
(Balaenoptera musculus)

SPERM WHALE
(Physeter catodon)

MALE BAIRD'S BEAKED WHALE
(Berardius bairdi)

MALE KILLER WHALE
(Orcinus orca)

MALE NARWHAL
(Monodon monoceros)

**INTERNAL ANATOMY OF
A MALE DOLPHIN**

Spinal cord   *Stomach*

Kidney

Intestine

Blowhole (nostril)   *Brain*   *Aorta*

Bladder

Nasal plug

Buccal cavity

Anus

Rectum

Tongue

Liver   *Penis*

Esophagus

Testis

Trachea

Lung

Urinogenital opening

Heart

205

Marsupials and Monotremes

MARSUPIALS AND MONOTREMES are two orders of mammals that differ from other mammalian groups in the ways that their young develop. The order Marsupalia, the pouched mammals, is made up of kangaroos and their relatives. Typically, marsupials give birth to their young at a very early stage of development. The young then crawls to the mother's pouch (which is on the outside of her abdomen), where it attaches itself to a nipple and remains until fully developed. Most marsupials live in Australia, although the opossums—which are classified as marsupials despite not having a pouch—live in the Americas. The order Monotremata is made up of the platypus and its relatives (the echidnas, or spiny anteaters). The monotremes are primitive mammals that lay eggs, which the mother incubates. The monotremes are found only in Australia and New Guinea.

SKELETON OF A KANGAROO

Skull
Mandible
Cervical vertebrae
Scapula
Clavicle
Humerus
Sternum
Radius
Ulna
Thoracic vertebrae
Lumbar vertebrae
Carpals
Metacarpals
Phalanges
Rib
Femur
Sacrum
Caudal vertebrae
Tibia
Fibula
Pelvis
Tail
Tarsals
Metatarsals
Phalanges

SKELETON OF A PLATYPUS

Skull
Orbit
Scapula
1st cervical vertebra
Phalanges
Metacarpals
Carpals
Ulna
Radius
Humerus
1st thoracic vertebra
Rib
1st lumbar vertebra
Femur
Fibula
Tarsals
Metatarsals
Phalanges
Tibia
Patella
Pelvis
1st caudal vertebra

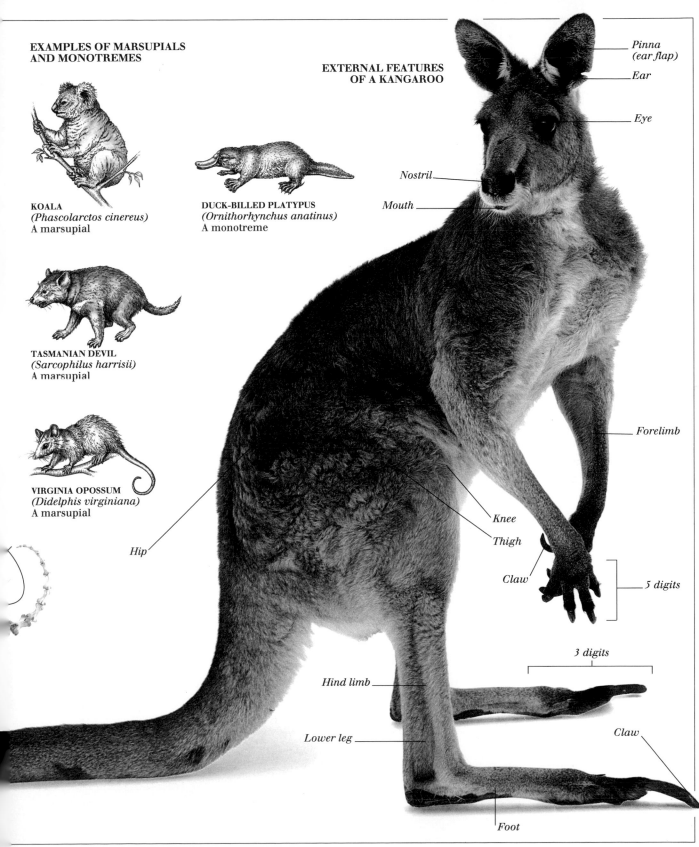

**EXAMPLES OF MARSUPIALS
AND MONOTREMES**

**EXTERNAL FEATURES
OF A KANGAROO**

KOALA
(Phascolarctos cinereus)
A marsupial

DUCK-BILLED PLATYPUS
(Ornithorhynchus anatinus)
A monotreme

TASMANIAN DEVIL
(Sarcophilus harrisii)
A marsupial

VIRGINIA OPOSSUM
(Didelphis virginiana)
A marsupial

*Pinna
(ear flap)*

Ear

Eye

Nostril

Mouth

Forelimb

Knee

Thigh

Claw

5 digits

Hip

3 digits

Hind limb

Lower leg

Claw

Foot

207

THE HUMAN BODY

Body features

ALTHOUGH THERE IS enormous variation between the external appearances of humans, all bodies contain the same basic features. The outward form of the human body depends on the size of the skeleton, the shape of the muscles, the thickness of the fat layer beneath the skin, the elasticity or sagginess of the skin, and the person's age and gender. Males tend to be taller than females, with broader shoulders, more body hair, and a different pattern of fat deposits under the skin; the female body tends to be less muscular and has a shallower and wider pelvis to allow for childbirth.

Ear

Nape of neck

Shoulder

Scapula
(shoulder blade)

Upper arm

Elbow

Loin

Waist

Forearm

Natal
cleft

Buttock

Gluteal fold

Popliteal fossa

Back

Arm

Hand

Leg

Calf

Foot

Heel

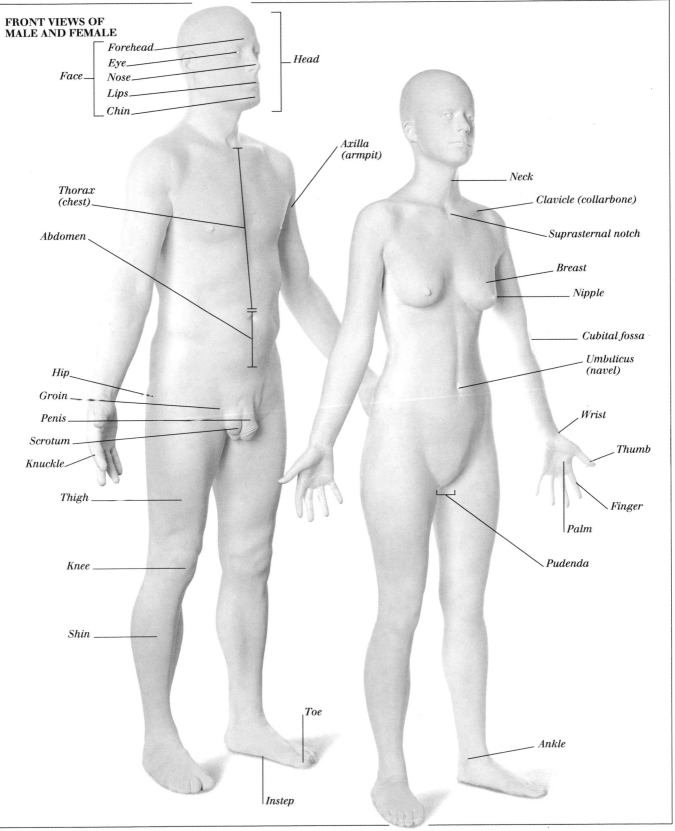

**FRONT VIEWS OF
MALE AND FEMALE**

Forehead

Eye

Face

Nose

Lips

Chin

Head

Axilla
(armpit)

Neck

Clavicle (collarbone)

Suprasternal notch

Thorax
(chest)

Breast

Nipple

Abdomen

Cubital fossa

Umbilicus
(navel)

Hip

Groin

Penis

Wrist

Scrotum

Thumb

Knuckle

Finger

Thigh

Palm

Pudenda

Knee

Shin

Toe

Ankle

Instep

Head

In a newborn baby, the head accounts for one quarter of the total body length; by adulthood, the proportion has reduced to one eighth. Contained in the head are the body's main sense organs: eyes, ears, olfactory nerves that detect smells, and the taste buds of the tongue. Signals from these organs pass to the body's great coordination center: the brain, housed in the protective, bony dome of the skull. Hair on the head insulates against heat loss, and adult males also grow thick facial hair. The face has three important openings: two nostrils through which air passes, and the mouth, which takes in nourishment and helps form speech. Although all heads are basically similar, differences in the size, shape, and color of features produce an infinite variety of appearances.

SIDE VIEW OF EXTERNAL FEATURES OF HEAD

Crown (vertex)

Forehead

Eyebrow

Eyelash

Eye

Nose

Cheek

Lip

Mouth

Chin

Jaw

Ear

Throat

SECTION THROUGH HEAD

Superior sagittal sinus

Cerebrum

Frontal sinus

Sphenoidal sinus

Superior concha

Middle concha

Inferior concha

Vestibule

Maxilla (upper jaw)

Hard palate

Soft palate

Tongue

Uvula

Mandible (lower jaw)

Palatine tonsil

Epiglottis

Trachea

Esophagus

Skull

Pineal body

Pituitary gland

Cerebellum

Pons

Medulla oblongata

Pharynx

Cervical vertebra

Spinal cord

Intervertebral disk

**FRONT VIEW OF EXTERNAL
FEATURES OF HEAD**

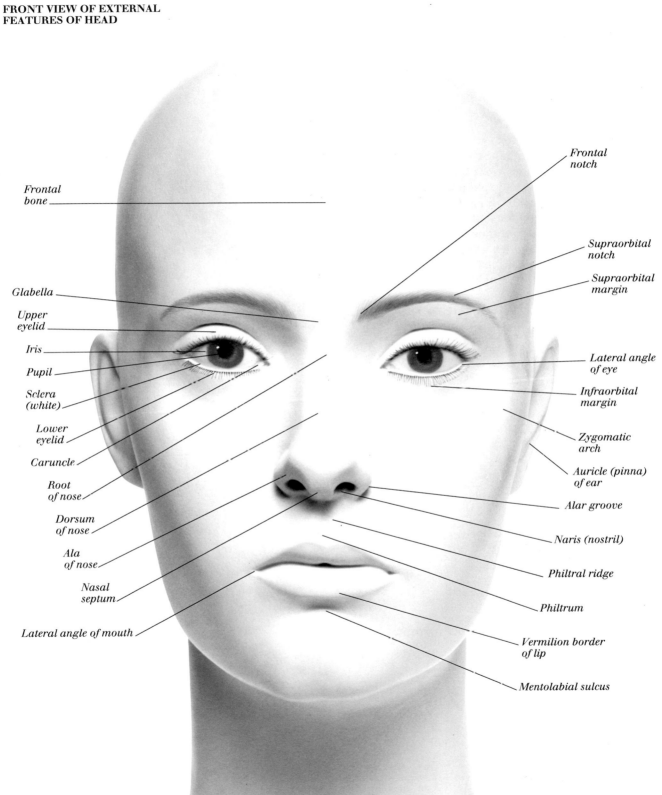

*Frontal
notch*

*Supraorbital
notch*

*Supraorbital
margin*

*Frontal
bone*

Glabella

*Upper
eyelid*

Iris

Pupil

*Sclera
(white)*

*Lower
eyelid*

Caruncle

*Root
of nose*

*Dorsum
of nose*

*Ala
of nose*

*Nasal
septum*

Lateral angle of mouth

*Lateral angle
of eye*

*Infraorbital
margin*

*Zygomatic
arch*

*Auricle (pinna)
of ear*

Alar groove

Naris (nostril)

Philtral ridge

Philtrum

*Vermilion border
of lip*

Mentolabial sulcus

Body organs

ALL THE VITAL BODY ORGANS except for the brain are enclosed within the trunk or torso (the body apart from the head and limbs). The trunk contains two large cavities separated by a muscular sheet called the diaphragm. The upper cavity, known as the thorax or chest cavity, contains the heart and lungs. The lower cavity, called the abdominal cavity, contains the stomach, intestines, liver, and pancreas, which all play a role in digesting food. Also within the trunk are the kidneys and bladder, which are part of the urinary system, and the reproductive organs, which hold the seeds of new human life. Modern imaging techniques, such as contrast X-rays and different types of scans, make it possible to see and study body organs without the need to cut through their protective coverings of skin, fat, muscle, and bone.

MAJOR INTERNAL STRUCTURES

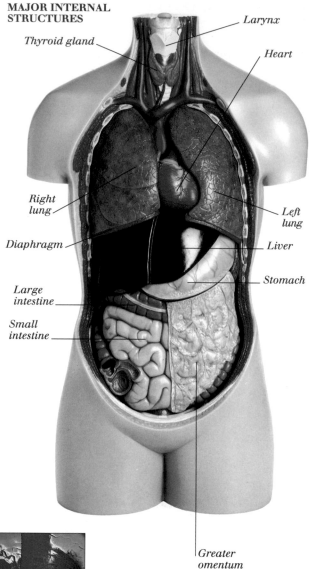

Thyroid gland

Larynx

Heart

Right lung

Left lung

Diaphragm

Liver

Large intestine

Stomach

Small intestine

Greater omentum

IMAGING THE BODY

SCINTIGRAM OF HEART CHAMBERS

ANGIOGRAM OF RIGHT LUNG

CONTRAST X-RAY OF GALLBLADDER

SCINTIGRAM OF NERVOUS SYSTEM

DOUBLE CONTRAST X-RAY OF COLON

ULTRASOUND SCAN OF TWINS IN UTERUS

ANGIOGRAM OF KIDNEYS

ANGIOGRAM OF ARTERIES OF HEAD

CT SCAN THROUGH FEMALE CHEST

THERMOGRAM OF CHEST REGION

ANGIOGRAM OF ARTERIES OF HEART

MRI SCAN THROUGH HEAD AT EYE LEVEL

214

**CHEST AND ABDOMINAL
CAVITIES WITH SOME
ORGANS REMOVED**

Right common carotid artery

Right jugular vein

*Right
subclavian
artery*

*Right
lung*

*Upper
lobe*

*Middle
lobe*

*Lower
lobe*

Heart

Left atrium

Right atrium

Left ventricle

Right ventricle

Right adrenal gland

Right kidney

Duodenum

Right ureter

Inferior vena cava

Common iliac vein

Rectum

External iliac vein

Larynx

Thyroid gland

Trachea

Superior vena cava

Aorta

Left lung

Primary bronchus

Secondary bronchus

Tertiary bronchus

Diaphragm

Esophagus

Spleen

Left adrenal gland

Pancreas

Left kidney

Left ureter

Abdominal aorta

Common iliac artery

Internal iliac artery

External iliac artery

Colon

Bladder

*Adipose
(fat) tissue*

Body cells

EVERYONE IS MADE UP OF BILLIONS OF CELLS, which are the basic structural units of the body. Bones, muscles, nerves, skin, blood, and all other body tissues are formed from different types of cells. Each cell has a specific function but works with other types of cells to perform the enormous number of tasks needed to sustain life. Most body cells have a similar basic structure. Each cell has an outer layer (called the cell membrane) and contains a fluid material (cytoplasm). Within the cytoplasm are many specialized structures (organelles). The most important organelle is the nucleus, which contains vital genetic material and acts as the cell's control center.

Microvillus

Adenine

Thymine

Vacuole

Nucleolus

Nuclear membrane

Cytosine

Guanine

Phosphate/sugar band

Smooth endoplasmic reticulum

Secretory vesicle

Nucleoplasm

THE DOUBLE HELIX
Diagrammatic representation of DNA, which is structured like a spiral ladder. DNA contains all the vital genetic information and instruction codes necessary for the maintenance and continuation of life.

GENERALIZED HUMAN CELL

Cytoplasm

Lysosome

Cell membrane

Mitochondrial crista

Nucleus

Rough endoplasmic reticulum

Microfilament

Pore of nuclear membrane

Ribosome

Centriole

Mitochondrion

Microtubule

Peroxisome

Pinocytotic vesicle

Golgi complex (Golgi apparatus; Golgi body)

TYPES OF CELLS

BONE-FORMING CELL

NERVE CELLS IN SPINAL CORD

SPERM CELLS IN SEMEN

SECRETORY THYROID GLAND CELLS

ACID-SECRETING STOMACH CELLS

CONNECTIVE TISSUE CELLS

MUCUS-SECRETING DUODENAL CELLS

RED AND TWO WHITE BLOOD CELLS

FAT CELLS IN ADIPOSE TISSUE

EPITHELIAL CELLS IN CHEEK

Skeleton

THE SKELETON IS A MOBILE FRAMEWORK made up of 206 bones, approximately half of which are in the hands and feet. Although individual bones are rigid, the skeleton as a whole is remarkably flexible and allows the human body a huge range of movement. The skeleton serves as an anchorage for the skeletal muscles, and as a protective cage for the body's internal organs. Female bones are usually smaller and lighter than male bones, and the female pelvis is shallower and has a wider cavity.

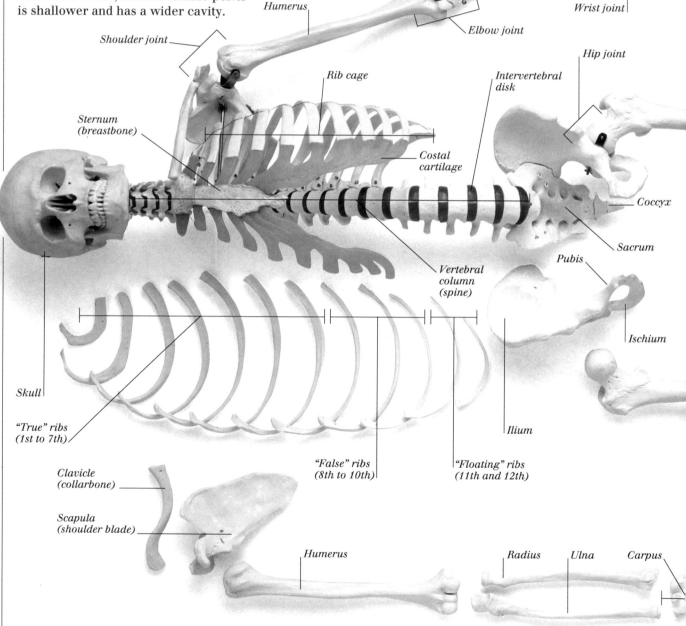

Metacarpal

Carpus

Ulna

Radius

Humerus

Elbow joint

Wrist joint

Shoulder joint

Hip joint

Rib cage

Intervertebral disk

Sternum (breastbone)

Costal cartilage

Coccyx

Sacrum

Pubis

Ischium

Vertebral column (spine)

Ilium

Skull

"True" ribs (1st to 7th)

"False" ribs (8th to 10th)

"Floating" ribs (11th and 12th)

Clavicle (collarbone)

Scapula (shoulder blade)

Humerus

Radius

Ulna

Carpus

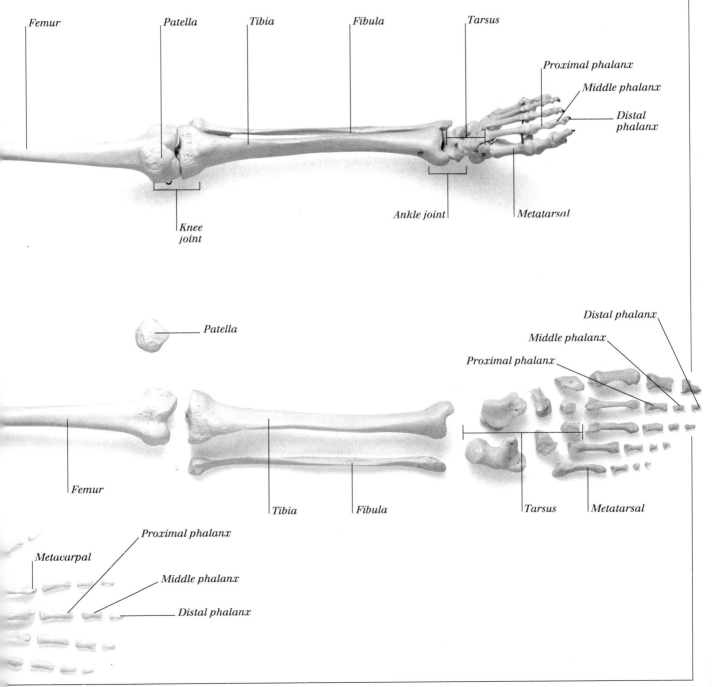

Distal phalanx

Middle phalanx

Proximal phalanx

Femur

Patella

Tibia

Fibula

Tarsus

Proximal phalanx

Middle phalanx

Distal phalanx

Knee joint

Ankle joint

Metatarsal

Patella

Distal phalanx

Middle phalanx

Proximal phalanx

Femur

Tibia

Fibula

Tarsus

Metatarsal

Proximal phalanx

Metacarpal

Middle phalanx

Distal phalanx

Skull

THE SKULL is the most complicated bony structure of the body—but every feature serves a purpose. Internally, the main hollow chamber of the skull has three levels that support the brain, with every bump and hollow corresponding to the shape of the brain. Underneath and toward the back of the skull is a large round hole, called the foramen magnum, through which the spinal cord passes. To the front of this are many smaller openings through which nerves, arteries, and veins pass to and from the brain. The roof of the skull is formed from four thin, curved bones that are firmly fixed together from the age of about two years. At the front of the skull are two orbits, which contain the eyeballs, and a central hole for the airway of the nose. The jawbone hinges on either side of the skull at ear level.

RIGHT SIDE VIEW OF A FETAL SKULL

Anterior fontanelle

Parietal bone

Coronal suture

Frontal bone

Nasal bone

Mental symphysis

Lambdoid suture

Occipital bone

Sphenoidal fontanelle

Mastoid fontanelle

External auditory meatus

RIGHT SIDE VIEW OF SKULL

Greater wing of sphenoid bone

Coronal suture

Frontal bone

Parietal bone

Frontozygomatic suture

Squamous suture

Supraorbital margin

Orbital cavity

Nasal bone

Anterior nasal spine

Maxilla (upper jaw)

Lambdoid suture

Mandible (lower jaw)

Occipital bone

Temporal bone

External auditory meatus

Styloid process

Mastoid process

Condyle

Zygomatic bone

Zygomatic arch

Coronoid process

Mental foramen

Posterior border of vomer

Concha

Mandible (lower jaw)

VIEW OF SKULL FROM BELOW

External occipital crest

Foramen magnum

Occipital condyle

Carotid canal

Mastoid process

Pharyngeal tubercle

Pterygoid plate

Pterygoid hamulus

Greater palatine foramen

Posterior nasal aperture

FRONT VIEW OF SKULL

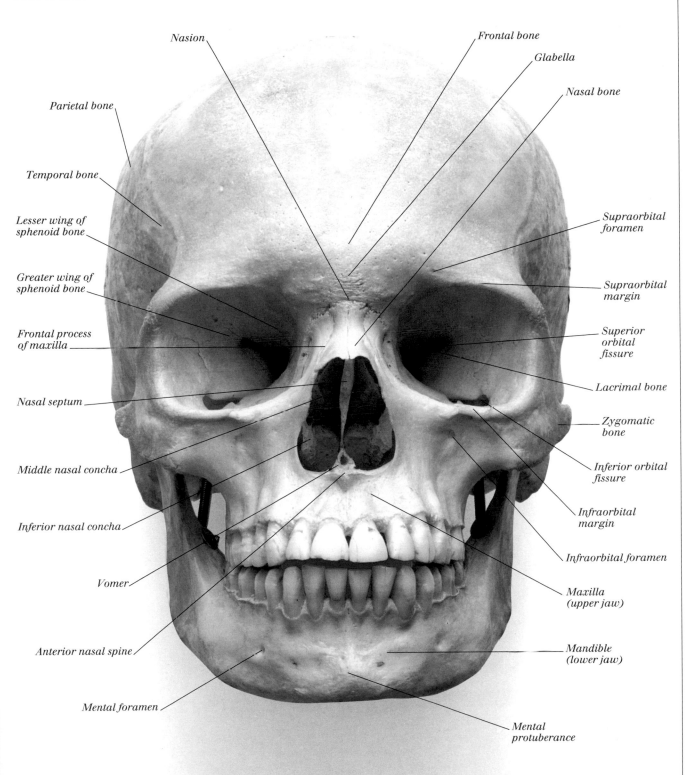

Nasion

Frontal bone

Glabella

Nasal bone

Parietal bone

Temporal bone

Lesser wing of
sphenoid bone

Greater wing of
sphenoid bone

Frontal process
of maxilla

Nasal septum

Middle nasal concha

Inferior nasal concha

Vomer

Anterior nasal spine

Mental foramen

Supraorbital
foramen

Supraorbital
margin

Superior
orbital
fissure

Lacrimal bone

Zygomatic
bone

Inferior orbital
fissure

Infraorbital
margin

Infraorbital foramen

Maxilla
(upper jaw)

Mandible
(lower jaw)

Mental
protuberance

Spine

THE SPINE (OR VERTEBRAL COLUMN) has two main functions: it serves as a protective surrounding for the delicate spinal cord and forms the supporting back bone of the skeleton. The spine consists of 24 separate differently shaped bones (vertebrae) with a curved, triangular bone (the sacrum) at the bottom. The sacrum is made up of fused vertebrae; at its lower end is a small tail-like structure made up of tiny bones collectively called the coccyx. Between each pair of vertebrae is a disc of cartilage that cushions the bones during movement. The top two vertebrae differ in appearance from the others and work as a pair: the first, called the atlas, rotates around a stout vertical peg on the second, the axis. This arrangement allows the skull to move freely up and down, and from side to side.

SPINE DIVIDED INTO VERTEBRAL SECTIONS   FRONT

Cervical vertebrae

Thoracic vertebrae

Lumbar vertebrae

Sacral vertebrae

Coccygeal vertebrae

TYPES OF VERTEBRAE (VIEWED FROM ABOVE)

ATLAS

Anterior arch

Anterior tubercle

Vertebral foramen

Transverse process

Lateral mass with superior articular facet

Posterior arch

Posterior tubercle

Transverse foramen

AXIS

Facet

Dens

Vertebral foramen

Spinous process

Lamina

Transverse process and foramen

CERVICAL VERTEBRA

Body

Anterior tubercle

Posterior tubercle

Superior articular process

Spinous process

Vertebral foramen

Transverse foramen

SKULL AND SPINE

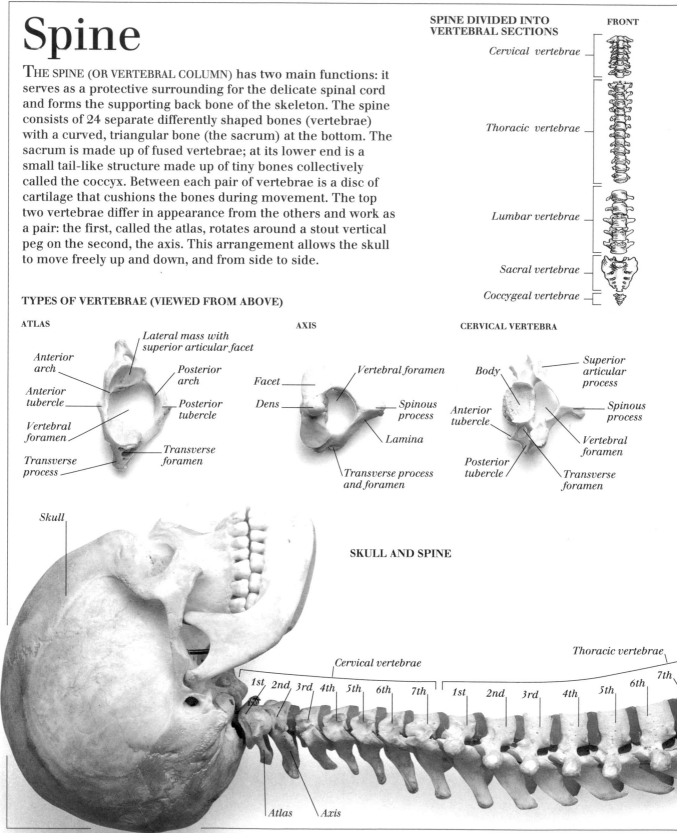

Skull

Cervical vertebrae

1st 2nd 3rd 4th 5th 6th 7th

Thoracic vertebrae

1st 2nd 3rd 4th 5th 6th 7th

Atlas Axis

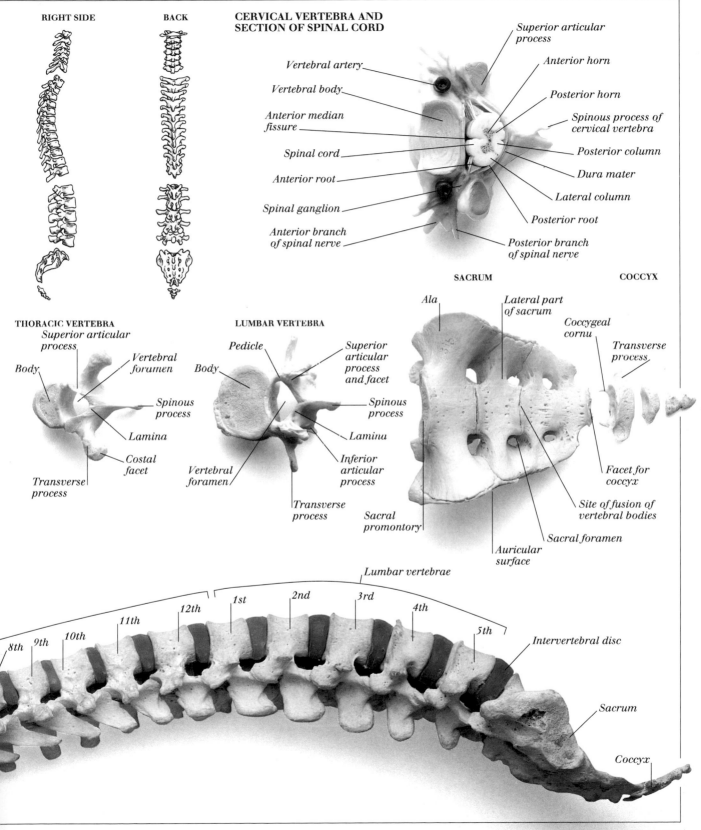

RIGHT SIDE

BACK

CERVICAL VERTEBRA AND SECTION OF SPINAL CORD

Superior articular process

Vertebral artery

Anterior horn

Vertebral body

Posterior horn

Anterior median fissure

Spinous process of cervical vertebra

Spinal cord

Posterior column

Anterior root

Dura mater

Spinal ganglion

Lateral column

Anterior branch of spinal nerve

Posterior root

Posterior branch of spinal nerve

THORACIC VERTEBRA

Superior articular process

Vertebral forumen

Body

Vertebral forumen

Spinous process

Lamina

Costal facet

Transverse process

LUMBAR VERTEBRA

Pedicle

Superior articular process and facet

Body

Spinous process

Lamina

Inferior articular process

Vertebral foramen

Transverse process

SACRUM

Ala

Lateral part of sacrum

Sacral promontory

Auricular surface

Sacral foramen

Site of fusion of vertebral bodies

COCCYX

Coccygeal cornu

Transverse process

Facet for coccyx

Lumbar vertebrae

1st   2nd   3rd   4th   5th

8th   9th   10th   11th   12th

Intervertebral disc

Sacrum

Coccyx

Bones and joints

BONES FORM the body's hard, strong skeletal framework. Each bone has a hard, compact exterior surrounding a spongy, lighter interior. The long bones of the arms and legs, such as the femur (thigh bone), have a central cavity containing bone marrow. Bones are composed chiefly of calcium, phosphorus, and a fibrous substance known as collagen. Bones meet at joints, which are of several different types. For example, the hip is a ball-and-socket joint that allows the femur a wide range of movement, whereas finger joints are simple hinge joints that allow only bending and straightening. Joints are held in place by bands of tissue called ligaments. Movement of joints is facilitated by the smooth hyaline cartilage that covers the bone ends and by the synovial membrane that lines and lubricates the joint.

LIGAMENTS SURROUNDING HIP JOINT

Iliac crest

Iliac fossa

Pubofemoral ligament

Iliac spine

Greater trochanter of femur

Obturator canal

Superior ramus of pubis

Iliofemoral ligament

Body of pubis

Intertrochanteric line

Obturator membrane

Lesser trochanter of femur

Ischial tuberosity

Femur

Ischium

SECTION THROUGH LEFT FEMUR

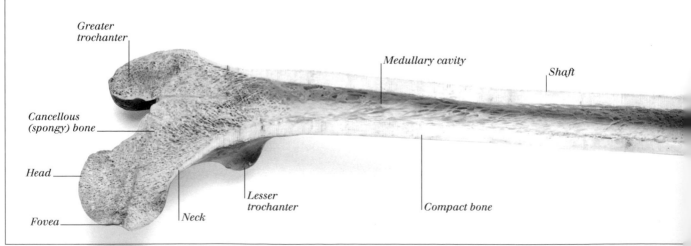

Greater trochanter

Medullary cavity

Shaft

Cancellous (spongy) bone

Head

Lesser trochanter

Compact bone

Fovea

Neck

SECTION THROUGH HIP JOINT

Psoas major muscle

Iliacus muscle

Iliac crest

External iliac artery

Hyaline cartilage of acetabulum

Hyaline cartilage of head of femur

Ligament of head of femur

Femoral artery

Articular cavity

Gluteus minimus muscle

Gluteus medius muscle

Acetabular labrum

Head of femur

Greater trochanter of femur

Neck of femur

Vastus lateralis muscle

Pectineus muscle

Shaft of femur

Adductor longus muscle

Iliacus muscle

Vastus medialis muscle

SECTION OF COMPACT BONE

Parallel rows of concentric bony layers make up this strong material.

BONE MARROW CELLS

Composed mainly of red and white blood cells, marrow fills the cavities of bones.

SECTION THROUGH LONG BONE

Lateral epicondyle

Patellar surface

Adductor tubercle

Medial epicondyle

Osteon (haversian system)

Osteocyte (bone cell)

Intermediate lamella

Endosteum

Volkmann's vessel

Lacuna

Haversian canal

Haversian lamella

Outer lamella

Sharpey's fiber

Periosteum

Muscles 1

THERE ARE THREE MAIN TYPES OF MUSCLE: skeletal muscle (also called voluntary muscle because it can be consciously controlled); smooth muscle (also called involuntary muscle because it is not under voluntary control); and the specialized muscle tissue of the heart. Humans have more than 600 skeletal muscles, which differ in size and shape according to the jobs they do. Skeletal muscles are attached either directly or indirectly (via tendons) to bones, and work in opposing pairs (one muscle in the pair contracts while the other relaxes) to produce body movements as diverse as walking, threading a needle, and an array of facial expressions. Smooth muscles occur in the walls of internal body organs and perform actions such as forcing food through the intestines, contracting the uterus (womb) in childbirth, and pumping blood through the blood vessels.

SOME OTHER MUSCLES IN THE BODY

Iris

Pupil

IRIS
The muscle fibers contract and dilate (expand) to alter pupil size.

TONGUE
Interlacing layers of muscle allow great mobility.

ILEUM
Opposing muscle layers transport semidigested food.

SUPERFICIAL SKELETAL MUSCLES

FRONT VIEW

Brachioradialis

Flexors of forearm

Frontalis

Brachialis

Orbicularis oculi

Temporalis

Sternocleidomastoid

Trapezius

Pectoralis major

Deltoid

Serratus anterior

Rectus abdominis

Biceps brachii

Linea alba

External oblique

Tensor fasciae latae

Iliopsoas

Pectineus

Adductor longus

Rectus femoris

Vastus lateralis

Gracilis

Sartorius

Vastus medialis

Gastrocnemius

Tibialis anterior

BACK VIEW

Extensors
of hand

Flexors
of hand

MOVEMENT OF THE FOREARM
Controlled movement of the limbs relies
on coordinated relaxation and contraction
of opposing muscles. To raise the forearm,
the biceps (two-rooted muscle) contracts
and shortens while the triceps (three-
rooted muscle) relaxes; the reverse occurs
when the forearm is lowered.

Temporalis

Sternocleidomastoid

Trapezius

Deltoid

Triceps
brachii

Teres minor

Teres major

Infraspinatus

Rhomboideus major

Latissimus dorsi

Gluteus
maximus

Adductor
magnus

Gracilis

Biceps femoris

Semitendinosus

Gastrocnemius

Soleus

Peroneus
brevis

Triceps in
resting phase

Biceps in
resting phase

Forearm
at rest

Triceps
relaxes

Biceps
contracts

Forearm
half raised

Triceps fully
relaxed

Biceps fully
contracted

Forearm
fully raised

Triceps
contracts

Biceps
relaxes

Forearm
half lowered

Triceps back in
resting phase

Biceps back in
resting phase

Forearm
back at rest

227

Muscles 2

SKELETAL MUSCLE FIBER

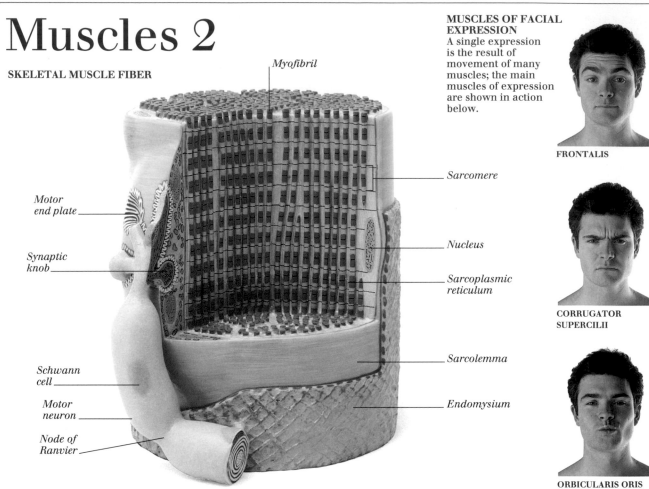

Myofibril

Motor end plate

Synaptic knob

Schwann cell

Motor neuron

Node of Ranvier

Sarcomere

Nucleus

Sarcoplasmic reticulum

Sarcolemma

Endomysium

FRONTALIS

CORRUGATOR SUPERCILII

ORBICULARIS ORIS

ZYGOMATICUS MAJOR

DEPRESSOR ANGULI ORIS

TYPES OF MUSCLE

CARDIAC MUSCLE

SKELETAL MUSCLE

SMOOTH MUSCLE

CONTRACTION OF SKELETAL MUSCLE

RELAXED STATE

CONTRACTED STATE

**MUSCLES OF
HEAD AND NECK**

Frontalis

Procerus

Temporalis

Corrugator
supercilii

Orbicularis
oculi

Levator labii
superioris

Nasalis

Zygomaticus
major

Orbicularis oris

Buccinator

Masseter

Risorius

Levator anguli oris

Depressor labii
inferioris

Platysma

Mentalis

Depressor anguli oris

Thyrohyoid

Scalenus medius

Sternocleidomustoid

Sternohyoid

Omohyoid

Cricothyroid

Trapezius

Hands

THE HUMAN HAND is an extremely versatile tool, capable of delicate manipulation as well as powerful gripping actions. The arrangement of its 27 small bones, moved by 37 skeletal muscles that are connected to the bones by tendons, allows a wide range of movements. Our ability to bring the tips of our thumbs and fingers together, combined with the extraordinary sensitivity of our fingertips due to their rich supply of nerve endings, makes our hands uniquely dextrous.

X-RAY OF LEFT HAND OF A YOUNG CHILD

Area of ossification in phalanx

Area of ossification in metacarpal

Area of ossification in wrist

Epiphysis of ulna

Epiphysis of radius

Areas of cartilage in the wrist and at the ends of the finger bones are the sites of growth and have still to ossify.

BONES OF HAND

Ring finger

Middle finger

Index finger

Little finger

Distal phalanx

Middle phalanx

Proximal phalanx

2nd metacarpal

3rd metacarpal

4th metacarpal

5th metacarpal

Hamate

Pisiform

Capitate

Triquetral

Lunate

Ulna

Head

Shaft

Base

Trapezium

Trapezoid

Scaphoid

Radius

Distal phalanx of thumb

Proximal phalanx of thumb

1st metacarpal

**STRUCTURES UNDERLYING SKIN
OF PALM OF HAND**

*Flexor pollicis
brevis muscle*

*Opponens
pollicis
muscle*

*Abductor
pollicis
brevis
muscle*

*Flexor
retinaculum*

*Radial
artery*

Adductor pollicis muscle

2nd lumbrical muscle

Digital artery *Digital nerve*

Flexor digitorum tendon

*Opponens
digiti
minimi
muscle*

*Abductor
digiti
minimi
muscle*

*Ulnar
nerve*

*Ulnar
artery*

*Palmaris
longus
tendon*

EXTERNAL FEATURES OF BACK OF HAND

*Distal
interphalangeal joint*

Little finger

*Proximal
interphalangeal joint*

*Extensor digitorum
tendon*

Head of ulna

Ring finger

*Middle
finger*

Cuticle

Lunule

*Index
finger*

Nail

*Metacarpophalangeal
joint*

Wrist

*Distal end
of radius*

Thumb

231

Feet

THE FEET AND TOES are essential elements in body movement. They bear and propel the weight of the body during walking and running, and also help to maintain balance during changes of body position. Each foot has 26 bones, more than 100 ligaments, and 33 muscles, some of which are attached to the lower leg. The heel pad and the arch of the foot act as shock absorbers, providing a cushion against the jolts that occur with every step.

BONES OF FOOT

2nd toe

Hallux (big toe)

3rd toe

Distal phalanx of hallux

4th toe

Proximal phalanx of hallux

5th (little) toe

Distal phalanx

Middle phalanx

Proximal phalanx

1st metatarsal

2nd metatarsal

3rd metatarsal

4th metatarsal

5th metatarsal

1st cuneiform

2nd cuneiform

3rd cuneiform

Navicular

Cuboid

Talus

Calcaneus

LIGAMENTS OF FOOT

Posterior cuneonavicular ligament

Articular capsule of interphalangeal joint

Plantar calcaneonavicular ligament

Articular capsule of metatarsophalangeal joint

Posterior tarsometatarsal ligament

Talonavicular ligament

Bifurcate ligament

Deltoid ligament

Fibula

Tibia

Calcanean (Achilles) tendon

Interosseous ligament

STRUCTURES UNDERLYING SKIN OF FOOT

Extensor hallucis longus tendon

1st dorsal interosseous muscle

Inferior extensor retinaculum

Medial malleolus

Tibialis anterior muscle

Tibia

Flexor hallucis longus muscle

Flexor digitorum longus muscle

Soleus muscle

Calcanean (Achilles) tendon

Extensor digitorum longus tendon

Abductor digiti minimi muscle

Extensor hallucis brevis muscle

Extensor digitorum brevis muscle

Peroneus brevis tendon

Lateral malleolus

Tibialis posterior muscle

Peroneus brevis muscle

Fibula

Peroneus longus muscle

EXTERNAL FEATURES OF FOOT

Toenail

Hallux (big toe)

Interphalangeal joint

Extensor hallucis longus tendon

Extensor digitorum longus tendon

Medial malleolus

2nd toe

3rd toe

4th toe

5th (little) toe

Lateral malleolus

Skin and hair

SKIN IS THE BODY'S LARGEST ORGAN, a waterproof barrier that protects the internal organs against infection, injury, and harmful sun rays. The skin is also an important sensory organ and helps to control body temperature. The outer layer of the skin, known as the epidermis, is coated with keratin, a tough, horny protein that is also the chief constituent of hair and nails. Dead cells are shed from the skin's surface and are replaced by new cells from the base of the epidermis, the region that also produces the skin pigment, melanin. The dermis contains most of the skin's living structures, and includes nerve endings, blood vessels, elastic fibers, sweat glands that cool the skin, and sebaceous glands that produce oil to keep the skin supple. Beneath the dermis lies the subcutaneous tissue (hypodermis), which is rich in fat and blood vessels. Hair shafts grow from hair follicles situated in the dermis and subcutaneous tissue. Hair grows on every part of the skin apart from the palms of the hands and soles of the feet.

SECTION OF HAIR

Medulla

Cortex

Melanin granule

Cell nucleus residue

Macrofibril

Cuticle

SECTIONS OF DIFFERENT TYPES OF SKIN

Sebaceous gland

Hair follicle

Enlarged sweat gland

Thickened epidermis

Sweat pore

Meissner's corpuscle

Follicle-rich dermis

Sweat gland

Pacinian corpuscle

SCALP

ARMPIT

SOLE OF FOOT

SECTION OF SKIN

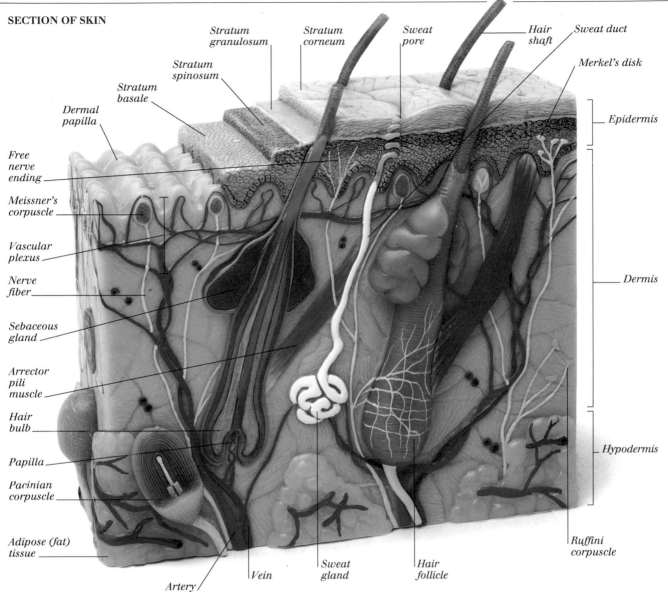

Stratum granulosum
Stratum spinosum
Stratum basale
Dermal papilla
Free nerve ending
Meissner's corpuscle
Vascular plexus
Nerve fiber
Sebaceous gland
Arrector pili muscle
Hair bulb
Papilla
Pacinian corpuscle
Adipose (fat) tissue
Artery
Vein
Stratum corneum
Sweat pore
Sweat gland
Hair follicle
Hair shaft
Sweat duct
Merkel's disk
Epidermis
Dermis
Hypodermis
Ruffini corpuscle

PHOTOMICROGRAPHS OF SKIN AND HAIR

SECTION OF SKIN
The flaky cells at the skin's surface are shed continuously.

SWEAT PORE
This allows loss of fluid as part of temperature control.

SKIN HAIR
Two hairs pushing through the outer layer of skin.

HEAD HAIR
The root and part of the shaft of a hair from the scalp.

Brain

THE BRAIN IS THE MAJOR ORGAN of the central nervous system and the control center for all the body's voluntary and involuntary activities. It is also responsible for the complexities of thought, memory, emotion, and language. In adults, this complex organ is a mere 3 lb (1.4 kg) in weight, containing over 10 thousand million nerve cells. Three distinct regions can easily be seen—the brainstem, the cerebellum, and the large cerebrum. The brainstem controls vital body functions, such as breathing and digestion. The cerebellum's main functions are the maintenance of posture and the coordination of body movements. The cerebrum, which consists of the right and left cerebral hemispheres joined by the corpus callosum, is the site of most conscious and intelligent activities.

MRI SCAN OF TRANSVERSE SECTION THROUGH BRAIN

White matter

Skull

Scalp

Gray matter

Lateral ventricle

Longitudinal fissure

Sagittal section

Coronal section

SAGITTAL SECTION THROUGH BRAIN

Central sulcus

Fornix

Cerebrum

Parietal lobe

Parieto-occipital sulcus

Pineal body

Occipital lobe

Aqueduct

Cerebellum

4th ventricle

Spinal cord

Corpus callosum

Thalamus

Frontal lobe

Hypothalamus

Optic chiasma

Pituitary gland

Mesencephalon (midbrain)

Pons

Medulla oblongata

Brainstem

SECTION THROUGH SKULL AND BRAIN

Scalp
Epicranial aponeurosis
Arachnoid granulation
Pericranium
Skull
Dura mater
Lateral lacuna
Arachnoid mater
Superior sagittal sinus
Pia mater
Falx cerebri
Subarachnoid space
Cerebral vessel
Cerebrum — Gray matter / White matter

EXTERNAL ANATOMY OF BRAIN

Parietal lobe
Parieto-occipital sulcus
Precentral gyrus
Postcentral gyrus
Central sulcus
Frontal lobe
Lateral sulcus
Occipital lobe
Temporal lobe
Cerebellum

SPECIFIC ROLES OF AREAS OF CEREBRUM

Skilled movements
Basic movements
Sensation
Visual recognition
Behavior and emotion
Speech
Vision
Hearing
Balance and muscle coordination

CORONAL SECTION THROUGH BRAIN

Corpus callosum
Longitudinal fissure
Gray matter
White matter
Cerebrum
Caudate nucleus
Lateral ventricle
Fornix
Lentiform nucleus
Internal capsule
Thalamus
Crus cerebri of midbrain
3rd ventricle
Pons
Medulla oblongata
Cerebellum

NERVE CELLS IN BRAIN

The dark cells are Purkinje cells, which are among the largest nerve cells in the body.

237

Nervous system

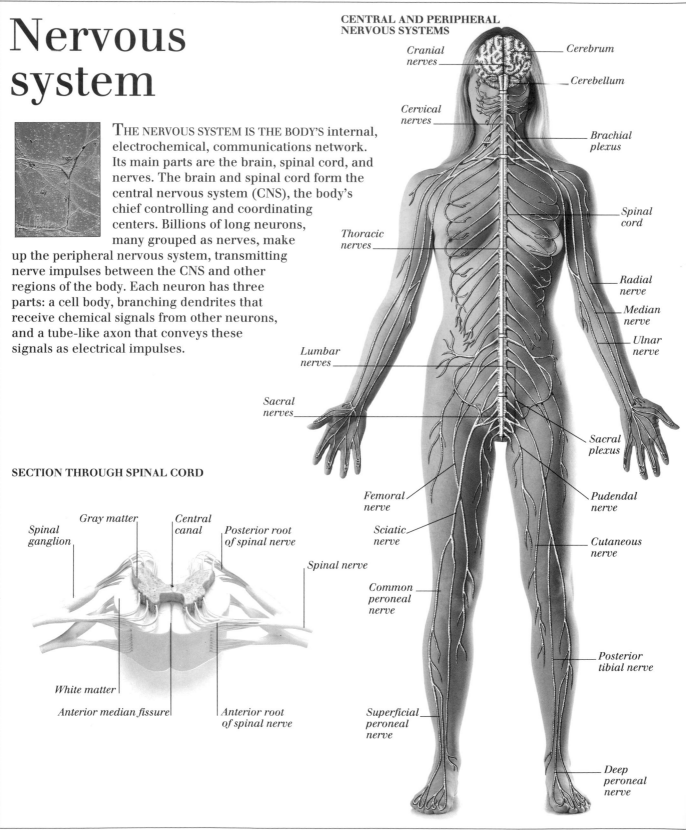

THE NERVOUS SYSTEM IS THE BODY'S internal, electrochemical, communications network. Its main parts are the brain, spinal cord, and nerves. The brain and spinal cord form the central nervous system (CNS), the body's chief controlling and coordinating centers. Billions of long neurons, many grouped as nerves, make up the peripheral nervous system, transmitting nerve impulses between the CNS and other regions of the body. Each neuron has three parts: a cell body, branching dendrites that receive chemical signals from other neurons, and a tube-like axon that conveys these signals as electrical impulses.

CENTRAL AND PERIPHERAL NERVOUS SYSTEMS

Cranial nerves

Cerebrum

Cerebellum

Cervical nerves

Brachial plexus

Spinal cord

Thoracic nerves

Radial nerve

Median nerve

Ulnar nerve

Lumbar nerves

Sacral nerves

Sacral plexus

Femoral nerve

Pudendal nerve

Sciatic nerve

Cutaneous nerve

Common peroneal nerve

Posterior tibial nerve

Superficial peroneal nerve

Deep peroneal nerve

SECTION THROUGH SPINAL CORD

Spinal ganglion

Gray matter

Central canal

Posterior root of spinal nerve

Spinal nerve

White matter

Anterior median fissure

Anterior root of spinal nerve

STRUCTURE OF A MOTOR NEURON

Cell body

Nucleus

Synaptic knob

Axon hillock

Axon

Dendrite

Nucleolus

Nissl body

Schwann cell

Node of Ranvier

Mitochondrion

Myelin sheath

TYPES OF NERVE ENDING

STRUCTURE OF A SYNAPTIC KNOB

Presynaptic axon

Microtubule

Neurofilament

Endoplasmic reticulum

Mitochondrion

Synaptic vesicle

Neurotransmitter

Presynaptic membrane

Myelin sheath

Axon

Cell body

Nucleus

Dendrite

TYPES OF NEURON

MULTIPOLAR

Motor end plate

Node of Ranvier

Schwann cell

Cell body

Nucleus

Receptor

UNIPOLAR

Dendrite

Axon

BIPOLAR

Dendrite

Axon

Cell body

Nucleus

Dendrite

FREE NERVE ENDING

MEISSNER'S CORPUSCLE

MERKEL'S DISK

RUFFINI CORPUSCLE

PACINIAN CORPUSCLE

Eye

THE EYE IS THE ORGAN OF SIGHT. The two eyeballs, protected within bony sockets called orbits and on the outside by the eyelids, eyebrows, and tear film, are directly connected to the brain by the optic nerves. Each eye is moved by six muscles, which are attached around the eyeball. Light rays entering the eye through the pupil are focused by the cornea and lens to form an image on the retina. The retina contains millions of light-sensitive cells, called rods and cones, which convert the image into a pattern of nerve impulses. These impulses are transmitted along the optic nerve to the brain. Information from the two optic nerves is processed in the brain to produce a single coordinated image.

Lateral rectus muscle

Vitreous humor

Macula

Central retinal vein

Central retinal artery

Pia mater

Arachnoid mater

Dura mater

Optic nerve

Area of optic disk

Retina

Choroid

Sclera

Retinal blood vessel

Medial rectus muscle

SECTION THROUGH LEFT EYE

Iris

Anterior chamber

Posterior chamber

} Aqueous humor

Conjunctiva

Pupil

Cornea

Lens

Sphincter muscle

Dilator muscle

Zonular ligament

Sinus venosus sclerae

Iridocorneal angle

Ciliary body

Ora serrata

LACRIMAL (TEAR-PRODUCING) APPARATUS

Lacrimal sac

Lacrimal canaliculus

Lacrimal gland

Middle meatus

Middle nasal concha

Nasal septum

Inferior nasal concha

Nasolacrimal duct

Lacrimal punctum

OPHTHALMOSCOPIC VIEW OF RETINA

Retinal blood vessel

Optic disk

Macula

The blind spot, where the optic nerve leaves the eye, can be clearly seen as a light circular area toward the center of the image.

MUSCLES SURROUNDING RIGHT EYE

Medial rectus

Superior oblique

Trochlea

Superior rectus

Levator palpebrae superioris

Annular tendon

Inferior rectus

Lateral rectus

Inferior oblique

Ear

THE EAR IS THE ORGAN OF HEARING AND BALANCE. The outer ear
consists of a flap called the auricle or pinna and the auditory canal.
The main functional parts—the middle and inner ears—are
enclosed within the skull. The middle ear consists of three tiny
bones, known as auditory ossicles, and the eustachian tube, which
links the ear to the back of the nose. The inner ear consists of the
spiral-shaped cochlea, and also the semicircular canals and the
vestibule, which are the organs of balance. Sound waves entering
the ear travel through the auditory canal to the tympanic membrane
(eardrum), where they are converted to vibrations that are
transmitted via the ossicles to the cochlea. Here, the vibrations are
converted by millions of microscopic hairs into electrical nerve
signals to be interpreted by the brain.

STRUCTURE OF EAR

Temporal bone

Cartilage
of auricle

Auricle
(pinna)

Auditory canal

Mastoid
process

Cartilaginous
part of meatus

Lobule

RIGHT AURICLE (PINNA)

Upper crux of
antihelix

Triangular
fossa

Scaphoid fossa

Lower crux
of antihelix

Concha

Helix

Antihelix

Antitragus

Tragus

Intertragic
notch

External
auditory
meatus

Lobule

OSSICLES OF MIDDLE EAR

INTERNAL STRUCTURE
OF AMPULLA

Membranous
portion

Cupula

Osseous
portion

Crista

Ampullar
nerve

Hair cell
of crista

MALLEUS (HAMMER)   INCUS (ANVIL)   STAPES (STIRRUP)

These three tiny bones connect to form a bridge between the
tympanic membrane and the oval window. With a system of
membranes they convey sound vibrations to the inner ear.

LABYRINTH

Utricle

Saccule

Vestibular nerve

Common crus

Tympanic canal

Anterior semicircular canal

Median canal

Vestibular canal

Lateral semicircular canal

Osseous (bony) part of meatus

Tympanic membrane (eardrum)

Semicircular canal

Ampulla

Cochlea

Vestibulocochlear nerve

Cochlea

Tensor tympani muscle

Cochlear nerve

Oval window

Posterior semicircular canal

SECTION THROUGH COCHLEA

Internal carotid artery

Organ of Corti

Median canal

Vestibular canal

Eustachian tube

Vestibular membrane

Spiral ganglion

Cochlear nerve

Hair cells

Styloid process

Tympanic canal

Basilar membrane

Nose, mouth, and throat

WITH EVERY BREATH, air passes through the nasal cavity down the pharynx (throat), larynx ("voice box"), and trachea (windpipe) to the lungs. The nasal cavity warms and moistens air, and the tiny layers in its lining protect the airway against damage by foreign bodies. During swallowing, the tongue moves up and back, the larynx rises, the epiglottis closes off the entrance to the trachea, and the soft palate separates the nasal cavity from the pharynx. Saliva, secreted from three pairs of salivary glands, lubricates food to make swallowing easier; it also begins the chemical breakdown of food, and helps to produce taste. The senses of taste and smell are closely linked. Both depend on the detection of dissolved molecules by sensory receptors in the olfactory nerve endings of the nose and in the taste buds of the tongue.

STRUCTURE OF TONGUE

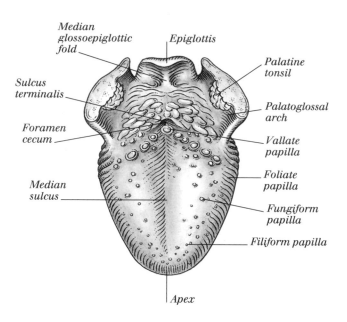

Median glossoepiglottic fold
Epiglottis
Palatine tonsil
Sulcus terminalis
Palatoglossal arch
Foramen cecum
Vallate papilla
Median sulcus
Foliate papilla
Fungiform papilla
Filiform papilla
Apex

STRUCTURES SURROUNDING PHARYNX

Lingual nerve
Tongue
Styloglossus muscle
Hyoglossus muscle
Sublingual gland
Hypoglossal nerve
Mandible (lower jaw)
Superior laryngeal nerve
Submandibular gland
Superior thyroid artery
Hyoid bone
Laryngeal prominence (Adam's apple)
Thyrohyoid muscle
Thyrohyoid membrane
Cricothyroid muscle
Cricothyroid ligament
Thyroid gland
Trachea

TASTE AREAS ON TONGUE

Bitter
Sour
Salt
Sweet

TYPES OF PAPILLAE

FILIFORM PAPILLAE   **FUNGIFORM PAPILLAE**   **VALLATE PAPILLAE**

SECTION THROUGH NOSE, MOUTH, AND THROAT

Frontal sinus

Superior nasal concha

Sphenoidal sinus

Middle nasal concha

Inferior nasal concha

Superior meatus

Middle meatus

Nasal cavity

Vestibule

Inferior meatus

Hard palate

Soft palate

Nasopharynx

Maxilla (upper jaw)

Incisive canal

Orbicularis oris muscle

Superior longitudinal muscle

Incisor

Apex of tongue

Genioglossus muscle

Sublingual fold

Sublingual salivary gland

Fibrous septum

Mandible (lower jaw)

Geniohyoid muscle

Myohyoid muscle

Uvula

Palatine tonsil

Oropharynx

Epiglottis

Lingual tonsil

Hyoid bone

Laryngeal prominence (Adam's apple)

Cricothyroid muscle

Cervical vertebra

Thyroid cartilage

Thyroid gland

Intervertebral disk

Esophagus

Trachea

ENDOSCOPIC VIEW OF VOCAL CORDS

Posterior part of tongue

Epiglottis

Vocal cord

Teeth

THE 20 PRIMARY TEETH (also called deciduous or milk teeth) usually begin to erupt when a baby is about six months old. They start to be replaced by the permanent teeth when the child is about six years old. By the age of 20, most adults have a full set of 32 teeth although the third molars (commonly called wisdom teeth) may never erupt. While teeth help people to speak clearly and give shape to the face, their main function is the chewing of food. Incisors and canines shear and tear the food into pieces; premolars and molars crush and grind it further. Although tooth enamel is the hardest substance in the body, it tends to be eroded and destroyed by acid produced in the mouth during the breakdown of food.

DEVELOPMENT OF TEETH IN A FETUS

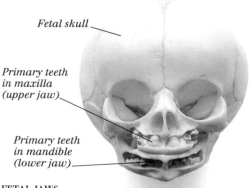

Fetal skull

Primary teeth in maxilla (upper jaw)

Primary teeth in mandible (lower jaw)

FETAL JAWS
By the sixth week of embryonic development areas of thickening occur in each jaw; these areas give rise to tooth buds. By the time the fetus is six months old, enamel has formed on the tooth buds.

DEVELOPMENT OF JAW AND TEETH

Maxilla (upper jaw)

Mandible (lower jaw)

A NEWBORN BABY'S JAWS
The primary teeth can be seen developing in the jawbones; they begin to erupt around the age of six months.

A FIVE-YEAR-OLD CHILD'S TEETH
There is a full set of 20 erupted primary teeth; the permanent teeth can be seen developing in the upper and lower jaws.

A NINE-YEAR-OLD CHILD'S TEETH
Most of the teeth are primary teeth but the permanent incisors and first molars have now emerged.

AN ADULT'S TEETH
By the age of 20, the full set of 32 permanent teeth (including the wisdom teeth) should be in position.

THE PERMANENT TEETH

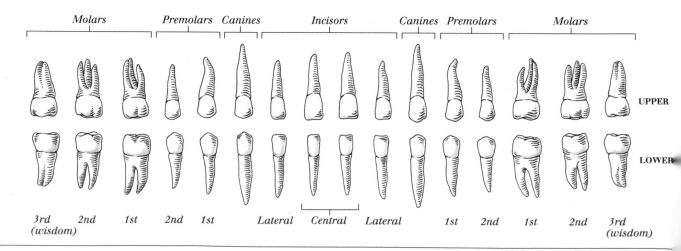

Molars   Premolars   Canines   Incisors   Canines   Premolars   Molars

UPPER

LOWER

3rd (wisdom)   2nd   1st   2nd   1st   Lateral   Central   Lateral   1st   2nd   1st   2nd   3rd (wisdom)

STRUCTURE OF A TOOTH

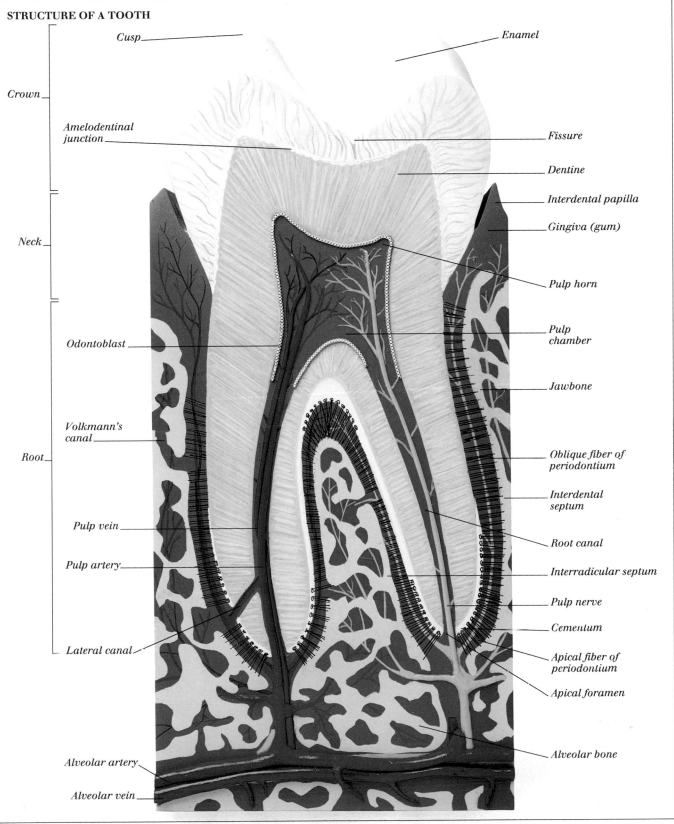

Cusp

Enamel

Crown

Amelodentinal junction

Fissure

Dentine

Interdental papilla

Neck

Gingiva (gum)

Pulp horn

Pulp chamber

Odontoblast

Jawbone

Volkmann's canal

Oblique fiber of periodontium

Root

Interdental septum

Pulp vein

Root canal

Pulp artery

Interradicular septum

Pulp nerve

Cementum

Lateral canal

Apical fiber of periodontium

Apical foramen

Alveolar artery

Alveolar bone

Alveolar vein

Digestive system

THE DIGESTIVE SYSTEM BREAKS DOWN FOOD into particles so tiny that blood can take nourishment to all parts of the body. The system's main part is a 30-foot (9 m) tube from mouth to rectum; muscles in this alimentary canal force food along. Chewed food first travels through the esophagus to the stomach, which churns and liquidizes food before it passes through the duodenum, jejunum, and ileum—the three parts of the long, convoluted small intestine. Here, digestive juices from the gallbladder and pancreas break down food particles; many filter out into the blood through tiny fingerlike villi that line the small intestine's inner wall. Undigested food in the colon forms feces that leave the body through the anus.

Stomach

Cardiac notch

Nasal cavity

Oral cavity

Maxilla (upper jaw)

Tooth

Mouth

Tongue

Mandible (lower jaw)

Uvula

Epiglottis

Trachea

Esophagus

Left lobe of liver

Falciform ligament

Hepatic artery

Cystic duct

Right lobe of liver

Gallbladder

ENDOSCOPIC VIEWS INSIDE ALIMENTARY CANAL

ESOPHAGUS

Mucosa

STOMACH ENTRANCE

Cardiac orifice

STOMACH

Ruga

STOMACH EXIT

Pylorus

ALIMENTARY CANAL

Fold of mucous membrane

Angular notch

Spleen

Pancreas

Peritoneum

Transverse colon

Tenia colica

Descending colon

Small intestine (jejunum and ileum)

Haustration of colon

Sigmoid colon

Anal sphincter muscle

Rectum

Pyloric sphincter muscle

Duodenum

Bile duct

Plica circulare

Ascending colon

Semilunar fold

Ileocecal fold

Cecum

Appendix orifice

Appendix

Terminal ileum

Anal canal

Anus

DUODENUM

Plica circulare

ILEUM

Villi of mucosa

COLON

Semilunar fold

Blood vessel

RECTUM

Mucosa

Heart

THE HEART IS A HOLLOW MUSCLE in the middle of the chest that pumps blood around the body, supplying cells with oxygen and nutrients. A muscular wall, called the septum, divides the heart lengthwise into left and right sides. A valve divides each side into two chambers: an upper atrium and a lower ventricle. When the heart muscle contracts, it squeezes blood through the atria and then through the ventricles. Oxygenated blood from the lungs flows from the pulmonary veins into the left atrium, through the left ventricle, and then out via the aorta to all parts of the body. Deoxygenated blood returning from the body flows from the vena cava into the right atrium, through the right ventricle, and then out via the pulmonary artery to the lungs for reoxygenation. At rest the heart beats between 60 and 80 times a minute; during exercise or at times of stress or excitement the rate may increase to 200 beats a minute.

ARTERIES AND VEINS SURROUNDING HEART

Aorta

Left coronary artery

Cardiac vein

Right coronary artery

Coronary sinus

Main branch of left coronary artery

SECTION THROUGH HEART WALL

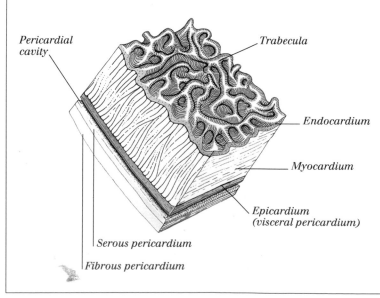

Pericardial cavity

Trabecula

Endocardium

Myocardium

Epicardium (visceral pericardium)

Serous pericardium

Fibrous pericardium

HEARTBEAT SEQUENCE

ATRIAL DIASTOLE

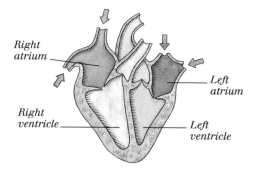

Right atrium

Left atrium

Right ventricle

Left ventricle

Deoxygenated blood enters the right atrium while the left atrium receives oxygenated blood.

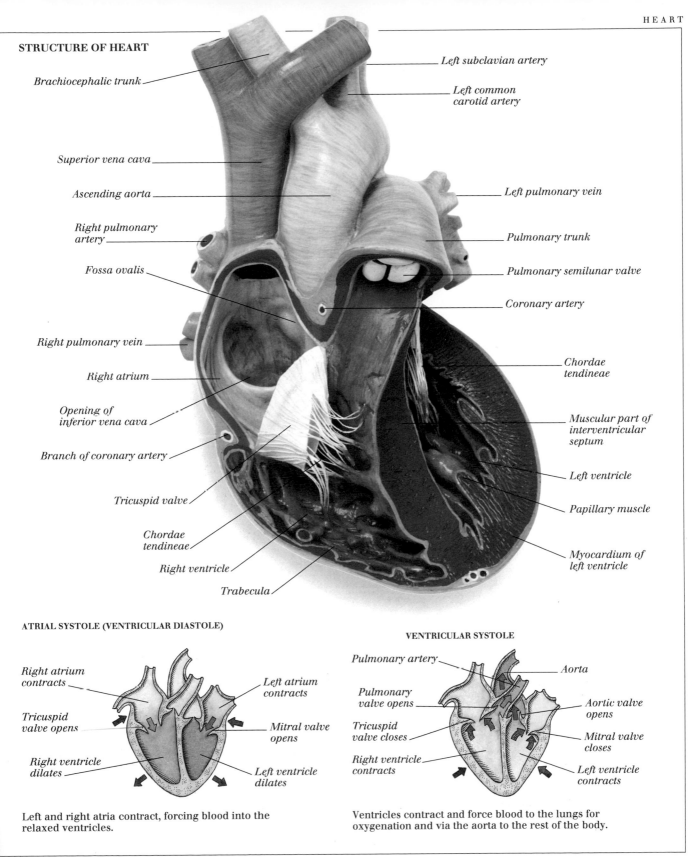

STRUCTURE OF HEART

Brachiocephalic trunk

Left subclavian artery

Left common carotid artery

Superior vena cava

Ascending aorta

Left pulmonary vein

Right pulmonary artery

Pulmonary trunk

Fossa ovalis

Pulmonary semilunar valve

Coronary artery

Right pulmonary vein

Right atrium

Chordae tendineae

Opening of inferior vena cava

Muscular part of interventricular septum

Branch of coronary artery

Left ventricle

Tricuspid valve

Papillary muscle

Chordae tendineae

Myocardium of left ventricle

Right ventricle

Trabecula

ATRIAL SYSTOLE (VENTRICULAR DIASTOLE)

Right atrium contracts

Left atrium contracts

Tricuspid valve opens

Mitral valve opens

Right ventricle dilates

Left ventricle dilates

Left and right atria contract, forcing blood into the relaxed ventricles.

VENTRICULAR SYSTOLE

Pulmonary artery

Aorta

Pulmonary valve opens

Aortic valve opens

Tricuspid valve closes

Mitral valve closes

Right ventricle contracts

Left ventricle contracts

Ventricles contract and force blood to the lungs for oxygenation and via the aorta to the rest of the body.

Circulatory system

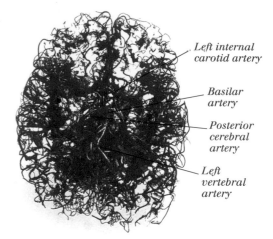

THE CIRCULATORY SYSTEM consists of the heart and blood vessels, which together maintain a continuous flow of blood around the body. The heart pumps oxygen-rich blood from the lungs to all parts of the body through a network of tubes called arteries, and smaller branches called arterioles. Blood returns to the heart via small vessels called venules, which lead in turn into larger tubes called veins. Arterioles and venules are linked by a network of tiny vessels called capillaries, where the exchange of oxygen and carbon dioxide between blood and body cells takes place. Blood has four main components: red blood cells, white blood cells, platelets, and liquid plasma.

ARTERIAL SYSTEM OF BRAIN

- Left internal carotid artery
- Basilar artery
- Posterior cerebral artery
- Left vertebral artery

CIRCULATORY SYSTEM OF LIVER

- Inferior vena cava
- Portal vein
- Common bile duct
- Hepatic artery
- Gallbladder

CIRCULATORY SYSTEM OF HEART AND LUNGS

- Superior vena cava
- Aorta
- Right ventricle
- Left ventricle

SECTION OF MAIN ARTERY

- Tunica media
- Collagen and elastic fibers
- External elastic lamina
- Tunica adventitia
- Internal elastic lamina
- Tunica intima
- Endothelium
- Arteriole

SECTION OF MAIN VEIN

- Tunica media
- Collagen and elastic fibers
- External elastic lamina
- Tunica adventitia
- Valve cusp
- Internal elastic lamina
- Tunica intima
- Endothelium

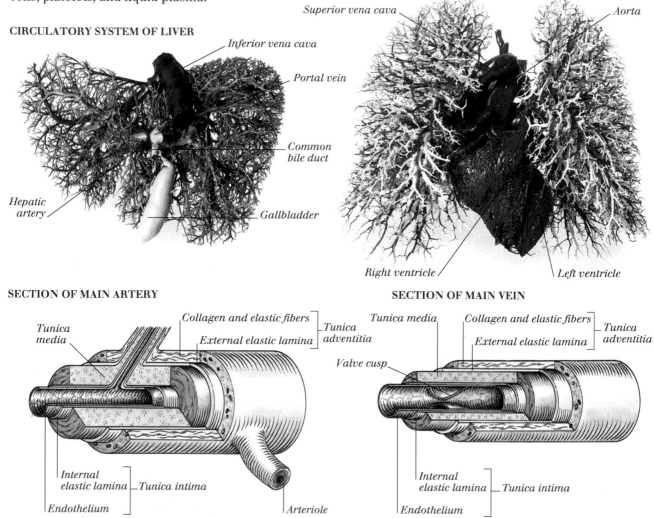

PRINCIPAL ARTERIES AND VEINS OF CIRCULATORY SYSTEM

Common carotid artery

Subclavian artery

Arch of aorta

Axillary artery

Pulmonary artery

Coronary artery

Brachial artery

Gastric artery

Hepatic artery

Splenic artery

Superior mesenteric artery

Radial artery

Ulnar artery

Palmar arch

Digital artery

Common iliac artery

External iliac artery

Internal iliac artery

Femoral artery

Popliteal artery

Peroneal artery

Anterior tibial artery

Posterior tibial artery

Lateral plantar artery

Dorsal metatarsal artery

Internal jugular vein

Brachiocephalic vein

Subclavian vein

Axillary vein

Cephalic vein

Superior vena cava

Pulmonary vein

Basilic vein

Hepatic portal vein

Median cubital vein

Inferior vena cava

Anterior median vein

Gastroepiploic vein

Palmar vein

Digital vein

Inferior mesenteric vein

Superior mesenteric vein

Common iliac vein

External iliac vein

Internal iliac vein

Femoral vein

Great saphenous vein

Short saphenous vein

Dorsal venous arch

Digital vein

TYPES OF BLOOD CELLS

RED BLOOD CELLS
These cells are biconcave in shape to maximize their oxygen-carrying capacity.

WHITE BLOOD CELLS
Lymphocytes are the smallest white blood cells; they form antibodies against disease.

PLATELETS
Tiny cells that are activated whenever blood clotting or repair to vessels is necessary.

BLOOD CLOTTING

Filaments of fibrin enmesh red blood cells as part of the process of blood clotting.

Respiratory system

THE RESPIRATORY SYSTEM supplies the oxygen needed by body cells and carries off their carbon dioxide waste. Inhaled air passes via the trachea (windpipe) through two narrower tubes, the bronchi, to the lungs. Each lung comprises many fine, branching tubes called bronchioles that end in tiny clustered chambers called alveoli. Gases cross the thin alveolar walls to and from a network of tiny blood vessels. Intercostal (rib) muscles and the muscular diaphragm below the lungs operate the lungs like bellows, drawing air in and forcing it out at regular intervals.

BRONCHIOLE AND ALVEOLI

Bronchial nerve
Branch of pulmonary vein
Terminal bronchiole
Bronchial vein
Visceral cartilage
Mucosal gland
Branch of pulmonary artery
Elastic fibers
Interalveolar septum
Alveolus
Connective tissue
Capillary network
Epithelium

SEGMENTS OF BRONCHIAL TREE

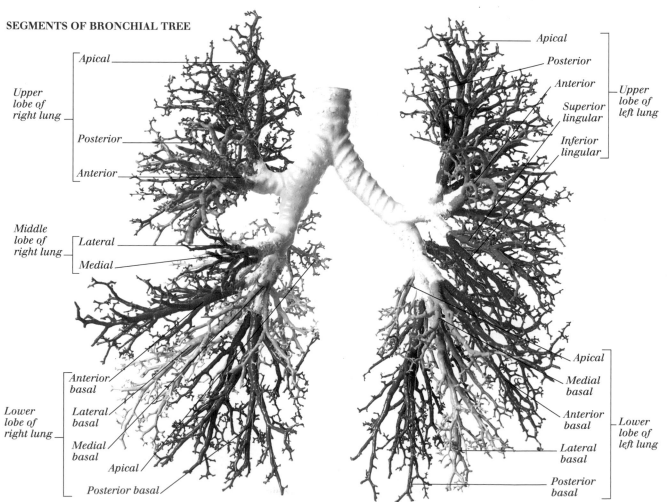

Apical
Upper lobe of right lung
Posterior
Anterior

Middle lobe of right lung
Lateral
Medial

Lower lobe of right lung
Anterior basal
Lateral basal
Medial basal
Apical
Posterior basal

Apical
Posterior
Anterior
Superior lingual
Inferior lingual
Upper lobe of left lung

Apical
Medial basal
Anterior basal
Lateral basal
Posterior basal
Lower lobe of left lung

STRUCTURES OF THORACIC CAVITY

GASEOUS EXCHANGE IN ALVEOLUS

Epiglottis

Hyoid bone

Thyroid cartilage

Thyroid gland

Apex of lung

Superior vena cava

Upper lobe of right lung

Horizontal fissure

Oblique fissure

Cricoid cartilage

Trachea

Aorta

Upper lobe of left lung

Pulmonary trunk

Left pulmonary artery

Heart

Lower lobe of left lung

Secondary bronchus

Tertiary bronchus

Muscular wall of diaphragm

Lower lobe of right lung

Middle lobe of right lung

Right crus of diaphragm

Abdominal aorta

Left crus of diaphragm

Esophagus

Oxygen diffuses into blood

Oxygenated blood

Alveolus

Deoxygenated blood rich in carbon dioxide

Carbon dioxide diffuses from blood into alveolus

MECHANISM OF RESPIRATION
INSPIRATION

Lung expands

Air drawn into lungs

Diaphragm contracts and flattens

Intercostal muscles contract

EXPIRATION

Lung contracts

Air forced out of lungs

Diaphragm relaxes and moves up

Intercostal muscles relax

Urinary system

THE URINARY SYSTEM FILTERS WASTE PRODUCTS from the blood and removes them from the body via a system of tubes. Blood is filtered in the two kidneys, which are fist-sized, bean-shaped organs. The renal arteries carry blood to the kidneys; the renal veins remove blood after filtering. Each kidney contains about one million tiny units called nephrons. Each nephron is made up of a tubule and a filtering unit called a glomerulus, which consists of a collection of tiny blood vessels surrounded by the hollow Bowman's capsule. The filtering process produces a watery fluid that leaves the kidney as urine. The urine is carried via two tubes called ureters to the bladder, where it is stored until its release from the body through another tube called the urethra.

ARTERIAL SYSTEM OF KIDNEYS

Aorta

Celiac trunk

Superior mesenteric artery

Right renal artery

Left renal artery

Right ureter

Left ureter

SECTION THROUGH LEFT KIDNEY

Interlobular vein

Collecting tubule

Medullary pyramid

Bowman's capsule

Interlobular artery

Nephron

Cortex

Medulla

Loop of Henlé

Renal artery

Renal vein

Renal pelvis

Renal sinus

Ureter

Major calyx

Minor calyx

Renal papilla

Fibrous capsule

Renal column

SECTION OF KIDNEY

Interlobular artery

Collecting tubule

Interlobular vein

Distal convoluted tubule

Nephron

Glomerulus

Cortex

Bowman's capsule

Proximal convoluted tubule

Medulla

Collecting duct

Loop of Henlé

Duct of Bellini

Vasa recta

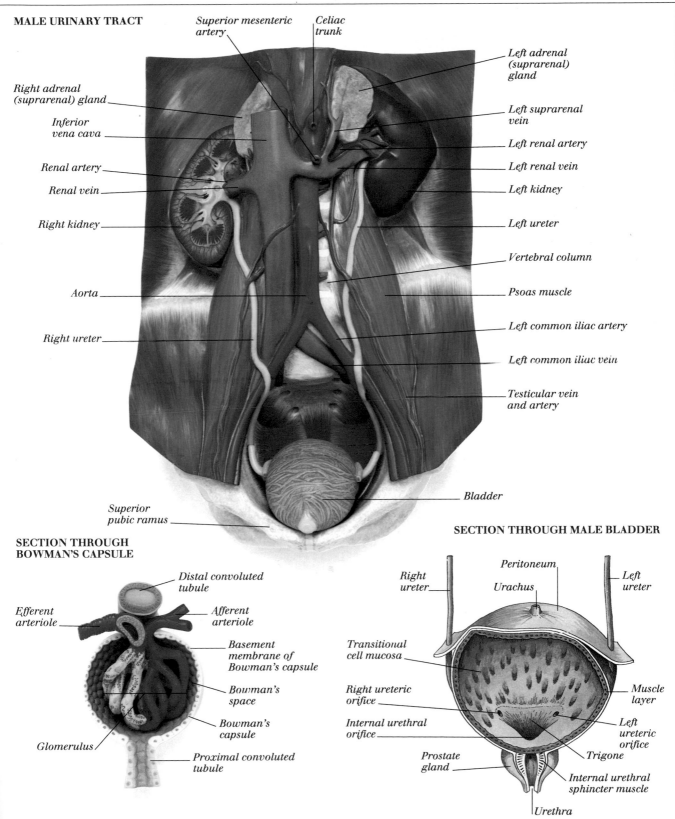

MALE URINARY TRACT

Superior mesenteric artery

Celiac trunk

Left adrenal (suprarenal) gland

Right adrenal (suprarenal) gland

Inferior vena cava

Left suprarenal vein

Left renal artery

Renal artery

Left renal vein

Renal vein

Left kidney

Right kidney

Left ureter

Vertebral column

Aorta

Psoas muscle

Right ureter

Left common iliac artery

Left common iliac vein

Testicular vein and artery

Bladder

Superior pubic ramus

SECTION THROUGH BOWMAN'S CAPSULE

Distal convoluted tubule

Efferent arteriole

Afferent arteriole

Basement membrane of Bowman's capsule

Bowman's space

Bowman's capsule

Glomerulus

Proximal convoluted tubule

SECTION THROUGH MALE BLADDER

Right ureter

Peritoneum

Urachus

Left ureter

Transitional cell mucosa

Muscle layer

Right ureteric orifice

Internal urethral orifice

Left ureteric orifice

Prostate gland

Trigone

Internal urethral sphincter muscle

Urethra

Reproductive system

SEX ORGANS LOCATED IN THE PELVIS create new human lives. Each month a ripe egg is released from one of the female's ovaries into a fallopian tube leading to the uterus (womb), a muscular pear-sized organ. A male produces minute tadpole-like sperm in two oval glands called testes. When the male is ready to release sperm into the female's vagina, many millions pass into his urethra and leave his body through the fleshy penis. The sperm travel up through the vagina into the uterus and one sperm may enter and fertilize an egg. The fertilized egg becomes embedded in the uterus wall and starts to grow into a new human being.

SECTION THROUGH OVARY

Corpus albicans

Fallopian tube

Corpus luteum

Mature ruptured follicle

Primary follicle

Germinal epithelium

Graffian follicle

Oocyte (egg)

Secondary follicle

SECTION THROUGH FEMALE PELVIC REGION

Ovary

Fundus of uterus

Uterus (womb)

Cervix (neck of uterus)

Os

Rectum

Vagina

Anus

Perineum

Introitus (vaginal opening)

Ureter

Ampulla of fallopian tube

Fimbria of fallopian tube

Isthmus of fallopian tube

Bladder

Pubic symphysis

Urethra

Clitoris

External urinary meatus

Labia minora

Labia majora

258

FEMALE REPRODUCTIVE ORGANS

Fallopian tube
Ovarian ligament
Ovary
Body of uterus (womb)
Os
Vagina
Fundus of uterus
Isthmus of fallopian tube
Ampulla of fallopian tube
Fimbria of fallopian tube
Cervix (neck of uterus)

MALE REPRODUCTIVE ORGANS

External spermatic fascia
Cremasteric fascia
Internal spermatic fascia
Epididymis
Testis (testicle)
Scrotum
Glans penis
Prostate gland
Ductus vas deferens
Seminal vesicle
Bulbourethral gland
Urethra
Corpus spongiosum
Corpus cavernosum
Prepuce (foreskin)
Urethral opening

SECTION THROUGH MALE PELVIC REGION

Intervertebral disk
Ureter
Colon
Sacrum
Seminal vesicle
Ejaculatory duct

EXTERNAL STRUCTURE OF SPERM

Acrosomal cap
Mitochondrial sheath
Head
Terminal ring
Tailpiece
Flagellum

Bladder
Pubis of pelvis
Prostate gland
Penis
Corpus cavernosum
Corpus spongiosum
Urethra
Epididymis
Glans penis
Testis (testicle)
Scrotum

259

Development of a baby

A FERTILIZED EGG IS NOURISHED AND PROTECTED as it develops into an embryo and then a fetus during the 40 weeks of pregnancy. The placenta, a mass of blood vessels implanted in the uterus lining, delivers nourishment and oxygen, and removes waste through the umbilical cord. Meanwhile, the fetus lies snugly in its amniotic sac, a bag of fluid that protects it against any sudden jolts. In the last weeks of the pregnancy, the rapidly growing fetus turns head down: a baby ready to be born.

EMBRYO AT FIVE WEEKS

Rudimentary ear

Rudimentary eye

Rudimentary mouth

Heart bulge

Arm bud

Rudimentary liver

Tail bud

Leg bud

Rudimentary vertebra

Amniotic fluid

Umbilicus (navel)

Uterine wall

Fetus

SECTION THROUGH PLACENTA

Umbilical cord

Umbilical vein

Amnion

Umbilical artery

Fetal blood vessels

Chorionic plate

Chorion

Trophoblast

Chorionic villus

Pool of maternal blood

Septum

Decidual plate

Maternal blood vessel

Myometrium

**SECTION THROUGH PELVIS IN
NINTH MONTH OF PREGNANCY**

THE DEVELOPING FETUS

Placenta

Uterine wall

Fallopian
tube

Fetus

SECOND MONTH
All the internal
organs have
developed by
this stage.

Intervertebral
disk

Vertebra

Spinal cord

Umbilical
cord

THIRD MONTH
The fetus is
fully formed
and now
begins a
period of rapid
growth.

FIFTH MONTH
Although the fetus
here is in breech
(bottom down)
position, it
will probably
turn by 180°
before birth. By
the fifth month
the baby is moving
actively and responds
to sound.

Cervix

Bladder

Cervix

Rectum

Anus

Pubic
bone

Vagina

Urethra

SEVENTH MONTH
The internal organs
are maturing in
preparation for life
outside the uterus.
The baby has grown
to such a size that
there is less room
for movement
within the uterus.

Placenta

GEOLOGY, GEOGRAPHY, AND METEOROLGY

Earth's physical features

MOST OF THE EARTH'S SURFACE (about 70 percent) is covered with water. The largest single body of water, the Pacific Ocean, alone covers about 30 percent of the surface. Most of the land is distributed as seven continents; these are (from largest to smallest) Asia, Africa, North America, South America, Antarctica, Europe, and Australasia. The physical features of the land are remarkably varied. Among the most notable are mountain ranges, rivers, and deserts. The largest mountain ranges—the Himalayas in Asia and the Andes in South America—extend for thousands of miles. The Himalayas include the world's highest mountain, Mount Everest (29,029 feet). The longest rivers are the River Nile in Africa (4,160 miles) and the Amazon River in South America (4,000 miles). Deserts cover about 20 percent of the total land area. The largest is the Sahara, which covers nearly a third of Africa. The Earth's surface features can be represented in various ways. Only a globe can correctly represent areas, shapes, sizes, and directions, because there is always distortion when a spherical surface like the Earth's is projected onto the flat surface of a map. Each map projection is therefore a compromise: some aspects of global features are shown accurately by allowing others to be distorted. Even satellite mapping does not produce completely accurate maps, although they can show physical features with great clarity.

EXAMPLES OF MAP PROJECTIONS

CYLINDRICAL PROJECTION

CYLINDRICAL-PROJECTION MAP

SATELLITE MAPPING OF THE EARTH

Satellite takes photographs of the Earth

Solar panel

Earth's rotation

Antenna

Earth

Polar orbit of satellite

Area of Earth's surface on each photograph

Composite picture of Earth created from thousands of separate images

180° 160° 120° 80°

Great Slave Lake
Great Bear Lake
Lake Superior
Greenland
Mackenzie-Peace River
Hudson Bay
Baffin Island
Bering Sea
NORTH AMERICA
Rocky Mountains
Mississippi-Missouri River
Lake Huron
Lake Ontario
Lake Erie
Lake Michigan
Sonoran Desert
Sierra Madre
Appalachian Mountains
ATLANTIC OCEAN
Gulf of Mexico
Chihuahuan Desert
Caribbean Sea
Guiana Highlands
Amazon River
Brazilian Highlands
PACIFIC OCEAN
Andes
Atacama Desert
Gran Chaco
Mato Grosso
Parana River
Pampas
Patagonia

180° 160° 120° 80°

WEST OF GREENWICH MERIDIAN

CONICAL
PROJECTION

CONICAL-
PROJECTION MAP

AZIMUTHAL
PROJECTION

AZIMUTHAL-
PROJECTION MAP

MODIFIED
AZIMUTHAL-PROJECTION MAP

SATELLITE MAP OF THE EARTH

160° 180°
120°
80°
40°
0°

ARCTIC
OCEAN

Aral Sea
Caucasus
Carpathians
Alps
Pyrenees

EUROPE

Black Sea

...as
...untains

...ara

Mediterranean
Sea

AFRICA

Red
Sea

Ural
Mountains

Kara
Kum

River
Ob-Irtysh

River
Lena

ASIA

River
Amur

Lake Baikal

Sea of
Japan

Honshu

Gobi Desert

Yellow River
(Huang He)

Yangtze
River (Chang
Jiang)

South
China
Sea

Pamirs

Caspian
Sea

Thar
Desert

Himalayas

Arabian
Desert

River Nile

Lake Victoria

Lake
Tanganyika

Takla Makan
Desert

River
Mekong

Borneo

New Guinea

Sumatra

INDIAN
OCEAN

Australian
Desert

AUSTRALASIA

River Congo
(Zaire)

Madagascar

Namib
Desert

Lake Nyasa

Kalahari
Desert

Drakensberg

New Zealand

ANTARCTICA

ARCTIC CIRCLE
(66° 52'N)

TROPIC OF
CANCER
(25° 50'N)

PACIFIC
OCEAN

EQUATOR
(0°)

TROPIC OF
CAPRICORN
(25° 50'S)

ANTARCTIC CIRCLE
(66° 52'S)

0°
40°
80°
120°
160° 180°

GREENWICH
MERIDIAN

EAST OF GREENWICH
MERIDIAN

The rock cycle

THE ROCK CYCLE IS A CONTINUOUS PROCESS through which old rocks are transformed into new ones. Rocks can be divided into three main groups: igneous, sedimentary, and metamorphic. Igneous rocks are formed when magma (molten rock) from the Earth's interior cools and solidifies (see pp. 274-275). Sedimentary rocks are formed when sediment (rock particles, for example) becomes compressed and cemented together in a process known as lithification (see pp. 276-277). Metamorphic rocks are formed when igneous, sedimentary, or other metamorphic rocks are changed by heat or pressure (see pp. 274-275). Rocks are added to the Earth's surface by crustal movements and volcanic activity. Once exposed on the surface, the rocks are broken down into rock particles by weathering (see pp. 282-283). The particles are then transported by glaciers, rivers, and wind and are deposited as sediment in lakes, deltas, deserts, and on the ocean floor. Some of this

HEXAGONAL BASALT COLUMNS, ICELAND

sediment undergoes lithification and forms sedimentary rock. This rock may be thrust back to the surface by crustal movements or forced deeper into the Earth's interior, where heat and pressure transform it into metamorphic rock. The metamorphic rock in turn may be pushed up to the surface or may be melted to form magma. Eventually, the magma cools and solidifies—below or on the surface—forming igneous rock. When the sedimentary, igneous, and metamorphic rocks are exposed once more on the Earth's surface, the cycle begins again.

THE ROCK CYCLE

Igneous rock

Cooling and solidification (crystallization)

Weathering, transport, and deposition

Sediment

Heat and pressure (metamorphism)

Weathering, transport, and deposition

Weathering, transport, and deposition

Compression and cementation (lithification)

Magma

Melting

Heat and pressure (metamorphism)

Metamorphic rock

Sedimentary rock

STAGES IN THE ROCK CYCLE

Magma extruded as lava, which solidifies to form igneous rock

Lava flow

Vent

Main conduit

Secondary conduit

Lava

Ash

Rock surrounding magma changed by heat to form metamorphic rock

Intense heat of rising magma melts some of the surrounding rock

Sedimentary rock crushed and folded to form metamorphic rock

IGNEOUS ROCK

Pyroxene crystal

Olivine crystal

Plagioclase feldspar

Coarse-grained texture

Dark pyroxene crystal

PHOTOMICROGRAPH OF GABBRO

PIECE OF GABBRO

SEDIMENTARY ROCK

Mud groundmass (matrix)

Brown coloring from iron oxides

Ammonite shell

Fine-grained texture

Ammonite shell embedded in rock

PHOTOMICROGRAPH OF SHELLY LIMESTONE

PIECE OF SHELLY LIMESTONE

METAMORPHIC ROCK

Garnet crystal (pink)

Quartz and feldspar crystal (gray)

Red garnet crystal

Wavy foliation

PHOTOMICROGRAPH OF GARNET-MICA SCHIST

PIECE OF GARNET-MICA SCHIST

Mountain

Glacier erodes rocks and carries rock particles to river

Waterfall erodes rock

River erodes valley floor and carries rock particles downstream

Rock particles deposited as sediment in lake

Rock particles deposited by wind to form sand dunes

Rock particles deposited in delta

Larger rock particles deposited on continental shelf

Continental shelf

Continental slope

Finer rock particles collect on ocean floor to form layers of sediment

Layers of sediment compressed and cemented to form sedimentary rock

267

Minerals

A MINERAL IS A NATURALLY OCCURRING SUBSTANCE that has a characteristic chemical composition and specific physical properties, such as habit and streak (see pp. 270-271). A rock, by comparison, is an aggregate of minerals and need not have a specific chemical composition. Minerals are made up of elements (substances that cannot be broken down chemically into simpler substances), each of which can be represented by a chemical symbol. Minerals can be divided into two main groups: native elements and compounds. Native elements are made up of a pure element. Examples include gold (chemical symbol Au), silver (Ag), copper (Cu), and carbon (C); carbon occurs as a native element in two forms, diamond and graphite. Compounds are combinations of two or more elements. For example, sulfides are compounds of sulfur (S) and one or more other elements, such as lead (Pb) in the mineral galena, or antimony (Sb) in the mineral stibnite.

NATIVE ELEMENTS

Dendritic (branching) copper

Limonite groundmass (matrix)

COPPER
(Cu)

Dendritic (branching) gold

Quartz vein

GOLD
(Au)

White diamond

Kimberlite groundmass (matrix)

DIAMOND
(C)

Hexagonal graphite crystal

GRAPHITE
(C)

SULFIDES

Cubic galena crystal

GALENA
(PbS)

Prismatic stibnite crystal

Quartz groundmass (matrix)

STIBNITE
(Sb_2S_3)

Perfect octahedral pyrites crystal

Quartz crystal

PYRITES
(FeS_2)

OXIDES/HYDROXIDES

Milky quartz groundmass (matrix)

Smoky quartz crystal

SMOKY QUARTZ
(SiO_2)

Rounded bauxite grains in groundmass (matrix)

BAUXITE
(FeO(OH) and $Al_2O_3.2H_2O$)

Mass of specular hematite crystals

SPECULAR HEMATITE
(Fe_2O_3)

Parallel bands of onyx

ONYX
(SiO_2)

Kidney ore hematite

Specular crystals of hematite

KIDNEY ORE HEMATITE
(Fe_2O_3)

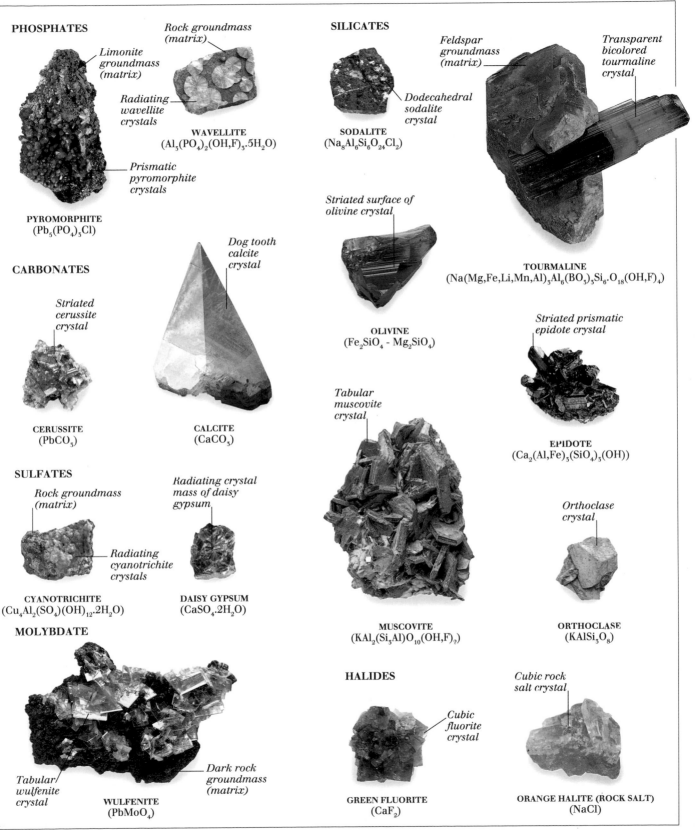

PHOSPHATES

Limonite groundmass (matrix)

Rock groundmass (matrix)

Radiating wavellite crystals

WAVELLITE
$(Al_5(PO_4)_2(OH,F)_3.5H_2O)$

Prismatic pyromorphite crystals

PYROMORPHITE
$(Pb_5(PO_4)_3Cl)$

CARBONATES

Striated cerussite crystal

Dog tooth calcite crystal

CERUSSITE
$(PbCO_3)$

CALCITE
$(CaCO_3)$

SULFATES

Rock groundmass (matrix)

Radiating crystal mass of daisy gypsum

Radiating cyanotrichite crystals

CYANOTRICHITE
$(Cu_4Al_2(SO_4)(OH)_{12}.2H_2O)$

DAISY GYPSUM
$(CaSO_4.2H_2O)$

MOLYBDATE

Tabular wulfenite crystal

Dark rock groundmass (matrix)

WULFENITE
$(PbMoO_4)$

SILICATES

Feldspar groundmass (matrix)

Transparent bicolored tourmaline crystal

Dodecahedral sodalite crystal

SODALITE
$(Na_8Al_6Si_6O_{24}Cl_2)$

Striated surface of olivine crystal

TOURMALINE
$(Na(Mg,Fe,Li,Mn,Al)_3Al_6(BO_3)_3Si_6.O_{18}(OH,F)_4)$

OLIVINE
$(Fe_2SiO_4 - Mg_2SiO_4)$

Striated prismatic epidote crystal

Tabular muscovite crystal

EPIDOTE
$(Ca_2(Al,Fe)_3(SiO_4)_3(OH))$

Orthoclase crystal

MUSCOVITE
$(KAl_2(Si_3Al)O_{10}(OH,F)_2)$

ORTHOCLASE
$(KAlSi_3O_8)$

HALIDES

Cubic rock salt crystal

Cubic fluorite crystal

GREEN FLUORITE
(CaF_2)

ORANGE HALITE (ROCK SALT)
$(NaCl)$

Mineral features

MINERALS CAN BE IDENTIFIED BY STUDYING features such as fracture, cleavage, crystal system, habit, hardness, color, and streak. Minerals can break in different ways. If a mineral breaks in an irregular way, leaving rough surfaces, it possesses fracture. If a mineral breaks along well-defined planes of weakness, it possesses cleavage. Specific minerals have distinctive patterns of cleavage. For example, mica cleaves along one plane. Most minerals form crystals that can be categorized into crystal systems according to their symmetry and number of faces. Within each system, several different but related forms of crystal are possible; for example, a cubic crystal can have six, eight, or twelve sides. A mineral's habit is the typical form taken by an aggregate of its crystals. Examples of habit include botryoidal (like a bunch of grapes) and massive (no definite form). The relative hardness of a mineral may be assessed by testing its resistance to scratching. This property is usually measured using Mohs' scale, which increases in hardness from 1 (talc) to 10 (diamond). The color of a mineral is not a dependable guide to its identity as some minerals have a range of colors. Streak (the color the powdered mineral makes when rubbed across an unglazed tile) is a more reliable indicator.

CLEAVAGE

Cleavage in one direction

CLEAVAGE ALONG ONE PLANE

Cleavage in three directions, forming a block cube

CLEAVAGE ALONG THREE PLANES

Horizontal cleavage

Vertical cleavage

CLEAVAGE ALONG TWO PLANES

Cleavage in four directions, forming a double-pyramid crystal

CLEAVAGE ALONG FOUR PLANES

CRYSTAL SYSTEMS

Cubic iron pyrites crystal

Tetragonal idocrase crystal

Representation of tetragonal system

TETRAGONAL SYSTEM

CUBIC SYSTEM

Representation of cubic system

Hexagonal beryl crystal

Representation of hexagonal/trigonal system

HEXAGONAL/TRIGONAL SYSTEM

Orthorhombic barite crystal

Representation of orthorhombic system

ORTHORHOMBIC SYSTEM

FRACTURE

Fire opal with conchoidal (shell-like) fracture

Nickel-iron with hackly (jagged) fracture

CONCHOIDAL FRACTURE

HACKLY FRACTURE

Orpiment with uneven fracture

Garnierite with splintery fracture

UNEVEN FRACTURE

SPLINTERY FRACTURE

Monoclinic selenite crystal

Representation of monoclinic system

Triclinic axinite crystal

Representation of triclinic system

MONOCLINIC SYSTEM

TRICLINIC SYSTEM

HABIT

Kunzite with prismatic habit

Silver with twisted wire habit

TWISTED WIRE HABIT

PRISMATIC HABIT

Wollastonite with fibrous habit

Hematite with tabular habit (flattened structure)

TABULAR HABIT

FIBROUS HABIT

Chalcedony with botryoidal habit (like a bunch of grapes)

Carnallite with massive habit (no definite shape)

BOTRYOIDAL HABIT

MASSIVE HABIT

STREAK

COLOR OF MINERAL

COLOR OF STREAK

Yellow orpiment — *Golden-yellow*

Brown hematite — *Red-brown*

Red-brown crocoite — *Yellow*

Gold chalcopyrite — *Black*

Black-red cinnabar — *Red*

Silver molybdenite — *Gray*

COLOR

Rose-colored crystal of rose quartz

ROSE, PINK

Translucent white-gray crystal of milky quartz

WHITE-GRAY

Translucent crystal of orange citrine

Transparent glassy crystal of rock crystal

ORANGE

BEIGE, TRANSPARENT

MOHS' SCALE OF HARDNESS

TALC	GYPSUM	CALCITE	FLUORITE	APATITE	ORTHOCLASE	QUARTZ	TOPAZ	CORUNDUM	DIAMOND
1	2	3	4	5	6	7	8	9	10

Volcanoes

VOLCANOES ARE VENTS OR FISSURES IN THE EARTH'S crust through which magma (molten rock that originates from deep beneath the crust) is forced onto the surface as lava. They occur most commonly along the boundaries of crustal plates; most volcanoes lie in a belt called the "Ring of Fire," which runs along the edge of the Pacific Ocean. Volcanoes can be classified according to the violence and frequency of their eruptions.

Nonexplosive volcanic eruptions generally occur where crustal plates pull apart. These eruptions produce runny basaltic lava that spreads quickly over a wide area to form relatively flat cones. The most violent eruptions take place where plates collide. Such eruptions produce thick rhyolitic lava and may also blast out clouds of dust and pyroclasts (lava fragments). The lava does not flow far before cooling and therefore builds up steep-sided, conical volcanoes. Some volcanoes produce lava and ash eruptions, which build up composite volcanic cones. Volcanoes that erupt frequently are described as active, those that erupt rarely are termed dormant, and those that have stopped erupting altogether are termed extinct. Besides the volcanoes themselves, other features associated with volcanic regions include geysers, hot mineral springs, solfataras, fumaroles, and bubbling mud pools.

Folded, rope-like surface

PAHOEHOE
(ROPY LAVA)

HORU GEYSER,
NEW ZEALAND

VOLCANO TYPES

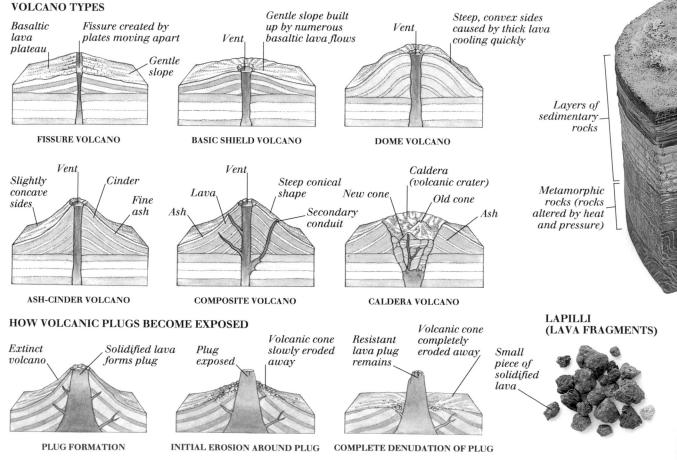

Basaltic lava plateau *Fissure created by plates moving apart* *Gentle slope*

FISSURE VOLCANO

Gentle slope built up by numerous basaltic lava flows *Vent*

BASIC SHIELD VOLCANO

Vent *Steep, convex sides caused by thick lava cooling quickly*

DOME VOLCANO

Slightly concave sides *Vent* *Cinder* *Fine ash*

ASH-CINDER VOLCANO

Vent *Lava* *Ash* *Steep conical shape* *Secondary conduit*

COMPOSITE VOLCANO

Caldera (volcanic crater) *New cone* *Old cone* *Ash*

CALDERA VOLCANO

Layers of sedimentary rocks

Metamorphic rocks (rocks altered by heat and pressure)

HOW VOLCANIC PLUGS BECOME EXPOSED

Extinct volcano *Solidified lava forms plug*

PLUG FORMATION

Plug exposed *Volcanic cone slowly eroded away*

INITIAL EROSION AROUND PLUG

Resistant lava plug remains *Volcanic cone completely eroded away*

COMPLETE DENUDATION OF PLUG

LAPILLI (LAVA FRAGMENTS)

Small piece of solidified lava

TYPES OF LAVA

Scoria (sharp, angular chunks)

Driblets of lava from roof of tunnel

AA (BLOCKY LAVA)

REMELTED LAVA

LOCATION OF VOLCANOES

▲ Volcano

╘┼┼┼ Plate boundary

STRUCTURE OF A VOLCANO

Steeply sloping cone consisting of numerous layers of ash and lava

Vent

Plug (solidified lava)

Main conduit

Volcanic ash

Cinder cone

Parasitic cone

Mineral spring

Laccolith

Secondary conduit

Magma reservoir

Lava flow

Groundwater

VOLCANIC FEATURES

Sulfurous gases

SOLFATARA

Jet of hot water and steam

Water heated by hot rocks

Steam pressure builds up

GEYSER

Hot water

Mud and surface deposits mixed with hot water

MUD POOL

Superheated water

Steam

FUMAROLE

Igneous and metamorphic rocks

BASALT COLUMNS

IGNEOUS ROCKS ARE FORMED WHEN MAGMA (molten rock that originates from deep beneath the Earth's crust) cools and solidifies. There are two main types of igneous rock: intrusive and extrusive. Intrusive rocks are formed deep underground, where magma is forced into cracks or between rock layers to form structures including sills, dikes, and batholiths. The magma cools slowly to form coarse-grained rocks such as gabbro and pegmatite. Extrusive rocks are formed above the Earth's surface from lava (magma that has been ejected in a volcanic eruption). The molten lava cools quickly, producing fine-grained rocks such as rhyolite and basalt. Metamorphic rocks are those that have been altered by intense heat (contact metamorphism) or extreme pressure (regional metamorphism). Contact metamorphism occurs when rocks are changed by heat from, for example, an igneous intrusion or lava flow. Regional metamorphism occurs when rock is crushed in the middle of a folding mountain range. Metamorphic rocks can be formed from igneous rocks, sedimentary rocks, or even other metamorphic rocks.

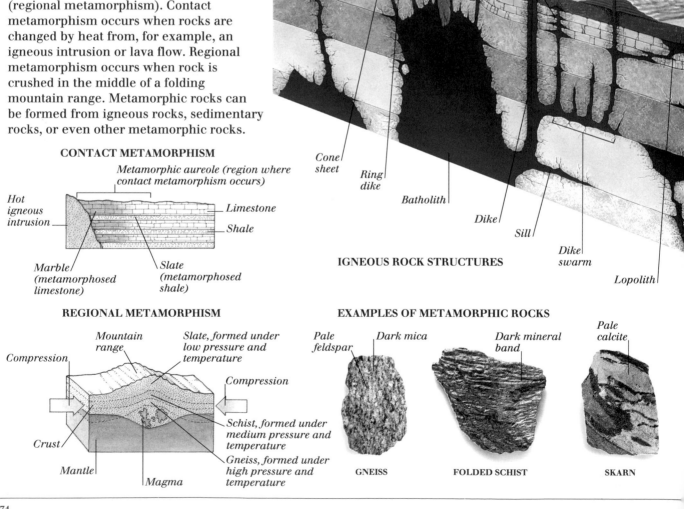

CONTACT METAMORPHISM

Metamorphic aureole (region where contact metamorphism occurs)

Hot igneous intrusion

Limestone

Shale

Marble (metamorphosed limestone)

Slate (metamorphosed shale)

IGNEOUS ROCK STRUCTURES

Cinder cone

Large eroded lava flow

Cedar tree laccolith

Butte

Plug

Cone sheet

Ring dike

Batholith

Dike

Sill

Dike swarm

Lopolith

REGIONAL METAMORPHISM

Mountain range

Slate, formed under low pressure and temperature

Compression

Compression

Schist, formed under medium pressure and temperature

Gneiss, formed under high pressure and temperature

Crust

Mantle

Magma

EXAMPLES OF METAMORPHIC ROCKS

Pale feldspar

Dark mica

Dark mineral band

Pale calcite

GNEISS

FOLDED SCHIST

SKARN

EXAMPLES OF EXTRUSIVE IGNEOUS ROCKS

Porphyritic texture

Fine-grained crystals

Elongated vesicles (gas cavities)

Fine-grained groundmass (matrix)

Conchoidal fracture

Glassy luster

RHYOLITE

BASALT

PUMICE

PORPHYRITIC ANDESITE

OBSIDIAN

Mesa (flat-topped plateau)

Extinct geyser

Lake

Caldera

Sea

Lava flow

Vent

Active juvenile volcano

Parasitic volcano

Main conduit

Sagging caused by weight of volcano

Magma reservoir

Eroded plug of extinct volcano

Batholith

Laccolith

EXAMPLES OF INTRUSIVE IGNEOUS ROCKS

Dark groundmass (matrix)

KIMBERLITE

Plagioclase feldspar

OLIVINE GABBRO

Amphibole crystals

White feldspar

FELDSPAR PEGMATITE

Fine groundmass (matrix)

Pyrites crystal

Chiastolite crystal

Green calc-silicate mineral

High quartz content

Amphibole crystal

SLATE WITH PYRITES

CHIASTOLITE HORNFELS

GREEN MARBLE

HALLEFLINTA

SYENITE

Sedimentary rocks

SEDIMENTARY ROCKS ARE FORMED BY THE ACCUMULATION and consolidation of sediments (see pp. 266-267). There are three main types of sedimentary rock: clastic sedimentary rocks, such as breccia or sandstone, are formed from other rocks that have been broken down into fragments by weathering (see pp. 282-283), which have then been transported and deposited elsewhere; organic sedimentary rocks, such as coal (see pp. 280-281), are derived from plant and animal remains; and chemical sedimentary rocks are formed by chemical processes. For example, rock salt is formed when salt dissolved in water is deposited as the water evaporates. Sedimentary rocks are laid down in layers called beds, or strata. Each new layer is laid down horizontally over older ones. There are usually some gaps in the sequence, called unconformities. These represent periods in which no new sediments were being laid down, or when earlier sedimentary layers were raised above sea level and eroded away.

THE GRAND CANYON, U.S.A.

EXAMPLES OF UNCONFORMITIES

Early beds tilted and eroded

Later beds horizontal

ANGULAR UNCONFORMITY

No bedding in early rocks

Later beds horizontal

NONCONFORMITY

Early beds folded and eroded

Later beds horizontal

DISCONFORMITY

SEDIMENTARY LAYERS OF THE GRAND CANYON REGION

Wasatch formation
Kaiparowits formation
Wahweap sandstone
Tropic formation
Dakota sandstone
Carmel formation
Pink Cliffs
Bryce Canyon
Zion Canyon
Gray Cliffs
Sevier fault
White Cliffs
Pipe Spring

Temple Cap sandstone | Navajo sandstone | Kayenta formation | Moenave formation | Chinle formation | Shinarump member | Moenkopi formation | Kaibab limestone | Toroweap formation | Coconino sandstone | Hermit shale

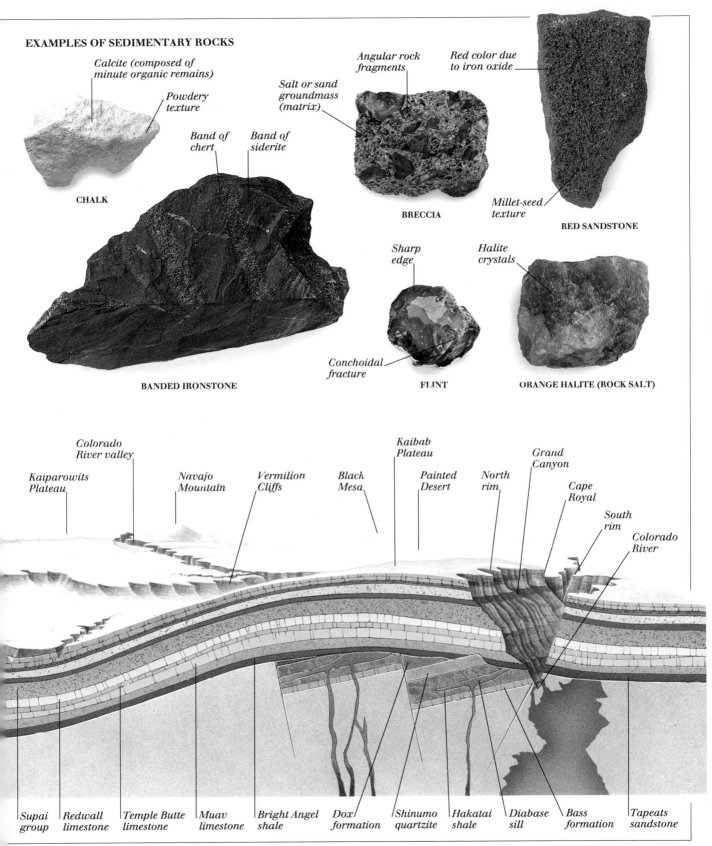

EXAMPLES OF SEDIMENTARY ROCKS

Calcite (composed of minute organic remains)

Powdery texture

CHALK

Band of chert

Band of siderite

BANDED IRONSTONE

Angular rock fragments

Salt or sand groundmass (matrix)

BRECCIA

Red color due to iron oxide

Millet-seed texture

RED SANDSTONE

Sharp edge

Conchoidal fracture

FLINT

Halite crystals

ORANGE HALITE (ROCK SALT)

Colorado River valley

Kaiparowits Plateau

Navajo Mountain

Vermilion Cliffs

Black Mesa

Kaibab Plateau

Painted Desert

North rim

Grand Canyon

Cape Royal

South rim

Colorado River

Supai group

Redwall limestone

Temple Butte limestone

Muav limestone

Bright Angel shale

Dox formation

Shinumo quartzite

Hakatai shale

Diabase sill

Bass formation

Tapeats sandstone

Fossils

FOSSILS ARE THE REMAINS of plants and animals that have been preserved in rock. A fossil may be the preserved remains of an organism itself, an impression of it in rock, or preserved traces (known as trace fossils) left by an organism while it was alive, such as organic carbon outlines, fossilized footprints, or droppings. Most dead organisms soon rot away or are eaten by scavengers. For fossilization to occur, rapid burial by sediment is necessary. The organism decays, but the harder parts—bones, teeth, and shells, for example—may be preserved and hardened by minerals from the surrounding sediment. Fossilization may also occur even when the hard parts of an organism are dissolved away to leave an impression called a mold. The mold is filled by minerals, thereby creating a cast of the organism. The study of fossils (paleontology) not only can show how living things have evolved, but can also help reveal the Earth's geological history—for example, by aiding in the dating of rock strata.

PROCESS OF FOSSILIZATION

Sea
Ammonite
Seabed

ANIMAL DIES

Sea
Shell
Seabed

SOFT PARTS ROT

Sea
Shell
Sediment
Seabed

SHELL BURIED

Shell dissolved away and replaced by minerals
Sea
Sediment
Sediment
Seabed

SHELL FOSSILIZED

EXAMPLES OF FOSSILS

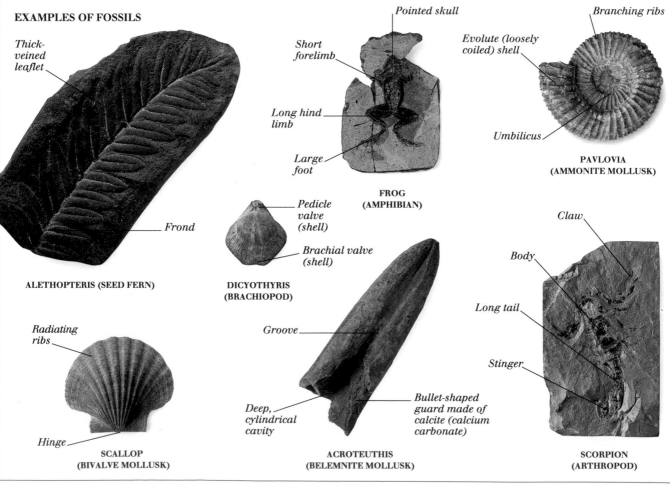

Thick-veined leaflet

Frond

ALETHOPTERIS (SEED FERN)

Radiating ribs

Hinge

SCALLOP (BIVALVE MOLLUSK)

Pointed skull

Short forelimb

Long hind limb

Large foot

FROG (AMPHIBIAN)

Pedicle valve (shell)

Brachial valve (shell)

DICYOTHYRIS (BRACHIOPOD)

Groove

Deep, cylindrical cavity

Bullet-shaped guard made of calcite (calcium carbonate)

ACROTEUTHIS (BELEMNITE MOLLUSK)

Branching ribs

Evolute (loosely coiled) shell

Umbilicus

PAVLOVIA (AMMONITE MOLLUSK)

Claw

Body

Long tail

Stinger

SCORPION (ARTHROPOD)

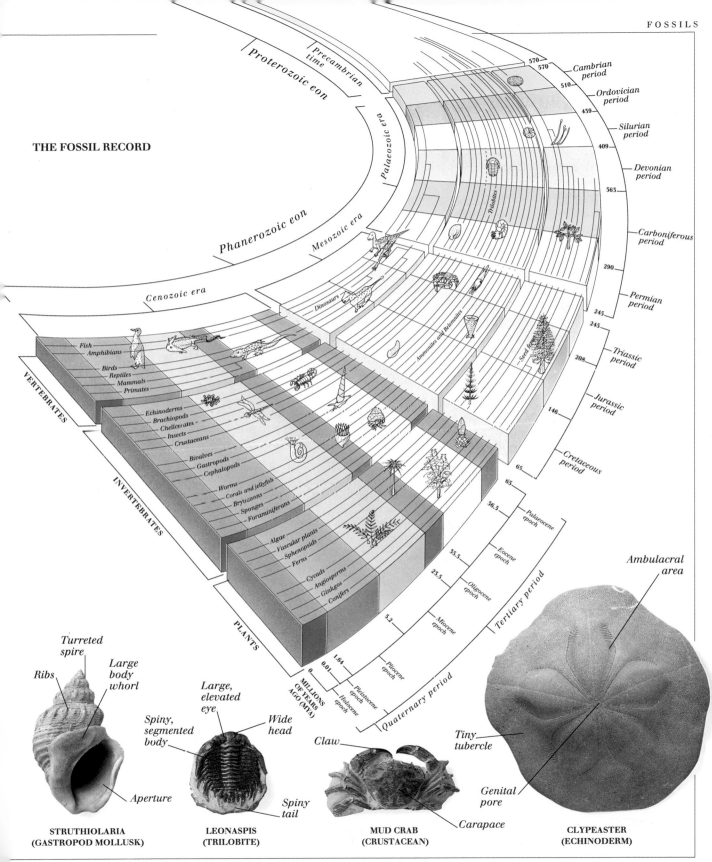

THE FOSSIL RECORD

Precambrian time

Proterozoic eon

Palaeozoic era

Phanerozoic eon

Mesozoic era

Cenozoic era

Cambrian period
Ordovician period
Silurian period
Devonian period
Carboniferous period
Permian period
Triassic period
Jurassic period
Cretaceous period
Tertiary period
Quaternary period

570
570
510
439
409
363
290
245
245
208
146
65
65
56.5
35.5
25.5
5.2
1.64
0.01
0

Palaeocene epoch
Eocene epoch
Oligocene epoch
Miocene epoch
Pliocene epoch
Pleistocene epoch
Holocene epoch

MILLIONS OF YEARS AGO (MYA)

VERTEBRATES
INVERTEBRATES
PLANTS

Fish
Amphibians
Birds
Reptiles
Mammals
Primates

Echinoderms
Brachiopods
Chelicerates
Insects
Crustaceans
Bivalves
Gastropods
Cephalopods
Worms
Corals and jellyfish
Bryozoans
Sponges
Foraminiferans

Algae
Vascular plants
Sphenopsids
Ferns
Cycads
Angiosperms
Ginkgos
Conifers

Trilobites
Dinosaurs
Ammonites and Belemnites
Seed ferns

Turreted spire
Ribs
Large body whorl
Aperture

STRUTHIOLARIA (GASTROPOD MOLLUSK)

Spiny, segmented body
Large, elevated eye
Wide head
Spiny tail

LEONASPIS (TRILOBITE)

Claw
Carapace

MUD CRAB (CRUSTACEAN)

Ambulacral area
Tiny tubercle
Genital pore

CLYPEASTER (ECHINODERM)

Mineral resources

MINERAL RESOURCES CAN BE DEFINED AS naturally occurring substances that can be extracted from the Earth and are useful as fuels and raw materials. Coal, oil, and gas—collectively called fossil fuels—are commonly included in this group, but are not strictly minerals, because they are of organic origin. Coal formation begins when vegetation is buried and partly decomposed to form peat. Overlying sediments compress the peat and transform it into lignite (soft brown coal). As the overlying sediments accumulate, increasing pressure and temperature eventually transform the lignite into bituminous and hard anthracite coals. Oil and gas are usually formed from organic molecules that were deposited in marine sediments. Under the effects of heat and pressure, the compressed organic molecules undergo complex chemical changes to form oil and gas. The oil and gas percolate upward through water-saturated permeable rocks. They may rise to the Earth's surface, or accumulate below an impermeable layer of rock that has been folded or faulted to form a trap—an anticline (upfold) trap, for example. Minerals are inorganic substances that may consist of a single chemical element, such as gold, silver, or copper, or combinations of elements (see pp. 268-269). Some minerals are concentrated in mineralization zones in rock associated with crustal movements or volcanic activity. Others may be found in sediments as placer deposits—accumulations of high-density minerals that have been weathered out of rocks, transported, and deposited (on riverbeds, for example).

OIL RIG, NORTH SEA

STAGES IN THE FORMATION OF COAL

Stalk   Leaf

PLANT MATTER

Decayed plant matter

About 60% carbon   PEAT

About 70% carbon

Crumbly texture   LIGNITE (BROWN COAL)

Powdery texture

About 80% carbon

Shiny surface   BITUMINOUS COAL   About 95% carbon

ANTHRACITE COAL

HOW COAL IS FORMED

Vegetation

Increasing layers of overlying sediment

Increasing pressure and temperature

Increasing layers of overlying sediment

Increasing pressure and temperature

Peat (about 60% carbon)

Lignite (about 70% carbon)

Bituminous coal (about 80% carbon)

PEAT   LIGNITE (BROWN COAL)   BITUMINOUS COAL

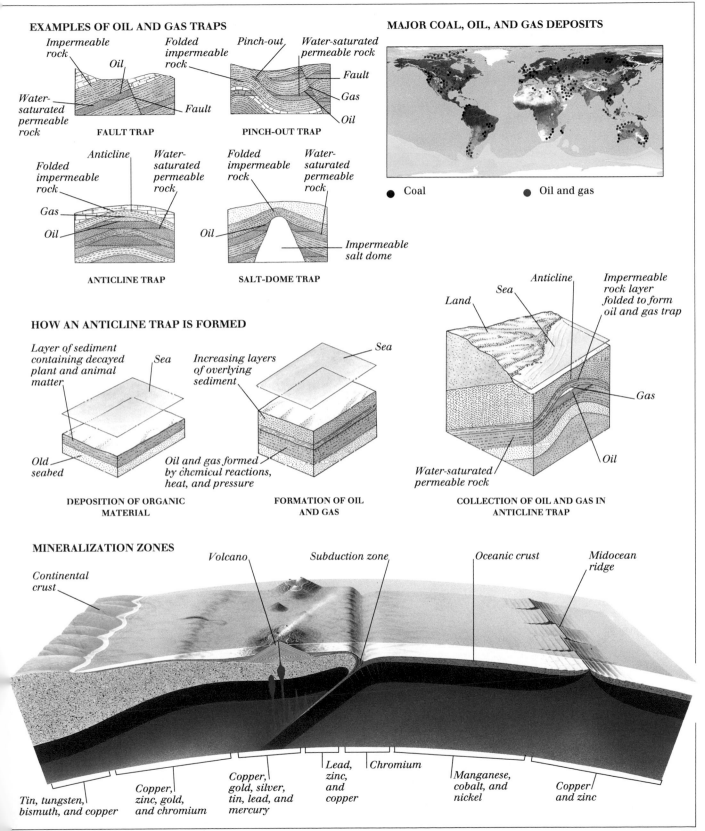

EXAMPLES OF OIL AND GAS TRAPS

Impermeable rock
Oil
Water-saturated permeable rock
FAULT TRAP
Fault

Folded impermeable rock
Pinch-out
Water-saturated permeable rock
Fault
Gas
Oil
PINCH-OUT TRAP

Folded impermeable rock
Anticline
Water-saturated permeable rock
Gas
Oil
ANTICLINE TRAP

Folded impermeable rock
Water-saturated permeable rock
Oil
Impermeable salt dome
SALT-DOME TRAP

MAJOR COAL, OIL, AND GAS DEPOSITS

● Coal   ● Oil and gas

HOW AN ANTICLINE TRAP IS FORMED

Layer of sediment containing decayed plant and animal matter
Sea
Old seabed
DEPOSITION OF ORGANIC MATERIAL

Increasing layers of overlying sediment
Sea
Oil and gas formed by chemical reactions, heat, and pressure
FORMATION OF OIL AND GAS

Land
Sea
Anticline
Impermeable rock layer folded to form oil and gas trap
Gas
Oil
Water-saturated permeable rock
COLLECTION OF OIL AND GAS IN ANTICLINE TRAP

MINERALIZATION ZONES

Continental crust
Volcano
Subduction zone
Oceanic crust
Midocean ridge

Tin, tungsten, bismuth, and copper
Copper, zinc, gold, and chromium
Copper, gold, silver, tin, lead, and mercury
Lead, zinc, and copper
Chromium
Manganese, cobalt, and nickel
Copper and zinc

281

Weathering and erosion

WEATHERING IS THE BREAKING DOWN of rocks on the Earth's surface. There are two main types: physical (or mechanical), and chemical. Physical weathering may be caused by temperature changes, such as freezing and thawing, or by abrasion from material carried by winds, rivers, or glaciers. Rocks may also be broken down by the actions of animals and plants, such as the burrowing of animals and the growth of roots. Chemical weathering causes rocks to decompose by changing their chemical composition. For example, rainwater may dissolve certain minerals in a rock. Erosion is the wearing away and removal of land surfaces by water, wind, or ice. It is greatest in areas of little or no surface vegetation, such as deserts, where sand dunes may form.

FORMATION OF A ROCK PAVEMENT (HAMADA)

Wind blows away small particles

Larger particles aggregate

Rock pavement forms

FIRST STAGE **SECOND STAGE** **FINAL STAGE**

FEATURES OF WEATHERING AND EROSION

FEATURES PRODUCED BY WIND ACTION

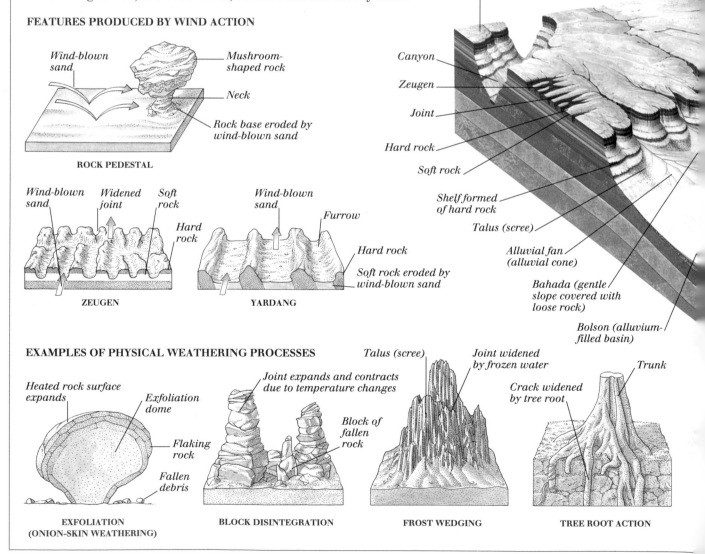

Wind-blown sand

Mushroom-shaped rock

Neck

Rock base eroded by wind-blown sand

ROCK PEDESTAL

Wind-blown sand

Widened joint

Soft rock

Hard rock

ZEUGEN

Wind-blown sand

Furrow

Hard rock

Soft rock eroded by wind-blown sand

YARDANG

Mesa (flat-topped plateau)

Canyon

Zeugen

Joint

Hard rock

Soft rock

Shelf formed of hard rock

Talus (scree)

Alluvial fan (alluvial cone)

Bahada (gentle slope covered with loose rock)

Bolson (alluvium-filled basin)

EXAMPLES OF PHYSICAL WEATHERING PROCESSES

Heated rock surface expands

Exfoliation dome

Flaking rock

Fallen debris

EXFOLIATION (ONION-SKIN WEATHERING)

Joint expands and contracts due to temperature changes

Block of fallen rock

BLOCK DISINTEGRATION

Talus (scree)

Joint widened by frozen water

FROST WEDGING

Crack widened by tree root

Trunk

TREE ROOT ACTION

SECTION THROUGH A BARKHAN DUNE

Strong wind

Weak wind

Direction of wind-blown sand

Windward face

Direction of sand movement

Slip face

Foreset strata

Cross-bed set

Topset strata

Bottomset strata

EXAMPLES OF SAND DUNES

Wind direction

Crescent-shaped dune

BARKHAN DUNE

Wind direction

Dune at right angle to wind

TRANSVERSE DUNE

Wind direction

Point where sand ridges meet

STAR DUNE

Wind direction

Parallel dunes

SEIF (LINEAR) DUNE

Canyon

Wadi (dry wash)

Mesa (flat-topped plateau)

Talus (scree)

Butte (flat-topped mesa remnant)

Eroded arch

Residual hill on pediment

Rock pavement (hamada)

Rock pedestal

Barkhan dune

Parabolic dune

Transverse dune

Seif (linear) dune

Inselberg (isolated, steep-sided hill)

Playa (dry lake bed of salt or desiccated clay)

Faultline

Freshwater lake

Fertile oasis

Deflation hollow (created by wind erosion)

Hogback (steep ridge)

Hard sandstone

Fault plane

Cuesta (asymmetric ridge)

Hard granite

Caves

CAVES COMMONLY FORM in areas of limestone, although on coastlines they also occur in other rocks. Limestone is made of calcite (calcium carbonate), which dissolves in the carbonic acid naturally present in rainwater, and in humic acids from the decay of vegetation. The acidic water trickles down through cracks and joints in the limestone and between rock layers, breaking up the surface terrain into clints (blocks of rock), separated by grikes (deep cracks), and punctuated by sinkholes (also called swallow holes or potholes) into which surface streams may disappear. Underground, the acidic water dissolves the rock around crevices, opening up a network of passages and caves, which can become large caverns if the roofs collapse. Various features are formed when the dissolved calcite is redeposited. For example, it may be redeposited along an underground stream to form a gour (series of calcite ridges), or in caves and passages to form stalactites and stalagmites. Stalactites develop where calcite is left behind as water drips from the roof; where the drops land, stalagmites build up.

STALACTITE WITH RING MARKS

Ring mark

MERGED STALACTITE

SURFACE TOPOGRAPHY OF A CAVE SYSTEM

Doline (depression caused by collapse of cave roof)

Sinkhole

Gorge where cave roof has fallen in

Porous limestone

Resurgence

Limestone terrain with clints and grikes

Impermeable rock

STALAGMITE FORMATIONS

Calcite (calcium carbonate) crystalized under water

Thin encrustations of calcite (calcium carbonate)

CRYSTALLINE STALAGMITIC FLOOR

CALCAREOUS TUFA

Scar of bare rock

Former water table

Permeable limestone

Encrustations on dead stems of small plants

Calcite (calcium carbonate)

Calcite (calcium carbonate)

Encrustations with fungoid structure

Resurgence

STALAGMITIC FLOOR

STALAGMITIC BOSS

Layer of impermeable rock

Present water table

CAVES

DEVELOPMENT OF A CAVE SYSTEM

Impermeable rock

Joint

Bedding plane

Impermeable rock

STRUCTURE OF LIMESTONE STRATA

Permeable limestone

Water seeps through cracks in rock

Calcite (calcium carbonate) deposits begin to form

Stream enters permeable rock

Resurgence

Tunnel

INITIAL CAVE

Underground stream

Doline caused by collapse of cave roof

Sinkhole

Stalactite

Stalagmite

Gorge

Resurgence

EXTENDED CAVE SYSTEM

Cave

Dry gallery

INTERCONNECTED CAVE SYSTEM

Stalactite

Pillar (column)

Gorge

Stalactite

Dry gallery (former course of underground stream)

Gour (series of calcite ridges) deposited by running water

Stalagmite

Joint in rock enlarged by water

Bedding plane

Curtain of deposited calcite (calcium carbonate)

Tunnel

Cave

Passage

Cavern

Gour (series of calcite ridges)

285

Glaciers

GLACIER BAY, ALASKA

A VALLEY GLACIER IS A LARGE MASS OF ICE that forms on land and moves slowly downhill under its own weight. It is formed from snow that collects in cirques (mountain hollows also known as corries), compressing into ice as more and more snow accumulates. The cirque is deepened by frost wedging and abrasion (see pp. 282-283), and arêtes (sharp ridges) develop between adjacent cirques. Eventually, so much ice builds up that the glacier begins to flow. As the glacier moves it collects moraine (debris), which may range in size from particles of dust to large boulders. The rocks at the base of the glacier erode the glacial valley, giving it a U-shaped cross section. Under the glacier, *roches moutonnées* (eroded outcrops of hard rock) and drumlins (rounded mounds of rock and clay) are left behind on the valley floor. The glacier ends at a terminus (the snout), where the ice melts as fast as it arrives. If the temperature increases, the ice melts faster than it arrives, and the glacier retreats. The retreating glacier leaves behind its moraine and also erratics (isolated single boulders). Glacial streams from the melting glacier deposit eskers and kames (ridges and mounds of sand and gravel) but carry away the finer sediment to form a stratified outwash plain. Lumps of ice carried on to this plain melt, creating holes called kettles.

VALLEY GLACIER

POST-GLACIAL VALLEY

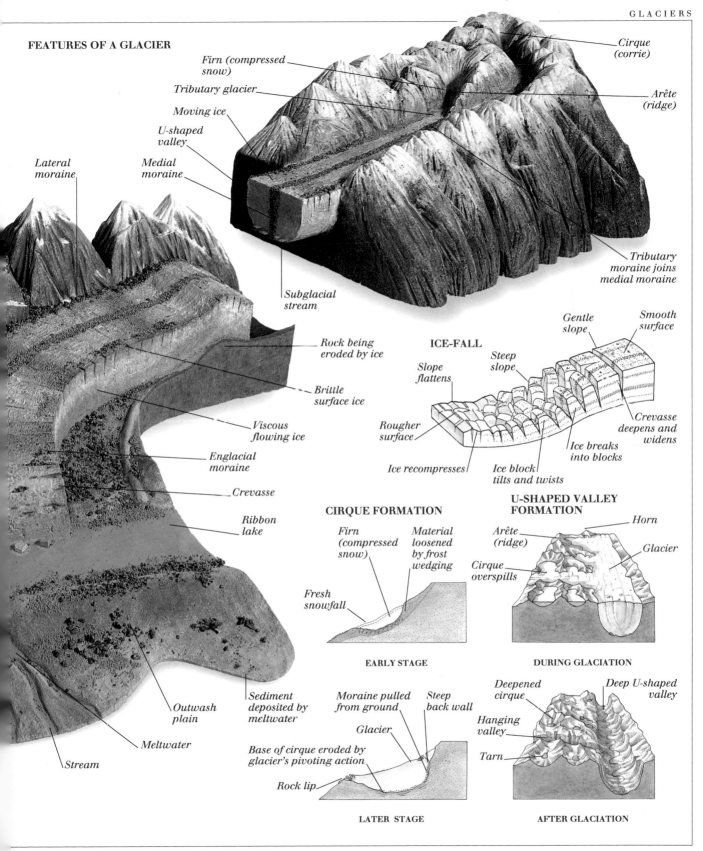

FEATURES OF A GLACIER

Cirque (corrie)

Firn (compressed snow)

Tributary glacier

Arête (ridge)

Moving ice

U-shaped valley

Medial moraine

Lateral moraine

Tributary moraine joins medial moraine

Subglacial stream

Rock being eroded by ice

ICE-FALL

Gentle slope

Smooth surface

Slope flattens

Steep slope

Brittle surface ice

Viscous flowing ice

Rougher surface

Crevasse deepens and widens

Englacial moraine

Ice breaks into blocks

Crevasse

Ice recompresses

Ice block tilts and twists

Ribbon lake

CIRQUE FORMATION

U-SHAPED VALLEY FORMATION

Firn (compressed snow)

Material loosened by frost wedging

Arête (ridge)

Horn

Glacier

Fresh snowfall

Cirque overspills

Outwash plain

Deepened cirque

Deep U-shaped valley

Sediment deposited by meltwater

Moraine pulled from ground

Steep back wall

Hanging valley

Meltwater

Glacier

Tarn

Stream

Base of cirque eroded by glacier's pivoting action

Rock lip

EARLY STAGE

LATER STAGE

DURING GLACIATION

AFTER GLACIATION

287

Rivers

RIVERS FORM PART of the water cycle—the continuous circulation of water between the land, sea, and atmosphere. The source of a river may be a mountain spring, or lake, or a melting glacier. The course that the river subsequently takes depends on the slope of the terrain and on the rock types and formations over which it flows. In its early, upland stages, a river tumbles steeply over rocks and boulders and cuts a steep-sided V-shaped valley. Farther downstream, it flows smoothly over sediments and forms winding meanders, eroding sideways to create broad valleys and plains. On reaching the coast, the river may deposit sediment, forming an estuary or delta (see pp. 290-291).

RIVER CAPTURE

Tributary erodes headward

River

River flow decreases

River

EARLY STAGE

Dry valley

River captured by tributary

River flow increases

LATER STAGE

THE WATER CYCLE

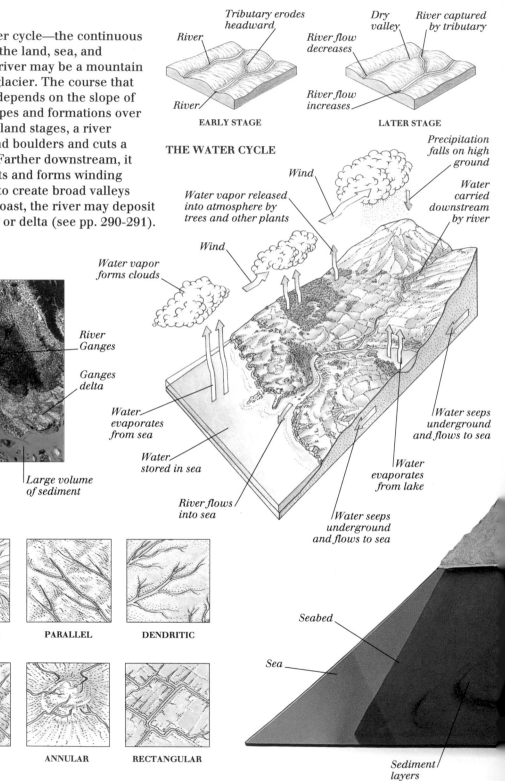

Precipitation falls on high ground

Wind

Water carried downstream by river

Water vapor released into atmosphere by trees and other plants

Wind

Water vapor forms clouds

Water evaporates from sea

Water stored in sea

River flows into sea

Water seeps underground and flows to sea

Water evaporates from lake

Water seeps underground and flows to sea

Seabed

Sea

Sediment layers

SATELLITE IMAGE OF GANGES RIVER DELTA, BANGLADESH

River Ganges

Ganges delta

Infertile swampland

Distributary

Large volume of sediment

RIVER DRAINAGE PATTERNS

RADIAL

CENTRIPETAL

PARALLEL

DENDRITIC

DERANGED

TRELLISED

ANNULAR

RECTANGULAR

288

STAGES IN A RIVER'S DEVELOPMENT

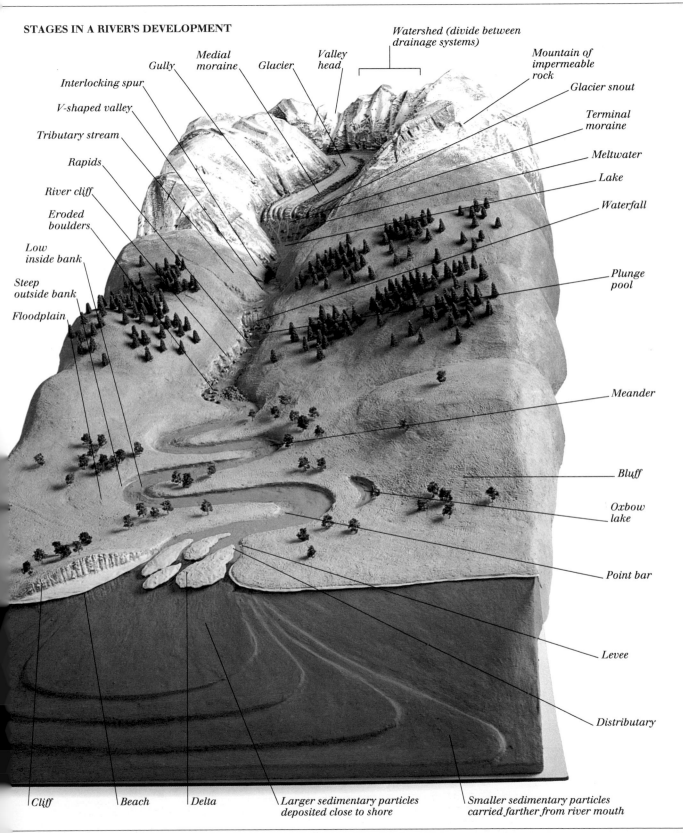

Watershed (divide between drainage systems)

Gully

Medial moraine

Interlocking spur

Glacier

Valley head

V-shaped valley

Mountain of impermeable rock

Tributary stream

Glacier snout

Rapids

Terminal moraine

River cliff

Meltwater

Eroded boulders

Lake

Low inside bank

Waterfall

Steep outside bank

Plunge pool

Floodplain

Meander

Bluff

Oxbow lake

Point bar

Levee

Distributary

Cliff

Beach

Delta

Larger sedimentary particles deposited close to shore

Smaller sedimentary particles carried farther from river mouth

River features

RIVERS ARE ONE OF THE MAJOR FORCES that shape the landscape. Near its source, a river is steep (see pp. 288-289). It erodes downward, carving out V-shaped valleys and deep gorges. Waterfalls and rapids are formed where the river flows from hard rock to softer, more easily eroded rock. Farther downstream, meanders may form and there is greater sideways erosion, resulting in a broad river valley. The river sometimes erodes through the neck of a meander to form an oxbow lake. Sediment deposited on the valley floor by meandering rivers and during floods helps to create a floodplain. Floods may also deposit sediment on the banks of the river to form levees. As a river spills into the sea or a lake, it deposits large amounts of sediment, and may form a delta. A delta is an area of sand bars, swamps and lagoons through which the river flows in several channels called distributaries—the Mississippi delta, for example. Often, a rise in sea level may have flooded the river mouth to form a broad estuary, a tidal section where seawater mixes with fresh water.

HOW WATERFALLS AND RAPIDS ARE FORMED

Hard rock

Plunge pool

Softer rock

WATERFALL

Hard rock

River erodes softer rocks to form rapids

Softer rock

Gently sloping rock strata

RAPIDS

A RIVER VALLEY DRAINAGE SYSTEM

Headward erosion

Waterfall

Gorge

Steep gorge cut by river

Mountain

GORGE

Floodplain

Stream

Sediment bar

BRAIDING

Entrenched meander

Braiding

Lake

River terrace

Levee

River erodes headward

HEADWARD EROSION

River erodes downward

Natural bridge

Meander

Steep cliffs

ENTRENCHED MEANDER

Old meander

Bridge

River

NATURAL BRIDGE

Oxbow lake

Lake

River mouth

Sediment deposited on seabed

290

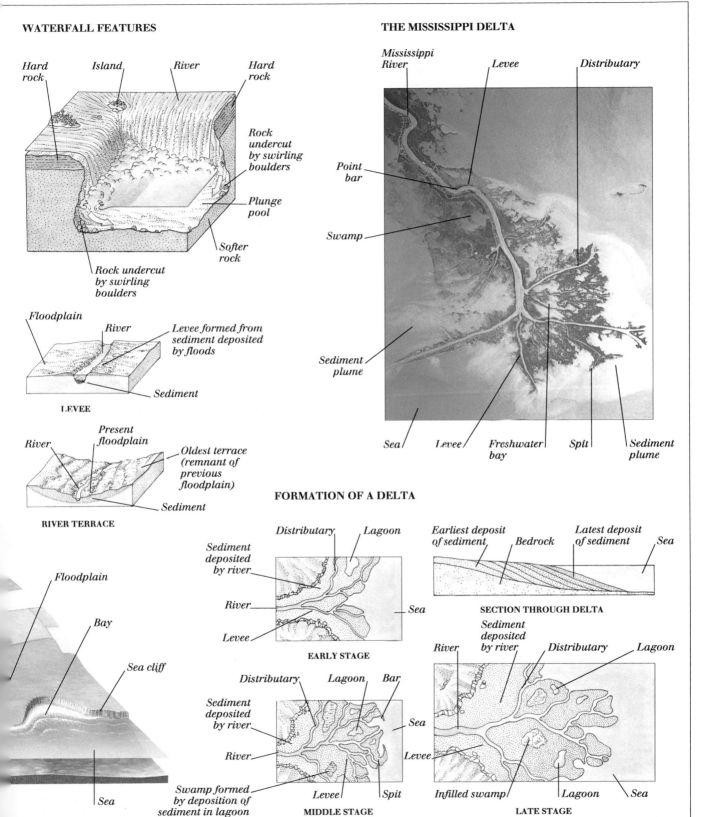

WATERFALL FEATURES

Hard rock
Island
River
Hard rock
Rock undercut by swirling boulders
Plunge pool
Softer rock
Rock undercut by swirling boulders

Floodplain
River
Levee formed from sediment deposited by floods
Sediment

LEVEE

River
Present floodplain
Oldest terrace (remnant of previous floodplain)
Sediment

RIVER TERRACE

Floodplain
Bay
Sea cliff
Sea

THE MISSISSIPPI DELTA

Mississippi River
Levee
Distributary
Point bar
Swamp
Sediment plume
Sea
Levee
Freshwater bay
Spit
Sediment plume

FORMATION OF A DELTA

Distributary
Lagoon
Sediment deposited by river
River
Levee
Sea

EARLY STAGE

Earliest deposit of sediment
Bedrock
Latest deposit of sediment
Sea

SECTION THROUGH DELTA

Distributary
Lagoon
Bar
Sediment deposited by river
River
Levee
Spit
Sea
Swamp formed by deposition of sediment in lagoon

MIDDLE STAGE

Sediment deposited by river
River
Distributary
Lagoon
Levee
Infilled swamp
Lagoon
Sea

LATE STAGE

Lakes and groundwater

NATURAL LAKES OCCUR WHERE a large quantity of water collects in a hollow in impermeable rock or is prevented from draining away by a barrier, such as moraine (glacial deposits) or solidified lava. Lakes are often relatively short-lived landscape features, because they tend to become silted up by sediment from the streams and rivers that feed them. Some of the more long-lasting lakes are found in deep rift valleys formed by vertical movements of the Earth's crust (see pp. 58-59)— for example, Lake Baikal in Russia, the world's largest freshwater lake, and the Dead Sea in the Middle East, one of the world's saltiest lakes. Where water is able to drain away, it sinks into the ground until it reaches a layer of impermeable rock, then accumulates in the permeable rock above it. This water-saturated permeable rock is called an aquifer. The saturated zone varies in depth according to seasonal and climatic changes. In wet conditions, the water stored underground builds up, while in dry periods it becomes depleted. Where the upper edge of the saturated zone—the water table—meets the ground surface, water emerges as springs. In an artesian basin, where the aquifer is below an aquiclude (layer of impermeable rock), the water table throughout the basin is determined by its height at the rim. At the center of such a basin, the water table is above ground level. The water in the basin is thus trapped below the water table and can rise under its own pressure along fault lines or well shafts.

LAKE BAIKAL, RUSSIA

EXAMPLES OF SPRINGS

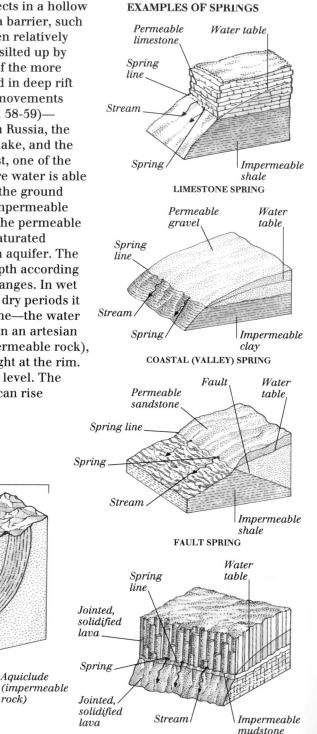

LIMESTONE SPRING

COASTAL (VALLEY) SPRING

FAULT SPRING

LAVA SPRING

STRUCTURE OF AN ARTESIAN BASIN

FEATURES OF A GROUNDWATER SYSTEM

Lake

Stream

Zone of aeration

Marsh

Layer of soil moisture

Zone of aeration

Capillary fringe

Water table

Saturated zone

CLOSE-UP OF SURFACE LAYER

Dry-season water table

Present water table (wet season)

Temporarily saturated zone (saturated only in wet season)

Permanently saturated zone (saturated in wet and dry seasons)

EXAMPLES OF LAKES

Glacial deposits

Lake in kettle (former site of ice block)

Oxbow lake (cut-off river meander)

River

KETTLE LAKE

OXBOW LAKE

Caldera (collapsed crater)

Volcanic lake

Movement along strike-slip (lateral) fault

Strike-slip (lateral) fault

Lake in elongated hollow

VOLCANIC LAKE

STRIKE-SLIP (LATERAL) FAULT LAKE

Rift valley

Steep back wall eroded by frost and ice

Moraine or rock lip damming lake

High valley walls

Sinking graben (block fault)

Tarn (circular mountain lake)

GRABEN (BLOCK-FAULT) LAKE

TARN

THE DEAD SEA, ISRAEL/JORDAN

River Jordan

Dead Sea

Steep rift-valley walls

Salt left by evaporation

Israel

Shallow flats

Jordan

293

Coastlines

COASTLINES ARE AMONG THE MOST RAPIDLY changing landscape features. Some are eroded by waves, wind, and rain, causing cliffs to be undercut and caves to be hollowed out of solid rock. Others are built up by waves transporting sand and small rocks in a process known as longshore drift and by rivers depositing sediment in deltas. Additional influences include the activities of living organisms such as coral, crustal movements, and sea-level variations due to climatic changes. Rising land or a drop in sea level creates an emergent coastline, with cliffs and beaches standing above the new shoreline. Sinking land or a rise in sea level produces a drowned coastline, typified by fjords (submerged glacial valleys) or submerged river valleys.

FEATURES OF A SEA CLIFF

Cliff top
Cliff face
High tide level
Low tide level
Offshore deposits
Wave-cut platform
Undercut area of cliff

FEATURES OF WAVES

Wave height
Crest
Wavelength
Trough
Shorter wavelength near beach
Circular orbit of water and suspended particles
Orbit deformed into ellipse as water gets shallower

LONGSHORE DRIFT

Pebble
Backwash
Movement of material along beach
Buildup of material against groyne
Beach
Groyne
Waves approaching shore at an oblique angle
Swash zone
Swash

Mature river
Headland
Bedding plane
Sea cliff
Remnants of former headland
Estuary

DEPOSITIONAL FEATURES OF COASTLINES

Bay head beach
Wave direction
Headland

Wave direction
Tombolo
Island

Wave direction
Cuspate foreland

Wave direction
Barrier beach
Lagoon

BAY HEAD BEACH   **TOMBOLO**   **CUSPATE FORELAND**   **BARRIER BEACH**

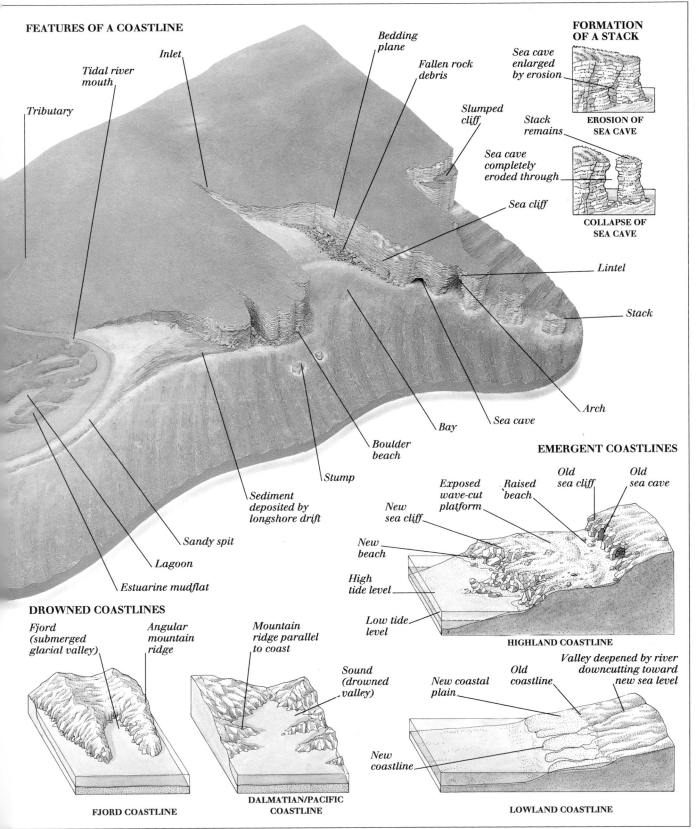

FEATURES OF A COASTLINE

Tributary

Tidal river mouth

Inlet

Bedding plane

Fallen rock debris

Slumped cliff

FORMATION OF A STACK

Sea cave enlarged by erosion

EROSION OF SEA CAVE

Stack remains

Sea cave completely eroded through

COLLAPSE OF SEA CAVE

Sea cliff

Lintel

Stack

Arch

Sea cave

Bay

Boulder beach

Stump

Sediment deposited by longshore drift

Sandy spit

Lagoon

Estuarine mudflat

EMERGENT COASTLINES

Exposed wave-cut platform

Raised beach

Old sea cliff

Old sea cave

New sea cliff

New beach

High tide level

Low tide level

HIGHLAND COASTLINE

DROWNED COASTLINES

Fjord (submerged glacial valley)

Angular mountain ridge

Mountain ridge parallel to coast

Sound (drowned valley)

FJORD COASTLINE

DALMATIAN/PACIFIC COASTLINE

Valley deepened by river downcutting toward new sea level

Old coastline

New coastal plain

New coastline

LOWLAND COASTLINE

Oceans and seas

OCEANS AND SEAS COVER ABOUT 70 PERCENT of the Earth's
surface and account for about 97 percent of its total
water. These oceans and seas play a crucial role
in regulating temperature variations and
determining climate. Their waters absorb
heat from the Sun, especially in tropical
regions, and the surface currents distribute
it around the Earth, warming overlying
air masses and neighboring land in
winter and cooling them in summer.
The oceans are never still. Differences
in temperature and salinity drive
deep current systems, while surface
currents are generated by winds
blowing over the oceans. All currents
are deflected—to the right in the
Northern Hemisphere, to the left in
the Southern Hemisphere—as a result
of the Earth's rotation. This deflective
factor is known as the Coriolis force.
A current that begins on the surface is
immediately deflected. This current in
turn generates a current in the layer of water
beneath, which is also deflected. As the movement
is transmitted downward, the deflections form an
Ekman spiral. The waters of the oceans and seas are
also moved by the constant ebb and flow of tides. These
are caused by the gravitational pull of the Moon and Sun.
The highest tides (Spring tides) occur at full and new Moon;
the lowest tides (neap tides) occur at first and last quarter.

SURFACE CURRENTS

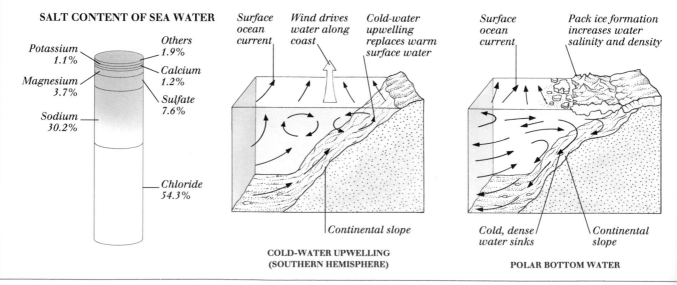

SALT CONTENT OF SEA WATER

Potassium
1.1%

Others
1.9%

Calcium
1.2%

Magnesium
3.7%

Sulfate
7.6%

Sodium
30.2%

Chloride
54.3%

OFFSHORE CURRENTS

Surface
ocean
current

Wind drives
water along
coast

Cold-water
upwelling
replaces warm
surface water

Continental slope

**COLD-WATER UPWELLING
(SOUTHERN HEMISPHERE)**

Surface
ocean
current

Pack ice formation
increases water
salinity and density

Cold, dense
water sinks

Continental
slope

POLAR BOTTOM WATER

EFFECT OF CORIOLIS FORCE

North Pole

Coriolis force

Winds and currents deflected to right in Northern Hemisphere

Equator

Winds and currents deflected to left in Southern Hemisphere

Original direction of wind or current

Actual direction of wind or current

South Pole

EKMAN SPIRAL (NORTHERN HEMISPHERE)

Wind

Surface current caused by wind

Subsurface current slightly deflected by Coriolis force

Deep current at 180° to surface current

Midwater current further deflected by Coriolis force

ARCTIC CIRCLE
(66° 32'N)

TROPIC OF
CANCER
(25° 50'N)

Oyashio Current

Kuroshio Current

North Equatorial Current

Equatorial Countercurrent

South Equatorial Current

EQUATOR
(0°)

North Equatorial Current

Equatorial Countercurrent

South Equatorial Current

Northeast Monsoon Drift

Agulhas Current

SOUTH
INDIAN
GYRE

West Australian Current

East Australian Current

TROPIC OF
CAPRICORN
(25° 50'S)

ANTARCTIC
CIRCLE
(66° 52'S)

HOW TIDES ARE CAUSED

HIGH
SPRING TIDE

New Moon

LOW
NEAP TIDE

Last quarter

Moon's gravitational pull

HIGH
SPRING TIDE

Full Moon

Earth's orbit   *Earth*

Tidal bulge caused by Sun's gravitational pull

Tidal bulge caused by Moon's gravitational pull

Sun's gravitational pull

Sun's gravitational pull reinforces centrifugal effect, producing large tidal bulge

Sun

Sun's gravitational pull diminishes Moon's effect

Equal and opposite tidal bulge produced by centrifugal effect due to Earth's spin

LOW
NEAP TIDE

First quarter

Moon's orbit

Tidal bulge where Moon's gravitational pull is strongest

Moon

The atmosphere

JET STREAM

THE EARTH IS SURROUNDED BY ITS ATMOSPHERE, a blanket of gases that enables life to exist on the planet. This layer has no definite outer edge, gradually becoming thinner until it merges into space, but over 80 percent of atmospheric gases are held by gravity within about 10 miles of the Earth's surface. The atmosphere blocks out much harmful ultraviolet solar radiation, and insulates the Earth against extremes of temperature by limiting both incoming solar radiation and the escape of re-radiated heat into space. This natural balance may be distorted by the greenhouse effect, as gases such as carbon dioxide have built up in the atmosphere, trapping more heat. Close to the Earth's surface, differences in air temperature and pressure cause air to circulate between the equator and poles. This circulation, together with the Coriolis force, gives rise to the prevailing surface winds and the high-level jet streams.

ATMOSPHERIC CIRCULATION AND WINDS

- Exosphere (altitude above about 300 miles)
- Corona
- North Pole (high pressure)
- Rotation of Earth
- Polar cell
- Polar easterlies
- Ferrel cell
- Low-pressure zone
- Polar jet stream
- Westerlies
- Subtropical jet stream
- High-pressure zone
- Hadley cell
- Northeast trade winds
- Equator
- Intertropical convergence zone (low pressure)
- Warm equatorial air rises and flows toward pole
- Southeast trade winds
- Thermosphere (altitude about 60–300 miles)
- Air cools and sinks
- High-pressure zone
- Westerlies
- Ozone layer absorbs ultraviolet radiation from Sun
- South Pole (high pressure)
- Low-pressure zone
- Polar easterlies

FORMATION OF ROSSBY WAVES IN THE JET STREAM

- Long Rossby wave develops in polar jet stream
- Cold air
- Rossby wave becomes more pronounced
- Fully developed Rossby wave
- Mesosphere (altitude about 30–60 miles)
- Warm air
- Stratosphere (altitude about 6–30 miles)
- Troposphere (altitude up to about 6 miles)

| INITIAL UNDULATION | DEEPENING WAVE | DEVELOPED WAVE |

STRUCTURE OF THE ATMOSPHERE

GLOBAL WARMING

Solar radiation re-radiated as heat

Some re-radiated heat escapes into space

Sun

Some re-radiated heat reflected back to Earth

Incoming solar radiation

Earth

Atmosphere

NATURALLY MODERATED GREENHOUSE EFFECT

Meteor (shooting star) burns up as it passes through atmosphere

Less re-radiated heat escapes

Solar radiation re-radiated as heat

More re-radiated heat reflected back to Earth

Aurora

Surface temperature rises

"Greenhouse gases" accumulate in atmosphere

UNBALANCED GREENHOUSE EFFECT

Incoming solar radiation

14% of incoming solar radiation absorbed by atmosphere

COMPOSITION OF THE LOWER ATMOSPHERE

7% of incoming solar radiation reflected by atmosphere

Other elements less than 0.1%

24% of incoming solar radiation reflected by clouds

Argon 0.93%

Cosmic rays (high-energy particles from space) penetrate to stratosphere

Oxygen 21%

Some absorbed heat re-radiated by atmosphere

4% of incoming solar radiation reflected by oceans and land

Nitrogen 78%

51% of incoming solar radiation absorbed by Earth's surface

Some absorbed heat re-radiated by clouds

301

Weather

WEATHER IS DEFINED AS THE ATMOSPHERIC CONDITIONS at a particular time and place; climate is the average weather conditions for a given region over time. Weather conditions include temperature, wind, cloud cover, and precipitation, such as rain or snow. Good weather is associated with high-pressure areas, where air is sinking. Cloudy, wet, changeable weather is common in low-pressure zones with rising, unstable air. Such conditions occur at temperate latitudes, where warm air meets cool air along the polar fronts. Here, spiraling low-pressure cells known as depressions (mid-latitude cyclones) often form. A depression usually contains a sector of warmer air, beginning at a warm front and ending at a cold front. If the two fronts merge, forming an occluded front, the warm air is pushed upward. An extreme form of low-pressure cell is a hurricane (also called a typhoon or tropical cyclone), which brings torrential rain, and exceptionally strong winds.

TYPES OF CLOUD

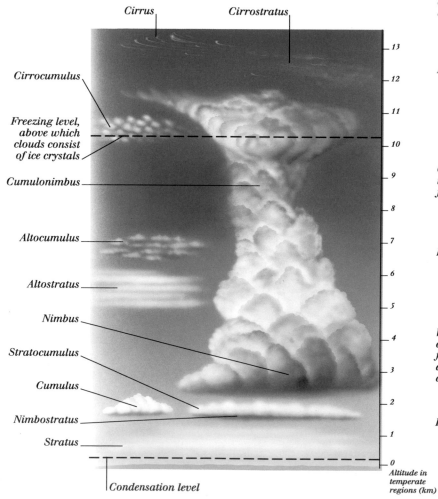

TYPES OF OCCLUDED FRONT

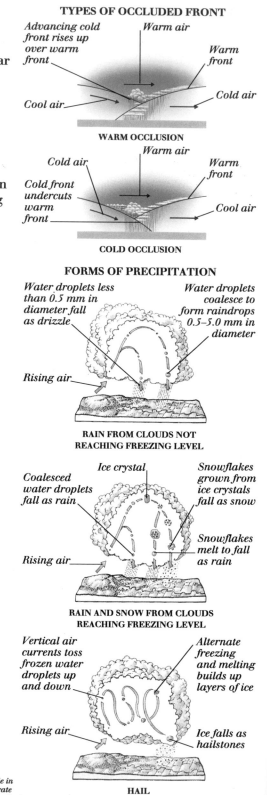

WARM OCCLUSION

COLD OCCLUSION

FORMS OF PRECIPITATION

RAIN FROM CLOUDS NOT REACHING FREEZING LEVEL

RAIN AND SNOW FROM CLOUDS REACHING FREEZING LEVEL

HAIL

STRUCTURE OF A HURRICANE

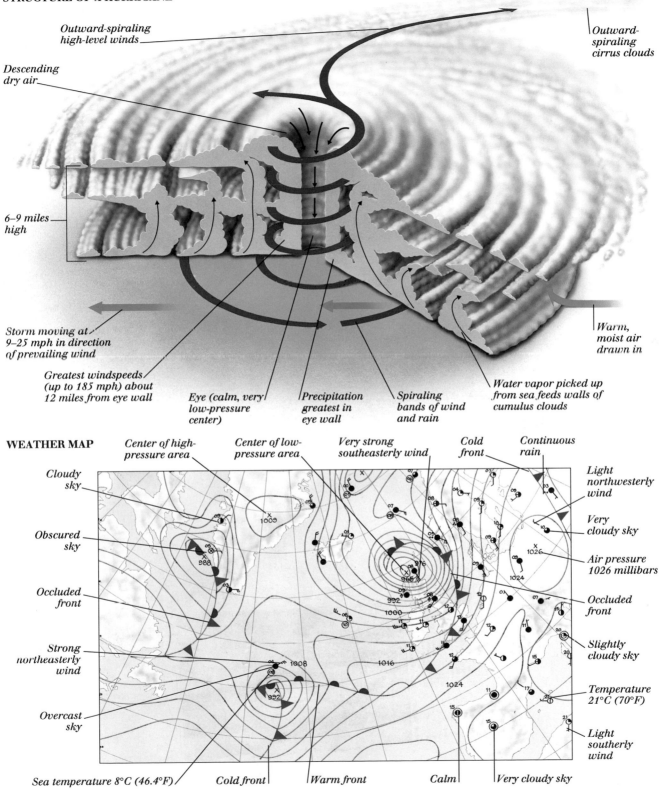

Outward-spiraling high-level winds

Outward-spiraling cirrus clouds

Descending dry air

6–9 miles high

Storm moving at 9–25 mph in direction of prevailing wind

Greatest windspeeds (up to 185 mph) about 12 miles from eye wall

Eye (calm, very low-pressure center)

Precipitation greatest in eye wall

Spiraling bands of wind and rain

Water vapor picked up from sea feeds walls of cumulus clouds

Warm, moist air drawn in

WEATHER MAP

Center of high-pressure area

Center of low-pressure area

Very strong southeasterly wind

Cold front

Continuous rain

Cloudy sky

Light northwesterly wind

Obscured sky

Very cloudy sky

Occluded front

Air pressure 1026 millibars

Occluded front

Strong northeasterly wind

Slightly cloudy sky

Overcast sky

Temperature 21°C (70°F)

Light southerly wind

Sea temperature 8°C (46.4°F)

Cold front

Warm front

Calm

Very cloudy sky

303

Physics and Chemistry

The variety of matter

**PLANT AND INSECT
(LIVING MATTER)**

MATTER IS ANYTHING THAT OCCUPIES SPACE. It includes everything from natural substances, such as minerals or living organisms, to synthetic materials. Matter can exist in three distinct states—solid, liquid, and gas. A solid is rigid and retains its shape. A liquid is fluid, has a definite volume, and will take the shape of its container. A gas (also fluid) fills a space, so its volume will be the same as the volume of its container. Most substances can exist as a solid, a liquid, or a gas: the state is determined by temperature. At very high temperatures, matter becomes plasma, often considered to be a fourth state of matter. All matter is composed of microscopic particles, such as atoms and molecules (see pp. 308-309). The arrangement and interactions of these particles give a substance its physical and chemical properties, by which matter can be identified. There is a huge variety of matter because particles can arrange themselves in countless ways, in one substance or by mixing with others. Natural glass, for example, seems to be a solid but is, in fact, a supercool liquid: the atoms are not locked into a pattern and can flow. Pure substances known as elements (see p. 310) combine to form compounds or mixtures. Mixtures called colloids are made up of larger particles of matter suspended in a solid, liquid, or gas, while a solution is one substance dissolved in another.

TYPES OF COLLOID

HAIR GEL (SOLID IN LIQUID)

**SHAVING CREAM
(AIR IN LIQUID)**

**MIST
(LIQUID IN GAS)**

EXAMPLES OF MATTER

The element silicon in pure crystalline form

Polythene is made by combining natural materials in new ways

Low pressure gases

Streaks of plasma (mixture of electrons and charged atoms)

Voltage tears electrons from atoms of low pressure gases inside

Central electrode

**POLYTHENE
(SYNTHETIC POLYMER)**

**PURE SILICON
(SEMICONDUCTOR)**

**BALL CONTAINING
HIGH-TEMPERATURE GAS
(PLASMA)**

Obsidian is molten volcanic rock that cools quickly, so atoms cannot form a regular pattern

Solid crystals dissolve in liquid water

Water

Potassium permanganate crystals

Azurite is found naturally with deposits of copper ore

**OBSIDIAN
(NATURAL GLASS)**

**AZURITE
(CRYSTALLINE MINERAL)**

**POTASSIUM PERMANGANATE AND WATER
(SOLUTION)**

STATES OF MATTER

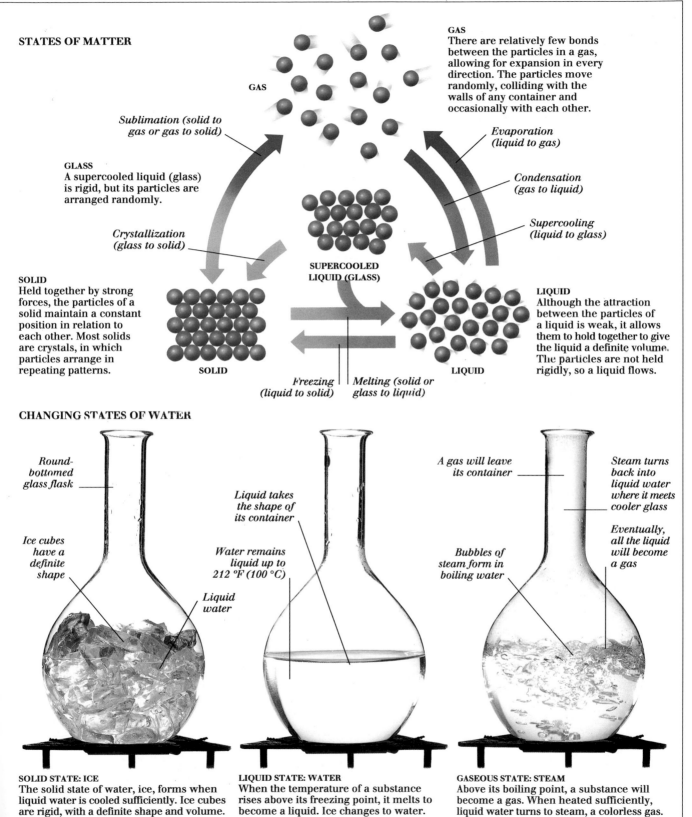

GAS
There are relatively few bonds between the particles in a gas, allowing for expansion in every direction. The particles move randomly, colliding with the walls of any container and occasionally with each other.

GAS

Sublimation (solid to gas or gas to solid)

Evaporation (liquid to gas)

Condensation (gas to liquid)

GLASS
A supercooled liquid (glass) is rigid, but its particles are arranged randomly.

Crystallization (glass to solid)

Supercooling (liquid to glass)

SUPERCOOLED LIQUID (GLASS)

SOLID
Held together by strong forces, the particles of a solid maintain a constant position in relation to each other. Most solids are crystals, in which particles arrange in repeating patterns.

LIQUID
Although the attraction between the particles of a liquid is weak, it allows them to hold together to give the liquid a definite volume. The particles are not held rigidly, so a liquid flows.

SOLID

LIQUID

Freezing (liquid to solid)

Melting (solid or glass to liquid)

CHANGING STATES OF WATER

Round-bottomed glass flask

Ice cubes have a definite shape

Liquid water

Liquid takes the shape of its container

Water remains liquid up to 212 °F (100 °C)

A gas will leave its container

Bubbles of steam form in boiling water

Steam turns back into liquid water where it meets cooler glass

Eventually, all the liquid will become a gas

SOLID STATE: ICE
The solid state of water, ice, forms when liquid water is cooled sufficiently. Ice cubes are rigid, with a definite shape and volume.

LIQUID STATE: WATER
When the temperature of a substance rises above its freezing point, it melts to become a liquid. Ice changes to water.

GASEOUS STATE: STEAM
Above its boiling point, a substance will become a gas. When heated sufficiently, liquid water turns to steam, a colorless gas.

Atoms and molecules

FALSE-COLOR IMAGE
OF ACTUAL GOLD
ATOMS

ATOMS ARE THE smallest individual parts of an element (see pp. 310-311). They are tiny, with diameters in the order of one ten-thousand-millionth of a meter (10^{-10} m). Two or more atoms join together (bond) to form a molecule of a substance known as a compound. For example, when atoms of the elements hydrogen and fluorine join together, they form a molecule of the compound hydrogen fluoride. So molecules are the smallest individual parts of a compound. Atoms themselves are not indivisible —they possess an internal structure. At their center is a dense nucleus consisting of protons, which have a positive electric charge (see p. 316), and neutrons, which are uncharged. Around the nucleus are negatively charged electrons. It is the electrons that give a substance most of its physical and chemical properties. They do not follow definite paths around the nucleus. Instead, electrons are said to be found within certain regions, called orbitals. These are arranged around the nucleus in "shells," each containing electrons of a particular energy. For example, the first shell (1) can hold up to two electrons, in a so-called s-orbital (1s). The second shell (2) can hold up to eight electrons in s-orbitals (2s) and p-orbitals (2p). If an atom loses an electron, it becomes a positive ion (cation). If an electron is gained, an atom becomes a negative ion (anion). Ions of opposite charges will attract and join together in a type of bonding known as ionic bonding. In covalent bonding, the atoms bond by sharing their electrons in what become molecular orbitals.

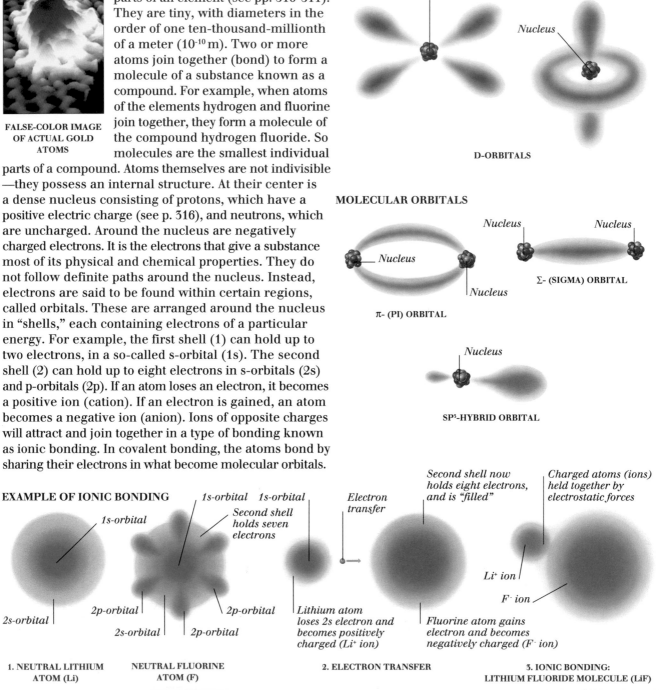

ATOMIC ORBITALS

S-ORBITAL

Nucleus

P-ORBITAL

Nucleus

Nucleus

D-ORBITALS

MOLECULAR ORBITALS

Nucleus

Nucleus

Nucleus

π- (PI) ORBITAL

Nucleus   *Nucleus*

Σ- (SIGMA) ORBITAL

Nucleus

SP³-HYBRID ORBITAL

EXAMPLE OF IONIC BONDING

1s-orbital

1s-orbital   1s-orbital

2s-orbital

2p-orbital   2s-orbital   2p-orbital

Second shell
holds seven
electrons

2p-orbital

*Electron
transfer*

Lithium atom
loses 2s electron and
becomes positively
charged (Li⁺ ion)

Second shell now
holds eight electrons,
and is "filled"

Fluorine atom gains
electron and becomes
negatively charged (F⁻ ion)

Charged atoms (ions)
held together by
electrostatic forces

Li⁺ ion

F⁻ ion

1. NEUTRAL LITHIUM
ATOM (Li)

NEUTRAL FLUORINE
ATOM (F)

2. ELECTRON TRANSFER

3. IONIC BONDING:
LITHIUM FLUORIDE MOLECULE (LiF)

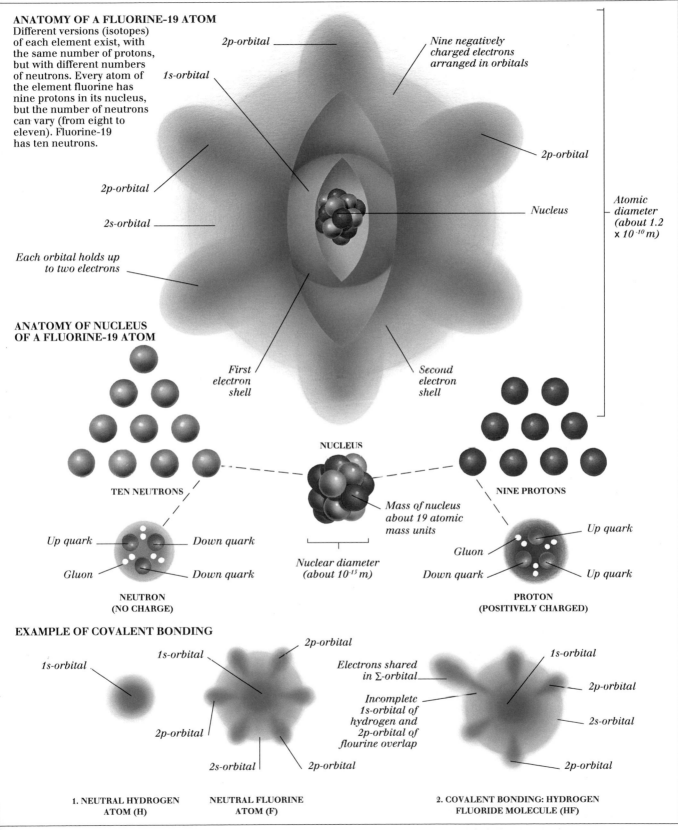

ANATOMY OF A FLUORINE-19 ATOM
Different versions (isotopes) of each element exist, with the same number of protons, but with different numbers of neutrons. Every atom of the element fluorine has nine protons in its nucleus, but the number of neutrons can vary (from eight to eleven). Fluorine-19 has ten neutrons.

2p-orbital

Nine negatively charged electrons arranged in orbitals

1s-orbital

2p-orbital

2p-orbital

Nucleus

2s-orbital

Atomic diameter (about 1.2 x 10^{-10} m)

Each orbital holds up to two electrons

ANATOMY OF NUCLEUS OF A FLUORINE-19 ATOM

First electron shell

Second electron shell

NUCLEUS

TEN NEUTRONS

NINE PROTONS

Mass of nucleus about 19 atomic mass units

Up quark

Down quark

Gluon

Down quark

Nuclear diameter (about 10^{-15} m)

Up quark

Gluon

Down quark

Up quark

NEUTRON (NO CHARGE)

PROTON (POSITIVELY CHARGED)

EXAMPLE OF COVALENT BONDING

2p-orbital

1s-orbital

1s-orbital

1s-orbital

Electrons shared in Σ-orbital

2p-orbital

Incomplete 1s-orbital of hydrogen and 2p-orbital of flourine overlap

2s-orbital

2p-orbital

2p-orbital

2s-orbital

2p-orbital

1. NEUTRAL HYDROGEN ATOM (H)

NEUTRAL FLUORINE ATOM (F)

2. COVALENT BONDING: HYDROGEN FLUORIDE MOLECULE (HF)

The periodic table

AN ELEMENT is a substance that consists of atoms of one type only. The 92 elements that occur naturally, and the 17 elements created artificially, are often arranged into a chart called the periodic table. Each element is defined by its atomic number—the number of protons in the nucleus of each of its atoms (it is also the number of electrons present). Atomic numbers increase along each row (period) and down each column (group). The shape of the table is determined by the way in which electrons arrange themselves around the nucleus: the positioning of elements in order of increasing atomic number brings together atoms with a similar pattern of orbiting electrons (orbitals). These appear in blocks. Electrons occupy shells of a certain energy (see pp. 308-309). Periods are ordered according to the filling of successive shells with electrons, while groups reflect the number of electrons in the outer shell (valency electrons). These outer electrons are important—they decide the chemical properties of the atom. Elements that appear in the same group have similar properties because they have the same number of electrons in their outer shell. Elements in Group 0 have filled shells, where the outer shell holds its maximum number of electrons, and are stable. Atoms of Group I elements have just one electron in their outer shell. This makes them unstable—and ready to react with other substances.

METALS AND NON-METALS
Elements at the left-hand side of each period are metals. Metals easily lose electrons and form positive ions. Non-metals, on the right of a period, tend to become negative ions. Semi-metals, which have properties of both metals and non-metals, are between the two.

Atomic number is number of protons in each nucleus

Atomic number goes up by one along each period

RELATIVE ATOMIC MASS
Atomic mass (formerly atomic weight) is the mass of each atom of an element. It is equal to the number of protons plus the number of neutrons (electrons have negligible mass). The figures given are the averages for all the different versions (isotopes) of each element, measured relative to the mass of carbon-12.

1st transition metals

s-block

Two series always separated out from the table to give it a coherent shape

d-block

Soft, silvery, and highly reactive metal

SODIUM: GROUP 1 METAL

Silvery, reactive metal

MAGNESIUM: GROUP 2 METAL

Hard, silvery metal

CHROMIUM: 1ST TRANSITION METAL

Radioactive metal

PLUTONIUM: ACTINIDE SERIES METAL

TYPES OF ELEMENT KEY:

- Alkali metals
- Alkaline earth metals
- Transition metals
- Lanthanides (rare earths)
- Actinides
- Poor metals
- Semi-metals
- Non-metals
- Noble gases

ALLOTROPES OF CARBON
Some elements exist in more than one form —these are known as allotropes. Carbon powder, graphite, and diamond are allotropes of carbon. They all consist of carbon atoms, but have very different physical properties.

Bright yellow crystal

IODINE: GROUP 7 SOLID NON-METAL

Purple-black solid turns to gas easily

DIAMOND

SULFUR: GROUP 6 SOLID NON-METAL

Group 0

GRAPHITE

CARBON POWDER

Boron and carbon groups

Nitrogen and oxygen groups

Halogens

						2
						He
						Helium 4.0

Period

2nd transition metals

3rd transition metals

Group III	*Group IV*	*Group V*	*Group VI*	*Group VII*	
5 **B** Boron 10.8	6 **C** Carbon 12.0	7 **N** Nitrogen 14.0	8 **O** Oxygen 16.0	9 **F** Fluorine 19.0	10 **Ne** Neon 20.2

Short period

13 **Al** Aluminum 27.0	14 **Si** Silicon 28.1	15 **P** Phosphorus 31.0	16 **S** Sulfur 32.1	17 **Cl** Chlorine 35.5	18 **Ar** Argon 40.0

26 **Fe** Iron 55.9	27 **Co** Cobalt 58.9	28 **Ni** Nickel 58.7	29 **Cu** Copper 63.5	30 **Zn** Zinc 65.4	31 **Ga** Gallium 69.7	32 **Ge** Germanium 72.6	33 **As** Arsenic 74.9	34 **Se** Selenium 79.0	35 **Br** Bromine 79.9	36 **Kr** Krypton 83.8
44 **Ru** Ruthenium 101.0	45 **Rh** Rhodium 102.9	46 **Pd** Palladium 106.4	47 **Ag** Silver 107.9	48 **Cd** Cadmium 112.4	49 **In** Indium 114.8	50 **Sn** Tin 118.7	51 **Sb** Antimony 121.8	52 **Te** Tellurium 127.6	53 **I** Iodine 126.9	54 **Xe** Xenon 131.3
76 **Os** Osmium 190.2	77 **Ir** Iridium 192.2	78 **Pt** Platinum 195.1	79 **Au** Gold 197.0	80 **Hg** Mercury 200.6	81 **Tl** Thallium 204.4	82 **Pb** Lead 207.2	83 **Bi** Bismuth 209.0	84 **Po** Polonium 210.0	85 **At** Astatine 210.0	86 **Rn** Radon 222.0
108 **Uno** Unniloctium (265)	109 **Une** Unnilennium (266)									

Long period

d-block

p-block

Atomic mass is estimated, as element exists fleetingly

Shiny semi-metal

Unreactive, colorless gas glows red in discharge tube

NOBLE GASES
Group 0 contains elements that have a filled (complete) outer shell of electrons, which means the atoms do not need to lose or gain electrons by bonding with other atoms. This makes them stable and they do not easily form ions or react with other elements. Noble gases are also called rare or inert gases.

Yellow, unreactive precious metal

Soft, shiny, reactive metal

NEON: GROUP 0 COLORLESS GAS

GOLD: 3RD TRANSITION METAL

TIN: GROUP 4 POOR METAL

ANTIMONY: GROUP 5 SEMI-METAL

61 **Pm** Promethium 147.0	62 **Sm** Samarium 150.4	63 **Eu** Europium 152.0	64 **Gd** Gadolinium 157.3	65 **Tb** Terbium 158.9	66 **Dy** Dysprosium 162.5	67 **Ho** Holmium 164.9	68 **Er** Erbium 167.3	69 **Tm** Thulium 168.9	70 **Yb** Ytterbium 173.0	71 **Lu** Lutetium 175.0
93 **Np** Neptunium 237.0	94 **Pu** Plutonium 242.0	95 **Am** Americium 243.0	96 **Cm** Curium 247.0	97 **Bk** Berkelium 247.0	98 **Cf** Californium 251.0	99 **Es** Einsteinium 254.0	100 **Fm** Fermium 253.0	101 **Md** Mendelevium 256.0	102 **No** Nobelium 254.0	103 **Lr** Lawrencium 257.0

f-block

311

Chemical reactions

A CHEMICAL REACTION TAKES PLACE whenever bonds between atoms are broken or made. In each case, atoms or groups of atoms rearrange, making new substances (products) from the original ones (reactants). Reactions happen naturally, or can be made to happen; they may take years, or only an instant. Some of the main types are shown here. A reaction usually involves a change in energy (see pp. 314-315). In a burning reaction, for example, the making of new bonds between atoms releases energy as heat and light. This type of reaction, in which heat is given off, is an exothermic reaction. Many reactions, like burning, are irreversible, but some can take place in either direction, and are said to be reversible. Reactions can be used to form solids from solutions: in a double decomposition reaction, two compounds in solution break down and re-form into two new substances, often creating a precipitate (insoluble solid); in displacement, an element (eg. copper) displaces another element (eg. silver) from a solution. The rate (speed) of a reaction is determined by many different factors, such as temperature, and the size and shape of the reactants. To describe and keep track of reactions, internationally recognized chemical symbols and equations are used. Reactions are also used in the laboratory to identify matter. An experiment with candle wax, for example, demonstrates that it contains carbon and hydrogen.

BURNING MATTER

Ammonium dichromate
$((NH_4)_2Cr_2O_7)$

Flame

In this burning reaction, atoms form simpler substances and give off heat and light

Ammonium dichromate $((NH_4)_2Cr_2O_7)$ converts to chromium oxide (Cr_2O_3)

Nitrogen monoxide (NO) and water vapor (H_2O) given off as colorless gases

THE REACTION
When lit, ammonium dichromate combines with oxygen from air.
$(NH_4)_2Cr_2O_7 + O_2 \rightarrow Cr_2O_3 + 4H_2O + 2NO$

A REVERSIBLE REACTION

Flat-bottomed glass flask

Potassium chromate solution (K_2CrO_4)

Bright yellow solution contains potassium and chromate ions

1. THE REACTANT
Potassium chromate dissolves in water to form potassium ions and chromate ions.
$K_2CrO_4 \rightarrow 2K^+ + CrO_4^{2-}$

Pipette

Hydrochloric acid (HCl) added in drops

Acid causes reaction to take place

Chromate ions converted to orange dichromate ions

Potassium dichromate (KCr_2O_7) forms

2. THE REACTION
Addition of hydrochloric acid changes chromate ions into dichromate ions.
$2CrO_4^{2-} \rightarrow Cr_2O_7^{2-}$

Sodium hydroxide (NaOH) neutralizes the acid

Solution turns to bright orange of potassium dichromate

Potassium dichromate (KCr_2O_7) re-forms to potassium chromate (K_2CrO_4)

3. REVERSING
Addition of sodium hydroxide changes dichromate ions back into chromate ions.
$Cr_2O_7^{2-} \rightarrow 2CrO_4^{2-}$

SALT FORMATION (ACID ON METAL)

Glass beaker

Hydrogen gas (H_2) given off

Zinc (Zn) replaces hydrogen (H) in acid (HCl) to form zinc chloride solution $(ZnCl_2)$

Hydrogen in acid driven off when acid meets a reactive metal

Zinc metal chippings (Zn)

Hydrochloric acid (HCl)

Effervescence

Zinc metal chippings (Zn)

THE REACTION
Hydrochloric acid added to zinc produces zinc chloride and hydrogen.
$Zn + 2HCl \rightarrow ZnCl_2 + H_2$

DISPLACEMENT

Copper metal (Cu)

Silver nitrate solution $(AgNO_3)$

Two metals compete for nitrate ions

Glass flask

Copper (Cu) ions displace silver (Ag) ions from silver nitrate solution $(AgNO_3)$

Blue solution of copper nitrate $(Cu(NO_3)_2)$ forms

Needles of silver metal (Ag) form

THE REACTION
Copper metal added to silver nitrate solution produces copper nitrate and silver metal.
$Cu + 2AgNO_3 \rightarrow Cu(NO_3)_2 + 2Ag$

Pipette

Sodium hydroxide (NaOH) added in drops

Solution returns to original bright yellow color

FERMENTATION

Yeast converts sugar into alcohol (C_2H_5OH) and carbon dioxide gas (CO_2)

Airtight stopper

Flat-bottomed glass flask

Yeast mixed with warm water and sugar ($C_6H_{12}O_6$)

Carbon dioxide bubbles (CO_2)

THE REACTION
Yeast converts sugar and warm water into alcohol and carbon dioxide.
$$C_6H_{12}O_6 \rightarrow 2C_2H_5OH + 2CO_2$$

DOUBLE DECOMPOSITION

Potassium iodide solution (KI)

Lead nitrate solution ($Pb(NO_3)_2$)

Two solutions swap partners

Potassium iodide solution added to lead nitrate solution

Lead iodide (PbI_2), a yellow solid, forms

Potassium nitrate solution (KNO_3) forms

1. THE REACTANTS
Potassium iodide in water (KI) and lead nitrate in water ($Pb(NO_3)_2$) each form colorless solutions.

2. THE REACTION
When the solutions are mixed, lead iodide, a precipitate, and potassium nitrate solution are formed.
$$2KI + Pb(NO_3)_2 \rightarrow PbI_2 + 2KNO_3$$

TESTING CANDLE WAX, AN ORGANIC COMPOUND

Clamp stand

Burning produces carbon dioxide gas (CO_2) and water vapor (H_2O)

Delivery tube

Delivery tube

Gases are trapped in funnel

Stopper

Stopper

Tube connection to pump that sucks gases through

Unburned carbon forms soot particles

U-tube

Stopper

Thistle funnel

Flame

Test tube

Burning candle wax

Water vapor condenses to form liquid water (H_2O)

Clamp

Calcium hydroxide solution (lime water, $Ca(OH)_2$)

Candle wax ($C_{18}H_{38}$), a hydrocarbon, contains the elements carbon and hydrogen

Water vapor trapped by solid drying agent, anhydrous copper sulfate ($CuSO_4$)

Anhydrous copper sulfate ($CuSO_4$)

Carbon dioxide gas (CO_2) given off

Calcium hydroxide ($Ca(OH)_2$) and carbon dioxide (CO_2) form insoluble calcium carbonate ($CaCO_3$): lime water becomes milky

Anhydrous copper sulfate crystals ($CuSO_4$) combine with water vapor (H_2O) to form darker blue hydrated copper sulfate ($CuSO_4 . 10H_2O$)

1. THE BURNING REACTION
Burning wax produces carbon dioxide gas and water vapor.
$$2C_{18}H_{38} + 55O_2 \rightarrow 36CO_2 + 38H_2O$$

2. TESTING FOR WATER VAPOUR
A solid drying agent traps water vapor, proving the presence of hydrogen in the candle wax.
$$CuSO_4 + 10H_2O \rightarrow CuSO_4 . 10H_2O$$

3. TESTING FOR CARBON DIOXIDE
Calcium hydroxide in solution reacts with carbon dioxide, forming a carbonate and turning milky.
$$Ca(OH)_2 + CO_2 \rightarrow CaCO_3 + H_2O$$

Energy

ANYTHING THAT HAPPENS—from a pin drop to an explosion —requires energy. Energy is the capacity for doing work (making something happen). Various forms of energy exist, including light, heat, sound, electrical, chemical, nuclear, kinetic, and potential energies. The Law of Conservation of Energy states that the total amount of energy in the Universe is fixed—energy cannot be created or destroyed, it can only change from one form to another (energy transfer). For example, potential energy is energy that is stored, and can be used in the future. An object gains potential energy when it is lifted; as the object is released, potential energy changes into the energy of motion (kinetic energy). During transference, some of the energy converts into heat. A combined heat and power station can put some of the "waste" heat to useful effect in local schools and housing. Most of the Earth's energy is provided by the Sun, in the form of electromagnetic radiation (see pp. 316-317). Some of this energy transfers to plant and animal life, and ultimately to fossil fuels, where it is stored in chemical form. Our bodies obtain energy from the food we eat, while energy needed for other tasks, such as heating and transportation, can be obtained by burning fossil fuels —or by harnessing natural forces like wind or moving water—to generate electricity. Another source is nuclear power, where energy is released by reactions in the nucleus of an atom. All energy is measured by the international unit, the joule (J). As a guide, one joule is about equal to the amount of energy needed to lift an apple one yard.

SANKEY DIAGRAM SHOWING ENERGY FLOW IN A COAL-FIRED COMBINED HEAT AND POWER STATION

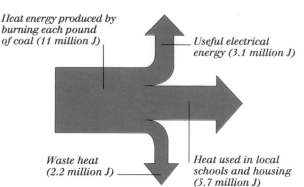

Heat energy produced by burning each pound of coal (11 million J)

Useful electrical energy (3.1 million J)

Waste heat (2.2 million J)

Heat used in local schools and housing (5.7 million J)

CROSS-SECTION OF HYDROELECTRIC POWER STATION WITH FRANCIS TURBINE

Transformer

Insulator

High voltage cable

Switch gear including circuit braker

Bushing

Rotor house

Generator unit

Gate

Generator rotor turned by turbine

Shaft

Francis turbine

Curved blade

Gate

Afterbay

Screen

Water in reservoir

Tailrace

Potential energy of water intake turns turbine

Penstock

Draft tube

Water that flows out has lost some energy

CROSS-SECTION OF NUCLEAR POWER STATION WITH PRESSURIZED WATER REACTOR

Steam generator

Concrete shielding

Water pressurizer

Steel girder framework

Control rod

Reactor core

Pump

Moderator (water)

Enriched uranium fuel

Coolant (water) takes heat from reactor core to heat exchanger

Water in heat exchanger turns to steam

Steam drives turbine

Heat exchanger

Water pumped back into steam generator

Pump

Turbine shaft turns generator

Generator produces electric current at 25,000 volts

Water cools used steam

Steam loses energy to turbine and condenses back to water

Transformer increases voltage to 300,000 volts

High voltage cable

Pylon carries high voltage electricity

Hot water to cooling tower

Cold water from cooling tower

ENERGY SYSTEMS

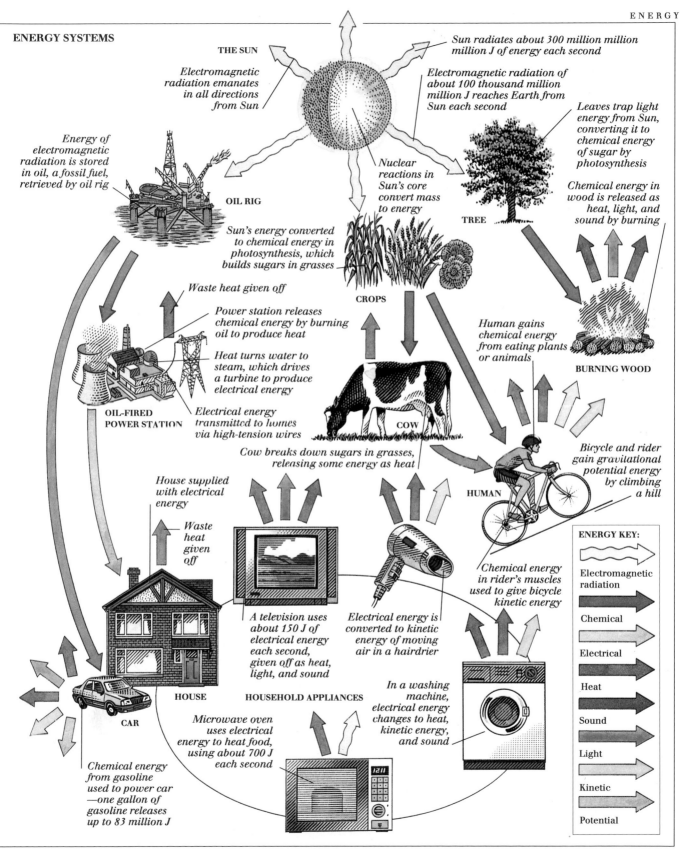

THE SUN

Electromagnetic radiation emanates in all directions from Sun

Sun radiates about 300 million million million J of energy each second

Electromagnetic radiation of about 100 thousand million million J reaches Earth from Sun each second

Nuclear reactions in Sun's core convert mass to energy

Energy of electromagnetic radiation is stored in oil, a fossil fuel, retrieved by oil rig

OIL RIG

Leaves trap light energy from Sun, converting it to chemical energy of sugar by photosynthesis

Chemical energy in wood is released as heat, light, and sound by burning

TREE

Sun's energy converted to chemical energy in photosynthesis, which builds sugars in grasses

CROPS

Human gains chemical energy from eating plants or animals

BURNING WOOD

Waste heat given off

Power station releases chemical energy by burning oil to produce heat

Heat turns water to steam, which drives a turbine to produce electrical energy

Electrical energy transmitted to homes via high-tension wires

OIL-FIRED POWER STATION

COW

Cow breaks down sugars in grasses, releasing some energy as heat

HUMAN

Bicycle and rider gain gravitational potential energy by climbing a hill

House supplied with electrical energy

Waste heat given off

A television uses about 150 J of electrical energy each second, given off as heat, light, and sound

Electrical energy is converted to kinetic energy of moving air in a hairdrier

Chemical energy in rider's muscles used to give bicycle kinetic energy

HOUSE

HOUSEHOLD APPLIANCES

In a washing machine, electrical energy changes to heat, kinetic energy, and sound

CAR

Chemical energy from gasoline used to power car —one gallon of gasoline releases up to 83 million J

Microwave oven uses electrical energy to heat food, using about 700 J each second

ENERGY KEY:

Electromagnetic radiation

Chemical

Electrical

Heat

Sound

Light

Kinetic

Potential

Electricity and magnetism

ELECTRICAL EFFECTS result from an imbalance of electric charge. There are two types of electric charge: positive (carried by protons) and negative (carried by electrons). If charges are opposite (unlike), they attract one another, while like charges repel. These forces of attraction and repulsion (electrostatic forces) exist between any two charged particles. Matter is normally uncharged, but if electrons are gained, an object will gain an overall negative charge; if they are removed, it becomes positive. Objects with an overall negative or positive charge are said to have an imbalance of charge, and exert the same forces as individual negative and positive charges. On this larger scale, the forces will always act to regain the balance of charge. This causes static electricity. Lightning, for example, is produced by clouds discharging a huge excess of negative electrons. If charges are free—in a wire or material that allows electrons to pass through it—the forces cause a flow of charge called an electric current. Some substances exhibit the strange phenomenon of magnetism—which also produces attractive and repulsive forces. Magnetic substances consist of small regions called domains. Normally unmagnetized, they can be magnetized by being placed in a magnetic field. Magnetism and electricity are inextricably linked, a fact put to use in motors and generators.

LIGHTNING

VAN DE GRAAFF (ELECTROSTATIC) GENERATOR

Positive charges at many thousands of volts

Metal dome

Rotation of belt

Positively charged belt strips negative charges (electrons) from dome via metal comb, giving dome a positive charge

Pulley wheel

Moving rubber belt gains a positive charge

Insulating column prevents charges leaking away

Positive metal comb strips negative charges (electrons) from belt

Negatively charged metal plate

Connection to positive electrical supply

Pulley wheel

Connection to negative electrical supply

Rotation of belt

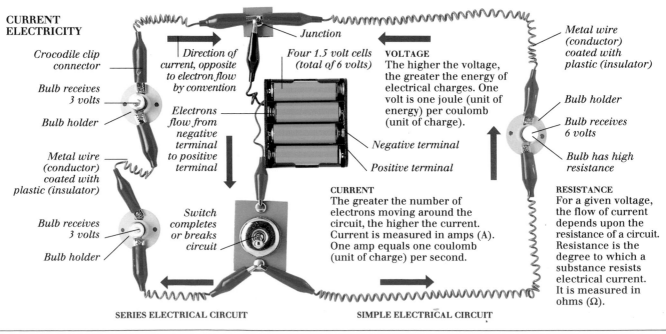

CURRENT ELECTRICITY

Crocodile clip connector

Bulb receives 3 volts

Bulb holder

Metal wire (conductor) coated with plastic (insulator)

Bulb receives 3 volts

Bulb holder

Junction

Direction of current, opposite to electron flow by convention

Electrons flow from negative terminal to positive terminal

Switch completes or breaks circuit

Four 1.5 volt cells (total of 6 volts)

VOLTAGE
The higher the voltage, the greater the energy of electrical charges. One volt is one joule (unit of energy) per coulomb (unit of charge).

Negative terminal

Positive terminal

CURRENT
The greater the number of electrons moving around the circuit, the higher the current. Current is measured in amps (A). One amp equals one coulomb (unit of charge) per second.

Metal wire (conductor) coated with plastic (insulator)

Bulb holder

Bulb receives 6 volts

Bulb has high resistance

RESISTANCE
For a given voltage, the flow of current depends upon the resistance of a circuit. Resistance is the degree to which a substance resists electrical current. It is measured in ohms (Ω).

SERIES ELECTRICAL CIRCUIT   SIMPLE ELECTRICAL CIRCUIT

MAGNETIC FIELDS AND FORCES

Iron filings

Profile of magnetic field

Bar magnet

North-seeking pole

North-seeking pole

Like poles repel

North-seeking pole

Unlike poles attract

North-seeking pole

South-seeking pole of electromagnet

North-seeking pole

South-seeking pole

Unlike poles attract

Direction of force

South-seeking pole

South-seeking pole

Like poles repel

Electromagnet

Wire to battery

MAGNETIC DOMAINS

Domain

Direction of magnetization within domain is random

Domain boundary

UNMAGNETIZED IRON

Direction of magnetization within domain has aligned

Domain aligned with magnetization has grown

Domain not aligned with magnetization has shrunk

Direction of overall magnetization

MAGNETIZED IRON IN A MAGNETIC FIELD

GENERATING MAGNETISM FROM ELECTRICITY

Direction of magnetic field (from north pole to south pole)

Magnetic field

Coil carries electric current

Direction of current

Metal wire (conductor) coated with plastic (insulator)

Negative terminal

Positive terminal

Electric current produces magnetic field

Four 1.5 volt cells (total of 6 volts)

CIRCUIT WITH ELECTROMAGNET

GENERATING ELECTRICITY FROM MAGNETISM

Terminal box

Coil of wire

Permanent magnet

Bearing

Non-drive end

Coil of wire

Terminal

Stator

Main rotor turns in magnetic field produced by coil of wire in stator

Fan

Drive end

Coil of wire

Shaft

Secondary (exciter) rotor

ELECTRIC GENERATOR
In a generator, the rotor rotates within the magnetic field of the stator to produce an electric current.

Coil of wire rotates within magnetic field of permanent magnet

Permanent magnet

Steel casing

Iron core

Coated copper winding

Commutator

Terminal

Spindle

End of shaft

Terminal

ELECTRIC MOTOR
In a motor, magnetic forces between the winding and permanent magnet produce a rotary motion.

Light

INFRARED IMAGE OF A HOUSE

LIGHT IS A FORM OF ENERGY. It is a type of electromagnetic radiation, like X rays or radio waves. All electromagnetic radiation is produced by electric charges (see pp. 316-317): it is caused by the effects of oscillating electric and magnetic fields as they travel through space. Electromagnetic radiation is considered to have both wave and particle properties. It can be thought of as a wave of electricity and magnetism. In that case, the difference between the various forms of radiation is their wavelength. Radiation can also be said to consist of particles, or packets of energy, called photons. The difference between light and X rays, for instance, is the amount of energy that each photon carries. The complete range of radiation is referred to as the electromagnetic spectrum, extending from low energy, long wavelength radio waves to high energy, short wavelength gamma rays. Light is the only part of the electromagnetic spectrum that is visible. White light from the Sun is made up of all the visible wavelengths of radiation, which can be seen when it is separated by using a prism. Light, like all forms of electromagnetic radiation, can be reflected (bounced back) and refracted (bent). Different parts of the electromagnetic spectrum are produced in different ways. Sometimes visible light— and infrared radiation—is generated by the vibrating particles of warm or hot objects. The emission of light in this way is called incandescence. Light can also be produced by fluorescence, a phenomenon in which electrons gain and lose energy within atoms.

MAXWELLIAN DIAGRAM OF ELECTROMAGNETIC RADIATION AS WAVES

Oscillating electric field

Wavelength

Oscillating magnetic field

Two fields at right angles

Direction of travel

ELECTROMAGNETIC RADIATION AS PARTICLES

Photon thought of as wave packet of energy

Red light has long wavelength

Blue light has about twice the energy of red light

Blue light has shorter wavelength: waves are more tightly packed

PHOTON OF RED LIGHT

PHOTON OF BLUE LIGHT

SPLITTING WHITE LIGHT INTO THE SPECTRUM

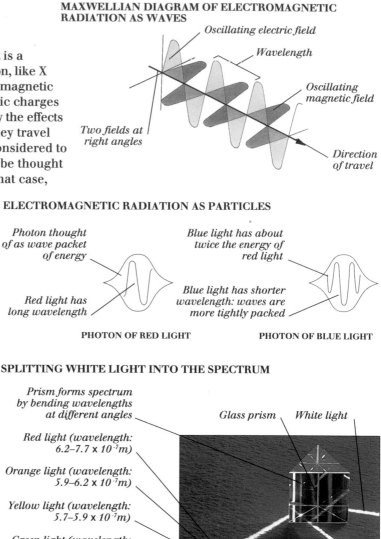

Prism forms spectrum by bending wavelengths at different angles

Glass prism   White light

Red light (wavelength: $6.2–7.7 \times 10^{-7}m$)

Orange light (wavelength: $5.9–6.2 \times 10^{-7}m$)

Yellow light (wavelength: $5.7–5.9 \times 10^{-7}m$)

Green light (wavelength: $4.9–5.7 \times 10^{-7}m$)

Blue light (wavelength: $4.5–4.9 \times 10^{-7}m$)

Violet light (wavelength: $3.9–4.5 \times 10^{-7}m$)

THE ELECTROMAGNETIC SPECTRUM

ENERGY (JOULES) 10^{-28}| 10^{-27}| 10^{-26}| 10^{-25}| 10^{-24}| 10^{-23}| 10^{-22}| 10^{-21}| 10^{-20}|

WAVELENGTH (METERS) 10^{4}| 10^{3}| 10^{2}| 10| 1| 10^{-1}| 10^{-2}| 10^{-3}| 10^{-4}| 10^{-5}|

Long-wave radio   Medium-wave radio   Shortwave radio   Very high-frequency (VHF) radio   Microwaves   Infrared radiation

Radio waves

ARTIFICIAL LIGHT SOURCES

FLUORESCENT TUBE

Glass tube filled with mercury vapor

Coiled tungsten filament

Ceramic end-piece

Electrical contact

Glass support

Filament heated and negatively charged electrons emitted

Electrons accelerate from one coil to the other

Electrons collide with mercury atoms

Mercury atom

Free electron

INCANDESCENT LIGHT BULB

SECTION OF FILAMENT OF INCANDESCENT LIGHT BULB: HOW INCANDESCENT LIGHT IS PRODUCED

Energy from collision produces ultraviolet light (shortwave radiation)

Phosphor coating

Glass

Moving electrons collide with metal atoms

Action of ultraviolet light on phosphor produces visible light (long-wave radiation)

Lead-in wire

Glass bulb

Seal

Glass support

Screw fitting

Electrical contact

Hot filament gives out light

Vibration of metal atoms increases temperature

Coiled tungsten filament

Mixture of unreactive gases at low pressure

Electrical contact

SECTION OF PHOSPHOR COATING OF FLUORESCENT TUBE: HOW FLUORESCENT LIGHT IS PRODUCED

REFLECTION OF LIGHT

Incident laser light

Mirror

Mirror support

Light strikes smooth surface at an angle, which reflects it at the same angle

Reflected light

REFRACTION OF LIGHT

Glass (transparent substance)

Incident laser light

Light enters substance

Light slows down and bends as it passes from air to glass

Light speeds up as it leaves glass

Refracted (bent) light

10^{-18} 10^{-17} 10^{-16} 10^{-15} 10^{-14} 10^{-13} 10^{-12} 10^{-11} 10^{-10} 10^{-9} 10^{-8}

10^{-7} 10^{-8} 10^{-9} 10^{-10} 10^{-11} 10^{-12} 10^{-13} 10^{-14} 10^{-15} 10^{-16} 10^{-17}

Visible light | Ultraviolet radiation | X rays | Gamma rays

Force and motion

FORCES ARE PUSHES OR PULLS that change the motion of objects. To make a stationary object move, or a moving object stop, a force is needed. A force is also required to change the speed or direction of an object. This change in speed or direction is known as acceleration. Acceleration depends on the size (magnitude) of the force, and on the mass of the object. The effects of forces were first summarized by Isaac Newton in his three laws of motion. The international unit of force, named after him, is the newton (N), which is approximately equal to the weight of one apple. Gravity—the force of attraction between any two masses—can be measured using a newton meter (spring balance). Forces are put to useful effect in machines. A simple machine, such as a wheel and axle, is a device that changes the size or direction of an applied force. It allows an applied force (the effort) to produce another force (the load). A lever uses a bar that turns on a fulcrum to exert force. In all simple machines, there is a relationship between force and distance. A small force (in a compound pulley, for instance) moves through a large distance to lift a heavy object a small distance. This is called the Law of Simple Machines.

SIMPLE MACHINES

Single-pulley system (simple pulley)

Pulley wheel

Simple pulley only changes direction of a force

Effort is the same size as the load (10 N) and is pulled the same distance

One rope attached to load

Load of 10 N

Two-pulley system (simple pulley)

Pulley wheel

Effort is half the load (5 N), but the rope must be pulled twice the distance

Two ropes share the force and distance

Pulley wheel

Load of 10 N

Four-pulley system (compound pulley)

Two pulley wheels

Effort is one quarter of the load (2.5 N), but the rope must be pulled four times the distance

Four ropes share the force and distance

SIMPLE AND COMPOUND PULLEYS

Two pulley wheels

Load of 10 N

NEWTON METERS (SPRING BALANCES)

Weight is measured using a spring

When weight pulls downward, pointer moves along scale and measures force

Weight is 10 N

Weight is 20 N

Mass of 1 kg

Mass of 2 kg

WEIGHT AND MASS
The mass of an object is a measure of the quantity of matter that it possesses. Mass is usually measured in grams (g) or kilograms (kg). The weight of an object is the force exerted on the object's mass by gravity. Since weight is a force, its unit is the newton (N).

Wheel and axle multiplies the effort

Force is transmitted to the wheels by the chain

Pedal

Effort, provided by cyclist's muscles, is smaller than the load, but moves through a greater distance

Crank

A larger force, the load, is produced at the axle

WHEEL AND AXLE

A screw, acting like a wedge wrapped around a shaft, multiplies the effort

Effort, a turning force supplied through a screwdriver

Pitch (the angle of the screw thread)

The smaller the angle of pitch, the less force is required, but more turns are needed to move it through a greater distance

A larger force, the load, pulls the screw into wood

SCREW

Effort pushes axe into wood

A larger force, the load, moves through a smaller distance to push wood apart

Axe blade has wedge shape

Wedge multiplies effort

WEDGE

NEWTON'S THREE LAWS OF MOTION

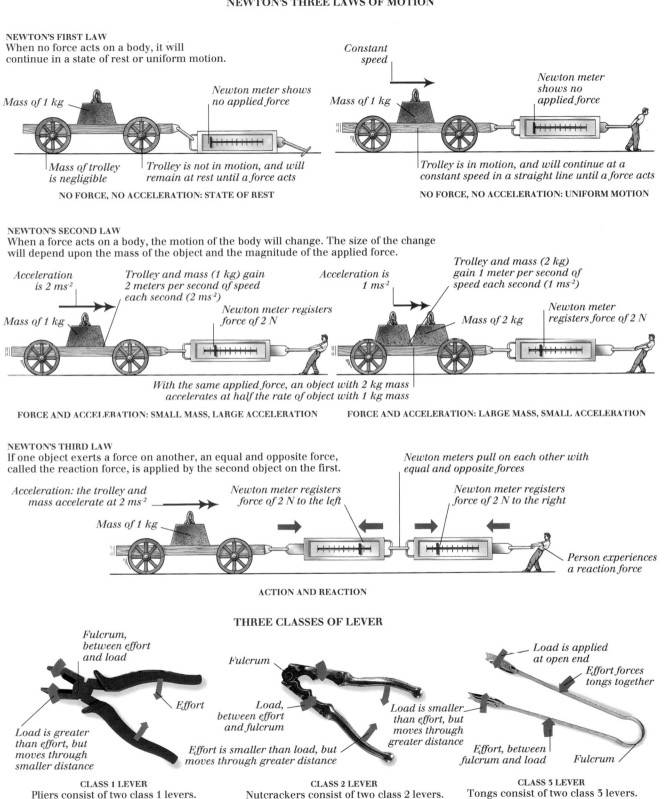

NEWTON'S FIRST LAW
When no force acts on a body, it will continue in a state of rest or uniform motion.

Mass of 1 kg

Newton meter shows no applied force

Mass of trolley is negligible

Trolley is not in motion, and will remain at rest until a force acts

NO FORCE, NO ACCELERATION: STATE OF REST

Constant speed

Mass of 1 kg

Newton meter shows no applied force

Trolley is in motion, and will continue at a constant speed in a straight line until a force acts

NO FORCE, NO ACCELERATION: UNIFORM MOTION

NEWTON'S SECOND LAW
When a force acts on a body, the motion of the body will change. The size of the change will depend upon the mass of the object and the magnitude of the applied force.

Acceleration is 2 ms^{-2}

Trolley and mass (1 kg) gain 2 meters per second of speed each second (2 ms^{-2})

Mass of 1 kg

Newton meter registers force of 2 N

Acceleration is 1 ms^{-2}

Trolley and mass (2 kg) gain 1 meter per second of speed each second (1 ms^{-2})

Mass of 2 kg

Newton meter registers force of 2 N

With the same applied force, an object with 2 kg mass accelerates at half the rate of object with 1 kg mass

FORCE AND ACCELERATION: SMALL MASS, LARGE ACCELERATION

FORCE AND ACCELERATION: LARGE MASS, SMALL ACCELERATION

NEWTON'S THIRD LAW
If one object exerts a force on another, an equal and opposite force, called the reaction force, is applied by the second object on the first.

Newton meters pull on each other with equal and opposite forces

Acceleration: the trolley and mass accelerate at 2 ms^{-2}

Mass of 1 kg

Newton meter registers force of 2 N to the left

Newton meter registers force of 2 N to the right

Person experiences a reaction force

ACTION AND REACTION

THREE CLASSES OF LEVER

Fulcrum, between effort and load

Effort

Load is greater than effort, but moves through smaller distance

CLASS 1 LEVER
Pliers consist of two class 1 levers.

Fulcrum

Load, between effort and fulcrum

Effort is smaller than load, but moves through greater distance

CLASS 2 LEVER
Nutcrackers consist of two class 2 levers.

Load is applied at open end

Effort forces tongs together

Load is smaller than effort, but moves through greater distance

Effort, between fulcrum and load

Fulcrum

CLASS 3 LEVER
Tongs consist of two class 3 levers.

RAIL AND ROAD

Steam locomotives

WAGONS THAT ARE PULLED along tracks have been used to transport material since the 16th century, but these trains were drawn by men or horses until the invention of the steam locomotive. Steam locomotives enabled the basic railroad system to realize its true potential. In 1804, Richard Trevithick built the world's first working steam locomotive in South Wales. It was not entirely successful, but it encouraged others to develop new designs. By 1829, the British engineer Robert Stephenson had built the Rocket, considered to be the forerunner of the modern locomotive. The Rocket was a self-sufficient unit, carrying coal to heat the boiler and a water supply for generating steam. Steam passed from the boiler to force the pistons back and forth, and this movement turned the driving wheels, propelling the train forward. Used steam was then expelled in characteristic puffs. Later steam locomotives, like Ellerman Lines and the Mallard, worked in a similar way, but on a much larger scale. The simple design and reliability of steam locomotives ensured that they changed very little in 120 years of use, before being replaced in the 1950s by more efficient diesel and electric power (see pp. 326-329).

ROCKET STEAM LOCOMOTIVE, 1829

Chimney

Smokebox

Pipe takes steam from boiler to cylinder

Remains of firebox

Leaf spring

Regulator (throttle)

Valve chest

Rocket nameplate

Wrought iron boiler

Valve setting control

Wooden buffer beam

Wooden driving wheel

Metal tire

Ballast

Rail chair

Wooden sleeper

Piston rod

Carrying wheel

Axle

Wrought iron rail

Cylinder

Driver's platform

ELLERMAN LINES, 1949 (CUTAWAY VIEW)

Stay

Vacuum reservoir

Panel brace

Water tank

Coal space

Tender hand brake

Cab

Firebox

Brick arch

Water filler

Panel sheeting

Hand rail

Buffer

Brake vacuum pipe

Wheel guard

Axle

Axle box

Tender wheel

Brake rigging

Water float to indicate water level

Water float lever

Step

Axle box cover

Coupling

Footplate

Coil spring

Trailing wheel

Grate

Fire drawn into fire tubes

TENDER

CAB INTERIOR OF MALLARD EXPRESS STEAM LOCOMOTIVE, 1938

Steam sanding control

Blower isolator valve

Pressure gauge isolator valve

Vacuum brake isolator valve

Steam heating isolator valve

Steam chest pressure gauge

Sliding roof vent

Vacuum brake pressure gauge

Boiler pressure gauge

Blower control

Gauge glass to show level of water in boiler

Regulator controls flow of steam to cylinders

Exhaust steam water injector control

Cab side window

Steam heating pressure gauge

Vacuum brake lever

Glass deflector

Live steam water injector control

Whistle lever

Manual sanding lever

Cylinder drain lever

Reverser handle

Control valve for hot water hose

Driver's seat

Fireman's seat

Steam-operated reversing shaft lock control

Steam heat safety valve

Oil can warming tray

Firebox

Firehole

Firebox door

Fire tube

Steam dome

Mechanical lubricator

Pipe takes steam from boiler to cylinder

Chimney

Thermal siphon

Regulator valve

Superheater tube inside flue tube

Boiler

Blast pipe

Smoke box

Smoke box door

Lubricating pipe

Piston valve

Buffer

Brake shoe

Expansion lever

Slide bar

Screw coupling

Brake rigging

Driving wheel

Crank

Connecting rod

Combination lever

Piston, linked to connecting rod

Leading wheel

Coupling rod

Cylinder

STEAM LOCOMOTIVE

Diesel trains

RUDOLF DIESEL FIRST DEMONSTRATED the diesel engine in Germany in 1898, but it was not until the 1940s that diesel locomotives were successfully established on both passenger and freight services in the U.S. Early diesel locomotives like the Union Pacific were more expensive to build than steam locomotives, but were more efficient and cheaper to operate, especially where oil was plentiful. One feature of diesel engines is that the power output cannot be coupled directly to the wheels. To convert the mechanical energy produced by diesel engines, a transmission system is needed. Almost all diesel locomotives have electric transmissions, and are known as diesel-electric locomotives. The diesel engine works by drawing air into the cylinders and compressing it to increase its temperature; a small quantity of diesel fuel is then injected into it. The resulting combustion drives the generator (more recently an alternator) to produce electricity, which is fed to electric motors connected to the wheels. Diesel-electric locomotives are essentially electric locomotives that carry their own power plants, and are used worldwide today. The Deltic diesel-electric locomotive, similar to the one shown here, replaced classic express steam locomotives, and ran at speeds up to 100 mph.

FRONT VIEW OF UNION PACIFIC DIESEL-ELECTRIC LOCOMOTIVE, 1950s

Exhaust vent   *Windshield wiper*   *Horn*   *Cab front window*   *Headlight*

Cab door   *Name of operating railroad*

Illuminated locomotive unit number

Railroad crest

Cab step   *Step*   *Motor-driven bogie axle*   *Air-brake coupling hose*   *Center buck-eye coupler*

PROTOTYPE DELTIC DIESEL-ELECTRIC LOCOMOTIVE, 1956

Engine room vent   *Inspection hatch*   *Engine exhaust port*   *Radiator fan*   *Engine room window*   *Engine room vent*

DELTIC

Fuel tank   *Water for heating boiler*   *Inspection socket*   *Folding step*   *Drain for radiator coolant*   *Radiator coolant*   *Sand box*   *Telescopic damper*   *Drain for control reservoir*

**DIESEL ENGINE OF BRITISH RAIL CLASS 20
DIESEL-ELECTRIC LOCOMOTIVE**

Exhaust vent

Cylinder head
(V-four configuration)

Turbo-charged diesel
engine drives generator

Generator
cooling fan

Generator
compartment
vent

Auxiliary
generator

Main generator
produces
electricity that
drives wheels

Main chassis
member

Innermost
wheel set on
cab-end bogie

Air brake pipe

Brake
rigging

Battery
box

Engine crankcase

Air reservoir and
isolator valves

Lubricating oil
primary pump and
fuel supply pump

EXAMPLES OF FREIGHT CARS

BOX CAR

HOPPER CAR

REFRIGERATOR CAR

LIVESTOCK CAR

FLAT CAR WITH BULKHEADS

AUTOMOBILE CAR

Cab
door

Driver's seat

Cab

Warning horn

Windshield

Windshield wiper

Cab window

Manufacturer's
logo

Cab vent

Indicator
light

Sand box

Buffer

Brake cylinder

Roller-bearing
axle box

Brake
shoe

Brake
actuating chain

Transverse leaf spring
secondary suspension

Coil spring primary
suspension

Electric and high-speed trains

THE FIRST ELECTRIC LOCOMOTIVE ran in 1879 in Berlin, Germany. In Europe, electric trains developed as a more efficient alternative to the steam locomotive and diesel-electric power. Like diesels, electric trains employ electric motors to drive the wheels but, unlike diesels, the electricity is generated externally at a power station. Electric current is picked up either from a catenary (overhead cable) via a pantograph, or from a third rail. Since it does not carry its own power-generating equipment, an electric locomotive has a better power-to-weight ratio and greater acceleration than its diesel-electric equivalent. This makes electric trains highly suitable for urban routes with many stops. They are also faster, quieter, and cause less pollution. The latest electric French TGV (Train à Grande Vitesse) reaches 186 mph; other trains, like the London to Paris and Brussels Eurostar, can run at several voltages and operate between different countries. Simpler electric trains perform special duties—the "People Mover" at Gatwick Airport, London, runs between terminals.

HOW ALTERNATING CURRENT (AC) ELECTRIC TRAINS WORK

Running rail for return current
Feeder station provides current
Catenary
Vacuum circuit breaker
Thyristor converter converts current (ac) to direct current (dc)
Pantograph collects current
Traction motor turns wheel
Control circuit
Transformer steps down voltage
Axle brush

FRONT VIEW OF ITALIAN STATE RAILWAYS CLASS 402 ELECTRIC LOCOMOTIVE

FRONT VIEW OF PARIS METRO

Route number
Windshield wiper
Unit number
Operator's initials (Régie Autonome des Transports Parisien)
Rubber running wheel
Guard for rubber wheel

Door open/shut indicator light
Driver's seat
Handle
Front light (white)
Rear light (red)
Buffing pad
Rubber guide wheel

Collector strip for electric current
Double-arm pantograph
Headlight
Windshield wiper
Italian State Railways crest
Number of electric (E) locomotive (class 402 No. 5)
Buffer
Jumper cable
Conventional hook-screw coupling
Front light (white)
Rear light (red)

SIDE VIEW OF GATWICK EXPRESS "PEOPLE MOVER"

Pneumatic rubber wheel
Concrete track
Automatic door
No driver (train controlled by central computer)

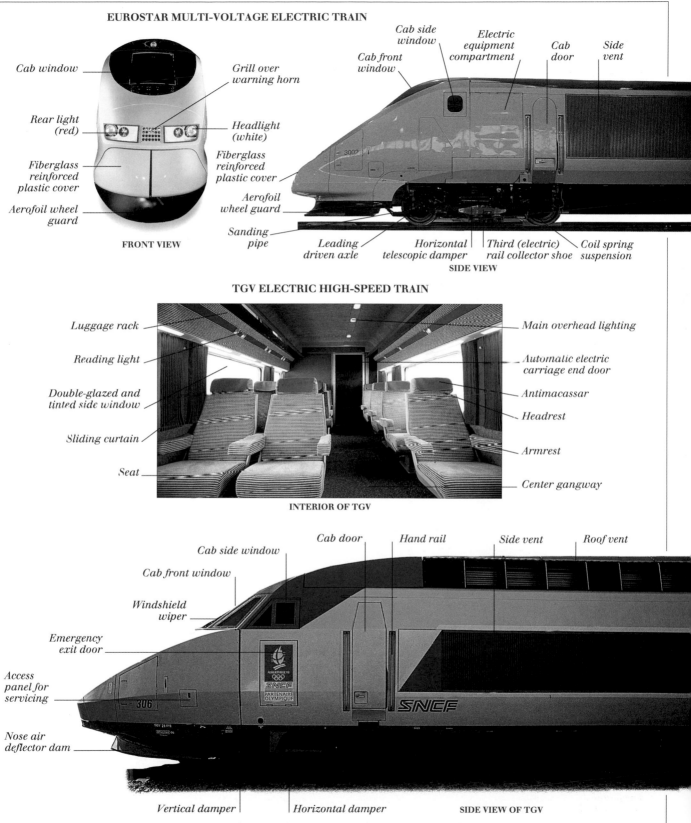

EUROSTAR MULTI-VOLTAGE ELECTRIC TRAIN

Cab window

Grill over
warning horn

Rear light
(red)

Headlight
(white)

Fiberglass
reinforced
plastic cover

Fiberglass
reinforced
plastic cover

Aerofoil wheel
guard

FRONT VIEW

Cab side
window

Electric
equipment
compartment

Cab
door

Side
vent

Cab front
window

3002

Aerofoil
wheel guard

Sanding
pipe

Leading
driven axle

Horizontal
telescopic damper

Third (electric)
rail collector shoe

Coil spring
suspension

SIDE VIEW

TGV ELECTRIC HIGH-SPEED TRAIN

Luggage rack

Main overhead lighting

Reading light

Automatic electric
carriage end door

Double-glazed and
tinted side window

Antimacassar

Sliding curtain

Headrest

Seat

Armrest

Center gangway

INTERIOR OF TGV

Cab side window

Cab door

Hand rail

Side vent

Roof vent

Cab front window

Windshield
wiper

Emergency
exit door

ALBERTVILLE 92
SNCF
PARTENAIRE
OLYMPIQUE

Access
panel for
servicing

306

SNCF

Nose air
deflector dam

Vertical damper

Horizontal damper

SIDE VIEW OF TGV

Train equipment

MODERN RAILROAD TRACK consists of two parallel steel rails clipped onto a support called a sleeper. Sleepers are usually made of reinforced concrete, although wood and steel are still used. The distance between the inside edges of the rails is the track gauge. It evolved in Britain, which uses a gauge of 4 ft 8½ in (1,435 mm), known as the standard gauge. As engineering grew more sophisticated, narrower gauges were adopted because they cost less to build. The loading gauge, which is equally important, determines the size of the largest loaded vehicle that may pass through tunnels and under bridges with adequate clearance. Safe train operation relies on following a signaling system. At first, signaling was based on a simple time interval between trains, but it now depends on maintaining a safe distance between successive trains traveling in the same direction. Most modern signals are colored lights, but older mechanical semaphore signals are still used. On the latest high-speed lines, train drivers receive control instructions by electronic means. Signaling depends on reliable control of the train by effective braking. For fast, modern trains, which have considerable momentum, it is essential that each vehicle in the train can be braked by the driver or by a train control system, such as Automatic Train Protection (ATP). Braking is achieved by the brake shoe acting on the wheel rim (rim brakes), by disc brakes, or, increasingly, by electrical braking.

MECHANICAL SEMAPHORE SIGNAL

Red, square-ended arm in raised position means "all clear"

Red glass

Green glass

Actuating lever system

Motor operating "home" stop signal

Green glass

Yellow glass

Yellow, "distant" warning arm in horizontal position means "caution"

Tubular steel post

Ladder

Electrical relay box

FOUR-ASPECT COLORED LIGHT SIGNAL

Glass (yellow)

Glass (green)

Yellow glass (lit)

Glass (red)

FRONT VIEW

Lifting lug

Lamp shield

Clip

Base

SIDE VIEW

HOW A MODERN MAIN-LINE SIGNALING SYSTEM WORKS

Red "stop" light instructs next train not to enter this section of track

Green "all clear" light instructs train B to proceed into this section of track

Green "all clear" light instructs train B to proceed into this section of track

Green "all clear" light instructs train B to proceed into this section of track

Pantograph

Catenary

Train B

Track

EXAMPLES OF INTERNATIONAL TRACK GAUGES

3 ft 3½ in
(1,000 mm)
*East Africa,
India,
Malaysia,
Chile, and
Argentina*

3 ft 6 in
(1,067 mm)
*Japan, Australia,
Sudan, West Africa,
South Africa, and
New Zealand*

4 ft 8½ in
(1,435 mm)
*U.S., Canada, China,
Egypt, Turkey, Iran,
Japan, Peru, Britain,
Europe, Australia,
Brazil, and Mexico*

5 ft 0 in
(1,524 mm)
*Russia, Spain,
Portugal, and
Finland*

5 ft 3 in
(1,600 mm)
*Ireland, Australia,
and Brazil*

5 ft 6 in
(1,676 mm)
*India, Pakistan,
and Argentina*

EXAMPLES OF INTERNATIONAL LOADING GAUGES

KEY:

Britain: 9 ft 0 in (2.75 m) x 12 ft 11 in (3.95 m)

Europe: 10 ft 2 in (3.1 m) x 14 ft 9 in (4.5 m)

U.S.: 10 ft 10 in (3.3 m) x 16 ft 2 in (4.9 m)

Russia: 11 ft 2 in (3.4 m) x 17 ft 4 in (5.3 m)

4 ft 8½ in
(1,435 mm)
*Standard track
gauge*

5 ft 0 in
(1,524 mm)
*Track gauge of Russia,
with largest loading gauge*

FLAT-BOTTOMED RAIL

Flat-bottomed steel rail

Steel spring secures
rail to sleeper

Synthetic
insulating
pad

Sleeper supports
track and
maintains
gauge

BULL-HEAD RAIL

Wooden "key" secures
rail in chair

Steel tapered
screw fastens
chair to
sleeper

Bull-head pattern
steel rail

Cast-iron chair

Wooden
sleeper

DISC BRAKES ON MODERN WAGON BOGIE

Base of wagon

Airbag secondary
suspension

HOT BOX
TEST VALVE

Brake
disc

Brake calliper

Damper

Hand
brake
wheel

Wheel

Axle

Two yellow "preliminary
caution" lights instruct train
B that it must stop in two
signals time

Yellow "caution" light
instructs train B that it
must stop at next signal

Green "all clear" light
instructs train A to proceed
into this section of track

Red "stop" light instructs
train B not to enter
this section of track

Braking distance

Train A

Trolleys and buses

WHEN CITY POPULATIONS exploded in the 1800s, there was an urgent need for mass transportation. Trolleys were an early solution. The first trolleys, like buses, were horse-drawn, but in 1881, electric streetcars appeared in Berlin, Germany. Electric trolleys soon became widespread throughout Europe and North America. Trolleys run on rails along a fixed route, using electric motors that receive power from overhead cables. As road networks developed, motorized buses offered a flexible alternative to trolleys. By the 1930s, they had replaced trolley systems in many cities. City buses typically have doors at both the front and rear to make loading and unloading easier. Double-decker designs are popular, occupying the same amount of street space as single-decker buses but able to transport twice the number of people. Buses are also commonly used for inter-city travel and touring. Tour buses have reclining seats, large windows, luggage space, and toilets. Recently, as city traffic has become increasingly congested, many city planners have designed new electric streetcar routes to run alongside bus routes as part of an integrated transport system.

METROLINK TROLLEY, MANCHESTER, BRITAIN

EARLY TROLLEY, c.1900

Trolley boom
Trolley head
Trolley base
Drop window
Upper deck
Quarter light
Brake
Stair
Lower deck
Underframe
Platform
Controller
Truck
Lifeguard

MCW METROBUS, LONDON, ENGLAND

Window vent
Upper deck windshield
Route information
Destination screen
Side mirror
Asymmetric windshield
Windshield wiper
Sidelight
Headlight
Grill
Fog light
License plate
Manufacturer's logo

Upper deck air intake
Route number

FRONT VIEW

Square roof dome
Mirror for driver to see upstairs
Operator's logo
Destination screen
Side mirror
Front bumper
Entrance door
Emergency door control
Turning indicator

Side mirror
Permit holder
Turning indicator

LONDON NORTHERN
Hornsey Rise Crouch End
Turnpike Lane
West Green Road
41
ARCHWAY STN.

PAY DRIVER
MCW
KYV 739X

LONDON NORTHERN

SINGLE-DECKER BUS, NEW YORK CITY, NEW YORK

Wheelchair access

Sliding window

Sloped roof dome

Tinted glass

Air intake

Tire

Axle

Exit door

Access panel

Sidelight

Entrance door

SIDE VIEW

Marker light

Repeater indicator

Entrance door

Route number

Side mirror

Headlight

Turning indicator

License plate

Bumper

Bumper

FRONT VIEW

DOUBLE-DECKER TOUR BUS, PARIS, FRANCE

Tinted glass

Air intake

Access panel

Skirt

Access door

Twin rear axle

Side entrance

Single front axle

Tire

Paris Vision

CAREUX

Raked windshield

Panoramic window

Turning indicator

Bumper

Plug-style entrance door

Sliding window vent

Upper saloon window

Advertising panel

Air intake

Lower saloon window

Fleet number

Engine access panel

Rear bumper

Skirt

Emergency door control

Two-leaf style exit door

Legal lettering

London Buses logo

Tire

Axle

NO ENTRY

NO ENTRY

HT

LONDON BUSES

LONDON NORTHERN BUS COMPANY LIMITED.
HOBSON HOUSE,
155 GOWER STREET,
LONDON WC1E 6LB.

Uw10267kg

M1041

SIDE VIEW

The first cars

THE EARLIEST ROAD VEHICLE powered by an engine, the Cugnot steam traction engine, was built in 1770. More practical steam carriages, such as the Bordino, were available in the early 19th century, but they were heavy and cumbersome. Restrictive laws and the introduction of railways, faster and able to carry more passengers, saw the decline of "cars" powered by steam. It was not until 1860 that the first practical power unit for road vehicles was developed with the invention of the internal combustion engine by the Belgian Étienne Lenoir. By around 1890, Karl Benz and Gottlieb Daimler in Germany and Albert de Dion and Armand Peugeot in France were building cars for sale to the public. These early cars, despite being primitive, expensive, and produced in limited numbers, heralded the age of the automobile.

STEAM-POWERED CUGNOT "FARDIER," 1770

Twin cylinder engine
Steam pipe
Rocking beam
Steering tiller
Chimney
Brake pedal
Seat
Wooden frame
Wooden wheel (artillery wheel)
Load space
Haystack boiler
Carrying fork
Piston rod
Ratchet wheel
Single front driving wheel
Step
Log basket
Broad, rough tire

BORDINO STEAM CARRIAGE, 1854

Chimney
Top iron (landau iron)
Landau body
Drop-down window
Leather top
Fire-tube boiler
Sprung chassis
Water tank
Safety valve
Safety valve weight
Coal hopper
Chauffeur's seat (stoker's seat; spider seat; tiger seat)
Step
Tie bar
Full-elliptic leaf spring
Iron tire
Wooden spoke
Wooden wheel (artillery wheel)
Hub
Unsprung chassis
Tie rod
Connecting rod
Steam chest
Twin-cylinder steam engine
Steam distributor valve

SIDE VIEW OF GASOLINE-DRIVEN BENZ MOTORWAGEN, 1886

Steering tiller
Brake quadrant
Brake lever
Cooling water tank
Steering column
Full-elliptic leaf spring
Steering rack
Bevel gear
Steering link
Final drive sprocket
Steering head
Seat spring
Driven pulley
Wheel fork
Tubular chassis
Driving chain
Driving sprocket
Hub
Solid rubber tire
Tangent-spoked wire wheel

REAR VIEW OF BENZ MOTORWAGEN, 1886

Pinion
Lubricator
Cooling tank
Crown wheel
Driving pulley
Fuel tank
Drive belt
Big-end bearing
Groove for rope starter
Crankshaft
Flywheel
Seat cushion

Candle lamp
Driver's seat
Steering tiller
Brake lever
Dashboard
Headlight
Round pin
Splinter bar
Towing hook
Forecarriage
Steam pipe
Spoke
Frame

OVERHEAD VIEW OF BENZ MOTORWAGEN, 1886

Steering link
Footboard (floorboard)
Steering tiller
Brake lever
Tool and battery box
Trembler coil box
Intake pipe
Single cylinder
Fuel tank
Cooling water tank
Oil-filled lubricator
Flywheel
Crown wheel
Crankshaft
Driving pulley
Drive belt

Elegance and utility

DURING THE FIRST DECADE OF THIS CENTURY, the motorist who could afford it had a choice of some of the finest cars ever made. These handbuilt cars were powerful and luxurious, using the finest wood, leather, and cloth, and bodywork made to the customer's individual requirements. Some had six-cylinder engines as big as 15 liters. The price of such cars was several times that of an average house, and their yearly running costs were also very high. As a result, basic, utilitarian cars became popular. Costing perhaps one-tenth of the price of a luxury car, these cars had very little trim and often had only single-cylinder engines.

1904 OLDSMOBILE SINGLE-CYLINDER ENGINE

Oil bottle dripfeed
Crankcase
Starting handle bracket
Exhaust pipe
Cylinder head
Cylinder
Starter cog
Carburetor
Engine timing gear
Crankshaft
Gear band
Flywheel

FRONT VIEW OF 1906 RENAULT

Canopy
Mahogany-framed windshield
Cast aluminum wheel spider
Rear window
British Automobile Association badge
Bedford cord upholstery
Window blind
British Royal Automobile Club badge
Blind pull
Window lift strap
Rearview mirror
Broad lace trim
Lamp bracket
Windshield support
Oil side lamp
Fender
Dashboard radiator
Brass bevel
Access panel
Hood catch
Bail handle
Lifting handle
Mirror reflector
Acetylene headlight
Steering spindle
Elliott steering knuckle
Chevron-tread tire
Dumb iron
Screwdown greaser
Front axle
Starting handle
Tie rod

SIDE VIEW OF 1906 RENAULT

Luggage grid
Button-quilted upholstery
Mahogany-framed plate glass window
Round-corner single limousine coachwork
Rear oil lamp
Shock absorber
Hub
Hubcap
Beaded edge tire
Tire security bolt

1904 OLDSMOBILE TRIM AND BODYWORK

Reflector

Seat back rest frame

Rear lamp

Dashboard

Engine cover handle

Tiller

Engine cover

Brake pedal

Throttle pedal

Fender

Mirror

Fender stay

Ignition switch

Seat cushion (squab)

1904 OLDSMOBILE CHASSIS

Front steering tie rod

Front spring

Brake rod

Full-elliptic steering spring

Steering wiffletree

Rear spring

Front axle

Starting handle bracket

Combined spring and chassis unit

Non-skid tire

Brass scrollwork

Blind pull

Canopy

Openable windshield

Brass bevel

Division

Dashboard

Hood

Broad lace trim

Handbrake

Oil side lamp

Leather upholstery

Steering wheel

Water pipe

Gear lever

Plug lead conduit

Acetylene headlight

Fuel/air intake pipe

Bi-block engine

Bulb horn

Spare tire

Dashboard radiator

Jump seat (opera seat; strapontin)

Rim clamp

Tire carrier

Running board

Leather valance

Tire strap

Hood support

Exhaust manifold

Starting handle

Wooden artillery wheel

Mass production

THE FIRST CARS WERE HAND-ASSEMBLED from individually built parts, a time-consuming procedure that required skilled mechanics and made cars very expensive. This problem was solved, in America, by a Detroit car manufacturer named Henry Ford. He introduced mass production by using standardized parts, and later combined these with a moving production line. The work was brought to the workers, each of whom performed one simple task in the construction process as the chassis moved along the line. The first mass-produced car, the Ford Model T, was launched in 1908. At first it was available in a limited range of body styles and colors. However, when the production line was introduced in 1914, the color range was cut back; the Model T became available, as Henry Ford said, in "any color you like, so long as it's black." Ford cut the production time for a car from several days to about 12 hours, and eventually to minutes, making cars much cheaper than before. As a result, half the cars in the world were Model T Fords by 1920.

FRONT VIEW OF 1913 FORD MODEL T

Throttle lever
Openable windshield
Steering wheel
Ignition lever
Windshield stay
Dashboard
Side lamp
Bulb horn
Spring shock absorber
Fender
Headlight
Radiator
Front transverse leaf spring
License plate
Starting handle
Steering knuckle
Front axle
Steering spindle connecting-rod

STAGES OF FORD MODEL T PRODUCTION

Left half of differential housing
Pinion
Hub bolt
Rear leaf spring (cross-member)
Steering arm
King pin
Removable wheel
Hub brake shoe
Tie rod
Steering wheel
Pinion housing
Front transverse leaf spring
Differential housing
Chassis frame
Rear spring perch
Radius rod
Rear axle
Front cross-member
Battery carrier
Body mount
Bearing sleeve
King pin
Half-shaft
Crown wheel
Bevel pinion
Front axle
Removable wheel
Radius rod
Torque tube
Right half of differential housing
Rear axle bearing
Running board support
Hub brake shoe

SIDE VIEW OF 1913 FORD MODEL T

Top

Rear seat

Top frame

Rear door

Front seat

Steering wheel

Horn bulb

Steering column

Windshield

Side lamp

Hood

Radiator filler cap

Radiator filler neck

Front fender

Spring shock absorber

Rear fender

Tire valve

Wooden-spoked wheel

Hub cap

Running board

Valance

Spare tire

Drain plug

Dummy front door

Horn

Radius rod

Steering column

Drag link

Removable wheel

Bun lamp burner

Fuel sediment bowl

Running board bracket

Light switch

Starter switch

Radiator shell

Headlight rim

Headlight

Starter

Tie rod

Ruckstell axle

Rear cross-member

Brake drum

Hood clip

Steering gearbox

Handbrake

Radiator hose

Transmission casing

Drop arm

Drag link

Crank handle

Cylinder block

Radiator apron

Torque tube

Greaser

Brake rod

Tank support

Front wing support

Carburetor

Radiator

Removable wheel

Steering arm

Clincher wheel

Battery strap

Reflector

Hood clip

Handbrake quadrant

Running board support

Detachable rim

Headlight shell

Running board

Fender eye bolt

The "people's car"

WORKING PARTS OF VOLKSWAGEN BEETLE

THE MOST POPULAR CAR in the history of car manufacture is the Volkswagen Beetle, originally called the KdF Wagen. The car was developed in Germany in the 1930s by Dr. Ferdinand Porsche. At that time, Germany had only half the number of cars of Britain or France, and Adolf Hitler took a personal interest in the development of the Volkswagen ("people's car"). The intention was to provide a new industry, new jobs, and a car so inexpensive that anyone with a job could afford it. Dr. Porsche designed a car that was cheap to build and run; its rear-mounted, air-cooled engine cut down the number of parts needed and also reduced weight. However, few civilians managed to obtain the Beetle before the outbreak of the Second World War in 1939. After the war, the Beetle proved so popular that eventually more than 20 million were sold.

CUSTOMIZED VOLKSWAGEN BEETLE

FLAT-FOUR CYLINDER ARRANGEMENT

Fuel tank

Fuel tank sender unit

Steering tie-rod

Fuel filler neck

Windshield-wiper motor assembly

Steering box assembly

Steering idler

Frame head

Anti-roll bar

Suspension strut

Brake back plate

Track control arm

Pedal cluster

Strut cartridge (shock absorber)

Dust shroud

Front suspension top mount

Gear lever knob

Front road spring

Taillight

Air scoop

Vent window

Luggage compartment lid

Seat mount

Front suspension top mount

Handbrake

Floor pan (platform chassis)

Turn signal and parking light

Torsion bar cover

Tail pipe

Pressed steel wheel

Fuel filler cap

Rear brake drum

Trailing arm

Tire

Sports wheel

Rear shock absorber

Drive shaft

Counterweight

Piston

Transaxle (gearbox and final drive)

Heat exchanger

Clutch and flywheel

Starter motor

Crankshaft

Flat-four engine

Big end

Connecting rod (con-rod)

Air filter

Tail pipe

BODY SHELL OF VOLKSWAGEN BEETLE

Front bumper

Release handle

Left side headlight unit

Chrome trim strip

Right side headlight unit

Left front parking light and turn signal lens

Right front parking light and turn signal lens

Luggage compartment lid

Left front fender

Right front fender

Front fender piping

Spare-wheel well

Hood hinge

Front fender piping

Blade

Right side running board

Vent window

Arm

Mirror

Windshield wiper

Left side running board

Door catch

Wind deflector (baffle)

Steering column

Quarter light

Door handle

Sun roof

Passenger door

Window winder handle

Body shell

Window winder regulator

Drop glass

Rear fender piping

Rear fender piping

Rear fender piping

Air intake vents

Rear valance

Engine lid (engine cover)

Air intake vents

Left side rear fender

License plate light

License plate

Right taillight

Right rear fender

Left taillight

Rear bumper

WRV 408L

Early engines

STEAM AND ELECTRICITY were used to power cars until early this century, but neither power source was ideal. Electric cars had to stop frequently to recharge their heavy batteries, and steam cars gave smooth power delivery but were too complicated for the average motorist to use. A rival power source, the internal combustion engine, was invented in 1860 by Étienne Lenoir (see pp. 334-335). This engine converted the force of an explosion into rotary motion to turn the wheels of a vehicle. Early variations on this basic model included sleeve valves, separately cast cylinders, and the two-stroke combustion cycle. Today, all combustion engines, including the Wankel rotary and diesels (see pp. 346-347), use the four-stroke cycle, first demonstrated by Nikolaus Otto in 1876. The Otto cycle has proved the best method of ensuring that the engine turns over smoothly and that exhaust emissions are controllable.

BERSEY ELECTRIC CAB, 1896

Mounting for tray of 40 batteries

Housing for electric motors

TROJAN TWO-STROKE ENGINE, 1927

Port linking combustion chambers of upper and lower cylinders

Water connection

Upper paired cylinder

Spark plug

Wide piston-ring

Transfer port

Wire gauze pad

Upper piston

Flywheel

Flexible, forked connecting-rod

Counterweight

Big end

Crankcase

SECTIONED WHITE STEAM CAR, 1903

Steering wheel

Throttle wheel

Brake lever

Reverse lever

Automatic cylinder lubricator

Flash steam generator

Lamp bracket

High-pressure cylinder

Rocking lever

Exhaust pipe

Water pump

Condenser

Low-pressure cylinder

Fuel tank

Semi-elliptic spring

Brake drum

Spiral tubes

Steel-reinforced wooden chassis

Steering drop arm

Water tank

Drag link

Dumb iron

CYCLE OF A FOUR-STROKE INTERNAL COMBUSTION ENGINE

INDUCTION STROKE

Exhaust port closed
Intake valve
Intake port opens
Piston moves downward
Fuel and air (the "charge") sucked into cylinder
Counterweight
Crankshaft
Crankpin

COMPRESSION STROKE

Exhaust port closed
Charge compressed by piston
Intake port closed
Connecting rod (con-rod)
Piston moves upward

POWER STROKE

Spark plug
Intake port closed
Exhaust port closed
Charge ignited by spark plug
Explosion pushes piston downward
Big end

EXHAUST STROKE

Exhaust valve
Intake port closed
Exhaust port opens
Burned gases forced out of cylinder
Piston moves upward

16-HORSEPOWER HUMBER ENGINE, 1911

Brass housing for ignition cable
Intake port
Water pipe
Valve cap
Spark plug
Side valve (inlet valve)
Cylinders (cast in pairs)
Water jacket
Fan bracket
Tappet
Valve spring
Timing chain
Timing cover
Crankcase
Starting handle
Flywheel
Camshaft
Oil pump
Oil pan

DAIMLER DOUBLE-SLEEVE VALVE ENGINE, 1910

Spark plug socket
Junk ring
Cylinder head
Intake port
Exhaust port
Intake manifold
Outer sleeve valve
Water jacket
Cylinder wall
Inner sleeve valve
Piston
Carburetor
Engine bearer
Flywheel

OUTER SLEEVE VALVE

Oil groove

INNER SLEEVE VALVE

Sleeve port
Eye for connecting con-rods to secondary crankshaft

Modern engines

TODAY'S GASOLINE ENGINE WORKS on the same basic principles as the first car engines of a century ago, although it has been greatly refined. Modern engines, often made from special metal alloys, are much lighter than earlier engines. Computerized ignition systems, fuel injectors, and multi-valve cylinder heads achieve a more efficient combustion of the fuel/air mixture (the charge) so that less fuel is wasted. As a result of this greater efficiency, the power and performance of a modern engine are increased, and the level of pollution in the exhaust gases is reduced. Exhaust pollution levels today are also lowered by the increasing use of special filters called catalytic converters, which absorb many exhaust pollutants. The need to produce ever more efficient engines means that it can take up to seven years to develop a new engine for a family car, at a cost of many millions of dollars.

FRONT VIEW OF A FORD COSWORTH V6 12-VALVE

Idle control valve
Plenum chamber
Valve rocker
Power steering pump reservoir
Oil dipstick
Steering pump pulley
High-tension ignition lead (spark plug lead)
Cogged drive belt
Fan
Alternator
Crankshaft pulley
Viscous coupling
Oil pan

FRONT VIEW OF A FORD COSWORTH V6 24-VALVE

Idle control valve
Plenum chamber
Exhaust gas recirculation valve
Camshaft timing gear
Steering pump drive pulley
Camshaft chain
Belt tensioner
Air-conditioning compressor
Alternator cooling fan
Oil pan
Drive belt
Crankshaft pulley

SECTIONED VIEW OF A JAGUAR STRAIGHT 6

Cam follower (bucket tappet)
Valve spring
Cam lobe
Cam
Combustion chamber
Compression ring
Camshaft
Cam cover
Distributor
Cylinder head
Fan
Valve stem
Air-conditioning refrigerant pipe
Exhaust valve
Suspension self-leveling pump
Cylinder liner
Water jacket
Power steering pump
Piston
Swash plate
Connecting rod (con-rod)
Drive belt
Main bearing housing
Big end
Compressor piston
Transmission adaptor plate
Air-conditioning compressor
Crankshaft counterweight
Oil pan
Oil pick-up pipe
Anti-surge baffle
Crankcase
Oil-control ring (scraper ring)

FRONT VIEW OF A JAGUAR V12

Air cleaner

Camshaft sprocket

Distributor

Fuel injector nozzle

Intake manifold tract

Piston

Crankshaft

Plenum chamber

Camshaft

Cam follower

Piston ring land

Piston ring groove

Exhaust manifold

Piston skirt

STRAIGHT 4 CYLINDER ARRANGEMENT

Coolant outlet

Cam cover

Viscous coupling

Wrist pin

Cooling fan

Fan drive shaft

Belt pulley

Counterweight

Connecting rod (con-rod)

V12 CYLINDER ARRANGEMENT

Alternator

Alternator pulley

SECTIONED VIEW OF A JAGUAR V12

Distributor drive shaft

Throttle butterfly

Fuel pipe

Intake manifold

Ignition amplifier

Throttle linkage

Air inlet

Exhaust valve

Inlet valve

Cam cover

Timing chain

Oil feed pipe

Piston crown

Cylinder head

Piston ring land

Water outlet

Water pump

Piston

Exhaust heat shield

Exhaust manifold

Oil pipe banjo

Accessory drive pulley

Timing chain drive sprocket

Drive plate

Connecting rod (con-rod)

Starter ring

Counterweight (balance weight)

Main bearing

Crankcase

Pipe to oil cooler

Oil pan

Oil filter

Alternative engines

THE MOST COMMON TYPE OF ALTERNATIVE ENGINE is the diesel engine. Instead of igniting the compressed fuel/air mixture with a spark, the diesel engine uses compression alone, which heats the mixture to the point where it explodes. A diesel engine's fuel consumption is low in comparison with similarly sized piston engines, despite its heavier, reinforced moving parts and cylinder block. Another type of engine is the rotary-combustion, first successfully developed by Felix Wankel in the 1950s. Its two trilobate (three-sided) rotors revolve in housings shaped in a fat figure eight. The four sequences of the four-stroke cycle, which occur consecutively in a piston engine, occur simultaneously in a rotary engine, producing power in a continuous stream.

ROTARY-ENGINED MAZDA RX-7 TURBO II

Aerodynamic windshield
Headrest
Top boot
Front spoiler (chin spoiler)
Side marker lamp
Body-side molding
Cast alloy wheel

WANKEL ROTARY ENGINE

OIL-PUMP HOUSING
Distributor fixing point (drive point)
FRONT SIDE HOUSING
Intake port
FRONT ROTOR CHAMBER
Trailing spark plug hole
Dipstick tube
Oil filler
INTERMEDIATE HOUSING
Intake port
REAR ROTOR CHAMBER
Aluminum alloy backing

Oil-pump drive
Coolant passage
Exhaust port
Water drain bolt
Leading spark plug hole
Leading spark plug hole
Trailing spark plug hole
Leading spark plug hole

THE WANKEL ROTARY CYCLE

Exhaust port
Intake port
Fuel/air mixture being compressed
Exhaust port closed
Vacuum sucks in fuel/air mixture
Burned gas exhausts
Burned gas continues to exhaust
Output shaft turns
Gas continues to expand
Water passage
Trilobate rotor
Rotor gear
Fuel/air mixture continues to enter
Compression begins
Burning gas expands
Stationary gear (fixed gear)
Compression continues
Compressed gas ignites
Burned gas begins to expand

FORD TURBOCHARGED DIESEL ENGINE

Engine lifting bracket

Valve cover

Baffle plate

Intake track

Turbo impeller (inlet rotor)

Turbo propeller (exhaust rotor)

Exhaust

Bell housing

Oil filler cap

Cam follower

Valve return spring

Water jacket

Water pump pulley

Compression ring

Oil-control ring

Piston

Accessory drive belt

Water jacket

Oil cooler

Oil cooler matrix

Oil filter

Engine block

Oil pan

Oil return pipe for turbocharger

REAR SIDE HOUSING

Chrome plating

Exhaust port

ROTOR AND SEALS

Outer oil seal

Inner oil seal spring

Inner oil seal

Corner seal spring

Rotor bearing

Corner seal insert

Rotor gear

Corner seal

Side gear

Rotor

Balancing drilling

Apex seal

Apex seal spring

Inner oil seal groove

Outer oil seal groove

Hole for output shaft

Apex seal groove

Outer oil seal spring

Side seal

Side seal spring

Side seal groove

OUTPUT SHAFT

Front counterweight

Front eccentric rotor journal

Oil passage

Rear stationary gear (fixed gear)

V-belt pulley

Front stationary gear (fixed gear)

Main journal

Eccentric shaft

Rear eccentric rotor journal

Oil jet

Flywheel with balance weight

347

Modern bodywork

RENAULT LOGO

THE BODY OF A MODERN MASS-PRODUCED CAR is built on the monocoque (single-shell) principle, in which the roof, side panels, and floor are welded into a single integral unit. This bodyshell protects and supports the car's internal parts. Steel and glass are used to construct the bodyshell, creating a unit that is both light and strong. Its lightness helps to conserve energy, while its strength protects the occupants. Modern bodywork is designed with the aid of computers, which are used to predict factors such as aerodynamic efficiency and impact resistance. High technology is also employed on the production line, where robots are used to assemble, weld, and paint the body.

BODYWORK OF A RENAULT CLIO

Door handle

Door lock

Left-hand door glass

Left-hand quarter glass

Tailgate support strut (rear hatch support strut)

Window washer jet

Heating element contact

Rear window glass

Tailgate support strut (rear hatch support strut)

Tailgate

Rear bumper

Bodyshell

Fuel cap

Zinc phosphating

Degreased bare metal

Right-hand quarter glass

Primer

Base coat color

Cataphoresic coating

Right-hand door glass

Clear coat

Chrome passivation

Door key and lock

Door handle

Left-hand door

Left-hand mirror assembly

Door hinge

Electric window motor

Radio antenna

Rear hatch

Side marker lamp

SIDE VIEW OF A RENAULT CLIO

Spoiler bumper

Hood-release cable

Hood

Hood catch

Hood hinge

Window winder cable

Window winder handle

Door hinge

Right-hand door

Right-hand mirror assembly

Windshield glass

Front bumper

Hood

Headrest

Headlight

H746 FBK

Spoiler bumper

Fog light

FRONT VIEW OF A RENAULT CLIO

Modern components

A TYPICAL MODERN CAR has several thousand individual mechanical components. These are assembled to form the car's various mechanical systems: engine and exhaust, transmission, steering, suspension, and brakes. To ensure that each system functions properly, components are manufactured to extremely fine tolerances—to within about one ten-thousandth of an inch in some cases.

Alloy wheel

Hubcap

Hub nut

Hub seal

Exhaust downpipe

Muffler

Catalytic converter

Suspension spring

Torsion bar

Handbrake

Left rear suspension arm

Anti-roll bar

Gear lever

Steering wheel

Steering rack

Rear muffler

Fuel tank

Right rear suspension arm

Steering column

Vent pipe

Shock absorber

Clutch pedal

Hub and brake drum

Electric fuel pump

Brake cylinder (wheel cylinder)

Brake pedal

Brake shoe

Accelerator pedal

Hub seal

Brake backplate

Hub nut

Clutch cable

Fuel tank filler neck

Accelerator cable

Hubcap

Wheel cover

Steel wheel

**MECHANICAL COMPONENTS
OF A RENAULT CLIO, 1991**

Brake shield

Alloy wheel

Clutch throw-out
bearing

Brake
disc

Hub

Left drive
shaft

Clutch pressure
plate

Tie-rod
end

Upper
suspension
arm

Brake hose

Power
steering
pump

Clutch
center
plate

Top
radiator
hose

Tie
rod

Brake
pad

Bottom radiator
hose

Gearbox
(transmission)

Lower
suspension
arm

Gear-
change rod

Flywheel

Anti-roll
bar

Starter
motor

Fan
motor

Subframe

Power steering
belt

Exhaust
manifold

Electronic
ignition unit

Brake
cylinder
(wheel
cylinder)

Intake
manifold

Brake
power-
assist
servo

Water
pump

Fan motor
support bracket

Alternator
belt

Alternator

Distributor

Engine

Brake caliper
fixing bolt

Suspension
strut

Brake caliper
locking plate

Air cleaner

Brake
caliper

Right drive
shaft

Radiator

Hub
carrier

Brake
hose

Lock nut and washer

Brake disc

Front hub
bearing

Water bottle

Brake shield

Steel wheel

Wheel cover

Modern trim

A MODERN CAR HAS TWO TYPES OF TRIM, according to the materials used: hard (chrome and plastics) and soft (upholstered materials). Safety and comfort are priorities in the trim's design: seats help the occupants maintain a comfortable posture, rubber seals keep out dirt and moisture, and headlights light the way. Older cars had interior or leather paneling cut and fitted by craftsmen; modern cars use precisely molded plastics and seat fabrics cut by robot-controlled lasers to reduce costs and production time. Doors are now assembled off the production line so that complex wiring can be built in.

TRIM OF A RENAULT CLIO, 1991

Rear quarter trim panel

Inner roof trim

Roof seal

Quarter trim panel

Quarter panel molding

Rear seat belt

Center seat belt

Rear seat belt stalk (catch)

Gear lever surround

Rear tire

Split, folding rear seat assembly

Rear shelf radio speaker

Rear shelf radio speaker

Rear shelf

Tailgate trim

Rear wiper blade

Tailgate seal

Rear wiper arm

License plate light

Rear turn signal and stop lamp assembly

Wheel cover (rear wheel embellisher)

Untrimmed headrest

Rear seat belt

Quarter panel molding

Rear tire

Quarter trim panel

HALOGEN HEADLIGHT BULB

SPOTLIGHT BULB

Filament

MARKER LIGHT BULB

Filament

FESTOON BULB

Rear quarter trim panel

Roof seal

Inner roof trim

Roof molding

Contact

Bayonet fixing

Contact

Contact

Window winder handle

Door seal

Front tire

Wheel cover (front wheel embellisher)

Door lock handle

Door pull handle

Turn signal lamp

Fog light

Inner sill trim

Door molding (rubbing strip)

Inner windshield molding

Front seat belt

Front door radio speaker

Dash radio speaker

Headlight

Front seat assembly

Sun visor

Dash panel (instrument panel)

Windshield wiper bracket and spindles

Windshield wiper blade

Interior light

Radio

Heater unit

Washer jet

Fan blade

Rearview mirror

Center console

Steering wheel

Fascia (dash)

Windshield seal

Front seat frame

Sun visor

Headlight

Windshield wiper arm

Front seat belt

Control stalk

Dash radio speaker

Front door radio speaker

Inner windshield molding

Door trim panel

Inner sill trim

Door molding (rubbing strip)

Door seal

Fog light

Door pull handle

Window winder handle

Turn signal lamp

Door lock handle

Front tire

Wheel cover (front wheel embellisher)

All-terrain vehicles

THE MODERN ALL-TERRAIN VEHICLE has its origins in the American military Jeep of the 1940s and the British Land Rover. Such vehicles have been used for a wide range of purposes, from safari travel to fire fighting. The principal special features of such cars—including four- or six-wheel drive, high ground clearance, and toughened braking, suspension, and transmission systems—are designed to enable driving under the most difficult off-road conditions. The vehicle shown here is equipped for safari travel and carries a comprehensive range of survival gear.

COOKING EQUIPMENT

TWO–BURNER ALCOHOL STOVE

Handle for all pans

Flame regulator

Wick

Zipper

Mosquito netting

Ventilation flap

Tie

Cooking pot

Locking fuel filler cap

Raised air intake

Dust filter

Guard

SIDE VIEW OF PINZGAUER TURBO D

HAND WINCH

Folding rooftop tent

Galvanized roof-rack

Steel body

Jerrycan

Spare wheel and tire

Bodyside molding (rub strip)

TIRE PUMP

Pressure gauge

TIRE IRON

Heavy-duty shovel

Tubular backbone chassis

Fuel tank

Metal jerrycan for fuel

Plastic jerrycan for water

LEFT-HAND
TREAD PLATE

RIGHT-HAND
TREAD PLATE

TOW STRAP

HEAVY-DUTY
SHACKLE

SAFETY WINDSHIELD CLAMPS

WASHING BUCKET

Radio aerial

Observation
roof hatch

Grab
handle

Rearview
mirror

Windshield
washer
bottle

Wrap-
around
bumper

Access step

SECURITY
CHAIN

FRONT VIEW OF PINZGAUER TURBO D

Observation
roof hatch

Radio aerial

Galvanized
roof-rack

Laminated
windshield

Air vent

Rearview
mirror

Indicator

Headlight
guard

Radiator
grille

Headlight

External
step

Indcpendent
swing axle

Locking
differential

Towing
loop

All-terrain
tire

REAR VIEW OF PINZGAUER TURBO D

Roof-rack

Observation
platform

External
step for roof

Jerrycan

Jerrycan
carrier

Spare
wheel

Bodyside
molding (rub
strip)

Rear
bumper

Offset door
hinge

Rear light
cluster

Door and
wheel
support
frame

Mudflap

Off-road
tire

Locking
differential

Independent swing axle

Racing cars

SINCE MOTORING BEGAN, racing cars have been a major focus of innovation in car design. Features that are now commonplace, such as disc brakes, turbochargers, and even safety belts, were used first on competition cars. Research into racing cars has contributed to a new understanding of engine performance, aerodynamics, and tire adhesion, and has led to the development of ultra-light materials such as carbon-fiber for car bodies. Like the 1937 Bugatti Type 57S below, a modern Williams Formula One car has a low, streamlined body and an open cockpit. Unlike its forerunner, it also has a front wing that pushes the front wheels firmly onto the track, huge slick tires for extra grip, and electrical sensors that continually relay information to the pits about the car's performance.

1937 BUGATTI TYPE 57S

Diffuser

Bodywork bracket

Heat shield

Forward radius arm

Rear wing upper mainplane

Slot

Upper flap

Half shaft

Rear radius arm

Temperature-sensitive sticker

Aeroquip pipe union

Oil tank

Constant velocity joint cover

Rear wing end-plate

Diffuser

Rear brake duct

Oil feed to engine

Fuel injection trumpet guard (debris guard)

Fuel injector

Cam cover

Cylinder head

Gearbox fixing stud

Tail pipe

Stressed cylinder block

Harmonically tuned exhaust pipe

Mounting point

Electronic control-unit connector

Water outlet

RENAULT V10 RS1 ENGINE

ENGINE COWLING

Dzus fastener

356

SIDE FAIRING

Slick racing tire

Steering link

Nose cover

Front wing end-plate

Front wing

Suspension push-rod

Rearview mirror

Lower wishbone

Front lower wishbone

Brake pipe

Water rail

Engine cooling radiator

Master electrical switch

Anchor nut

Radiator air duct

Electrical connectors to engine

Exhaust

Chassis electrical plug

Fuel injection air-intake trumpet

Lifting hook

Emergency electricity cut-off

Fuel filler

Fuel breather

Safety harness

Emergency air hose for driver

Driver's radio antenna

Single-point safety harness release

Upper wishbone

Push-rod adjuster

Air intake

FRONT VIEW OF WILLIAMS 1990 FORMULA ONE RACING CAR

Rear wing upper mainplane

Engine air intake

Driver's radio aerial

Rear wing end-plate

Rearview mirror

Upper wishbone

Rear brake duct

Suspension push-rod

Slick racing tire

Radiator air intake

Front wing end-plate

Steering link

Front wing

End-plate aerodynamic skirt

Bicycle anatomy

THE BICYCLE IS A TWO-WHEELED, lightweight machine, which is propelled by human power. It is efficient, cheap, easily manufactured, and one of the world's most popular forms of transportation. The first pedal-driven bicycle was built in Scotland in 1839. Since then the basic design—of a frame, wheels, brakes, handlebars, and a saddle—has been gradually improved, with the addition of a chain, gear system, and pneumatic tires (tires inflated with air). The recent invention of the mountain bike (all-terrain bike) has been an important development. With its strong, rugged frame, wide tires, and 21 gears, a mountain bike enables riders to reach rough and hilly areas that were previously inaccessible to cyclists.

REAR WHEEL

Tire

Spoke

Hub

Rim

Saddle (seat)

Seat post

Seat post quick release bolt

Cable guide

Straddle wire

Seat tube

Rear cantilever brake

Seat stay

Rear dropouts

Front derailleur

Rear hub quick release spindle

Bottom bracket shell

Bottom bracket axle

Crank bolt

Washer

17-tooth sprocket

13-tooth sprocket

Adjustable cup

Fixed cup

Bottom bracket sleeve

Caged ball bearings

Lock washer

Lock ring

Freewheel lock nut

Jockey wheel

Chain

Lock washer

Rear derailleur

Derailleur cage plate

Jockey wheel

46-tooth chain ring

23-tooth sprocket

Toe clip

Sprocket spacer

GEAR SYSTEM

30-tooth sprocket

Spider

Spoke guard

FREEWHEEL SPROCKETS

Toe strap

Pedal

Right arm

Gear cable

Gearshift

Gearshift

Handlebar

Handlebar
stem

Handlebar
grip

Expander
bolt

Top tube

Lock
nut

Rear brake
cable

Brake lever

Top race

Lock
washer

Brake
lever

Cable guide

Head
tube

Top cup

Front brake
cable

Hub

Spoke

**BICYCLE
FRAME**

Down
tube

Bottom
cup

Caged ball
bearings

Rubber
bearing
seal

Steerer
tube

Straddle wire

Bottom
race

Toe clip

Front
cantilever
brake

Cantilever
brake boss

Rim

Inner tube

Toe
strap

Pedal

Fork blade

Left arm

24-tooth
chain ring

Front hub
quick release
spindle

36-tooth
chain ring

Handlebar

Valve cap

Saddle

Frame

Brake lever
and gearshift

Valve

Pedal

Tire

FRONT WHEEL

Chain

Bicycles

ALTHOUGH ALL BICYCLES are made up of the same basic components, they can vary greatly in design. A racing bike, such as the Eddy Merckx model, with its light frame and steep head- and seat-angles, is built for speed. Its design forces the rider to adopt the aero tuck, a crouched, aerodynamic position. While a touring bike resembles a racing bike in many respects, it is designed for comfort and stability on long-distance journeys. Touring bikes are characterized by more relaxed frame angles, heavy chain stays that support the rear panniers, and a long wheelbase (the distance between the wheel axles) for reliable handling. All-purpose bicycles, known as hybrids, combine the light weight and speed of sports bikes with the rugged durability of mountain bikes (see pp. 358-359). Bicycles that are not designed for conventional road use include time-trial bikes, which have a short head tube, sloping top tube, aero handlebars, and aerodynamic tubing. Most Human Powered Vehicles (HPVs) are recumbents—the rider has a recumbent position—which maximize power output and minimize drag (resistance). Essential to the safety of all riders are helmets, and both front and rear lights; locks protect against theft.

FRONT AND REAR LIGHTS

HELMET

Hard outer shell

Red rear light

Air vent

White front light

Polystyrene padding

Quick-release strap

EDDY MERCKX RACING BICYCLE

Saddle (seat)

Saddle clamp

Seat post

Seat-post bolt

Cable guide

Rear brake cable

Brake-block bolt

Top tube (crossbar)

Steel frame

Brake block

Seat stay

Seat tube

Down tube

Tire

Water-bottle cage

Tire tread

Front derailleur

Tire wall

Wheel rim

Freewheel sprocket

STEEL LOCK

Key

Hardened steel

Pick-proof lock

Rear derailleur

Pulley bolt

Tension pulley

Chain

Chain stay

Chain ring

Crank bolt

Crank

Spider

Pedal

Toe clip

CANNONDALE SH600 HYBRID BICYCLE

Gel-filled saddle

Lightweight frame

Straight handlebar

Brake bridge

Cantilever brake

All-surface tire

CANNONDALE ST1000 TOURING BICYCLE

Rear fender

Water bottle

Drop handlebar

Front fender

Rear pannier

Rear pannier

Long chain stay

Large diameter aluminum tubing

Front pannier

Headset

Stem

Binder bolt

Handlebar

Front brake cable

Brake lever

Head tube

Brake pivot bolt

Brake pad

Fork

Hub quick-release lever

Spoke

Spoke nipple

Presta valve

Hub

ROSSIN ITALIAN TIME-TRIAL BICYCLE

Aero handlebar

Sloping top tube

Steep seat tube

Hollow disk wheel

Short head tube

Narrow tire

Clipless pedal

Tri-spoke wheel

WINDCHEETAH SL MARK VI "SPEEDY" RACING HPV BICYCLE

Fleecy headrest

Fiberglass bucket seat

Joystick

Brake lever

53-tooth chain ring

7-speed freewheel

Aluminum tubing

Drum brake

Clipless pedal

Extended racing chain

The motorcycle

THE MOTORCYCLE HAS EVOLVED from a motorized cycle—a basic bicycle with an engine—into a sophisticated, high-performance machine. In 1901, the Werner brothers established the most viable location for the engine, positioning it low in the center of the chassis (see pp. 364-365): the new Werner became the basis for the modern motorcycle. Motorcycles are used for many purposes —for commuting, delivering messages, touring, and racing—and different machines have been developed to suit the demands of different types of riders. The Vespa scooter, for instance, which is small-wheeled, economical, and easy-to-ride, was designed to meet the needs of the commuter. Sidecars provided transportation for the family until the arrival of cheap cars caused their popularity to decline. Serious riders generally favor larger capacity machines that are capable of greater performance and offer more comfort. Four-cylinder machines have been common since the Honda CB750 appeared in 1969. Despite advances in motorcycle technology, many riders are attracted to the traditional look of motorcycles like the twin-cylinder Harley-Davidson. Harley-Davidson Glides exploit the style of the classic American V-twin engine, where the cylinders are placed in a V-formation.

1901 WERNER MOTORCYCLE

Vacuum-operated inlet valve

Bicycle-type saddle

Pulley rim rear brake

Fuel tank

Electric ignition control

Inlet-over-exhaust (IOE) engine

Alloy crankcase

Twisted rawhide drive belt

Cast iron cylinder barrel

1988 HARLEY-DAVIDSON FLHS ELECTRA GLIDE

Backrest

Saddlebag

Luggage rack

Licence plate

Taillight

Indicator

Side reflector

Silencer

Silencer bracket

Disc brake

Crash bar

Exhaust clamp

Passenger seat

Passenger grab rail

1965 BMW R/60 WITH 1952 STEIB CHAIR

Handlebar

Adjustable link

Headlight

Mirror

Windshield

Sidecar

Side light

Fender

Sidecar chassis rail

Sidecar wheel

Sidecar lower link

Exhaust pipe

Fuel tank

Horizontally opposed engine

Square-section tire

FRONT VIEW

Fender

Canvas shroud

Speedometer

Ignition lock

Taillight

Grab rail

Tool tray

Fender clamp

Lockable luggage trunk

Suspension linkage

Bullet-shaped sidecar body

Knock-off wheel nut

SIDE VIEW

Drum brake

Long leading-link fork (Earles fork)

1969 HONDA CB750

Taillight
Seat
Mirror
Front brake lever
Seat strap
Indicator
Shock absorber
Oil tank
Telescopic fork
Fender clamp
Disc brake
Clutch cover
Single overhead camshaft engine
Mirror
Heat shield
Passenger footrest
Brake master cylinder
Exhaust pipe
Handgrip
Front brake lever
Padded seat
Light switch
Manufacturer's logo
Oil tank filler cap
Fuel tank
Oil tank
Gearbox
Air filter
Passenger foot rest
45° V-twin engine
Exhaust pipe
Foot rest
Crash bar
Duplex tubular cradle frame
Brake pedal

1963 VESPA GRAND SPORT 160 MARK 1

Twist grip gear change
Monocoque chassis
Seat strap
Throttle
Front brake lever
Clutch lever
Engine cover
Seat
Headlight
Cooling grille
Horn
Taillight
Choke
Shock absorber
Gas tap
Kick-starter
Center stand
Foot brake
Silencer
Rubber foot mat
Drum brake
Single-sided trailing-link fork
Windshield
Clutch cable
Throttle cable
Windshield adjustor
Headlight
Fog lamp
Indicator
Telescopic fork
Side reflector
Fender
Brake calliper
Disc brake
Cast alloy wheel

363

The motorcycle chassis

THE MOTORCYCLE CHASSIS is the main "body" of the motorcycle, to which the engine is attached. Consisting of the frame, wheels, suspension, and brakes, the chassis performs various functions. The frame, which is built from steel or alloy, keeps the wheels in line to maintain the handling of the motorcycle, and serves as a structure for mounting other components. The engine and gearbox unit is bolted into place, while items such as the seat, the fenders, and the fairing are more easily removable. Suspension cushions the rider from irregularities in the road surface. In most suspension systems, coil springs controlled by an oil damper separate the main mass of the motorcycle from the wheels. At the front, the spring and damper are usually incorporated in a telescopic fork; the rear employs a pivoted swing arm. The suspension also helps to retain maximum contact between the tires and the road, necessary to effective braking and steering. Drum brakes were common until the 1970s, but modern motorcycles use disc brakes, which are more powerful.

1985 HONDA VF750 WITH BODYWORK

Racing number plate

Frame-mounted fairing

Fuel tank

Telescopic fork

Dual seat

Fender

Disc brake

Box-section swing arm

V4 engine unit

Box-section tubular cradle frame

Floating disc brake

1985 HONDA VF750 WITH BODYWORK REMOVED

Brake master cylinder

Headstock

Bracing tube

Shock absorber top mounting

Engine mounting plate

Square-section steel tubing

Rear sub-frame

Bodywork mounting point

Exhaust mounting strap

Shock absorber

Exhaust pipe

Light alloy wheel

Axle adjustor

Disc brake

Disc brake calliper

Box-section swing arm

Brake torque arm

Brake master cylinder

Foot rest hanger

Brake pedal

Swing arm pivot

Multiplate clutch

Oil level window

Oil sump

Engine cover

Engine mounting bolt

V4 engine unit

Radiator

Oil cooler

Radiator pipe

DRUM BRAKE

EXTERIOR OF DRUM BRAKE

Bolt hole
Torque arm
Air cooling scoop
Axle hole
Cooling fin
Speedometer drive
Cable stop
Brake plate
Operating arm

INTERIOR OF DRUM BRAKE

Torque arm
Bolt hole
Brake shoe
Pivot
Brake shoe return spring
Operating cam
Brake shoe return spring
Axle hole
High-friction material

OPERATING PARTS OF DISC BRAKE SYSTEM

Brake-fluid reservoir
Master cylinder
Push-rod
Piston
Hydraulic brake fluid
Calliper assembly
Wheel disc
Piston
Brake pad

Clutch cable
Hydraulic brake hose
Telescopic fork leg
Fork slide
Light alloy wheel
Floating disc brake
Axle
Brake calliper

SPRING/DAMPER UNIT

Rubber mounting bush
Twin rate spring
Damper rod
Damper body
Pre-load adjustor
Rubber mounting bush

HOW A SPRING/DAMPER UNIT WORKS

Rubber mounting bush
Spring
Damper rod
Nonreturn valve
Hydraulic fluid
Compressible gas
Hydraulic fluid chamber
Rubber mounting bush

TYPES OF TIRE

RACING SLICK
No tread pattern

TUBELESS SPORTS
Radial groove

TRIALS
Knobby tread pattern

STANDARD
Hard-wearing rubber compound

Motorcycle engines

MOTORCYCLE ENGINES must be lightweight and compact, and have a good power output. They have between one and six cylinders, can be cooled by air or water, and the capacity of the combustion chamber varies from 49cc (cubic centimeters) to 1500cc. Two types of internal combustion engine are common: the four-stroke, which is used in cars (see pp. 342-343), and the two-stroke. A basic two-stroke engine has only three moving parts—the crankshaft, the connecting rod, and the piston—but the power output is high. The engine fires every two strokes (rather than every four), giving a "power stroke" every revolution (see p. 343). Power is conveyed from the engine to the rear wheel by the transmission system. This usually consists of a clutch, a gearbox, and a final drive system. Clutches are multiplate devices, which run in oil. Gearboxes have five or six speeds and are operated by foot pedal. Shaft and belt drive systems are used in some cases, but chain drive to the rear wheel is most common.

EXTERIOR OF STANDARD TWO-STROKE ENGINE

Spark plug cap

Fuel tap

Carburetor mounting

Kick-starter

Carburetor

Cylinder head

Cooling fin

Exhaust port

Case screw

Clutch activating arm

Engine cover

Gear lever

TRANSMISSION SYSTEM

GEARBOX

Gear lever selector shaft

5th gear

2nd gear

1st gear

6th gear

4th gear

3rd gear

Input shaft

Splines for mounting gear lever

Bearing

Output shaft

Splines for mounting final drive sprocket

Gear tooth

Selector fork

Copper oil feed pipe

Aluminum outer casing

MULTIPLATE CLUTCH

Fiber plate

Outer clutch drum, connected to engine

Pressure plate, connected to inner clutch drum

Springs force plates together

Metal plate

Key locks fiber plate to outer drum

Straight-cut primary-drive gear

MODERN O-RING DRIVE CHAIN

Small front sprocket

Roller with sealed-in lubricant

Large rear sprocket

Mounting hole

Sprocket tooth

Hole for retaining bolt

Plate

**VELOCETTE OVERHEAD
VALVE (OHV) ENGINE**

*Screw and lock nut
tappet adjustor*

Rocker arm

*Rocker cover
retaining bolt*

Oil feed pipe

Cylinder head

Inlet port

Exhaust port

Spark plug lead

Cylinder head

Combustion chamber

Cam follower

Cooling fin

Piston

Push rod

Magneto drive

Valve lifter

Camshaft gear

Timing gear

*Engine
mounting
bolt hole*

*Engine
mounting
bolt hole*

Oil passageway

Crankcase

Crankshaft

Oil pump

Mounting lug

Nonreturn valve

Oil sump

Competition motorcycles

THERE ARE MANY TYPES of motorcycle sports and in each, a special machine has evolved to perform to specific requirements. Races take place on roads or tracks or "off-road," in fields, dirt tracks, and even the desert. "Grand Prix" world championships in roadracing exist for 125cc, 250cc, and 500cc classes, as well as for sidecars. The latest racing sidecars have more in common with racing cars than motorcycles. The rider and passenger operate within an all-enclosing, aerodynamic fairing. The Suzuki RGV500 shown here, like other Grand Prix machines, carries advertising, which promotes the manufacturer and helps to cover the cost of developing motorcycle technology. In Speedway, which originated in the U.S. in 1902, motorcycles operate without brakes or a gearbox. Off-road competition motorcycles have less emphasis on high power output. In Motocross, for example, which is held on rough terrain, they must have high ground clearance, flexible long-travel suspension, and tires with a chunky tread pattern, to allow them to grip in sand or mud.

1992 HUSQVARNA MOTOCROSS TC610

Throttle cable
Handlebar brace
Long seat
Racing number
Hand protector
Radiator air vent
Flexible plastic fender
Light-weight exhaust system
Telescopic fork
Plastic guard
Axle
Overhead camshaft engine
Gear lever
Shock absorber
Disc brake
Knobby tire
Disc brake
Brake calliper
Alloy swing arm
Shock absorber linkage

1992 SUZUKI RGV500
SIDE VIEW

Exhaust pipe
Racing number
Air vent
One-piece seat and tail unit
Shock absorber
Minimal seat padding
Arched alloy swing arm

Exhaust pipe
Vent
Silencer
Shock absorber mounting
Three-spoke alloy wheel
Exhaust pipe
Axle adjustor
Disc brake
Brake pedal
Disc brake master cylinder
Foot rest
Rear brake calliper
Slick racing tire
Drive chain
Lightweight alloy frame

Exhaust pipe
Handlebar
Foot rest
Rear brake pedal
Drive chain
Wide, slick tire

REAR VIEW

1981 WESLAKE SPEEDWAY

Throttle

Throttle cable

Carburetor cover

Fuel cap

Oil cap

Fender

Seat

Fuel tank

Fender

Wheel cover

Telescopic fork

Narrow tire

Wide tire

Brakeless wheel hub

Silencer

Foot rest

Oil pump

Overhead valve engine

Tubular open cradle frame

Fairing stay

Throttle cable

Fuel tank breather

Fuel tank

Throttle

Front brake lever

Telescopic fork

Fender

Sponsor's logo

Air vent

Braided steel hydraulic hose

Brake calliper

Carbon-fiber disc brake

Three-spoke alloy wheel

Slick racing tire

Quickly detachable (QD) fairing

1968 KIRBY BSA RACING SIDECAR

FRONT VIEW

Rev counter

Windshield

All-enclosing fairing

Fuel tank

Battery

Wheel guard

Square-section tire

Passenger windshield

Passenger grab rail

SIDE VIEW

Throttle cable

Exhaust pipe

Rev counter

All-enclosing fairing

Sidecar chassis

Fuel cap

Engine

Fiberglass wheel guard

Windshield

Racing number

Clutch lever

Fairing

Radiator

Front brake lever

Hydraulic brake hose

Fender

Axle

Slick tire

FRONT VIEW

369

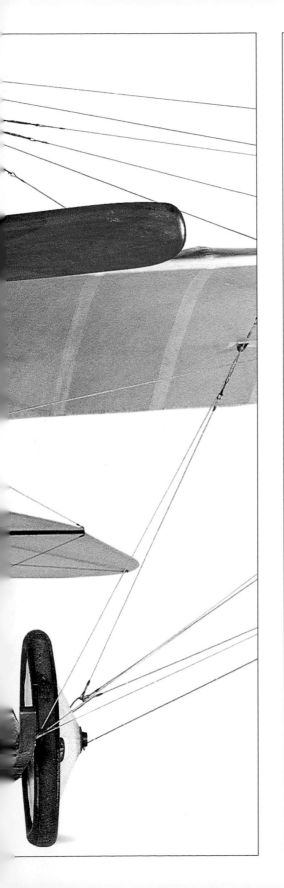

SEA AND AIR

Ships of Greece and Rome

ROMAN ANCHOR

Stock

Shank

Palm

Acutely angled arm

Ring

Crown

IN THE EXPANSIVE EMPIRES OF GREECE AND ROME, powerful fleets were needed for battle, trade, and communication. Greek galleys were powered by a sail and many oars. A new armament, the embolos (ram), was fitted on to the galley bow. As ramming duels required fast and maneuverable boats, extra rows of oarsmen were added, culminating in the trireme. During the fifth and fourth centuries B.C., the trireme dominated the Mediterranean. It was powered by 170 oarsmen, each pulling one oar, and ranged on three levels, as the model opposite shows. The trireme also carried archers and soldiers for boarding enemy craft. Galleys were pulled out of the water when not in use, and were kept in dockyard ship-sheds. The merchant ships of the Greeks and Romans were mighty vessels, too. The full-bodied Roman corbita, for example, could hold up to 400 tons of cargo, such as spices, gems, silk, and animals. The construction of these boats was based on a stout hull with planking secured by mortice and tenon. Some of these ships made long trading voyages, sailing even as far as India. To make them easier to steer, corbitas set a foresail called an "artemon." It flew from a forward-leaning mast that was the forerunner of the long bowsprits carried by the great clipper ships of the 19th century.

ATTIC VASE SHOWING A GREEK GALLEY

Bronze mast truck

Kalos (brailing rope)

Keraia (yard)

Mast

Embolos (ram; beak)

Kubernetes (helmsman)

Sternpost

Ophthalmos (eye)

Pedalia (twin rudder)

Oar port sleeve

Kope (oar)

Double halyard **ROMAN CORBITA**

Antenna (yard)

Bullseye

Fore mast

Buntline

Brace

Artemon (fore sail)

Oculus (eye)

Tabling

Bolt rope

Prow

Windlass

Roband (rope band)

Ceruchi (lift)

Heraldic device

Ring

Ruden (brail line)

Fore stay

Anchor

Sheet

Scala (ladder)

Catena (riding bitt)

Ancorale (anchor rope; anchor rode)

Hatch board

Deck beam

Zosteres (rubbing strake)

Cargo hold

Masthead

Single clump block

Malus (mast)

Rope parrel

Bullet block

Antenna (yard)

Timber fairlead

Shroud

Leather reinforcing strip

Main double halyard

Main brace

Scala (ladder)

Velum (main sail)

Sheer pole

Deadeye

Lanyard

Poop break

Poop deck

Main sheet

Hole and peg joint

Poop deck house

Clavus (tiller)

Swan neck ornament

Stern balustrade

Ring bolt

Sternpost

Gubernator (helmsman)

Wale

Planking

Shaft

Blade

Gubernacula (rudders)

Clew

Midships fence

Constratum (deck)

Bitt

Oar lanyard

ROWING POSITIONS ON A GREEK TRIREME (TRIERE)
The katastroma (deck) has been removed from this model to show the positions taken by oarsmen on a trireme.

Thranite (upper level oarsman)

Zygian (middle level oarsman)

Deck rail

Tropeter (leather grommet)

Paraxeiresia (outrigger)

Kope (oar)

Stanchion

Zugon (thwart; seat)

Thalamian (lower level oarsman)

Hyperesion (oarsman's cushion)

Pine hull

MORTICE-AND-TENON FASTENINGS FOR HULL PLANKS

Mortice

Gomphoi (dowel)

Tenon

Hull plank

A ship of the line

THE 74-GUN THIRD-RATER WAS A MAINSTAY of British and French battlefleets in the late 18th and early 19th centuries. (The biggest ships in the fledgling American navy of the time were 44-gun frigates.) The length of such a man-of-war was determined by the number of guns needed for each deck, allowing room for crews to man them. The gun deck of this vessel was about 170 ft (52 m) long. Her decks had to be strong to carry the weight of the guns. The deck planks have been removed in the model below to illustrate the number of beams needed to make the hull strong enough. Only timber with perfect grain was used. The upper deck was open at the waist, but forward and aft were officers' cabins. The forecastle (foc's'l) and quarterdeck carried light guns and provided platforms for handling the rigging and for reconnaissance. The ship's longboats, or launches, were carried on skids between the gangways.

LONGBOAT

Truck
Flag halyard
Mast
Backstay
Jib halyard
Topping lift
Fore stay halyard
Peak halyard
Shrouds
Main sheet
Fore staysail halyard
Gaff
Boom
Parrel
Bowsprit
Traveler
Stem
Waterline
Deadeyes
Oar
Side bench

Thole pins
Windlass bar
Transom
Tiller
Planking
Rabbit line
Sheerplank
Frame
Keel
Rudder
Floor
Thwart (seat)

UPPER DECK OF A 74-GUN SHIP

Stock
Hoop
Cathead
Ring
Knightheads
Head (privy)
Figurehead
Head beam
Steam grating
Timber head
Fore bitts
Galley stove chimney
Belfry
Waterway
Deadeye
Gangway
Capstan

Head rail
Roundhouse (privy)
Boomkin
Anchor cable
Arm
Sheave for cat tackle
Deck beam
Fluke
Hoop
Stock
Foremast hole
Breastwork
Forked beam
Pawl
Skid beam
Carling (carline)
Bulwark
Main companion way

Head
Forecastle (foc's'l)
Waist

BOW

Figurehead
Main rail
Headboard
Middle rail
Lower rail
Head rail
Supporter
Eiking
Cat block
Side counter timber
Cheek
Counter timber
Tuck
Catted anchor
Main wale
Riband
Frame
Hawse piece
Hawse hole
Side step
Stempost
Deadwood

STERN

Cove
Taffrail
Screen bulkhead
Balcony
Upper counter rail
Drop
Lower counter rail
Gunport lid
Filling transom
Tuck rail
Wing transom
After fashion piece
Timber under transom
Cant frame

Eye bolt
Main bitts
Ledge (batten)
Companion ladder
Hatch coaming/ shot garland
Spirketting
Backstay stool
Master's sea cabin
Mizzen mast hole
Great cabin (captain's cabin)
Pilaster
Screen bulkhead
Channel
Coaming
Ledge (batten)
Standard knee

Stern carving
Poop rail
Necking
Taffrail
Gunport drip (eyebrow; rigol)
Wardroom
Upper finishing
Main mast hole
Grating
Gunport lid
Rail at break of poop deck
Mizzen bitts
Mast partners
Lodging knee
Clerk's cabin
Quarter gallery

Quarterdeck
Poop deck

Rigging

MOST SAILING SHIPS HAVE TWO TYPES OF RIGGING. Standing rigging—kept taut by turnbuckles or old-fashioned lanyards and deadeyes—refers to the ropes, wires, and chains that support the masts and yards (horizontal spars). Running rigging, which includes types of block and tackle, halyards, and sheets, is used to hoist, lower, or trim sails.

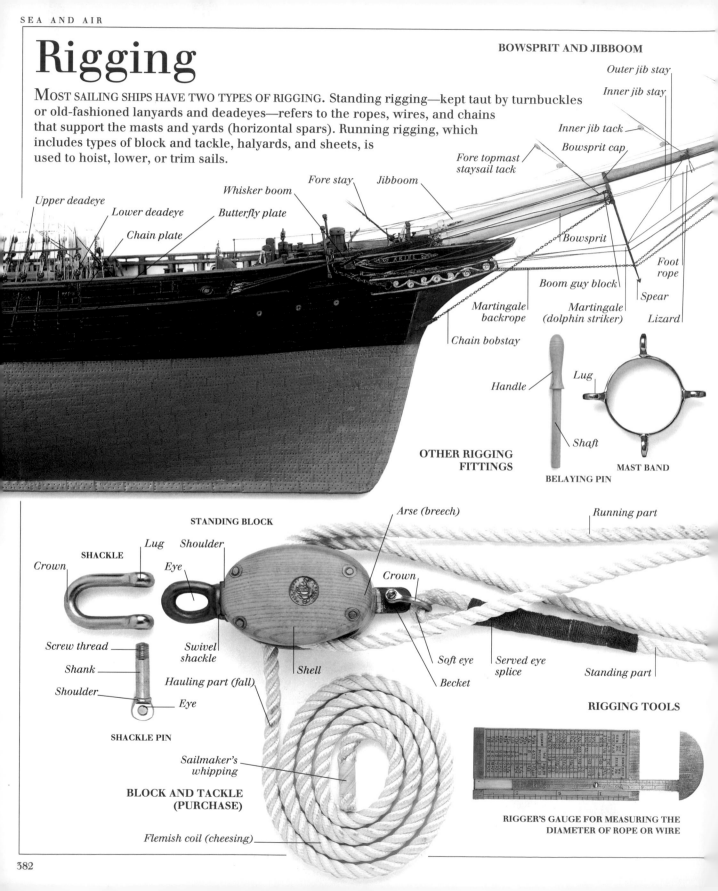

BOWSPRIT AND JIBBOOM

Outer jib stay

Inner jib stay

Inner jib tack

Fore topmast staysail tack

Bowsprit cap

Fore stay

Jibboom

Whisker boom

Upper deadeye

Lower deadeye

Butterfly plate

Chain plate

Bowsprit

Foot rope

Boom guy block

Spear

Martingale backrope

Martingale (dolphin striker)

Lizard

Chain bobstay

OTHER RIGGING FITTINGS

Handle

Lug

Shaft

BELAYING PIN

MAST BAND

STANDING BLOCK

Arse (breech)

Running part

SHACKLE

Crown

Lug

Shoulder

Eye

Shoulder

Crown

Screw thread

Shank

Shoulder

Eye

Swivel shackle

Shell

Soft eye

Served eye splice

Standing part

Becket

SHACKLE PIN

Hauling part (fall)

RIGGING TOOLS

Sailmaker's whipping

BLOCK AND TACKLE (PURCHASE)

Flemish coil (cheesing)

RIGGER'S GAUGE FOR MEASURING THE DIAMETER OF ROPE OR WIRE

Fore royal stay

Flying jib tack

Outer jib tack

Outer martingale stay

Middle martingale stay

Inner martingale stay

Eye

SCORED BULLSEYE FAIRLEAD

Eye

Strap

SHEET LEAD

Base

RUNNING BLOCK

Double rope becket

DUTCH TRIPLE FIDDLE BLOCK

Flat seizing

Swallow

Strop

Sheave

Back

Shank

HOOK

Crown

Fixed lug

Bill

SPLICING FID

ROPE SERVING MALLET

Cheek

Pin cover plate

HEAVER FOR WIRE SERVING

PRICKERS

HOLLOW SPIKE FOR WIRE

MARLINESPIKE

LANYARD AND DEADEYES

Leather parceling

Turk's head

Hitched hauling end

UPPER DEADEYE

Standing part

LANYARD

LOWER DEADEYE

Grooving (scone)

Binding

Bolt

Face

Nut

TURNBUCKLE (RIGGING SCREW)

Shroud

Marline serving

Flat wire seizing

Solid heart thimble

Cotter pin

Fork end

Tail

Right hand screw

Open body

Left hand screw

Safe working load mark

Seizing

Shoulder

Eye

Crown

383

Sails

THERE ARE TWO MAIN TYPES OF SAILS: Old-fashioned square sails hang from yards at right angles to the mast, and are powerful drivers with following winds; fore-and-aft sails are set parallel to the length of the boat, with the luff (leading edge) of the sail attached to a mast or a stay. They are more efficient for all-round sailing, and almost all modern sailboats are rigged this way. Some fore-and-aft sails have a gaff at the head; Marconi-rig sails are pointed at the top (below). The bottom (foot) of the sail is on a boom. Sails are made of strips of cloth sewn together. Cotton and flax are traditional sail materials but synthetic fabrics are now more often used.

TOP OF A MARCONI SAIL

Seizing LUFF (LEADING EDGE) *Luff slide* *Bolt rope* Head

Round thimble

Rope strand

Grommet

Head cringle

LEECH
(LEACH)

Flat seam

*Synthetic flax
(duradon)*

Tabling

Rat's tail

SERVING MALLET

*Groove for
spunyarn (twine)*

Flatboard

NEEDLES AND SAIL TWINE

Handle

Sharp
point

Grip

SAILMAKER'S FID

Sail twine

Needle packet

Needle

SAILCLOTHS

KEVLAR
ON FLEX
FILM

HEAVYWEIGHT
NYLON CLOTH

MYLAR

NYLON
AND
SILICON
CLOTH

SYNTHETIC
FLAX
(DURADON)

DACRON

SAIL HOOK

Crown

Bill *Shank*

SAILMAKER'S PALM

Strap

Thumbhole

*Metal
needle pad*

Cowhide
face

BEESWAX

*Groove made
by thread*

Handle

SAILMAKER'S MALLET

Cheek

Whipping

Hide grip

Seizing

Copper
face

SAILMAKING TOOLS

Mizzen gaff topsail

Main sail

Main gaff topsail

Fore staysail

Jib

Mizzen sail

KETCH

Lugger topsail

Lug foresail

Lug mainsail

LUGGER

SAILS AND RUNNING RIGGING OF A DOUBLE TOPSAIL SCHOONER

Upper topsail lift

Lower topsail brace

Main topsail halyard

Fore upper topsail

Triatic stay

Flying jib halyard

Foot rope

Upper topsail brace

Outer jib halyard

Fore peak halyard

Lower topsail clewline

Fore yard lift

Fore lower topsail

Inner jib halyard

Fore throat halyard

Yard

Head

Gaff

Fore staysail halyard

Fore sail

Mast hoop (parrel)

Inner jib downhaul

Outer jib downhaul

Outer jib sheet

Flying jib sheet

Inner jib sheet

Flying jib downhaul

Luff

Boom

Foot

Flying jib

Outer jib

Reef point

Fore staysail

Inner jib

Fore staysail sheet

Fisherman's staysail

FORE-AND-AFT SAILING RIGS

Main gaff topsail

Fore sail

Main sail

Fore staysail

Jib

GAFF-HEADED SCHOONER

Mooring and anchoring

IN MOST HARBORS AND PORTS, a ship can moor (tie up or "make fast") directly to a pier, wharf, or quay (pronounced "key"), using heavy hawsers and docking lines attached to bitts or bollards. Hawsers are tied to each other with knots called bends. In open water, however, ships that are not under way must drop an anchor, which attaches the ship securely to the seabed. The earliest anchors were simply heavy stones. Later, various anchor designs were developed for different uses. Most small vessels today use Danforth or plow anchors, which dig deeply into the sea bottom. A permanent mooring is an anchor set in the bottom to which a ship can tie up without using its own anchor. On old sailing ships, anchors were pulled up, or "weighed," by sailors pushing against bars that turned a capstan, which wound up the anchor cable. Now, most capstans are powered by electricity.

STONE ANCHOR (KILLICK)

Rope hole

TYPES OF ANCHOR

CLOSE-STOWING ANCHOR

CQR ANCHOR (PLOW ANCHOR)

BRITISH ADMIRALTY ANCHOR TYPE ACII

YACHTSMAN'S ANCHOR (KEDGE)

STOCKLESS ANCHOR

MUSHROOM ANCHOR (PERMANENT MOORING ANCHOR)

ANCHOR CHAIN

End link | *Common link* | *Patent link*

SHACKLE, SWIVELS, AND LINK

DANFORTH ANCHOR

Shank

Pea (bill)

Fluke (palm)

Stock

Tripping palm

Crown

Throat

Crown

Bolt

Lug

GALVANIZED "D" SHACKLE

MOORING SWIVEL

CHAIN SWIVEL

Screw thread

SCREW LINK

TWIN BOLLARDS (BITTS), WITH RAKED PILLARS AND A HAWSER (HEAVY ROPE)

Flat

Rim

Base

BERTHING ROPES (HAWSERS)

Ship
Bitts
Stern line
Stern breast line
Quayside
After spring
Bollard
Fore spring
Bow line
Bow breast line

MOORING ROPE BENDS

HAWSER BEND (TWO BIGHTS WITH DOUBLE HALF HITCHES)

Standing part
Seizing
Seizing

CARRICK BEND

Seizing

SINGLE SHEET BEND (BECKET BEND)

Bare end
Standing part
Thin rope
Thick rope

Three-strand hawser belayed with figure of eight turns

Outboard end
Pillar
Foundry plug
Horn
Bolt hole
Cross piece
Bitter end (inboard end)

Bar hole (pigeon hole)
Cap
Strengthening chock
Barrel
Trenail (treenail)
Strengthening chock
Pawl slot
Whelp
Lignum vitae bearing
Tapered spindle

WOOD CAPSTAN WITH A VERTICAL SPINDLE

Pin

Ropes and knots

ALL KINDS OF ROPES ARE USED AT SEA, from thin twines and yarn to thick hawsers. Synthetic fibers are much in use today. Nylon ropes stretch, and so are ideal for anchoring; polyester (frequently called by the trade name Dacron) has little stretch and is used for halyards and sheets. Different knots have different uses. Knots that join two ropes are often called bends; hitches join a rope to another object. Ropes, usually called "lines" on board ship, can also be joined by seizing (lashing them together side by side) or splicing (unraveling the ends and weaving them together).

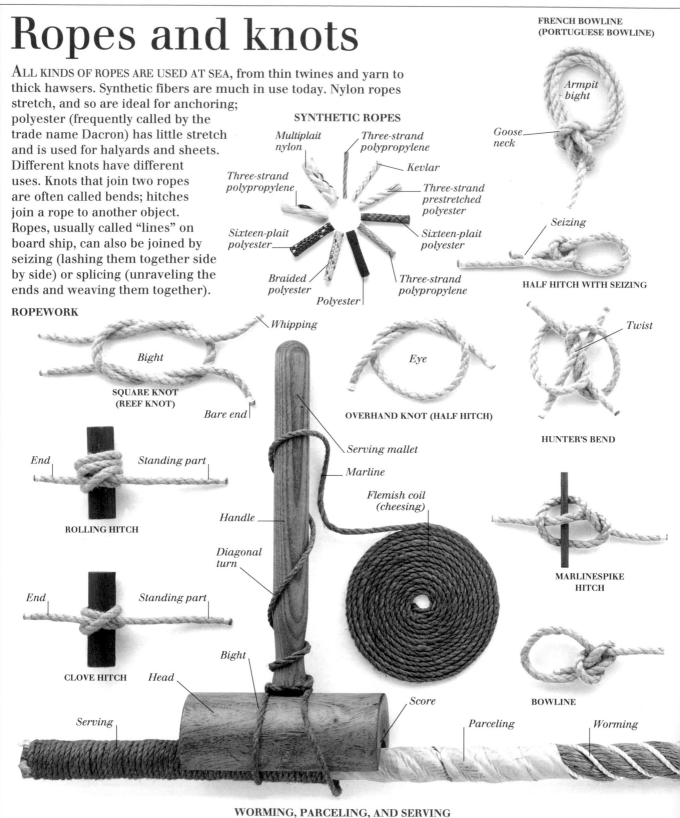

FRENCH BOWLINE (PORTUGUESE BOWLINE)

Armpit bight

Goose neck

SYNTHETIC ROPES

Multiplait nylon

Three-strand polypropylene

Kevlar

Three-strand polypropylene

Three-strand prestretched polyester

Sixteen-plait polyester

Sixteen-plait polyester

Braided polyester

Three-strand polypropylene

Polyester

Seizing

HALF HITCH WITH SEIZING

ROPEWORK

Whipping

Bight

SQUARE KNOT (REEF KNOT)

Bare end

Eye

OVERHAND KNOT (HALF HITCH)

Twist

HUNTER'S BEND

End

Standing part

ROLLING HITCH

Serving mallet

Marline

Flemish coil (cheesing)

Handle

Diagonal turn

MARLINESPIKE HITCH

End

Standing part

CLOVE HITCH

Head

Bight

Score

BOWLINE

Serving

Parceling

Worming

WORMING, PARCELING, AND SERVING

THUMB KNOT

SPANISH BOWLINE

**ROUND SEIZING
(FLAT SEIZING)**

DOUBLE CARRICK BEND

LIGHTERMAN'S HITCH

End

Frapped turn

Heaving line knot

HEAVING LINE BEND

Standing part

**JURY MAST KNOT
(MAST HEAD BEND)**

**SHEET BEND
(BECKET BEND)**

**MANHARNESS KNOT
(BUTTERFLY KNOT;
ARTILLERY LOOP)**

Flemish coil (cheesing)

Marlinespike

HEAVING LINE

PINNED SHEEPSHANK

Rat tail

Jaw

*Hawser laid three-strand manila
rope with right-handed lay*

Paddle wheels and propellers

THE INVENTION OF THE STEAM ENGINE IN THE 18TH CENTURY made mechanically driven ships fitted with paddle wheels or propellers a viable alternative to sails. Paddle wheels have fixed or feathered floats, and the model shown below features both types. Feathered floats give more propulsive power than fixed floats because they are almost upright at all times in the water. Paddle wheels were superseded by the propeller on oceangoing vessels in the mid-19th century. Propellers are more efficient, work better in rough water, and are less vulnerable in collisions. The first propellers were two-bladed, but later three- and four-bladed versions are more powerful; the shape and pitch of the blades have also been refined over the years. At the beginning of the 18th century, tillers were replaced on many larger ships by the ship's wheel as a means of steering.

SHIP'S WHEEL

King spoke handle

Handle

Spoke

Rim plate

Felloe (rim section)

Maker's name

Nave plate

Nave

PADDLE WHEEL WITH FIXED FLOATS

Wrist pin

Limb

Fixed float

Hub

Deck beam

OSCILLATING STEAM ENGINE

Slip eccentric for slide valve

Ahead/astern controls

Slide valve

Main crank

THREE-BLADED PROPELLER

Blade

Tapered shaft hole

Hub

Keyway

Strut

Frame

Piston rod (tail rod)

Stuffing box

Oscillating cylinder

Bottom plate (bedplate)

Slide valve rod

Control platform

Pitch

Propeller blade tip trace

Blade

Hub

Propeller hub trace

Propeller diameter

PROPELLER ACTION

DESIGN FOR A STEAMBOAT WITH PADDLE WHEELS

Connecting rod

Truss

Rim

Paddle float

Safety valve

Funnel

Drive to air pump

Tiller

Boiler

Flat bottom with no keel

Shallow, carvel-built hull

Bell crank (triangle)

Flywheel

Hub

Air pump

Paddle shaft

PADDLE WHEEL WITH FEATHERED FLOATS

TYPES OF PROPELLER

Crank for air pipe

Disengaging catch

Cylinder cover

Gland

Crankshaft

Outer rim

Drag link

Spoke

Inner rim

Paddle shaft

Hub

Paddle wheel box

Main steam supply pipe

Eccentric rod (drive for pump)

Pump piston

Feed bilge pump

Guardrail

Exhaust

Air pump

Keelson

Feathered float

FROUDE'S EARLY TEST PROPELLER

TUG PROPELLER

THREE-BLADED PROPELLER

Shroud ring

SHROUD RING PROPELLER

PROPULSION SYSTEM OF A 19TH CENTURY PADDLESTEAMER

Anatomy of an iron ship

IRON PARTS WERE USED IN WOODEN SHIPS AS EARLY AS 1675, often in the same form as the wooden parts that they replaced. Eventually, as on the tea clipper Cutty Sark (below), iron standing rigging was found to be stronger than the traditional rope. The first "ironclads" were warships whose wooden hulls were protected by iron armor plates. Later ironclads actually had iron hulls. The model opposite is based on the British warship HMS Warrior, launched in 1860, the first battleship built entirely of iron. The plan of an iron paddlesteamer (bottom), built somewhat later, shows that the craft had the masts and bowsprit of a sailing ship; but it also boasted a steam propulsion plant amid ships that turned two side paddlewheels. Early iron plates were painstakingly riveted together (below), but by the 1940s, steel vessels were welded together, whole sections at a time. The Liberty ships built in America during World War II are prime examples of such "production-line" vessels.

Steel yard **Iron wire stay**

Steel lower mast

Steel bowsprit

TEA CLIPPER

Wooden planking with copper sheathing

Forged iron anchor

RIVETED PLATES

Pan head rivet

Plate

Button head rivet (snap head)

Seam

LIBERTY SHIP

Gun section

Accommodation section

Cargo derrick

Weld line

Stern section **Midships section** **Cargo hold** **Bow section**

PLAN OF AN IRON PADDLESTEAMER

Crankshaft **Paddle wheel**

Steam whistle **Guardrail**

Mizzen mast **Main mast** **After funnel** **Eccentric** **Connecting rod**

Steering position **Poop deck** **Lounge** **Deck lantern** **State room**

Guardrail **Binnacle** **Skylight**

Steering gear

Stern

Vertical frame ladder

Mast step

Rudder

Rudder post

Heel of rudder post

Bar keel **Afterpeak** **Tank** **Main mast step** **Box boiler** **Reversing wheel** **Side lever**

Cabin

Stern framing **Donkey boiler** **Foundation** **Bottom plate** **Cylinder**

CUTAWAY SECTION OF AN "IRONCLAD"

Bulwark cap

Bulwark

Upper sheer strake

Teak backing

Topside strake

Wrought iron armor plate

Main sheer strake

Main deck tie plate

Lower deck tie plate

Frame

Bilge stringer

Bilge strake

Bilge keelson

Side keelson

Bottom plating

Garboard strake

Waterway

Scupper

Deck planking

Upper deck stringer (tie) plate

Upper deck beam

Upper deck pillar (stanchion)

Main deck beam

Main deck pillar (stanchion)

Lower deck beam

Pillar (hold stanchion)

Centerline keelson

Limber hole

Floor

Keel

Lighting hole

Angle bar (I bar)

Box sister keelson

Forward funnel

Fore mast

Skylight

Ventilator cowl

Capstan

Chimney

Hatch

Bowsprit

Main deck

Hawse pipe

Stem

Beam

Chain locker

Bulkhead stiffener

Deep floor

Forefoot

Deck beam

Smoke box

Combustion chamber

Cabin

'Tween decks ladder

Lower deck

Center girder

Forepeak

393

The battleship

IN THE EARLY YEARS OF THE 20TH CENTURY, sea warfare—attacking enemy vessels or defending a ship—was revolutionized by the introduction of Dreadnought-type battleships like the Brazilian vessel below. These new ships combined the latest advances in steam propulsion, gunnery, and armor plating. Their gun turrets, protected by armor up to 12 in (30 cm) thick, were designed to fire shells over great distances. The ship shown here, the Minas Geraes, was 500 ft (152 m) long. It was built at Elswick, England, and launched in 1908. Its chief armament was of 12 in (30 cm) guns (firing shells with a 12 in diameter). Other naval weapons developed in the 20th century include the torpedo—as portrayed on the upper cigarette card (right). This was a self-propelled underwater missile, often steered by gyro-control. Depth charges were designed in the First World War for use against submerged U-boats. They are canisters filled with explosives that are detonated by depth-sensitive pistols. The lower cigarette card shows depth charges being fired by a "thrower," fired from a torpedo tube, and rolled from the stern. Ship's shields were fitted to warships from the late 19th century onwards. The shield shown opposite depicts a traditional ship's cannon.

20TH CENTURY WEAPONRY

Torpedo tube

Warhead

Sight

TORPEDOES

DEPTH
CHARGES

Side-thrown
canister

Stern-rolled
canister

Torpedo-fired
canister

Boat handling
derrick

BRAZILIAN BATTLESHIP

Rangefinder

Forward
funnel

Light screen

Lifeboat

Compass

Compass and rangefinder
platform

Ship's wheel

Navigating bridge

Conning tower

Captain's shelter/
chart house

Weather shutter
for gun

"F" turret

Arms of
Brazil

Jack staff

12 in (30 cm)
gun

Skylight

Gunnery
spotting top

Purchase wire

Searchlight

Searchlight
platform

Leading block

Tripod mast

Boat
winch

Stem
(false ram bow)

Porthole

Belt
armor

Forward
accommodation
ladder

Sighting
hood

"A" turret

Turret barbette

Open gun mounting

Steam launch

4.7 in (12 cm) gun

Guest boat boom

SHIP'S SHIELD

Rope molding

Muzzle molding

Swell of muzzle

Chase

Reinforce

Ogee

Astragal

Trunnion

Lion crest

Radio antenna

Upper wireless and telegraphy yard (Upper W/T yard)

Topgallant mast

Wireless and telegraphy yard (W/T yard)

Lower yard

Signal gear

Ladder way

Brake slip

Davit

Clump cathead

Guardrail

Hawser fairlead

Sheet anchor

Starboard bower anchor

Lifeboat davit

Breakwater

Cable holder

Anchor chain

Bollard

Hawse pipe

Boat boom

Towing fairlead

Port bower anchor

Exhaust pipe

Searchlight

Vedette boat

Gig

After funnel

Funnel stay

Searchlight platform

After compass platform

After bridge

3 pound (1.3 kg) gun ("three pounder")

"X" turret

"Y" turret

Officer's accommodation ladder

Davit for whaler

Whaler

Flagmast

Stern walk

Scarph

Stern anchor

Propeller

Propeller shaft boss

Propeller shaft

Rudder

Life buoy

"P" turret

Ash chute

Hen coop

Bilge keel

Gun battery

Torpedo net boom

Turret roof rail

Torpedo net

Frigates and submarines

Fʀᴏᴍ ᴛʜᴇ ᴍɪᴅ-19ᴛʜ ᴄᴇɴᴛᴜʀʏ, ᴀʀᴍᴏʀᴇᴅ ꜱʜɪᴘꜱ provided a new challenge to enemy craft. In response, huge revolving gun turrets were developed. These could shoot in any direction, were loaded quickly from the breech, and fired exploding shells. Today's fighting ships, like the Royal Navy frigate opposite, also carry missile launchers and helicopters. Submarines operate underwater, have great speed, and some can fire missiles while submerged. A nuclear sub can operate for several years without refueling.

Stabilizer fin

Aft hydroplane

Propeller

Lower rudder

Rangefinder

Look out periscope

Local control cabinet

Breech wheel

Breech block

Loading arm

Slide locking lever

Slide

Sighting hood

Recoil cylinder

Elevating wheel

Guide for gun loading cage

Rammer lever

Gun loading cage

Training rack gearing

Blast bag (breeches)

Floor of gun house

Turret roller

Roller path

Working chamber

Training gear

Rammer

Waiting position

Roller path support

Floor

"Walking pipe" (hydraulic supply)

GUN TURRET
In this turret for two 15 in (37 cm) guns carried on the British "Queen Elizabeth class" battleship, shells are carried in a hoisting cage. The shell is rammed into the gun, followed by the propellant (charge). Once the breech is closed, the gun is ready for firing. The whole operation requires around 70 sailors.

Barbette (armor)

Main hoisting cage

Cordite handling room

Cordite supply shuttle

Cordite case

Turret trunk

Ensign staff

Lynx helicopter

SONAR torpedo decoy

Rudder

Variable pitch propeller

Accommodation ladder

Practice projectile

High-explosive projectile

Shell bogie

Shell room

Hydraulic grab

Shell-handling gear

Steam pipework

Machinery raft

Main turbine

Conning tower

Machinery control room

Switchboard room

Snorkel mast

Electronic warfare mast

Periscope

Control room

Sonar room

Galley

ROYAL NAVY NUCLEAR "HUNTER-KILLER" SUBMARINE

Officers' mess

SONAR transducer array

Main engine steam condenser

Distiller

Diesel motor compartment

Reactor space

Muzzle

Barrel

Wireless office

Junior enlisted men's mess

Carbon dioxide scrubber compartment

Torpedo compartment

Torpedo tube

Forward hydroplane

Junior enlisted men's bunk space

Senior enlisted men's mess

6 in (15 cm) SHELL
This shell is designed to burst in the air above its target.

Bursting charge (explosive)

Flash tube

Body

Wooden packing

Expelling plate

Driving band

SHELL CASE

CROSS SECTION OF THE SHELL

Transit plug

Bullet (shrapnel)

FRIGATE HMS ALACRITY

Surveillance RADAR

Navigation/helicopter control RADAR antenna

RADAR for gunnery and missile control

Motor whaler

Mast

Signaling lamp

Jack staff

Seacat missile launcher

Vent

Aerial rig

Oerlikon gun position

Stern gallery

Funnel

Enclosed bridge

Aerial

Exocet missile launcher

Gun turret

4.5 in (11 cm) gun

F174

RADAR for gunnery and missile control

Stabilizer

Liferaft cylinder

Triple "chaff" rocket launcher

Signal flag compartment

Bilge keel

Reel

SONAR bulge

Pennant number

Porthole

Fairlead

Breakwater

Bollard

Anchor

Draft mark

Anti-submarine torpedo tube

Pioneers of flight

Fᴌɪɢʜᴛ ʜᴀs ꜰᴀsᴄɪɴᴀᴛᴇᴅ ᴍᴀɴᴋɪɴᴅ for centuries, and countless unsuccessful flying machines have been designed. The first successful flight was made by the French Montgolfier brothers in 1783, when they flew a balloon over Paris. The next major advance was the development of gliders, notably by the Englishman Sir George Cayley, who in 1845 designed the first glider to make a sustained flight, and by the German Otto Lilienthal, who became known as the world's first pilot because he managed to achieve controlled flights. However, powered flight did not become a practical possibility until the invention of lightweight, gas-driven internal-combustion engines at the end of the 19th century. Then, in 1903, the American brothers Orville and Wilbur Wright made the first powered flight in their Wright Flyer biplane, which used a four-cylinder, gas-driven engine. Aircraft design advanced rapidly, and in 1909 the Frenchman Louis Blériot made his pioneering flight across the English Channel (see pp. 400-401). The American Glenn Curtiss also achieved several "firsts" in his Model-D Pusher and its variants, most notably winning the world's first competition for airspeed at Reims in 1909.

Biplane elevator

Pusher propeller (rear-mounted propeller)

Chain drive to starboard propeller

Fuel tank

Propeller-shaft bracing strut

Offset pilot's cradle

Takeoff and landing skid

Side-mounted engine to balance pilot's weight

SIDE VIEW OF CURTISS MODEL-D PUSHER, 1911

Nine-cylinder Salmson radial engine

Pusher propeller (rear-mounted propeller)

Aileron operating arm

Wing strut

Body cradle that pivots to control ailerons

Fuel filler cap

Oil filler cap

Fuel and oil tank

Rudder control wheel

Elevator wire for diving

Seatbelt

Control column

Throttle

Nose wheel brake

Footrest

Aileron

Turnbuckle

Fuel pipe

Pneumatic tire

Elevator wire for climbing

Thin, cambered lower wing

Starboard main landing gear

Rubber-tired nose wheel

Seat support strut

Pilot's seat

Wing-protecting skid

Engine and propeller thrust frame

SIDE VIEW OF WRIGHT FLYER, 1903

Plain cotton fabric

Interplane strut

Water-filled radiator

Wing warping wire

Chain drive

Pusher propeller (rear-mounted propeller)

Front diagonal strut

Rigid leading edge

Elevator drive wheel

Steel hub

Water pipe

Steel propeller shaft

Front-mounted biplane elevator

Rudder

Bracing wire

Landing skid

Elevator control cable

Pilot's cradle

Magneto

Rudder control cable

Braced rudder strut

Warping connection strut

Four-cylinder 12-HP engine

Propeller-shaft bracing strut

Softwood strut

Tail plane

Elevator control wire

Laminated wooden boom

Rudder

Rudder bracing wire

Curtiss

Elevator operating arm

Elevator

FRONT VIEW OF CURTISS MODEL-D PUSHER, 1911

Rudder control wheel

Fuel and oil tank

Nine-cylinder Salmson radial engine

Elevator operating arm

Anti-lift wire

Aileron operating arm

Starboard aileron

Port aileron

Carved interplane strut

Wing-protecting skid

Wing-protecting skid

Lift wire

Control column

Seat beam

Tubular steel leg

Interplane strut pin-jointed to front spar

Footrest

Axle

Main landing gear lateral brace

Early monoplanes

MONOPLANES HAVE ONE WING on each side of the fuselage. The principal disadvantage of this arrangement in early wooden-framed aircraft was that single wings were weak. They required strong wires to brace them to king posts above and below the fuselage. However, single wings also had advantages: they experienced less drag than multiple wings, allowing greater speed; they also made aircraft more maneuverable because single wings were easier to warp (twist) than double wings, and warping the wings was how pilots controlled the roll of early aircraft. By 1912, the French pilot Louis Blériot had used a monoplane to make the first flight across the English Channel, and the Briton Robert Blackburn and the Frenchman Armand Deperdussin had proved the greater speed of monoplanes. However, a spate of crashes caused by broken wings discouraged monoplane production, except in Germany, where all-metal monoplanes were developed in 1917. The wings of all-metal monoplanes did not need strengthening by struts or bracing wires, but despite this, such planes were not widely adopted until the 1930s.

RUMPLER MONOPLANE, 1908

FRONT VIEW OF BLACKBURN MONOPLANE, 1912

Taut fabric

Carved wooden propeller

King post

Hub bolted to propeller

Nose ring

Pilot's viewing aperture

Gnome seven-cylinder rotary engine

Exhaust valve push-rod

Elevator hinge

Elevator

Landing gear rear cross-member

Wheel fairing

Rubber-sprung wheel

Tailskid

Landing gear front strut

Axle

Landing skid

Landing gear rear strut

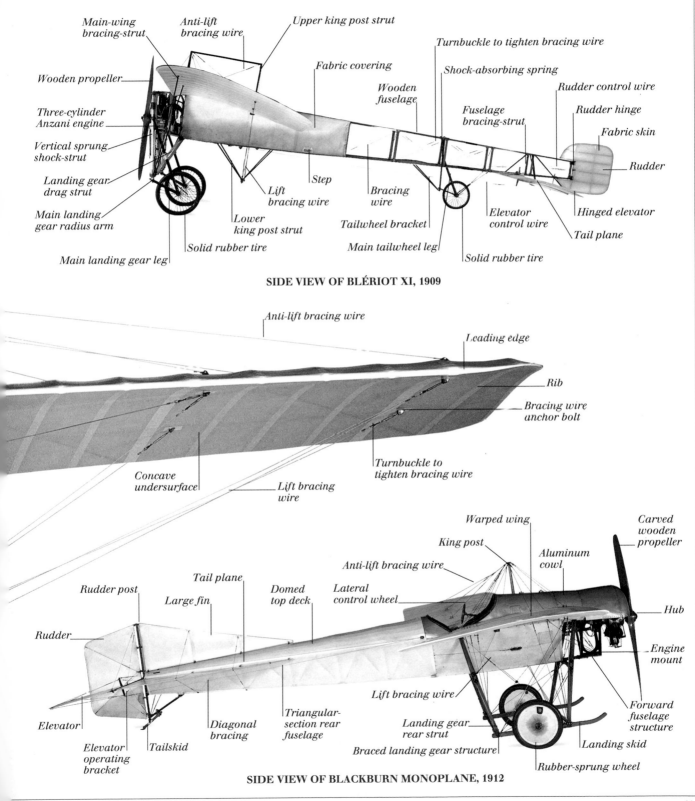

Main-wing bracing-strut

Anti-lift bracing wire

Upper king post strut

Fabric covering

Turnbuckle to tighten bracing wire

Shock-absorbing spring

Wooden fuselage

Rudder control wire

Rudder hinge

Wooden propeller

Fabric skin

Three-cylinder Anzani engine

Fuselage bracing-strut

Rudder

Vertical sprung shock-strut

Landing gear drag strut

Lift bracing wire

Step

Main landing gear radius arm

Bracing wire

Hinged elevator

Main landing gear leg

Solid rubber tire

Lower king post strut

Tailwheel bracket

Elevator control wire

Tail plane

Main tailwheel leg

Solid rubber tire

SIDE VIEW OF BLÉRIOT XI, 1909

Anti-lift bracing wire

Leading edge

Rib

Bracing wire anchor bolt

Concave undersurface

Lift bracing wire

Turnbuckle to tighten bracing wire

Warped wing

Carved wooden propeller

King post

Aluminum cowl

Anti-lift bracing wire

Lateral control wheel

Rudder post

Tail plane

Domed top deck

Large fin

Hub

Rudder

Engine mount

Elevator

Lift bracing wire

Forward fuselage structure

Elevator operating bracket

Tailskid

Diagonal bracing

Triangular-section rear fuselage

Landing gear rear strut

Braced landing gear structure

Landing skid

Rubber-sprung wheel

SIDE VIEW OF BLACKBURN MONOPLANE, 1912

Biplanes and triplanes

BIPLANES DOMINATED AIRCRAFT DESIGN until the 1930s, largely because some early monoplanes (see pp. 400-401) were too fragile to withstand the stresses of flight. The struts between biplanes' wings made the wings strong compared with those of early monoplanes, although the greater surface area of biplanes' wings increased drag and reduced speed. Many aircraft designers also developed triplanes, which had a particular advantage over biplanes: more wings meant a shorter wingspan to achieve the same lifting power, and a shorter wingspan gave greater maneuverability. Triplanes were most successful as fighters during World War I, the German Fokker triplane being a notable example. However, the greater maneuverability of triplanes was no advantage for normal flying, so most manufacturers continued to make biplanes. Many other aircraft designs were attempted. Some were quadruplanes, with four pairs of wings. Some had tandem wings (two pairs of monoplane wings, one behind the other). One of the most bizarre designs was by the Englishman Horatio Phillips; it had 20 sets of narrow wings and looked rather like a Venetian blind.

LAMINATED PROPELLER

Rudder hinge

RAF Central Flying School badge

Rudder

Fin

Navigation light

K 3215

Elevator

Rudder cable

Tail plane

Tailwheel

Bracing strut

SIDE VIEW OF AVRO TRIPLANE IV, 1910

Valve rocker

Air cooling baffle

Magneto

Crankcase breather pipe

Directly driven propeller

Main front strut to engine mount

Skid upper bracing strut

Wing strut

Fuel tank

Throttle

Harness

Pilot's seat

Limit of fuselage skin

Ash skid

Rubber cord suspension

Axle

Turnbuckle

Skid rear strut

Lateral bracing strut

Rubber tire

Wire wheel

Wheel rim

AVRO TUTOR BIPLANE, 1931

Aileron hinge strut

Pin joint

Navigation light

Slat-arm fairing

Aileron control wire

Lift bracing wire

Instructor's cockpit

Wooden-domed deck

Padded coaming

Engine cowl

Student's cockpit

Propeller hub

RAF roundel

Laminated-wood, fixed-pitch propeller

Metal leading edge

X 3215

Exhaust collector ring

Exhaust pipe

Main landing gear leg

Aircraft registration code

Inspection cover

Radius rod

Inflation valve

Fabric-covered steel-tube fuselage

Fabric-covered aluminum and steel wing

Manufacturer's logo

Recessed nose of aileron

FRONT VIEW OF AVRO TRIPLANE IV, 1910

Unpainted, varnished fabric

Leading edge

Fuel filler and vent

Fixed-pitch wooden propeller

Anti-lift bracing wire

Top wing

Wing strut

Middle wing

Rib

Bottom wing

Landing skid

Axle

Elevator

Tail plane

Triangular-section fuselage

Lift bracing wire

Triangular-section fuselage

Fuselage bracing wire

Rudder control cable

Lateral bracing strut

Tail plane

Rudder

Metal plate anchorage

Elevator control cable

Longeron

Rubber cord suspension

Tailskid pivot

Tailskid

Elevator

World War I aircraft

WHEN WORLD WAR I STARTED in 1914, the main purpose of military aircraft was reconnaissance. The British-built BE 2, of which the BE 2B was a variant, was well suited to this duty; it was very stable in flight, allowing the occupants to study the terrain, take photographs, and make notes. The BE 2 was also one of the first aircraft to drop bombs. One of the biggest problems for aircraft designers during the war was mounting machine guns. On aircraft that had front-mounted propellers, the field of fire was restricted by the propeller and other parts of the aircraft. The problem was solved in 1915 by the Dutchman Anthony Fokker, who designed an interrupter gear that prevented a machine gun from firing when a propeller blade passed in front of the barrel. The German LVG CVI had a forward-firing gun to the right of the engine, as well as a rear-cockpit gun, and bombing capability. It was one of the most versatile aircraft of the war.

FLYING HELMET

PORT WINGS FROM A BE 2B

Interplane-strut attachment
Intermediate leading-edge rib
Leading edge
Airspeed-indicator tube
Wingtip
Airspeed-indicator tube
Main rib
Root
Interplane strut
Trailing edge
Airspeed pitot tube
Interplane-strut attachment
Upper side of lower wing
Attachment lug

BE 2B, 1914

Observer's windshield
Cabane strut fairing
Top-wing center section
Engine air intake (ram scoop)
Cabane strut
Wooden propeller
Lift bracing wire
Pilot's windshield
Air-cooled V8 engine
Plywood skin
Crankcase
Control column
Padded coaming
Buffed metal cowling
Silencing heat exchanger
Exhaust pipe
Landing gear front strut
Elevator rocking arm
Ash skid
Step
Step
Bomb rack
Lateral control wire
Reconnaissance camera bracket
Pneumatic rubber tire
Wheel cover
V-strut
Lower-wing attachment
112 lb (51 kg) bomb

SIDE VIEW OF LVG CVI, 1917

Pilot's cockpit

Cold-water pipe

Observer's cockpit

Exhaust pipe

Starboard aileron

230-HP Benz six-cylinder water-cooled engine

7.92-mm Parabellum machine gun

Rudder

Fin

Rudder control wire

Laminated wooden propeller

Elevator

Air ventilator inlet

Steel-drive bracket

Pitot head

Pivoted sprung tailskid

Interplane strut

Pneumatic rubber tire

Aircraft registration code

Aileron control cable

Axle

Elevator control wire

Aircraft type

Bracing wire

Tire inflation aperture

FRONT VIEW OF LVG CVI, 1917

Lozenge-patterned fabric

Forward-firing machine gun

Exhaust stack

230-HP Benz six-cylinder water-cooled engine

Wooden propeller

Pitot head

Interplane strut

Anti-lift bracing wire

Lift bracing wire

Main fuel tank

Turnbuckle

Pneumatic rubber tire

Axle

Gravity-feed fuel tank

Multiple rubber-cord suspension

Tailskid

Landing gear strut

Fixed tail plane

Fabric covering

Elevator

Rib

Rudder

Elevator hinge

Fabric lacing

Steel lug

Tail plane attachment

Rudder post

Aircraft registration code

Spar

Shock-absorbing spring

Steel V-strut

Trailing edge

Pivoted tailskid

National marking

Leading edge

Rib

HORIZONTAL TAIL OF A BE 2B

405

Early passenger aircraft

FRONT VIEW OF LOCKHEED ELECTRA, 1934

UNTIL THE 1930s, most passenger aircraft were biplanes, with two pairs of wings and a wooden or metal framework covered with fabric or, sometimes, plywood. Such aircraft were restricted to low speeds and low altitudes because of the drag on their wings. Many had an open cockpit, situated behind or in front of an enclosed—but unpressurized—cabin that carried a maximum of 10 people. The passengers usually sat in wicker chairs that were not bolted to the floor, and the journey could be bumpy when flying through turbulence. Warm clothing, and earplugs to reduce the effects of prolonged noise, were often required. During the 1930s, powerful, streamlined, all-metal monoplanes, such as the Lockheed Electra shown here, became widespread. By 1939, the advent of pressurized cabins allowed fast flights at high altitudes, where there is less turbulence. Flying boats were still necessary on many routes until 1945 because of inadequate runways and the frequency of emergency sea landings. World War II, however, resulted in enough good runways being built for land planes to become standard on all major airline routes.

Green starboard navigation light
Flush-riveted metal-skinned wing
Leading edge
Fuel-jettison valve
Static discharge wick
Split flap in landing position

PASSENGER CABIN TRIM PANELS

Roof trim panel
Forward bulkhead upper panel
Passenger service panel aperture
Ashtray
Starboard wall forward panel
Cockpit door panel
Forward bulkhead lower panel
Starboard wall mid-forward panel

SIDE VIEW OF LOCKHEED ELECTRA, 1934

Cockpit windshield
Sliding window
Emergency escape hatch
Oil tank
Steel firewall
Passenger window
Air intake
Ventilator exit
Nose
Propeller pitch-change cylinder
Blade counterweight
Spinner mounting disk
Variable-pitch propeller
Exhaust collector ring
Pratt & Whitney nine-cylinder radial engine
Red port navigation light
Landing gear door
Exhaust pipe
Electrically driven split flap
Passenger door
Main landing gear
Brake pipe
Aileron
Static discharge wick
Aluminum wheel
Mudguard
Metal-skinned wing

Cylinder-cooling gills

Variable-pitch propeller

Cockpit windshield

High-visibility tip

Streamlined spinner

Pratt & Whitney nine-cylinder radial engine

Valve push-rod tube

Inner wing containing fuel tank

Fixed landing light

Red filter signal light

Exhaust pipe

Single-leg main landing gear

Pitot mast

Tank drain tap

Single-leg main landing gear

Landing gear door

Landing gear fork

Battery compartment

Electrical service compartment

Brake pipe

Axle

Pneumatic rubber tire

Brake pipe

Inspection cover

Tailwheel

Disc brake

Landing gear fork

Axle

Pneumatic rubber tire

Starboard wall aft panel

Roof trim

PASSENGER SEAT

Bulkhead starboard trim

Backrest

Document panel

Seat button

Seat belt

Armrest

Bulkhead port trim

Starboard wall mid-aft panel

Seat anchor bolt hole

Interior cabin trim for aft bulkhead between cabin and luggage hold

Wall anchor

Seat cushion

Floor anchor

PORT ENGINE COWLS

Rotating beacon

Starboard rudder

Inspection door

Fixed tail plane

Starboard trim tab

Tail plane

Port fin

Aluminum flush-riveted skin

120° cowl segment

Propeller-hub spinner

Port trim tab

NC517IN

Ventilator exit

Tail plane tip

Aircraft registration code

Swiveling rubber-tired tailwheel

120° cowl panel

Joining latch

407

World War II aircraft

WHEN WORLD WAR II began in 1939, air forces had already replaced most of their fabric-skinned biplanes with all-metal stressed-skin monoplanes. Aircraft played a far greater role in military operations during World War II than ever before. The wide range of aircraft duties and the introduction of radar tracking and guidance systems put pressure on designers to improve aircraft performance. The main areas of improvement were speed, range, and engine power. Bombers became larger and more powerful—converting from two to four engines—in order to carry a heavier bomb load; the U.S. B-17 Flying Fortress could carry up to 6 tons of bombs over a distance of about 2,000 miles (3,200 km). Some aircraft increased their range by using drop tanks (fuel tanks that were jettisoned when empty to reduce drag). Fighters needed speed and maneuverability: the Hawker Tempest shown here had a maximum speed of 435 mph (700 kph) and was one of the few Allied aircraft capable of catching the German jet-powered V1 "flying bomb." By 1944, Britain had introduced its first turbojet-powered aircraft, the Gloster Meteor fighter, and Germany had introduced the fastest fighter in the world, the turbojet-powered Me 262, which had a maximum speed of 540 mph (868 kph).

PROPELLER

High-visibility yellow tip

Light-alloy propeller spinner

Variable-pitch aluminum-alloy blade

COMPONENTS OF A HAWKER TEMPEST MARK V, c.1943

Radiator-access cowling

STARBOARD ENGINE COWLINGS

Lower side cowling

Upper side cowling

Cowling fastener

2,400-HP Napier Sabre 24-cylinder engine

Cartridge starter

Propeller governor

Radiator header tank

Propeller drive shaft

Distributor

Ejector exhaust

Magneto

Starter motor

Engine top cowling

Cowling fastener

Upper side cowling

Lower side cowling

Radiator-access cowling

PORT ENGINE COWLINGS

SECTIONED B-17G FLYING FORTRESS BOMBER, c.1943

Astronavigation dome

Hand-held gun

Plastic nose

Pilot's seat

Oxygen bottle

Upper gun turret

1,000 lb (454 kg) bomb

Radio operator's seat

Waist gun

Ammunition belt

Ammunition box

Dorsal fin

Fin

VHF antenna

Rudder

"Cheyenne-type" tail-gun turret

Tail gunner's compartment

Ammunition feed

Chin gun turret

HF radio antenna

Bombardier's viewing panel

Bomb door

Direction-finding-antenna fairing

Navigator's seat

Sperry ball gun turret

Ammunition feed

Entrance door

Oxygen bottle

Retracted tailwheel

PORT WING UNDERSIDE

Flap

Cockpit starboard access panel

Starboard tail plane

Landing gear door

Wing front fillet panel

Wing rear fillet panel

Elevator hinge

Starboard elevator

Wing fillet panel

Leading edge

Elevator control rod

Canopy rail

Seat pan

Harness strap

FUSELAGE

Canopy rail

VHF radio whip antenna

Fin

Tail fairing

Trim tab operating rod

Rudder

Flat, bulletproof windshield

Armored seat back

Dorsal fin

Tail plane root

Gyroscopic gunsight

Plastic cockpit canopy

Cockpit front belly panel

Cockpit center belly panel

Tail band

Tail plane front attachment bracket

Tail plane rear attachment bracket

RAF C1-type roundel

Port elevator trim tab

Rear spar trunnion

Cockpit rear belly panel

Trailing edge

Wing fillet panel

Camouflage

Wing front fillet panel

Wing rear fillet panel

Port tail plane

TAIL

Outboard ammunition-feed blister

Cockpit port access panel

Trailing edge

Wing upper surface

HAWKER TEMPEST MARK V FIGHTER, c.1943

Aileron

Hispano Mark V 20-mm cannon

Armor-plated seat back

Squadron code

Rudder

Dorsal fin

Exhaust pipe

Headrest

Gyroscopic gunsight

RAF C1-type roundel

Propeller spinner

RAF B-type roundel

Engine air intake

Radiator

Radiator outlet

Pitot head

Instant-identification "invasion" stripes

Retracted tailwheel

Rudder trim tab

Yellow-painted leading edge

PORT WING

Wingtip

Modern piston aircraft engines

PISTON ENGINES today are used mainly to power the vast numbers of light aircraft and ultralights, as well as crop sprayers and crop dusters, small helicopters, and fire-bombers (which dump water on large fires). Virtually all heavier aircraft are now powered by jet engines. Modern piston aircraft engines work on the same basic principles as the engine used by the Wright brothers in the first powered flight in 1903. However, today's engines are more sophisticated than earlier engines. For example, modern aircraft engines may use a two-stroke or a four-stroke combustion cycle; they may have from one to nine air- or liquid-cooled cylinders, which may be arranged horizontally, in-line, in V formation, or radially; and they may drive the aircraft's propeller either directly or through a reduction gearbox. One of the more unconventional types of modern aircraft engine is the rotary engine shown here, which has a trilobate (three-sided) rotor spinning in a chamber shaped like a fat figure-eight.

MID WEST TWO-STROKE, THREE-CYLINDER ENGINE

MID WEST 75-HP TWO-STROKE, THREE-CYLINDER ENGINE

Spark plug

Coolant outlet

Cylinder head

Piston

Cylinder barrel

Exhaust manifold

Exhaust port

Cylinder liner

Upper crankcase

Pump drive belt

Coolant pump

Reduction gearbox

Driven gear

Gearbox drive splines

Connecting rod (con-rod)

Small end

Generator rotor

Propeller drive flange

Big end

Counterweight

Torsional vibration damper

Sprag clutch

Crankshaft

Stator

Ignition trigger housing

Gearbox mounting plate

Lower crankcase

Engine mounting plate

ROTOR AND HOUSINGS OF A MID WEST SINGLE-ROTOR ENGINE

Propeller bolt hole

Propeller drive flange

Dowel

Stud

Coolant jacket

Inlet tract

Roller

Stud hole

Eccentric-shaft bearing

Stud hole

Propeller shaft rear bearing

Coolant jacket

Dowel hole

Dowel

Rotor chamber

Exhaust tract

GEARBOX CASE

FRONT HOUSING (FRONT END PLATE)

TROCHOID HOUSING

MID WEST 90-HP TWIN-ROTOR ENGINE

Propeller-bolt collar

Propeller drive flange

Reduction gearbox

Lubricating oil feed

Engine front mounting plate

Blanking plate over air inlet

Upper rubber anti-vibration engine mount

Carburetor

Rotor-cooling air duct

Pipe clamp joint

Rotor-cooling air pump

Upper rotor-cooling air duct

Generator housing

Electric cable

Front bearing mount

Oil pump drive shaft cover

Torsional vibration damper

Fuel pipe inlet connection

Blanking plate over exhaust port

Fuel drip tray

Exhaust pipe flange

Engine rear mounting plate

Lower rubber anti-vibration engine mount

Starter motor

Flywheel

OUTPUT SHAFT OF A MID WEST ROTARY ENGINE

Balance weight

Drive gear

Front bearing

Drive gear spline

Flywheel retaining thread

Eccentric shaft

Rotor bearing

Rear bearing

Flywheel

Starter-ring teeth

Oil seal spacer ring

Corner bolt

Rotor tip seal

Tip seal groove

Rotor-gear teeth

Rotor bearing

Cooling fins

Rotor tip spring

Balancing drilling

Rotor side seal

Side seal spring

Side seal groove

ROTOR AND SEALS

Fixed gear (stationary gear)

Engine mounting

Stud hole

Dowel hole

Coolant jacket

REAR HOUSING (REAR END PLATE)

Outlet manifold

Pump drive shaft

Fixing stud

Bolt hole

Inlet manifold

Water pump cover and oil pump housing

Thermostat

Oil pump

WATER-PUMP HOUSING

Modern jetliners 1

BAE 146 JETLINER

MODERN JETLINERS HAVE ENABLED ordinary people to travel to places where once only the wealthy could afford to go. Compared with the first jetliners (which were introduced in the 1940s), modern jetliners are much quieter, burn fuel more efficiently, and produce less air pollution. These advances are largely due to the replacement of turbojet engines with turbofan engines (see pp. 418-419). The greater power of turbofan engines at low speeds enables modern jetliners to carry more fuel and passengers than turbojet aircraft; a modern Boeing 747-400 (popularly known as a "jumbo jet") can fly 400 people for 8,500 miles (13,700 km) without needing to refuel. Jetliners fly at high altitudes, typically cruising at 26,000-36,000 ft (8,000-11,000 m), where they can use fuel efficiently and usually avoid bad weather. The pilot always controls the aircraft during takeoff and landing, but at other times the aircraft is usually controlled by an autopilot. Autopilots are complex onboard mechanisms that detect deviations from an aircraft's route and make appropriate adjustments to the flight controls. Flight decks are also equipped with radar that warns pilots of approaching hazards, such as mountain ranges, bad weather, and other aircraft.

Shoulder nacelle

Engine pylon

Hinged nacelle panel

Nose cowling

Fire extinguisher discharge indicator

Oil-filler door

Push-in door for hand-held fire extinguisher

Oil-filler door for integrated-drive generator

Drain mast

Fan duct nozzle

Core-engine jet pipe

TURBOFAN ENGINE COWLING

STRUCTURAL COMPONENTS OF A BAE 146 JETLINER

FUSELAGE NOSE-SECTION

FUSELAGE MID-SECTION

Electrically heated, birdproof windshield

Side window

Anchor for open door

Rain gutter

Hinge

Peephole

Finger recess

Static air-pressure plate

Forward main door aperture

Passenger window aperture

VHF omni-range and instrument-landing-system antennas

Light-alloy door frame

Main external operating handle

Multiple-pinned lock

Floor level

Radome

Toilet service connector

Air temperature probe

Stall-warning vane

Pitot head for dynamic air pressure

FORWARD MAIN DOOR

Anchor for open door

Overwing
fuel-filler cap

Systems
connector

Overwing fuel-
filler cap

Fuel contents
indicator

**STARBOARD
WING
ASSEMBLY**

Center-line (spine)
of aircraft

Single-piece skin
over inboard wing

Rubber sealing strip

Rubber sealing strip

Trailing edge

Trailing edge
of fixed wing

Spoiler anchorage

Hydraulic actuator
attachment

Pivot point

Flap-track fairing

Screw
joint

Aft section

Hinge

**INBOARD LIFT
SPOILERS**

Stainless-steel
flap seal

MOVABLE FLAP TRACK AND FAIRING

Upper carriage
attached to flap

Track roller

Tab hinge line

FOWLER FLAP

Leading edge

Anchor
bearing

Track

Root

Gearbox
mount

Bellcrank
lever

Gearbox unit

Carriage
drive nut

Flap drive
screw

Lower carriage

Skin lap-
joint

Leading
edge

Main spar
bridge

Root rib

Wing-root mount
containing central
fuel tank

Inboard
tab

Attachment structure for
wing-to-fuselage fillet

Cabin air-pressure
discharge valve

Floor
level

Fairing of
landing gear bay

Fairing of landing
gear pivot

Yellow anti-
corrosion paint

Modern jetliners 2

Landing and taxiing light

Heated deicing leading edge

Roll-spoiler hinge

Roll-spoiler hydraulic actuator attachment

STARBOARD WING

Fixed trailing edge

Aileron hinge

Starboard navigation light

Hinge

Hydraulic actuator attachment

Spoiler arm

Aerodynamic balance

Horn balance

Hinge bracket

Recessed hinge

INTERMEDIATE LIFT SPOILER

Flap seal

OUTBOARD ROLL SPOILER

AILERON

Trim tab

MAIN FOWLER FLAP

Static discharge wick attachment

Leading edge

Flap tip

FUSELAGE SPINE FAIRING

Tab-hinge line

Outboard tab

Landing gear door

Hydraulic brake line

Main pivot

Finger recess

Peephole

Hot-air deicing duct

Skin lap joint

Electrical harness

Oleo lock-jack

Direction bar

Passenger window aperture

Light-alloy beam

Brake line

Main external operating handle

Hinge

Side brace and retraction jack trunnions

Shock-strut bearing

Pneumatic tire

Outer wheel axle

Hinge

Lower pivot

Wheel hub

Pivoted trailing-link arm

Hydraulic brake line

Anchor for open door

Cabin air-discharge aperture

STARBOARD TWIN-WHEEL MAIN LANDING GEAR

AFT MAIN DOOR

BAE 146 MODERN JETLINER

Tail plane

Logo

Rudder

Fin

Starboard aft service door

Flap-track fairing

Core-engine jet pipe

Main landing-gear fairing

Landing light

VHF antenna

VHF radio antenna

Forward door for crew and service

Radome

Water-drain mast

STARBOARD ELEVATOR

Horn balance

Tab hinge

Aerodynamic balance

Recessed hinge

Center line (spine)

Root

Trim tab

Servo-tab

TAIL PLANE FAIRINGS

Intermediate fairing (fin tip)

Aft fairing

Fin trailing edge

Forward fairing

Side fairing

Elevator chassis box

Tail plane attachment bracket

FIN

Heated deicing leading edge

Forward spar

Fairing panel

Fin-attachment skin

Aft spar

Access to yaw dampers and rudder trim jack

Rain gutter

Fin leading-edge attachment

Auxiliary power unit (APU) inlet

Heated deicing leading edge

Operating arm

TAIL PLANE

Elevator hinge

Auxiliary power unit (APU) vent

Oil-cooler duct

Hinge

Skin lap joint

Trailing edge

Tail plane tip

Aft main door aperture

Heated drain mast

FUSELAGE TAIL SECTION

STARBOARD AIR BRAKE

Supersonic jetliners

SUPERSONIC AIRCRAFT FLY FASTER than the speed of sound
(Mach 1). There are many supersonic military aircraft, but only
two supersonic passenger-carrying aircraft (also called SSTs, or
supersonic transports) have been produced: the Russian Tu-144,
and the Concorde, produced jointly by Britain and France.
The Tu-144 had a greater maximum speed than
the Concorde but was withdrawn in
1978, after only seven months in service. The Concorde has
remained in service since 1976. It features many innovations,
including a droop nose, which is lowered during takeoff and
landing to aid visibility from the cockpit, and the pumping of fuel
between forward and aft trim tanks to help stabilize the aircraft.
The Concorde has a narrow fuselage and short-span wings to reduce drag during
supersonic flight. Its noisy turbojet engines with afterburners enable it to carry
100 passengers at a cruising speed of Mach 2 at 50,000-60,000 ft (15,000-18,000 m).
Once an aircraft is flying faster than Mach 1, it produces a continuous air-pressure
wave, which is heard as a "sonic boom."

COMPUTER-
DESIGNED SST

FRONT VIEW OF CONCORDE

OVERHEAD VIEW
OF CONCORDE

SECTIONED VIEW OF CONCORDE

Fire-suppression bottle access panel

Cold-air unit

Static discharge wick

HF radio antennas fairing

Auxiliary power unit

Upper rudder

Tail cone

Pressurized keel box

Elevon (combined elevator and aileron)

VHF omni-range antenna

Fuel tank

Cabin air duct

Emergency oxygen cylinders

Lower-rudder power control unit

Main air duct

Inspection panel

Emergency exit

Flight-control mixing unit

Servo control-unit fairing

Fuel-jettison pipe

Twin-wheel tail bumper

Air-conditioning duct

Rear bulkhead

Aft galley unit

Rear emergency door

Tank inspection access

Inboard elevon (combined elevator and aileron)

Landing gear hydraulics

Port main landing-gear leg well

Variable nozzle

Nozzle actuator

Heat exchanger exhaust

Elevon power control unit

Spar

Fuel pipe

Forward ramp drive

Rib

VHF antenna

Four-wheel bogie

Main landing gear cross beam

Leading edge

Fuel tank

Honeycomb elevon structure

Middle passenger door

Port engine fuel pumps

Port main landing gear leg

Upper lip of port engine air intakes

Heat exchanger

Rolls-Royce Olympus Mark 610 turbojet

Retraction jack

Engine front support link

SIDE VIEW OF CONCORDE

VHF antenna

Emergency exit

Passenger window

Flight deck windshield

Retracted visor

Nose in drooped position

Standby pitot head

Nose gear leg

Nose leg telescopic strut

Aerodynamic strake

Starboard forward door

Radome

Steerable twin-wheel nose gear

417

Modern military aircraft

MODERN MILITARY AIRCRAFT ARE AMONG THE MOST SOPHISTICATED and expensive products of the 20th century. Fighters need computer-operated controls for maneuverability, powerful engines, and effective air-to-air weapons. Most modern fighters also have guided missiles, radar, and passive, infrared sensors. These developments enable today's fighters to engage in combat with adversaries who are outside visual range. Bombers carry a large weapon load and enough fuel for long-range flights. A few military aircraft, such as the Tornado and the F-14 Tomcat, have variable-sweep ("swing") wings. During takeoff and landing their wings are fully extended, but for high-speed flight and low-level attacks the wings are pivoted fully back. A recent development is the "stealth" bomber, which is designed to absorb or deflect enemy radar in order to remain undetected. Earlier bombers, such as the Tornado, use terrain-following radars to fly so close to the ground that they avoid enemy radar detection.

FRONT VIEW OF A PANAVIA TORNADO

Instrument landing system antenna

Birdproof windshield

Air data probe

Port variable-incidence air intake

Wing-root glove fairing

Starboard inboard stores pylon

Taileron

Starboard main landing-gear door

Main landing-gear leg

Laser ranger and marked-target seeker

Starboard nose gear door

Steerable twin-wheel nose gear

Radome containing ground-mapping, attack, and terrain-following radars

Taxiing light

Wing extended for takeoff and landing

Wing pivoted back for high-speed flight

SWING-WING F-14 TOMCAT FIGHTER

SIDE VIEW OF A PANAVIA TORNADO GR1A (RECONNAISSANCE VERSION), 1986

Pilot's cockpit

Navigator's instrument console

Navigator's cockpit

Single canopy over both cockpits

Engine air intake

Navigation light

Flat, birdproof windshield

High-velocity air duct to disperse rain

Upper "request identification" antenna

Air data probe

Radome containing ground-mapping, attack, and terrain-following radars

UHF antenna

Angle-of-attack probe

Tacan (tactical air navigation) antenna

Emergency canopy release handle

Nose gear door

Steerable nose gear leg

Twin nose-wheel

Pitot head

Window covering infrared reconnaissance camera

Hinged auxiliary air intake

Cold-air intake (ram scoop)

Heat exchanger exhaust duct

NORTHROP B-2 ("STEALTH" BOMBER), 1989

Starboard split rudder

Inboard elevons (combined elevators and ailerons)

Refractory (heat-resistant) skin behind exhaust outlet

Variable-incidence gust alleviator

Wing leading edge coated with radar-absorbent material

Port wingtip rudder

Outboard elevon (combined elevator and aileron)

Leading-edge antenna

Engine aft bulkhead

Wing containing fuel tank

Weapon-bay rear bulkhead

Flight refueling receptacle

Auxiliary air intake

Weapon-bay front bulkhead

Air intake coated with radar-absorbent material

Space for extra crew member

Ejector-seat roof hatches

Two-seater cockpit

Port navigation light

Port outboard stores pylon

Fin tip antenna fairing

Radar warning receiver looking forward

Instrument landing system antenna

Heat exchanger air intake (ram scoop)

Wing-root glove fairing

Extended port air brake

Fin

Radar warning receiver looking rearward

Wing-root pneumatic seal

Rudder

Fin-root antenna fairing

Heat exchanger hot-air exhaust

Air brake jack

Spine end fairing

Thrust-reverser (closed)

Port fully variable afterburner nozzle

Port flap

Port taileron (combined tail plane and aileron)

Wingtip antenna fairing

Port navigation light

Lower "request identification" antenna

Port inboard stores pylon

Hydraulic hand pump

Powered leading-edge slat

Main-gear door

Port main landing gear

Port outboard stores pylon

Helicopters

HELICOPTERS USE ROTATING BLADES for lift, propulsion, and steering. The first machine to achieve sustained, controlled flight using rotating blades was the autogiro built in the 1920s by Juan de la Cierva of Spain. His machine had unpowered blades above the fuselage that relied on the flow of air to rotate them and provide lift while the autogiro was driven forward by a conventional propeller. Then, in 1939, the Russian-born American Igor Sikorsky produced his VS-300, the forerunner of the modern helicopter. Its engine-driven blades provided lift, propulsion, and steering. It could take off vertically, hover, and fly in any direction, and had a tail rotor to prevent the helicopter body from spinning. The introduction of gas turbine jet engines to helicopters in 1955 produced quieter, safer, and more powerful machines. Because of their versatility in flight, helicopters are used today for many purposes, including crop spraying, traffic surveillance, and transporting crews to deep-sea oil rigs, as well as acting as gunships, air ambulances, and air taxis.

BELL 47G-3B1

BELL 47G-3B1

SCHWEIZER 300C

Blade-root attachment

Three-blade main rotor

Ventilator

Outside air-temperature gauge

Flight-control rod

Anti-collision beacon

Anti-torque tail rotor

Magnetic compass

Main rotor mast

Automatic direction-finding antenna

Plastic canopy

Navigation antenna

Cyclic-pitch lever

Fuel tank

G-SAND

Tubular bracing strut

Tail boom

Engine air intake

Tail-rotor drive shaft

Vertical stabilizer

Tail rotor guard

Pitot head

Tail-boom support strut

Anti-collision beacon

Exhaust silencer

Landing skid

Landing gear damper

Transmission drive-pulley cover

Landing light

Transponder antenna

Lycoming four-cylinder engine

High-visibility tip

Twin-blade main rotor

Anti-torque tail rotor

Tail rotor hub

Anti-collision beacon

Triangular-section, unskinned rear fuselage

Elevator upper control wire

Synchronized elevator

Tail rotor gearbox

Tubular tail rotor guard

G-BGID

Elevator lower control wire

Tail rotor pitch control wire

Small fixed fin

Main rotor blade

Droop stop

Main rotor hub

Allison 250-C20J turboshaft engine

Anti-collision beacon

Blade-root attachment

Jet pipe

Main rotor mast

Horizontal stabilizer

Upper fin

VHF antenna

Anti-torque tail rotor

Air temperature probe

Lower fin

Forward-hinged door

Flush-riveted aluminum fuselage

Tail boom

Transponder antenna

Boarding step

Baggage compartment door

BELL 206 JETRANGER

Landing skid

Rear cross-tube

423

Light aircraft

Port wingtip

LIGHT AIRCRAFT, SUCH AS THE ARV SUPER 2 shown here, are small, lightweight, and of simple construction. More than a million have been built since World War I, mainly for recreational use by private owners. Virtually all light aircraft have piston engines, most of which are air-cooled, although some are liquid-cooled. Open cockpits, almost universal in the 1920s, have now been replaced by enclosed cabins. The cabins of high-wing aircraft have one or two doors, while those of low-wing aircraft usually have a sliding or hinged canopy. Most modern light aircraft are made of aluminum alloy, although some are made of wood or of fiber-reinforced materials. Light aircraft today also usually have navigational instruments, an electrical system, cabin heating, wheel brakes, and a two-way radio.

Aileron mass balance

Aileron torque tube

Port aileron

PORT MAIN LANDING GEAR

Inner tube

Tire

Hub

Brake disk

Stub axle

Landing gear leg

Brake mount

Brake pipe

Hydraulic brake caliper

Dorsal fin

Rear fuselage top skin

Elevator

TAIL PLANE AND RUDDER

Rudder tip fairing

Rudder mass balance

Fin tip fairing

Rudder

Fin

Elevator trim tab

Drive pillar

Attachment plate

Coolant outlet

Aluminum radiator

Air scoop

Coolant intake

Tail plane

Rear fuselage bottom skin

REAR FUSELAGE

Longeron

Frame

Battery box

Diaphragm

Side skin

"Skin-grip" pin

Rear attachment-bracket for wing

CONTROL RODS AND CABLES

Elevator push-rod

Elevator push-rod

Flap torque tube

Aileron rod

Rocking elevator arm

Navigational antenna

Aileron torque tube

Rudder cable

Flap drive-rod

Flap drive-rod

SIDE VIEW OF ARV SUPER 2

Spinner

Canopy

Wing

Communications antenna

Fin

Dorsal fin

Rudder

Engine cowling

G-BNHB

Elevator

Nose gear

Radiator

Tail plane

Step

Wing strut

Tailskid

Venturi for instruments

Main landing gear

Aircraft registration code

STARBOARD MAIN LANDING GEAR

Brake caliper

Brake mount

Brake pipe

Landing gear leg

Brake disk

Inner tube

Stub axle

Tire

Hub

PORT WING

Port top-wing fairing

SEAT ASSEMBLY

Seat cushion

CANOPY

Direct-vision panel

Pressurized strut

Hinge

Port underwing fairing

Headrest

Backrest

Seatbelt

Quick-release mechanism

Seatbelt length adjuster

Leading-edge fairing

Canopy latch

Wing strut

Port flap

Pitot head

Airspeed-indicator tube

Molded plastic

Outside air-temperature gauge

Bolted anchor

COCKPIT

Fiberglass canopy frame

Fuel tank top skin

Rudder pedal

Cockpit coaming

THREE-CYLINDER ENGINE

Port engine cowling

PROPELLER

Forward attachment bracket for wing

Control-column aperture

Semi-bulkhead

Engine mount

Air intake box

Water outlet

Carburetor

Backplate

Spinner

Fiberglass fuel tank

Bulkhead

Seatbelt attachment bracket

"Skin-grip" pin

Nose leg upper mount

Firewall

Cylinder head

Exhaust manifold

Gearbox

Fuel hose

Propeller drive flange

Flanged plate

CONTROL COLUMN AND FLAP LEVER

Torque tube assembly

Throttle lever

Brake lever

Starboard engine cowling

INSTRUMENT PANEL

Flight instruments

Engine instruments

Elevator arm

Control column

Flap lever

Elevator trim tab lever

NOSE GEAR

Steering stop

Elevator push-rod

Flap lever detent box

Release button

Carburetor hot air lever

Glove compartment

Nose leg down tube

Rubber bungee shock absorber

Bearing assembly

Pilot's handgrip

Radio plugs

Damper unit

Hoop

STARBOARD WING

Pivoted fork

Axle bolt

Nose wheel

Wing strut

Starboard underwing fairing

Starboard top-wing fairing

Gliders, hang gliders, and ultralights

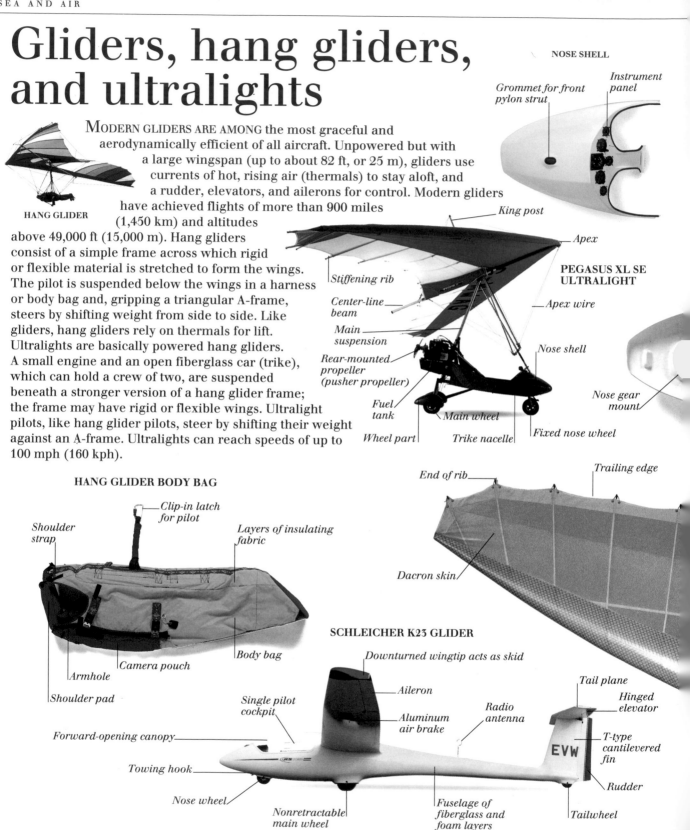

HANG GLIDER

MODERN GLIDERS ARE AMONG the most graceful and aerodynamically efficient of all aircraft. Unpowered but with a large wingspan (up to about 82 ft, or 25 m), gliders use currents of hot, rising air (thermals) to stay aloft, and a rudder, elevators, and ailerons for control. Modern gliders have achieved flights of more than 900 miles (1,450 km) and altitudes above 49,000 ft (15,000 m). Hang gliders consist of a simple frame across which rigid or flexible material is stretched to form the wings. The pilot is suspended below the wings in a harness or body bag and, gripping a triangular A-frame, steers by shifting weight from side to side. Like gliders, hang gliders rely on thermals for lift. Ultralights are basically powered hang gliders. A small engine and an open fiberglass car (trike), which can hold a crew of two, are suspended beneath a stronger version of a hang glider frame; the frame may have rigid or flexible wings. Ultralight pilots, like hang glider pilots, steer by shifting their weight against an A-frame. Ultralights can reach speeds of up to 100 mph (160 kph).

NOSE SHELL

Grommet for front pylon strut

Instrument panel

King post

Apex

PEGASUS XL SE ULTRALIGHT

Apex wire

Stiffening rib

Center-line beam

Main suspension

Rear-mounted propeller (pusher propeller)

Nose shell

Fuel tank

Main wheel

Wheel part

Trike nacelle

Fixed nose wheel

Nose gear mount

HANG GLIDER BODY BAG

Clip-in latch for pilot

Shoulder strap

Layers of insulating fabric

Armhole

Camera pouch

Body bag

Shoulder pad

End of rib

Trailing edge

Dacron skin

SCHLEICHER K23 GLIDER

Downturned wingtip acts as skid

Single pilot cockpit

Aileron

Radio antenna

Tail plane

Hinged elevator

Aluminum air brake

Forward-opening canopy

T-type cantilevered fin

EVW

Towing hook

Rudder

Nose wheel

Nonretractable main wheel

Fuselage of fiberglass and foam layers

Tailwheel

SOLAR WINGS PEGASUS QUASAR ULTRALIGHT

Foot throttle

Passenger's steering bar and footrest

Seat belt

Fuel tank filler nozzle

Wheel part

Pilot's steering bar

Engine mount

Pylon fairing

Aircraft name

Air outlet

Rear engine cowling

Pylon strut

Footbrake

Pylon-strut strap

Main wing strut

Pilot's seat

Hand throttle

Passenger's seat

TRIKE UNIT

TWIN-CYLINDER ENGINE

Leading edge

Trailing edge

Propeller-drive gearbox

Sealed lid

Twin carburetors

Air filter

Dual ignition plugs

Air-cooling fan

Exhaust connection

Engine rear mount

Metal hub

Waterproof stowage box

TRIKE NACELLE

EXHAUST PIPE

PROPELLER

WINGFRAME

After muffler

Main exhaust muffler

Eyelet tensioning trailing edge to rib

Bracing cable

Center-line beam

King post

Rib

Single spar

Leading edge

Semirigid fiberglass skin

Lift bracing wire

427

THE VISUAL ARTS

Drawing

DRAWINGS CAN BE FINISHED WORKS OF ART, or preparatory studies for paintings and other visual arts. They can be made using a wide variety of drawing instruments such as pencils, graphite sticks, chalks, charcoal, pens and inks, and silver wires. The most common drawing instrument is the graphite pencil. A graphite pencil consists of a thin rod of graphite mixed with clay, encased in wood. Charcoal is one of the oldest drawing instruments. It is produced by firing twigs of willow, vine, or other woods at high temperatures in airtight containers. Erasers can be used to rub out marks made by drawing materials such as graphite pencils or charcoal, or to achieve a particular effect—such as smudging. Fixative is often applied—using a mouth diffuser or aerosol spray fixative—to prevent smudging once a drawing is finished. Silver lines can be produced by drawing silver wire across specially prepared paper— a technique known as silverpoint. The lines are permanent and cannot be erased. In time the silver lines oxidize and turn brown.

FIXATIVE AND MOUTH DIFFUSER

Hinge

Liquid fixative consisting of dissolved resin

Fixative is sucked into tube and sprayed onto drawing

CHALK, CRAYON, AND CHARCOAL

Calcite (calcium carbonate) mixed with pigment

BLUE CHALK

Iron oxide mixed with chalk

SANGUINE CRAYON

Carbonized wood

WILLOW CHARCOAL

ERASERS

Hard texture

PLASTIC ERASER

Soft texture

KNEADED ERASER

DRAWING INSTRUMENTS

Medium-soft, light line

2B GRAPHITE PENCIL

Very soft, dark line

8B GRAPHITE PENCIL

SILVER WIRE IN A METAL HOLDER

DRAWING BOARD

DRAWING MATERIALS

Graphite stick

Binder clip

Colored pencil

Dip pen

Drawing board

Paper

Drawing clip

Pencil sharpener

Sketch book

Ink bottle

Silver lines
oxidize to a
light brown
color

Vanishing
point located
on head of
man riding
rearing horse

Figures drawn
in ink on top
of lines

Lines of
squared
pavement slabs
recede toward
a single
vanishing
point

Line drawn
in silverpoint
using a ruler

Complex perspective
drawing done as a
preparatory study
for a painting

Paper prepared
with size (glue)
and pigment

EXAMPLE OF A SILVERPOINT DRAWING
The Adoration of the Magi, Leonardo da Vinci, 1481
Pen and ink over silverpoint on paper
6½ x 11½ in (16.5 x 29.2 cm)

Handmade, tinted
paper

One of a series
of drawings
recording
London during
1944–1945

Charcoal lines
softened by
rubbing and
smudging

Broad charcoal
mark

Lines rapidly
drawn on site

Charcoal
gives strong,
expressive lines

EXAMPLE OF A CHARCOAL DRAWING
St. Paul's and the River, David Bomberg, 1945
Charcoal on paper
20 x 25⅛ in (50.8 x 65.8 cm)

431

Tempera

THE TERM TEMPERA is applied to any paint
in which pigment is tempered (mixed) with
a water-based binding medium—usually
egg yolk. Egg tempera is applied to a
smooth surface such as vellum (for
illuminated manuscripts) or more
commonly to hardwood panels prepared
with gesso—a mixture of chalk and size
(glue). Bristle brushes are used to apply the gesso.
A layer of gesso grosso (coarse gesso) is followed by
successive layers of gesso sotile (fine gesso) that are
sanded between coats to provide a smooth, yet absorbent
ground. The paint is applied with fine sable brushes in
thin layers, using light brushstrokes. Tempera dries
quickly to form a tough skin with a satin sheen. The
luminous white surface of the gesso combined with
the overlaid paint produces the brilliant crispness
and rich colors particular to this medium. Egg
tempera paintings are frequently gilded
with gold. Leaves of finely beaten gold are
applied to a bole (reddish-brown clay) base
and polished by burnishing.

MATERIALS FOR GILDING

Parchment for
protecting gold
leaf from drafts

Brush

Bowl
containing
diluted bole

Gold leaf

Gilder's knife

Gilder's tip
for picking
up gold leaf

Gilder's cushion

Gold leaf smoothed and
polished with a burnisher

Surface
prepared
with gesso

Gold leaf applied in
overlapping layers

Bole brushed
onto gesso

Burnisher

Agate tip

MATERIALS FOR TEMPERA PANEL PAINTING

Yolk

EGG

White

SIZE (GLUE)

GESSO

Lip

Mortar

MORTAR AND
PESTLE

Pestle for
crushing
and
grinding
pigments

EGG YOLK BINDING MEDIUM

EXAMPLES OF BRUSHES

FLAT
BRISTLE
BRUSH

SABLE
BRUSH
NO. 6

SABLE
BRUSH
NO. 1

EXAMPLE OF A TEMPERA PAINTING
Presentation in the Temple, Ambrogio Lorenzetti, 1342
Tempera on wood, 8 ft 5⅛ in x 5 ft 6⅛ in (257 x 168 cm)

PIGMENTS FOR
FLESH-COLOR
PAINTING

Altarpiece
commissioned for
Siena Cathedral, Italy

Textured gold ornament made
by punching motifs into the
gilded surface

The red tinge of
the bole is just
visible beneath
the gold

Edge of a sheet
of gold leaf

VERDACCIO

Crisp edge
characteristic of
tempera painting

Vine black used
to create the
dim cathedral
interior

VERMILION AND
LEAD WHITE

Highlights on
the beard made
by applying thin
layers of white
over dried paint

Red drapery
painted in
vermilion

Raised right hand
and pointing finger
is the gesture of
prophecy

VERMILION

Receding floor
tiles create the
impression of
depth

Patch of discolored
varnish, left from
last cleaning

RED EARTH
(IRON OXIDE)

EXAMPLES OF PIGMENTS

Warm flesh
tones achieved
by layering
vermilion and
white over an
undercoat of
verdaccio

Patterned gold
halo glitters in
candlelight

MALACHITE

ULTRAMARINE
LAPIS LAZULI

Ultramarine
lapis lazuli, as
costly as gold,
was reserved for
significant
figures such as
the Virgin Mary

Craquelure
(pattern of
cracks in
the paint)

VINE BLACK

LEAD TIN YELLOW

**DETAIL FROM "PRESENTATION
IN THE TEMPLE"**

Fresco

FRESCO IS A METHOD OF WALL PAINTING. In buon fresco (true fresco), pigments are mixed with water and applied to an intonaco (layer of fresh, damp lime-plaster). The intonaco absorbs and binds the pigments as it dries making the picture a permanent part of the wall surface. The intonaco is applied in sections called giornate (daily sections). The size of each giornata depends on the artist's estimate of how much can be painted before the plaster sets. The junctions between giornate are sometimes visible on a finished fresco. The range of colors used in buon fresco are limited to lime-resistant pigments such as earth colors (below). Slaked lime (burnt lime mixed with water), bianco di San Giovanni (slaked lime that has been partly exposed to air), and chalk can be used to produce fresco whites. In fresco secco (dry fresco), pigments are mixed with a binding medium and applied to dry plaster. The pigments are not completely absorbed into the plaster and may flake off over time.

CROSS-SECTION SHOWING FRESCO LAYERS

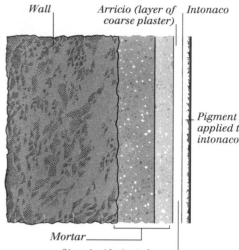

Wall

Arricio (layer of coarse plaster)

Intonaco

Pigment applied to intonaco

Mortar

Sinopia (design) drawn on surface of arricio

EXAMPLES OF EARTH COLOR PIGMENTS

RAW UMBER

RED EARTH (IRON OXIDE)

GREEN EARTH

RAW SIENNA

EXAMPLES OF FRESCO BRUSHES

Round bristle brush

Rust-resistant twine binding

Dome-shaped bristle brush

Pointed bristle brush

TONDO

MUCCINI

RIGA

INGREDIENTS FOR FRESCO WHITES

Marble slab for mixing ingredients

Bianco di San Giovanni

Slaked lime

Chalk

EXAMPLE OF A FRESCO
The Expulsion of the Merchants from the Temple, Giotto, c.1306
Fresco, 78 x 72 in (200 x 185 cm)

One of a series of frescoes in the Arena Chapel, Padua, Italy

Temple acts as a backdrop for the action

Bianco di San Giovanni often used for fresco whites

Patches of azurite blue have turned green due to reaction with carbon dioxide

Gold leaf applied to apostle's halo

Hairline junction between giornate is visible

Green earth pigment applied to robe

Red earth pigment applied in buon fresco has retained rich hue

Child painted on top of apostle's robe

Azurite blue applied in fresco secco has flaked off to reveal the plaster beneath

Dry, matt surface characteristic of buon fresco

Paint applied in buon fresco to child's face

Artist has to finish giornata before plaster dries

Junction between giornate

White dove represents the Holy Ghost

A fresco was generally worked in zones from the top down

Area with little detail can be painted quickly, allowing a larger giornata to be completed

Paint applied in fresco secco to child's body has flaked off

Sinopia (design) sketched in red earth

Highly detailed area takes a longer time to paint, restricting the size of the giornata

DETAIL FROM "THE EXPULSION"

GIORNATE (DAILY SECTIONS) IN "THE EXPULSION"

Oils

KIDNEY-SHAPED PALETTE

OIL PAINTS ARE MADE BY MIXING and grinding pigment with a drying vegetable oil such as linseed oil. The paint can be applied to many different surfaces and textures—the most common being canvas. Before painting, the canvas is stretched on a wooden frame and its surface is prepared with layers of size (glue) and primer. The two main types of brushes used in oil painting are stiff hog hair bristle brushes—generally used for covering large areas; and soft hair brushes made from sable or synthetic material—generally used for fine detail. Other tools, including painting knives, can also be used to achieve different effects. Oil paint can be applied thickly (a technique known as impasto), or can be thinned down using a solvent such as turpentine. Varnishes are sometimes applied to finished paintings to protect their surface and to give them a matt or gloss finish.

DAMMAR RESIN VARNISH

Crystals are dissolved and applied to painting to protect its surface

COMMERCIAL OIL PAINTS

CADMIUM RED

Lightfast opaque color

ULTRAMARINE

Transparent color

LINSEED OIL

Oil derived from seeds of flax plant

EXAMPLES OF PIGMENTS

CADMIUM RED

CERULEAN BLUE

DOUBLE DIPPER (PALETTE ATTACHMENT)

Screw-top lid

Container for storing solvent or drying oil

EXAMPLES OF BRUSHES

SYNTHETIC BRUSH

SABLE BRUSH

BRISTLE BRUSHES

Filbert bristle brush

Flat bristle brush

Flat bristle brush

Filbert bristle brush

Round bristle brush

Long, wooden handle

Protective, plastic case

EQUIPMENT FOR MAKING OIL PAINT

Airtight jar for storing paint

Palette knife for mixing drying oil and pigment

Glass muller for grinding drying oil and pigment

Glass slab with abrasive surface

PAINTING KNIVES

TROWEL-SHAPED PAINTING KNIFE

DIAMOND-SHAPED PAINTING KNIFE

Blade

Blade

Cranked, steel shank

Cranked, steel shank

EXAMPLE OF AN OIL PAINTING
Fritillarias, Vincent van Gogh, 1886
Oil on canvas, 29 x 24 in (73.5 x 60.5 cm)

Artist's signature scratched in wet paint with the end of the brush

Background enlivened by dabs of white and green

Each leaf painted in a single, rapid stroke

Orange and blue (complementary colors) placed together to give maximum contrast and enhance one another to appear brighter

Impasto (deep ridges of paint applied in thick strokes)

Strong directional brushstrokes on table draw attention to the vase

Features of vase highlighted by generous touches of yellow

STUDIO EASEL

Top sliding-block adjusts to canvas height

Canvas support

Height adjustment key

Angle adjustment key

Tripod

CANVAS STRETCHED ON WOODEN FRAME (VIEWED FROM THE BACK)

Staple

Canvas prepared with glue (size) and primer

Wooden frame

Unprimed canvas

EXAMPLES OF CANVASES

COTTON DUCK

FINE LINEN

COARSE LINEN

Watercolor

WATERCOLOR PAINT IS MADE OF GROUND PIGMENT mixed with a water-soluble binding medium, usually gum arabic. It is usually applied to paper using soft hair brushes such as sable, goat hair, squirrel, and synthetic brushes. Watercolors are often diluted and applied as overlaying washes (thin, transparent layers) to build up depth of color. Washes can be laid in a variety of ways to create a range of different effects. For example, a wet-in-wet wash can be achieved by laying a wash on top of another wet wash. The two washes blend together to give a fused effect. Sponges are used to modify washes by soaking up paint so that areas of pigment are lightened or removed from the paper. Watercolors can also be applied undiluted—a technique known as dry brush—to create a broken-color effect. Watercolors are generally transparent and allow light to reflect from the surface of the paper through the layers of paint to give a luminous effect. They can be thickened and made opaque by adding body color (Chinese white).

GUM ARABIC

Natural sap from acacia tree

NATURAL SPONGE

ANATOMY OF A SABLE BRUSH

Soft red sable hair

Toe (tip)

Wooden handle

SOFT HAIR BRUSHES

ROUND SABLE BRUSH (NO. 6)

ROUND SABLE BRUSH (NO. 1)

Hair trimmed and cemented into ferrule

Round ferrule

Hair tied with clove hitch knot

SYNTHETIC WASH BRUSH

TUBES OF WATERCOLOR PAINT

WINSOR GREEN

SQUIRREL MOP WASH BRUSH

CADMIUM YELLOW

PORTABLE BOX OF WATERCOLOR PAINTS

Painted color swatch

Chinese white

Pan of watercolor paint

Lid can be used for mixing colors

LARGE GOAT HAKE WASH BRUSH

EXAMPLE OF A WATERCOLOR
Burning of the Houses of Parliament, Turner, 1834
Watercolor on paper, 11½ x 17½ in (29.2 x 44.5 cm)

Transparent washes laid on top of each other to create tonal depth

Transparent washes allow light to reflect off the surface of the paper to give a luminous effect

Highlight scratched out with a scalpel

Paper shows through thin wash to give flames added highlight

Crowd painted with thin strokes laid over a pale wash

Undiluted paint applied, then partly washed out, to create the impression of water

EXAMPLES OF WATERCOLOR PAPERS

SMOOTH-TEXTURED PAPER

EXAMPLES OF WASHES

WASH OVER DRY BRUSH
Wash laid over paint applied with dry brush gives two-tone effect

GRADED WASH
Strong wash applied to tilted paper gives graded effect

DRY BRUSH
Undiluted paint dragged across surface of paper gives broken effect

MEDIUM-TEXTURED PAPER

WET-IN-WET
Two diluted washes left to run together to give fused effect

COLOR WHEEL OF WATERCOLOR PAINTS

ROUGH-TEXTURED PAPER

Yellow (primary color)

Secondary colors made by mixing yellow and blue

Secondary colors made by mixing red and yellow

Blue (primary color)

Red (primary color)

Secondary colors made by mixing blue and red

Pastels

PASTELS ARE STICKS OF PIGMENT made by mixing ground pigment with chalk and a binding medium, such as gum arabic. They vary in hardness depending on the proportion of the binding medium to the chalk. Soft pastel—the most common form of pastel—contains just enough binding medium to hold the pigment in stick form. Pastels can be applied directly to any support (surface) with sufficient tooth (texture). When a pastel is drawn over a textured surface, the pigment crumbles and lodges in the fibers of the support. Pastel marks have a particular soft, matt quality and are suitable for techniques such as blending, scumbling, and feathering. Blending is a technique of rubbing and fusing two or more colors on the support using fingers or various tools such as tortillons (paper stumps), soft hair brushes, kneaded erasers, and soft bread. Scumbling is a technique of building up layers of pastel colors. The side or blunted tip of a soft pastel is lightly drawn over an underpainted area so that patches of the color beneath show through. Feathering is a technique of applying parallel strokes of color with the point of a pastel, usually over an existing layer of pastel color. A thin spray of fixative can be applied— using a mouth diffuser (see pp. 430-431) or aerosol spray fixative—to a finished pastel painting, or in between layers of color, to prevent smudging.

EQUIPMENT FOR MAKING PASTELS

Glass muller

Chalk

Glass slab with abrasive surface *Gum arabic* *Ivory-black pigment* *Cobalt-blue pigment*

EXAMPLES OF SOFT PASTELS

COBALT-BLUE HALF PASTEL

VERMILION HALF PASTEL

OLIVE-GREEN FULL PASTEL

MAUVE FULL PASTEL

BOXED PASTEL SET

EQUIPMENT USED WITH PASTELS

Boxed set containing a mixture of portrait and landscape colors

Foam compartments protect the pastels

Soft pastel

Wooden tray

AEROSOL SPRAY FIXATIVE

KNEADED ERASER

SOFT HAIR BRUSH

BREAD

Soft bread suitable for erasing and blending

TORTILLONS (PAPER STUMPS)

Soft point used for blending

Tight roll of paper

EXAMPLE OF A PASTEL PAINTING
Woman Drying her Neck, Edgar Degas, c.1898
Pastel on cardboard, 24½ x 25½ in (62.5 x 65.5 cm)

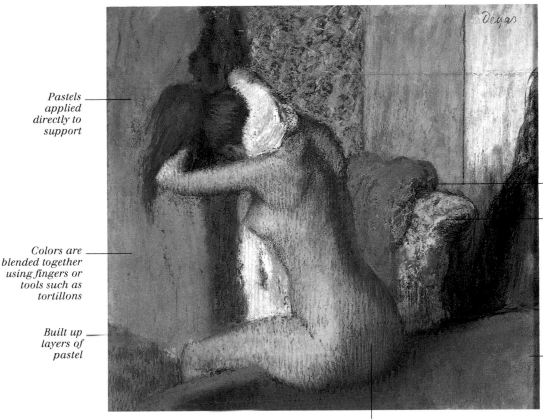

Pastels applied directly to support

Rich color of fabric created by overlaying yellows and oranges

Broken colors, characteristic of scumbling technique

Colors are blended together using fingers or tools such as tortillons

Built up layers of pastel

Toned color of paper visible beneath thinly applied pastels

Pure bright colors laid side by side produce strong contrasts

DETAIL FROM "WOMAN DRYING HER NECK"

Feathering technique used to produce skin tones

EXAMPLES OF TEXTURED PAPERS AND PASTEL BOARDS

WATERCOLOR PAPER (ROUGH TEXTURE)

GLASS PAPER

WATERCOLOR PAPER (MEDIUM TEXTURE)

INGRES PAPER

FLOCKED PASTEL BOARD

CANSON PAPER

EXAMPLES OF COLORED AND TINTED PAPERS

Printmaking 2

EXAMPLE OF A LITHOGRAPHIC STONE AND PRINT
Crown Gateway 2, Mandy Bonnell, 1987
Lithograph, 19½ x 15¾in (50 x 40 cm)

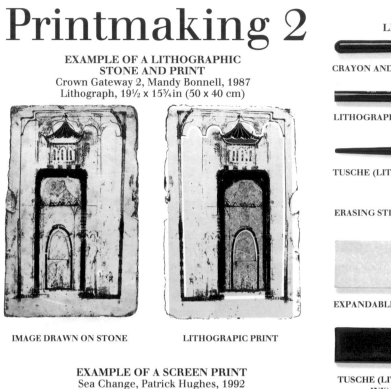

IMAGE DRAWN ON STONE   LITHOGRAPIC PRINT

EXAMPLE OF A SCREEN PRINT
Sea Change, Patrick Hughes, 1992
Screen print, 30 x 37 in (77 x 94.5 cm)

SCREEN AND SQUEEGEE

Squeegee

Rubber blade

Mesh

Wooden frame

EQUIPMENT USED IN LITHOGRAPHIC PRINTING

CRAYON AND HOLDER

LITHOGRAPHIC PENCIL

TUSCHE (LITHOGRAPHIC INK) PEN

ERASING STICK

EXPANDABLE SPONGE

TUSCHE (LITHOGRAPHIC INK) STICK

RUBBING INK

INK ROLLER

MILD ACIDIC SOLUTION   GUM ARABIC SOLUTION

WATER-BASED SCREEN PRINTING INKS

BLUE ACRYLIC INK   RED ACRYLIC INK   BROWN TEXTILE INK

EQUIPMENT USED IN RELIEF PRINTING

V-SHAPED GOUGE

INK ROLLER

Rubber roller

LINOLEUM AND WOODCUT BLOCK

U-SHAPED GOUGE

GRAVER

Linoleum

KNIFE

SCORPER

Side-grain wood block

WOOD ENGRAVING

END-GRAIN WOOD BLOCK

INKED-UP ENGRAVED BLOCK

WOOD ENGRAVING PRINT

RELIEF-PRINTING PRESS

Tympan lowered onto printing block

Printed image

Printing block

Bed is rolled under platen

Drum handle

Counterweight

Rail

Drum (rounce)

Pillar (post)

Foot

Spiral spring

Crown

Piston

Bar (pressure handle)

Staple (frame)

Platen

Leg

Mosaic

MOSAIC IS THE ART OF MAKING patterns and pictures from tesserae (small, colored pieces of glass, marble, and other materials). Different materials are cut into tesserae using different tools. Smalti (glass enamel) and marble are cut into pieces using a hammer and a hardy (a pointed blade) embedded in a log. Vitreous glass is cut into pieces using a pair of pliers. Mosaics can be made using a direct or indirect method. In the direct method, the tesserae are laid directly into a bed of cement–based adhesive. In the indirect method, the design is drawn in reverse on paper or cloth. The tesserae are then stuck face down on the paper or cloth using water-soluble glue. Adhesive is spread with a trowel onto a solid surface—such as a wall—and the back of the mosaic is laid into the adhesive. Finally, the paper or cloth is soaked off to reveal the mosaic. Gaps between tesserae can be filled with grout. Grout is forced into gaps by dragging a grouting squeegee across the face of the mosaic. Mosaics are usually used to decorate walls and floors, but they can also be applied to smaller objects.

EXAMPLE OF A MOSAIC (DIRECT METHOD)
Seascape, Tessa Hunkin, 1993
Smalti mosaic on board
31½ in (80 cm) diameter

EQUIPMENT FOR BREAKING MARBLE

Strip of marble, ready for breaking into cubes

Mosaic hammer

PLIERS

Hardwearing, tungsten carbide tip

Alicante (red marble) pieces

Hardy (pointed blade) embedded in a log

SMALTI (GLASS ENAMEL)

RED SMALTI

Handle with rubber grip

MOSAIC TOOLS

CEMENT-BASED ADHESIVE

GROUT

YELLOW SMALTI

BLUE SMALTI

Gold-leaf smalti

TROWEL

Notch

Wooden handle

Steel blade

Wooden handle

GROUTING SQUEEGEE

Wooden handle

Rubber blade

Nicobond

STAGES IN THE CREATION OF A MOSAIC (INDIRECT METHOD)

MOSAIC POT

Geometric design

Grout

COLOR SKETCH
A color sketch is drawn
in oil pastel to give a clear
impression of how the finished
mosaic will look.

REVERSE IMAGE
Tesserae are glued face down
on reverse image on paper.
Mosaic is then attached to solid
surface and paper is removed.

MOSAIC MOSQUE DESIGN

Floral design

Geometric border

*Andamenti
(line along
which tesserae
are laid)*

*Grout fills
the gaps
between the
tesserae*

*Mosaic
mounted
on board*

*Vitreous
glass cut into
triangular
shape with
pliers*

*Gold tessera
with ripple
finish*

*Gold tessera
placed upside-
down*

VITREOUS GLASS

**GREEN VITREOUS
GLASS WITH GOLD LEAF**

*Plain
finish*

*Ripple
finish*

**RED VITREOUS
GLASS**

**BLUE VITREOUS
GLASS**

SHEETS OF VITREOUS GLASS

FINISHED MOSAIC
Goldfish, Tessa Hunkin, 1993
Vitreous glass mosaic on board
14 x 10 in (35.5 x 25.5 cm)

*Border of square
vitreous glass*

Sculpture 1

THE TWO TRADITIONAL SCULPTURE METHODS are carving and modeling. A carved sculpture is made by cutting away the surplus from a block of hard material such as stone, marble, or wood. The tools used for carving vary according to the material being carved. Heavy steel points, claws, and chisels that are struck with a lump hammer are generally used for stone and marble. Sharp gouges and chisels that are struck with a wooden mallet are used for wood. Sculptures formed from hard materials are generally finished by filing with rasps, rifflers, and other abrasive implements. Modeling is a process by which shapes are built up, using malleable materials such as clay, plaster, and wax. The material is cut with wire-ended tools and modeled with the fingers or a variety of hardwood and metal implements. For large or intricate modeled sculptures an armature (frame), made from metal or wood, is used to provide internal support. Sculptures formed in soft materials may harden naturally or can be made more durable by firing in a kiln. Modeled sculptures are often first designed in wax or another material to be cast later in a metal (see pp. 454-455) such as bronze. The development of many new materials in the 20th century has enabled sculptors to experiment with new techniques such as construction (joining preformed pieces of material such as machine components, mirrors, and furniture) and kinetic (mobile) sculpture.

EXAMPLES OF MARBLE-CARVING TOOLS

2½ lb (1.1 kg) iron head

Ash handle

LUMP HAMMER

WIDE MARBLE CLAW

NARROW MARBLE CLAW

POINT

FLAT CHISEL

BULLNOSE CHISEL

Surface for sharpening stone-carving tools

DIAMOND WHETSTONE

CALLIPERS

Curved leg

Gap measures distance between two points on a sculpture

Wing nut

EXAMPLES OF WOOD-CARVING TOOLS

CABINET RASP

STRAIGHT GOUGE

SALMON BEND GOUGE

CHISEL

Stone for sharpening wood-carving tools

Cedar box

ARKANSAS HONE-STONE

CARVING MALLET

EXAMPLES OF RIFFLERS (FOR STONE, MARBLE, AND WOOD)

12 IN (30 CM) RIFFLER

6 IN (15 CM) RIFFLER

Tiny holes along the hairline made with a point

Soft skin texture tooled with a fine-toothed marble claw

DETAIL OF SLAVE'S HEAD

EXAMPLE OF A CARVED WOOD SCULPTURE
Mary Magdalene, Donatello, 1454-1455
Poplar wood, height 6 ft 2 in (188 cm)

EXAMPLE OF A CARVED MARBLE SCULPTURE
The Rebel Slave, Michelangelo, 1513-1516
Marble, height 7ft (213 cm)

Hair worked with a narrow claw

Delicately modeled hand carved with a chisel

Hair highlighted with gold leaf

Translucent white marble, quarried at Carrara, Italy

Figure cut from single length of poplar

Deep ridges of hair cut with a gouge

Surface rubbed smooth with rifflers and pumice

Strut gives added support to long slender limb

Wood prepared with gesso (chalk and glue) and painted

Base scored with jagged parallel cuts made with point and lump hammer

Series of tiny punch holes, made with a fine point, outline the form

Foot carved in deep relief

Rough surface made by driving a point into the marble at an oblique angle

The dimensions of the marble block determine the size of the sculpture

DETAIL OF SLAVE'S FOOT

Sculpture 2

EXAMPLES OF MODELING TOOLS

WIRE-ENDED CUTTING TOOL

CURVED MOLDING TOOL

SPATULA-ENDED WAX MODELING TOOL

ROUNDED WAX MODELING TOOL

EXAMPLES OF BRONZE FINISHING TOOLS

HOOKED RIFFLER

POINTED RIFFLER

ALCOHOL BURNER (FOR HEATING WAX MODELING TOOLS)

Wick

Brass holder

Glass bowl

Denatured alcohol

STAGES IN THE LOST-WAX METHOD OF CASTING
Based on Mars, Giambologna, c.1546

Wax-covered wire armature

Wax riser (vertical, hollow rod)

Chaplet (iron nail)

Wax runner (horizontal, hollow rod)

Fire-resistant clay

ORIGINAL MODEL
An original, solid wax model is made and preserved so that numerous replicas can be cast.

HOLLOW WAX FIGURE IS CAST
A new, hollow wax model is cast from the original model. It is filled with a plaster core that is held in place with nails. Wax runners and risers are attached.

FIGURE IS BAKED IN CASTING MOLD
The model is encased in clay and baked. The wax melts away (through the channels made by the wax rods) and is replaced by molten bronze.

MODELING STAND AND ARMATURE

Aluminum wire figure

Fixed iron armature support

Marine ply modeling board

Screw-hole for fastening the iron to modeling board

Rotating table top

Aluminum table stand

Height adjustor

Tripod

EXAMPLE OF A CLAY MODEL
Madonna and Child, Henry Moore, 1943
Terracotta, height 7¼ in (18.4 cm)

Clay smoothed to create the effect of soft skin

Maquette (small sketch) modeled from a solid lump of clay

Terracotta clay, fires at 1,832°F to 1,922°F (1,000°C to 1,050°C)

Incision made with serrated tool

Model for a much larger bronze sculpture

Strips of clay, added to the model, give the effect of folded drapery

Roughly worked clay

Metal riser

Metal runner

Golden brown color of untreated bronze

Stump left by rod will be filed down

Dark brown patina

Hole left by nail will be plugged with bronze

STATUE IS STRIPPED OF CLAY
When the bronze has cooled, the clay mold is broken open to reveal the bronze statue with solid metal runners and risers.

STATUE IS FINISHED
The nails are pulled out and a large hole is made to remove the plaster core. When the metal rods have been sawn off, the sculpture is filed to refine the surface.

STATUE IS CLEANED
Finally the work is cleaned and polished. An artificial patina (coloring) is achieved by treating the surface with chemicals.

ARCHITECTURE

Ancient Egypt

THE CIVILIZATION OF THE ANCIENT EGYPTIANS (which lasted from about 3100 BC until it was finally absorbed into the Roman empire in 30 BC) is famous for its temples and tombs. Egyptian temples were often huge and geometric, like the Temple of Amon-Re (below and right). They were usually decorated with hieroglyphs (sacred characters used for picture writing) and painted reliefs depicting gods, Pharaohs (kings), and queens. Tombs were particularly important to the Egyptians, who believed that the dead were resurrected in the afterlife. The tombs were often decorated—for example, the surround of the false door opposite— in order to give comfort to the dead. The best-known ancient Egyptian tombs are the pyramids, which were designed to symbolize the rays of the sun. Many of the architectural forms used by the ancient Egyptians were later adopted by other civilizations. For example, columns and capitals were later used by the ancient Greeks (see pp. 460-461) and ancient Romans (see pp. 462-465).

Cornice decorated with cavetto molding

Campaniform (open papyrus) capital

Architrave

Papyrus-bud capital

Socle

Side aisle | Central nave | Side aisle

SIDE VIEW OF HYPOSTYLE HALL, TEMPLE OF AMON-RE, KARNAK, EGYPT, c.1290 BC

Horus, the sun-god

Architrave

Stone slab forming flat roof of side aisle

Kepresh crown with disc

Chons, the moon-god

Amon-Re, king of the gods

Hathor, the sky-goddess

Papyrus motif

Cartouche (oval border) containing the titles of the Pharaoh (king)

Socle

Aisle running north–south

LIMESTONE FALSE DOOR WITH HIEROGLYPHS, TOMB OF KING TJETJI, GIZA, EGYPT, c.2400 BC

Hieroglyph representing a house

Lintel

Disc representing sun or light

Eroded image of Tjetji

Limestone stela (slab)

Hoe-shaped hieroglyph representing "mr" sound

Head of false door

Image of Tjetji's wife

Image of Tjetji's daughter

PLANT CAPITAL OF THE PTOLEMAIC-ROMAN PERIOD, EGYPT, 332-30 BC

Palm leaf

Papyrus flower

Papyrus leaf

Papyrus stem

Lotus bud *Lotus stem*

Cornice decorated with cavetto molding

Bead molding

Trellis window

Rectangular pier decorated with hieroglyphs

Elevated roof of central nave

Clerestory

Disc representing sun or light

Architrave

Square abacus

Papyrus-bud capital

Papyriform column

Shaft

Scene depicting a Pharaoh (king) paying homage to the god Amon-Re

Central nave

ANCIENT EGYPTIAN BUILDING DECORATION

DECORATED WINDOW, MEDINET HABU, EGYPT, C.1198 BC

ROPE AND PATERAE DECORATION

CAPITAL WITH THE HEAD OF THE SKY-GODDESS HATHOR, TEMPLE OF ISIS, PHILAE, EGYPT, 283-47 BC

LOTUS AND PAPYRUS FRIEZE DECORATION

Ancient Greece

THE CLASSICAL TEMPLES OF ANCIENT GREECE were built according to the belief that certain forms and proportions were pleasing to the gods. There were three main ancient Greek architectural orders (styles), which can be distinguished by the decoration and proportions of their columns, capitals (column tops), and entablatures (structures resting on the capitals). The oldest is the Doric order, which dates from the seventh century BC and was used mainly on the Greek mainland and in the western colonies, such as Sicily and southern Italy. The Temple of Neptune, shown here, is a classic example of this order. It is hypaethral (roofless) and peripteral (surrounded by a single row of columns). About a century later, the more decorative Ionic order developed on the Aegean Islands. Features of this order include volutes (spiral scrolls) on capitals and acroteria (pediment ornaments). The Corinthian order was invented in Athens in the fifth century BC and is typically identified by an acanthus leaf on the capitals. This order was later widely used in ancient Roman architecture.

Abacus
Echinus
Annulet
Trachelion (neck)

DORIC CAPITAL, THE PROPYLAEUM (GATEWAY), THE ACROPOLIS, ATHENS, GREECE, 449 BC

Coussinet (cushion)
Abacus
Lesbian leaf pattern
Cyma reversa profile
Volute
Eye
Palmette
Echinus with egg and dart decoration

IONIC CAPITAL, THE PROPYLAEUM (GATEWAY), TEMPLE OF ATHENA POLIAS, PRIENE, GREECE, c.334 BC

Mask
Abacus
Volute
Cauliculus
Acanthus leaf
Bell-shaped core

CORINTHIAN CAPITAL FROM A STOA (PORTICO), PROBABLY FROM ASIA MINOR

TEMPLE OF NEPTUNE, PAESTUM, ITALY, c.460 BC

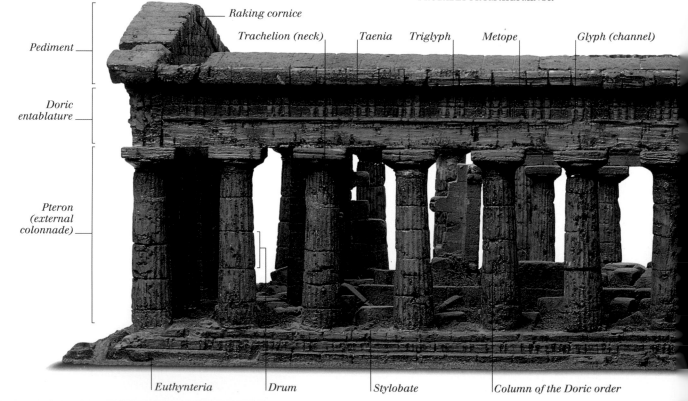

Pediment
Raking cornice
Trachelion (neck)
Taenia
Triglyph
Metope
Glyph (channel)
Doric entablature
Pteron (external colonnade)
Euthynteria
Drum
Stylobate
Column of the Doric order

PLAN OF THE TEMPLE OF NEPTUNE, PAESTUM

Pronaos (vestibule)

Naos wall

Anta (pilaster terminating naos wall)

Naos (cella)

Peristyle

Opisthodomos (rear portico)

Pteron (external colonnade)

Hexastyle pteron (colonnade of six columns)

ANCIENT GREEK BUILDING DECORATION

Volute

FACADE, TREASURY OF ATREUS, MYCENAE, GREECE, 1350-1250 BC

Meander

FRETWORK, PARTHENON, ATHENS, GREECE, 447-436 BC

ACROTERION, TEMPLE OF APHAIA, AEGINA, GREECE, 490 BC

Griffon (gryphon)

Raking cornice

ANTEFIXA, TEMPLE OF APHAIA, AEGINA, GREECE, 490 BC

Palmette

Volute

Regula (short fillet beneath taenia)   Eaves

Cornice

Frieze

Architrave

Capital

Shaft

Crepidoma (stepped base)

Entasis (slight curve of a column)   Intercolumniation   Fluting

Ancient Rome 1

IN THE EARLY PERIOD OF THE ROMAN EMPIRE extensive use was made of ancient Greek architectural ideas, particularly those of the Corinthian order (see pp. 460-461). As a result, many early Roman buildings—such as the Temple of Vesta (opposite)—closely resemble ancient Greek buildings. A distinctive Roman style began to evolve in the first century AD. This style developed the interiors of buildings (the Greeks had concentrated on the exterior) by wing arches, vaults, and domes inside the buildings and by ornamenting internal walls; many of these features can be seen in the Pantheon. Exterior columns were often used for decorative rather than structural purposes, as in the Colosseum and the Porta Nigra (see pp. 464-465). Smaller buildings had timber frames with wattle-and-daub walls, as in the mill (see pp. 464-465). Roman architecture remained influential for many centuries, with some of its principles being used in the 11th century in Romanesque buildings (see pp. 468-469) and also in the 15th and 16th centuries in Renaissance buildings (see pp. 474-477).

ANCIENT ROMAN BUILDING DECORATION

FESTOON, TEMPLE OF VESTA, TIVOLI, ITALY, C.80 BC

RICHLY DECORATED ROMAN OVUM

INTERIOR OF THE PANTHEON, ROME, ITALY, 118-c.128

Inner dome, following the curve of a depressed arch

Outer saucer dome

Entablature

Curved cornice

Lesene

Cornice

Triangular pediment

Concave niche

Marble veneer — *Segmental pediment* — *Pedestal*

Series of concentric, steplike rings

Oculus

Outer saucer dome

Dentil ornament

Intermediate block

Engaged pediment

Entablature with inscription

Raking cornice

Pediment

Rotunda

Octastyle portico (eight-column portico)

FRONT VIEW OF THE PANTHEON

SIDE VIEW OF THE PANTHEON

Entablature

Intermediate block

Upper cornice

Pitched roof

Eaves

Relieving arch

Opening for ventilation

Cornice

Colonnade

Ornamental band decorated with festoons

Attached fluted pilaster

TEMPLE OF VESTA, TIVOLI, ITALY, c.80 BC

Circular naos (cella) Architrave Ceiling Fascia
Corinthian entablature Corinthian capital
Pteron (colonnade) Naos (cella) window
Opus incertum (concrete wall faced with irregularly shaped stones)
Egg and dart decoration
Upper torus
Scotia
Jamb with corrugated surface Naos (cella) door Cornice Podium Lower torus
Threshold

FRIEZE, FORUM OF TRAJAN, ROME, ITALY, 98-113

KEYSTONE, ARCH OF TITUS, ROME, ITALY, 81

Oculus illuminating interior of rotunda
Coffer
Stepped side of coffer
Frieze decorated with arabesques, urns, and winged horses
Steplike ring
Barrel vault
Passageway
Coffer
Engaged pediment
Monolithic shaft (shaft made from a single stone)
Barrel vault
Raking cornice
Pediment
Entablature
Corinthian column
Corinthian capital

Entablature Aedicule (tabernacle) Festoon Fluting Corinthian pilaster Base
Rotunda Portico

463

Ancient Rome 2

SIDE VIEW OF A ROMAN MILL

Principal rafter
Lath
Pantile
Verge
Wall plate
Eaves
Wall post
Plain fascia
Top plate
Floorboard
Plaster coating
Intermediate floor joist
Sill
Stud
Foundation
Grille
Joist
Boarding

FRONT VIEW OF A ROMAN MILL, 1ST CENTURY BC

Half-round ridge tile
King strut
Lath
Pitched roof
Principal rafter
Ashlar post
Tie beam
Plain fascia
Wall plate
Flat soffit
Intermediate floor joist
Mill wheel
Top plate
Wall post
Sill
Binder
Wattle-and-daub with plaster coating
Supporting post
Floor joist
Foundation post

THE COLOSSEUM (FLAVIAN AMPHITHEATER), ROME, ITALY, 70–82

Bracket for velarium (awning)
Crowning cornice
Barrel vault
Horizontal gangway
Arcade
Third floor
Corinthian pilaster
Round arch
Second floor
Corinthian half-column
Entablature
Ionic half-column
First floor
Doric half-column
Ground floor
External travertine shell
Intermediate shell
Inner shell

PORTA NIGRA, TRIER, GERMANY, c.240-260

Crowning cornice

Impost

Semicircular tower

Parapet

Keystone

Arcaded passageway

Round-arched window

Lesene

Voussoir

Semicircular tower

Cornice

Entablature

Frieze

Relieving arch

Architrave

Arcading

Apse (added in Middle Ages)

Attached column

Courtyard

Round arch

Entrance to town

Capital

Shaft

Base

Facade

ROMAN WATTLE-AND-DAUB WALL, 1ST CENTURY BC

Opening to staircase

Maenianum summum) (gallery)

Hazel twig framework

Clay mixture

Rectangular window

String course

Paintwork

Plaster

Cuneus (wedge of seating)

Opus quadratum (square masonry)

Arched opening to staircase

Radiating, wedge-shaped chamber

Radial wall

Opus incertum (concrete wall faced with irregularly shaped stones)

Cornice

Ambulatory corridor

Attached rectangular pier

Keystone

Impost

Tuscan capital

Voussoir

Tuscan pilaster

465

Medieval castles and houses

WARFARE WAS COMMON IN EUROPE in the Middle Ages, and many monarchs and nobles built castles as a form of defense. Typical medieval castles have outer walls surrounding a moat. Inside the moat is a bailey (courtyard), protected by a chemise (jacket wall). The innermost and strongest part of a medieval castle is the keep. There are two main types of keep: towers called donjons, such as the Tour de César and Coucy-le-Château in France, and rectangular keeps ("hall-keeps"), such as the Tower of London. Castles were often guarded by salients (projecting fortifications), like those of the Bastille. Medieval houses typically had timber cruck (tent-like) frames, wattle-and-daub walls, and pitched roofs, like those on medieval London Bridge (opposite).

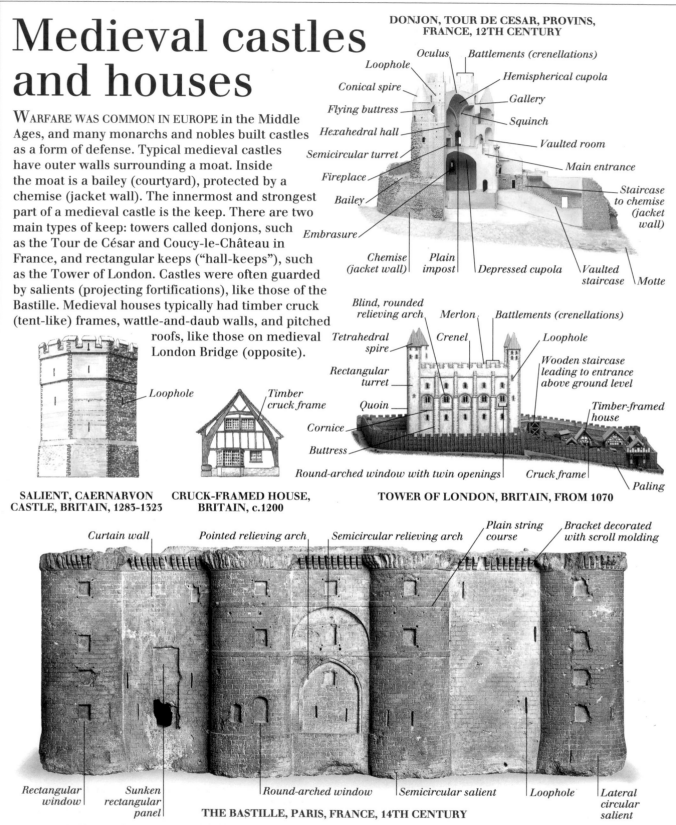

DONJON, TOUR DE CESAR, PROVINS, FRANCE, 12TH CENTURY

Oculus
Loophole
Conical spire
Flying buttress
Hexahedral hall
Semicircular turret
Fireplace
Bailey
Embrasure
Chemise (jacket wall)
Plain impost
Battlements (crenellations)
Hemispherical cupola
Gallery
Squinch
Vaulted room
Main entrance
Staircase to chemise (jacket wall)
Depressed cupola
Vaulted staircase
Motte

SALIENT, CAERNARVON CASTLE, BRITAIN, 1283-1323

Loophole

CRUCK-FRAMED HOUSE, BRITAIN, c.1200

Timber cruck frame

TOWER OF LONDON, BRITAIN, FROM 1070

Blind, rounded relieving arch
Tetrahedral spire
Rectangular turret
Quoin
Cornice
Buttress
Round-arched window with twin openings
Merlon
Crenel
Battlements (crenellations)
Loophole
Wooden staircase leading to entrance above ground level
Timber-framed house
Cruck frame
Paling

THE BASTILLE, PARIS, FRANCE, 14TH CENTURY

Curtain wall
Pointed relieving arch
Semicircular relieving arch
Plain string course
Bracket decorated with scroll molding
Rectangular window
Sunken rectangular panel
Round-arched window
Semicircular salient
Loophole
Lateral circular salient

**MEDIEVAL LONDON BRIDGE, BRITAIN, 1176 (WITH 14TH-CENTURY
BATTLEMENTED BUILDING, NONESUCH HOUSE, AND TWO-TOWERED GATE)**

Gate-house

Battlemented building

Chapel pier

Railing

Onion-shaped dome

Pitched roof

Shaped gable

Crypt of Becket Chapel

Starling

Two-towered gate

Oriel window

Timber framing with ornamental woodwork

Nonesuch House

Pier

Pointed Gothic stone arch

Timber framing

DONJON, COUCY-LE-CHATEAU, AISNE, FRANCE, 1225-1245

Cornice

Pointed arch

Loophole

Round arch

Parapet

Gallery

Passageway

Pointed arch

Inner hall

Tribune (elevated platform)

Springing point of rib vault

Dodecahedral second floor

Projecting rectangular pier

Engaged colonette

Window opening

Chimney shaft

Dodecahedral first floor

Rectangular opening

Fireplace

Embrasure

Archivolt decorated with torus and fascia

Bridge to castle entrance

Steps

Dodecahedral ground floor

Mezzanine (entresol) housing drawbridge windlass

Entrance

Moat

Passageway inside structure of outer wall

Four-centered relieving arch

Niche

Corbel with sculptural decoration

Capital

String course

Ruin of segmental ramp leading to chemise (jacket wall)

Medieval churches

ABBEY OF ST. FOI, CONQUES, FRANCE, c.1050–c.1130

LARGE NUMBERS OF CHURCHES were built in Europe in the Middle Ages. European churches of this period typically have high vaults supported by massive piers and columns. In the 10th century, the Romanesque style developed. Romanesque architects adopted many Roman or early Christian architectural ideas, such as cross-shaped ground plans—like that of Angoulême Cathedral (opposite)—and the basilican system of a nave with a central vessel and side aisles. In the mid-12th century, flying buttresses and pointed vaults appeared. These features later became widely used in Gothic architecture (see pp. 470–471). Bagneux Church (opposite) has both styles: a Romanesque tower and a Gothic nave and choir.

CHURCH ROOF BOSS, BRITAIN

ROMANESQUE CAPITALS

"THE FLIGHT INTO EGYPT" CAPITAL, CATHEDRAL OF ST. LAZARE, AUTUN, FRANCE, 1120–1130

"CHRIST IN MAJESTY" CAPITAL, BASILICA OF ST. MADELEINE, VEZELAY, FRANCE, 1120–1140

Finial

Incline

Circular staircase-turret

Loophole

Octahedral spire

Octahedral crossing tower

Round-arched window

Series of archivolts decorated with torus

Series of jambs decorated with colonettes

Pitched roof

Tribune (elevated platform)

Semicircular transverse arch

Vaulting shaft

Attached half-column

Round arcade arch

Romanesque capital

Arcade

Square central shaft

Twin opening of gallery bays

Compound pier

Barrel vault

Lean-to roof

Transept

Quadrant arch

Colonette

Round stilted arch

Attached half-column

Side aisle

Main vessel

Side aisle

GROUND PLAN OF ANGOULEME CATHEDRAL, FRANCE, FROM c.1105

Crossing

Transept chapel

Heavily molded transverse arch

Chevet (choir with round apse and chapels)

Transept

Engaged column

Dome

Buttress

Nave

Transverse arch with plain fascia

Nave bay

Clustered column

Vestibule

CHOIR, CHURCH OF ST. SERGE, ANGERS, FRANCE, c.1215-1220

Historiated boss

Longitudinal ridge rib

Loophole

Diagonal rib with torus molding

Cell

Gable

Domed rib-vault

Transverse arch

Lierne

Historiated keystone

Formeret

Round-arched window

Tas-de-charge

Cubic abacus

Polyhedral abacus

Attached colonette

Foliated capital

Embrasure

Rectangular apse

Cornice

Vaulting shaft

Rectangular side-chapel

Impost with foliated frieze

Arcade column

Bay of main vessel

Octahedral socle

BAGNEUX CHURCH, FRANCE, 1170-1190

Molded rib with an arris between two tori

Flying buttress

Cell

Polyhedral abacus

Transverse arch

Roof space

Oculus

Tower vault

Square-roofed pinnacle

Lean-to roof

Exterior wall

Triforium

Tower

Foliated capital

Pointed arch

Triple vaulting-shaft

Torus molding

Quadripartite vault

Colonette

Formeret

Tower-vault oculus

Attached compound pier

Recessed panel

Corbel

Round arch

Pier buttress

Impost

Embrasure

Pier supporting tower

Weathering

Side aisle

Attached half-column

Base

Square socle

Intrados of arch with flat band between two tori

Nave column

Compound pier

Arcade

Nave

Choir

Octahedral socle

Bay

Attached colonette

469

Gothic 2

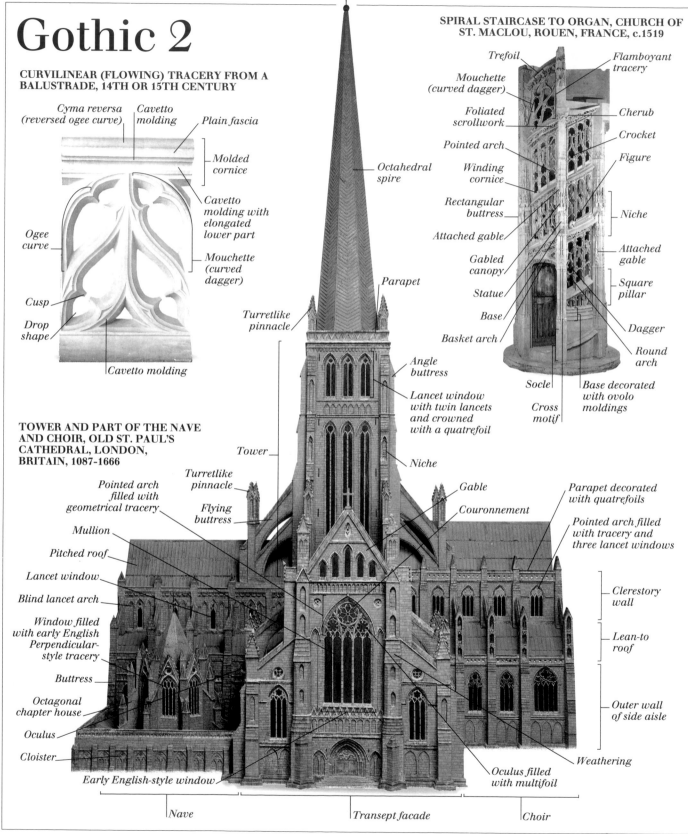

CURVILINEAR (FLOWING) TRACERY FROM A BALUSTRADE, 14TH OR 15TH CENTURY

Cyma reversa (reversed ogee curve)

Cavetto molding

Plain fascia

Molded cornice

Cavetto molding with elongated lower part

Mouchette (curved dagger)

Ogee curve

Cusp

Drop shape

Cavetto molding

SPIRAL STAIRCASE TO ORGAN, CHURCH OF ST. MACLOU, ROUEN, FRANCE, c.1519

Trefoil

Mouchette (curved dagger)

Foliated scrollwork

Pointed arch

Winding cornice

Rectangular buttress

Attached gable

Gabled canopy

Statue

Base

Basket arch

Flamboyant tracery

Cherub

Crocket

Figure

Niche

Attached gable

Square pillar

Dagger

Round arch

Socle

Cross motif

Base decorated with ovolo moldings

TOWER AND PART OF THE NAVE AND CHOIR, OLD ST. PAUL'S CATHEDRAL, LONDON, BRITAIN, 1087-1666

Octahedral spire

Parapet

Turretlike pinnacle

Angle buttress

Lancet window with twin lancets and crowned with a quatrefoil

Tower

Niche

Pointed arch filled with geometrical tracery

Turretlike pinnacle

Flying buttress

Mullion

Pitched roof

Lancet window

Blind lancet arch

Window filled with early English Perpendicular-style tracery

Buttress

Octagonal chapter house

Oculus

Cloister

Early English-style window

Gable

Couronnement

Parapet decorated with quatrefoils

Pointed arch filled with tracery and three lancet windows

Clerestory wall

Lean-to roof

Outer wall of side aisle

Weathering

Oculus filled with multifoil

Nave

Transept facade

Choir

**SPIRE AND TRANSEPT
ROOF, CATHEDRAL OF
NOTRE DAME DE PARIS,
FRANCE, c.1163-1250**

Ridge

Common
rafter

Architrave of
window zone,
also acting as
collar beam

Principal

Attached baluster

Attached column

Strut

Raised surface

Hammer-post

Beveled edge

Arched brace

Wooden panel

Hammer-beam

Gothic
window
tracery

Collar beam
decorated with
pearl motif

Gothic
window

Arched brace

Arched brace

Brace

Bracket

Impost

**TRUSS OF HAMMER-BEAM ROOF,
THE UPPER FRATER (LATER
BLACKFRIARS' PLAYHOUSE),
LONDON, BRITAIN, PROBABLY
14TH CENTURY**

TYPICAL GOTHIC FEATURES

**FLYING BUTTRESS OVER
SIDE AISLES, MILAN
CATHEDRAL, ITALY, C.1385-1485**

**GARGOYLE, HORSLEY CHURCH,
DERBYSHIRE, BRITAIN, C.1450**

**HAMMER-BEAM ROOF, CHURCH
OF ST. BOTOLPH, TRUNCH,
NORFOLK, BRITAIN, 1360-1380**

Rafter

Straight
brace

Beam

Gable

Round arch

Pinnacle

Oculus

Blind trefoil

Lancet
arch

Trefoil arch

Cusp

Quatrefoil

Colonette

Pointed
arch

Lesene

Lancet arch

Balustrade

Mullion

Triangular cornice

Cornice
with
chamfered
edge

Geometrical tracery

Trefoil arch

Stud

Balustrade

Scissor
brace

Upper collar

Ridge board

Principal
rafter

Common rafter

Octahedral
spire

Roof
truss of
nave
and
transept

Vertical strut

Intermediate collar

Raised
valley-rafter

Beam

Jack-rafter

Clasped purlin

Queen
post

Lower collar

King post

Scissor-beam

Tie beam

Passing brace

Renaissance 1

THE RENAISSANCE was a period in European history—lasting roughly from the 14th century to the mid-17th century—during which the arts and sciences underwent great changes. In architecture, these changes were marked by a return to the classical forms and proportions of ancient Roman buildings. The Renaissance originated in Italy, and the buildings most characteristic of its style can be found there, such as the Palazzo Strozzi shown here. Mannerism is a branch of the Renaissance style that distorts the classical forms; an example is the Laurentian Library staircase. As the Renaissance style spread to other European countries, many of its features were incorporated into the local architecture. For example, the Château de Montal in France (see pp. 476-477) incorporates aedicules (tabernacles).

FACADE ON TO PIAZZA, PALAZZO STROZZI

Crowning cornice

Arched window

Round arch

Light

Rustication

Arched doorway

Rectangular window

SIDE VIEW OF PALAZZO STROZZI, FLORENCE, ITALY, 1489 (BY G. DA SANGALLO, B. DA MAIANO, AND CRONACA)

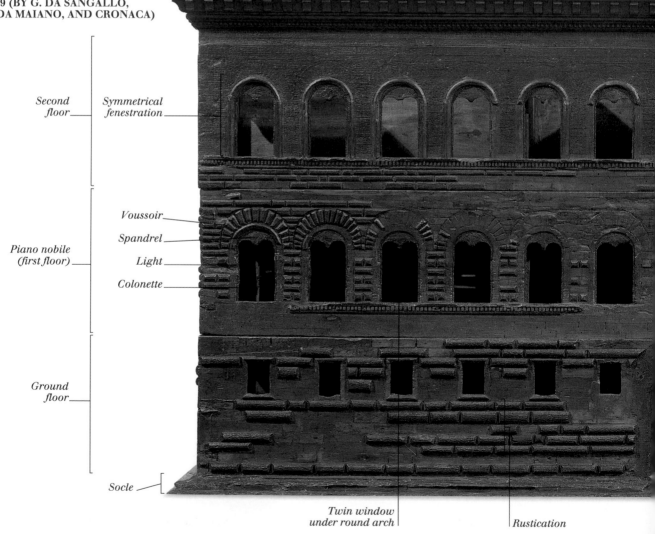

Second floor

Symmetrical fenestration

Piano nobile (first floor)

Voussoir

Spandrel

Light

Colonette

Ground floor

Socle

Twin window under round arch

Rustication

DETAILS FROM ITALIAN RENAISSANCE BUILDINGS

PANEL FROM DRUM OF DOME,
FLORENCE CATHEDRAL, 1420-1436

COFFERING IN DOME,
PAZZI CHAPEL,
FLORENCE, 1429-1461

STAIRCASE,
LAURENTIAN LIBRARY,
FLORENCE, 1559

PORTICO, VILLA ROTUNDA,
VICENZA, 1567-1569

Cymatium

Dentil ornament

Modillion (bracket)

Torus molding

Fillet

Crowning cornice

Corona

Cyma recta (ogee molding)

Round arch

Cornice

Torus molding

Diamond-shaped block

Rustication

Dentil ornament

Fillet

Rectangular window

Arched doorway

Cushion block

Splayed windowsill

Bowtell molding (roll molding)

Renaissance 2

DETAILS FROM EUROPEAN RENAISSANCE BUILDINGS

STONE WALL, QUOINS, AND SHELL DECORATION, CASA DE LAS CONCHAS, SALAMANCA, SPAIN, 1475–1483

SPIRAL-STAIRCASE TOWER, CHATEAU DE BLOIS, FRANCE, 1514–1530

CONICAL DOME, CHATEAU DE CHAMBORD, FRANCE, 1519–1547

PAIR OF CHIMNEY STACKS, PALAIS DE FONTAINEBLEAU, FRANCE, FROM 1528

Chimney stack

Ridge of half-round tiles

Pitched roof

Finial

Medallion

Pinnacle

Foliated volute with dolphin head

Gable

Head-shaped keystone

Dormer window

Frieze with shell-pattern decoration

Finial

Ionic capital with head-shaped decoration

Putto holding candelabrum

Blind pediment

Grotesque figure

Medallion with bust of Robert de Montal

Lesene decorated with paterae

Frieze decorated with sculptural wreaths, tendrils, and grotesque figures

Lesene

Pedestal

Dado

Plinth   Cornice   Architrave   Portal   Pilaster

Hipped roof

Conical spire of turret

Fish-scale tile

Belvedere

Keystone decorated with scroll ornament

Cornice decorated with fascias and an ogee molding

Rectangular window

Transom

Aedicule (tabernacle)

Double pilaster

Mullion

Shell

Concave arched niche

Small pier decorated with statuette in concave niche

Cornice

Frieze with scroll motif

Pseudo-Corinthian capital

NORTH WING STAIRCASE, CHATEAU DE MONTAL

Hipped roof

Conical spire

Turret

Eaves with oversailing fascias and fillets

Loophole

Cornice with fascias and ogee moldings

Rib vault

Column

Second-floor landing

Conical corbel

First-floor landing

Flight of stairs

Lesene

Pier supporting flight of stairs

Handrail

Pier supporting first-floor landing

Riser

Tread

CAMPANILE, CHURCH OF ST. EUSTACHE, PARIS, FRANCE, 1532-1640

Weather vane

Orb

Fish-scale tile

Hemispherical dome

Semicircular torus molding

Fillet

Weathering

Plain fascia

Ogee molding

Small architrave

Archivolt

Volute

Plain fascia

Emphasized keystone

Cavetto molding

Cincture

Capital

Zinc plating

Fillet

Square column

GLOBE THEATER, LONDON, BRITAIN, 1599

Hipped roof

Timber-framed hut housing windlass

Turret

Ornamental paneling

Pitched roof

Music gallery

Balustrade

Balcony stage

Stage cover

Light curtain

Ornamental paneling with concave brace decoration

Thatched roof

Door to dressing-rooms

Loft used as storage room

Box (gentlemen's room)

Window stage

Upper gallery (twopenny gallery)

Outer wall

Railing

Middle gallery

Post supporting bay window

Upper-gallery support

Stage-door

Standing room

Lower gallery

Bench

Round pillar (stage post)

Square, carved base

Study (inner stage) with traverse (crossing)

Platform stage

Paling

Low balustrade

Door to tiring house

Partition separating galleries from boxes

Baroque and neoclassical 1

THE BAROQUE STYLE EVOLVED IN THE EARLY 17TH CENTURY in Rome. It is characterized by curved outlines and ostentatious decoration, as can be seen in the Italian church details (right). The baroque style was particularly widely favored in Italy, Spain, and Germany. It was also adopted in Britain and France, but with adaptations. The British architects Sir Christopher Wren and Nicholas Hawksmoor, for example, used baroque features—such as the concave walls of St. Paul's Cathedral and the curved buttresses of the Church of St. George in the East (see pp. 480-481)—but they did so with restraint. Similarly, the curved buttresses and volutes of the Parisian Church of St. Paul-St. Louis are relatively plain. In the second half of the 17th century, a distinct classical style (known as neoclassicism) developed in northern Europe as a reaction to the excesses of baroque. Typical of this new style were churches such as the Madeleine (a proposed facade is shown below), as well as secular buildings such as the Cirque Napoleon (opposite) and the buildings of the British architect Sir John Soane (see pp. 482-483). In early 18th century France, an extremely lavish form of baroque developed, known as rococo. The balcony from Nantes (see pp. 482-483) with its twisted ironwork and head-shaped corbels is typical of this style.

SCROLLED BUTTRESS, CHURCH OF ST. MARIA DELLA SALUTE, VENICE, 1631-1682

STATUE OF THE ECSTASY OF ST. THERESA, CHURCH OF ST. MARIA DELLA VITTORIA, ROME, 1645-1652

PROPOSED FACADE, THE MADELEINE (NEOCLASSICAL), PARIS, FRANCE, 1764 (BY P. CONTANT D'IVRY)

CIRQUE NAPOLEON (NEOCLASSICAL), PARIS, FRANCE, 1852 (BY J.I. HITTORFF)

EXTERIOR

Rectangular panel

Small polyhedral roof

Attached colonette

Polyhedral iron roof

Projecting entablature

Palmette

Sculpted frieze

Cornice

Pedestal

Smooth, vertical rustication

Smooth rustication

Statue of Amazon on horseback

Dado (die)

Plinth

Hanging wreath

Projecting pedestal

Eagle carrying festoons

INTERIOR

King post

Statue of Minerva

Tie beam

Orb

Painted inner roof

Brace

Polyhedral lantern

Roll molding

Strut

Straight brace

Projecting entablature

Crest

Projecting socle

Outer wall

Attached Corinthian column

Frieze painted with scenes from classical mythology

Circle (auditorium)

Finial with cavetto molding

Foliated panel

Transverse arch

Crowning cornice

Window hood-mold

Volute

Fascia

Barrel vault

Dentil

Clerestory level

Rectangular door leading to roofed space

Groin vault

Raised window jamb

Curved buttress

Semi-parabolic curve

Short pilaster

Gallery level

Modillion (bracket)

Cornice

Semicircular arched window

Pier-shaped pinnacle

Corinthian capital

Architrave decorated with oversailing fascias

Gallery

Cornice

Depressed arch

Foliated frieze

Small cupola

Balustrade

Pendentive

Oeil-de-boeuf ("ox-eye") window

Keystone decorated with scroll ornament

Archivolt

Formeret (wall rib)

Cornice

Archivolt decorated with plain fascias

Window jamb

Arcade

Round arch

Windowsill

Arcade level

Buttress

Round arch

Outer wall

Re-entrant corner

Base

Socle

Doorway connecting chapels

Side chapels

Main vessel

Side chapels

NAVE, CHURCH OF ST. PAUL-ST. LOUIS (FRENCH BAROQUE), PARIS, FRANCE, FROM 1627 (BY E. MARTELLANGE)

Baroque and neoclassical 2

ARABESQUE

Volute
Palmette
Tendril
Cornucopia

BAY LEAF GARLAND

Bayberry
Bay leaf

PATERA

Petal
Fillet
Rosette
Ovolo (quarter-round) molding

DECORATIVE MOLDINGS FROM ENGLISH NEOCLASSICAL BUILDINGS

Raking cornice
Representation in bas-relief of conversion of St. Paul

TRIANGULAR PEDIMENT, WEST FACADE, ST. PAUL'S CATHEDRAL

MODEL BUILT IN 1674 OF PROPOSED EXTERIOR OF ST. PAUL'S CATHEDRAL (ENGLISH BAROQUE), LONDON, BRITAIN (BY C. WREN)

Cross
Orb
Small dome
Entablature
Pedestal
Arcade
Gallery with balustrade
Lantern
Convex molding
Circular lucarne window
Dome
Plat lesene
Curved buttress
Round arch
Corinthian pilaster
Rectangular pier
Sunken lunette
Raking cornice
Sunken panel
Pediment
Plain pilaster
Attic story
Entablature
Architrave
Cornice
Small pilaster
Pedestal
Semicircular cornice
Plinth
Concave, arched niche
Attached Corinthian column
Freestanding Corinthian column
Projecting side portal

CHURCH OF ST. GEORGE IN THE EAST (ENGLISH BAROQUE), LONDON, BRITAIN, 1714-1734 (BY N. HAWKSMOOR)

SOUTH SIDE

WEST FACADE

Fluted circular pinnacle

Fluted capital

Pierced parapet

Plain buttress

Semicircular window

Urn

Platband

Sunken panel

Octahedral dome

Round-arched window

Triple keystone

Oeil-de-boeuf ("ox-eye") window

Cornice

Lateral pilaster-strip

Semicircular crypt window

Plain pedestal

Square post

Label mold

Octahedral turret

Plain frieze

East pediment

Semicircular apse

Emphasized keystone

Emphasized quoin

Side entrance

Steeple

Cornice

Stepped archivolt

Octahedral lantern

Parapet

Square stone block

Set-back buttress

Three-tier belfry

Cornice decorated with ogee molding and fascias

Pepper-pot lantern

Finial

Broken pediment

Volute

Raking cornice

Ionic capital

Continuous hood-mold

Triple band

Platband

Dog-leg staircase set in oval stone walls

Curved buttress

Ionic twin columns

Attic of drum

Drum

Arcade

Pedestal

Stepped tetrahedral roof

Statuette

Urn

Entablature

Rectangular window

Twin columns

Cruciform pedestal

Lantern

Circular lucarne window

Dome

Triangular lesene

Stepped cornice

Cornice

Raking cornice of facade pediment

Dentil ornament

Frieze

Corinthian capital

Corinthian twin pilasters

Dado

Round-arched window

Re-entrant

Doorway

Architrave

Rectangular vestibule

Concave wall

Emphasized keystone

Crepidoma (stepped base)

Corinthian capital

Baroque and neoclassical 3

DETAILS FROM BAROQUE, NEOCLASSICAL, AND ROCOCO BUILDINGS

CORNER OF THE NEW STATE PAPER OFFICE (NEOCLASSICAL), LONDON, BRITAIN, 1830-1831 (BY J. SOANE)

PORTICO, THE VYNE, HAMPSHIRE, BRITAIN, 1654 (NEOCLASSICAL)

GILT IRONWORK FROM SCREEN, PALAIS DE VERSAILLES, FRANCE, 1669-1674 (FRENCH BAROQUE)

WINDOW, PALAZZO STANGA, CREMONA, ITALY, EARLY 18TH CENTURY (ROCOCO)

ATLAS (MALE CARYATID), UPPER BELVEDERE, VIENNA, AUSTRIA, 1721 (GERMAN-STYLE BAROQUE)

BALCONY, NANTES, FRANCE, 1730-1740 (ROCOCO)

MASONRY OF A NICHE IN THE ROTUNDA (NEOCLASSICAL), BANK OF ENGLAND, LONDON, BRITAIN, 1794 (BY J. SOANE)

Scoop-pattern concave molding

Keystone

Frieze

Spandrel

Semidome

Voussoir

Rotunda wall

Flat, rectangular niche

Rounded niche

Flat, square niche

Classical-style entablature

Cornice

Frieze

Architrave

Pantile (S-shaped roofing tile)

Fascia

Eaves

Scroll-shaped corbel

Curved corbel

Smooth rustication

Second-floor window

Cornice

Drip-cap

Cornice

Frieze

Window architrave

Window jamb

First-floor window

Windowsill in the form of a frieze

Ground-floor window

Splayed windowsill

Vermiculated rustication

TYRINGHAM HOUSE (NEOCLASSICAL), BUCKINGHAMSHIRE, BRITAIN, 1793-1797 (BY J. SOANE)

ROOF LEVEL (ATTIC LEVEL)

Space for illumination above unroofed central hall

Chimney stack

Space above unroofed main staircase

Flat roof

Oculus illuminating secondary staircase

Parapet rail

Balustrade

Baluster

Cornice

Attic story of convex portico

Cornice

FIRST-FLOOR LEVEL (CHAMBER FLOOR)

Upper level of central hall, open to floor below

Main staircase

Secondary staircase

Abacus

Triangular pilaster

Pilaster capital

Attached Tuscan twin pilasters

First-floor story of convex portico

Windowsill

Bow front

GROUND-FLOOR LEVEL (PRINCIPAL FLOOR)

Withdrawing room

Central hall

Library and breakfast room

Main staircase

Water closet (toilet)

Eating room

Secondary staircase

Segmented lintel course

Band incised with Greek-style fret ornament

Windowsill

Window architrave

Window jamb

Base

Basement

Plinth

Horizontal rustication

Vestibule (entrance hall)

Ground-floor storey of convex portico

FACADE OF TYRINGHAM HOUSE

Chimney stack

Voussoir

Rail

Baluster

Parapet

Balustrade

Cornice

Entablature

Capital

Basement window

Shaft

Ionic column

Entrance door

Circular entrance steps

Base

PROSTYLE COLONNADE

Arches and vaults

PARTS OF AN ARCH

Voussoir   *Keystone*   *Crown*   *Abutment*

Abutment

Keystone

Extrados

Intrados (soffit)

Haunch

Abutment

Impost

Intrados (soffit)

Springing point

Abutment

Span

FRONT   **SIDE**

ARCHES ARE CURVED STRUCTURES used to bridge spans and to support the weight of upper parts of buildings, such as domes, as in St. Paul's Cathedral (below) and the historical temple (opposite). The voussoirs (wedge-shaped blocks) that form an arch (right) support each other and convert the downward force of the weight of the building into an outward force. This outward force is in turn transferred to buttresses, piers, or abutments. A vault is an arched roof or ceiling. There are four main types of vault (opposite). A barrel vault is a single vault, semicircular in cross-section; a groin vault consists of two barrel vaults intersecting at right angles; a rib vault is a groin vault reinforced by ribs; and a fan vault is a rib vault in which the ribs radiate from the springing point (where the arch begins) like a fan.

ARCHES AND BASE OF DOME, ST. PAUL'S CATHEDRAL, LONDON, BRITAIN, 1675-1710 (BY C. WREN)

Inner dome

Colonnade

Pilaster

Passageway

Base

Cornice

Pendentive

Opening to passageway

Pedestal of outer dome

"Whispering Gallery"

Triangular buttress

Upper arch (concealing difference in heights between main arch and minor arches)

Molded bracket

Round arch

Semidome

Extrados

Upper barrel-vaulted passage opening onto side aisle

Intrados (soffit)

Springing point

Barrel vault

Impost

Abutment

Passage leading to side aisle

Strut built into masonry to strengthen pier (added in the 20th century)

Minor arch leading to side aisle

Main arch leading to nave

Pier

Minor arch

TYPES OF ARCH

HORSESHOE ARCH (MOORISH ARCH), GREAT MOSQUE, CORDOBA, SPAIN, 785

BASKET ARCH (SEMI-ELLIPTICAL ARCH), PALATINE CHAPEL, AIX-LA-CHAPELLE, FRANCE, 790-798

TUDOR ARCH, TOWER OF LONDON, BRITAIN, C.1086-1097

LANCET ARCH, WESTMINSTER ABBEY, LONDON, BRITAIN, 1503-1519

TREFOIL ARCH, BEVERLEY MINSTER, YORKSHIRE, BRITAIN, C.1300

TYPES OF VAULT

Transverse rib

Temporary brace

Horizontal abutment

Temporary structure used to center vault

BARREL VAULT (TUNNEL VAULT; WAGON VAULT)

Barrel vault

Right-angled intersection

Voussoir

Groin

GROIN VAULT

Transverse ridge-rib

Longitudinal ridge-rib

Transverse arch

Diagonal rib

RIB VAULT

Tierceron (secondary rib)

Ridge rib

Springing point

Concave-sided lozenge

Panel

FAN VAULT

COMPOSITE MODEL OF HISTORICAL FRENCH TEMPLE

Coved dome

Lesene

Series of plain fascias

Re-entrant angle

Cavetto molding

Fillet

Cornice

Plain frieze

Architrave

Ionic capital

Chamfered corner

Keystone decorated with scroll

Plain Ionic column

Shaft

Scotia

Plinth

Dado

Base

Pedestal of lantern

Archivolt decorated with plain fascias

Abutment

Dentil

Round arch

Cornice

Horizontal band

Twisted vertical band

Naos (cella)

Intercolumniation

Lantern

Coved dome

Pedestal of dome

Entablature

Fluted Ionic column

Pedestal of column

Ionic column with twisted vertical bands (wreaths) and horizontal bands

ENGLISH BOND BRICKWORK OF GROIN VAULT AND RIB VAULT

Right-angled intersection

Groin

Header

Stretcher

Cell of barrel vault

Springing point

EXTRADOS OF GROIN VAULT

Stretcher

Header

Cell

Extrados of diagonal rib

Springing point

EXTRADOS OF RIB VAULT

INTERIOR DECORATION OF COFFERED VAULT

Compass

Square

Hammer

Coffer (square sunken panel)

Chamfered edge

Arris molding

Mason's tools

Domes

A DOME IS A CONVEX ROOF. Domes are categorized according to the shapes of both the base and the section through the center of the dome. The base may be circular, square, or polygonal (many-sided), depending on the plan of the drum (the walls on which the dome rests). The section of a dome may be the same shape as any arch (see pp. 484-485). Various types of dome are illustrated here: a hemispherical dome, which has a circular base and a semicircular section; a saucer dome, which has a circular base and a segmental (less than a semicircle) section; a polyhedral dome, which is a dome on a polygonal base whose sides meet at the top of the dome; and an onion dome, which has a circular or polygonal base and an ogee-shaped section. Many domes have a lantern (a turret with windows) to provide light inside.

LANTERN AND UPPER DOME TIMBERING, ST. PAUL'S CATHEDRAL

DOME TIMBERING, CHURCH OF THE SORBONNE, PARIS, FRANCE, 1635-1642 (BY J. LEMERCIER)

Ogee-curved dome
Straight brace
Window zone
Deeply projecting pier buttress
Cornice
Pedestal
Depressed hood mold
Circular lucarne window
Floorboard
Ashlar piece
Floor joist
Pin
Hood mold
Short strut
Waisted-oval lucarne window
Mortise and tenon joint
Principal rafter
Ogee-curved window frame
Straight brace
Vertical post
Tie beam
Circular baseplate
Common rafter
Shaft connecting lantern and church interior

ROOF WITH LANTERN AND ONION DOME

Weather vane
Ellipsoid orb
Onion dome
Keeled lesene
Fish-scale tile
Octahedral base
Sloping roof
Round arch
Oversailing fascia
Attached pillar
Tetrahedral capital
Vertical band
Return
Window
Oversailing fascia
Torus
Octahedral base of lantern
Fillet
Lantern
Tetrahedral roof

REPRESENTATION OF DOME METALING, CHURCH OF THE SORBONNE

Cross
Orb
Square rib
Inverted ovolo (quarter-round)
Astragal
Fillet
Volute
Plain fascia
Roll molding
Lantern
Round-arched window
Buttress
Ovolo (quarter-round)
Volute
Cornice
Fillet
Dome on a circular base
Projecting pier buttress
Fish-scale tile
Inverted demi-heart torus molding
Hood mold
Waisted-oval lucarne window
Small volute
Gutter
Parapet
Semicircular torus molding
Small roll
Fillet
Plain fascia
Triple lesene

TYPES OF DOME

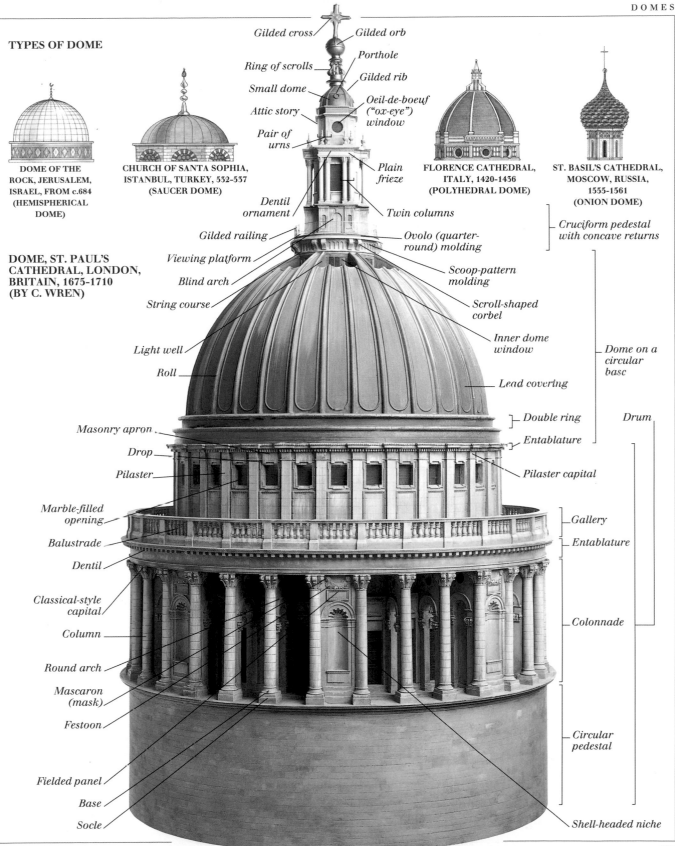

DOME OF THE ROCK, JERUSALEM, ISRAEL, FROM c.684 (HEMISPHERICAL DOME)

CHURCH OF SANTA SOPHIA, ISTANBUL, TURKEY, 532-537 (SAUCER DOME)

FLORENCE CATHEDRAL, ITALY, 1420-1436 (POLYHEDRAL DOME)

ST. BASIL'S CATHEDRAL, MOSCOW, RUSSIA, 1555-1561 (ONION DOME)

DOME, ST. PAUL'S CATHEDRAL, LONDON, BRITAIN, 1675-1710 (BY C. WREN)

Gilded cross

Gilded orb

Porthole

Ring of scrolls

Gilded rib

Small dome

Oeil-de-boeuf ("ox-eye") window

Attic story

Pair of urns

Plain frieze

Dentil ornament

Twin columns

Gilded railing

Ovolo (quarter-round) molding

Viewing platform

Scoop-pattern molding

Blind arch

Scroll-shaped corbel

String course

Inner dome window

Light well

Roll

Lead covering

Masonry apron

Double ring

Drop

Entablature

Pilaster

Pilaster capital

Marble-filled opening

Gallery

Balustrade

Entablature

Dentil

Colonnade

Classical-style capital

Column

Round arch

Mascaron (mask)

Festoon

Circular pedestal

Fielded panel

Base

Socle

Shell-headed niche

Cruciform pedestal with concave returns

Dome on a circular base

Drum

487

Islamic buildings

OPUS SECTILE MOSAIC DESIGN

THE ISLAMIC RELIGION was founded by the prophet Mohammed, who was born in Mecca (in present-day Saudi Arabia) about 570 AD. During the next three centuries, Islam spread from Arabia to North Africa and Spain, as well as into India and much of the rest of Asia. The worldwide influence of Islam remains strong today. Common characteristics of Islamic buildings include ogee arches and roofs, onion domes, and walls decorated with carved stone, paintings, inlays, or mosaics. The most important type of Islamic building is the mosque—the place of worship—which generally has a minaret (tower) from which the muezzin (official crier) calls Muslims to prayer. Most mosques have a mihrab (decorative niche) that indicates the direction of Mecca. As figurative art is not allowed in Islam, buildings are ornamented with geometric and arabesque motifs and inscriptions (frequently Koranic verses).

Budlike onion dome
Depressed arch surrounding mihrab
Painted roof pavilion
Turkish crescent finial
Lotus flower pendentive
Arabic inscription
Crest
Painted minaret with censer (incense burner)
Spandrel
Series of recessed arches
Semidome
Arched niche within a niche
Mural resembling tomb
Polyhedral niche
Recessed colonettes

MIHRAB, JAMI MASJID (PRINCIPAL OR CONGREGATIONAL MOSQUE), BIJAPUR, INDIA, c.1636

Tablet flower
Shield
Herringbone pattern
Spandrel with floral design
Ogee arch
Carved stone
Undulating band
Cusp
Volute
Impost
Capital with stylized floral design
Panel with fret pattern
Band with Arabic inscriptions praising Allah (God)
Column shaft
Attached colonette
Jali (latticed screen) with geometrical patterns

ARCH, THE ALHAMBRA, GRANADA, SPAIN, 1333-1354

Enameled turquoise earthenware tile
Trigon
Cube with chamfered corners
Polygonal capital
Niche
Enameled white earthenware tile
Arabesques of stylized plants
Enameled lapis blue earthenware tile

MIHRAB WITH COLUMN, EL-AINYI MOSQUE, CAIRO, EGYPT, 15TH CENTURY

EXAMPLES OF ISLAMIC MOSAICS, EGYPT AND SYRIA

Star-shaped motif

Triangle of yellow marble

Rhombus of black marble

Stone band

Greek cross of red marble

STAR AND GREEK CROSS MOSAIC

Mosaic tessellation

Stone

Black marble

Turquoise glass

Tessera (small mosaic piece)

FRET-PATTERN MOSAIC

Greek cross of black and yellow marble

Star-shaped motif

Stone band

Rhombus of red marble

STAR AND GREEK CROSS MOSAIC

Parallelogram of black marble

Triangle of yellow marble

Rhombus of red marble

Symmetrical quadrilateral of stone

Star-shaped motif

MOSAIC OF HEXAGONS, TRIANGLES, AND SYMMETRICAL QUADRILATERALS

Hexagonal design

Band of black marble

Band of stone

HEXAGON AND BAND MOSAIC

Triangle of turquoise glass

Parallelogram of mother-of-pearl

DANCETTE (ZIG-ZAG)-PATTERN MOSAIC

Symmetrical quadrilateral of black marble

Hexagon of red marble

Triangle of stone

MOSAIC OF HEXAGONS, TRIANGLES, AND SYMMETRICAL QUADRILATERALS

MARBLE TOMB OF ITIMAD-UD-DAULA, AGRA, INDIA, c.1622-1628

Kalasa finial (finial with orbs)

Padmakosa (lotus petal)

Ogee-curved roof

Chajya (deep eaves)

Domed roof

Circular top of minaret

Parapet decorated with latticework

Balcony

Roof pavilion

Cusped arch

Pietra dura inlay (slices of semiprecious stone laid in sockets)

Cornice

Bracket

Octahedral base of minaret

Spandrel decorated with arabesque

Star-pattern inlay

Sandstone plinth

Sandstone parapet decorated with latticework

Jali (latticed screen) with geometrical patterns

Depressed entrance arch

Sandstone stairway

Opus sectile mosaic (geometric mosaic) of stone, tile, glass, and enamel

South and east Asia

THE TRADITIONAL ARCHITECTURE of south and east Asia has been profoundly influenced by the spread from India of Buddhism and Hinduism. This influence is shown by both the abundance and by the architectural styles of temples and shrines in the region. Many early Hindu temples consist of rooms carved from solid rock faces. However, freestanding structures began to be built in southern India from about the eighth century AD. Many were built in the Dravidian style, like the Temple of Virupaksha (opposite), with its characteristic antarala (terraced tower), perforated windows, and numerous arches, pilasters, and carvings. The earliest Buddhist religious monuments were Indian stupas, which consisted of a single hemispherical dome surmounted by a chattravali (shaft) and surrounded by railings with ornate gates. Later Indian stupas and those built elsewhere were sometimes modified. For example, in Sri Lanka, the dome became bell-shaped, and was called a dagoba. Buddhist pagodas, such as the Burmese example (right), are multistoried temples, each story having a projecting roof. The form of these buildings probably derived from the yasti (pointed spire) of the stupa. Another feature of many traditional Asian buildings is their imaginative roof forms, such as gambrel (mansard) roofs, and roofs with angle rafters (below).

DETAILS FROM EAST ASIAN BUILDINGS

KASUGA-STYLE ROOF WITH SUMIGI (ANGLE RAFTERS), KASUGADO SHRINE OF ENJOJI, NARA, JAPAN, 12TH-14TH CENTURY

TERRACES, TEMPLE OF HEAVEN, BEIJING, CHINA, 15TH CENTURY

GAMBREL (MANSARD) ROOF WITH UPSWEPT EAVES AND UNDULATING GABLES, HIMEJI CASTLE, HIMEJI, JAPAN, 1608-1609

CORNER CAPITAL WITH ROOF BEAMS, POPCHU-SA TEMPLE, POPCHU-SA, SOUTH KOREA, 17TH CENTURY

SEVEN-STORIED PAGODA IN BURMESE STYLE, c.9TH-10TH CENTURY

Gilded band

Gilded iron hti (crown)

Dubika (mast)

Arrow motif

Torus molding with spiral carving

Decorative eaves board

Ogee-arched motif with decorative carvings

Ogee-arched motif forming horn

Hip rafter

Pentroof

Undulating molding

Engaged pillar

Baluster finial

Arched entrance

Balustrade

Rectangular window

Pillar

Baluster

Straight brace

PERFORATED STONE WINDOWS, TEMPLES OF VIRUPAKSHA AND MALLIKARJUNA, PATTADAKAL, INDIA, 8TH CENTURY

Tablet flower

Fret motif

Chain motif

Floral pattern

Leaf

Scroll motif

Sickle motif

Semicircle

DAGOBA STUPA, KANDY, SRI LANKA, c.2ND CENTURY BC- 7TH CENTURY AD

Chattra (umbrella)

Hanging ornament

Chattravali (shaft)

Ring with indentations symbolizing chattras

Ornamental metalwork

Yasti (tee; pointed spire)

Harmika (stylized square railing)

Auda (bell-shaped dome)

Trimala (series of three circular courses)

Circular base

SIDE VIEW AND PLAN VIEW, TEMPLE OF VIRUPAKSHA, PATTADAKAL, INDIA, c.746

Stupica (small stupa) of the Dravidian order

Dravidian finial

Blind chataya arch

Perforated window

Gopuram finial (wagonlike finial)

Bracketed capital

Small gopuram (gate head)

Parapet

Roll cornice

Antarala (terraced tower)

Niche with statue

Gate

Plan view

Panel with bas-relief carving

Pillar

Twin pilasters

Shrine

Niche

Mandapa (pillared hall)

Pradakshina (circumambulatory passage around shrine)

Shrine chamber

Gate

The 19th century

BUILDINGS OF THE 19TH CENTURY are characterized by the use of new materials and by a great diversity of architectural styles. From the end of the 18th century, iron and steel became widely used as alternatives to wood for the framework of buildings, as in the flax-spinning mill shown here. Built in Britain in 1796, this mill exemplifies an architectural style that became common throughout the industrialized world for more than a century. The Industrial Revolution also brought mass production of building parts—a development that enabled the British architect Sir Joseph Paxton to erect London's Crystal Palace (a building made entirely of iron and glass) in only nine months, ready for the Great Exhibition of 1851. The 19th century saw a widespread revival of older architectural styles. For example, in the United States and Germany, Neo-Greek architecture was fashionable; in Britain and France, Neo-Baroque, Neo-Byzantine, and Neo-Gothic styles (as seen in the Palace of Westminster and Tower Bridge, London) were dominant.

**FLAX-SPINNING MILL,
SHREWSBURY, BRITAIN,
1796 (BY C. BAGE)**

Cast-iron wall plate

Pitched roof

Ridge

Verge

Gutter

Machinery space

Cast-iron mortise and tenon joint

Anchor joint

Inverted T-section cast-iron beam

Drain pipe

Segmentally arched brick vault

End flange

Concrete floor

Tapering part of column

Paved ground floor

Strengthened central column

Multi-gabled roof (ridge and furrow roof)

Ridge

Furrow

Verge

Timber rafter

Cast-iron wall plate

Gutter

Gable

Drain pipe

Tapering part of column

Three courses of stretchers

Segmentally arched brick vault

Course of headers

Cast-iron mortise and tenon joint

Course of decorative headers

Tie-rod

Cast-iron lattice window

Cast-iron cruciform column

Cast-iron tenon

Anchor joint

Inverted T-section cast-iron beam

Strengthened central column

Bonded brick wall

Stone foundation

Quoin

Jamb

Gauged arch (segmental arch of tapered bricks)

CLOCK TOWER ("BIG BEN"), PALACE OF WESTMINSTER, LONDON, BRITAIN, 1836-1868 (BY C. BARRY AND A.W.N. PUGIN)

Finial

Spire

Skylight

Cornice decorated with shields

Iron railing

Small orb

Orb

Iron tracery

Dormer window

Round arch filled with open tracery

Tetrahedral spire

Bell chamber

Balustrade

Ogee tracery arch filled with trefoil

Flying buttress

Pinnacle

Spandrel

Octahedral shaft with billet decoration

Dial

Cornice

Molded corbel

Star-shaped corner buttress

Paneled field filled with tracery

Slender diagonal buttress

Narrow window

String course

Carved panel

Stepped storys

Octahedral column

Side exit

DETAILS FROM BUILDINGS IN REVIVALIST STYLES

CUPOLA, MERCHANTS' EXCHANGE, PHILADELPHIA, USA, 1832-1834 (NEO-GREEK)

SCULPTURE AND PEDIMENT, OPERA HOUSE, PARIS, FRANCE, 1861-1874 (NEO-BAROQUE)

DOMED TURRET, WESTMINSTER CATHEDRAL, LONDON, BRITAIN, 1894-1903 (NEO-BYZANTINE)

Tetrahedral spire

Finial

Finial

Spire

Cornice

Archway

Dormer head (gable) filled with blind tracery

Parapet

High-level footbridge

Latticework

Heraldic shield

Cast-iron tracery

Cast-iron paneling

Drawbridge (bascule)

Steel brace

Circular turret/buttress

Archway

Parapet of balcony

Octahedral upper turret

Wedge-shaped corbel

Molded corbel

String course

Stone panel

Pier

TOWER BRIDGE, LONDON, BRITAIN, 1886-1894 (BY H. JONES)

CRYSTAL PALACE EXHIBITION HALL, LONDON, BRITAIN, 1851 (BY J. PAXTON)

Longitudinal girder

Window

Cast-iron ornamental arch-plate

Ridge and furrow glass roof-windows

Crest

Arched facade

Semicircular barrel vault

Cast-iron trapezium

Sheet-iron louver

Strengthened support

Entrance

493

The early 20th century

ARCHITECTURE OF THE EARLY 20TH CENTURY is notable for radical new types of steel and glass buildings—particularly skyscrapers—and the widespread use of steel-reinforced concrete. The steel-framed skyscraper was pioneered in Chicago in the 1880s but did not become widespread until the first decades of the 20th century. As construction techniques were refined, skyscrapers became higher and higher. For example, the Empire State Building (right) of 1929-1931 has 102 storys. Many buildings of this period were constructed from lightweight concrete slabs that could be supported by cantilever beams or by pilotis (stilts), as in the Villa Savoye (below). The early 20th century also produced a great variety of architectural styles, some of which are illustrated opposite. Despite their diversity, the styles of this period generally had one thing in common: they were completely new, with few links to past architectural styles. This originality is in marked contrast to 19th-century architecture (see pp. 492-493), much of which was revivalist.

EMPIRE STATE BUILDING, NEW YORK, USA, 1929-1931 (BY R. H. SHREVE, T. LAMB, AND A. L. HARMON)

- Radio mast
- Circular lantern
- Art Deco splayed seashell form
- Stepped plinth
- Chamfered corner
- Colonnaded storey
- Ornamentation
- Ziggurat-style step-back
- Set-back
- Steel mullion
- Flush window
- Vertical pier
- Regular fenestration
- Solid-panel infill
- Fanlike Art Deco decoration
- Stone structure line
- Decorated stone lintel
- Limestone and granite cladding
- Flat roof
- Stepped cornice
- Parapet
- Plinth
- Ground-floor entrance
- Base
- Square bay

VILLA SAVOYE, POISSY, FRANCE, 1929-1931 (BY LE CORBUSIER)

TOP VIEW

- Fixed table
- Parapet
- Slab floor
- Screen
- Ramp
- Handrail
- Windowsill
- Flat roof
- Curved wall
- Flat roof
- Directional skylight
- Terrace
- Raised planting bed

SIDE VIEW

- Terrace
- Cement-rendered wall of lightweight slabs
- Solarium
- Sliding pane of glass
- Mullion
- Piano nobile (first floor)
- Reinforced-concrete pilotis (stilt)
- Rooms for staff
- Ribbon window of long living room
- Curved glazing
- Covered driveway

MIDWAY GARDENS, CHICAGO, USA, 1914 (BY F. L. WRIGHT)

Flagpole

Plain coping stone

Main floor

Decorated cement frieze

Projecting balustrade

Ornamental light

Arcade

Main pavilion

Terrace

Ornamental sculpture

Stone plinth

Tiled frieze

Deep-set window

Brick pier

Stepped flat roofs

Ornamented coping stone

Terrace

Steps

Stage

Orchestra shell

Tiled, shallow pitched roof

Ridge

Hip

Octagonal window

Flat roof

Cantilevered latticed shade

Planting bed

Slit window

Terrace

EAST SIDE

NORTH SIDE

EARLY 20TH-CENTURY ARCHITECTURAL STYLES

DORMER WINDOW, STUDIO ELVIRA, MUNICH, GERMANY, 1902 (ART NOUVEAU)

AEG TURBINE HALL, BERLIN, GERMANY, 1909 (DEUTSCHER WERKBUND)

ROBIE HOUSE, CHICAGO, USA, 1909-1910 (PRAIRIE STYLE)

GRUNDTVIG CHURCH, COPENHAGEN, DENMARK, 1920 (EXPRESSIONIST)

VERTEX, CHRYSLER BUILDING, NEW YORK, USA, 1928-1930 (ART DECO)

TOWER, TOWN HALL, HILVERSUM, NETHERLANDS, 1930 (DUTCH CUBIST)

CASA DEL FASCIO, COMO, ITALY, 1932-1936 (GRUPPO SEVEN CUBIST)

MOTIF ABOVE DOORWAY, HOOVER FACTORY, LONDON, BRITAIN, 1933 (ART DECO)

Modern buildings 1

KAWANA HOUSE, JAPAN, FROM 1987 (BY N. FOSTER)

ARCHITECTURE SINCE ABOUT THE 1950s is generally known as modern architecture. One of its main influences has been functionalism—a belief that a building's function should be apparent in its design. Both the Centre Georges Pompidou (below and opposite) and the Hong Kong and Shanghai Bank (see pp. 498-499) are functionalist buildings. On each, elements of engineering and the building's services are clearly visible on the outside. In the 1980s, some architects rejected functionalism in favor of postmodernism, in which historical styles—particularly neoclassicism—were revived, using modern building materials and techniques. In many modern buildings, walls are made of glass or concrete hung from a frame, as in the Kawana House (right); this type of wall construction is known as curtain walling. Other modern construction techniques include the intricate interlocking of concrete vaults—as in the Sydney Opera House (see pp. 498-499)—and the use of high-tension beams to create complex roof shapes, such as the paraboloid roof of the Church of St. Pierre de Libreville (see pp. 498-499).

Solar panel
Concrete frame
Pile foundation
Raft
Composite cladding panel
SIDE VIEW

Rocker beam
Curtain walling
Lattice beam
Floor-beam connection
Floor
FRONT VIEW

SERVICES FACADE, CENTRE GEORGES POMPIDOU, PARIS, FRANCE, 1977 (BY R. PIANO AND R. ROGERS)

Metal-faced fire-resistant panel
Air-conditioning duct
Cooling tower
Water pipe

Grand gallery level
Main gallery levels
Library level
Administrative level
Mezzanine gallery level
Reception level

Staircase to grand hall
Electrical plant
Water-cooled fire-resistant column
Continuous glazing
Tinted glass
Services entrance

PRINCIPAL FACADE, CENTRE GEORGES POMPIDOU

Gallery space

External walkway

Electronically operated roller blind

Cooling tower

Continuous glazing

Steel lattice beam

Terrace

Main truss

Cradle support for escalator

Gerberette (cast-steel rocker beam)

Cross-bracing

Suspended fire-resistant glass curtain

Double fire escape staircase

Reinforced-concrete and steel floor plate

Double floor height

Main entrance

Glazed escalator tube

Node

Water-cooled fire-resistant steel column

Exposed "plug-in" services

Steel lattice beam

Dual air-conditioning unit for roof

Elevator

Elevator-motor room

Vertical-duct distribution zone

Metal sandwich-panel (insulating panel)

Gerberette (cast-steel rocker beam)

Rose connection

Outer tension-column

External steel-lattice mullion

Water-cooled fire-resistant cross-beam

Double fire escape staircase

Water storage tank

Cross-bracing

Open gallery floor

Water pipe

Steel-framed services column

Double cross-bracing

Modern buildings 2

HONG KONG AND SHANGHAI BANK, HONG KONG, 1981-1985 (BY N. FOSTER)

Inverted top truss
Mast
Illuminated fascia
Curved glazing
External maintenance crane
Cockpit
Counterweight
Soffit
Boom
Circular access platform
Sunshade louver
Steel column
Mullion
Face panel
Hanger
Handrail
Composite cladding panel
Top beam
Outer diagonal beam
Escalator
Outer bottom boom
Inner diagonal beam
Fire escape staircase
Inner bottom boom
External staircase
Pin joint
Double floor height
Refuge terrace
Full-height glazing
Hanger
Sun scoop
Glazed curtain wall
Two-story stability truss (coat hanger truss)
Flange
Vertical glazed typhoon screen
Lightweight, column-free steel and concrete floor
Entrance lobby
Plaza
Glazed soffit

SOUTH FACADE

Helicopter landing pad
Soffit
Navigation light
Stepped elevation
Face panel
Horizontal window
Vertical window
External maintenance crane
Cross-bracing
Service shaft
Double floor height
Sun scoop
10-floor-high atrium
Internal bridge

EAST SIDE

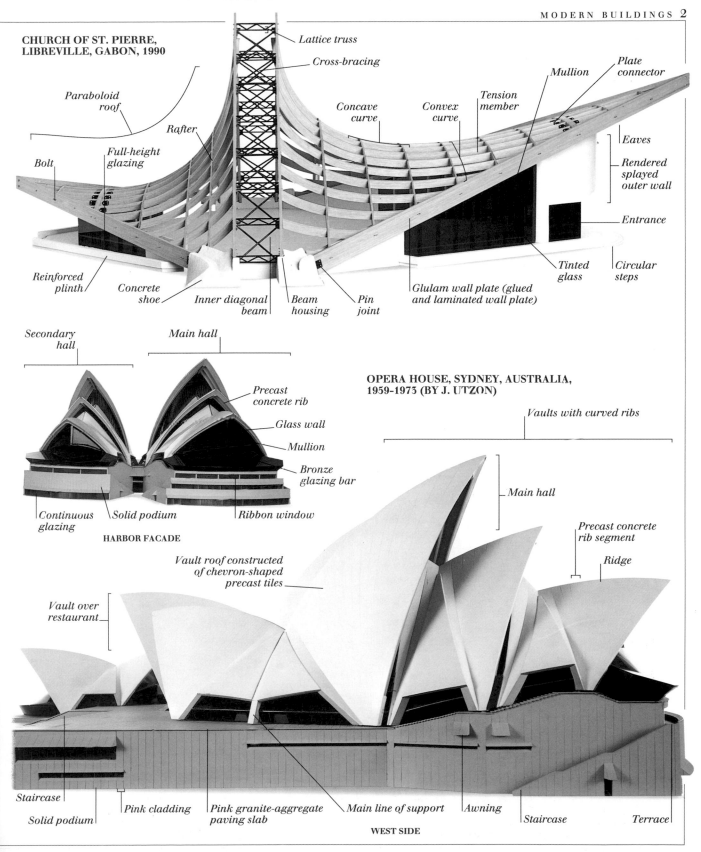

CHURCH OF ST. PIERRE, LIBREVILLE, GABON, 1990

Lattice truss

Cross-bracing

Paraboloid roof

Rafter

Concave curve

Convex curve

Tension member

Mullion

Plate connector

Full-height glazing

Eaves

Rendered splayed outer wall

Bolt

Entrance

Tinted glass

Circular steps

Reinforced plinth

Concrete shoe

Inner diagonal beam

Beam housing

Pin joint

Glulam wall plate (glued and laminated wall plate)

Secondary hall

Main hall

OPERA HOUSE, SYDNEY, AUSTRALIA, 1959-1973 (BY J. UTZON)

Precast concrete rib

Glass wall

Mullion

Bronze glazing bar

Vaults with curved ribs

Main hall

Precast concrete rib segment

Ridge

Continuous glazing

Solid podium

Ribbon window

HARBOR FACADE

Vault roof constructed of chevron-shaped precast tiles

Vault over restaurant

Staircase

Solid podium

Pink cladding

Pink granite-aggregate paving slab

Main line of support

Awning

Staircase

Terrace

WEST SIDE

499

MUSIC

Musical notation

MUSICAL NOTATION IS ANY METHOD by which sounds are written down so that they can be read and performed by others. The present-day conventional system of notation uses a five-line stave (staff)—divided by vertical lines into sections known as bars—on which notes, rests, clefs, key signatures, time signatures, accidentals, and other symbols are written. A note indicates the duration of a sound and, according to its position on the stave, its pitch. Notes can be arranged on the stave in order of pitch to form a scale. A silence in the music is indicated by a rest. The clef, which is placed at the begininng of a stave, fixes the pitch. The key signature, which is placed after the clef, indicates the key. The time signature, placed after the key signature, shows the number of beats in a bar. Accidentals are used to indicate the raising or lowering of the pitch of a note.

ELEMENTS OF MUSICAL NOTATION

CLEFS

Treble (or G) clef

Alto (or C) clef

Bass (or F) clef

TIME SIGNATURES

Six-eight time

Three-four time

NOTES

Breve
Minim
Quaver
Semibreve
Crotchet
Semiquaver

RESTS

Breve rest
Minim rest
Quaver rest
Semibreve rest
Crotchet rest
Semiquaver rest

SCALE

C D E F G A B C

ACCIDENTALS

Sharp
Natural
Double sharp
Flat
Double flat
Key signature

Moderately fast and quiet

Tie (bind)

Repeat the previous bar

Treble clef

Bass clef

Four-four time (common time)

Key signature

Stave (staff)

Alto clef

Treble voice

Alto voice

Tenor voice

Bass voice

Organ part for right hand

Organ part for left hand

Organ pedal line

Instruments of the orchestra written in Italian

Bar line

Bass clef

Bar

Crotchet

FLUTES

OBOES

CLARINETS IN A

BASSOONS

HORNS IN D

TRUMPETS IN D

TIMPANI IN D AND A

FIRST AND SECOND VIOLINS

VIOLAS

VOICES

CELLOS

DOUBLE BASSES

ORGAN

Accidental sharp

Tie (bind)

Accidental natural

Unison (both clarinets play the same note)

Semibreve

Crotchet

Semibreve rest

Accidental sharp

Slur

Piano (play softly)

Pianissimo (play very softly)

Crotchet rest

Orchestras

An ORCHESTRA IS A GROUP of musicians that plays music written for a specific combination of instruments. The number and type of instruments included in the orchestra depends on the style of music being played. The modern orchestra (also known as a symphony orchestra) is made up of four sections of instruments—stringed, woodwind, brass, and percussion. The stringed section consists of violins, violas, cellos (violoncellos), double basses, and sometimes a harp (see pp. 510-511). The main instruments of the woodwind section are flutes, oboes, clarinets, and bassoons—the piccolo, cor anglais, bass clarinet, saxophone, and double bassoon (contrabassoon) can also be included if the music requires them (see pp. 508-509). The brass section usually consists of horns, trumpets, trombones, and the tuba (see pp. 506-507). The main instruments of the percussion section are the timpani (see pp. 518-519). The snare drum, bass drum, cymbals, tambourine, triangle, tubular bells, xylophone, vibraphone, gong (tam-tam), castanets, and maracas can also be included in the percussion section (see pp. 516-517). The musicians are usually arranged in a semi-circle—strings spread along the front, woodwind and brass in the center, and percussion at the back. A conductor stands in front of the musicians and controls the tempo (speed) of the music and the overall balance of the sound, ensuring that no instruments are too loud or too soft in relation to the others.

TUBULAR BELLS

TAM-TAM (GONG)

VIBRAPHONE

XYLOPHONE

CASTANETS

TAMBOURINE

MARACAS

TRIANGLE

TRUMPETS

HORNS

CLARINETS

BASS CLARINET

SAXOPHONE

PICCOLO

HARP

SECOND VIOLINS

FIRST VIOLINS

CYMBALS   SIDE DRUM   BASS DRUM

TIMPANI

EXAMPLE OF A LAYOUT OF THE
INSTRUMENTS FOR A MODERN
(SYMPHONY) ORCHESTRA

TROMBONES

TUBA

BASSOONS

DOUBLE BASSOON

DOUBLE BASSES

FLUTES   OBOES   COR ANGLAIS

VIOLAS

Score

CONDUCTOR'S
STAND

CELLOS

505

Brass instruments

BRASS INSTRUMENTS ARE WIND INSTRUMENTS that are made of metal, usually brass. Although they appear in many different shapes and sizes, all brass instruments have a mouthpiece, a length of hollow tube, and a flared bell. The mouthpiece of a brass instrument may be cup-shaped, as in the cornet, or cone-shaped, as in the horn. The tube may be wide or narrow, mainly conical, as in the horn and tuba, or mainly cylindrical, as in the trumpet and trombone. The sound of a brass instrument is made by the player's lips vibrating against the mouthpiece, so that the air vibrates in the tube. By changing lip tension, the player can vary the vibrations and produce notes of different pitches. The range of notes produced by a brass instrument can be extended by means of a valve system. Most brass instruments, such as the trumpet, have piston valves that divert the air in the instrument along an extra piece of tubing (known as a valve slide) when pressed down. The total length of the tube is increased and the pitch of the note produced is lowered. Instead of valves, the trombone has a movable slide that can be pushed away from or drawn toward the player. The sound of a brass instrument can also be changed by inserting a mute into the bell of the instrument.

BUGLE

Brace

Tuning slide

Counterbalancing weight

SIMPLIFIED DIAGRAM SHOWING HOW A PISTON VALVE SYSTEM WORKS

Piston valves at rest

Air bypasses piston valves

PISTON VALVES AT REST

First piston valve pressed down

Second and third piston valves at rest

Air diverted through first valve slide

PISTON VALVE PRESSED DOWN

TRUMPET

Finger button

First piston valve

Spring returns piston valve to rest position

Second piston valve

Third piston valve

Holes divert air into valve slides

Little finger support

Music stand holder

Narrow, cylindrical tube

Flared bell

Cup-shaped mouthpiece

Mouthpiece receiver

Tuning slide

First valve slide

Tuning slide water key

First valve slide thumb hook

Third valve slide finger ring

Third valve slide

Third valve slide water key

Second valve slide

SECTIONS OF A TROMBONE

EXAMPLES OF MUTES

Flared bell

CUP MUTE

TENOR MUTE

ALTO MUTE

Inner tube

Outer tube of slide

Cup-shaped mouthpiece

Mouthpiece brace held by the left hand

Slide brace held by the right hand

Narrow, cylindrical tube

Water key

TROMBONE

Flared bell

Outer tube of slide

Cup-shaped mouthpiece

FLUGELHORN

Little finger support

Piston valves

Flared bell

Cup-shaped mouthpiece

Conical tube

Valve slide

HORN

Cone-shaped mouthpiece

Finger key

Rotary valves

Narrow, conical bore

Large, flared bell

CORNET

Little finger support

Piston valves

Flared bell

Cup-shaped mouthpiece

Bore widens after valves

Valve slide

TUBA

Large, flared bell

Piston valves

Cup-shaped mouthpiece

Valve slide

Wide, conical tube

507

Woodwind instruments

WOODWIND INSTRUMENTS ARE wind instruments that are generally made of wood, although some are made of metal or plastic. The sound of a woodwind instrument is produced by the vibration of air in a hollow tube. The air is made to vibrate by blowing across a blow hole—as in the flute and piccolo— or by blowing through a single reed— as in the clarinet and saxophone— or a double reed—as in the bassoon, cor anglais, and oboe. The pitch of a woodwind instrument can be changed by opening or closing holes cut into the tube of the instrument.

Bell

Bell joint

Double reed

Curved crook

Double reed

Crook

Cylindrical, metal tube

Key

Body joint

Blow hole

Head joint

Lip plate

PICCOLO

Conical, wooden tube

Tenor joint

Conical, wooden tube

Upper joint

Bass joint

Key

Double reed

Cork

Upper joint

Finger hole

Foot joint

Key

Mouthpiece with single reed

Right-hand rest

Key

Upper joint

Key

Body joint

Ligature

Barrel joint

Butt

Key

Middle joint

Middle joint

Cylindrical, metal tube

Cylindrical, wooden tube

Upper joint

BASSOON

Finger hole

Key

Bell joint

Conical, wooden tube

Finger hole

Lip plate

Head joint

Middle joint

Bulb-shaped bell

COR ANGLAIS

Bell joint

Blow hole

Bell joint

Flared bell

Flared bell

OBOE

FLUTE

CLARINET

TENOR SAXOPHONE

Mouthpiece with single reed

Conical, metal tube

Upturned, flared bell

SECTIONS OF A TENOR SAXOPHONE

Mouthpiece with single reed

Ligature

Upper octave key

Neck

Key rod

KEYS FOR THE LEFT THUMB

Lower octave key

Key

Key

Key rod

KEYS FOR THE LEFT HAND

Key rod

Key

Mother-of-pearl touchpiece (button)

KEYS FOR THE RIGHT HAND

Key

Key rod

MAIN BODY OF SAXOPHONE

Conical, metal tube

Tone hole

Mother-of-pearl touchpiece (button)

KEYS FOR THE RIGHT PALM

KEYS FOR THE LEFT PALM

Upturned, flared bell

Tone hole

Pad made up of layers of felt and cork

Roller

Cup

Key rod

Key guard

Key

Metal center of pad reflects sound

Padded key

Key guard

KEYS FOR THE RIGHT LITTLE FINGER

KEYS FOR THE LEFT LITTLE FINGER

Key guard

Stringed instruments

STRINGED INSTRUMENTS PRODUCE SOUND by the vibration of stretched strings. This may be done by drawing a bow across the strings, as in the violin; or by plucking the strings, as in the harp and guitar (see pp. 512-513). The four modern members of the bowed string family are the violin, viola, cello (violoncello), and double bass. Each consists of a hollow, wooden body, a long neck, and four strings. The bow is a wooden stick with horsehair stretched across its length. The vibrations made by drawing the bow across the strings are transmitted to the hollow body, and this itself vibrates, amplifying and enriching the sound produced. The harp consists of a set of strings of different lengths stretched across a wooden frame. The strings are plucked by the player's thumbs and fingers—except the little finger of each hand—which produces vibrations that are amplified by the harp's sound board. The pitch of the note produced by any stringed instrument depends on the length, weight, and tension of the string. A shorter, lighter, or tighter string gives a higher note.

Scroll eye

Scroll

Peg hole

Ebony tuning pegs

Neck made of maple wood

Strings

Fingerboard

Rounded shoulder

Belly (sound board)

Waist

Head

Point

Bridge

Stick

Scroll

Scroll eye

Peg box

Tuning peg

Horsehair

Nut

String

Fingerboard

Rounded shoulder

Belly (sound board)

Purfling

Sound hole

Waist

Sound hole

Bridge

Rib

Tuning adjustor

Purfling

Tailpiece

Frog

Chin rest

Tailpiece

Screw

Chin rest

Tailpiece loop fits around end pin

VIOLIN BOW

VIOLIN

SECTIONS OF A VIOLIN

End pin (tail pin)

HARP

Crown
Tuning peg
Neck (string arm)
Shoulder
String
Sound board
Pillar
Pedestal
Foot
Pedal

DOUBLE BASS BOW

Head
Point
Inward-curving stick
Horsehair
Frog
Screw

CELLO (VIOLONCELLO)

Scroll
Scroll eye
Peg box
Tuning peg
Nut
Fingerboard
String
Belly (sound board)
Rounded shoulder
Sound hole
Waist
Bridge
Tuning adjustor
Tailpiece
Spike

DOUBLE BASS

Scroll
Scroll eye
Tuning pegs at back of peg box
Nut
Fingerboard
String
Sloping shoulder
Belly (sound board)
Purfling
Waist
Bridge
Rib
Sound hole
Tailpiece
Spike

VIOLA

Scroll
Scroll eye
Tuning peg
Peg box
Nut
Fingerboard
Belly (sound board)
String
Rounded shoulder
Purfling
Waist
Bridge
Sound hole
Tuning adjustor
Tailpiece
Chin rest

Guitars

THE GUITAR IS A PLUCKED stringed instrument (see pp. 510-511). There are two types of guitar—acoustic and electric. Acoustic guitars have hollow bodies and six or twelve strings. Plucking or strumming the strings produces vibrations that are amplified by their hollow bodies. Electric guitars usually have solid bodies and six strings. Pick-ups placed under the strings convert vibrations into electronic signals that are magnified by an amplifier, and sent to a loudspeaker where they are converted into sounds (see pp. 520-521). Electric bass guitars are very similar in structure to electric guitars, and produce sound in the same way, but have four heavier-gage strings and play lower pitched notes.

ACOUSTIC GUITAR

Hollow body

String

Fret

Machine head

Neck

Headstock

Sound hole

Bridge

B string

G string

D string

A string

Low E string

Maker's label

Lining glued along top and bottom edge of rib

Rib

End block

Strap peg

Joint

Transverse (crosswise) strut strengthens back

Back made of two pieces of cherry wood joined together

Saddle

Bridge pin

Bridge

Binding

EXAMPLES OF ACOUSTIC GUITARS

Rose

Sound hole

Hollow body

String

Machine head

Bridge

Neck

Headstock

Scratch plate

WASHBURN TWELVE-STRING

Hollow, metal body

Sound hole

Tailpiece

String

Machine head

Neck

Headstock

Resonator

DOBRO RESONATOR

COMPONENTS OF AN ACOUSTIC GUITAR

Machine heads

Truss rod cover

Top E string

Nut

Screws

Headstock

Machine head

Truss rod slot

Truss rod

Fingerboard

Fretwire slot

Position marks

Fretwire

Sound hole

Bracing

Sound board made of two pieces of spruce joined together

EXAMPLES OF ELECTRIC GUITARS

Pick-up

Scratch plate

Solid body

String

Machine head

Bridge

Neck

Headstock

Output socket

Vibrato arm

FENDER STRATOCASTER

Pick-up

Pick-up selector

Solid body

String

Machine head

Bridge

Neck

Headstock

Scratch plate

GIBSON LES PAUL

Pick-up

Solid body

String

Machine head

Bridge

Neck

Headstock

Output socket

Scratch plate

FENDER JAZZ BASS

Keyboard instruments

KEYBOARD INSTRUMENTS are instruments that are sounded by means of a keyboard. The organ and piano are two of the principal members of the keyboard family. The organ consists of pipes which are operated by one or more keyboards and foot pedals. The pipes are lined up in rows (known as ranks or registers) on top of a wind chest. The sound of the organ is made when air is admitted into a pipe by pressing a key or pedal. The piano consists of wire strings stretched over a metal frame, and a keyboard and pedals that operate hammers and dampers. The piano frame is either vertical—as in the upright piano—or horizontal—as in the grand piano. When a key is at rest, a damper lies against the string to keep it from vibrating. When a key is pressed down, the damper moves away from the string as the hammer strikes it, causing the string to vibrate and sound a note.

ORGAN PIPE

UPRIGHT PIANO

Muffler felt
Pressure bar
Tuning pin
Pin block
Hammer
Hammer rail
88–note keyboard
Wooden case
Keybed
Metal frame
Sound board
String
Hitch pin
Treble bridge
Bass bridge
Una corda (soft) pedal
Sostenuto pedal
Damper (sustaining) pedal

ORGAN CONSOLE

Pipe
Pedal stop
Music stand
Swell stop
Choir stop
Swell manual (keyboard)
Great stop
Great manual (keyboard)
Thumb piston
Choir manual (keyboard)
Toe piston
Pedal board
Foot pedal
Swell pedal

UPRIGHT PIANO ACTION

KEY AT REST

String
Hammer
Damper lies against string, and keeps it from vibrating
Hammer rest
Back check
Damper lever
Action lever
Jack
Capstan screw
Key released

KEY PRESSED DOWN

String
Hammer strikes string
Damper moves away from string, allowing it to vibrate
Hammer rest
Back check
Damper lever
Action lever
Jack
Capstan screw
Key pressed down

CONCERT GRAND PIANO (VIEWED FROM ABOVE)

CONCERT GRAND PIANO (FRONT VIEW)

Sound board

Bass bridge

Hitch pin

Metal frame

Single bass note string

Long bridge

Tenor note strings (two strings for each note)

Treble note strings (three strings for each note)

Wooden case

Hammer

Tuning pin

Wrest plank

Keyboard lid

Lid

String

Wooden case

Keyboard

Una corda (soft) pedal

Sostenuto pedal

Damper (sustaining) pedal

88-note keyboard

Percussion instruments

TEMPLE BLOCKS

PERCUSSION INSTRUMENTS are a large group of instruments that produce sound by being struck, shaken, scraped, or clashed together. Some percussion instruments—such as the gong (tam-tam), cymbals, and maracas—do not have a definite pitch and are used for rhythm and impact, and the distinctive timber (color) of their sound. Other percussion instruments—such as the xylophone, vibraphone, and tubular bells—are tuned to a definite pitch and can play melody, harmony, and rhythms. The xylophone and vibraphone each have two rows of bars that are arranged in a similar way to the black and white keys of a piano. Metal tubes are suspended below the bars to amplify the sound. The vibraphone has electrically operated fans that rotate in the tubes and produce a vibrato (wavering pitch) effect.

TUBULAR BELLS

Tube struck with mallet

Hollow, metal tube

Damper bar

Metal frame

Mechanism linking pedal and damper bar

Row of tubes graduated in length and pitch

Damper pedal

EXAMPLES OF MALLETS

SOFT-HEADED MALLET   *Felt-covered head*

HARD-HEADED MALLET   *Rosewood head*

HAMMER MALLET   *Leather-covered head*

Row of bars graduated in length and pitch

XYLOPHONE

Wooden bar struck with hard-headed mallet

Hollow, metal tube

Metal stand

GONG (TAM-TAM)

Tam-tam struck in center with soft-headed mallet

Cord

Metal frame

Rim

Large, metal disk

CYMBALS

Leather strap fits around player's hand

Pad protects hands from vibrations

Thin, convex disk of copper and tin alloy

Zildjian

SECTIONS OF A MARACA

Wooden handle

Lead beads

Hollow, wooden head

TRIANGLE

Steel rod bent into triangular shape

Steel wand

CLAVES

Hardwood sticks clashed together to give a sharp crack

CASTANETS

Cord

Hollowed wood

VIBRAPHONE

Row of bars graduated in length and pitch

Metal bar struck with soft-headed mallet

MUSSER

Metal frame

Damper pedal

Metal tube containing electrically operated fan that produces vibrato (wavering pitch) effect

Electric cable

Drums

A DRUM IS A percussion instrument that consists of a drumhead, made of skin or plastic, stretched over one or both ends of a hollow vessel (the body shell). Drums are played in most parts of the world and are made in a number of different shapes and sizes. They can be divided into three groups according to the shape of the

TAMBOURINE

body shell: frame drums (e.g., tambourines), bowl-shaped drums (e.g., timpani), and tubular drums (e.g., congas). Drums are usually sounded by striking the drumhead with the hands or with mallets, such as a hard-headed stick. The drumhead vibrates, and its vibrations are amplified by the hollow body shell. The snare drum has wires—known as snares—stretched across the lower drumhead; the snares vibrate against the lower drumhead when the drum is played. Most drums, such as congas, do not have a definite pitch and can play only rhythms (see pp. 516-517). Other drums, such as timpani, have a definite pitch and can play melody, harmony, and rhythms. They can be tuned by adjusting the tension of the drumhead. Different types of drum can be combined together with other percussion instruments to form a drum kit. The basic components of the drum kit are bass drum, tom-toms, floor tom (tenor drum), snare drum, and cymbals.

DRUM KIT

Crash cymbal

Tension key

Tension rod

Tom-tom

Lug

Hi-hat cymbal

Snare drum

Tripod stand

Chain

Tension screw

Felt-covered mallet

Pedal

Pedal

SNARE DRUM (VIEWED FROM BELOW)

Snare mounting

Adjustable damper

Lug

Transparent lower drumhead

Upper drumhead

Snare

Stick

Snare release lever

EXAMPLES OF STICKS

Acorn

HARD-HEADED STICK

Taper

SOFT-HEADED STICK

Felt-covered head

WIRE BRUSH

Wire bristles

Ride cymbal

Tension key

Tom-tom

Height adjustment key

Tension rod

Lug

Floor tom (tenor drum)

Tension rod

Lug

Wooden body shell

Height adjustment key

Leg

Bass drum

Rubber foot

CONGAS

Metal hoop

Drumhead

Tension rod

Wooden body shell

Tripod stand

Leg

TIMPANUM (KETTLE DRUM)

Drumhead

Tension rod

Metal hoop

Tuning gauge

Copper body shell

Strut

Crown

Tension rod

Tuning pedal

Castor

519

Electronic instruments

ELECTRONIC INSTRUMENTS generate electronic signals that are magnified by an amplifier, and sent to a loudspeaker where they are converted into sounds. Synthesizers, and other electronic instruments, simulate the characteristic sounds of conventional instruments, and also create entirely new sounds. Most electronic instruments are keyboard instruments, but electronic wind and percussion instruments are also popular. A digital sampler records and stores sounds from musical instruments or other sources. When the sound is played back, the pitch of the original sound can be altered. A keyboard can be connected to the sampler so that a tune can be played using the sampled sounds. With a MIDI (Musical Instrument Digital Interface) system, a computer can be linked with other electronic instruments, such as keyboards and electronic drums, to make sounds together or in sequence. It is also possible, using music software, to compose and play music on a home computer.

ELECTRONIC DRUMS

Drum pad

Height adjustment key

Tripod

HOME KEYBOARD

Power button *Volume control* *Function display* *Sequence record button* *Tone editor control*

Demonstration tune button

Modulation wheel *Multi-accompaniment system control* *Tone and rhythm pattern selector* *Key*

SYNTHESIZER

Memory card slot *Joystick* *Function display* *Edit control* *Data entry key pad*

Sound waveform selection guide

Volume control

Modulation wheel *Sound selection control* *Key*

WIND SYNTHESIZER

Keys for left hand

Mouthpiece

WIND CONTROLLER

Keys for right hand

DIGITAL SAMPLER

Contrast control

Function display

Power button

Data increment control

POWER PACK

MIDI (Musical Instrument Digital Interface) cable

Connecting cable

SOUND MODULE

Record trigger

Floppy-disk drive

Play button

Data entry key pad

Microphone input

Store button

Data entry key pad

Input connector socket

Volume control

HOME COMPUTER SYSTEM

VISUAL DISPLAY UNIT

Music sequencing software

Score for selected instrument

Edit control

Play button

Function display

Effect balance control

SPEAKER

Hard-disk drive

Floppy-disk drive

SOUND MODULE

SPEAKER

Volume control

Volume and tone controls

Volume control

KEYBOARD

Data entry key pad

Mouse pad

Mouse

SPORTS

Soccer

GAMES INVOLVING KICKING A BALL have a long history and were recorded in China as early as 300 BC; in medieval Europe, street football was banned as a menace to the public; only in 1863 were the rules established, specifically banning carrying the ball for all players except the goalkeeper, and separating rugby from soccer. Soccer, also known as association football, is a team sport in which players attempt to score goals by passing and dribbling the ball down the field past opposing defenders, and kicking or heading the ball into the goal net, outwitting the defending goalkeeper or "goalie." Each team consists of ten outfield players (defenders, midfielders, and strikers) and a goalkeeper. Players from the opposing team may challenge the player in possession of the ball, but an illegal or foul tackle results in a penalty if a foul occurs inside the penalty area or a free kick if outside the penalty area. The round ball used in soccer is more easily controlled than the oval balls used in American, Canadian, and Australian rules football and in rugby. The result is a more "open" or flowing game which is played and watched by millions of people worldwide.

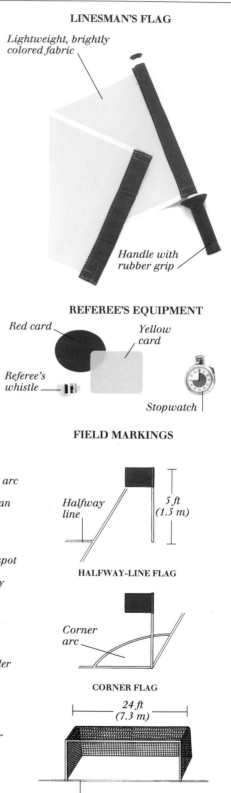

LINESMAN'S FLAG

Lightweight, brightly colored fabric

Handle with rubber grip

REFEREE'S EQUIPMENT

Red card

Yellow card

Referee's whistle

Stopwatch

FIELD MARKINGS

Halfway line

5 ft (1.5 m)

HALFWAY-LINE FLAG

Corner arc

CORNER FLAG

24 ft (7.3 m)

Goal line

GOAL

SOCCER FIELD

150–300 ft (46–91 m)

Goal line

Corner flag

Corner arc

Penalty area

Penalty mark

Referee

Halfway-line flag

Striker

Striker

Left midfielder

Central midfielder

Left back

Touch line

Central defender

Penalty arc

Linesman

Center circle

Center spot

Halfway line

Striker

Right midfielder

Right back

Central defender

Goal area

Goal

Goalkeeper

GOALKEEPER

Goalkeeper's shirt

Glove

Shin guard

Shorts

Sock

Soccer shoe

SOCCER UNIFORM

Open-neck collar

Lightweight, man-made fabric team shirt

Team logo

Manufacturer's logo

Ribbed welt

Sponsor's logo

lotto

Motta

MAKING A SOCCER BALL

Hole punched in panel for stitching

Mitre

F.I.F.A. APPROVED

MULTIPLEX

Waxed thread

Needle

Ball size number

Manufacturer's name

Edge cut to fit perfectly

Mitre
MULTIPLEX

8¹⁄₂–9 in (22–23 cm)

Bladder valve

Bladder made from latex rubber

Panels sewn together with ball inside out

Laminated panel

Long cotton sock

Club crest

Team shorts

Synthetic shoelace

Interchangeable nylon stud

SOCCER SHOE

Football

IN AMERICAN AND CANADIAN FOOTBALL, the object of the game is to get the ball across the opponent's goal line, either by passing or carrying it across (a touchdown), or by kicking it between their goalposts (a field goal). An American football team has 11 players on the field at a time, although up to 40 players can appear for each side in a single game. The agile offense tries to score points, and the heavy hitting defense holds back the opposition. When in possession of the ball, a team has four chances (downs), to move it at least ten yards up the field to make a first down. The opposition gains possession if they fail, or by tackling and intercepting the ball. Canadian football is played on a larger field, with 12 men on each side. A team has only three chances, instead of four, to achieve a first down. Otherwise, the game is very similar to American football. Helmets, face masks, and layers of body padding are worn by the players for protection.

AMERICAN FOOTBALL FIELD

Goalpost
End line
Goal line
Inbound line
Sideline
Players' bench
Referee
Umpire
Back judge
End zone
Line judge

160 ft 6 in
(49 m)

GOALPOST

30 ft
(9.2 m)

AMERICAN FOOTBALL PLAYING FORMATION

Right safety
Middle linebacker
Left safety
Right defensive tackle
Left defensive tackle
Right cornerback
Inside linebacker
Left cornerback
Outside linebacker
Right defensive end
Center
Left defensive end
Tight end
Split end
Left tackle
Right tackle
Right guard
Left guard
Quarterback
Left halfback
Right halfback
Fullback

CANADIAN FOOTBALL FIELD

Goalpost
Goal line
Players' bench
Referee
Umpire
Field judge
Yardsman
Head linesman
Yardsman
Sideline
End zone

195 ft
(59.5 m)

GOALPOST

30 ft
(9.2 m)

CANADIAN FOOTBALL PLAYING FORMATION

Right defensive back
Middle linebacker
Safety
Left defensive back
Left defensive tackle
Right cornerback
Left cornerback
Left outside linebacker
Right outside linebacker
Left defensive end
Right defensive end
Right guard
Wide receiver
Wide receiver
Right defensive tackle
Right tackle
Flanker
Running back
Left guard
Center
Left tackle
Quarterback
Fullback
Halfback

PLAYER

Team logo

Helmet

Wrist pad

Player's number

Thigh pad

Pants

Studded shoe

PROTECTIVE EQUIPMENT

11 in (28 cm)

Painted white ring

Lace

Brown pebbled leather

FOOTBALL

HELMET

Non-breakable plastic

Rubber-coated plastic

Shock absorber

SHOULDER PAD

Tie to shoulder pads

BIKE

AIR·LITE

BLUE LASER 40-42

Chest protector weight up to 5 lb 8 oz (2.5 kg)

RIB PADS

Strap ties onto shoulder pad

UPPER ARM PAD

BIKE

REFEREE'S SIGNALS

TIME OUT

TOUCHDOWN OR FIELD GOAL

PERSONAL FOUL

OFFSIDE OR ENCROACHMENT

HOLDING

ILLEGAL MOTION

FIRST DOWN

PASS INTERFERENCE

ELBOW PAD

FINGERLESS GLOVE

Screw-in stud

PONY

FOOTWEAR

Fold-over leather tongue

Tail bone pad

Foam-sponge filling

BIKE AL60

BIKE AL60

HIP PAD

Rigid plastic covering

BIKE AL82

BIKE AL82

THIGH PAD

PANTS

KNEE PAD

Australian rules and Gaelic football

VARIETIES OF FOOTBALL have developed all over the world and Australian rules football is considered to be one of the roughest versions, allowing full body tackles although participants wear no protective padding. Two teams of 18 players play on a large, oval pitch. Players can kick or punch the ball, which is shaped like a rugby ball, but cannot throw it. Running with the ball is permitted, as long as the ball touches the ground at least once every ten meters. The full backs defend two sets of posts. Teams try to score goals (six points) between the inner posts or behinds (one point) inside the outer posts. Each game has four quarters of 25 minutes, and the team with the most points at the end of the allotted time is the winner. In Gaelic football, an Irish version of soccer (see pp. 524–525), a size 5 association football is used. Each team can have 15 players on the field at a time. Players are allowed to catch, fist, and kick the ball, or dribble it using their hands or feet, but cannot throw it. Teams are awarded three points for getting the ball into the net, and one point for getting it through the posts above the crossbar. Gaelic football is rarely played outside of Ireland.

START OF PLAY

Field umpire

Center circle

SCORING

GOAL (6 POINTS)

BEHIND (1 POINT)

AUSTRALIAN RULES FOOTBALL FIELD

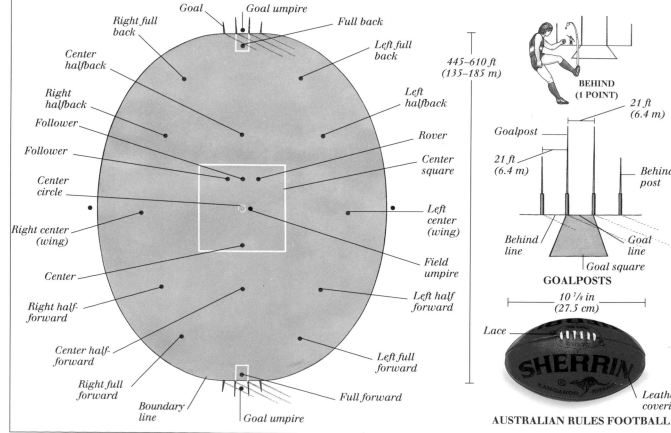

Goal

Goal umpire

Right full back

Full back

Left full back

Center halfback

Right halfback

Left halfback

Follower

Rover

Follower

Center square

Center circle

Left center (wing)

Right center (wing)

Center

Field umpire

Right half-forward

Left half forward

Center half-forward

Left full forward

Right full forward

Full forward

Boundary line

Goal umpire

445–610 ft (135–185 m)

21 ft (6.4 m)

Goalpost

21 ft (6.4 m)

Behind post

Behind line

Goal line

Goal square

GOALPOSTS

10 ⁷⁄₈ in (27.5 cm)

Lace

Leather covering

AUSTRALIAN RULES FOOTBALL

AUSTRALIAN RULES FOOTBALL SKILLS

RUNNING WITH THE BALL

KICKING

TACKLING

TAKING A MARK

PASSING THE BALL

AUSTRALIAN RULES FOOTBALL UNIFORM

Australian Football League logo

Team colors

Sleeveless team guernsey

Sock

Shorts

GAELIC FOOTBALL PITCH

Corner flag

Goalkeeper

Goal umpire

Goal area

Right fullback

Left fullback

Fullback

Right halfback

Left halfback

Center halfback

Center flag

Linesman

Linesman

Left midfielder

Right midfielder

Midfield line

Referee

Left half-forward

Right half-forward

Right full-forward

Center half-forward

Full forward

Left full-forward

260–295 ft
(80–90 m)

CONTROLLING THE BALL

SCORING IN GAELIC FOOTBALL

GOAL (3 POINTS)

POINT (1 POINT)

8 1/2–9 in
(22–23 cm)

21ft
(6.4 m)

Goalpost

Crossbar

Parallelogram

GOAL

Oneills all-ireland

GAELIC FOOTBALL

Rugby

RUGBY IS PLAYED WITH AN OVAL BALL which may be carried, thrown, or kicked. There are two types of rugby. Rugby Union is an amateur game played by two teams of 15 players. Players can score points in two ways: by placing the ball behind the opponents' goal line (a try, scoring four points) or by kicking it over the crossbar of the opponent's goal (a conversion, scoring two points; a penalty kick, scoring three points; or a drop-kick, scoring three points). Rugby League developed from the Union game but is played by 13 players at amateur and professional levels. In League games, a try scores four points; a conversion scores two points; a drop goal scores three points, and a penalty kick scores two points. In both forms of the game, whenever a rule is broken, play is resumed with a scrum. In a scrum, each team's forwards bind together facing each other and fight for possession of the ball.

RUGBY UNION SCRUM

Loose-head prop
Hooker
Tight-head prop
Scrum-half
Flanker
Flanker
Lock forward
Lock forward
Number 8

RUGBY LEAGUE SCRUM

Blind-side prop
Hooker
Open-side prop
Scrum-half
Second-row forward
Second-row forward
Loose forward

18 ft (5.5 m)
Upright
Crossbar
Protective padding
9 ft 10 in (3 m)
RUGBY UNION GOALPOST

18 ft (5.5 m)
Upright
Crossbar
Protective padding
RUGBY LEAGUE GOALPOST

RUGBY UNION FIELD

Goal
Dead-ball line
Touch in-goal line
Goal line
5 m line
Scrum-half
10 m line
Loose-head prop
Flanker
Lock forward
Center
Left wing
Center
Full back
Touch-line
Referee
Hooker
Tight-head prop
Linesman
Flanker
Lock forward
Right wing
Number 8
Fly-half
In-goal area
225 ft (68 m) maximum

RUGBY LEAGUE FIELD

Goal
Dead-ball line
Touch in-goal
Goal line
10 m line
Referee
Blind-side prop
Linesman
Second-row forward
Loose forward
Left wing
Full back
Touch in-goal line
Touch-line
Hooker
Open-side prop
Linesman
Second-row forward
Scrum-half
Stand-off half
Center
Center
Right wing
225 ft (68 m) maximum

RUGBY SCORING AND SKILLS

GOAL

Goal line

TRY

PASS

PLACE KICK

FLYING TACKLE

RUGBY UNION PLAYER

Shirt in team color

Knee-high sock

Team shorts

Studded boot

RUGBY UNION BALL

Four-panel construction

Laminated leather panel covered with textured plastic

Mitre MULTIPLEX

11–12 in (28–30 cm)

RUGBY LEAGUE BALL

Four-panel construction

Laminated leather panel covered with smooth plastic

Mitre MULTIPLEX 2

11 in (28 cm)

RUGBY LEAGUE SHIRT

Team crest

Official logo of the British Rugby Football League

Three-quarter sleeve

RUGBY UNION SHIRT

Button-up collar

Team crest

Long sleeve

RUGBY SHOE

Ankle support

Circular stud

Team color

RUGBY SHIRTS

Basketball

BASKETBALL IS A BALL GAME for two teams of five players, originally devised in 1890 by James Naismath for the Y.M.C.A. in Springfield, Massachusetts. The object of the game is to take possession of the ball and score points by throwing the ball into the opposing team's basket. A player moves the ball up and down the court by bouncing it along the ground or "dribbling"; the ball may be passed between players by throwing, bouncing, or rolling. Players may not run with or kick the ball, although pivoting on one foot is allowed. The game begins with the referee throwing the ball into the air and a player from each team jumping up to try and "tip" the ball to a teammate. The length of the game and the number of periods played varies at different levels. There are amateur, professional, and international rules. No game ends in a draw. As many extra periods as necessary are played to break the tie. In addition to the five players on court, each team has up to seven substitutes, but players may only leave the court with the permission of the referee. Basketball is a noncontact sport and fouls on other players are penalized by a throw-in awarded against the offending team; a free throw at the basket is awarded when a player is fouled in the act of shooting. Basketball is a fast-moving game, requiring both physical and mental coordination. Skillful tactical play matters more than simple physical strength and the agility of the players makes the game an excellent spectator sport.

BASKETBALL SKILLS

CHEST PASS

DRIBBLE

OVERHEAD PASS

INTERNATIONAL BASKETBALL COURT

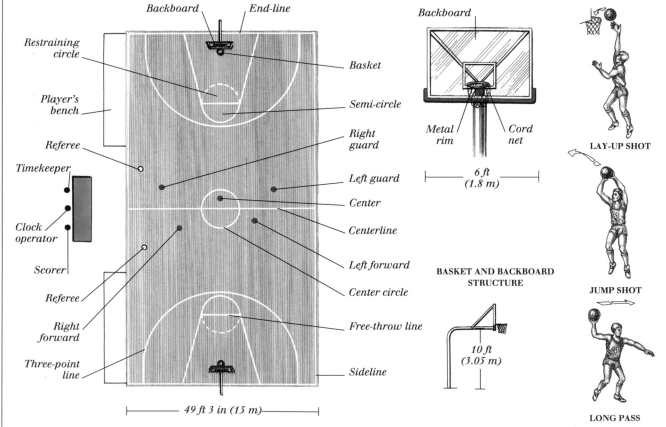

Backboard

End-line

Restraining circle

Player's bench

Referee

Timekeeper

Clock operator

Scorer

Referee

Right forward

Three-point line

Basket

Semi-circle

Right guard

Left guard

Center

Centerline

Left forward

Center circle

Free-throw line

Sideline

49 ft 3 in (15 m)

BASKET AND BACKBOARD

Backboard

Metal rim

Cord net

6 ft (1.8 m)

BASKET AND BACKBOARD STRUCTURE

10 ft (3.05 m)

LAY-UP SHOT

JUMP SHOT

LONG PASS

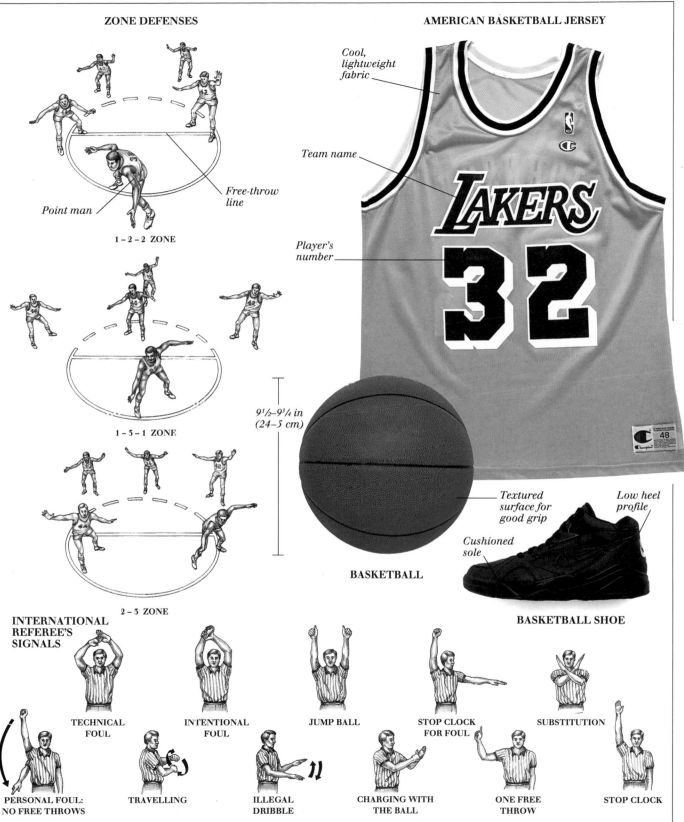

ZONE DEFENSES

Point man

Free-throw line

1 – 2 – 2 ZONE

1 – 3 – 1 ZONE

2 – 3 ZONE

AMERICAN BASKETBALL JERSEY

Cool, lightweight fabric

Team name

Player's number

LAKERS

32

Champion 48

9¹/₂–9³/₄ in (24–5 cm)

Textured surface for good grip

Low heel profile

Cushioned sole

BASKETBALL

BASKETBALL SHOE

INTERNATIONAL REFEREE'S SIGNALS

TECHNICAL FOUL

INTENTIONAL FOUL

JUMP BALL

STOP CLOCK FOR FOUL

SUBSTITUTION

PERSONAL FOUL: NO FREE THROWS

TRAVELLING

ILLEGAL DRIBBLE

CHARGING WITH THE BALL

ONE FREE THROW

STOP CLOCK

Volleyball, netball, and handball

VOLLEYBALL, NETBALL, AND HANDBALL are fast-moving team sports played with balls, usually on courts with a hard surface. In volleyball, the object of the game is to hit the ball over a net strung across the center of the court so that it touches the ground on the opponent's side. The team of six players can take three hits to direct the ball over the net, although the same player cannot hit the ball twice in a row. Players can hit the ball with their arms, hands or any other part of their upper body. Teams score points only while serving. The first team to score 15 points, with a two-point margin over their opponent, wins the game. Netball is similar to basketball (see pp. 532–533), but is played on a slightly larger court with seven players instead of five. A team moves the ball toward the goal by throwing, passing, and catching it with the aim of throwing the ball through the opponents' goal net. Players are confined by their playing position to specific areas of the court. Team handball is one of the world's fastest games. Each side has seven players. A team moves the ball by dribbling, passing, or bouncing it as they run. Players may stop, catch, throw, bounce, or strike the ball with any part of the body above the knees. Each team tries to score goals by directing the ball past the opposition's goalkeeper into the net, which is similar to a soccer goal net (see pp. 524–525).

VOLLEYBALL SHOTS

OVERHAND SERVE   SPIKE (SMASH)

UNDERHAND SERVE   FOREARM PASS (DIG)

VOLLEYBALL KIT

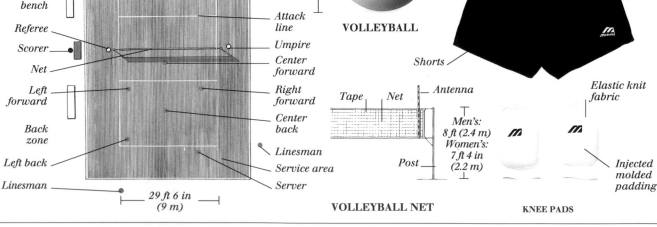

Team colors

Ribbed cuff

Cotton-knit jersey

Leather covering

Elastic waist

VOLLEYBALL COURT

End line

Linesman

Clear space

8 in (21 cm)

Linesman

Sideline

Players' bench

Referee

Scorer

Net

Left forward

Back zone

Left back

Linesman

Attack zone

Attack line

VOLLEYBALL

Umpire

Center forward

Right forward

Center back

Linesman

Service area

Server

29 ft 6 in (9 m)

Shorts

Elastic knit fabric

Tape   Net   Antenna

Men's: 8 ft (2.4 m)
Women's: 7 ft 4 in (2.2 m)

Post

VOLLEYBALL NET

Injected molded padding

KNEE PADS

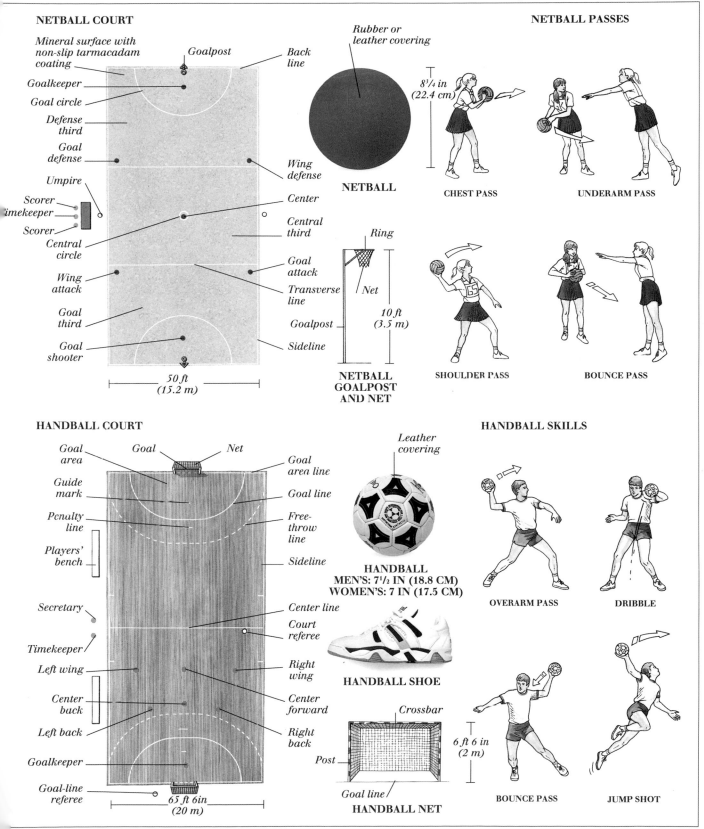

NETBALL COURT

Mineral surface with non-slip tarmacadam coating

Goalpost

Back line

Goalkeeper

Goal circle

Defense third

Goal defense

Wing defense

Umpire

Center

Scorer

Timekeeper

Central third

Scorer

Central circle

Goal attack

Transverse line

Wing attack

Goal third

Goal shooter

Sideline

50 ft (15.2 m)

NETBALL PASSES

Rubber or leather covering

8³/₄ in (22.4 cm)

NETBALL

CHEST PASS

UNDERARM PASS

Ring

Net

10 ft (3.5 m)

Goalpost

NETBALL GOALPOST AND NET

SHOULDER PASS

BOUNCE PASS

HANDBALL COURT

Goal area

Goal

Net

Goal area line

Guide mark

Goal line

Penalty line

Free-throw line

Players' bench

Sideline

Secretary

Center line

Court referee

Timekeeper

Left wing

Right wing

Center back

Center forward

Left back

Right back

Goalkeeper

Goal-line referee

65 ft 6in (20 m)

HANDBALL SKILLS

Leather covering

**HANDBALL
MEN'S: 7¹/₂ IN (18.8 CM)
WOMEN'S: 7 IN (17.5 CM)**

HANDBALL SHOE

Crossbar

6 ft 6 in (2 m)

Post

Goal line

HANDBALL NET

OVERARM PASS

DRIBBLE

BOUNCE PASS

JUMP SHOT

Baseball

BASEBALL IS A BALL GAME for two teams of nine players. The batter hits the ball thrown by the opposing team's pitcher, into the area between the foul lines. He then runs round all four fixed bases in order to score a run, touching or "tagging" each base in turn. The pitcher must throw the ball at a height between the batter's armpits and knees, a height which is called the strike zone. A ball pitched in this area that crosses over the home plate is called a "strike" and the batter has three strikes in which to try to hit the ball (otherwise he has "struck out"). The fielding team tries to get the batting team out by catching the ball before it bounces, tagging a player of the batting team who is running between bases with the ball, or by tagging a base before the player has reached it. Members of the batting team may stop safely at a base as long as it is not occupied by another member of their team. When the batter runs to first base, his teammate at first base must run onto second – this is called a force play. A game consists of nine innings and each team will bat once during an inning. When three members of the batting team are out, the teams swap roles. The team with the most runs wins the game.

BATTER'S HELMET

Plastic shell

Peak

Foam padding

Wire coated in strong nylon

Plastic-coated foam padding

CATCHER'S MASK

BASEBALL FIELD

Center field

Center fielder

Warning track

Left fielder

Right fielder

Left field

Second baseman

Right field

Foul line

Outfield

Shortstop

First baseman

Umpire

Third baseman

First base

Third base

Infield

Coach's box

Home run

Second base

Dugout

On-deck circle

Pitcher's mound

325 ft (100 m) minimum

PITCHER'S MOUND

Pitcher

Pitcher's rubber

HOME PLATE

Batter

Home plate

Catcher

Home-plate umpire

MAKING A BASEBALL

Wool yarn

Rubber inner casing

Horsehide strip

CUSHION CORK
5 OZ
9 IN
TAIWAN
LEATHER COVER

Cork center

Cooper
63

Cotton thread outer casing

Wool strand

Red outer stitching

BASEBALL EQUIPMENT

Webbed pocket

Fingers laced together

Strap

Thumb

Palm

STEERHIDE LEATHER

Leather stitching

Heel

FIELDER'S GLOVE AND BALL

PONY

Metal heel plate

AMERICAN BASEBALL SHOE

Metal toe plate

THE PITCHING SEQUENCE

THE WINDUP 1 **THE WINDUP 2** **THE WINDUP 3**

THE WINDUP 4 **THE RELEASE** **THE FOLLOW-THROUGH**

UMPIRING SIGNALS

BALL **INFIELD** **STRIKE**

FAIR BALL **RUNNER IS SAFE** **FOUL TIP**

Batter's helmet

Bat

Batting glove

Team shirt

Undershirt

Pants

Spiked shoe

BATTER

Hitting area

Official Baseball

Crest

3 ft 6 in (1.1 m) maximum

Handle

Knob

BAT

Cricket

CRICKET IS A BALL GAME PLAYED by two teams of eleven players on a pitch with two sets of three stumps (wickets). The bowler bowls the ball down the pitch to the batsman of the opposing team, who must defend the wicket in front of which he stands. The object of the game is to score as many runs as possible. Runs can be scored individually by running the length of the playing strip, or by hitting a ball which lands outside the boundary (six), or which lands inside the boundary but bounces or rolls outside (four); the opposing team will bowl and field, attempting to dismiss the batsmen. A batsman can be dismissed in one of several ways: by the bowler hitting the wicket with the ball ("bowled"); by a fielder catching the ball hit by the batsman before it touches the ground ("caught"); by the wicket-keeper or another fielder breaking the wicket while the batsman is attempting a run and is therefore out of his ground ("stumped" or "run out"); by the batsman breaking the wicket with his own bat or body ("hit wicket"); by a part of the batsman's body being hit by a ball that would otherwise have hit the wicket ("leg before wicket" ["lbw"]). A match consists of one or two innings and each innings ends when the tenth batsman of the batting team is out, when a certain number of overs (a series of six balls bowled) have been played, or when the captain of the batting team "declares" ending the innings voluntarily.

POSSIBLE FIELD POSITIONS FOR AN AWAY SWING BOWLER TO A RIGHT-HANDED BATSMAN (IN RED) AND OTHER FIELD POSITIONS

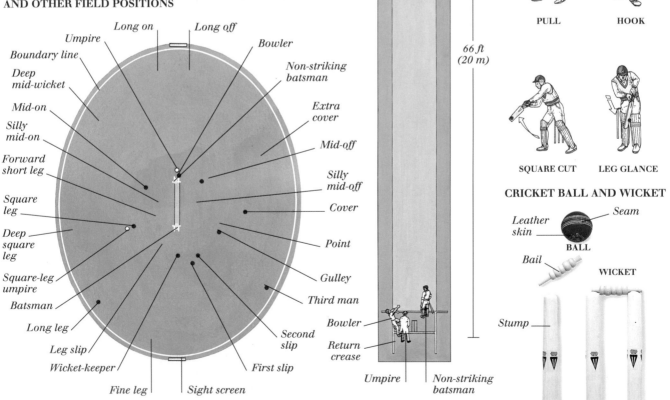

FORWARD DEFENSIVE STROKE

BACKWARD DEFENSIVE STROKE

ON-DRIVE

OFF-DRIVE

PULL

HOOK

SQUARE CUT

LEG GLANCE

CRICKET BALL AND WICKET

Leather skin

Seam

BALL

Bail

WICKET

Stump

Long on
Umpire
Long off
Bowler
Boundary line
Deep mid-wicket
Non-striking batsman
Mid-on
Extra cover
Silly mid-on
Forward short leg
Mid-off
Silly mid-off
Square leg
Cover
Deep square leg
Point
Square-leg umpire
Gulley
Batsman
Third man
Long leg
Leg slip
Second slip
Wicket-keeper
First slip
Fine leg
Sight screen

CRICKET PITCH

Wicket-keeper
Batsman
Wicket
Bowling crease
66 ft (20 m)
Bowler
Return crease
Umpire
Non-striking batsman

MAKING A BAT HANDLE

Sarawak cane

Twine wrapped around handle

Rubber strip

LAMINATING THE WOOD

BINDING THE HANDLE

MAKING A BAT BLADE

Kiln-dried willow

SEASONING THE TIMBER

V-shaped splice

Blade planed by hand

CUTTING THE SPLICE

PROTECTIVE CLOTHING

Slit in leather for greater flexibility

Padding protects knuckles from injury

Mesh covering for ventilation

BATTING GLOVE

Dimpled rubber improves grip

Wrist strap

WICKET-KEEPER'S GLOVES

Polycarbonate shell with cloth covering

Peak

Foam cheek-piece for comfort and good fit

Protective plastic ear piece

HELMET

ADDING THE HANDLE TO THE BAT

Rubber grip

Grip rolled onto handle

Shoulder of bat

Handle glued into splice

Scoop

Toe of the bat shaped

FITTING THE HANDLE

GRAYNICOLLS

Sanded and polished bat

FINISHING TOUCHES

Bat

BATSMAN

Padded glove

Cap

Wristband

White shirt

White sweater

Stripes in team colors

Thigh pad under white pants

Knee roll

Cricket shoe

Leg pad

Dimpled rubber sole

539

Field hockey, lacrosse, and hurling

ALL OVER THE WORLD, TEAM GAMES have evolved which require that a ball be struck or carried, and tossed at the end of a stick. Early forms of these games include hurling, shinty, bandy, and pelota. Field hockey is played by men and women: two teams of eleven players try to gain and keep possession of the ball and score goals by using the hockey stick to propel the ball into their opponents' goal net. Skills such as passing, pushing, or hitting the ball by slapping or lifting it in a flicking movement, and shooting at the goal are crucial. Field hockey is played indoors and outdoors on grass or synthetic fields. Lacrosse is played internationally as a 12-a-side game for women and as 10-a-side game for men. The women's field has no absolute boundaries but the men's has clearly defined sidelines and end lines. The ball is kept in play by being carried, thrown or batted with the crosse, and rolled or kicked in any direction. In men's and women's lacrosse, play can continue behind the marked goal areas. Similar skills are required in hurling – a Gaelic field game played on the same pitch as Gaelic football (see pp. 528–529), using the same goalposts and net. In hurling, the ball may be struck with or carried on the hurley and, when off the ground, may be struck with the hand or kicked. Goals (three points) are scored when the ball passes between the posts and under the crossbar; one point is scored when the ball passes between the posts and over the crossbar.

GOALKEEPER'S EQUIPMENT

Air vent

Hard shell

Face mask

Cooper XL7

HELMET

Strap

Rigid palm

Padded wrist

PRO spec

GAUNTLET

FIELD HOCKEY STICK AND BALL

Steam-bent ash head

Blade

Stitched seam

STICK

Handle

Tape

Slazenger FLEXI

2¾–3 in (7–7.5 cm)

3 ft (91 cm)

BALL

FIELD HOCKEY FIELD

Center forward

Inside right

Right wing

Right half

Right back

Sideline

Corner flag

Shooting circle

Goal

Penalty spot

Five yard mark

Goal line

Inside left

Left wing

Umpire

Center half

Left half

Left back

Goalkeeper

180 ft (55 m)

Protective overshoe

Padding protects toes against the hard ball

Strap

GOALKEEPER'S BOOT

7 ft (2.1 m)

FIELD HOCKEY GOAL

MEN'S LACROSSE FIELD

Defender
Goalkeeper
Defender
Midfielder
Midfielder
Referee
Attacker
Attacker
Corner flag
Goal
Goal circle
Defender
Midfielder
Chief bench official
Scorer
Penalty timekeeper
Attacker
Timekeeper
180 ft (55 m)

WOMEN'S LACROSSE FIELD

Center
Left wing defense
Left wing attack
Third home
Second home
First home
Third man
15 m fan
Hash mark
Goalkeeper
Goal circle
Point
Cover point
Right wing defense
Timekeeper
Scorer
Penalty timekeeper
Right wing attack
Umpire
200 ft (60 m) approx.

CROSSE AND BALL

Butt
Handle
Lacing
Guardstop
Throat
Net made from rawhide or cord
Pocket
Wall
Head

HURLER

Helmet
Team shirt
Hurley
Team shorts
Sock
Shoe

LACROSSE SKILLS

CRADLING
THROWING
SIDE-SHOOTING

LACROSSE GOALKEEPER

Goalkeeper's stick
Helmet
Face mask
Team shirt
Leather glove
Sweat pants
Player's number
Solid rubber lacrosse ball
6 ft (1.8 m)
Crossbar
Post
Peg

LACROSSE NET

SCORING AT HURLING

GOAL (3 POINTS)
POINT (1 POINT)
23 ft (7 m)

Leather cover around a cork center
HURLING BALL

HURLEY AND HURLING BALL

Grip
HURLEY
Boss
3 ft (91 cm)

Track and field

THE SPORTS that make up athletics are divided into two main groups: track events – which include sprinting, middle, and long distance running, relay running, hurdling, and walking – and field events which require jumping and throwing skills. Contests designed to test the speed, strength, agility, and stamina of athletes were held by the ancient Greeks over 4,000 years ago. However, the abolition of the Olympic Games in 393 AD meant that track and field events were neglected until the revival of large-scale competitions in the mid-nineteenth century. Modern stadiums offer areas reserved for the long jump, triple jump, and pole vault usually situated outside the running track. The javelin, shot, hammer, and discus are thrown within the track area. Most athletes specialize in one or two events but, in the heptathlon, women compete in seven events, held over two days: 200 m and 800 m races, 100 m hurdles, javelin, shot put, high jump, and long jump. In the decathlon, men compete in ten events over two days: 100 m, 400 m, and 1,500 m races, 110 m hurdles, javelin, discus, shot put, pole vault, high jump, and long jump.

FIELD EVENT EQUIPMENT

Steel wire

Head

Body

Swivel

Metal rim

Center weight

DISCUS
MEN'S: 4 LB 7 OZ (2 KG)
WOMEN'S: 2 LB 3 OZ (1 KG)

Hammer handle

HAMMER
16 LB (7 KG)

Rubber coating

Shot pellet filling

5 in (12.7 cm)

4 in (10 cm)

MEN'S SHOT
16 LB (7 KG)

WOMEN'S SHOT
8 LB 12 OZ (4 KG)

JAVELIN   Cord grip   Shaft   Tip

Men: 8 ft 6 in (2.6 m)
Women: 7 ft 6 in (2.3 m)

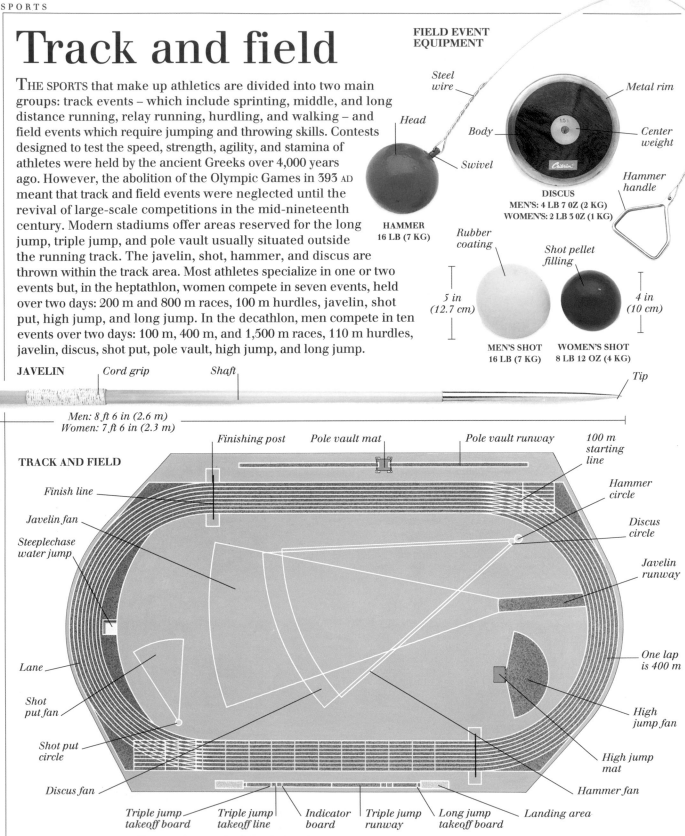

TRACK AND FIELD

Finishing post   Pole vault mat   Pole vault runway   100 m starting line

Finish line

Javelin fan

Steeplechase water jump

Lane

Shot put fan

Shot put circle

Discus fan

Triple jump takeoff board   Triple jump takeoff line   Indicator board   Triple jump runway   Long jump takeoff board   Landing area

Hammer circle

Discus circle

Javelin runway

One lap is 400 m

High jump fan

High jump mat

Hammer fan

RELAY BATONS

Hollow plastic tube

TYPES OF SHOE

Lightweight construction

Spiked sole

TRACK SHOE

Air "pumping" device for comfort and fit

Reflective side strip

Wedge heel

Air-cushioned sole

RUNNING SHOE

DISCUS THROW

Swing — *Shift* — *Twist* — *Release*

SHOT PUT

Crouch — *Shift* — *Thrust* — *Release*

HAMMER THROW

Swing — *Entry* — *Lift* — *Release*

JAVELIN THROW

Withdrawal stride — *Halfturn* — *Step* — *Drive forward* — *Release*

HIGH JUMP

Approach — *Takeoff* — *Drive* — *Arch* — *Landing*

LONG JUMP

Takeoff — *Flight* — *Hitch kick* — *Stretch* — *Landing*

Takeoff board

POLE VAULT

Plant — *Takeoff* — *Hang* — *Rock-back* — *Push-pull* — *Handstand* — *Release* — *Landing*

TRIPLE JUMP

Takeoff — *Hop* — *Skip* — *Jump*

Takeoff board — *Land on foot used for takeoff* — *Land on opposite foot*

Racket sports

PROTECTIVE
EYEWEAR

THE OBJECT OF ALL RACKET SPORTS is to make shots the opponent cannot return. Games are played by two players (singles) or four players (doubles). Racket shape and size is tailored to each sport, but all rackets are constructed of wood, plastic, aluminum, or high-performance materials such as fiberglass and carbon graphite. Racket strings are usually synthetic, although natural gut is still used. Tennis is played on a court divided by a low net. Opposing players serve alternate games. At least six games must be won to gain a set, and two or sometimes three sets are needed to win a match. Tennis courts may be concrete, grass, clay, or synthetic, each surface requiring a different style of play. Badminton is an indoor sport that is played with light, flexible rackets and a birdie on a court with a high net. Players can score points only on their serve. The first to reach 15 points (11 points for women's singles) wins the game. Two games are needed to win a match. Squash and racketball are both played in enclosed courts. One player hits the ball against the front wall, and the other tries to return it before it bounces on the floor more than once. Squash rackets have smaller, rounder heads and stiffer frames than badminton rackets. International courts are wider than those in the U.S., where a much harder ball is used. Squash games are played to nine points (international) or 15 points (U.S.). In racketball, players use a ball that is larger and bouncier than a squash ball. The racketball racket is thick and sturdy, with a large head, short handle, and a strap that loops around the wrist. Points can be won only when serving, and the first player to reach 21 points wins.

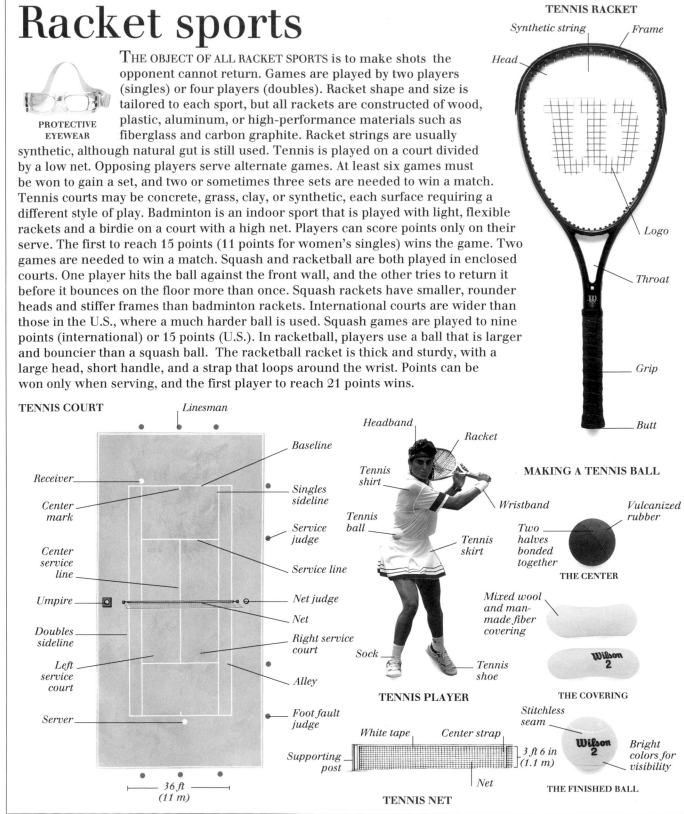

TENNIS RACKET
Synthetic string
Frame
Head
Logo
Throat
Grip
Butt

TENNIS COURT
Linesman
Baseline
Receiver
Singles sideline
Center mark
Service judge
Center service line
Service line
Umpire
Net judge
Net
Doubles sideline
Right service court
Left service court
Alley
Server
Foot fault judge
36 ft
(11 m)

TENNIS PLAYER
Headband
Racket
Tennis shirt
Wristband
Tennis ball
Tennis skirt
Sock
Tennis shoe

TENNIS NET
White tape
Center strap
Supporting post
Net
3 ft 6 in
(1.1 m)

MAKING A TENNIS BALL
Vulcanized rubber
Two halves bonded together
THE CENTER
Mixed wool and man-made fiber covering
Wilson 2
THE COVERING
Stitchless seam
Wilson 2
Bright colors for visibility
THE FINISHED BALL

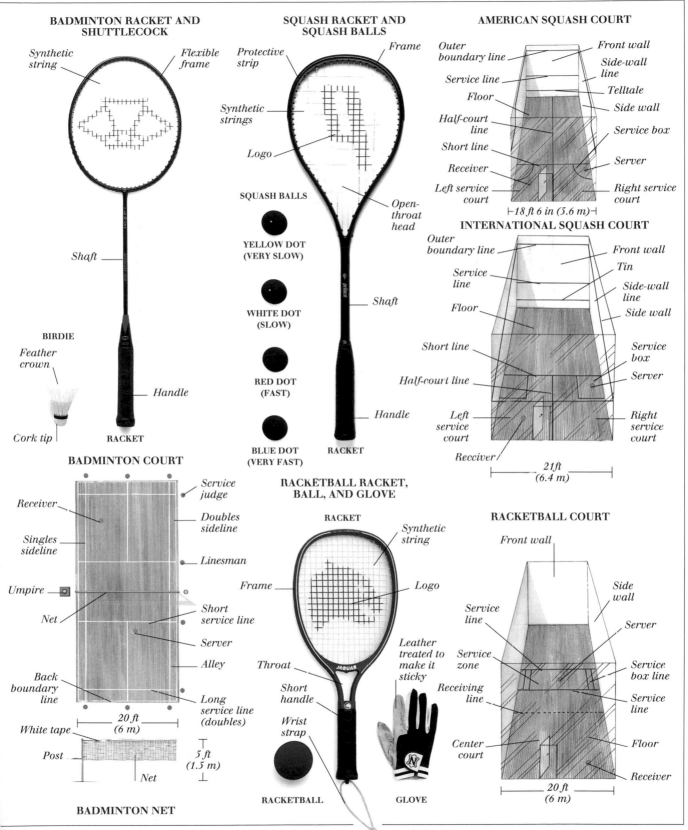

BADMINTON RACKET AND SHUTTLECOCK

Synthetic string

Flexible frame

Shaft

Handle

BIRDIE

Feather crown

Cork tip

RACKET

BADMINTON COURT

Receiver

Singles sideline

Umpire

Net

Back boundary line

Service judge

Doubles sideline

Linesman

Short service line

Server

Alley

Long service line (doubles)

20 ft (6 m)

White tape

Post

Net

5 ft (1.5 m)

BADMINTON NET

SQUASH RACKET AND SQUASH BALLS

Protective strip

Frame

Synthetic strings

Logo

SQUASH BALLS

YELLOW DOT (VERY SLOW)

WHITE DOT (SLOW)

RED DOT (FAST)

BLUE DOT (VERY FAST)

Open-throat head

Shaft

Handle

RACKET

RACKETBALL RACKET, BALL, AND GLOVE

RACKET

Synthetic string

Frame

Logo

Throat

Short handle

Wrist strap

Leather treated to make it sticky

RACKETBALL

GLOVE

AMERICAN SQUASH COURT

Outer boundary line

Service line

Floor

Half-court line

Short line

Receiver

Left service court

Front wall

Side-wall line

Telltale

Side wall

Service box

Server

Right service court

18 ft 6 in (5.6 m)

INTERNATIONAL SQUASH COURT

Outer boundary line

Service line

Floor

Short line

Half-court line

Left service court

Receiver

Front wall

Tin

Side-wall line

Side wall

Service box

Server

Right service court

21 ft (6.4 m)

RACKETBALL COURT

Front wall

Side wall

Service line

Service zone

Receiving line

Center court

Server

Service box line

Service line

Floor

Receiver

20 ft (6 m)

Golf

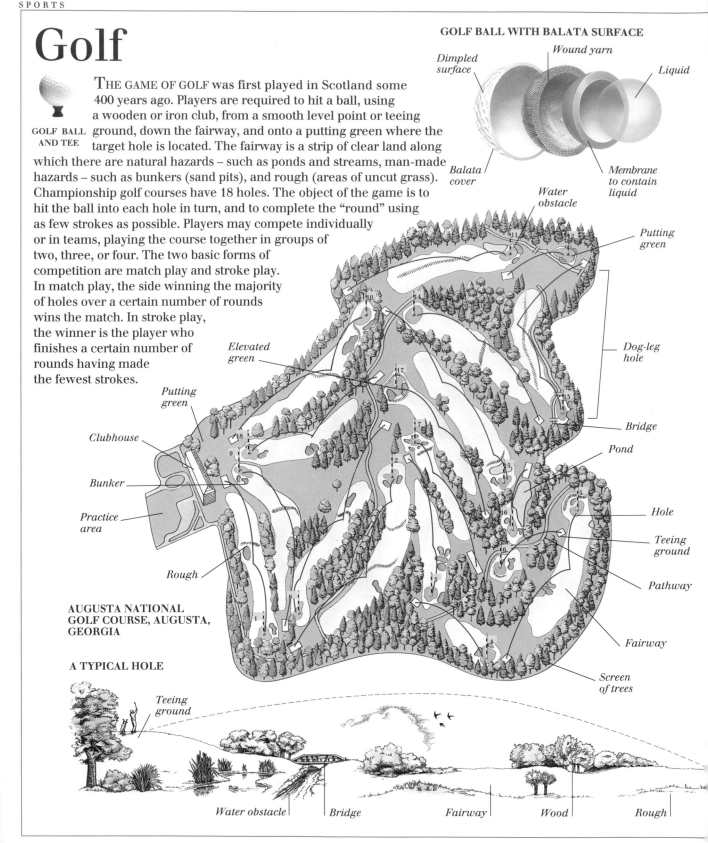

GOLF BALL AND TEE

THE GAME OF GOLF was first played in Scotland some 400 years ago. Players are required to hit a ball, using a wooden or iron club, from a smooth level point or teeing ground, down the fairway, and onto a putting green where the target hole is located. The fairway is a strip of clear land along which there are natural hazards – such as ponds and streams, man-made hazards – such as bunkers (sand pits), and rough (areas of uncut grass). Championship golf courses have 18 holes. The object of the game is to hit the ball into each hole in turn, and to complete the "round" using as few strokes as possible. Players may compete individually or in teams, playing the course together in groups of two, three, or four. The two basic forms of competition are match play and stroke play. In match play, the side winning the majority of holes over a certain number of rounds wins the match. In stroke play, the winner is the player who finishes a certain number of rounds having made the fewest strokes.

GOLF BALL WITH BALATA SURFACE

Dimpled surface

Wound yarn

Liquid

Balata cover

Membrane to contain liquid

Water obstacle

Putting green

Dog-leg hole

Bridge

Pond

Hole

Teeing ground

Pathway

Fairway

Screen of trees

Elevated green

Putting green

Clubhouse

Bunker

Practice area

Rough

AUGUSTA NATIONAL GOLF COURSE, AUGUSTA, GEORGIA

A TYPICAL HOLE

Teeing ground

Water obstacle

Bridge

Fairway

Wood

Rough

MAKING A WOODEN CLUB

Close grain of wood

Streamlined back

Plastic insert on face

Sand, stain, and varnish finish

Persimmon wood

Slot cut for plate

Metal sole plate protects the wood

Outline of head

RAW MATERIAL

CREATING THE BASIC SHAPE

ADDING THE LEAD WEIGHT

THE FINISHED CLUB HEAD

RANGE OF WOODEN CLUBS

10 degree loft

15 degree loft

21 degree loft

DRIVER

3-WOOD

5-WOOD

RANGE OF IRON CLUBS

22 degree loft

26 degree loft

3-IRON

4-IRON

30 degree loft

34 degree loft

38 degree loft

42 degree loft

46 degree loft

50 degree loft

56 degree loft

5-IRON

6-IRON

7-IRON

8-IRON

9-IRON

PITCHING WEDGE

SAND WEDGE

GOLF ACCESSORIES

BALL MARKERS

SCORECARD AND PENCIL

GOLF TEES

PITCHMARK REPAIRER

PRACTICE BALL

Spiked sole

LIGHTWEIGHT SHOE

Flag pole or pin

Green

Bunker (sand pit)

PUTTER, WOOD, AND IRON

WOOD

Textured vulcanized rubber grip

IRON

PUTTER

Shaped pistol grip

Stainless steel shaft

Steel shaft

Steel shaft

33 in (85 cm)

37 in (97 cm)

43 in (109 cm)

Neck

Angled neck

Neck

Face

Heel

Heel

Toe

Toe

Blade

Toe

Groove

Sole

Heel

Archery and shooting

TARGET SHOOTING AND ARCHERY EVOLVED as practice for hunting and battle skills. Modern bows, although designed according to the principles of early hunting bows, use laminates, fiberglass, dacron, and carbon, and are equipped with sights and stabilizers. Competitors in target archery shoot over distances of 100 ft (30 m), 165 ft (50 m), 230 ft (70 m), and 300 ft (90 m) for men, and 100 ft (30 m), 165 ft (50 m), 200 ft (60 m), and 230 ft (70 m) for women. The closer the shot is to the center of the target, the higher the score. The individual scores are added up, and the archer with the highest total wins the competition. Crossbows are used in match competitions over 33 ft (10 m), and 100 ft (30 m). Rifle shooting is divided into three categories: smallbore, bigbore, and air rifle. Contests take place over a variety of distances and further subdivisions are based on the type of shooting position used; prone, kneeling, or standing. The Olympic biathlon combines cross-country skiing and rifle shooting over a course of approximately 12^1/$_2$ miles (20 km). Additional magazines of ammunition are carried in the butt of the rifles. Bigbore rifles fitted with a telescopic sight can be used for hunting and running game target shooting. Pistol shooting events, using rapid-fire pistols, target pistols, and air pistols, take place over 33 ft (10 m), 82 ft (25 m), and 165 ft (50 m) distances. In rapid-fire pistol shooting, a total of 60 shots are fired from a distance of 82 ft (25 m).

CROSSBOW AND BOLT

Laminated fiberglass bow

Bolt

Bolt rest

1³/₄ in (45 mm)

CROSSBOW TARGET

Bolt

Stirrup held between feet when drawing bow

Sight

Hardwood laminate limb

Dacron string

Sight

MODERN BOW

Pressure button

Grip

V-bar stabilizers

Magnesium riser

Plastic fletch

Nock

Forearm guard

Finger hole

Aluminum shaft

BRACER

FINGER TAB

Strap

Wristband

ARCHER'S GLOVE

Weight

Waistband

Accessory pouch

Velcro fastening

ARCHERY EQUIPMENT

QUIVER

SMALLBORE BIATHLON RIFLE

Rifle sight without magnifying lens

Fore sight

Barrel

Trigger

Trigger guard

Extra magazine stored in rifle butt

0.22 in (5.6 m) caliber bullet

Magazine

6 in (155 m)

SMALLBORE FREE RIFLE TARGET FOR 165 FT (50 M) RANGE

BIGBORE HUNTING RIFLE

Bolt handle

Bolt

Telescopic sight

Open sight

Open sight

Sling fixing point

0.3 in (7.62 mm) calibre bullet

39 in (1 m)

BIGBORE RIFLE TARGET FOR 1000 FT (300 M) RANGE

AIR PISTOL

Wooden grip shaped to fit the hand

Cocking lever and barrel

Piston

TARGET PISTOL

Back sight

Fore sight

Hammer

Firing pin

Sight pin

Sight ring attachment

Magazine

0.35 in (9 mm) calibre bullet

7³/₄ in (197 mm)

PISTOL TARGET FOR 60 FT (18 M) RANGE

Trigger

Air-pistol pellet

6 in (155 mm)

AIR-PISTOL TARGET FOR 33 FT (10 M) RANGE

Nock

FIELD ARROW

Metal tip

Feathering

Wooden shaft

Straw butt

White inner 2 points

Aluminum longrod stabilizer

Blue outer 5 points

Yellow inner 10 points (bull's-eye)

ARCHERY TARGET

Ice hockey

ICE HOCKEY IS PLAYED by two teams of six players on an ice rink, with a goal net at each end. The object of this fast, and often dangerous, game is to hit a frozen rubber puck into the opposing team's net with an ice hockey stick. The game begins when the referee drops the puck between the sticks of two players from opposing teams, who face off. The rink is divided into three areas: defending, neutral, and attacking zones. Players may move with the puck and pass it to one another along the ice, but the puck should not travel more than two zones across the rink markings. A goal is scored when the puck entirely crosses the goal-line between the posts and under the crossbar of the goal. A team may field up to 20 players although only six players are allowed on the ice at one time; substitutions occur frequently. Each game consists of three periods of 20 minutes, divided by breaks of 15 minutes.

GOALKEEPER

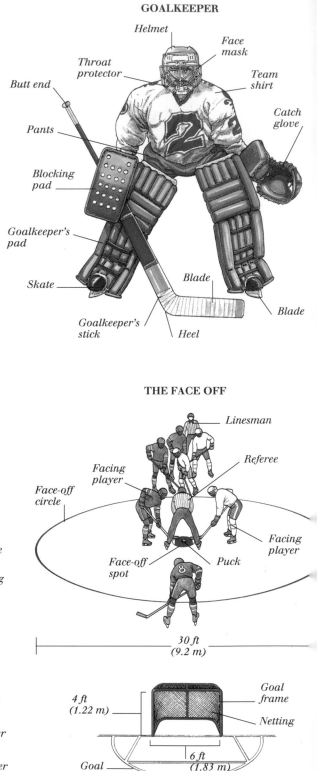

Helmet

Face mask

Throat protector

Team shirt

Butt end

Pants

Catch glove

Blocking pad

Goalkeeper's pad

Blade

Skate

Goalkeeper's stick

Heel

Blade

ICE HOCKEY RINK

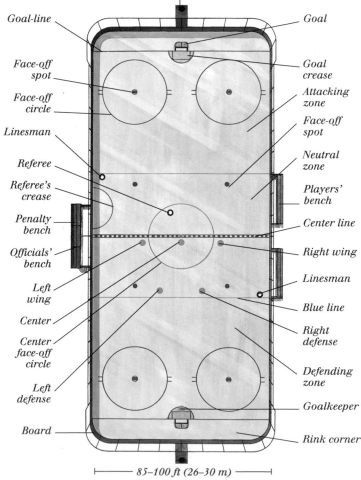

Goal judge

Goal-line

Goal

Face-off spot

Goal crease

Face-off circle

Attacking zone

Linesman

Face-off spot

Referee

Neutral zone

Referee's crease

Players' bench

Penalty bench

Center line

Officials' bench

Right wing

Left wing

Linesman

Center

Blue line

Center face-off circle

Right defense

Left defense

Defending zone

Goalkeeper

Board

Rink corner

85–100 ft (26–30 m)

THE FACE OFF

Linesman

Facing player

Referee

Face-off circle

Facing player

Face-off spot

Puck

30 ft (9.2 m)

4 ft (1.22 m)

Goal frame

Netting

Goal crease

6 ft (1.83 m)

ICE HOCKEY GOAL

GOALKEEPER'S HELMET

Customized paint

Face guard

Chin protection

PLAYER'S BODY ARMOR

Air vents

Rigid plastic shell

Manufacturer's logo

Foam padding

Chin strap

PLAYER'S HELMET

Shoulder padding

ELBOW PADS

ICE HOCKEY STICKS

GOALKEEPER'S STICK

OUTFIELD PLAYER'S STICK

SHOULDER AND CHEST PADDING

MADE IN FINLAND

TORSPO

Pro 5000

TORSPO

Pro 500

4 ft 9 in (147 cm)

Strap

DR
Daignault - Rolland
4355 M
DÉFENSE · PRO · DEFENCE

Chest padding

Wrist protection

Heavy padding

Flexible gusset

Rigid finger cap

GLOVE

DAIGNAULT LLAND
3075N
GRAND / LARGE

LEG PROTECTOR

Knee protection

Rigid plastic casing

DR
Daignault - Rolland
16.5" 43cm
CENTURION·J

Thick foam backing

Leg pad

Wide lower shaft

TORSPO

Thin shaft

TORSPO

Vulcanized rubber

3 in (7.62 cm)

FROZEN PUCK

Ankle support

Blade

SKATE

501

Safety heel tip

Puck stopper

15 in (39 cm)

12¹/₂ in (32 cm)

Thick blade

Heel

Alpine skiing

COMPETITIVE ALPINE SKIING is divided into four disciplines: downhill, slalom, giant slalom, and super-giant slalom (Super-G). Each one tests different skills. In downhill skiing, competitors race down a slope marked out by control flags, known as "gates," and are timed on a single run only. Competitors wear crash helmets, one-piece Lycra suits, and long skis with flattened tips to minimize air resistance. Slalom and giant slalom skiers negotiate a twisting course requiring balance, agility, and quick reactions. Courses are defined by pairs of gates. Racers must pass through each pair of gates to complete the course successfully. Competitors are timed on two runs over different courses, and the skier who completes the courses in the shortest time wins. The equipment and protective guards used by slalom skiiers are shown opposite. In Super-G races, competitors ski a single run that combines the technical challenge of slalom with the speed of downhill. The course requires skiers to complete medium-to-long radius turns at high speed, and contain up to two jumps. Clothing is the same as for downhill, but slightly shorter skis are used.

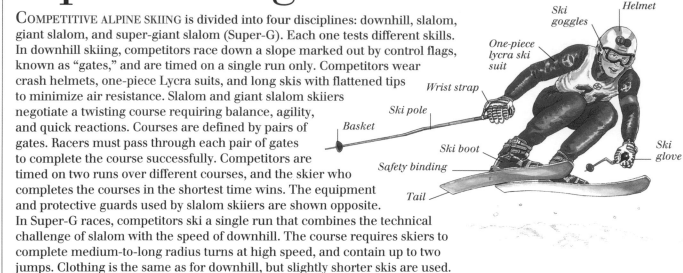

Ski goggles · Helmet · One-piece lycra ski suit · Wrist strap · Ski pole · Basket · Ski boot · Safety binding · Tail · Ski glove

ALPINE SKI SLOPE COURSES

Downhill start · Downhill racing control flag · Super-G start · Pine forest · Giant slalom start · Giant slalom gate · Slalom start · Slalom gate · Finish line · Safety barrier

SKI BOOT

Polyamide inner boot · Tongue · Upper cuff · Upper strap · Buckle · Adjusting catch · Power bar · Tension control · Sole · Lower shell of boot · Heel grip

SAFETY BINDING

Toe piece · Heel piece · Blind release lever · Wing · Anti-friction pad · Housing · Release adjustment screw · Base plate · Brake arm

SLALOM CLOTHING AND EQUIPMENT

GOGGLES

Elastic strap

Anti-glare lens

SLALOM HELMET

Hard nylon shell

Padding

Strap

Chin guard

SKI GLOVE

Extended cuff

Wrist strap

Rigid pad for hand protection

High collar

Double-knit wool and polyester fabric

Adjustable shoulder strap

Ribbed cuff

Zip pocket

Front zip fastening

Waterproof fabric

Cuff fits over ski boot

PADDED SKI PANTS

PADDED SWEATER

HAND GUARD

Moulded polypropylene

Wrist strap

Grip

Shock-absorbing platform under boot

Edge

74–80 in (188–203 cm)

Tough polypropylene shell deflects the shaft of the slalom gate

Velcro strap

LEG GUARD

Shaft

Basket

SLALOM SKI POLE

Tail

Tip

SLALOM SKI

Equestrian sports

EQUESTRIAN SPORTS HAVE TAKEN place throughout the world for centuries: events involving mounted horses were recorded in the Olympic Games of 642 BC. Show jumping, however, is a much more recent innovation, and the first competitions were held at the beginning of the 1900s. In this sport, horse and rider must negotiate a course of variable, unfixed obstacles, making as few mistakes as possible. Show-jumping fences consist of wooden stands, known as standards or wings, that support planks or poles. Parts of the fence are designed to collapse on impact, preventing injury to the horse and rider. Judges penalize competitors for errors, such as knocking down obstacles, refusing jumps, or deviating from the course. Depending on the type of competition, the rider with the fewest faults, most points, or fastest time wins. There are two basic forms of horse racing – flat races and races with jumps, such as steeplechase or hurdle races. Thoroughbred horses are used in this sport, because they have great strength and stamina and can achieve speeds of up to 40 mph (65 kph). Jockeys wear silks – caps and jackets designed in distinctive colors and patterns which help identify the horses. In harness racing, the horse is driven from a light, two-wheeled carriage called a sulky. Horses are trained to trot and to pace, and different races are held for each of these types of gait. In pacing races, the horses wear hobbles to prevent them from breaking into a trot or gallop. Breeds such as the Standard-bred and the French Trotter have been developed especially for this sport.

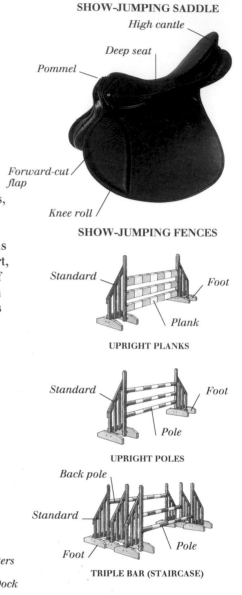

SHOW-JUMPING SADDLE

High cantle

Deep seat

Pommel

Forward-cut flap

Knee roll

SHOW-JUMPING FENCES

Standard

Foot

Plank

UPRIGHT PLANKS

Standard

Foot

Pole

UPRIGHT POLES

Back pole

Standard

Pole

Foot

TRIPLE BAR (STAIRCASE)

Standard

Pole

Foot

HOG'S-BACK

Pillar

Wooden block painted to resemble a brick

WALL

Hard hat

Riding jacket

Browband

Throat-latch

Rein

Jodhpurs

Cheek-piece

Show-jumping saddle

Hindquarters

Dock

Running martingale

Noseband

Brushing boot

Sheepskin numnah

Girth

Stirrup iron

Riding boot

Gaskin

Hock joint

Pillar

Hoof

SHOW-JUMPING HORSE WITH RIDER

Fetlock joint

Pastern

Coronet

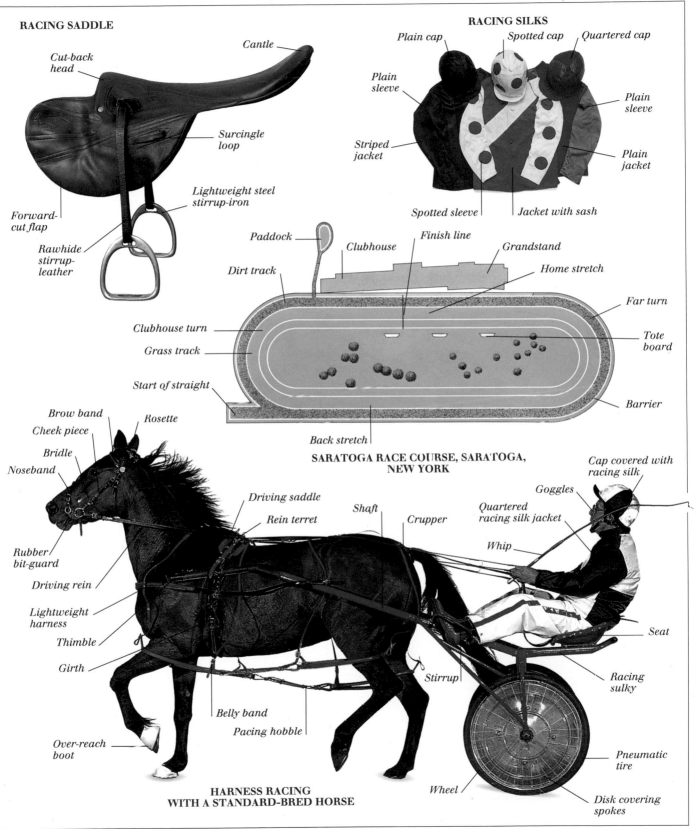

RACING SADDLE

Cut-back head

Cantle

Surcingle loop

Lightweight steel stirrup-iron

Forward-cut flap

Rawhide stirrup-leather

RACING SILKS

Plain cap

Spotted cap

Quartered cap

Plain sleeve

Plain sleeve

Striped jacket

Plain jacket

Spotted sleeve

Jacket with sash

Paddock

Finish line

Grandstand

Clubhouse

Home stretch

Dirt track

Far turn

Clubhouse turn

Tote board

Grass track

Start of straight

Barrier

Back stretch

SARATOGA RACE COURSE, SARATOGA, NEW YORK

Brow band

Rosette

Cheek piece

Bridle

Noseband

Driving saddle

Rein terret

Shaft

Crupper

Cap covered with racing silk

Goggles

Quartered racing silk jacket

Whip

Rubber bit-guard

Driving rein

Lightweight harness

Thimble

Seat

Girth

Racing sulky

Belly band

Stirrup

Pacing hobble

Over-reach boot

Pneumatic tire

Wheel

Disk covering spokes

HARNESS RACING WITH A STANDARD-BRED HORSE

Judo and fencing

COMBAT SPORTS ARE BASED ON THE SKILLS used in fighting. In these sports, the competitors may be unarmed – as in judo and boxing – or armed – as in fencing and kendo. Judo is a system of unarmed combat developed in the East. Translated from the Japanese the name means "the gentle way." Students learn how to turn an opponent's force to their own advantage. The usual uniform is loose white pants and a jacket, fastened with a cloth belt. The color of belt indicates the student's level of expertise, from white-belted novices to the expert black belts. Competitions take place on a mat or "shiaijo," 30 or 33 ft (9 or 10 m) square in size, bounded by "danger" and "safety" areas to prevent injury. Competitors try to throw, pin, or master their opponent by applying pressure to the arm joints or neck. Judo matches are strictly monitored, and competitors receive points for superior technique, not for injuring their opponent. Fencing is a combat sport using swords, which takes place on a narrow piste or strip 46 ft (14 m) long. Competitors try to hit specific target areas on their opponent with their sword or foil while avoiding being touched themselves. The winner is the one who scores the greatest number of hits. Fencers wear uniforms made from strong white material, which affords maximum protection while allowing freedom of movement, steel mesh masks with padded bibs to protect the fencer's neck, and a long white glove on their sword hand. Fencing foils do not have sharpened blades, and their tips end in a blunt button to prevent injuries. Three types of swords are used – foils, épées, and sabres. Official foil and épée competitions always use an electric scoring system. The sword tips are connected to lights by a long wire that passes underneath each fencer's jacket. A bulb flashes when a hit is made.

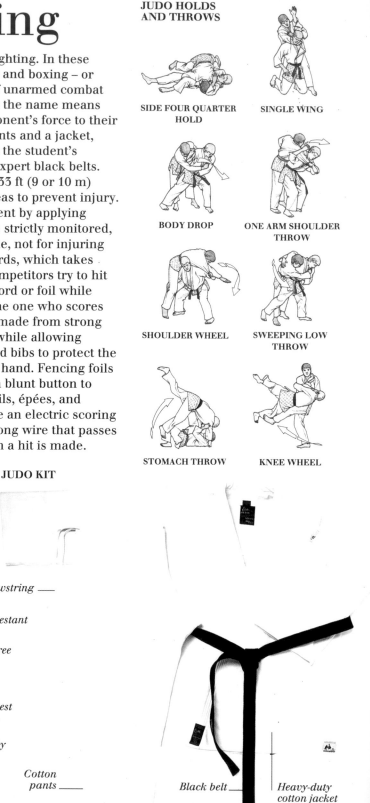

JUDO HOLDS AND THROWS

SIDE FOUR QUARTER HOLD

SINGLE WING

BODY DROP

ONE ARM SHOULDER THROW

SHOULDER WHEEL

SWEEPING LOW THROW

STOMACH THROW

KNEE WHEEL

JUDO KIT

Drawstring

Contestant

Referee

Contest area

Safety area

Cotton pants

Black belt

Heavy-duty cotton jacket

JUDO MAT

52 ft 6 in
(16 m)

Judge

Scorer

Holding timekeeper

Timekeeper

Danger area

Contestant

FENCING STRIP

Rear limit line

46 ft
(14 m)

Sabre
and épéé
warning
line

Scorer

Electrical
scoring
apparatus

Center
line

President

Time-
keeper

On-guard
line

Body
wire

Reel

FENCING EQUIPMENT

Steel
wire
mesh

Padded
bib

MESH MASK

Woven
metal
thread

METALLIC JACKET

Cuff

GAUNTLET

THE SABRE

THE FOIL

Martingale

THE EPEE

Button

Blade

Glove

**PARTS
OF THE
SWORD**

Guard

Tang

Leather
pad

Alternative
pistol-grip
handle

Brass
screw

Steel foil pommel

**TARGET AREAS ON
THE UPPER BODY**

Mask

Wire
mesh

Bib

Under
plastron

Tierce

Sixte

Quinte

Quarte

Primc

Septime

Gauntlet

Seconde

Octave

Metallic
over-jacket

Knickers

Stocking

Fencing
shoe

FENCING TARGET AREAS

SABREUR

FOILIST

EPEEIST

Swimming and diving

SWIMMING GOGGLES

SWIMMING WAS INCLUDED in the first modern Olympic Games in 1896 and diving events were added in 1904. Swimming is both an individual and a team sport and races take place over a predetermined distance in one of the four major categories of stroke – freestyle (usually front crawl), butterfly, breaststroke, and backstroke. Competition pools are clearly marked for racing and anti-turbulence lane lines are used to separate the swimmers and help keep the water calm. The first team or individual to finish the race is the winner. Competitive diving is divided into men's and women's springboard and platform (highboard) events. There are six official groups of dives: forward dives, backward dives, armstand dives, twist dives, reverse dives, and inward dives. Competitors perform a set number of dives and after each one a panel of judges awards marks according to the quality of execution and the degree of difficulty.

STYLES OF DIVES

Starting position

Hands above head

Legs fully stretched

Flight

Arched back

Toes pointed

Entry

Feet together

Hands close together

Entry

FORWARD DIVE

BACKWARD DIVE

SWIMWEAR

Latex rubber molds to shape of head

CAPS

Rubber-covered wire

NOSE CLIP

Molded rubber

EARPLUG

High neckline

Man-made stretch fabric

Drawstring

High-cut leg

Strong seam

SWIMSUIT

TRUNKS

SWIMMING POOL

Swimmer

Lane number

Starting block

Lane timekeeper

Chief timekeeper

Placing judge

End wall

Starter

Recorder

Side wall

Backstroke marker 49 ft (15 m) from end of pool

Anti-turbulence lane line

Referee

Stroke judge

Backstroke turn indicator 16 ft (5 m) from end of pool

Bottom line

Turning judge

Turning wall

Lane

75 ft 6 in (23 m)

Perfectly steady armstand

Arms and legs align throughout flight and entry

ARMSTAND DIVE

Arms spread wide apart

Body and legs straighten for flight and entry

TWIST DIVE

Pike position

Height of dive

Shoulders fall backward for vertical entry

REVERSE PIKE DIVE

Pike position

Hands touch toes

Feet lift up for straight entry

INWARD PIKE DIVE

FRONT CRAWL
Flutter kick

Arm pulls like a paddle

Arrowlike position

Body rolls on a central axis

FULL BODY STRETCH

LOWER ARM PULL

STREAMLINED ARM ENTRY

SIDE-TO-SIDE BODY ROLL

BREASTSTROKE
Straight leg

Knees together

Elbows tucked in

Arm fully extended

BODY GLIDE

DOUBLE ARM PULL

SQUEEZING THE WATER

FROG KICK

BACKSTROKE Little finger enters first

Arm comes up straight

Recovering hand

Shoulder exits water first

BODY ROLL

PULLING THROUGH

STRAIGHTENING OUT

SHOULDER LIFT

BUTTERFLY Palm turned outward

Legs ready to kick down

Head clears the water

Shoulders power the stroke

CATCHING THE WATER

DOUBLE ARM PULL

KICKING DOWN

WHOLE BODY UNDULATION

Kayaking, rowing, and sailing

WATERBORNE SPORTS are as varied as the crafts used. There are two disciplines in rowing; sweep rowing, in which each rower has one oar, and sculling, in which rowers use two oars. There are a number of different Olympic and competitive rowing events for both men and women. The number of rowers and weight classes vary. Some rowing events use a coxswain; a steersman who does not row but directs the crew. Kayaks are used in straight sprint and slalom races. Slalom races take place over a course consisting of 20 to 25 gates, including at least six upstream gates. In yacht racing, competitors must complete prescribed courses, organized by the race committees, in the shortest possible time, using sail power only. Olympic events include classes for keel boats, dinghies, catamarans, and windsurfers.

SAILING GEAR

Sleeveless long johns

Personal flotation device

Long-sleeved jacket

Neoprene material

Belt

GLOVE

Bootlace

Ribbed top

Non-slip sole

BOOT

ONE-PERSON KAYAK AND PADDLE

Blade

Rim

Shaft

Nose cone

Right rail

Cockpit

Back strap

Stern

High density polythene

Grab loop

Bow

Left rail

Seat

Cockpit rim

SINGLE SCULL AND OARS (WITH CLOTH DECKING REMOVED)

Oarlock

Neck

Collar

Shaft

Port-side oar

Spoon

Blade

Colors

Gate

Grip

Starboard oar

Button

Loom

Rigger

Stretcher

Sycamore beam

Water shoot

Keel

Bung

Aft shoulder

Shoe

Stern deck

Spruce beam

Diagonal frame

Aluminum beam

Keelson

PERSONAL FLOTATION DEVICE

Backstrap/ rescue strap

Reinforced seam

Neck opening

Whistle

Topping- up valve

Lanyard

Waistband

SAILING DINGHY

Boom

Rudder

Mast

Mainsheet

Standing rigging

Spreader

Stern

Bow

Tiller

Hiking strap

Centerboard

Cockpit

Shroud

SCULLS

Jib fairlead

DOUBLE SCULL

SINGLE SCULL

Non-slip deck surface

SWEEP-ROWING BOATS

Sliding track

Wheel

FOUR WITHOUT COXSWAIN

PAIR WITH COXSWAIN

PAIR WITHOUT COXSWAIN

Sliding seat

Main deck

Saxboard

EIGHT

FOUR WITH COXSWAIN

Wheel spacer

Hatch

Breakwater

Bowball

Bowclip

Angling

ANGLING MEANS FISHING WITH A ROD, reel, line, and lure. There are several different types of angling: freshwater coarse angling, for members of the carp family and pike; freshwater game angling, for salmon and trout; and sea angling, for sea fish such as flatfish, bass, and mackerel. Anglers use a variety of methods of catching fish. These include bait fishing, in which bait (food to allure the fish) is placed on a hook and cast into the water; fly fishing, in which a natural or artificial fly is used to lure the fish; and spinning, in which a lure that looks like a small fish revolves as it is pulled through the water. The angler uses the rod, reel, and line to cast the lure over the water. The reel controls the line as it spills off the spool and as it is wound back. Weights may be fixed to the line so that it will sink. Swivels are attached to prevent the line from twisting. When a fish bites, the hook must become embedded in its mouth and remain there while the catch is reeled in.

BUTT SECTION

Keeper ring

Drag spindle

Handgrip

Disk drag

Drag washer

Disk spring

Gear retainer

Dual click gear

Retaining screw

Check pawl cover

Check pawl

Check slide

Check spring

REELS

Plate-nut

Spool-release button

Reel foot (reel scoop)

Click mechanism

Mechanical brake

Side plate

Centrifugal brake

Spool

Handle

Star drag

Level-wind system

BAITCASTER

Unskirted spool

Reel foot (reel scoop)

Handle

Line

Tension nut (drag adjustment)

Ratchet (anti-reverse device)

Handgrip

Reel

Bail arm

SPINNING REEL

HOOKS, SWIVELS, AND WEIGHTS

Eye

Shank

Gap

ANATOMY OF A HOOK

Bend

Throat

Point

Barb

TREBLE HOOK

ABERDEEN HOOK

REVERSED BEND HOOK

EXAMPLES OF BARREL SWIVELS

HILLMAN ANTI-KINK WEIGHT

FLY ROD AND REEL

Intermediate ring

TIP SECTION

Reel seat

Screw locking nut

Tip-top

Butt cap

Disk drag housing

Reel foot (reel scoop)

Line

Drag knob screw

Butt extension

Release lever

Spool screw

Clicker plate

Drag knob

DragonFly 100

Disc Drag

Spool cover

Release spring

Spool-release button

ARTIFICIAL FLIES

Line guide

DUNKELD WET FLY

Tail

Body

Cheek

Head

Line guide cover

Hackle

Handle

Retaining screw

Ribbing

ARTIFICIAL LURES

DEVON MINNOW

Fin

Eye

Treble hook

Swivel

Tulip mount

DEER HOPPER DRY FLY

Front hackle

Eye

Tail

Hook

Wing

Head

JOINTED PLUG

Adjustable vane

Joint

Treble hook

Everyday Things

Drills

THE ELECTRICALLY POWERED MOTOR OF A POWER DRILL, cooled by a fan, turns a shaft at high speed. The shaft connects, in turn, to a system of gears that rotates a chuck even faster. Clamped by the chuck, a sharp drill bit cuts out the hole, and at the same time the bit's screw-shaped grooves channel the waste out of the hole. For drilling hard materials, many power drills have a hammer mechanism; when this is operated a ratchet in the gearcase causes the chuck and bit to pound in and out as they drill. A hand drill, although slower and less forceful than a power drill, is easier to control. For cutting wide holes, carpenters often prefer a brace-and-bit. This acts like a lever: the bowed handle of the brace moves a larger distance than the bit, turning the bit with extra force.

MOTOR ASSEMBLY

Commutator

Armature

Armature spindle

Fan

Motor case

Motor case

Field

Brush spring

Screw

Washer

Brush

Lead wire to motor

Brush holder

Top insert blank

Hammer mechanism actuator

Screw hole

Electromagnetic induction capacitor

Switch

Chuck key holder

Screw

INTERNAL VIEW OF HOUSING COVER

Hammer actuator position

Gearcase position

Motor position

Trigger position

Lock button

Switch trigger

Cable cordset

Washer

Spring

TRIGGER MECHANISM

GEAR MECHANISM

Thrust plate

Bearing

Spindle gear

Spindle

Gearcase cover

Chuck key

Jaw

Drill bit

Gearcase

Washer

Thrust washer

Gearcase cover screw

Chuck key pilot hole

Gearcase screw

POWER DRILL

Hammer mechanism actuator

Chuck

Switch trigger

Chuck key holder

Cable

HAND DRILL

Main handle

Turning handle

Side handle

Drive wheel

Pinion

Chuck

Jaw

Drill bit

EXTERNAL VIEW OF HOUSING COVER

Screw hole

Air intake slot

Air exhaust slot

Housing cover screw

BRACE-AND-BIT

Quill

Head

Crank

Handle

Ratchet

Chuck

Jaw

Drill bit

Shoes

WELL MADE SHOES PROTECT THE FEET and are also comfortable and long lasting. The best shoemakers use a wood or plastic mold, called a last, which matches the shape of the customer's foot. The different parts of a shoe are stitched and glued together around the last; rivets and nails are used only in the heel, which is built up from layers of leather and rubber. The steel shank gives support to the arch of the foot and, with the seat lift, helps the wearer maintain posture. The layers of the sole give strength, while the soft insole cushions the foot. The leather welt sewn between the leather uppers and the sole ensures a strong join.

Inside quarter

Quarter lining

Wing cap and vamp backer

Quarter backer

Inner sock

Counter

Tongue

Shoelace

Outside quarter

Vamp

Box toe

Punchhole

Welt

Perforated wing cap

Wing cap

Wing cap backer

Vamp

CROSS SECTION OF FINISHED SHOE

Tongue

Tongue lining

Cuff

Heel grip

Counter

Seat lift

Heel

Tongue

Vamp

Wing cap

Welt

Insole

Bottom filler

Outsole

Lining

Steel shank

Quarter backer

Outside quarter

Shoelace

Eyelet

Tag

Counter

Counter stiffener

Quarter and counter lining

Cone

LAST

Thimble (jack-locating hole)

Vamp backer

Hinge

Back lining

Bottom filler

Outsole

Shank

Seat lift

Insole with ribbing

Welt

Thread

Quarter tip

Inner sock

Seat rivet

Heel nail

Heel

569

Clock

MECHANICAL CLOCKS HAVE TWO essential elements: a mainspring and a pendulum. When the clock is wound with the key, the mainspring is tightened. As the mainspring unwinds, it turns the gears, which move the minute and hour hands at different speeds around the face of the clock. The pendulum ensures that the hands move at a regular pace. At the top of the pendulum are two hooks called pallets. As the pendulum swings, the pallets allow the escape wheel to turn slowly and evenly.

CLOCK CASE

Steady pin hole

Screw hole

Pallet arbor position

Barrel pivot hole

Wood peg

Fusee pivot hole

Pillar

Winding key

Ratchet screw

Ratchet pawl

Click wheel

PENDULUM ASSEMBLY

Barrel arbor hook

Mainspring barrel arbor

Suspension spring

Mainspring barrel cap

Pendulum rod

Crutch screw

Crutch

Pallet cock screw

Pallet cock

CLOCK TRAIN

Pallet arbor

Pallet screw

Pallet

Escape wheel

FRONT PLATE

Pinion

Third wheel

Pinion

Pinion

Center wheel

Fusee

Fusee chain

Mainspring

Mainspring barrel

Lenticular bob

Pivot hole

Fusee stop screw

Fusee stop

Tension spring screw

Tension spring

Rating nut

Side inspection door

Wood peg

Back plate

Bottom door key

Back box

Bottom door

Minute hand

Screw hole

Minute wheel cock

Cock screw

Minute wheel

Dial washer

Hour hand screw

Hand collet

Cannon pinion

Hour wheel

Pin

Bridge

Bridge screw

Pin

Dial foot hole

Pillar hole

Hour hand

Dial

Wood bezel

CLOCK FACE

Hinged brass bezel

Minute track

Hour marker

Roman numeral

CAMERER. KUSS & C:
56 New Oxford St

Maker's name

Center hole

Winding hole

LONDON

Lamp

THE FIRST SPRING-TENSIONED, adjustable work lamp was designed in 1934 by George Carwardine. This type of lamp imitates the human arm in the way that it can be kept in a fixed position or moved easily and precisely. In the arm, such control is achieved by coordinating the opposing action of paired muscles (e.g., when the biceps contracts, the triceps relaxes and the arm bends). In the work lamp, one muscle of a pair is represented by the springs that pull on the rigid bars of the lamp; the other muscle is represented by the nuts, bolts, screws, and washers in the lamp's joints that resist the pull of the springs. By balancing the pull of the springs against the resistance in the joints, the lamp's height and angle can be adjusted with minimal pressure.

Cap nut

Switch enclosure cover

Push switch

Terminal screw

Bushing

Power supply cord

Insulation

End cap

Copper conductor

Switch enclosure

Pivot plate

Bracket

Metal shade

Dome

Body

Cap

LIGHT BULB

Connecting wire

Terminal screw

Nut

Fuse enclosure

Plunger contact

LAMP HOLDER

Support wire

Glass envelope

Skirt

Filament

Wing nut

SUPPORT ARM ASSEMBLY

Cheese head screw

Washer

Nut

Locking nut

Power supply cord

Pivot plate

End cap

Cheese head screw

Washer

Hexagon nut

Metal arm

Spring attachment

Coil tension spring

Bushing

Clamping screw

Arm coupling

Metal arm

Lamp holder coupling

Pivot

Spigot

Socket

Shade coupling

Power supply cord

Metal shade

Pivot plate

Metal arm

Washer

Spring attachment

Clamp upper jaw

Adjustment locking nut

Threaded rod

Metal arm

TABLE CLAMP ASSEMBLY

Coil tension spring

Coil tension spring

Cheese head screw

Washer

Nut

Threaded rod

Table clamp

Clamp lower jaw

End cap

Spring attachment bolt

Wing nut

Mini television

MINIATURIZED TELEVISION SETS are small enough to be held in the hand while being watched. A signal sent by a broadcast transmitter is picked up by the television antenna and passed to an electron gun at the back of the television set. In response to the signal this gun produces an electron beam that is passed through a deflection yoke. The yoke contains magnets and coils that cause the beam to scan across the screen in a series of lines. The screen is coated with phosphor, which glows when hit by the beam. As the beam scans the screen, its strength is varied so that the phosphor glows with different intensities in different parts of the screen. A continuous sequence of 25 black-and-white pictures per second appears on the screen so rapidly that the illusion of a moving picture is created.

Antenna connector
Tuner
Rear cabinet
Electrolytic capacitor

Dial pointer

Keystone (East-West) amplifier integrated circuit

CATHODE RAY TUBE (CRT)

CRT cover

Tuning drive gear

Earphone jack

Direct current jack

Metal shield

Tuning dial

Battery compartment

Screw

Tuning printed circuit board

Deflection coil

CRT bracket

Battery case lid

Tape

Positive pole

Electron gun

Mounting bracket

TUBE NECK

Nipple

Scan coil clamp

BATTERY CONTACTS

SCAN COIL DEFLECTION YOKE

Connecting pin

Positive pole

CRT socket

Centering magnet

Positive pole

Negative pole

Positive pole

Screw

Antenna holder

Intermediate frequency coil

PRINTED CIRCUIT BOARD

Plastic sheath

Ornamental strip

Choke

Coil

Glue

Horizontal frequency adjustment

Window

Capacitor

Volume control dial

Power switch

Power dial

Filter

Fly-back transformer

Plastic cap

SONY

Focus control

21 30 40 50 60 68 UHF

FD-250B

Extra-high tension lead

Filter ornament

Speaker

Front cabinet

575

Chair

A TRADITIONALLY MADE DINING CHAIR, such as the Regency-style carver shown here, is held together, not by nails or bolts, but by snugly fitting joints, screws, dowels, and glue. Its curved arms and top splats, as well as its tapering legs, are cut from seasoned—that is, dried—mahogany. Mortice slots in the back legs receive the tenon tongues of the top and bottom splats; angled grooves at the top of the back legs, called rebates, take the curved arm rail. Though the various joints are so tight-fitting that they could produce a solid frame on their own, screws and glue are used to give the joints added strength. The comfortable, upholstered seat pad shown here consists of a patterned cover, calico lining, and foam padding that has been treated for fire safety; it is supported by webbing stretched across a wood frame.

Top splat
Cross stick
Bottom splat
Arm
Head
Seat pad
Front rail
Back leg
Left front leg

Square brass line
Tenon
Tenon
Mortice
Arm
Washer
Groove
Top splat
Washer
Screw
Diamond
Screw
Dowel screw
Wood plug
Wood plug
Splat mortice
Cross stick
Head
Bottom splat
Tenon
Tenon
Side rail
Dowel
Back rail
Dowel
Dowel hole
Screw
Dowel
Dowel
Right front leg
Dowel
Dowel hole
Back leg
Front rail

CHAIR FRAME

SEAT UPHOLSTERY

Seat cover

Mortice

Webbing

Arm

Foam padding

Dowel screw

Splat mortice

Head

Tenon

Side rail

Dowel hole

Screw

Back leg

Bottom lining

Left front leg

Calico lining

Seat back rail

Tack

SEAT FRAME

Seat side rail

Dowel hole

Seat side rail

Seat front rail

Toaster

MOST ELECTRIC TOASTERS NOT ONLY GRILL slices of bread, they also pop them up when ready. While the slices rest on a spring-loaded rack, electric heating elements toast the bread. At the same time, a bimetallic strip heats and expands. One of the two metals in this strip expands more quickly than the other, causing the strip to curve. As it bends, it completes an electrical circuit and activates an electromagnet. The magnet attracts a catch, releasing the spring that holds the rack down in the toaster. The elements switch off, and the toasted slices pop up.

Terminal connections

Ejector bracket

Time switch

Variable time control knob

Selector switch

Screw

Screw

Switch end casting

Crumb tray

End baffle plate

Screw

Ground connection point

Cordset entry point

End element connecting link

End element

Foot

Base plate

End element wire guard

Screw

Washer

Power supply cord

Bolt

Nut

Strain release

Ejector knob

Screw

Spring

Nut

Ejector bracket

Ejector assembly

Center element
wire cage

Inner cage
assembly

End baffle
plate

Plain end
casting

Switch end
casting

Stainless steel
cover

Selector switch

Ejector lever

Variable time
control knob

Foot

Crumb tray

Fixing screw

Screw

Foot

Screw

Element
retaining stop

Nut

Washer

Screw

Stainless steel
cover

Plain end
casting

Foot

Screw

Element
connecting
link

End element

Nut

Washer

Screw

Center element

End element
wire guard

579

Lawnmower

THE SHARP BLADES OF A LAWNMOWER—whether driven by electrical, gasoline, or human power—shave grass close to the ground. The gasoline-powered type shown here has a small engine that is electrically ignited by a battery and spark plug. This engine rotates a horizontal blade at the base of the lawnmower, which then slices the grass against a fixed blade. A grass bag at the back of the machine collects the cuttings. As the engine rotates the blades, it also turns the rear wheels, moving the lawnmower forward. Gears ensure that the horizontal blade spins faster than the wheels so that all of the grass is cut neatly before the lawnmower moves on.

Rear tire

Wheel cover

Rear wheel

GEAR CASE ASSEMBLY

Upper gear case

Wheel bolt

Blower shroud

Fuel tank

Spring

Door

Drive shaft

Half pulley

Belt guard

Drive belt

Screw

Cap

Screw

Oil dipstick

Door seal

Bolt

ENGINE AND RECOIL ASSEMBLY

Oil fill tube

Screw

Flywheel

Recoil case

Starter cup

Housing

Screw

Screw

Muffler cover

Blade cover

Air filter

Muffler

Throttle guard

Air filter cover

Screw

Engine pulley

Front tire

Height adjuster

Shoulder screw

Front wheel

TORO

OHV

HOT

53 cm

Handle

Control panel

Grass bag

Fuel tank cap

Recoil case

Muffler cover

Latch handle

Rear wheel

Housing

Front wheel

Handle

Traction lever

Mower drive handle

Ground speed control knob

Throttle control lever

Control lever

Traction cable support

Control panel

TORO

KEY-LECTRIC

Battery

HANDLE AND TRACTION CONTROL ASSEMBLY

Battery retainer

Vertical panel

Cable support bracket

Latch handle

Screen panel

Door discharge

Grass bag

Traction cable

Screw

Blade

Blade retainer

Washer

Blade bolt

Grass bag frame

Battery connection

Wheel bolt

Saddle

THE FIRST HORSEBACK RIDERS HAD NO SADDLES; they sat bareback, clinging to the animal's mane. Next came a simple cloth saddle. The leather saddle, which was invented about 2,000 years ago by the warriors of the Asian steppes, revolutionized horseback riding. On this saddle, horsemen could gallop toward the enemy, fire arrows in all directions, and stay on their horses. Modern saddles are of two main types. The Western saddle is a heavy, working saddle used mainly by ranch hands in the United States. It has a metal horn at the front for securing a lasso and a high cantle at the back to keep the rider on the horse. The English saddle is much lighter. Designed for sport, it allows the horse to gallop fast. Its drawback is that it provides less stability; to stay on the horse, the rider must grip the animal with the knees.

ENGLISH SADDLE

Cantle

Leather seat

Pommel

Sloped head

Dee

Surcingle

Block flap

Girth

Stirrup leather

Stirrup

Facing

Strap bearing

Gullet

Point pocket

Stuffing hole

Knee roll

Top leather

Facing

Lining of underside of saddle

Knee cover

Gullet lining

Nylon rope

Flock stuffing

Tree

Cantle

Metal reinforcement

Spring tree

Stirrup bar

Web

Web

Flexible leather point

Gullet plate

Copper rivet

Point cover

Rivet

Belly nail

Brass nameplate nail

Screw

Tack

Stirrup buckle

Stirrup leather

SHAPED GIRTH

Girth buckle

Chape

Stirrup

Block flap

Plated nail

Dee

Buckle guard

Surcingle

Name-plate

Billet strap

Bar leather

Stirrup buckle

Forepiece

Belly nail

Dee

Skirt

Stirrup leather

Welt

Back

Leather seat

Canvas

Webbing

Canvas

Leather

Back

Rubber seat

Welt

Canvas

Skirt

Buckle guard

Lacing thread

3-cord linen thread

Belly nail

Bar leather

Leather belly

Beeswax

4-cord linen thread

Surcingle

Nameplate

Dee

Stirrup leather

Stirrup

Block flap

Plated nail

CD-ROM

A CD-ROM IS A TYPE OF COMPACT DISC (CD) that can be used to produce images on a computer screen. ROM stands for Read Only Memory, which means that the digitally recorded data registered in pits on the surface of the disc is fixed and cannot be altered or replaced. The CD is loaded into the CD-ROM player, where the data on the spinning disc is read by a laser. CD-ROMs are different from vinyl records in that they are not read along a spiral groove, from outer circumference to inner edge: instead each image or piece of information has a coordinate on the disc, which is located by the laser. Information picked up by the laser is relayed to the computer, where it is translated into the text and images that appear on screen. The information is relayed through a SCSI (Small Computer System Interface), which processes the electronic impulses between the disc drive and the computer system. The user can move around the program by clicking on different parts of the screen with a mouse (a hand-held tool with a clicking button whose movement on its pad is mimicked by an icon on the screen). The image in the viewing area (see opposite) can be changed by clicking on the active scrolling button: this moves a rectangular panel down the scrolling figure in the navigational panel. Clicking on active text will provide a new screen with more information, either in the form of text and diagrams, or as narrated animated sequences.

CD-ROM drive

CD loading tray

Caddy cover flap

Front bezel

Push button

CD-ROM CASING

CD-ROM drive motor

Laser

Connector

Film strip connector

Roller bearing

Guide post

Washer

Gearing mechanism

Spring

Insulating grommet

Power connector to CD-ROM

SCSI connectors

Connector clasp

SCSI selector switch

Ground connection to case

Power switch

Washer

Ground wire

Power supply screening cover

Surface-mounted integrated circuit

Mounting rail

Transistor

Power on/off LED (Light Emitting Diode)

CD-ROM disc

Screws

CD-ROM DISC DRIVE

CD-ROM LOADING MECHANISM

CONTENTS PAGE

THE ULTIMATE HUMAN BODY

BODY MACHINE

BODY ORGANS

BODY SYSTEMS

External speaker

Keyboard

Disc

Display monitor

Dorling Kindersley
MULTIMEDIA

Mouse

CD-ROM PLAYER

COMPUTER HARDWARE

Mouse pad

SCREEN FROM A
CD-ROM PROGRAM

Navigational panel

Help button

Index button

Back button

Pronunciation button on/off

Options button

Navigational figures

BODY MACHINE   BODY ORGANS   BODY SYSTEMS

Scrolling figure

Active scrolling button

BODY MACHINE

FIND OUT MORE

BODY MACHINE

Picon (pictorial icon)

BODY MACHINE

ABOUT THE BODY MACHINE

What happens when you sleep?

Why do you blink?

How do you hear?

How do you swallow?

Why do you chew your food?

How do reflex actions work?

How often does your heart beat?

Active text

How do your joints move?

What are you made of?

Viewing area

ZOOMING INTO MULTI-LAYERED INFORMATION

HEAD
YOUR HEAD contains your brain, which is protected by the strong interlocking bones of your skull. Most of your sensory organs are located in your head; these include your eyes, ears, mouth, and nose.

Hair, skull and scalp

Brain

Eye

Ear

Nose

Mouth and lip

INITIAL SCREEN UNDER BODY ORGANS MENU

EYES
THESE DELICATE ORGANS lie in pads of fat protected within bony sockets called orbits. On the outside they are protected from injury by your eyelids, thin folds of skin that can close rapidly. Each eye is moved by six muscles which are attached around the eyeball.

Around the eye   Inside the eye

Skin   Blood vessels   Bone

CLICKING ON "EYES" LABEL PRODUCES MORE INFORMATION

INSIDE THE EYE
THE EYE is a hollow sphere filled with gel-like fluids that help keep the eye in shape. Light rays entering the eye through the pupil, are focused by the cornea and lens to form an image on the retina. Here, millions of cells enable you to detect light and colors. The cells send messages to the brain, which then makes sense of what you see.

Conjunctiva (Thin, clear layer covering cornea)

Vitreous humous (Clear jelly that fills the space behind the lens)

Lens

Iris

Cornea

Vein

Optic nerve

Retina

EACH LABEL PRODUCES A FURTHER SCREEN

LENS
THE LENS of your eye is on the front surface of your eyeball. It is transparent and light passes through it to be focused onto the back of your eye. To focus on both objects that are near and those far away, the lens must change its shape. The many fibers around the lens allow this by pulling against the outer rim of the lens.

Lens

Fibers

THE FINAL IMAGE SHOWS MICROSCOPIC DETAIL

Books

THOUGH THE PROCESS OF BOOKBINDING today is usually mechanized, some books are still bound by hand. The pages of a book are printed on large sheets of paper called sections, or signatures. When folded, sections usually make 8, 16, or 32 pages. To assemble a hand-bound hardback book, the binder first places the folded sections in the correct order within the endpapers. Next, he or she sews the sections together along the spine edge using strong thread and then pastes them with glue for extra strength. After trimming the pages, the binder puts the book in a press and hammers the spine to shape it. The binder then glues one or more linings on the spine. The cover, or case, comes last. To make this, the bookbinder sticks cover boards to the endpapers, front and back, and then covers them with cloth or leather.

HALF-BOUND BOOK   **LEATHER-BOUND BOOK**

Corner piece

Spine

Fore edge

Rib

Spine

Tail

Marbleized paper

Joint

Leather cover

Tail

Ribbon

Gold tooling

HALF-BOUND BOOK

Marbleized paper

Buckram corner piece

Pastedown (endpaper)

Lining

Mull

Headband

Spine piece

Section (signature)

Tape

Front cover board

Tailband

Manila

LEATHER-BOUND BOOK

Pastedown (endpaper)

Headband

Rib

Tape

Leather cover

Back cover board

Section (signature)

Frontispiece

Thread

Front cover board

Ribbon

Lining

Mull

Tailband

Flyleaf (endpaper)

Buckram corner piece

Back cover board

Reverse of marbleized paper

Pastedown (endpaper)

Buckram corner piece

Pastedown (endpaper)

LEATHER-BOUND BOOK

Joint

Ribbon

Headband

Mull

Tape

Rib

Lining

Spine

Gold tooling

Fore edge

Flyleaf (endpaper)

Pastedown (endpaper)

Front cover board

Leather cover

Camera

A CAMERA IS AN INSTRUMENT used for recording images on photographic film. It consists of a light-tight box with a shutter, a lens containing a diaphragm, and a viewing system. When the shutter is released, the film is exposed to light from the subject that is being photographed. Adjusting the shutter speed alters the time for which the film is exposed to light. The diaphragm, by altering the aperture of the lens, controls the intensity of light entering the camera. The total amount of light entering the camera is called the exposure. The lens focuses the light onto the film. When there is insufficient light to produce an adequate image, a flashgun may be used to give extra light.

FRONT VIEW OF CAMERA

Shutter release button
Shutter speed dial
Film rewind/back cover release knob
Exposure counter
Strap lug
Lens lock release lever
X-flash sync terminal

FRONT BOARD ASSEMBLY

Lens mount
Left body covering
Right body covering
Lens lock release lever
X-flash sync cap

BOTTOM COVER ASSEMBLY

Tripod socket hole
Bottom cover
Battery
Battery chamber cap

REAR VIEW OF CAMERA

Film rewind crank
Viewfinder eyepiece
Film take-up spool
Film rewind/back cover release knob
Film roller
Film chamber
Back cover
Film rail
Film pressure plate
Film guide rail
Shutter curtain
Film sprocket spool

LENS BARREL ASSEMBLY

Ornament ring
Cover frame
Nameplate ring
Front lens frame retainer plate
Front lens group
Installing ring retainer plate
Retainer screw
Washer
Retainer screw
Retainer screw

TOP COVER ASSEMBLY

Shutter dial knob spring

Film speed indicator

Speed dial knob

Shutter speed dial

Retainer screw

Counter dial housing

Film wind lever

Rewind shaft

Film rewind/back cover release knob

Counter dial cover

Exposure counter dial

Wind lever install spring

Wind lever collar

Top cover

X-contact

Hot shoe

Retainer screw

Washer

Rewind shaft bushing

Window

Prism retainer plate

Shutter release button

Shutter speed index

Film rewind crank

MAIN BODY

Prism retainer spring

Pentaprism

Viewfinder eyepiece

Strap lug

Cover frame

Retainer screw

TOP VIEW OF CAMERA

Focusing ring

Aperture/distance index

Subject distance scale

Depth-of-field guide

ft m ∞ 10 15 3 8 26 1.5 4

22 16 11 8 5 6 4 3 4 4 10 22

A⌟ 22 16 11 8 5.6 4 2.8 2

Lens alignment node

Lens lock release lever

Shutter release button

Aperture auto-lock button

Hole for film rewind button

Shutter cocked indicator

Exposure counter

Retainer screw

Film rewind crank

Film rewind/back cover release knob

Hot shoe

X-contact

Shutter speed index

Film speed indicator

Shutter speed dial

Film wind lever

Supporter ring retainer plate

Supporter ring

Diaphragm blade

Installing ring

Main barrel assembly

Rear lens group

Opening and closing plate

Appendix: useful data

UNITS OF MEASUREMENT

U.S. unit	Equivalent
Length	
1 foot (ft)	12 inches (in)
1 yard (yd)	3 feet
1 rod (rd)	5.5 yards
1 mile (mi)	1,760 yards
Mass	
1 dram (dr)	27.344 grains (gr)
1 ounce (oz)	16 drams
1 pound (lb)	16 ounces
1 hundredweight (cwt) (long)	112 pounds
1 hundredweight (cwt) (short)	100 pounds
1 ton (long)	2,240 pounds
1 ton (short)	2,000 pounds
Area	
1 square foot (ft²)	144 square inches (in²)
1 square yard (yd²)	9 square feet
1 acre	4,840 square yards
1 square mile	640 acres
Volume	
1 cubic foot	1,728 cubic inches
1 cubic yard	27 cubic feet
Capacity (liquid and dry measures)	
1 fluidram (fl dr)	60 minims (min)
1 fluid ounce (fl oz)	8 fluidrams
1 gill (gi)	4 fluid ounces
1 pint (pt)	4 gills
1 quart (qt)	2 pints
1 gallon (gal)	4 quarts
1 peck (pk)	2 gallons
1 bushel (bu)	4 pecks

Metric unit	Equivalent
Length	
1 centimeter (cm)	10 millimeters (mm)
1 meter (m)	100 centimeters
1 kilometer (km)	1,000 meters
Mass	
1 kilogram (kg)	1,000 grams (g)
1 tonne (t)	1,000 kilograms
Area	
1 square centimeter (cm²)	100 square millimeters (mm²)
1 square meter (m²)	10,000 square centimeters
1 hectare	10,000 square meters
1 square kilometer (km²)	1,000,000 square meters
Volume	
1 cubic centimeter (cc)	1 milliliter (ml)
1 liter (l)	1,000 milliliters
1 cubic meter (m³)	1,000 liters
Capacity (liquid and dry measures)	
1 centiliter (cl)	10 milliliters (ml)
1 deciliter (dl)	10 centiliters
1 liter (l)	10 deciliters
1 decaliter (dal)	10 liters
1 hectoliter (hi)	10 decaliters
1 kiloliter (kl)	10 hectoliters

TEMPERATURE SCALES

To convert from Celsius (C) to Fahrenheit (F): $F = (C \times 9 \div 5) + 32$
To convert from Fahrenheit to Celsius: $C = (F - 32) \times 5 \div 9$
To convert from Celsius to Kelvin (K): $K = C + 273$
To convert from Kelvin to Celsius: $C = K - 273$

Celsius	-20	-10	0	10	20	30	40	50	60	70	80	90	100
Fahrenheit	-4	14	32	50	68	86	104	122	140	158	176	194	212
Kelvin	253	263	273	283	293	303	313	323	333	343	353	363	373

AREAS AND VOLUMES

Radius r
Diameter
d = 2 x r

CIRCLE
Circumference = 2 x π x r
Area = π x r²
(π = 3.1416)

Height h
Sides a, b, c

TRIANGLE
Perimeter = a + b + c
Area = ½ x b x h

Sides a, b

RECTANGLE
Perimeter = 2 x (a + b)
Area = a x b

Height h
Radius r

CYLINDER
Surface area = 2 x π x r x h
(excluding ends)
Volume = π x r² x h

Height h
Radius r
Side l

CONE
Surface area = π x r x l (excluding base)
Volume = ⅓ x π x r² x l

Sides a, b, c

RECTANGULAR BLOCK
Surface area = 2 x (a x b + b x c + a x c)
Volume = a x b x c

U.S. – METRIC CONVERSIONS

To convert	Into	Multiply by
Length		
Inches	centimeters	2.5400
Feet	meters	0.3048
Miles	kilometers	1.6090
Yards	meters	0.9144
Mass		
Ounces	grams	28.3500
Pounds	kilograms	0.4536
Long tons	tonnes	1.0160
Short tons	tonnes	0.9070
Area		
Square inches	square centimeters	6.4520
Square feet	square meters	0.0929
Acres	hectares	0.4047
Square miles	square kilometers	2.5900
Square yards	square meters	0.8361
Volume		
Cubic inches	cubic centimeters	16.3900
Cubic feet	cubic meters	0.0283
Capacity		
Pints (liquid)	liters	0.4730
Gallons (liquid)	liters	3.7850

METRIC – U.S. CONVERSIONS

To convert	Into	Multiply by
Length		
Centimeters	inches	0.3937
Meters	feet	3.2810
Kilometers	miles	0.6214
Meters	yards	1.0940
Mass		
Grams	ounces	0.0352
Kilograms	pounds	2.2050
Tonnes	long tons	0.9843
Tonnes	short tons	1.1025
Area		
Square centimeters	square inches	0.1550
Square meters	square feet	10.7600
Hectares	acres	2.4710
Square kilometers	square miles	0.3861
Square meters	square yards	1.1960
Volume		
Cubic centimeters	cubic inches	0.0610
Cubic meters	cubic feet	35.3100
Capacity		
Liters	pints (liquid)	2.1142
Liters	gallons (liquid)	0.2642

NUMBER SYSTEMS

Roman	Arabic
I	1
II	2
III	3
IV	4
V	5
VI	6
VII	7
VIII	8
IX	9
X	10
XI	11
XII	12
XIII	13
XIV	14
XV	15
XX	20
XXI	21
XXX	30
XL	40
L	50
LX	60
LXX	70
LXXX	80
XC	90
C	100
CI	101
CC	200
CCC	300
CD	400
D	500
DC	600
DCC	700
DCCC	800
CM	900
M	1,000
MM	2,000

PHYSICS SYMBOLS

Symbol	Meaning
α	alpha particle
β	beta ray
γ	gamma ray; photon
ε	electromotive force
η	efficiency; viscosity
λ	wavelength
μ	micro-; permeability
ν	frequency; neutrino
ρ	density; resistivity
σ	conductivity
c	velocity of light
e	electronic charge

MATHEMATICS SYMBOLS

Symbol	Meaning
$+$	plus
$-$	minus
$\pm$	plus or minus
$\times$	multiplied by
$\div$	divided by
$=$	equals
$>$	is greater than
$<$	is less than
$\geq$	is greater than or equal to
$\leq$	is less than or equal to
$\%$	per cent
$\sqrt{\ }$	root
π	pi (3.1416)
$\circ$	degree
∞	infinity
$\approx$	is approximately equal to
$\angle$	angle

CHEMISTRY SYMBOLS

Symbol	Meaning
$+$	plus; together with
$-$	single bond
$\bullet$	single bond; single unpaired electron; two separate parts or compounds regarded as loosely joined
$=$	double bond
$\equiv$	triple bond
R	group
X	halogen atom
Z	atomic number

BIOLOGY SYMBOLS

Symbol	Meaning
$\circ$	female individual (used in inheritance charts)
$\square$	male individual (used in inheritance charts)
$\female$	female
$\male$	male
$\times$	crossed with; hybrid
$+$	wild type
F_1	offspring of the first generation
F_2	offspring of the second generation

POWERS OF TEN USED WITH SCIENTIFIC UNITS

Factor	Name	Prefix	Symbol
10^{18}	quintillion	exa-	E
10^{15}	quadrillion	peta-	P
10^{12}	trillion	tera-	T
10^{9}	billion	giga-	G
10^{6}	million	mega-	M
10^{3}	thousand	kilo-	k
10^{2}	hundred	hecto-	h
10^{1}	ten	deca-	da
10^{-1}	one tenth	deci-	d
10^{-2}	one hundredth	centi-	c
10^{-3}	one thousandth	milli-	m
10^{-6}	one millionth	micro-	μ
10^{-9}	one billionth	nano-	n
10^{-12}	one trillionth	pico-	p
10^{-15}	one quadrillionth	femto-	f
10^{-18}	one quintillionth	atto-	a

Index

B

596

Acknowledgments

Dorling Kindersley would like to thank (in order of sections):

The Universe
(consultant editors – Sue Becklake, Gevorkyan Tatyana Alekseyevna):
John Becklake; the Memorial Museum of Cosmonautics, Moscow; The Cosmos Pavilion, Moscow; The United States Space and Rocket Centre, Alabama; Broadhurst, Clarkson and Fuller Ltd; Susannah Massey

Prehistoric Earth
(consultant editors – William Lindsay, Martyn Bramwell, Dr Ralph E. Molnar, David Lambert):
Dr Monty Reid, Andrew Neuman, and the staff of the Royal Tyrrell Museum of Palaeontology, Drumheller, Alberta; Dr Angela Milner and the staff of the Department of Palaeontology, the Natural History Museum, London; Professor W. Ziegler and the staff, in particular Michael Loderstaedt, of the Naturmuseum Senckenburg, Frankfurt; Dr Alexander Liebau, Axel Hunghrebüller, Reiner Schoch, and the staff of the Institut und Museum für Geologie und Paläontologie der Universität, Tübingen; Rupert Wild of the Institut für Paläontologie, Staatliches Museum für Naturkunde, Stuttgart; Dr Scheiber of the Stadtmuseum, Nördlingen; Professor Dr Dietrich Herm of Staatssammlung für Paläontologie und Historische Geologie, München; Dr Michael Keith-Lucas of the Department of Botany, University of Reading; Richard Walker; American Museum of Natural History, New York

Plants
(consultant editor – Richard Walker):
Diana Miller; Lawrie Springate; Karen Sidwell; Chris Thody; Michelle End; Susan Barnes and Chris Jones of the EMU Unit of the Natural History Museum, London; Jenny Evans of Kew Gardens, London; Kate Biggs of the Royal Horticultural Society Gardens, Wisley, Surrey; Spike Walker of Microworld Services; Neil Fletcher; John Bryant of Bedgebury Pinetum, Kent; Dean Franklin

Animals
(consultant editor – Richard Walker):
David Manning's Animal Ark; Intellectual Animals; Howletts Zoo, Canterbury; John Dunlop; Alexander O'Donnell; Sue Evans of the Royal Veterinary College, London; Dr Geoff Potts and Fred Frettsome of the Marine Biological Association of the United Kingdom, Plymouth; Jeremy Adams of the Booth Museum of Natural History, Brighton; Derek Telling of the Department of Anatomy, University of Bristol; the Natural History Museum, London; Andy Highfield of the Tortoise Trust; Brian Harris of the Aquarium, London Zoo; the Invertebrate Department, London Zoo; Dr Harold McClure of the Yerkes Regional Primate Research Center, Emory University, Atlanta, Georgia; Nielson Lausen of the Harvard Medical School, New England Regional Primates Research Centre, Southborough, Massachusetts; Dr Paul Hopwood of the Department of Veterinary Anatomy, University of Sydney; Dean Franklin

The Human Body
(consultant editors – Dr Frances Williams, Dr Fiona Payne, Richard Cummins FRCS):
Derek Edwards and Dr Martin Collins, British School of Osteopathy; Dr M.C.E. Hutchinson of the Department of Anatomy, United Medical and Dental Schools of Guy's and St Thomas' Hospitals, London. Models – Barry O'Rorke (Bodyline Agency) and Pauline Swaine (MOT Model Agency)

Geology, Geography, and Meteorology
(consultant editor – Martyn Bramwell):
Dr John Nudds of the Manchester Museum, Manchester; Dr Alan Wooley and Dr Andrew Clark of the Natural History Museum, London; Graham Bartlett of the National Meteorological Library and Archive, Bracknell; Tony Drake of BP Exploration, Uxbridge; Jane Davies of the Royal Society of Chemistry, Cambridge; Dr Tony Waltham of Nottingham Trent University, Nottingham; staff of the Smithsonian Institute, Washington; staff of the United States Geological Survey, Washington; staff of the National Geographic Society, Washington; staff of Edward Lawrence Associates (Export Ltd), Midhurst; John Farndon; David Lambert

Rail and Road
Rail (consultant editor – John Coiley)
Michael Ashworth of the London Transport Museum

Road (consultant editors – David Burgess-Wise, Hugo Wilson)
The National Motor Museum, Beaulieu; Alf Newell of Renault UK Ltd; David Suter of Cheltenham Cutaway Exhibits Ltd; Francesca Riccini of the Science Museum, London. Signore Amadelli of the Museo dell' Automobile Carlo Biscaretti di Ruffia; Paul Bolton of the Mazda MCL Group; Duncan Bradford of Reg Mills Wire Wheels; John and Leslie Brewster of Autocavan; David Burgess-Wise; Trevor Cass of Garrett Turbo Service; John Corbett of The Patrick Collection; Gary Crumpler of Williams Grand Prix Engineering Ltd; Mollie Easterbrooke and Duncan Gough of Overland Ltd; Arthur Fairley of the Vauxhall Motor Company; Paul Foulkes-Halbard of Filching Manor Motor Museum; Frank Gilbert of I. Wilkinson and Son Ltd; Paolo Gratton of Gratton Museum; Colvin Gunn of Gunn and Son; Judy Hogg of Ecurie Bertelli; Milton Holman of Dream Cars; Ian Matthews of IMAT Electronics; Eric Neal of Jaguar Cars Ltd; Paul Niblett, Keith Davidson, Mark Reumel, and David Woolf of Michelin Tyre plc; Doug Nye; Kevin O'Keefe of O'Keefe Cars; Seat UK; Roger Smith; Jim Stirling of Ironbridge Gorge Museum, Staffordshire; Jon Taylor; Doug Thompson; Martyn Watkins of Ford Motor Company Ltd; John Cattermole, Customer Services Manager at London Northern Buses; F. W. Evans Cycles Ltd; Trek UK Ltd (Bicycle); Sam Grimmer

Physics and Chemistry
(consultant editor – Jack Challoner)

Sea and Air
Sea (consultant editors – Geoff Hales and Harvey B. Loomis):
David Spence, Gillian Hutchinson, David Topliss, Simon Stephens, Robert Baldwin, Jonathan Betts, all of the National Maritime Museum, London; Ian Friel; Simon Turnage of Captain O.M. Watts of London Ltd; Davey and Company Ltd, Great Dunmow; Avon Inflatables Ltd, Llanelli; Musto Ltd, Benfleet; Peter Martin of Spencer Rigging Ltd, Southampton; Peter Rowson of Ratseys Sailmakers, Southampton; Swiftech Ltd, Wallingford; Colin Scattergood of the Barrow Boat Company Ltd, Colchester; Professor J.S. Morrison of the Trireme Trust, Cambridge; The Cutty Sark Maritime Trust; Adrian Daniels of Kelvin Hughes Marine Instruments, London; Arthur Credland of Hull City Council Museums and Art Galleries; The Hull Maritime Society; Gerald Clark; Peter Fitzgerald of the Science Museum, London; Alec Michael of HMB Subwork Ltd, Great Yarmouth, and Ray Ward of the OSEL Group, Great Yarmouth; Richard Bird of UWI, Weybridge; Walker Marine Instruments, Birmingham; The International Sailing Craft Association; The Exeter Maritime Museum; Jane Wilson of the Trinity Lighthouse Company, London; The Imperial War Museum Collections; Thorn Security Ltd; Michael Bach

Air (consultant editor – Bill Gunston):
Aeromega Helicopters, Stapleford; Aero Shopping, London; Avionics Mobile Services Ltd, Watford; Roy Barber and John Chapman of the RAF Museum, Hendon; Mitch Barnes Aviation, London; Mike Beach; British Caledonian Flight Training Ltd; Fred Coates of Helitech (Luton) Ltd; Michael Cuttell and CSE Aviation Ltd, Oxford; Dowty Aerospace Landing Gear, Gloucester; Guy Hartcup of the Airship Association; Anthony Hooley, Chris Walsh, and David Cord of British Aerospace Regional Aircraft Ltd; Ken Huntley of Mid-West Aero Engines Ltd; Imperial War Museum, Duxford; The London Gliding Club, Dunstable; Musée des Ballons, Calvados; Noel Penny Turbines Ltd; Andy Pavey of Aviation Scotland Ltd; Tony Pavey of Thermal Aircraft Developments, London; the Commanding Officer and personnel of RAF St Athan; the Commanding Officer and personnel of RAF Wittering; The Science Museum, London; Ross Sharp of the Science Museum, Wroughton; The Shuttleworth Collection; Skysport Engineering; Mike Smith; Solar Wings Ltd, Marlborough; Julian Temple of Brooklands Museum Trust Ltd; Kelvin Wilson of Flying Start

Architecture
(consultant editor – Alexandra Kennedy):
Stephen Cutler for advice and text; Gavin Morgan of the Museum of London, London; Chris Zeuner of the Weald and Downland Museum, Singleton, Sussex; Alan Hills and James Putnam of the British Museum, London; Dr Simon Penn and Michael Thomas of the Avoncroft Museum of Buildings, Bromsgrove,

Worcestershire; Christina Scull of Sir John Soane's Museum, London; Paul Kennedy and John Williamson of the London Door Company, London; Lou Davis of The Original Box Sash Window Company, Windsor; Goddard and Gibbs Studios Ltd, London, for access to stained glass windows; The Royal Courts of Justice, Strand, London; Charles Brooking and Peter Dalton for access to the doors and windows in the Charles Brooking Collection, University of Greenwich, Dartford, Kent; Clare O'Brien of the Shakespeare Globe Trust, Shakespeare's Globe Museum, Bear Gardens, Southwark, London; Ken Teague of the Horniman Museum, London; Canon Haliburton, Mike Payton, Ken Stones, and Anthony Webb of St Paul's Cathedral, London; Roy Spring of Salisbury Cathedral; Reverend Gillean Craig of the Church of St George in the East, London; the Science Museum, London; Dr Neil Bingham; Lin Kennedy of Historic Royal Palaces; Katy Harris of Sir Norman Foster and Partners; Production Design, Thames Television plc, London, for supplying models; Dominique Reynier of Le Centre Georges Pompidou, Paris; Denis Roche of Le Musée National des Monuments Français, Paris; Franck Gioria and students of Les Compagnons du Devoir, Paris, for access to construction models; Frank Folliot of Le Musée Carnavalet, Paris; Dr Martina Harms of Hessische Landesmuseums, Darmstadt; Jefferson Chapman of the University of Tennessee, Knoxville, for access to the model of the Hypostyle Hall, Temple of Amon-Re; staff of the Palazzo Strozzi, Florence; staff of the Sydney Opera House, Sydney; staff of the Empire State Building, New York; Nick Jackson; Ann Terrell

The Visual Arts
(consultant editor – Pip Seymour):
Rosemary Simmons; Michael Taylor of Paupers Press, London; Tessa Hunkin and Emma Biggs of Mosaic Workshop, London; John Tiranti, Jonathan Lyons of Alec Tiranti Ltd, London; Chris Hough; Dr Ashok Roy; Satwinder Sehmi of Alphabet Soup, London; Phillip Poole of Cornelissens, London; George Weil and Sons Ltd, London; The National Gallery, London; Chris Webster of the Tate Gallery, London; China Art Cultural Centre, London; London Graphic Centre, London; A.P. Fitzpatrick, London; Flowers Graphics, London; Intaglio Printmaker, London; Falkiner Papers, London; Edgar Udny and Co, London; John Green

Music
(consultant editor – Susan Sturrock):
Boosey and Hawkes Music Publishers Ltd, London, for permission to reproduce extract from The Prodigal Son by Arthur Sullivan; The Bass and Drum Cellar, London; Empire Drums and Percussion, London; Argents (part of World of Music), London; Bill Lewington Ltd, London; Frobenius organ at Kingston Parish Church, Surrey; Yamaha-Kemble Music (UK) Ltd, Tilbrook, Milton Keynes; Yamaha Atelier, London; Akai (UK) Ltd, Hounslow, Middlesex; Casio Electronics Co. Ltd, London; Roland (UK) Ltd, Fleet, Hampshire; Richard Schulman

Sports
The Sports Council Information Centre, London; The British Olympic Games Committee; Brian Crennell of Black's Leisure Group (First Sport); Lillywhites of Piccadilly, London; Mitre Sports International Ltd, Huddersfield; David Bloomfield of the Football Association; Denver Athletics Ltd, Norfolk; Greg Everest and Keith Birley of the British League of Australian Rules Football; Peter McNally of the Gaelic Athletic Association; Rex King of the Rugby Football Union, Twickenham; Neil Tunnicliffe of the Rugby Football League, Leeds; Wayne Patterson of the Basketball Hall of Fame, Springfield, Connecticut; Brian Coleman of the English Basketball Association; All American Imports, Northampton; George Bulman of the English Volleyball Association; Julie Longdon of Mizuno Mallory (UK) Ltd; Juliet Stanford of the All-England Netball Association; Jeff Rowland of the British Handball Association; Cally Melin of Adidas UK Ltd; Patrick Donnely of the Baseball Hall of Fame, Cooperstown, New York; Ian Lepage and Stephen Barlow of the Hockey Association, Milton Keynes; Alison Taylor and Anita Mason of the All England Women's Lacrosse Association; David Shuttleworth of the English Lacrosse Union; Les Barnett and Jock Bentley of the British Athletic Federation Ltd, Birmingham; Mike Gilks of the Badminton Association of England; Gurinder Purewall for advice on archery; Chris McCartney of the US Archery Association; Geoff Doe of the National Smallbore Rifle Association, Bisley, Surrey, for information and reference material on shooting; Fagan Sports Goods Distributors, Surrey; Konrad Bartelski for advice on skiing; The British Ski Federation, Edinburgh; Mike Barnett of Snow and Rock of London; Sally Spurway of Mast-Co. Ltd, Reading; Sarah Morgan for advice on equestrian sports; Steve Brown and the New York Racing Association Inc, New York; Danrho of London; Alan Skipp and James Chambers of the Amateur Fencing Association, London; Carla Richards of the US Fencing Association; Hamilton Bland and John Dryer of the Amateur Swimming Association, Loughborough; Cotswold Camping Ltd, London; Tim Spalton of Glyn Locke (Racing Shells) Ltd, Chalgrove; Terry Friel of the US Rowing Association; House of Hardy; Leeda Fishing Tackle

Everyday Things
City Clocks (Clocks); Christopher Cullen of Babber Electronics; Sony UK Ltd (Mini-television); Black and Decker Ltd (Drills); British Footwear Manufacturing Federation; Grenson Shoes Ltd (Shoes); The Folio Society; R S Bookbinders (Books); Pentax UK Ltd (Camera); F E Murdin of the Decorative Lighting Association; Habitat (Lamp); Chingford Reproductions Ltd (Chair); Dualit Ltd (Toaster); J B Dove; Toro Wheelhorse UK Ltd (Lawnmower); WandH Gidden Ltd (Saddle)

PHOTOGRAPHY:
M. Alexander; Peter Anderson; Charles Brooks; Jane Burton; Peter Chadwick; Simon Clay; John Coiley; Andy Crawford; Geoff Dann; Philip Dowell; John Downs; Mike Dunning; Torla Evans; David Exton; Robert and Anthony Fretwell of Fretwell Photography Ltd.; Philip Gatward; Anna Hodgson; Gary Kevin; J. Heseltine; Cyril Laubscher; John Lepine; Lynton Gardiner (American Museum of Natural History, New York); Steve Gorton; Michelangelo Gratton; Judith Harrington; Peter Hayman; Anna Hodgson; Colin Keates; Gary Kevin; Dave King; Bob Langrish; Brian D.Morgan; Nick Nicholls; Nick Parfitt; Tim Parmenter and Colin Keates (Natural History Museum, London); Tim Ridley; Dave Rudkin; Philippe Sebert; James Stevenson; Clive Streeter; Harry Taylor; Matthew Ward; Jerry Young

PHOTOGRAPHIC ASSISTANCE:
Kevin Zak; Gary Ombler

ILLUSTRATORS:
Julian Baum; Rick Blakeley; Kuo Kang Chen; Karen Cochrane; Simone End; Ian Fleming; Roy Flooks; Mark Franklin; David Gardner; Will Giles; Mick Gillah; David Hopkins; Selwyn Hutchinson; Mei Lim; Linden Artists; Nick Loates; Chris Lyon; Kathleen McDougall; Coral Mula; Sandra Pond; Dave Pugh; Colin Rose; Graham Rosewarne; John Temperton; John Woodcock; Chris Woolmer

MODEL MAKERS:
Roby Braun; David Donkin; Morrison Frederick; Gordon Models; John Holmes; Graham High and Jeremy Hunt of Centaur Studios; Richard Kemp; Kelvin Thatcher; Paul Wilkinson

ADDITIONAL DESIGN ASSISTANCE:
Stefan Morris; Ulysses Santos; Suchada Smith

ADDITIONAL EDITORIAL ASSISTANCE:
Helen Castle; Colette Connolly; Camela Decaire; Nick Harris; Andrea Horth; Stewart McEwen; Damien Moore; Melanie Tham

INDEX: Kay Wright

Picture credits:

Action Plus 530tc; Anglo Australian Telescope Board 11cl, 11cra, 11cbl, 12tr, 12bc, 13tl, 13bl, 14tl, 16b, 17tc, 17bl, 22tl/D.Malin 16tl, 26tr, 27tl; Austin Brown and the Aviation Picture Library 426tl; Baptistery, Florence/Alison Harris 453r; Biophoto Associates 217ca, 217cra, 228cbc, 228cbc 230tr; Paul Brierley 311bra; British Aerospace/Anthony Hooley 412tl, 415tl; British Aerospace (Commercial Aircraft) Ltd 416tl; By prmission of the British Library 432tl, 445bl; British Museum 459tl, 459tr, 460tr, 460tc, 460tb, 489b; BP Exploration 299; Duncan Brown 25tl; Frank Lloyd Wright, American, 1867-1959, Model of Midway Gardens, 1914, executed by Richard Tickner, mixed media, 1987, 41.9 x 81.3 x 76.2, 1989.48. view 1. Photography courtesy of the Art Intitute of Chicago 495t; J.A. Coiley 331cr; Bruce Coleman Ltd/Andy Price 272tl; Courtesy of the Board of Trustees of the Victoria and Albert Museum, London 454-455b; European Passenger Services 329tl; ESA /PLV 11bl; French Railways 329c; Geoscience Features 311cla; Robert Harding Picture Library 62tl; Michael Holford /British Museum 372bl, Michael Holford 374tr; Hutchison Picture Library 60cl; The Image Bank/Edward Bower 306tr; Jet Propulsion Laboratory 11cbr; 30bc; 31bc; 31bcr; 38tl; 42crb; 44cb; 44cbr; 44bc; 44br; 46tl; 46cr; 46cb; 46bc; 46br; 50tl; 50cra; 50cl; 50c; 50cr; 50br; KeyMed Ltd 248bl, 249bl, 249bcl; Department of Prints and Drawings, Uffizi, Florence/Philip Gatward 431tc/Uffizi, Florence/Philip Gatward 433tl; Dr D.N. Landon (Institute of Neurology) 228bl,br; Life Science Images/Ron Boardman 244bl, 244br; The Lund Observatory 15bc; Brian Morrison 329tl, 329tr; © The Henry Moore Foundation 455tr; Musée d'Orsay, Paris/Philippe Sebert 437tc, 441tc;

Musée du Louvre, Paris/Philippe Sebert 453tl, 453l, 453br; NASA/AUI 13tr; NASA/JPL 11 cbr, 11br, 30tl, 30bl, 30br, 30bc, 31bc, 31bcr, 31bl, 34cr, 38tl, 40tl, 40cr, 42cr, 44tl, 44cb, 44cbr, 44bc, 44br, 44cr, 46crb, 46tl, 46cr, 46cb, 46bc, 46br, 48tl, 48cra, 48bca, 48bc, 48br, 50tl, 50bc, 50bc, 50cbr, 50br, 50cr, 52cr; National Maritime Museum 373br, 392-393b; National Medical Slide Bank 217cr; Nature Photographers/Paul Sterry 286tl; Newage International 317bl; Oxford Scientific Films/Breck P. Kent 166tl; Planet Earth 274tr; Quadrant 326tr; Margaret Robinson 332tl; Giotto The Expulsion of the Merchants from the Temple Scala 435tc, 435bl, 435br; Science Photo Library 10bl, 13tr, 28tr, 214bcr, 214bl, 236tr/Michael Abbey 225tc/Agema Infrared Systems 318tl/AGFA 220tl/Biophoto Associates: 217crb/Dr Jeremy Burgess/Science Photo Library 132tr; Dr Jeremy Burgess 235bcl/CNRI 214tl, 214cl, 214c, 214cr, 214bl, 214clb, 214crb, 214blc, 214br, 217cb, 235bcr, 238tl, 249bcr, 253tr, 253cra, 256tl; Science Photo library /Earth Satellite Corporation 288cl, 293br/Dr Brian Eyden 228cbr/Professor C. Ferlaud 245bl/Vaughan Fleming 311tl/Simon Fraser/U.S. Dept.of Energy 214bcl, 266tl/Eric Grave 217br/Hale Observatories 32br/Max Planck Institute for Radio Astronomy 15tl/Jan Hinsch 225tc/Jodrell Bank 11 tr, 13c / Manfred Kage 217c, 235br, 237br/Dr William C. Keel 13br/Keith Kent 316tl/Russ Lappa 310bra/Astrid & Hans-Frieder Michler 217tr/Dennis Milon 52bl/NASA 11cla, 12tl, 15tr, 30c, 31br, 32tl, 35tl, 36tl, 36cl, 36cr, 36bc, 42br, 42tr, 44tl 52tl, 291tr, 300tl/National Optical Astro Observatory 52tr/NIBSC 253crb/Novosti Press Agency 42bc/Omikron 244bc/David Parker 63bl, 304-305, 308br/Philippe Plailly 308tl, Roussel-UCLAF/CNRI 217tc/Rev Ronald Royer 32cr/Royal Observatory, Edinburgh/D Malin

11tl, 11cr,12c, 16cl, 16cr, 17br/David Scharf 235bl/Dr Kaus Schiller 248bcl, 248bcr, 248br/Secchi-Lecaque/Roussel-UCLAF/CNRI 253br/H. Sochurek 214cb/Stammers/Thompson 230tl/Sheila Terry 234tl/US Department of Energy 310bc/U.S Geological Survey/Science Photo Library 8-9, 30bcr, 42tl, 42bl/Tom Van Sant/Geosphere Project, Santa Monica/Science Photo Library 273tr, 281tr, 296tr, 297tl/Dr Christopher B. Williams/(Saint Marks Hospital)249br; Oxford Scientific Films/Animals Animals/Breck P. Kent 167tl; Pratt & Whitney Canada 418-419b, 419t; Science Museum 306bl,306bcl. 306 bcr, 324t, 326-327b, 330tr, 331ct, 331 cb; Sporting Pictures 524tl, 544cr; Tony Stone Worldwide 280tl; David Bomberg St Pauls and River 1945/Dinora Davies-Rees/Tate Gallery 431bc; David Hockney A Bigger Splash 1967/ © David Hockney/Tate Gallery 443tc; J.M.W. Turner The Burning of the Houses of Parliament Tate Gallery 439tc; Vision 26tr, 27c; Jerry Young 306tl; Dr Robert Youngson 241cr; Zefa 217bc/Janicek 276tl/H. Sochurek 210tl, 250tl, 254tl,/G. Steenmans 292tl

Jacket:
Indianapolis Motor Speedway Foundation front cover bc; NASA background to 2001 on spine, front cover, front inside flap

(t=top, b=bottom, a=above, l-left, r=right, c=centre)

Every effort has been made to trace the copyright holders. Dorling Kindersley apologises for any unintentional omissions and would be pleased, in any such cases, to add an acknowledgment in future editions.

Some pages in this book previously appeared in the *Visual Dictionary* series published by Dorling Kindersley. Contributors to this series include:

Project Art Editors:
Duncan Brown, Ross George, Nicola Liddiard, Andrew Nash, Clare Shedden, Bryn Walls

Designers:
Lesley Betts, Paul Calver, Simone End, Ellen Woodward

Additional design assistance:
Sandra Archer, Christina Betts, Alexandra Brown, Nick Jackson, Susan Knight

Project Editors:
Fiona Courtney-Thompson, Paul Docherty, Tim Fraser, Stephanie Jackson, Mary Lindsay

Editorial Assistant:
Emily Hill

Additional editorial assistance:
Susan Bosanko, Edward Bunting, Candace Burch, Deirdre Clark, Jeanette Cossar, Danièle Guitton, Jacqui Hand, David Harding, Nicholas Jackson, Edwina Johnson, David Lambert, Gail Lawther, David Learmount, Paul Jackson, Christine Murdock, Bob Ogden, Cathy Rubinstein, Louise Tucker, Dr Robert Youngson

Picture Researchers:
Vere Dodds, Danièle Guitton, Anna Lord, Catherine O'Rourke, Christine Rista, Sandra Schneider, Vanessa Smith, Clive Webster

Series Editor:
Martyn Page

Series Art Editor:
Paul Wilkinson

Managing Art Editors
Philip Gilderdale, Steve Knowlden

Art Director
Chez Picthall

Managing Editor
Ruth Midgley

Production:
Jayne Simpson